JAINA
Philosophy and Religion

[English translation of *Jaina Darśana*
by Muniśrī Nyāyavijayajī]

JAINA is pleased to bring this book, Jaina Philosophy and Religion written by Muni Sri Nyayavijayaji and translated by Nagin J. Shah. The distribution of this book is funded by JAINA CHARITABLE TRUST. The book deals with all the Fundamentals of Jainism in a simple nonsectarian way as applicable to modern day living in a rational scientific age. JAINA believes this book will enrich your knowledge of our religion and serve as a ready reference to you and your family. JAINA sincerely thanks Shri. N.P. Jain, of Motilal Banarsidass for his kind cooperation in making this book available in time and at a reasonable cost.

Jai Jinendra !

JAINA

Muniśrī Nyāyavijayajī

SANSKRIT WORKS BY THE AUTHOR
MUNIŚRĪ NYĀYAVIJAYAJĪ

1. *Nyāyakusumāñjaliḥ*
2. *Ātmatattvaprakāśaḥ*
3. *Adhyātmatattvālokaḥ*
4. *Mahātmavibhūtiḥ*
*5. *Jīvanāmṛtam*
6. *Jīvanahitam*
7. *Jīvanabhūmiḥ*
8. *Anekāntavibhūtiḥ*
*9. *Dīnākrandanam*
*10. *Bhaktagītam*
*11. *Mahāmānava-Mahāvīra*
*12. *Kalyāṇabhāvanā*
*13. *Kalyāṇamārgamīmāṁsā*
14. *Vīravibhūtiḥ*
15. *Jīvanapāṭhopaniṣad*
16. *Bhaktabhārati*
*17. *Vidyārthijīvanaraśmi*
*18. *Ātmahitopadeśaḥ*
19. *Upadeśasāraḥ*
20. *Āśvāsanam*
21. *Ārtanādaḥ*
22. *Nyāyālaṅkāraḥ*
*23. *Kalyāṇabhāratī*

*These works are translated into English by the author himself.

BLII SERIES NO. 12

JAINA
Philosophy and Religion

[English translation of *Jaina Darśana* by Muniśrī Nyāyavijayajī]

Translated by
NAGIN J. SHAH

JOINTLY PUBLISHED BY

MOTILAL BANARSIDASS PUBLISHERS PRIVATE LIMITED
BHOGILAL LEHAR CHAND INSTITUTE OF INDOLOGY
MAHATTARĀ SĀDHVĪ ŚRĪ MRIGĀVATĪJĪ FOUNDATION
DELHI

First Published: Delhi, 1998
Reprinted : Delhi, 1999, 2001

ISBN: 81-208-1490-8 (Cloth)
ISBN: 81-208-1701-x (Paper)

Also available at:
MOTILAL BANARSIDASS
41 U.A. Bungalow Road, Jawahar Nagar, Delhi 110 007
8 Mahalaxmi Chamber, Warden Road, Mumbai 400 026
120 Royapettah High Road, Mylapore, Chennai 600 004
Sanas Plaza, 1302 Baji Rao Road, Pune 411 002
236, 9th Main III Block, Jayanagar, Bangalore 560 011
8 Camac Street, Kolkata 700 017
Ashok Rajpath, Patna 800 004
Chowk, Varanasi 221 001

Printed in India
BY JAINENDRA PRAKASH JAIN AT SHRI JAINENDRA PRESS,
A-45 NARAINA, PHASE-I, NEW DELHI 110 028
AND PUBLISHED BY BHOGILAL LEHAR CHAND INSTITUTE OF INDOLOGY
20 KM, G.T. KARNAL RAOD, DELHI 110 036

FOREWORD

The Bhogilal Leharchand Institute of Indology (BLII) has great pleasure, indeed, in publishing the English translation of Muniśrī Nyāvijayajī's (A.D. 1890-1970) original Gujarāti Work entitled 'Jaina Darśana' which has run into twelve editions. The Work reveals his stupendous scholarship, his positive approach, his non-sectarian outlook, his wisdom and competence in attempting synthesis of conflicting views, his mastery of Indian philosophical and religious thought, his insight into the heart of religion, his sensitivity to all aspects of a problem, and his spiritual craving. It is a comprehensive, competent and authoritative treatise on Jainism. It attempts to arouse sympathetic response to the ethical and spiritual aspirations of man. The author has made sincere and honest efforts to bring out the true significance of Jaina views on various subjects.

We are most thankful to Dr. Nagin J. Shah, an eminent scholar of Indian philosophy, for accepting our invitation to translate the original Gujarātī Work into English. He has successfully accomplished the task of producing an English version that would closely retain the meaning of the original text and yet be intelligible to the English-speaking readers. He catches the spirit of the original and takes great pains to match it with proper verbal expression. He attempts to be as lucid as possible.

It will be perfectly in place here to say some words about how the BLII was founded. The late revered Jain Āchārya Vijay Vallabh Sūrīshwarjī Mahārāj is well-known throughout India for his concern for the upliftment of the human race and his disciplined way of life.

To commemorate the teachings of the great visionary Āchārya, a beautiful Memorial (Smārak Complex) with a magnificent Shrine has come up at the 20th km Point, G.T. Karnal Road, Delhi. The Smārak is the brain-child of the late Mahattarā Vidushī Sādhvīśrī Mrigāvatījī, herself a scholar of Jaina Āgamas and a true disciple of Āchārya Vijay Vallabh Sūrīshwarjī Mahārāj.

The BLII was started through the munificent donations provided by the trusts of the Bhogilal Leharchand family and through Śri Ātma Vallabh Jaina Smārak Shikshaṇ Nidhi to sponsor and promote research in Indology and other aspects of Indian culture, objectives dear to revered Āchārya Vijay Vallabh Sūrīshwarjī Mahārāj, who had been advised by his guru Jain Āchārya Śrī Vijayānand Sūrīshwarjī Mahārāj in his last sermon:

"Temples to God have since been built; Now you
must build temples to Saraswatī."

The academic programme of the Institute is to initiate, organise and give a fillip to research in Indological subjects in general and Jainology in particular.

This English translation of the original Work in Gujarātī has been published in accordance with the true spirit of these aims and objects.

On this occasion, we respectfully remember revered Mahattarā Sādhavīśrī Mrigāvatījī Mahārāj. It was at her suggestion that this project was undertaken by the management of the Institute. She was deeply impressed by the intrinsic worth of the Work. It is really sad that she was no more to see this publication.

Our thanks are also due to Trustees of Śrī Ātma Vallabh Jaina Smārak Shikshaṇ Nidhi, for the deep interest they have shown in this publication. We express our sincere gratitude to the Mahattarā Sādhvīśrī Mrigāvatī Foundation for the financial help for the project.

It is hoped that the publication of this Work will be of immense value to the keen students of Jaina philosophy in particular and Indian philosophy in general.

B.L. Institute of Indology — **Jitendra B. Shah**
Delhi 110 036, January 3, 1999

CONTENTS

CHAPTER 2
JAINA PATH OF PURIFICATION (LIBERATION) 39-148

CHAPTER 3
REFLECTIONS ON SOME PROBLEMS OF METAPHYSICS, ETHICS AND SPIRITUAL DEVELOPMENT   149-265

CHAPTER 4
KARMA PHILOSOPHY
(LAW OF MORAL CAUSATION)

CHAPTER 5
JAINA LOGIC

TRANSLATOR'S NOTE

I was fortunate to have an opportunity to study Muni Nyayavijayaji's '*Jaina Darśana*' as a student of Shri Mahavir Jaina Vidyalaya, Ahmedabad in 1952-54, since it was included in our curriculum. I was impressed by the lucid, cogent and non-sectarian presentation. It had a lasting effect on my mind. That urged me to know about the author Muni Nyayavijayaji (A.D. 1890-1970). He was a worthy disciple of that internationally renowned saint scholar Rev. Vijayadharmasūri who aroused interest of Western scholars in Indian culture in general and Jainism in particular. He was an embodiment of learning and love. He was imbued with the spirit of non-absolutism (*anekānta*). His penetrating insight could see the truth inherent in each and every religion and system. This was the reason why he was respected by the great personages of other religions, and the non-Jaina communities too devotedly requested him to spend four months of rainy season in their town. Muni Punyavijayaji, an eminent indologist, held him in high esteem. Even Shrimanta Maharaja Sayaji Rao Gaekwad, the then ruler of Baroda State, had great respect for his elevating wisdom and lofty character, and consulted him in religious matters.

He wrote nearly thirty works in Sanskrit. *Nyāyakusumāñjali,* his work on logic and philosophy, earned him Nyāyaviśārada Degree. His *Adhyātmatattvāloka* was highly appreciated. It was praised by Mahavir Prasada Dvivedi, a noted man of literature, for its spiritual fervor and ideas. Pandits of Ujjain honoured him, praised his literary excellence and described him as an incarnation of Aśvaghoṣa and Kālidāsa. In his last years he composed *Kalyāṇabhāratī* in 534 Sanskrit verses. It expounds the philosophy of good living. Its appeal being universal, it won the praise of general readers, scholars and religious personages.

He wrote several works in Gujarātī. But the work entitled '*Jaina Darśana*' is his *magnum opus.* It is extremely interesting both for the general reader and for the specialist in Jainism. The first will undoubtedly appreciate the effort made by the author to explain clearly the principles and spirit of Jainism, whereas the second will learn much from the treatment of many aspects of Jainism by a scholar who is equally at home in both Jainism and other systems of Indian Philosophy. The work covers a wide variety of problems. It is so lucid, cogent and authentic that twelve editions sold out in no time. It got translated into Hindi but has come out in English only now. It evinces the author's close acquaintance with the tenets of Jainism, his keenness of arriving at right and rational conclusions, his insight into the essentials of religion, his positive and constructive approach, and his deep knowledge of the systems of Indian Philosophy. It won the praise of many including an Ārya Samājī Pt. Swami Premanandji and Muni Punyavijayaji.

Under the tutelage of Rev. Vijayadharmasūri he was able to invoke all those spiritual elements which he has woven into his writings. His forte is his spiritual and philosophical thinking and his contribution in the field is both substantial and distinctive. His exposition is neither sectarian nor dogmatic. His writings aim to enable his readers better evaluate the philosophical and ethical principles in the light of changing world. Freshness of interpretation of old texts, discretionary power, penetrating insight, spontaneous spiritual feelings and all-embracing love have been clearly manifested in his writings. He every now and then regrets that owing to sectarianism and narrowmindedness the religious atmosphere is greatly polluted.

It is my pleasant duty to express my sincere thanks to the management of B.L. Institute of Indology for providing me an opportunity to translate into English an important and interesting Gujarātī work on Jainism.

23, Valkeshvar Society **Nagin J. Shah**
Ambawadi,
Ahmedabad 380 015
October 2, 1996

INTRODUCTION

Philosophy (*darśana-śāstra*) imparts us knowledge of Reality. In other words, its subject-matter is Reality. On the other hand, science of religion (*dharma-śāstra*) treats of *dharma. Dharma* means good conduct and spiritual discipline. Though philosophy and science of religion are different sciences, the subject-matter of the latter is more or less dealt with in the former. It is so because it does not serve the purpose of life to know merely the subject-matter of philosophy alone. As a matter of fact, even after knowing any subject, it is quite necessary for man to know *dharma.* Why? The reason is that good of life is achieved by the practice of *dharma.* So it is necessary for all to know and understand *dharma* in its true nature. From this it is quite clear that the purpose of acquiring knowledge of *dharma,* the subject-matter of the science of religion, is the highest good (*niḥśreyas*). One can practise *dharma* truly, if one knows rightly as to what *dharma* is. And if one practises *dharma* truly, then and then only one can attain ultimate good. But the propounder of each system of Indian philosophy explicitly states at the beginning of his work that the object of his system is the highest good. He explains at the outset as to how his system serves the highest human end, Ultimate Release. So, when it is said that the purpose of the knowledge of philosophy is also the highest good, it means that knowledge of the science of religion and that of philosophy have some special relation. Knowledge of philosophy is useful to make knowledge of science of religion brilliant and sharp. The Yoga philosophy of Patañjali can be called philosophy and science of religion as well. Just as it presents a system of philosophy even so it imparts the religious teachings pertaining to non-violence, truthfulness, non-stealing, continence, non-possession, austerity, scriptural study, meditation on God or any holy personage, etc. Similarly, there are many well-known works on science of religion or science of spiritual evolution, which are fraught with philosophical discussions. So they can be called partly philosophical works. Take, for instance, *Dhammasaṃgahaṇi* by Ācārya Haribhadrasūri. As its title suggests, it is a collection of (discussions related to) *dharma.* In spite of this fact, it mainly contains philosophical discussions. In fact, religious (or spiritual) and philosophical subjects are so closely connected with one another that in a work dealing with religious (or spiritual) subject, the discussions pertaining to philosophical subject naturally and inevitably find their place, and *vice versa.*

The term '*darśana*' occurring in the title '*Jaina Darśana*' of the original Gujarātī work does not yield the sense of philosophy. It is employed in the sense of religious sect (*dharma-sampradāya*). The title, therefore, means "the work giving information about religious and philosophical thought of a religious sect known as '*Jaina-dharma*' ".

The tradition which rightly offers sacred knowledge or pure thought is called *sampradāya* (*sam + pra + dāya,* meaning that which offers rightly). None should understand that *sampradāya* in its true sense is only one in the whole world. It is good for the world, if it has as many *sampradāyas* as possible—*sampradāyas* which show pure Path of knowledge and wisdom. The greater the number of lamps, the more is the light we receive. But when *sampradāyas* are afflicted with narrow outlook, factional tendency and madness, are under the sway of fanaticism, are overpowered by attachment and aversion, and fight with one another, they no longer remain *sampradāya,* but turn into *sampradāha* (*sam + pra + dāha,* meaning that which burns causing great pains).

We may not mind if there is no *sampradāya* in the world, but there should be no *sampradāha* at all in it. And a serious thinker will unhesitatingly state that it does not matter if *sampradāyas* do not impart knowledge of other things; it is enough for worldly and other-worldly happiness if they rightly and nicely teach man the lessons of truthfulness, non-violence, friendliness, benevolence and self-control alone. If they desire to impart knowledge of other things for his intellectual development and pleasure, let them do so gently, affectionately and impartially without any quarrel or bitterness.

In the days of Mahāvīra and Buddha, Vedic and Śramaṇa cultures came into great conflict. These two great sages came out victorious on account of the force of their severe austerities. Some of the great Vedic scholars joined the Order of Mahāvīra, while some others that of Buddha. Besides Mahāvīra and Buddha, there were other five great personages among the chief propagators of *Śramaṇa* culture. Of them Gośālaka's name[1] repeatedly

1. The other four were Pūraṇakāśyapa, Ajitakeśakaṃbalī, Pakudhakātyāyana and Saṃjayabelaṭṭhīputta. Their sects or paths along with that of Gośālaka have become extinct.

occurs in the ancient *Śramaṇa* literature. He was the propounder of the *niyativāda* (predeterminism). According to it, what is destined to happen will certainly happen (*yad bhāvyaṃ tad bhaviṣyati*). Even today, it is found deeply rooted in the hearts of many Indians.

Readers will find in this work (see p. 427 ff.) the brief summary of the revolutionary teachings of Mahāvīra. The possible points of his programme can be succinctly stated as follows:

To remove blind faith prevailing among the people, to dissipate the atmosphere of violence, to propagate the principle of non-violence and universal friendliness, to effect synthesis of various religions and philosophies through awakening power of discretion and reason, and to disseminate the very important teaching that one's happiness is in one's own hands and that those who seek happiness in wealth, prosperity and possession certainly fail to attain it. Real happiness is within us. Mahāvīra, the great saint, set aside Sanskrit, the language of the elite and pundits, and adopted Prakrit, the language of the people, to propagate his teachings, because thereby he wanted to spread Truth among the people at large. (Buddha followed the same path. There is great similarity between languages and gospels of both Mahāvīra and Buddha. We notice similar altruistic tendencies and similar teachings of universal good in the ancient Jaina and Buddhist works). Mahāvīra emphatically declared: 'The greater good a man does to himself and the more he purifies himself, the greater good he can do to others'[1]. Some glimpses of his noble teachings which we find in the *Āgamas*, the Jaina canons, are presented in the closing part of this work. From this, readers will have some idea of his revolutionary, dynamic, sublime and elevating nature.

Mahāvīra was born in 599 B.C. And he died at the age of seventytwo. He was posterior to Pārśva, the penultimate *Tīrthaṅkara* of the current time-cycle. The historicity of Pārśva is proved by the modern historians and scholars.[2] The event of Mahāvīra's death took place two hundred fifty

---

1. "Let him that would move the world, first move himself."—Socrates.
2. Dr. Guerinot writes: "There can no longer be any doubt that Pārśva was a historical personage. According to the Jaina tradition he must have lived a hundred years and died 250 years before Mahāvīra. His period of activity, therefore, corresponds to the 8th century B.C.

   The parents of Mahāvīra were followers of the religion of Pārśva. . . There have appeared twenty-four prophets of Jainism. They are ordinarily called *Tīrthaṅkaras*. With the twenty-third Pārśvanātha we enter into the region of history and reality". [Introduction to his Essay on Jaina Bibliography].

years after Pārśva's death. From this we understand that Mahāvīra, who flourished 2,500 years ago, did not found a new religion but brought to the fore and developed the teachings which his preceding omniscient *Tīrthaṅkaras* had already taught. Thus Mahāvīra was not the founder of Jaina religion; he was rather the propagator of Jaina religion which had been taught by Pārśva and other omniscient teachers of his ever present and imperishable Jaina tradition. The actual study of its philosophy convinces us of the fact that this religious tradition or sect (*sampradāya*) is not a fanatic factional sect but is one which shows the path of universal happiness and the highest good (or which offers sacred knowledge and pure thought). A great Jaina Ācārya Haribhadra, a pre-eminently learned brāhmaṇa converted to a Jaina monk, states: *yasmād ete mahātmāno bhavavyādhibhiṣagvarāḥ* (Kapila, Buddha and other great saints were eminent physicians specialised in the cure of the disease of transmigratory existence). How great must be the peace and poise of his soul when he would have uttered and supported these brilliant words! Though he followed the practice of a particular religious sect (*sampradāya*) and took prominent part in philosophical discussions, he respected great sages of other sects and never lost sight of the goal of universal love. Whatever be the cultural tradition that led him towards the final goal of non-attachment and awakened in him the feeling of equanimity and universal friendliness, it really deserves our salutation and veneration.

Jaina literature is very vast and varied. It is rich in the works dealing with all possible subjects. Pointing out the importance of Jaina Sanskrit literature Dr. Hartel, a German scholar, observes: "Now what would Sanskrit Poetry be without the large Sanskrit literature of the Jainas! The more I learn to know it, the more my admiration rises". (*Jaina Śāsana* Vol. I, No. 21).

The followers of Jaina religion have been divided into two main branches, viz. Śvetāmbara and Digambara. Apart from some minor differences pertaining to the rituals and monastic practice, the religious and philosophical literature of both the branches is almost unanimous[1] on all points.

---

1. *śeṣaṃ śvetāmbarais tulyam ācāre daivate gurau /*
śvetāmbarapraṇītāni tarkaśāstrāṇi manvate //
syādvādavidyāvidyotāt prāyaḥ sādharmikā amī //

Rājaśekharasūri's *Ṣaḍdarśanasamuccaya*

The import is: 'Can women attain liberation?', 'Does an omniscient being in the embodied state engage in eating meals?'—these and some other are the minor

Regarding Jaina religion the Late Dr. Hermann Jacobi, a great German scholar, remarks: "In conclusion, let me assert my conviction that Jainism is an original system, quite distinct and independent from all others and that, therefore, it is of great importance for the study of philosophical thought and religious life in ancient India."

—Read in the Congress of History of Religions

[The Āgamas (the Jaina canonical works) which embody the teachings of Mahāvīra expound *karma* (moral causation), spiritual development, transmigratory journey of a soul from one birth to another, classes and aggregates of material atoms, six ultimate substances and nine principles. Looking to the systematic exposition of all these topics, one can conclude that the Jaina philosophical and religious tradition as presented in the *Āgamas* must have been the result of the efforts of many generations anterior to Lord Mahāvīra. The Jaina tradition is original, and different from and independent of Upaniṣadic and other traditions.]

Dr. L.P. Tessitory, an Italian scholar, extols Jaina religion and philosophy in following terms: "Jaina philosophy and religion is of a very high order. It is not only my inference but also my experience that its fundamental principles are based on science. As physics advances, it supports the principles of Jaina religion and philosophy."

Jaina literature has remained in the dark and fallen into oblivion. Again, Jaina works which are coming or have come to light are not properly exposed to the world. This is the reason why even great scholars are seen totally or partly ignorant of the principles of Jaina philosophy and religion. Apart from this, we also notice that those who are blinded

---

doctrinal points on which they are divided. Again, they are divided on some minor practical points like the one as to whether the practice of nudity is an absolute prerequisite to the mendicant's path. Apart from these minor differences, everything is almost the same in both the Śvetāmbara and Digambara *sampradāyas*. They accept one another's works on logic. *Syādvāda* (theory of relative judgement) is the fundamental theory of Jaina religion and philosophy; and both the branches support it with equal enthusiasm. So followers of both these branches are co-religionists (*sādharmika*).

[Great scholars and venerable saints have flourished in both the branches. The literature produced by either of them is equally vast and rich. There are all points that can very well urge them to live amicably with great love like two brothers born of the same mother. But it is a matter of regret that they do not live in harmony with one another. If they cooperate with one another and forge unity, they can very well elevate, with their joint strength, the holy religion of Lord Mahāvīra to a very lofty position.]

by fanaticism, deluded by undue attachment to their schools or sects and afflicted with narrow outlook, do not naturally have liberal tendency or outlook inducing them to read the philosophical and religious works of others and hence are deprived of reading the Jaina works containing wholesome, noble and salutary teaching.

I confidently express that the study of Indian philosophy remains utterly incomplete without the study of Jaina philosophy (and literature). Again, I impartially declare that the study of Jaina philosophical works is very useful in purifying and increasing one's fund of knowledge as also in finding the right path of spiritual poise and peace.

None has the right to own exclusively the field of philosophy. Nobody has monopoly on it. Anybody can acquire it. It is wrongly regarded as the exclusive possession of a particular group or sect. When a man respects only that system of philosophy, which he has acquired through family tradition, and does not cast even a glance at other systems of philosophy, he cannot be regarded as endowed with liberal attitude and catholicity of outlook. Development of knowledge and attainment of truth depend on the liberal attitude and wide study. The liberal attitude expresses itself in the words: 'Whatever is true is mine'. Truth is not confined to a particular race, class or sect. It is present everywhere without any obstruction. It is accessible to all irrespective of race, class, creed, sect, etc. Whose is Truth? It is his who realises it. Any literature permeated with and purified by Truth is the wealth which belongs to the whole world. Any man from whatever part of the world has the right to enjoy it.

Substance of the Work

Though all great men are seekers and cognisers of truth, their search of it and their presentation of it are not identical. The style of presentation, which Buddha[1] adopted is different from that which Mahāvīra had adopted. The special method Mahāvīra employed is called *anekāntavāda* (non-ab-

1. It was the nature of Buddha to remain aloof from the mutually conflicting doctrines. This is the reason why he at once called the current metaphysical questions presented before him as in a way 'untouchable' (i.e. inexplicable or unanswerable). For example, he could not call the soul eternal; and if he called it non-eternal, the doctrine of its complete destruction on the death of the body—the doctrine accepted by the materialists akin to Cārvākas—would force itself upon him. So, he called all such questions unanswerable and made the complete destruction of the cycle of birth and death the subject-matter of his teachings. On the other hand, it was the nature of

solutistic or non-one-sided method). It is difficult to gain the wholly true knowledge of a thing or Reality. Even those who have gained it find it difficult to express it in words in its entirety. Their descriptions or presentations of a thing differ from one another or look somewhat conflicting with one another on account of difference of time, place, circumstances, language, style, etc. This is inevitable.

Apart from the omniscient great personages, if we talk about the ordinary persons alone, there are persons among them also who love and speak truth, but they have only partial knowledge of a thing. They are incompetent to present even their partial knowledge perfectly. Imperfect knowledge is presented imperfectly. So the understanding of even truth-loving men sometimes differs. Added to it, the difference of their culture gives rise to even more mutual conflict. Thus, at last all truth-loving persons, omniscient and non-omniscient, automatically present the data or postulates differing from and conflicting with one another; or other persons obtain from them or create through them such data or postulates.

Taking into account this situation, Mahāvīra decided to invent such a method that those having incomplete or partial knowledge of Reality or a thing might not suffer injustice at the hands of others. If others' knowledge, though partial and even conflicting with ours, is true, and similarly our knowledge, though partial and conflicting with others, is true, then we should find out such a method that both may get justice. That method is non-one-sided way or outlook (*anekāntadṛṣṭi*).With the wonderful key

---

Mahāvīra to view and understand all the conflicting doctrines from their respective standpoints. He answered Buddha's 'unanswerable' questions from different standpoints. For example, he described the soul as permanent and impermanent, universe as eternal and non-eternal, soul and body as identical and different, from different standpoints. He logically resolved the apparent conflict in the different views. Answers which Mahāvīra gave from different standpoints are found in the original *Āgamas*. They testify to the all-comprehensive intellect of Mahāvīra. It is not that Buddha's was not a synthetic outlook. He too was in a sense the supporter of the doctrine of non-one-sidedness (*anekāntavāda*) under the guise of the doctrine called *Vibhajyavāda* (the doctrine which upholds that one can answer rightly certain questions by analysing and 'breaking up'). When Siṃha Senāpati asked him as to whether it was proper for the people to call him *akriyāvādin* (non-believer in action), he told him that as he taught the people to perform good and wholesome actions, he was *kriyāvādin* (believer in action) but that as he taught them to refrain from performing evil and unwholesome actions he was *akriyāvādin* (non-believer in action).

of this method Mahāvīra, a great saint, unlocked portals of the practical and theoretical problems pertaining to individual and social life. While formulating a system of thought and also a code of conduct, both useful in life, he applied the non-one-sided method under certain conditions; and he asked others who wanted to apply it to follow strictly those conditions. The conditions are as follows:

(1) One should not yield to the passions of attachment and aversion, and should remain calmly impartial and equanimous.
(2) So long as the tendency of equanimity or impartiality does not develop to its fulness, one should constantly keep before him the aim of achieving its perfection and entertain simply the desire to know Truth.
(3) One should reflect on one's own position or views. Similarly, he should reflect with honour and respect on the position or views of others. And one should critically examine one's own position just as one critically examines the position of others.
(4) One should cultivate liberality of accepting and synthesising discreetly all those aspects of one's own and others' experiences which are found considerably true—though they may seem conflicting. And with the growth of experience, if one finds any defect in the former synthesis, one should immediately correct it, abandoning false pride or self-conceit and should advance on this line.

Nayavāda (doctrine of standpoints) and *saptabhaṅgīvāda* (doctrine of sevenfold judgement) are the corollaries of *anekāntadṛṣṭi* (non-one-sided method or outlook). All the systems of thought, which were prevalent then, were given their due place in *nayavāda*. And all the conflicting views regarding one and the same thing which were prevalent then were given their due place in *saptabhaṅgīvāda*.

Man makes efforts to the last moment of his life for his own good and welfare. Even the great men who are constantly engaged in doing good to others desire to uncover, manifest and realise their Highest Self through that benevolent activity. The idea of one's own good has the chief place even in the activity of doing good to others. In other words, it is the end of one's own good that urges man to do good to others. The spiritually steadfast, peaceful and wise *yogī* too remains constantly engaged in the spiritual efforts with the conviction that he will certainly attain the state of Supreme Soul in future birth, if not in the present one.

How narrow will be the purpose of life, if we do not believe in the existence of soul even after the death of the body? And how limited will also be the field of action, then? No other idea can instil strength and energy in human heart as does the idea that he will certainly attain his ultimate goal in the future birth, if not in the present one. Taking into account all this one gets convinced of the existence of an independent eternal sentient substance called soul. It certainly experiences the fruits of good or evil actions which it performs knowingly or unknowingly. There is no escape from them. And on account of the karmic bondage it has to wander in the cycle of rebirth.

Ācārya Haribhadra observes in his *Yogabindu:*

daivaṁ nāmeha tattvena karmaiva hi śubhāśubham /
tathā puruṣakāraś ca svavyāpāro hi siddhidaḥ //319//
Meaning: The auspicious or inauspicious *karma* itself is destiny (*daiva*). And one's own successful activity is human effort (*puruṣakāra*).

vyāpāramātrāt phaladaṁ niṣphalaṁ mahato'pi ca /
ato yat karma tad daivaṁ citraṁ jñeyaṁ hitāhitam //322//
Meaning: That *karma* which bears fruit even with little effort and remains barren even with great efforts is called destiny or fate. It is either auspicious or inauspicious. Again, auspicious or inauspicious *karma* is of various kinds.

evaṁ puruṣakāras tu vyāpārabahulas tathā /
phalahetuniyogena jñeyo janmāntare'pi hi //323//
anyonyasaṁśrayāv eva dvāv apy etau vicakṣaṇaiḥ. . . //324//
Meaning: Similarly, human effort is nothing but much exertion which certainly gives its fruit even in future birth. *Karma* and human effort are mutually dependent.

After that in verse 326, he declares that *karma* does not give its fruit without human effort.

daivaṁ puruṣakāreṇa durbalaṁ hy upahanyate /
daivena caiṣo'pīty eta. . . //327//
Meaning: Human effort destroys weak destiny or fate. And strong destiny or fate destroys human effort. Stronger of the two destroys the other.

Attachment for sensual pleasures, indulgence in vices and unmindfulness cause bodily and other types of miseries that befall oneself and others.

It is proper to believe so. And this is also supported by scriptures. Hence, if man has to experience miseries on account of his foolishness, thoughtlessness, indulgence in injustice and cruelty, all these defects of his are certainly responsible for his miserable condition and he is guilty of all those evil activities. This is what the science of *karma* loudly proclaims.

Similarly, the science of *karma* emphatically declares that man should put forth enough effort to remove miseries, not only of his but also of others. This declaration, when considered with regard to oneself, requires one to achieve one's own welfare, and when considered with regard to others, inspires one to perform one's duty by behaving compassionately and affectionately with others. When a man's house is on fire and instead of making efforts to extinguish fire, if he simply sits and prays to God to send rains, what will you think of his attitude and behaviour? Will you approve of it? Will even God be pleased with his behaviour? God helps those who help themselves.

The science of *karma* never propagates such cruel and mean teaching as to leave those who are poor, humiliated, oppressed and miserable as also those who are entrapped and deceived by rascals, robbers and murderers to their *karma* (destiny). It only commands and enjoins people to put forth sincere efforts to relieve them of their miseries, to remove their poverty and distress, and to save them from calamities.

Do we not take immediate measures to save our relative or friend who has fallen from height, is wounded by a severe stroke of a weapon, bitten by a cobra or afflicted with an ailment? Do we pay any heed to his past *karma*? Not at all. We simply neglect his past *karma*. Similarly, it is our duty to make sincere efforts to emancipate the people from miseries, poverty, diseases and helplessness and to elevate those who are miserable, tortured, fallen, oppressed and exploited to the state of happiness, freedom and self-respect. And if we perform this duty, we generate auspicious *karmas*. On the other hand, if we remain indifferent to the miserable, neglect them though we have the ability to help them, and seek to excuse ourselves that they are miserable on account of their own past *karma*, it proves beyond doubt that we lack universal love, friendliness and compassion; such hard-hearted tendency and behaviour of ours are but sins no doubt and they generate inauspicious *karma*. If, in accordance with our ability, we put forth sincere efforts to uplift the miserable, then, as maintained by the science of *karma*, their misery-causing *karmas* would suffer a severe blow, and as a result of it we can remove or at least mitigate their miseries. These efforts of ours would generate our auspicious *karmas*. This is the holy essence of the religion of man. One should practise it to one's full capacity. It is what we call *dharma.* And by following it, we do good to ourselves as well as to the society. The assertion of the celebrated Vyāsa in the following couplet comprises universal truth.

na hīdṛśaṁ saṁvananaṁ triṣu lokeṣu vidyate /
dayā maitrī ca bhūteṣu dānaṁ ca madhurā ca vāk //

Meaning: Compassion and friendliness towards all living beings, charity and sweet words constitute the matchless charm or spell in the three worlds, which unfailingly wins over the hearts of all beings.

Nyayavijaya

CHAPTER 1

ESSENTIALS OF JAINA PHILOSOPHY

Introductory

How many reals are there in the world? There are two fundamental reals—the sentient and the insentient. There is no third fundamental real besides these two. They exhaust the entire universe. They are known by the common term 'substance'.

That which is devoid of sentience, feeling, is insentient. Contrary to it, that whose nature is sentience is sentient; it is soul. *Ātman, jīva* and *cetana* are synonymous words meaning soul. The defining characteristic of soul is cognitive faculty.

From the spiritual standpoint seven more reals are derived from these two, thus making the total of nine reals. Liberation being the ultimate goal to be achieved by living beings, those things whose understanding is absolutely necessary for the attainment of liberation are here considered to be reals. So the Jaina thinkers have extensively explained these nine reals.

Terms 'Jina' and 'Jaina'

The term '*Jaina*' is derived from the term '*Jina*'. And the term '*Jina*' is the common name for the supreme souls who are totally free from all the feelings of attachment, aversion, etc., that defile the soul. It is a noun formed from the Sanskrit verbal root '*ji*' meaning 'to conquer'. Thus, it meaningfully well applies to the supreme souls who have won victory over the feelings of attachment, aversion, etc. *Arhan* (the Worthy), *Vītarāga* (One free from attachment) and *Parameṣṭhī* (the Supreme Divinity) are synonyms of '*Jina*'. And devotees of *Jina* are called '*Jaina*'. And the Religion propounded by *Jina* is called 'Jaina Religion'. *Ārhata Dharma* (Religion propounded by the Worthy), *Anekāntadarśana* (Philosophy of Non-one-sidedness), *Nirgranthaśāsana* (Teachings of the Knotless),

Vītarāgamārga (Path made and enlightened by one who is free from attachment)—these are the terms employed for the Jaina Religion and Philosophy.

Tīrthaṅkara

A soul attains the full manifestation of its sentiency as soon as all the karmic veils are totally removed. And the karmic veils are totally removed when the practice of spiritual discipline reaches its highest point. The birth in which this event takes place is the last birth for that soul. And that soul is regarded as having become the supreme soul in that birth. Such supreme souls are divided into two broad classes. The first class comprises *tīrthaṅkaras* (Makers of *tīrtha*) who are from the very birth endowed with miraculous cognitive powers and extraordinary grandeur and sublimity. Many uncommon specialities are described as associated with them. We call a prince 'a king' even though he does not possess the kingdom, keeping in view the fact that he is going to possess it in future. Similarly, *tīrthaṅkaras* are not omniscient from their very birth and hence they do not actually and primarily have *tīrthaṅkara*hood from their very birth, yet they are called *tīrthaṅkara* from their very birth, keeping in view the fact that they are going to attain *tīrthaṅkara*hood in future in that very birth. Having renounced their household life and taken to monk life, when they, on the attainment of the highest plane of the spiritual discipline, completely remove the nature-obscuring karmic veils and as a result acquire manifestation of their natural omniscience, they establish *tīrtha*. What is the meaning of the term '*tīrtha*'? The term '*tīrtha*' here means the fourfold order of monks, nuns, laymen and laywomen. The principal direct disciples of a *tīrthaṅkara* compose scriptures on the basis of the preachings of the *tīrthaṅkara*. These scriptures are divided into twelve books which are known by a collective name '*Dvādaśāṅgī* (a group of twelve *Aṅga* works)'. The term '*Aṅga*' is a technical name given to each of these twelve works. *Aṅgas* are so called because they are 'limbs' of the entire body of the scripture. By the term '*tīrtha*' is also meant this group of twelve *Aṅga* works. Thus, *tīrthaṅkaras* are so called because they are the founders of the fourfold order as also because they are the authors of the meaning embodied in *Aṅga* works composed by their direct principal disciples.

The second class comprises the omniscient, attachment-free, supreme souls who lack the above-mentioned specialities. So, they are called 'ordinary omniscient ones' (*sāmānya-kevalins*).

In the Vedic tradition, *Dharmaśāstras* (Hindu Law Books) divide one Time-cycle into four divisions called *Yugas* (Ages); they are *Kṛtayuga, Tretāyuga, Dvāparayuga* and *Kaliyuga.* Each succeeding Age is having less duration than that of the immediately preceding one. It is also supposed that the regularly descending length of the Ages represents a corresponding physical and moral deterioration in the people who live during each Age, *Kṛta* being called the 'golden' and *Kali* or the present Age the 'iron' age. Similarly, according to the Jainas, Cycle of Time ceaselessly and eternally moves on. It consists of two halves. One half (called *utsarpiṇī*) represents the period of progress with the gradual increase in the life-span, physical strength, prosperity, happiness, etc. And the other half (called *avasarpiṇī*) represents the period of decadence with the gradual decrease in the life-span, etc. Either of these halves is divided into six parts called '*aras*'. At present India and other regions are in the fifth part of the descending half-cycle; this fifth part corresponds to *Kaliyuga. Tīrthaṅkaras* flourish in the third and the fourth parts of either half-cycle. *Tīrthaṅkaras* and the ordinary omniscient ones are never born again in this transmigratory world, once they attain the state of absolute freedom from embodiment. So, we have to understand that those who become *tīrthaṅkaras* are not different incarnations of one Supreme Soul or God, but that they are souls different from one another. The Jaina philosophy does not accept the principle that after having attained absolute freedom, a soul comes again in this world in the form of incarnation.

As already stated, nine reals constitute the subject-matter of the Jaina philosophical works. These nine reals are—*jīva* (soul), *ajīva* (non-soul), *puṇya* (auspicious karmic matter), *pāpa* (inauspicious karmic matter), *āsrava* (inflow of karmic matter), *saṁvara* (stoppage of the inflow of karmic matter), *bandha* (bondage of soul with the inflowed karmic matter), *nirjarā* (partial dissociation of the bound karmic matter from soul) and *mokṣa* (total and absolute dissociation of the bound karmic matter from soul).

SOUL (JĪVA)

Soul is not amenable to sense perception as the physical objects are. But it can be known through the simple experience of self-awareness. A body (being a statue made of physical elements, viz., earth, etc.) is insentient. Hence it cannot have feelings: 'I am happy', 'I am unhappy'. If the body be soul, then why does the body treated as a 'corpse' not have the light of cognition? And why is such a body not considered to be a sentient being? As a matter of fact, the qualities, viz., cognition, desire, feeling, etc., are not found in the dead body. This proves that the body is not the substratum of these qualities. So some other substratum should be there for these qualities to reside in. The name given to this other substratum is 'soul' (='*ātman*'), whereas the body constituted of elements of matter, viz., earth, etc.[1], is physical and hence insentient. The physical body being insentient cannot be the substratum of the qualities of cognition, desire, feeling, etc., just as the physical objects like pots, clothes, etc., being insentient cannot be the substrata of these qualities.

There are five sense-organs in a body. But the soul who uses them as instruments is different from them. It cognises colour, etc., through the instrumentality of the sense-organs. It sees colour with the eyes, experiences taste with the tongue, grasps smell with the nose, hears words with the ears and cognises touch with the skin. To illustrate, one makes a writing pen with a knife, but the maker and the knife are different; one cuts grass with a sickle, but the cutter and the sickle are different; one sees a pot with the instrumentality of a lamp, but the seer and the lamp are different. Similarly, the soul cognises colour, etc., with the sense-organs, but the cogniser, the soul, is different from the sense-organs which it uses as instruments of cognition. The soul requires the assistance of the sense-organs as instruments to cognise physical things but on that account the sense-organs, the instruments of cognition, and the soul having cognition through their instrumentality cannot be regarded as one. A dead body does have five sense-organs, yet it cognises nothing through them. Why? It is because the soul that cognises things through sense-organs is different from the sense-organs. Moreover, it should be borne in mind that there are five sense-organs in a body; now if we regard them as souls, there will be an undesirable contingency of there being five souls in one body.

We know that a blind man remembers the things seen by him in the past when he was not blind. If sense-organs were souls, this phenomenon will not be possible. Things seen by the visual sense-organ in the past can be remembered neither by the visual sense-organ nor by any other sense-organ—not by the visual sense-organ because it is not existent, nor by any other sense-organ because it is a rule that only the one who has seen

1. Earth, water, fire and air.

the things in the past can remember those things later on, and any other sense-organ has not seen the things in the past. To explain the phenomenon in point, we have to posit some entity that has seen the things in the past and remembers those very things later on. This entity is given the name 'soul'. Soul that has seen the thing in the past through the visual sense-organ remembers that very thing later on even when it is devoid of the visual sense-organ. Soul can remember the thing experienced in the past because the past experience has left behind its impressions which the soul continues to retain and carry with it, and it is these impressions, when revived, that give rise to the memory of the thing which was the object of that experience.

We do have the experience in the form 'I saw a particular thing, then I touched it, and after that I smelt and tasted it'. If we reflect a little on this experience, it will become quite clear to us that the one who saw the thing, the one who touched it, the one who smelt it and the one who tasted it are not different but one and the same. Who is that one? It cannot be a visual sense-organ, because its function is only to see and not to touch, etc., also. It cannot be a tactile sense-organ because its function is only to touch and not to see, etc., also. Similarly, it cannot be an olfactory sense-organ or a gustatory sense-organ, because the function of the former is to smell and that of the latter is to taste. This fact doubtlessly proves that the one who sees, touches, smells and tastes is different from sense-organs. And that is the soul.

Soul has no colour whatsoever. So like physical objects, it is not perceived by the visual sense-organ. But on that account it cannot be said that it does not exist. Though physical atoms are not amenable to visual sense perception, their existence is accepted on the basis of inference. Any gross physical object requires its material cause for its production. This material cause, itself being an effect, requires its own material cause for its production. This process will go on *ad infinitum*, if atoms are not posited as the ultimate cause of all physical effects. Thus is proved the existence of physical atoms. Similarly, means other than sense perception prove the existence of the soul. If atoms having physical qualities cannot be grasped by sense perception, how can one expect the soul bereft of physical qualities to be an object of sense perception?

Many times we observe that the acts performed by a person do not give their fruits to that person in his entire life and that the fruits he enjoyed in his entire life are not the fruits of the acts he performed. Many times we see that a good man suffers from poverty and miseries throughout his life, while a rascal wallows in luxuries throughout his life. We cannot account for this anomaly by the seen causes. So we are left with no other alternative but to posit on the one hand a previous life before the present birth, where lie the causes (good or bad acts) of the fruits he experienced in the present birth, as also to posit on the other hand a life beyond the death of the present body, where he will enjoy the fruits of the acts performed in the present birth. And we can easily understand that that which was in the previous birth, is in the present one and will be in the next one, can be neither the body nor the sense-organs, but is something else. This something else is a sentient substance, the soul. And we should also bear in mind that all acts do not bear their fruits in the birth in which they are performed. Acts are momentary. So, how can they give their fruits afterwards when they themselves are non-existent? Acts give their fruits through their impressions which serve as a link between acts and fruits. Though acts are momentary, they leave behind their impressions on the soul. These impressions remain associated with the soul till the soul enjoys their fruits at the destined time. These impressions are material and called '*karma*'.

In this world some are happy while others are miserable, some are intelligent while others are dull, some are rich while others are poor, and some are masters while others are servants. We observe infinite inequalities and differences of this type. These differences are not possible without their causes. Again, an intelligent person does not acquire the desired object in spite of his repeated attempts and strivings, while a dullard gets the desired object even without the least attempt. Innumerable such events happen before our eyes. Twin brothers born of the same mother differ in their growth and development and their life-styles differ widely. What is the cause of these anomalies and differences? They cannot be ungoverned and causeless. There must be some cause that governs all these seemingly causeless differences. This cause is *karma* (material impressions of the past acts). In this way, the wise philosophers have proved the existence of *karma*. And the existence of *karma* automatically proves the existence of soul. It is because *karma* (in the form of fine material particles), which causes happiness or misery to soul is associated with the soul from the beginningless time. And, because of its association with *karma*, the soul transmigrates from birth to birth in the world. Once we are convinced of the existence of soul and *karma* nothing is required to convince us of the existence of life after death (*paraloka*).

If the soul performs auspicious, wholesome and good acts in the present birth, its next birth will be good. On the other hand, if it performs inauspicious, unwholesome and bad acts in the present birth, its next birth will be bad. An auspicious or an inauspicious act leaves behind correspondingly an auspicious or an inauspicious impression upon the soul. This impression is a group of material atoms of a special type. It is called '*karma*'. So *karma* is a group of material atoms of a special type attracted towards and bound with the soul on account of its activity. New *karmas* (groups of material atoms of a special type) go on associating themselves with the soul and old *karmas* go on dissociating themselves from the soul after having given their proper and complete fruits to it. These two processes go on simultaneously every moment. *Karmas* bound with the soul simply continue to exist there inactive till the next birth or through many births without rising to give their fruits. And when they rise to give their fruits, they cause the soul to experience their good or bad fruits. There is a specific period of time within which the soul can completely experience the fruit of a particular *karma* once it has started to experience it. As soon as it completes the experience of the fruit, the *karma* of which it is the fruit gets dissociated from the soul. The present birth and the future births of the soul are governed and conditioned by the force of its accumulated *karmas*.

Thus we have proved the soul as an independent substance different from the body and the sense-organs on the basis of the above-stated logical reasons and arguments as also on the basis of the feeling 'I am happy, I am unhappy' experienced not by the body or the sense-organs but by our innermost self.

Infinite Souls in the World

At this juncture, there is a possibility of the following question to arise in our mind. From the total number of souls that are there in the world, many souls have attained liberation having totally dissociated themselves from the bound *karmas*, many are attaining it and others will attain it in future. Thus, every moment the number of souls in the world goes on decreasing. Will this not result, at one point of time, in the world becoming empty of souls?

Before answering this question, we should bear in mind that no system of Indian philosophy ever endorses a view that the world at some time will become empty of souls; and our mind too refuses to accept such a situation. On the other hand, we cannot even think that the liberated souls are again born in the world and subjected to the round of births and deaths. For, is not liberation an end of all the *karmas*? And if all the *karmas* have once ended, how can there be a return to bondage? If there is a fall from the state of liberation, this state will lose all its charm, greatness and importance, it will no longer remain an attractive goal. So, we should find out the solution of the question in such a way as neither of the two principles—one that the world never gets empty of souls and the other that the liberated souls are never born again in the world—suffers any harm. Scriptures state that the total number of souls in the world gets reduced by the number of souls that attain liberation, yet the world will never be empty of souls, because the souls in the world are *ananta* (infinite) in number. Though no new soul is added to the totality of souls in the world as also the souls in the world are incessantly decreasing in number, yet the number of the souls in the world are so *ananta* (infinite) that at no time in future the number of the souls in the world will become nil. The term '*ananta*' is explained in the scriptures as follows: The minutest indivisible unit of time is called '*samaya*' in the Jaina scriptures. *Samaya* is so minute a time-unit that it is impossible for us to know as to how many *samayas* pass in a second. If we take all the *samayas* of the past and the future time together, their number comes to infinite times infinite. The number of the souls in the world is equal to that of infinite-time-infinite *samayas*. Hence there is no possibility at all of the world becoming empty of souls at any time.

The Classification of Souls

Generally souls are divided into two classes, viz., *saṁsārī* (transmigratory) and *mukta* (liberated). Those who transmigrate in the world from birth to birth are called *saṁsārī*. The term '*saṁsāra*' is derived from the Sanskrit verbal root '*sṛ*' prefixed with the preposition '*sam*'. The meaning of the root '*sṛ*' is 'to go, to wander, to transmigrate'. The preposition '*sam*' prefixed to the root simply strengthens this meaning. So, the meaning of the term '*saṁsāra*' is 'wandering, transmigration'. To wander, to transmigrate in the eightyfour lakh birth-types (species) is *saṁsāra* and one who does so is called *saṁsārī*. Or, the meaning of the term '*saṁsāra*' can be 'eightyfour birth-types (species)' or 'four main birth-types (species)'[1].

1. Human existence, animal existence, celestial existence, infernal existence.

Moreover, even one name of the physical body is *saṁsāra.* And those who are attached to their bodies or births (*saṁsāra*) are called *saṁsārī.* The primary sense of the term '*saṁsāra*' being the soul's state of bondage with *karma,* we can very well understand as to what the defining characteristic of the *saṁsārī* (transmigratory) souls is.

We can classify the transmigratory souls in various ways. In one way, they are divided into two main classes—mobile (*trasa*) and immobile (*sthāvara*). Those who can voluntarily move from one place to another in order to seek pleasure and avoid pain are mobile. And those who cannot voluntarily move from one place to another in order to seek pleasure and avoid pain are immobile. The earth-bodied, the water-bodied, the fire-bodied, the air-bodied and the plant-bodied souls are included in the class of the immobile souls. These five types of immobile souls have one sense-organ only and that one sense-organ is invariably the tactile one. Therefore, they are called one-sensed souls. These one-sensed souls are again divided into two classes — the subtle and the gross (*bādara*). The subtle earth-bodied, the subtle water-bodied, the subtle fire-bodied, the subtle air-bodied and the subtle plant-bodied souls are present everywhere in the universe. As their bodies are very subtle, we cannot see them. The gross earth-bodied, the gross water-bodied, the gross fire-bodied, the gross air-bodied and the gross plant-bodied souls are amenable to visual perception. Souls whose bodies are various forms of earth, viz., stone, clay, etc., which have not suffered attacks of friction, collision, cutting, etc., are to be understood as gross earth-bodied souls. Souls whose bodies are various forms of water, viz., well-water, river-water, pond-water, stepwell-water, etc. which are not attacked by fire or not influenced by mixing some other substance with it are to be regarded as gross water-bodied souls. Similarly, souls whose bodies are lamp, fire, lightning, etc., are gross fire-bodied souls. Souls whose bodies are various forms of air that we experience with our skin are gross air-bodied souls. And a tree, its branches, sub-branches, twigs, leaves, flowers, fruits, roots, bulbous roots, etc., are gross plant-bodied souls.[1] When the above-mentioned forms

---

1. Jagdish Chandra Bose, a great Indian scientist, has proved that even plants, etc. have souls by demonstration in scientific experiments.
Modern scientists are of the opinion that all so-called empty spaces are filled with subtle living beings. This view is identical with the one upheld by the Jaina thinkers. Again, a well-known discovery made by the modern scientists long ago is that of a very subtle living being—it is so minute that on a point of a needle a lakh of them can rest easily. Such descriptions are on line with those found in the Jaina scriptures.

of living earth are attacked by cutting, colliding, piercing, baking, etc., souls depart from them leaving them dead and soulless. Similarly, when water is boiled or mixed with sugar, etc., it becomes dead and soulless. And even different forms of vegetation become dead and soulless when they are cut, burnt, etc.

The two-sensed souls have two sense-organs only and these two sense-organs are invariably the tactile and the gustatory. An intestinal worm, a microbe found in water, a leech, an earth worm, etc., fall in the group of two-sensed souls. The three-sensed souls have three sense-organs only and these three sense-organs are invariably the tactile, the gustatory and the olfactory. A louse, a bug, a large black ant, a large red ant, etc., are the instances of the three-sensed souls. The four-sensed souls have four sense-organs only and these four sense-organs are invariably the tactile, the gustatory, the olfactory and the visual. A fly, a mosquito, a locust, a scorpion, a bee, etc., are the instances of the four-sensed souls. The five-sensed souls have all the five sense-organs, that is, the above-mentioned four plus the auditory organ. These five-sensed souls are divided into four classes — a class of humans, that of animals including birds, reptiles, serpents, mongoose, etc., that of gods dwelling in heavens and that of infernal beings dwelling in hells.

The class of mobile souls[1] comprises the two-sensed, the three-sensed, the four-sensed and the five-sensed souls.

Thus, all the transmigratory souls are exhausted by the two classes, viz. one of the mobile souls and the other of the immobile souls, when both are taken together.

INSENTIENT REAL (AJĪVA)

All the objects that are bereft of sentiency fall under the class of insentient reals. There are five insentient reals — medium of motion (*dharma*),

1. The air-bodied and fire-bodied souls move from one place to another. Thus, in respect of motion they are similar to the souls having two or more sense-organs. So, sometimes they are figuratively or secondarily considered to be mobile. But primarily and actually they are not mobile, because though they exhibit motion, their motion is not purposive, that is, it is not undertaken by them with a specific purpose of attaining pleasure and avoiding pain. This purposive motion is possible only in the case of souls having two or more sense-organs. So, all one-sensed souls are immobile, because their motion is not voluntary. On the other hand, the souls having two or more sense-organs are mobile because they exhibit voluntary motion.

medium of rest (*adharma*), space (*ākāśa*), matter (*pudgala*) and time (*kāla*). These five are substances. Together with the sentient substance soul, they make six substances.

For the medium of motion and the medium of rest the Jaina thinkers use the terms '*dharma*' and '*adharma*' respectively, which ordinarily mean auspicious *karmas* (*puṇya*) and inauspicious *karmas* (*pāpa*) respectively. Medium of motion and medium of rest are two substances. Like space they pervade the entire universe and are devoid of physical qualities. These two substances are not even mentioned in any philosophical work of the non-Jaina systems of Indian philosophy. But the Jaina philosophical works treat of them. Just as all scholars recognise space as a substance whose special function is to give room to other substances, even so the Jaina thinkers posit these two substances to serve some specific purpose.

Medium of Motion (Dharma)

We observe physical objects and living beings moving from one place to another. Though they are inherently capable of motion, they cannot move without some assisting cause. And this assisting cause is the medium of motion. To illustrate, a fish has inherent capacity to move from one place to another, but it cannot do so without the assistance of water.

Medium of Rest (Adharma)

A tired traveller has inherent capacity to stop his motion but he will not stop on the way, unless he finds a shade of a tree. Here the shade of the tree serves as an assisting cause for his stoppage of motion. Similarly, though physical objects and living beings have inherent capacity to stop their motion, they cannot stop their motion without some assisting cause. And this assisting cause is the medium of rest.

Souls and physical objects are the independent agents of motion as also of stoppage-of-motion. They by their own nature move or rest. But that they require the assistance of some other force or principle is accepted by even the modern scientists. It is noteworthy that the Jaina thinkers have posited, from the very ancient times, the medium of motion and the medium of rest as two assisting causes of motion and rest respectively. It is to be borne in mind that according to the Jaina thinkers, the medium of motion does not itself impart motion to the physical objects and souls or set them in motion. Similarly, the medium of rest does not itself urge them to stop motion and to rest. But they passively assist them when the latter themselves undertake motion or rest.

Space (Ākāśa)

For the Jaina thinkers, space is an independent substance. It is devoid of colour, odour, taste and touch. It is infinite in extent. It is present everywhere, it stretches not only over the universe, but also far beyond it over the non-universe. All other substances are confined to the universe only. Thus, no substance is so extensive as the space substance is. The pervasiveness of space is infinite. Space is one in number. It is one and will remain one for ever. As it is present everywhere in the universe, the possibility of movement from one place to another is rejected in its case.

The function of space is to offer room to other substances. Other substances exist by their own nature. There is no doubt about it. But they require something to exist in. They do exist by themselves. But wherein do they exist? They exist in space. Their existence is not the same as space. Nor is space an aspect of them. It is a fundamental substance different from them. Thus, space is a universal container in which all other substances are contained.

That space which is related to the universe is called the universe-space (*lokākāśa*) and that which is beyond it is called the space-beyond-universe (*alokākāśa*). The special condition which gives rise to this division of space into the universe-space and the space-beyond-universe is the presence or otherwise of the two substances, viz. the medium of motion (*dharma*) and the medium of rest (*adharma*). These two substances are present in all directions and that region which is covered by their presence is given the name 'universe' ('*loka*'). And the region which falls outside this universe is given the name 'region-beyond-universe' ('*aloka*'). As already stated, it is only with the assistance of these two substances that souls and material objects move from place to place and rest. As these two substances are absent in the region-beyond-universe, there exists neither an atom nor a soul therein. And neither an atom nor a soul can cross the limit of the universe and move into the region-beyond-universe, because the region-beyond-universe is devoid of these two substances. Then, what is there in the region-beyond-universe? There is nothing in it. It is simply of the form of pure space. That pure space in which at no place is present either an atom or a soul or a physical object is the space-beyond-universe.

There is yet one more logical argument to prove the division of space into the universe-space and the space-beyond-universe through the presence or otherwise of the two substances, viz. the medium of motion and the medium of rest. It is as follows: The Jaina scriptural principle is that the soul moves upward as soon as it becomes completely free from all material karmic atoms. To illustrate this point, the Jaina scriptures give an instance of a gourd. The gourd pasted with clay, sunk in water, at once comes up on the surface of water as soon as the clay is completely washed away from it. Similarly, the soul bound with material karmic atoms becomes bodyless and moves upward as soon as it completely dissociates itself from all those material karmic atoms. But what is the limit of its upward motion? Where will this upward motion end? This is an important question. The answer to it cannot be found unless the division of space into the universe-space and the space-beyond-universe through the presence or otherwise of the medium of motion and the medium of rest is accepted. The acceptance of this division of space offers a solution of the problem posed. It is because now we can say that the medium of motion, the assisting cause of motion, is present in the upward direction up to the highest point of the universe, so the upward motion of the soul freed from material karmic atoms stops as soon as it reaches the highest upward limit of the universe and there it stays; beyond that limit the medium of motion being absent it cannot move further. If these two substances were non-existent and consequently no division of space into the universe-space and the space-beyond-universe were possible, then the questions as to where the upward motion of the liberated soul stops and as to where it rests could never be answered satisfactorily.

Matter (Pudgala)

All physical objects from an atom to the grossest object are given the technical name '*pudgala*'. This term '*pudgala*' is a compound formed from the two verbal roots, viz. '*pur*' and '*gala*', the meaning of the former is 'to fill, to augment', that is, 'to conjoin, to integrate', and that of the latter is 'to decay, to wane', that is, 'to disjoin, to disintegrate'. The two processes of integration and disintegration we experience in our bodies and physical objects are incessantly going on. Every moment some free atoms get integrated into an aggregate and simultaneously some integrated atoms get disintegrated from it. Again, this name '*pudgala*' is meaningfully applicable to even an atom as it integrates itself into and disintegrates itself from another atom or the aggregate.

An atom is the ultimate unit of matter (*pudgala*). The object that comes into being as a result of the combination of atoms is called an aggregate (*skandha*).

To have the physical qualities of touch, taste, smell and colour is the nature of matter. This constitutes its corporeality (*mūrtatā*). Corporeality means the state of an assemblage of all the four physical qualities, viz. touch, taste, smell and colour. For the corporeal, even the term '*rūpī*' ('one having *rūpa*') is used. But here '*rūpī*' does not mean 'one having *rūpa* (colour) alone'; here it means 'one having *rūpa* (colour), etc.'. From this it becomes quite clear that the reason why all the substances except matter are called *arūpī* (devoid of *rūpa*) is not that they are devoid of nature ('*rūpa*' also means 'nature'). If they were really devoid of any nature whatsoever, they would be absolutely non-existent and unreal like a hare's horn. As a matter of fact, each of them has its own specific nature, but it being bereft of four physical qualities is called *arūpī*.

Touch is admitted to be of eight types, viz. hard, soft, heavy, light, cold, hot, unctuous and arid. Taste is of five types, viz. pungent, bitter, astringent, sour and sweet. Smell is of two types, viz. good smell and bad smell. Colour is of five types, viz. black, green, red, yellow and white. Thus, the types of all the four physical qualities are twenty in all. But each of these twenty types of physical qualities again has numerable, innumerable and infinite sub-types when viewed from their different degrees of intensity.

Physical objects having soft touch do not exhibit the same degree of softness. They have different degrees of softness. On this account, though generally speaking the soft touch is one, it is divided into numerable, innumerable and infinite types according as the degrees of intensity it exhibits. Similarly, the same logic is applicable to the hard touch and the modes of taste, etc.

Sound, light, shadow, hot radiation and darkness are the forms of matter.

According to the Jaina thinkers, all atoms are qualitatively the same. There are no four classes of atoms. Atoms combine to form an aggregate when they manifest the required degrees of cohesiveness and aridness. The combinatory urge in atoms is not due to external agency but to their degrees of cohesiveness and aridness. Atomic combination is of two types —one giving rise to dimension and shape and the other not. The Jaina thinkers recognise the possibility of an aggregate occupying that much space which a free atom occupies.

Time (Kāla)

Time is experienced by all. A new thing becomes old, an old one decays and a decayed one is at last destroyed. A boy grows into a young man, a young man becomes old and an old man at last dies. A future event becomes present and a present one becomes past. All this is the result of time substance. Ever new forms, different transformations and varied changes are due to time. Time substance is posited to account for the incessant minute imperceptible changes as well as perceptible gross changes. Without it these changes would not take place as it is their auxiliary or assisting cause. Though other substances are by nature capable of undergoing changes, some auxiliary or general cause like time substance should be posited to help them undergo changes.

Space-Point (Pradeśa)

Medium of motion, medium of rest, space and matter — these four insentient substances and one sentient substance soul are possessed of many space-points. A space-point means the most subtle (that is, indivisible ultimate) unit. All understand that the ultimate indivisible units of physical objects like a pot, a piece of cloth, etc. are atoms. And these atoms are called space-points so long as they are integrated into the whole (*avayavī*). But when they are disintegrated from it and are free, they are called atoms. In other words, when atoms are in a free state, they are called atoms (*paramāṇu*); but when they are in an integrated state, they are called space-points (*pradeśa*). The space-points of the above-mentioned four non-physical substances are of a special type. They are mutually absolutely inseparable and form a perfect unity. They are never disintegrated or separated from their substances as those of a physical object like a pot are. They are identical with their substance; they together form an impartite unity. The four substances under consideration which have space-points of this type are eternal.

Substances of the Nature of a Collection of Space-points, i.e., Extended Substances (Astikāya)

A soul, medium of motion and medium of rest possess innumerable space-points, each. Space has infinite space-points. Space confined to the universe has innumerable space-points, while space which is there in the region-beyond-universe has infinite space-points. A physical object may have numerable, innumerable or infinite space-points. Thus, these five substances are of the form of a collection of space-points. Hence they are called '*astikāya*'. The term '*astikāya*' is formed of two words '*asti*' and '*kāya*'. Here '*asti*' means 'space-point' ('*pradeśa*') and '*kāya*' means 'a collection'. So, the meaning of the term '*astikāya*' is 'that which is of the nature of a collection of space-points'. In other words, it ultimately means 'that which has extension'.

Medium of motion, medium of rest and space are one, each. In other words, each of them has one individual or instance only. The sentient substance soul has infinite individuals or instances. All living beings have their different souls; each one has its own soul. Matter is a substance having infinite instances in the form of atoms.

Time is not of the nature of a collection of space-points. In its case 'a space-point' may mean a moment. There is no possibility of two moments existing simultaneously and hence there is no possibility of a collection of moments. A past moment has already been destroyed and a future one has not come into existence, only the present moment is existent. So, how could there be a collection of moments? It is quite impossible. All the divisions of time, viz. hour, day, night, month, year, etc. are made after having mentally collected the non-existent moments together. As time is but a moment, the term '*astikāya*' is not applicable to it. In other words, time is not an extended substance.

In all, there are six substances recognised in the Jaina philosophy — five extended and one non-extended, as described above. For those who do not regard time as an independent substance, there are five substances only.

AUSPICIOUS *KARMA* (*PUṆYA*) AND INAUSPICIOUS *KARMA* (*PĀPA*)

The term '*karma*' means mental, vocal or bodily act as also a trace or an impression that the act leaves behind on the soul. In the present context, the term '*karma*' has the latter meaning and consequently the meaning 'the karmic matter constituting the trace'. The trace is material in nature and bears its fruit in future in this or the next life. The karmic matter of the form of the trace gets bound to the soul on account of its mental, vocal or bodily acts and gets dissociated from it as soon as it bears its fruit. It remains bound with the soul till its fruition is fully experienced by it.

The formulation of *karma* theory is the result of the Jaina thinkers' sincere efforts to find answers to the following questions: All souls are equal by nature. What causes inequality in them? What explains the born diversity among different individuals? What is it that gives rise to unequal and vastly diverse states experienced by even one and the same individual at different times?

The consistency of the life of a soul — the life stretched in the three divisions of time — depends on *karma.* Again, the theory of rebirth is a natural corollary of the theory of *karma.* Every act must necessarily be followed by its consequence. If the consequences of our acts have not been experienced in the present life, they necessarily demand a future life for fruition.

The auspicious acts form and leave behind auspicious traces on the soul. The auspicious traces, material in nature, lead the soul to the attainment of the means of happiness, viz. health, wealth, fame, good family, long life, etc. On the other hand, the inauspicious acts form and leave behind inauspicious traces on the soul, and these inauspicious traces, material in nature, lead the soul to the attainment of the means of misery. The karmic matter constituting the auspicious traces is regarded as auspicious and the karmic matter constituting the inauspicious traces is regarded as inauspicious.

Karmic matter is classified into eight fundamental types. They are: knowledge-covering (*jñānāvaraṇa*) *karma*, vision-covering (*darśanāvaraṇa*) *karma*, feeling-producing (*vedanīya*) *karma*, deluding (*mohanīya*) *karma*, longevity-determining (*āyuḥ*) *karma*, body-making (*nāma*) *karma*, status-determining (*gotra*) *karma* and obstructive (*antarāya*) *karma.* We shall deal with them later on. Of these eight types, knowledge-covering *karma*, vision-covering *karma*, deluding *karma* and obstructive *karma* are inauspicious because knowledge-covering *karma* veils the faculty of knowledge, vision-covering *karma* obscures the faculty of vision, deluding *karma* deludes and confuses the soul — that is, obstructs right inclination and right conduct — and obstructive *karma* obstructs our attainment of the desired objects. Each of the remaining four types of *karmas* are auspicious or inauspicious. Body-making *karma* causing bad and repulsive bodily traits, longevity-determining *karma* causing longevity of the infernal class of beings, status-determining *karma* responsible for the low status, feeling-producing *karma* producing painful experiences — these are inauspicious *karmas*. Contrary to them, body-making *karma* causing good and attractive bodily traits, status-determining *karma* responsible for the high status, feeling-producing *karma* producing pleasant experiences and longevity-determining *karma* causing longevity of the heavenly class of beings, human class of beings and animal class of beings—these are auspicious *karmas*.[1]

INFLOW OF KARMIC MATTER (ĀSRAVA)

The entire universe is full of karmic matter. The inflow of karmic matter into a soul takes place on account of the soul's activities. So, these activities themselves are also regarded as the inflow of karmic matter.

Through soul's mental, vocal and bodily activities the karmic matter is attracted towards the soul, flows into it and gets bound with it. The auspicious activities cause the bondage of auspicious karmic matter, and the inauspicious activities cause the bondage of inauspicious karmic matter. The bodily operations like violence, theft, incontinence, etc. are cases of inauspicious bodily activities; those like mercy, donation, continence, etc. are cases of auspicious bodily activities. True but blameworthy speech, false speech, harsh speech and the like are cases of inauspicious vocal activities; blameless true speech, soft speech, civilised speech and the like are cases of auspicious vocal activities. Thinking ill of others, thinking of injuring others and the like are cases of inauspicious mental activities; thinking well of others, feeling happy on seeing others flourish and the like are cases of auspicious mental activities.

The auspicious or inauspicious character of bodily or vocal activities depends on the auspicious or inauspicious character of the accompanying mental operation or state. The main cause of the bondage of auspicious or inauspicious karmic matter with soul is mental activity. And the vocal and bodily activities are regarded as causes of bondage insofar as they assist mental activity.

STOPPAGE OF THE INFLOW OF KARMIC MATTER (SAṀVARA)

For the stoppage of the inflow of karmic matter into a soul, the Sanskrit term '*saṁvara*' is used. This term is formed from two words, viz. a prepo-

---

1. It is to be specially noted that not only the *karma* of auspicious type is regarded as auspicious but also that *karma* which undergoes the process of voluntary partial dissociation and thereby secures the reduction of the amount of karmic atoms is regarded as auspicious. Study the following statements of Ācārya Hemacandra.
   (i) *nirjarā saiva rūpam yasya tasmāt, puṇyād iti puṇyam na prakṛtirūpam, kintu karmalāghavarūpam, tasmāt/—Yogaśāstra, Vṛtti* on IV. 107.
   (ii) *puṇyataḥ karmalāghavalakṣaṇāt śubhakarmodayalakṣaṇāc ca/—Ibid., Vṛtti* on IV. 108.

sition '*sam*' and a verbal root '*vṛ*'. The verbal root '*vṛ*' prefixed with the preposition '*sam*' yields the meaning 'to stop, to prevent'. Highly spiritual internal states of the soul, causing control and restraint of the mental, vocal and bodily activities, effect the stoppage of the inflow of karmic matter. So, even those spiritual internal states as also the controlled and restrained threefold activities themselves are regarded as the stoppage of the inflow of karmic matter. The Sanskrit term '*āsrava*' is derived from the verbal root '*sṛ*' meaning 'to ooze', prefixed with the preposition '*ā*'. Hence, it means the inflow of the karmic matter into the soul, or the activities through which this inflow takes place. And the prevention of the inflow is called '*saṁvara*'. The higher the spiritual stage, the thinner is the inflow of karmic matter. The greater the cessation of the inflow of karmic matter, the higher is the spiritual plane attained by the soul.

BONDAGE OF THE KARMIC MATTER WITH SOUL (BANDHA)

Bondage is of the nature of interpenetration of karmic matter and soul like the interpenetration of milk and water in a mixture of the two. Karmic matter is present everywhere in the universe. The entire universe is thickly stuffed with it. There are numerous groupings of matter. From among them the grouping that has the capacity to undergo transformation of the form of *karma* is attracted towards itself by the soul through its threefold activities and then bound to itself by it. The karmic matter gets stuck to the soul due to its unctuousness of attachment, aversion and delusion.

At this juncture there arises a question: why should a naturally 'dry' (passionless), i.e., pure soul come to acquire an adventitious unctuousness of the passions of attachment and aversion? To find a satisfactory answer to this question it is necessary to ponder over it deeply and sharply. We cannot say that the soul had acquired this unctuousness at a certain point of time. It is because this involves the admission of the view that before the acquisition of the unctuousness the soul was in its pure and pristine natural state. But then there is no reason why a naturally pure, i.e., 'dry' (passionless) soul should come to acquire the adventitious unctuousness of passions. If we accept the possibility of a naturally pure, i.e., 'dry' (passionless) soul starting at some point of time to assume impure states of unctuousness of passions then why even the liberated souls who have attained perfect purity be not again infected with the impurities of attachment and aversion? How can we avert the undesirable contingency of the regeneration of the states of attachment and aversion in the soul who has attained the perfect purity in the state of liberation with the spiritual efforts, if we once concede that the soul in the past was pure and at some point of time it assumed the impure states of attachment and aversion? This proves that the impure states have not started at some point of time but are beginningless. The impure states of attachment and aversion are not natural to the soul in the sense that they depend on *karma.* This is because they rise in the soul bound with karmic matter. And this state of bondage is also beginningless.

One may ask: How can that which has no beginning have an end? The Jaina philosopher answers that this question has no force. It is a matter of experience that the dross found in an ore of gold is as old as gold itself, still it is found to be removed by the action of an alkaline substance or by calcination in a sealed vessel. Exactly like this, the removal of the karmic matter, though bound with the soul from beginningless time, is possible by the practice of spiritual discipline. The dross covers the natural glitter of gold from the beginningless time. Similarly, *karmas* (karmic matter) cover the pure sentience from the beginningless time. When the dust is removed from the glass with cloth, the glass shines. Similarly, when the karmic impurities are removed from the soul, it shines with pure light of sentience.

From this it follows that we cannot say that first the soul was alone and only afterwards the *karma* came into existence. Nor can we say that first the *karma* alone was there and only afterwards the soul came into existence because this will prove the soul to be producible and destructible, which idea is repugnant to the spiritual thinkers, also because the existence of *karma* is impossible in the absence of the soul. Thus, when these two alternatives are found untenable, the only third alternative that the soul and the *karma* both are bound together from the beginningless time gets automatically established. That is, in the remote past there was not a time when there was soul alone, nor the time when there was *karma* alone, but both were bound together from time immemorial.

Types of soul's activities govern the types of *karmas* (karmic matter). In the Jaina scriptures, eight basic types of *karmas* are enumerated. They are: knowledge-covering *karma,* vision-covering *karma,* feeling-producing *karma,* deluding *karma,* longevity-determining *karma,* body-making *karma,* status-determining *karma* and obstructive *karma.* Soul in its real nature is the highest spiritual light—the pure Existence, the pure Sentience and the pure Bliss. But on account of the coverings of the above-mentioned *karmas*, its original nature is not manifested. This results in soul's transmigratory wanderings and their attendant miseries and troubles.

Now let us describe eight basic types of *karma*:

1. Knowledge-covering *karma*, as its name suggests, covers soul's faculty of knowledge. The stronger this *karma,* the greater is the covering of the faculty of knowledge. The lesser or weaker this *karma*, the more developed is the intellect. The degree of intellect is in direct proportion of the degree of subsidence or elimination of this *karma*. Therefore, the intellectual diversity noticed in the world is due to the different degrees of subsidence or elimination of the karmic matter of this type. When the karmic matter of this type is totally eliminated from the soul, faculty of knowledge is manifested in its fullness or perfection — this is what we call omniscience.

2. Vision-covering *karma*, as its name suggests, covers the soul's faculty of vision. There is not much difference between knowledge and vision. The initial cognition that grasps the object concerned in a generic form is given the name 'vision' ('*darśana*'). It is like a cognition that a man has of an object when he sees it from a distance. And the cognition which, arising in the wake of vision, grasps that very object in a specific form is given the name 'knowledge' ('*jñāna*'). Sleep, blindness, deafness, etc. are the fruits of this *karma*.

3. Feeling-producing *karma*, as its name suggests, produces everchanging experiences of happiness and unhappiness through sense-organs and mind. Accordingly it has two sub-types, viz. the one producing experiences of happiness alone and the other producing experiences of unhappiness alone.

4. Deluding *karma* generates delusion in the soul with regard to wife, son, friend and the things it likes. This *karma* generates attachment and aversion towards worldly objects. Blinded by delusion and its attendant attachment and aversion the soul loses its sense of discrimination, it cannot differentiate the good from the evil, the auspicious acts from the inauspicious ones. It is like a man who is under the influence of liquor. The drunken man loses all his power of understanding the situation and as a result becomes infatuated and goes astray and does such despising and disgusting acts as he would not have done if he were not infatuated by liquor. Similarly, a living being greatly infected with delusion is unable to understand the reality as it is and under the sway of nescience and

wrong understanding gropes in the dark and in vain. Workings and designs of delusion are beyond the ken of our understanding. In support of this fact, one will come across in the world infinite queer and unintelligible instances. Of the eight *karmas*, this plays a leading role in blurring and perverting all-knowing all-seeing pure nature of the soul. This *karma* is of two types — one that obstructs soul's natural inclination towards what is real and good, and the other that hampers its good and wholesome conduct.

5. Longevity-determining *karma* has four types according as it determines the longevity of celestial beings, of human beings, of animal beings and of infernal beings. A man whose legs are bound with a chain cannot move to some other place till he is not freed from the chain. Similarly, a soul who is bound with a particular longevity-determined *karma* and born in a particular birth with longevity determined by that *karma* cannot transmigrate to another birth till it has not fully enjoyed that determined longevity of the present birth.

6. Body-making *karma* has many types and sub-types. In short, on this *karma* depends the beauty or ugliness of the body, good or bad bodily structure, fair or dark complexion, attractive or harsh voice, fame or infamy, etc. Again, on account of this *karma*, the soul is born in one of the four main species, viz. gods, humans, animals and hell-beings and in one of the five classes of beings, viz. the one-sensed up to the five-sensed. This *karma* creates varied bodily forms, colour-shades and structures just as a painter creates varied good or bad pictures. On account of the auspicious body-making *karma*, the soul acquires good body. And on account of the inauspicious body-making *karma*, it acquires bad body.

7. Status-determining *karma* is divided into two sub-types, viz. the higher-status-determining and the lower-status-determining. On account of this *karma*, the soul is born in the praiseworthy or blameworthy country, in the cultured or uncultured family.

8. Obstructive *karma* puts obstacles in soul's efforts to achieve various objectives. Though one knows religion and is rich, one cannot donate because of the operation of this *karma*. Though one is not free from attachment towards worldly objects and is rich and has all the means of pleasure at his disposal, one cannot enjoy those objects on account of this *karma*. Though one intelligently makes various attempts, one cannot succeed in his business or incurs losses on account of this *karma*. Though one possesses healthy body, one cannot make use of it and become

industrious on account of this *karma*.

In brief we have treated of *karma*. The degree of passions with which a soul performs an act determines the degree of stickiness of bondage of the karmic material atoms with the soul as well as the degree of goodness or otherwise of the fruit of the karmic material atoms bound with the soul. At the time of the formation of bondage of the karmic matter with soul, the duration, that is, how long this karmic matter will remain stuck to the soul, is also bound. We have not to understand that the *karma* rises to give its fruit as soon as it is bound. We all know that crop does not appear as soon as the seeds are sown. Similarly, *karma* rises to give its fruit after certain period of time since it is bound with the soul. And there is no rule as to how long this process of enjoying the fruit of a particular *karma* will continue because the bound duration changes according to the changes in the mental states.

Karma is bound not in one way only. Some *karma* is bound very tight, some tight, some moderately tight and some loose. That *karma* which is bound very tight is known by the name '*nikācita*' in the Jaina scriptures. Mostly one cannot escape from the enjoyment of the fruit of this *karma*. Regarding other *karmas*, one can free oneself from them even without enjoying their fruits, if one practises meditation and spiritual discipline.

Let us think somewhat more clearly about the bondage following the inflow.

There are numerous groupings of material atoms. From among them the grouping that possesses the capacity to undergo transformation of the form of *karma* is received into itself by a soul and is bound by it to its constituent units in a particular fashion. That is to say, even while being non-physical (*amūrta*) by nature a soul has become akin to something physical since it has been associated with physical *karma* from beginningless time; and it is as such that it receives into itself the karmic material atoms that are physical. The physical karmic atoms are attracted towards the soul through its mental, vocal and bodily activities; then they are stuck to it due to the unctuousness of passions as are the dust particles stuck to the wet leather when brought there by air. There takes place interpenetration of the karmic material atoms and the units of soul like the interpenetration of milk and water in a mixture of the two. This is called bondage. That the karmic material atoms received by the soul undergo transformation of the form of *karma* means that at that time four characteristics are produced in them, the four characteristics being nature, duration, intensity and quantity.

It is these characteristics that constitute the types of bondage. Thus, the types of bondage are four, viz. bondage in respect of nature (*prakṛtibandha*), bondage in respect of duration (*sthitibandha*), bondage in respect of intensity (*anubhāvabandha* or *rasabandha*), and bondage in respect of quantity (*pradeśabandha*). The nature of the karmic atoms—the nature to cover knowledge, the nature to cover vision, the nature to cause the experience of pleasure or pain, etc. — is generated in them in accordance with the nature of the activity undertaken by the soul. For instance, an act of destroying books, despising the learned, etc., generates the knowledge-covering nature in the karmic atoms bound on account of this act. Thus, the nature of the activity determines the nature of the karmic atoms inflowed into and bound with the soul as a result of this activity. The natures of the karmic atoms are invisible, but they can be known and enumerated simply on the basis of the observable effects produced by them. In one worldly soul or in many of them, innumerable effects are observed to have been produced by the *karmas*. The natures that produce these effects are really innumerable, yet on the basis of the summary classification they have been divided into eight types. Therefore, eight types of *karmas* are enumerated; as for instance, that karmic matter which has the nature to cover knowledge is called knowledge-covering *karma*, the karmic matter which causes the experiences of pleasure and pain is called feeling-producing *karma*.

As already stated, along with the generation of nature-characteristic in the karmic atoms, the duration-characteristic is also generated in those very karmic atoms as soon as they are bound with the soul. That is, a limitation as to time-period up to which the karmic atoms in question obstruct the concerned quality of the soul is produced in those atoms as soon as they are bound.

Again, along with a nature-characteristic there is produced in the karmic atoms the effect-intensity characteristic. In other words, as soon as the karmic atoms are bound, there is generated in them certain speciality on account of which their effect experienced by the concerned soul will have specific intensity — strong, moderate or mild.

All the karmic atoms that are being received by the soul get transformed into diverse natures and hence naturally undergo a corresponding quantitative distribution under each nature. This is what we mean by quantity-characteristic.

As already stated, the nature-characteristic is governed by the nature of activity. The quantity of karmic atoms depends on the degree or intensity of activity. This is so because even passion-free soul binds karmic atoms to itself due to its activities. On the other hand, duration of *karmas* and the intensity of their fruits depend on passions. The stronger the passions, the longer is the duration of *karmas* and the greater is the intensity of their fruits. In other words, the bondage in respect of nature and the bondage in respect of quantity depend on the activity concerned. But the bondage in respect of duration and the bondage in respect of intensity are due to passions. Thus, activity and passion are the two causes of bondage.

Going into the details, one finds five causes of bondage, viz. *mithyātva* (pervert inclination or faith), *avirati* (non-restraint), *pramāda* (carelessness), *kaṣāya* (passions) and *yoga* (activities). *Mithyātva* means lack of faith in the existence of soul or absence of spiritual reflection. *Avirati* means not to desist from vices, violence, etc. and to indulge in the enjoyment of worldly pleasures. *Pramāda* means self-forgetfulness, spiritual lethargy and lack of feeling of regard for virtuous acts. It also means not to remain awake to the memory of what has to be done and what has not to be done. *Kaṣāya* means passions like anger, greed, etc. *Yoga* means activity of mind, speech and body.

Through the mouth of a tunnel, etc., water enters a pond and when that mouth is closed the inflow of water stops. Water enters a boat through holes and when those holes are filled with some proper substance water stops entering the boat. Similarly, activities of mind, speech and body are the entrances through which karmic matter enters the soul, and when these entrances are shut, the karmic matter stops entering the soul. It is a common experience that when we shut windows and doors, the dust does not enter a room and settle on clothes hanging in it. Similarly, when the activities that serve as doors for the entry of the karmic matter are completely arrested, no karmic matter at all enters the soul and sticks to it. This event takes place in the life of the liberated-while-living-in-the-world (*jīvanmukta*) at the last moment when he enters the disembodied state of liberation. Before the attainment of the disembodied state of liberation, he does have a body and consequently activities of mind, speech and body. So through these activities karmic matter does enter his soul and get somewhat bound with it. But the bound karmic matter gets dissociated from his soul the moment it is bound with it, because his soul is completely liberated from passions and spiritual lethargy. It is like the sand which falls off from a dry stick the moment it comes in contact with the stick. It is only when the activities are defiled with passions that the karmic matter gets strongly bound with the soul and remains stuck to it for long. But the liberated-while-living-in-the-world is so called because though he lives in the world he is completely liberated from passions. And as he is absolutely free from passions, the bondage of *karmas* that takes place due to activities only, has almost nil duration and no fruit.

As stated above, though mainly there are two causes of bondage, viz. passions and activities, it is with a view to accounting for the greater or lesser number of *karma*-types bound down in the different *guṇasthānas* (the gradual stages of spiritual progress) that there have been mentioned the four causes of bondage, viz. *mithyātva, avirati, kaṣāya* and *yoga.* Thus, the greater the number of the causes of bondage from among these four present in a *guṇasthāna,* the greater is the number of *karma*-types bound in it; on the other hand, when the causes of bondage are fewer in number, then even the number of *karma*-types bound is also smaller. Adding *pramāda* to these four, the total number of causes comes to five. *Pramāda* is but a type of *asaṁyama* (non-restraint) and so is included in *avirati* or in *kaṣāya*; and it is from this point of view that we can say that the causes of bondage are four. Viewed minutely both *mithyātva* and *avirati* are not essentially different from *kaṣāya*; so in the last count *kaṣāya* and *yoga,* these two are the only causes of bondage.

The removal of the causes of bondage is achieved by the cultivation of their opposite qualities. *Mithyātva* is removed by *samyagdarśana,* that is, true view regarding soul; *avirati* by *virati,* that is, refrainment from vicious acts; *pramāda* by *apramāda,* that is, spiritual vigilance or alertness in the performance of acts one should perform; anger, pride, deceit and greed — these four *kaṣāyas* by forbearance, softness of heart (humility), straightforwardness and contentedness. Activities (*yoga*) of mind, speech and body turn auspicious and pure through restraint and culture, and at last at the highest stage of spiritual development these activities get arrested altogether. Thus, to remove the causes of bondage is called *saṁvara.* And the partial dissociation of the bound *karmas* from the soul is called *nirjarā.*

PARTIAL DISSOCIATION (NIRJARĀ)

The partial dissociation of the bound karmic matter takes place in two ways. One way is as follows: By force of austerity undertaken for a high spiritual objective, the bound karmic matter gets dissociated from the soul even before it has yielded its fruit. The other way is as follows: The dissociation of the bound karmic matter comes about through experiencing its fruit at the destined time. The former partial dissociation is voluntary (*sakāma*) and the latter involuntary (*akāma*). We all know that fruits naturally by themselves become ripe on the tree itself, whereas in a room they are being ripened quickly by employing certain means. Similarly, *karmas* too become ripe by themselves and get dissociated as soon as their fruits are experienced by the concerned soul, or they are made ripe by the heat of austerity and get burnt (dissociated) by the fire of austerity.

If the soul practises austerities with a view to dissociating the bound *karmas*, the latter do get dissociated from the former; otherwise, on the maturity of their time duration, the *karmas* yield their fruits and it is their nature to get dissociated from the soul as soon as their fruits are fully experienced by it. But while experiencing the fruits of *karmas*, if the soul is perturbed, constantly engages itself in bad thoughts and yields itself to passions, then it binds new *karmas*. Thus, this cycle will go on for a very long time or even for infinity. On the other hand, if the fruits of the bound *karmas* are experienced peacefully without yielding oneself to passions, then no new *karmas* are bound to one's soul. If one lives a life of equanimity and thereby gradually develops spiritual purity, then one binds no *karmas* and ultimately becomes totally free from them and consequently from miseries and attains liberation.

As already stated, *saṁvara* (stoppage or prevention) is the opposite of *āsrava* (inflow). It stops the inflow of karmic matter. It is of the nature of internal purity. This internal purity is achieved by means of *gupti, samiti, dharma, anuprekṣā, parīṣahajaya* and *cāritra. Gupti* means spiritually beneficial control of the activities of mind, speech and body. *Samiti* means careful activities inspired by a sense of discrimination. *Dharma* means meritorious qualities, viz., forbearance, softness of heart (humility, modesty), straightforwardness, contentedness, truthfulness, restraint, austerity, renunciation, non-attachment and continence. *Anuprekṣā* means spiritually beneficial deep-reflections. *Parīṣahajaya*[1] means endurance with equa-

1. To endure with equanimity hunger-thirst, honour-dishonour, disease-affliction, not to be carried away by temptations, not to be conceited by one's intelligence or learning, not to feel despair because of one's dull intellect, etc. are instances of *parīṣahajaya*.

nimity. *Cāritra* means the endeavour to remain steady in the state of equanimity by giving up all impure activities. By all these means stoppage of the inflow of the karmic matter is achieved. And the partial dissociation of the bound *karmas* is achieved by means of austerity. Spiritually motivated external and internal austerity leads to the partial dissociation. The internal austerity is divided into six types, viz., *prāyaścitta* (atonement with a view to making clean sweep of defects), *vinaya* (veneration), *vaiyāvṛttya* (rendering service), *svādhyāya* (self-study), *vyutsarga* (renouncement of attachment and other passions) and *dhyāna* (spiritually beneficial mental concentration). Like austerity, even the means of *saṁvara*, viz. *gupti*, etc. cause partial dissociation because they too are basically of the nature of austerity.

As already stated, the *karmas* get dissociated from the soul as soon as they yield their fruits completely and reach the limit of their time-duration. The process of partial dissociation of this type goes on incessantly in the case of worldly souls caught in the cycle of transmigration. But the spiritually beneficial 'partial dissociation' is that which takes place in association with the stoppage of the inflow. And when the process of the stoppage of the inflow of new *karmas* and that of the dissociation of the bound *karmas* reach their acme, the absolute and total dissociation of *karmas*, which characterises liberation, is attained.

Knowledge-covering *karma*, vision-covering *karma*, deluding *karma* and obstructive *karma* — these four *karma*-types are called '*ghāti-karma*' ('destructive *karma*') because they cover or adversely affect the natural qualities of soul. When these four *ghāti-karmas* are removed completely from the soul, the perfect knowledge (omniscience) manifests itself. And when this perfect knowledge manifests itself, the soul becomes perfect seer and perfect knower. Then the concerned soul, at the time of its life-span coming to its end, by its special efforts dissociates even the remaining four *karmas* designated '*aghāti*'[1] or '*bhavopagrāhī*'[2]. And the moment they are totally removed from the soul, the latter moves upward; and within a moment reaches the end of the universe and rests there. This state is called liberation (*mokṣa*).

1. '*Aghāti* is the opposite of '*ghāti*'.
2. '*Bhava*' means transmigratory cycle or body, and that which sustains it is '*bhavopagrāhī*'.

LIBERATION (MOKṢA)

On account of the removal of the causes of bondage as also on account of the dissociation of the bound *karmas*, there takes place the total and absolute dissociation of all *karmas*. This is liberation. In liberation the soul is totally and absolutely free from all *karmas* and consequently established in its pure and pristine state. To move upward on the total and absolute removal of all the *karmas* is the nature of soul. We have already given an instance of a gourd to explain this phenomenon. Moving upward when the soul reaches the end of the universe, it stops there and rests there. It cannot move further upward because beyond the upper limit of the universe there is no medium of motion, an assisting cause of motion, there. Nor can it move back downward, because it has no weight, nor sideways, because it is devoid of any urge generated by *karmas*.

In the state of liberation the soul is absolutely free from all *karmas*, the hampering and defiling adjuncts. And consequently it does not have body, sense-organs and mind altogether. So, bliss or happiness that the liberated experiences is not conditioned and perverted by them. It is eternal, infinite and pure. It is indescribable and matchless. All sensual pleasures taken together of all the three worlds are nothing before the highest natural bliss of the liberated. Some have doubt in their mind: How can there be any pleasure or happiness in the state of liberation because in that state there is total absence of all the means of sensual pleasure? In liberation, there are no gardens, no women, no vehicles, no sweet dishes, etc. But how can we forget that all the miseries a soul experiences in the world are due to its desire for sensual pleasures? Afflictions due to desire for sensual pleasures are the only afflictions that we find in the world. The reason why we enjoy sweet and delicious dishes is that we are afflicted with hunger. When one's belly is full, one does not like even the nectar-sweet food. We do not like to wear in scorching heat of the summer sun those very clothes which we like to wear in winter to remove sufferings due to cold. One who has sat for long, wishes to walk. And one who is tired of walking, wishes to sit and rest. Enjoyment of sensual pleasures at the end appears as unfavourable as it has appeared favourable in the beginning. How queer are the events in this world? Do the objects that we regard as means of happiness produce any positive happiness besides some relief? When a suppurated boil bursts we experience relief. But that is no real positive happiness. It is merely subsidence of pain. The pleasure we experience in sensual enjoyment is nothing but subsidence of pain and distress.[1] And how long does this sensual pleasure continue? It is perishable. It is momentary. Within a moment it disappears and again a whirl-wind of miseries, afflictions and distresses rises. And that slight sensual pleasure is not a positive state of happiness, but simply a negative condition of the absence of misery. Again, it is always mixed with grief and sorrow. Are there in this world only a few distresses and agonies due to attachment and aversion? Are there only a few griefs caused by desires and anger? Are there only a few attacks of diseases and sorrows? Are all these situations pleasant? Is the degree of distress and dissatisfaction not infinite times more than that of peace and satisfaction?

One who is suffering from eczema, experiences pleasure in scratching skin affected with it. Others do not have any desire to scratch skin, nor do they experience pleasure in doing so. Similarly, those who are afflicted with desires arising from delusion or nescience find pleasure in activities inspired by it. But how can others (i.e., those free from delusion, nescience and hence from attachment, or the liberated ones) find pleasure in such activities? Sensual pleasure experienced in the enjoyment of worldly objects is like the pleasure experienced in scratching skin affected with eczema. The liberated souls, who are completely cured of the disease of delusion, always remain blissfully engrossed in their pure natural state. Such bliss as is there in the absolutely pure state of soul (i.e., in liberation) is ultimately real, perfectly pure and completely unmixed with sorrow. The Indian philosophers have given to such supreme souls as are absolutely pure, supremely blissful and perfectly luminous (i.e., omniscient) various names, viz., Śuddha (the Pure), Buddha (the Enlightened), Siddha (the Perfected), Nirañjana (the Unstained), etc.

Liberation is attained through human body only. Heavenly gods are by nature lacking in restraint. So, it is not possible for them to attain the supreme state of liberation directly from their state of godhood. All worldly

---

1. *tṛṣā śuṣyaty āsye pibati salilaṁ svādu surabhi*
kṣudhārtaḥ san śālīn kavalayati śākādivalitān /
pradīpte kāmāgnau sudṛḍhataram āśliśyati vadhūṁ
pratīkāro vyādheḥ sukham iti viparyasyati janaḥ //

Great sage Bhartṛhari's *Vairāgyaśataka*

English rendering: A person drinks sweet fragrant water when his mouth is dry with thirst. He eats rice mixed with vegetables, etc., when he is afflicted with pain of hunger. He strongly embraces a woman, when he is burning with sex desire. He wrongly regards the subsidence of diseases (miseries) as positive happiness.

souls are divided into two, viz., the *bhavyas* and the *abhavyas*. The *bhavyas* are those who are capable of attaining liberation, whereas the *abhavyas* are those who are not capable of attaining liberation.

God (Īśvara)

According to the Jaina philosophical works, the definition of God is as follows: God is that soul who has completely removed all the *karmas*. Thus He is not in any way different from the liberated soul described above. The defining characteristic of Godhood is identical with that of liberation itself. To attain liberation is to attain Godhood. The meaning of the term '*Īśvara*' is 'powerful'. So, the term '*Īśvara*' can very well apply to the soul that has become powerful by attaining its perfectly pure nature constituted of four characteristics, viz., infinite knowledge, infinite vision, infinite power and infinite bliss.

The basic idea of God is one in which He is characterised by the fourfold features of infinite knowledge, infinite vision, infinite power and infinite bliss. Thus, the undisputable nature of God is constituted of these four qualities. We must recognise that every living being is essentially pure and has the capacity of fully developing its own nature. We must recognise, in other words, that every creature is God in potentiality and that when thus developed to perfection, this potential God in a living being appears in its true light, i.e., as a full-fledged God with His fourfold infinities.

Jaina philosophical works maintain that by constant practice of spiritual discipline spiritually right knowledge and right conduct, the means of liberation, gradually develop and ultimately attain perfection. And when they attain perfection, all the coverings get removed and all the bondages are cut off. As a result, the soul's natural qualities of knowledge, etc. get fully manifested. To attain this state is to attain Godhood.[1]

It is a Jaina doctrine that one who steadily advances on the path of spiritual development and makes right efforts to attain the state of absolute purity, i.e., liberation, can well become God. The Jaina thinkers do not

1. The position of a *tīrthaṅkara* is more exalted than that of an ordinary omniscient one (*sāmānyakevalin*), because the former is attended with miraculous events as a consequence of the bound auspicious *karmas* of a special type as also because he is a greatly powerful propounder of Religion. But they are on the same plane so far as the degree of their spiritual development is concerned. As they have attained omniscience and the state of highest purity, they are absolutely equal; hence both of them are supreme souls, Gods.

maintain that there is only one God. For them, there are many Gods. In spite of this, there are reasons for our regarding them as one. As all the perfected souls possess infinite knowledge, infinite vision, infinite power and infinite bliss, they are absolutely alike. And their absolute likeness is the cause of our considering them to be one as also of our applying the term 'one' to them. Again, all the perfected souls being uniformly formless, they interpenetrate with one another as do the lights of different lamps. Hence, they in their indistinguishable and undifferentiable collective form are viewed as one and consequently the term 'one' is applied to them. Waters collected from different rivers and wells, when mixed, interpenetrate with one another. So, we do not recognise their difference and treat them as one. Thus it is not contradictory and improper to regard many perfected souls as one God (*Īśvara* or *Bhagavān*) from this standpoint.

Liberation—Everlasting and Endless

There may arise a doubt in our mind: According to the law that a thing that is produced is necessarily destroyed some time, liberation too must end some time as it is produced; so its being eternal is implausible and untenable.

To remove this doubt from our mind, we should know that liberation is not something producible. Liberation is nothing but the complete removal of all *karmas* from the soul. No new thing (quality) is produced in it, so there is no question of its destruction or end. When the clouds move away, the bright sun shines in its fullness. Similarly, when all the coverings of *karmas* are removed from the soul, all its qualities get fully manifested, in other words, now the soul is manifested fully in its original nature which is luminous sentiency. This is liberation. Now tell us, what is produced here?

The soul that has attained absolute purity on the total removal of all *karmas* never again binds any *karma* and consequently is never born again in this world. Umāsvāti writes: "When a seed is completely burnt, no sprout is produced from it. Similarly, when the seed of *karma* is burnt, the sprout of birth does not grow out of it."[1]

1. *dagdhe bīje yathā'tyantaṁ prādurbhavati nāṅkuraḥ/*
karmabīje tathā dagdhe na rohati bhavāṅkuraḥ//—Tattvārthādhigamaśāstra
Compare with it the following statement from the *Chāndogya-Upaniṣad: na sa punar āvartate, na sa punar āvartate/*

The cycle of birth and death depends on soul's bondage with *karma*, and the bondage depends on the unctuousness of attachment, aversion and delusion. How can those who have become absolutely pure, absolutely free from the defilements of *karmas*, have the unctuousness of attachment, aversion and delusion? And how can there be any possibility of their being bound again with *karmas*? We cannot even imagine such a situation. And it is only on this account that the Jaina thinkers consider it to be absolutely impossible for the liberated soul to be born again in the world and thus to be caught again in the cycle of birth and death.

Total Removal of All Karmas Possible

At this juncture there arises a question: How can the beginningless bondage of *karmas* with soul be ended or destroyed? It is because there is a rule that the beginningless thing can have no end. In answer to this question we are told that every moment new *karmas* are bound and some old *karmas* get dissociated. This means that no bondage of an individual *karma* is beginningless, but the stream of bondages taking place at different consecutive moments has been flowing from beginningless time. In other words, the ever new karmic material atoms incessantly go on binding the soul and hence the stream of the ever new bondages is beginningless. But the bondage of a particular individual *karma* is having a beginning. And as it has a beginning, it is bound to have its end. In other words, the bound individual *karmas* are bound to get dissociated from the soul some time. Thus, no individual *karma* is bound with soul from beginningless time, and consequently no individual *karma* remain bound with it for ever, without end. From this follows that it is quite possible for the soul to dissociate all the bound *karmas* as well as to stop the inflow of the new *karmas* into it by the force of pure concentration. This ultimately makes possible for the soul to eradicate completely all the *karmas* and to become absolutely free from them.

Moreover, if we observe the worldly souls, we find that in some the degree of attachment and aversion is greater, in others it is less. Not only that but even in one and the same individual, at one time they are intense and at another time they are mild. The increase and decrease of any thing remain unaccounted for, unless some cause is posited for them. When the cause of its gradual decrease operates with all its force, the thing is destroyed completely. For instance, the intense cold of the month of Pauṣa gradually decreases as the heat of the sun gradually rises, and it completely disappears when the heat reaches its highest point. Similarly, if the cause of the gradual decrease of attachment and aversion is developed to its fullness, it will completely destroy attachment and aversion. Is there anything objectionable in this? The cause of the decrease of attachment and aversion is wholesome mental activity or reflection. When the wholesome mental reflections become very strong ultimately resulting in the purest mental concentration, then attachment and aversion get completely destroyed. And on their destruction, the soul attains the state absolutely free from the coverings of *karmas*. It is so because on the destruction of attachment and aversion, the knowledge-covering *karma*, the vision-covering *karma* and the obstructive *karma*—these three get completely eradicated. And on the attainment of perfect freedom from all the coverings of *karmas*, the infinite knowledge (omniscience) manifests itself. The whole palace of the worldly existence rests on the two pillars of attachment and aversion. Attachment and aversion are the roots of deluding *karma* or delusion. A kind of palm tree (*tāla-vṛkṣa*) dries up if it is simply pierced with a needle at its top. Similarly, if the roots of all *karmas*, viz., attachment and aversion are cut off, then the entire tree of *karmas* gets dried up and destroyed.

Establishment of the Existence of Omniscience

On the destruction of attachment and aversion, the deluding *karma* gets totally dissociated from the soul. And on the total dissociation of the deluding *karma*, the remaining three *ghātī karmas* get completely eliminated. As a result of this, infinite knowledge (omniscience) gets fully manifested. The following proof is offered for its existence. What does the varying degrees of knowledge observed in different individuals suggest? It suggests that the degree of the manifestation of knowledge is in direct proportion to the degree of the removal of the covering of the *karma*. The greater the degree of the removal of the covering, the greater is the manifestation of knowledge. And when the covering is totally removed, knowledge is manifested fully. Knowledge is not acquired. It is there in the soul. Infinite knowledge is the nature of the soul. Though infinite knowledge is present in all living beings, the degree of its manifestation varies due to the varying degree of the removal of the covering of the *karma*. Thus, the proof of omniscience follows from the proof of the necessity of the final consummation of the progressive development of knowledge. The progressive development must reach its completion somewhere, because this is the way of all progression. Just as magnitude is subject to varying degrees and consequently reaches its highest limit in the sky, so also knowledge which is subject to progressive development owing to various degrees of dissociation of the covering of the *karma*, reaches the highest limit (omniscience) in some person. That person is called 'omniscient' (*sarvajña*), 'all-seer' (*sarvadarśī*), and his knowledge is designated '*kevala-jñāna*' (pure knowledge). The soul can totally remove the defilements of attachment and aversion and consequently can gain absolute purity. And through this perfect purity the light of infinite knowledge manifests itself in all its infinity.

God is not World-creator

One of the Jaina doctrines is that God is not the creator of the world. The Jaina scriptures contend that in the worldly cycle of birth and death, revolving by the force of *karmas*, there can be no place for the creatorship of God, who, according to the Jaina, is absolutely free from attachment and desires. The entire world constituted of the sentient and insentient substances is governed by the laws of Nature. Pleasures and pains experienced by a living being depend on the material traces (*karmas*) left by the acts performed by it. Absolutely pure and attachment-free God is not pleased with some, nor is He displeased with others. This is because He is supreme soul with no taint or defilement whatsoever and absolutely free from attachment.

Worship of God Necessary

Regarding the doctrine of God as not world-creator, there arises a question: What is the use of worshipping such God? That is, if God is free from attachment and consequently is neither pleased nor displeased, then what is the use of worshipping Him? But the Jaina philosophers say that worship of God is not to please Him, but to purify one's own self. It is highly useful and spiritually beneficial to worship God who is absolutely free from attachment and aversion. One should worship such God in order to cleanse one's own soul of attachment and aversion—the only cause of all miseries. The soul is by nature as pure as a crystal. But it is highly tainted with the defilements of attachment, aversion, delusion and desires. The pure crystal assumes the red colour of the red flower placed in its vicinity. Similarly, the soul gets tainted with attachment and aversion as soon as it comes in contact with them. The degree of the influence of the taint depends on the degree of their contact. From this follows the necessity of our seeking and securing good purifying situations as also of our living through them. The nature of attachment-free God is absolutely pure and peaceful. Tainting influences of attachment and aversion are totally absent there. So, by worshipping Him, by contemplating on Him, the feeling of non-attachment arises in the worshipper and gradually advancing on this path, he can ultimately become attachment-free. It is a common experience that in the company of a beautiful woman one experiences feelings of a special type, the sight of a son or a friend generates a feeling of affection and that of an unperturbed and calm monk causes the experience of calmness and mental peace. The company of the good inculcates good qualities; and that of the bad, bad qualities. 'Good company, good influence; bad company, bad influence' so the saying goes. Now, imagine as to how beneficial the company of the attachment-free God can be. What is meant by His company? His company means to recall Him to one's mind, to contemplate on Him, to praise Him and to worship Him. His constant and close company has the purifying influence on the worshipper, with the result that the vicious feelings of attachment and aversion start subsiding. This is the prime and real fruit of worshipping God. He expects nothing from the worshipper, nor does He favour him with something. The devotee worships Him simply to elevate his soul spiritually. Making God an object of his worship and meditation, the devotee earns the proper fruit, viz., internal purity.

One who goes near fire is relieved of shivering pain due to cold simply on account of the nearness of fire. Fire does not call any person, nor does it give any fruit to anybody. Similarly, by the fire of meditation of God the cold of attachment by itself disappears and the fruit of spiritual development or internal purity is attained. Constant recalling of the good qualities of God to mind removes mental impurities, causes the development of internal purity and leads the soul on the path of spiritual progress. The devotee attains this fruit by his own spiritually elevating efforts, and not by the grace of God.

It is true that the person who passes his time in the company of a prostitute acquires bad desert. But who gives him bad desert? To regard the prostitute as a giver of the bad desert is not proper because firstly she does not know what the bad desert is and secondly no one is able to generate bad desert in another person. So, it is only the impurity of one's own mind that is the cause of one's bad desert. This is easily understandable. From this follows the principle that the cause of one's pleasure and pain is one's own *karma* which is ultimately governed by one's mental states. And the means by which one can make mental states good and wholesome, is the worship of God. By making mental states good and wholesome one can achieve spiritual progress and attain happiness and calmness. Thus, worship of God ultimately leads the devotee to spiritual welfare.

In short, according to the Jainas, God is not the creator of the world. For them, He is a perfected soul. He is absolutely pure. He has destroyed all passions and removed all impurities. As a result of this, He manifests infinite knowledge, infinite vision, infinite bliss and infinite power. This is the reason why he is regarded as God. By meditating on his pure qualities, the Jaina reminds himself daily of the possibility of attaining this highest state. He purifies his mind by the contemplation of the pure and strengthens his heart for the uphill journey to liberation. Worship, for the Jaina, is not seeking for mercy and pardon.

CHAPTER 2

JAINA PATH OF PURIFICATION (LIBERATION)

Introductory

We have already given in the first chapter a brief account of the nine reals. Among them the sentient and the insentient substances are the two fundamental reals. The third real is the inflow of the karmic material atoms into the sentient substance, the soul. The inflow takes place as a result of thought activity. The fourth real is the bondage which is nothing but a close connection of the soul and the karmic matter, that is, of the sentient and the insentient substances. The fifth and the sixth reals are the stoppage of the inflow of the karmic matter and the partial dissociation of the bound karmic matter respectively. They are caused by the elevated and bright spiritual states of the soul. The seventh real is the total and absolute dissociation of the karmic matter from the soul. It is called liberation; it is the perfect pure state of the soul. Thus, the five reals beginning with the inflow are covered by the two fundamental reals, viz. the sentient and the insentient substances. The eighth and the ninth reals are the auspicious karmic matter and the inauspicious karmic matter respectively. They are but the bound karmic matter. So, if we include them in the bondage, the total number of reals remains seven only. Just as there is a tradition of nine reals, so also there is a tradition of seven reals.[1] The inflow and the bondage are the causes of worldly existence, whereas the stoppage and the partial dissociation are the causes of liberation. The inflow of the karmic matter, which presents us the means of liberation, is regarded as auspicious. It is considered to be a religion.[2]

---

1. In the *Tattvārthasūtra* (I.4) of Vācaka Umāsvāti there is mention of seven reals.
2. There are three forms of religion (*dharma*), viz., its cause, its nature and its effect. Among them, the righteous activity is the cause of religion. The nature of religion

The knowledge of these nine reals is a must for those who are desirous of liberation. This is the reason why they are called '*tattvas*' ('reals') in the science of liberation. The Jaina philosophy indicates all the objects of the entire world through the mention of the two fundamental reals, the sentient and the insentient, declares liberation as the ultimate goal and shows as to what is conducive to liberation and what is detrimental to it. Bondage (*bandha*) and its cause the inflow (*āsrava*) are opposed to liberation, whereas the stoppage (*saṁvara*) and the partial dissociation (*nirjarā*) are the factors leading to liberation.

The brief treatment of the nine reals has presented the Jaina view about the soul, merit-demerit (*puṇya-pāpa*), life after death, liberation and God. It easily awakens our faith in the path of liberation, the soul, the supreme soul, merit-demerit and rebirth. It will not do to accept sense perception alone. Search of reality is not possible on the basis of sense perception alone. Even the upholder of the view that sense perception is the only means of knowledge has to accept inference of the presence of the unseen fire from the perception of smoke. It is not logical to assert the non-existence of a thing on the basis of its non-perception. There are many things which are beyond the ken of our sense perception. But on that account their non-existence can never be established. A bird is flying in the sky. It soars so high that we are not able to see it. But that does not prove its non-existence. We cannot see our forefathers. But on that account none can boldly declare that they never existed. Water mixed with milk is not seen. But that does not prove its non-existence. Stars are not seen in the sky in the bright light of the sun. But on that account we have no right to declare their non-existence then in the sky. From all

---

has two forms, viz., one form is the inflow of the karmic matter and the other form is the opposite of the inflow. Accumulation of the auspicious karmic matter in the soul is its nature of the form of the inflow. And the dissociation of the accumulated and bound karmic matter is its nature of the form of the opposite of the inflow. And the special good qualities that manifest on that account is the effect of religion. Study the following passages:

1. *dharmaḥ śubhāśrave saṁvare [nirjarāyāṁ] ca antarbhavati/—Yogaśāstra* of Ācārya Hemacandra, *Vṛtti* on II.2
2. *sāmānyena tāvad dharmasya trīṇy eva rūpāṇi draṣṭavyāni bhavanti/ tadyathā—kāraṇaṁ svabhāvaḥ kāryaṁ ca/ tatra sadanuṣṭhānaṁ dharmasya kāraṇam/ svabhāvaḥ punar dvividhaḥ—sāśrāvo'nāśravaś ca/ tatra sāśravo jīve śubhaparamāṇūpacayarūpaḥ, anāśravas tu pūrvopacitakarmaparamāṇuvilayamātralakṣaṇaḥ. . . . kāryaṁ punar dharmasya yāvanto jīvagatāḥ sundaraviśeṣāḥ/—Upamitibhavaprapañcā Kathā, Prathama Prastāva,* p.72.

this we can easily understand that in the world there do exist imperceptible objects just as there exist perceptible ones. To believe in what we ourselves have experienced and declare thoughtlessly false and fictitious what others have experienced is not proper. If someone having heard the description of prosperity of the cities of London, Paris, Berlin and New York by an impartial gentleman who has himself visited and seen them regards it as false and attempts to establish its falsity, then that will be improper on his part. Similarly, to declare as false the principles propounded by the great men more advanced in experience than the ordinary people like us, simply on account of our not seeing, experiencing or knowing them is an act of blasphemy, arrogance and impropriety. From this follows that taking into account the effects of the past meritorious and demeritorious acts, which we can see, and understanding the innumerable diversities of the world and the terrible consequences of delusion, man must try hard to remove the passional defects like anger, etc. He should steadily continue his journey on the path of purity, keeping constantly before his mind's eye the highest aim of spiritual welfare and liberation. Slowly but steadily moving on the right path, a living being never becomes depressed and miserable, but gradually progresses and at last attains the goal. Liberation, that is, the perfect development of the soul is the real aim or goal and everyone—be a layman or a monk—should constantly keep it before oneself and establish it on the centre of one's constant concentration. One should know the path that leads to that final destination. Shunning obstinacy and attachment to one's preconceived notions and cultivating love for the good qualities, one should examine the essence of the scriptures. If one studies scriptures with purely knowledge-seeking intellect and with pure aspiration for the spiritual welfare, one will surely find the spotless path leading to liberation. After knowing it, one should start one's journey on it. One should translate one's knowledge into practice. Knowledge without practice, that is, knowledge which is not put into practice, can never bear fruits. A man who knows theoretically all the movements a swimmer should undertake in water cannot himself swim in water, if he has not cared to put into practice his knowledge and he himself has not learnt those movements. Similarly, one who knows the means of crossing the ocean of worldly existence cannot cross the ocean if he himself does not employ those means. This is the reason why the Jaina thinkers use the aphorism '*samyakjñānakriyābhyāṁ mokṣaḥ*' ('right knowledge and right activity—these two combined are the means of liberation') to propound that liberation can be attained only when right knowledge and right conduct join together and cooperate. Though we know the path leading to the destination, we can never reach there if we do not walk on the path. How can we cure ourselves of the disease, if we do not take the required medicine, though known to us? If after laying foundations of faith and knowledge, a man stops there and does not proceed to construct the temple of spiritual welfare through right acts (conduct), then how can he have the finished temple of spiritual welfare?

Right Knowledge (samyak jñāna)

What is right knowledge? It means knowledge of the nature of soul as also of the means of spiritual welfare. In order to completely know the nature of soul, it is necessary to know even the material karmic coverings that affect it. Without knowing them we cannot understand the various states of the soul and consequently cannot easily achieve the spiritual good. As a matter of fact, without faith in, knowledge of and meditation on the soul, all our worldly knowledge is vain[1] and useless. All our miseries and distresses are due to our ignorance of the soul. What else except the constant knowledge of the soul could be the means to remove this ignorance? The sole secret teaching of the entire spiritual literature is that one should be inclined to the soul.

Right Conduct (samyak cāritra)

The fruit of the knowledge of reality is the refrainment from the vicious acts. And it alone is right conduct. The true meaning of 'right conduct' is to make one's life pure, keeping it aloof from vices and moral defilements, and to help others strive for the good according to one's ability. If a man follows instructions and teachings of the scriptures, it will help him very much in the practice of right conduct. Generally, right conduct is divided into two grades—right conduct for the mendicant and right conduct for the layman. Right conduct for the mendicant is called *sādhu-dharma* (the spiritual discipline for the mendicant). Right conduct for the layman is called *gṛhastha-dharma* (the spiritual discipline for the layman).

1. *ātmā vā are ! draṣṭavyaḥ śrotavyo mantavyo nididhyāsitavyaḥ / ātmano vā are! darśanena śravaṇena matyā vijñānena idaṁ sarvaṁ viditaṁ bhavati //*

Bṛhadāraṇyaka Upaniṣad

In the Jaina scriptures, we find detailed exposition of these two grades of the spiritual discipline.

Spiritual Discipline for the Mendicant (sādhu-dharma)

A man who performs acts beneficial to himself as well as to others is a *sādhu* (a saint, a mendicant)[1]. And the life-long vow of absolute non-attachment, which he accepts, setting his eye on the pure and holy objective of spiritual welfare is *sādhu-dharma* (spiritual discipline for the mendicant). It necessarily implies prior renunciation of all the worldly pleasures of wealth, woman, etc. and cutting off all the bonds of home, family and kin. The main and only object of his spiritual efforts is to subdue and conquer passions of attachment and aversion. Refraining from violence, refraining from lying of any sort, refraining from taking anything that is not given, refraining from sexual activities and refraining from possessions and attachment-for-possessions — these are the five major-scale vows. Observance of these five major-scale vows is the spiritual efforts constituting the life of the mendicant. Again, the prime characteristic of his life is the progressive curbing of the activities of mind, speech and body. His spiritual discipline is the life-long vow of universal brotherhood. Its fruit is liberation which, when negatively characterised, is the absence of all miseries, viz. birth, old age, death, mental distresses, physical pains and worldly troubles, and when positively characterised, is the infinite bliss. One can easily see how pure and luminous and at the same time how hard and difficult this *sādhu-dharma* is! But a man accepts and observes such a monastic discipline, only when he realises the emptiness of the worldly existence (transmigratory cycle) and consequently becomes free from all attachment to worldly pleasures as also experiences the awakening of irresistible aspiration for the attainment of liberation, that is, spiritual welfare and infinite bliss.

Those who are not qualified for the monastic discipline can make their lives fruitful by observing the spiritual discipline meant for the layman. The first requirement to qualify oneself for this discipline is honesty in the earning of wealth, and morality and integrity in one's behaviour and dealings with others. It is necessary for the layman to cultivate the quality of fearlessness on the strength of the faith in the existence of soul and to remain vigilant in the observance of proper self-control. Again, he

---

1. *sādhnoti svaparahitakāryāṇi iti sādhuḥ /*

should avail of the benefits of the company of the spiritually advanced persons in order to keep burning the fire of spiritual fervour.

Spiritual Discipline for the Layman (gṛhastha-dharma)

In the Jaina scriptures and philosophical works, the term '*gṛhastha-dharma*' and '*śrāvaka-dharma*' have the same meaning. A man and a woman who observe the *gṛhastha-dharma* are called '*śrāvaka*' and '*śrāvikā*' respectively. The term '*śrāvaka*' is derived from the verbal root '*śru*' (to hear, to listen to). Those who listen to with interest the discourses on the path of spiritual welfare are '*śrāvakas*' and '*śrāvikās*'. The term '*upāsaka*' is also employed in the sense of *śrāvaka*. In the works dealing with the spiritual discipline for the layman, there occurs the exposition of twelve vows. They are—gross vow of refraining from violence, gross vow of refraining from lying, gross vow of refraining from taking anything which is not given, gross vow of refraining from sexual activities, gross vow of limiting one's possessions, vow of limiting the area of unvirtuous acts, vow of limiting the quantity of things that could be used once as also of things that could be used repeatedly, vow to abstain from harmful activities that serve no useful purpose, vow of remaining completely equanimous for a fixed period of time, vow of reducing for a limited period of time the limits of area set forth in the sixth vow (*digvrata*), vow of observing fast and living like a monk for certain days and vow of sharing with a deserving guest. Among them, the first five vows are called '*aṇuvrata*' (atomised vows, minor-scale vows) as they are partial. Their nature of being partial and limited is suggested by the term '*sthūla*' ('gross') used as their qualifying adjective.

Gross vow of Refraining from Violence (Sthūla Prāṇātipātaviramaṇa)

For violence the term '*prāṇātipāta*' is used here. It literally means 'to destroy (*atipāta*) life forces (*prāṇa*) of living being'. The term '*viramaṇa*' means refrainment. Thus, '*prāṇātipātaviramaṇa*' means 'refrainment from destroying life forces of a living being'. In short, it is refrainment from violence. Violence is committed in three ways—by doing the act oneself, by urging or forcing others to do it or by approving it done by others. Similarly, lying, etc. are committed in three ways. A man who produces certain things commits acts of violence, while producing them. And those who use or enjoy those things, by doing so approve his acts of violence. Not only that, but they by using or enjoying those things directly or indirectly cause him to commit acts of violence while producing them. So, users or enjoyers of those things are defiled by violence involved in their production and trade. Not only the person who actually does the vicious or virtuous acts binds as a result the inauspicious or auspicious *karmas*, but also those who urge or force him to do those acts or those who approve his acts bind the respective *karmas*. Of course, it is possible that the mental state of the actual doer is more acute than that of the one who causes him to do the act or of the one who approves his act. But this is not the absolute statement. The mental state of the one who forces others to do the act is more acute than that of those who have to do the act helplessly under pressure. For instance, the degree of furiousness of an officer who forces a policeman to beat the accused is higher than that of the policeman who has to beat the accused helplessly. Similarly, the mental state of the person who praises, approves and strongly propagates the acts of violence is possibly more acute than the one who actually does them. Man being imperfect cannot know as to whose mental state is more acute. But this much is certain that all the three bind the *karmas* according to the acuteness of their mental states.

Life forces are ten—three channels of activity, viz., mind, speech and body, five sense-organs, the duration of life, and respiration. To destroy or injure, through negligence or ill-will, one or more life forces of one's own or of others is violence. From this follows that through negligence or ill-will to hurt the feelings of others, to insult others, to censure others, to speak ill of others behind their back, to cause fear or mental torture to others, in short, to do wrong to others or to wound their feelings is violence. Even in the absence of actual overt act of injuring the life forces of others, an evil act of violence is committed through mere entertaining ill-will or ill-thought. Lying, theft, dishonesty, cheating, and mental states of anger, greed, pride, jealousy, hatred, etc.,—all these are of the nature of violence and hence vices. Real cultivation or observance of non-violence consists in being ever vigilant and engaged in the acts of purifying mind by removing those mental defects and bad thoughts.

The following aphorism presents the definition of violence: '*pramattayogāt prāṇavyaparopaṇam hiṁsā*'[1], that is, 'the destruction of life due to an act involving negligence is violence'. The term '*pramāda*' yields two mean-

1. *Tattvārthasūtra*, VII.8.

ings: (1) mental state of attachment and aversion and (2) negligence. So, to destroy life of a living being through passions of attachment and aversion is violence; and to destroy life of a living being through negligence is also violence. The mental state of attachment and aversion as also of negligence is internal violence (*bhāva-hiṁsā*). And the actual overt act of destroying life of a living being is external violence (*dravya-hiṁsā*). Internal violence is by itself violence of evil nature, whereas external violence is not by itself violence of evil nature but it becomes so only when it is associated with internal violence.

For a householder total and absolute abstinence from violence is impossible. So, abstinence from violence for him is shown as limited and partial in the Jaina works on ethics. The types of limitations allowed are evident in the following statement of the vow: 'I shall not kill with determined intention[1] the gross (i.e., mobile) living beings when they are innocent'. Now let us understand the statement and thereby the limitactions. The one-sensed living beings, viz. earth, water, fire, air and plants are immobile; they are the things a householder uses once or repeatedly and in his daily life their constant use is inevitable. So, in his vow of non-violence, he is not required to refrain from killing them. This is the reason why the statement of his vow contains the words 'I shall not kill the gross (i.e., mobile, i.e., two-sensed, etc.) living beings'. This is how his vow of non-violence is made narrow and limited by leaving out the one-sensed living beings from its purview. But there is a possibility of killing even the gross (mobile, i.e., two-sensed, etc.) living beings like ants, etc. while constructing a house, performing agricultural activities, digging wells, step-wells and ponds, etc. So, it will not do to put the mere words 'I shall not kill the gross living beings' in the statement of his vow. Therefore, the words 'with determined intention' are inserted in the statement of his vow. Thus, now the statement is: 'I shall not kill with determined intention the gross living beings'. The killing of the gross living beings that takes place in constructing a house, performing agricultural activities, digging wells, etc. and performing acceptable and allowed occupations is not done with determined intention. Hence it does not go against the householder's vow of non-violence. Again, there arose a problem. In a difficult situation, he has to kill with determined inten-

---

1. *paṅgukuṣṭikuṇitvādi dṛṣṭvā hiṁsāphalaṁ sudhīḥ /*
nirāgastrasajantūnāṁ hiṁsāṁ saṅkalpatas tyajet //

Yogaśāstra, Ācārya Hemacandra, II. 19

tion the guilty while defending himself and others. He is allowed to do so. So, in the statement of his vow the words 'when they are innocent' are inserted. Now the complete statement of a householder's vow of non-violence is formulated thus: 'I shall not kill with determined intention the gross (mobile) living beings when they are innocent'.

Let us simplify the above exposition. The living beings are divided into the mobile and the immobile. A householder cannot take a vow to refrain from killing the latter. Regarding the mobile living beings, there is the killing of them with determined intention or without determined intention. He cannot take a vow to refrain from killing the mobile living beings without determined intention. Again, regarding the killing of the mobile living beings with determined intention there is the killing of the guilty or the innocent. Here too he cannot take a vow to refrain from killing the guilty mobile living beings with determined intention.

From the above discussion it follows that the gross violence is of four types: (1) intentional violence (*saṅkalpī hiṁsā*), (2) violence involved in the ordinary daily acts of a householder (*ārambhī hiṁsā*), (3) violence involved in occupations and industries (*udyogī hiṁsā*) and (4) return of violence in self-defence (*virodhī hiṁsā*). In cases where the act of violence to an innocent living being is actuated by an intention to injure it, we have the first type of violence (i.e., *saṅkalpī hiṁsā*). Killing of the mobile living beings that takes place in spite of utmost care and vigilance on the part of a householder while performing his daily acts of sweeping the floors of shop and house, washing his clothes, lighting up his oven, cooking his food, ploughing his field and so on is the second type of violence (i.e., *ārambhī hiṁsā*). Violence involved in the acts of earning wealth is of the third type (i.e., *udyogī hiṁsā*). In defence of one's own self as well as others against the violent attacks of a wicked person if a householder has to kill him, the violence committed is of the fourth type (i.e., *virodhī hiṁsā*).

Of the four types of violence one should give up the first type of violence, i.e., intentional violence. Of the remaining three types of violence, the second and the third types of violence, i.e., *ārambhī* and *udyogī hiṁsā* are naturally and necessarily associated with the life of a householder. And on rare occasion he is constrained to take recourse to the fourth type of violence, i.e., *virodhī hiṁsā.*

The difference between *ārambhī hiṁsā* and *saṅkalpī hiṁsā* is as follows. In *ārambhī hiṁsā* the main objective is to accomplish the acts of one's daily life, viz. cooking the food, performing agricultural activities, etc. In accomplishing these acts, no doubt living beings are killed, but the householder does not directly kill them. This means that he does not kill them intentionally, but performing his daily acts they are being killed without his intention to kill them. On the other hand, in the intentional violence (*saṅkalpī hiṁsā*) the main objective is the killing of living beings. There the act of killing is done intentionally. The killing done with intention is intentional violence. In a difficult situation, when one is violently attacked by a wicked person, the former is constrained to kill the latter with determined intention. But this intentional killing has a just cause. Hence it is differentiated from the intentional killing without a just cause (*saṅkalpī hiṁsā*), it is recognised as an independent type of violence and given a separate name '*virodhī hiṁsā*', and it is not to be avoided in the observance of the householder's vow of non-violence.

It goes without saying that violence committed without intention through mere negligence or carelessness should be avoided.

It is necessary to say something about the purpose of inserting the adjective 'innocent' in the statement of the householder's vow of partial or limited non-violence. If a wicked tyrant does not stop his oppressive, wrong, unjust and outrageous acts by non-violent means, a householder is free to resist and oppose him properly by other means and in doing so he does not do any harm to his vow of non-violence. On the contrary, it is his duty to do so. In such difficult times under special circumstances if even a monk becomes ready to take proper steps for the good of the people, his decision and consequent action are considered to be fair and just.

Entire universe is tightly filled with living beings. So, every activity involves violence. Though there does occur inevitable violence in the performance of activity, a man remains untouched by the defilement of violence provided his mind is permeated through and through with the feeling of non-violence and he undertakes activity with utmost care and vigilance. On the other hand, a negligent and careless person is soiled with the defilement of violence on account of his negligence and carelessness even though he may not actually commit violence (gross violence), while doing careless activity.

No activity is free from violence. This is the reason why more emphasis is laid on the renunciation of activity. The following seems to be the logic: Every activity involves violence. From this follows the principle—the less the activity performed, the less is violence committed. But how can we afford to reduce the activity of duty or the activity meant for the (spiritual) welfare of the people, simply in order to reduce violence in this way? We should not reduce such activity simply for fear of violence. No doubt the killing of or injury to living beings which is inevitable and natural in sustaining the body is committed without intention, while conducting such activities even with proper care, vigilance and discretion. But that defect of violence which we incur is very negligible. Not only that, but that very little defect melts away in the vast rushing stream of good and wholesome acts of duty.

Moreover, is it certain that by renouncing activity one will be free from violence? Mind is not bound to become calm simply by renouncing overt activity. It is possible that mind is excessively perturbed even when the body is inactive. Though on one side control over body is very great, yet on the other side furiousness of mind is so great that it may bind *karmas* causing birth in terrible hells. To illustrate this point, the Jaina works relate the well-known stories of Prasannacandra Rājarṣi, etc.

And if one concedes the activity of eating, drinking, etc., why should one stop the activity meant solely for social good and welfare as also the activity which duty demands?

Bondage and liberation depend on the mental states. Good and wholesome mental states direct the body to do good and wholesome acts. So, the important point one should bear in mind is that one should keep one's mind ever vigilant in order to prevent evil thoughts and feelings from stealthily entering the mind. Members of the society are required to perform such activities as are necessary for its maintenance and sustenance as well as for its happiness and comforts. And though there is no intention to kill or injure living beings, violence (external violence) is no doubt committed in such activities. So, in what way one should conduct such activities if one is required to conduct them for the happiness and comforts of the society? According to the Jaina works on religious conduct, the answer to the question is that if these activities are conducted with such care and vigilance that all avoidable and unnecessary violence is assiduously refrained from, then whatever violence that may take place in those activities should not be regarded as defilement and of evil nature. But if these activities are conducted without taking proper care for refraining from avoidable and unnecessary violence, then that violence due to carelessness and negligence becomes defect and defilement. In this case, if there may not be any external violence in the overt activities, even then on account of carelessness and negligence with which the activities are performed, the doer does incur the defilement of (internal) violence.

What is proper care? How can one decide that the care is proper? This depends upon the circumstances under which one conducts one's activities. It is quite obvious that a farmer while conducting agricultural activities in his field cannot observe that much care which a saint in his hermitage observes while conducting hermitage activities. All agree that while conducting agricultural activities many small living beings are injured or killed. Yet to prevent the calamity of great and terrible violence on account of the lack of agricultural products, it becomes our (farmers') inescapable duty to produce corns in the fields.[1] Violence committed on such occasions is considered to be very little, negligible and pardonable. If the activities involving violence are done with the sole objective of social welfare, then those activities turn good, wholesome and praiseworthy. Problem of the determinants of the different scales of violence is treated of in the third chapter of this book.

As for the householder it is not possible to abstain from the violence of the one-sensed beings, his vow of non-violence concedes the violence of the one-sensed beings. Yet he is required to avoid as far as possible the unnecessary violence of the one-sensed beings too. Again, in determining as to which living beings are to be considered innocent or guilty, one should use one's discretionary faculty. It is not proper to consider a snake or a scorpion to be guilty, simply because it has bitten us or our relatives. So, it is not proper to kill a snake or a scorpion that bites us or our relatives. Man's mind should be full of compassion and universal love. With his discretionary power he should weigh benefits and harms possible in each and every act he is going to perform. And only afterwards he should undertake any activity. The essence of humanity is good will towards all creatures.

Gross Vow of Refraining from Lying (Sthūla Mṛṣāvādaviramaṇa)

For the householder who cannot vow to refrain from subtle falsehoods

1. Ānanda, etc. were the ten well-known direct lay-disciples of Lord Mahāvīra. They had taken twelve vows of the householder. In the vow of limiting one's possessions, they had conceded to possess 500 ploughs, 500 carts for journey from country to country and 500 other carts for carrying load of grass, grains, sticks, etc. to places like home, etc.; again, some of them had one *vraja* (1 *vraja* = 10,000 cows), some four, some six and still some eight. See *Upāsakadaśāsūtra.*

too, there is a second vow of refraining from gross falsehoods. This is the vow of not telling lies about human beings, viz. a bride, a bridegroom, etc., about animals, viz., a bullock, a horse, a cow, a buffalo, etc., and about land, viz., houses, buildings, fields, trees, orchards, gardens, etc. This vow includes refraining from misappropriating the deposits left with one, bearing false witness in or out of court, and forging fake documents.[1] The observer of the vow should specifically bear in mind that if he practises treachery and fraud in business and under temptation indulges in boasting and spreading rumours, he puts his religion to shame and makes it an object of despise, mockery and ridicule. He should not forget that breach of confidence or trust and giving wrong advice are great sins. In short, he should understand that the secret of earning wealth is honesty and morality. And in morality lie the roots of one's own happiness, peace, mental health and also of others' welfare.

Those who observe this vow are trusted and liked by the people.

Gross Vow of Abstaining from Taking anything that is not given (Sthūla Adattādānaviramaṇa)

For the householder who cannot abstain from subtle acts of theft, there is a vow of abstaining from gross acts of theft.[2] The taking, with intent to steal, of objects which are not given by their owners is an act of theft. The householder should refrain from house-breaking, pick-pocketing, smuggling, buying or accepting stolen property, using false weights and measures, secretly adulterating commodities or substituting inferior ones for the original. He should not sell things at inequitable prices, i.e., practise black marketing, pick up things lost or forgotten by their owners, misappropriate deposits left with him, take away the wealth hidden by its owner, evade taxes and steal another person's property. He should not stealthily introduce changes in documents in his own favour, use another person's writings as his own (plagiarise) and declare the philanthropic work done with another person's money as his own. To abduct a man, his child, wife or daughter is the heinous type of theft. The householder should not commit such an act of theft. He should not do any act of theft

1. *kanyāgobhūmyalīkāni nyāsāpaharaṇaṁ tathā /*
kūṭasākṣyaṁ ca pañceti sthūlāsatyāny akīrtayan//
—*Yogaśāstra,* Ācārya Hemacandra, II.54

2. *patitaṁ vismṛtaṁ naṣṭam sthitaṁ sthāpitam āhitam/*
adattaṁ nādadīta svaṁ parakīyaṁ kvacit sudhīḥ//
—*Yogaśāstra,* Ācārya Hemacandra, II.66

that is punishable by the state and lowers him in the eyes of the people. Even an ordinary act of theft committed by man proves him a liar and dishonest person, makes him a target of public censure and his vow an object of ridicule, and shakes the faith of others in religion. The observer of this vow should always remember this.

The result of the observance of this vow is that you are trusted, and in that way you prosper. Also the character is developed. If the choice not to steal is not made, or if it is soiled, then the result is untrustworthiness, also there is legal punishment, also you cannot carry out your ideas on account of not being trusted.

Gross Vow of Refraining from all Illicit Sexual Contacts (Sthūla Maithunaviramaṇa)

This vow means to avoid any sexual contact with the wives of others. It covers even the avoidance of sexual contacts with harlots, widows and unmarried women. All sexual contacts, except the moderate[1] ones, with one's own wife should also be avoided[2]. Similarly, a woman should avoid

---

1. Moderate sexual contact generally means sexual intercourse undertaken with the objective of saving and protecting the valuable semen, that is, with the objective of not unnecessarily wasting it, and with the sole intention of procreation. Use of semen is not limited to procreation alone. It can also be used specially in enhancing the mental and bodily energy, in developing will-power and in preserving health, in short, in achieving the bodily, mental, material and spiritual progress. Blinded by sexual infatuation, man who indulges in excessive sexual activities invites ruin of his body and mind and this, in turn, makes him unfit for the enjoyment of material happiness as also for procreation; not only that but it (=excessive indulgence in the sexual acts) also destroys will-power which is absolutely necessary for the accomplishment of any act—even for the attainment of liberation—and throws him into the deep dark valley of degradation. Semen has creative power and its use can be made in noble acts other than procreation. Those who are engaged in study or creation of scientific and literary works and in the service of mankind, or those who are engrossed in meditation of the highest goal, in finding out the paths leading to it and in living a life in accordance with them have no time at all to think of sex. And it is such great men who can completely refrain from all sexual activities. To control any power (sex urge is also a power), the unfailing means is not its suppression. Like a spring the suppressed power springs up with great force. The true and unfailing means to control it is to divert it into the beneficial and wholesome acts, that is, to sublimate it. This is like channelising or diverting the rushing waters of flood into the canals before they play havoc in destroying lives and property. If it is not diverted in other elevating and noble acts, then in its flood one will be dragged away and drowned.
2. *ṣaṇḍhatvam indriyacchedaṁ vīkṣyābrahmaphalaṁ sudhīḥ/*
   bhavet svadārasantuṣṭo'nyadārān vā vivarjayet//—Yogaśāstra, Ācārya Hemacandra, II.76

all sexual contacts with all men except her husband.

Vow of Limiting One's Possessions (Parigrahaparimāṇa)

Desire has no end. It is limitless. In this vow there is an attempt to control it, to limit it. Possession of land, houses, silver, gold, diverse commodities, grains, livestock and furniture is called external possession. The attachment to and delusion of these things is internal possession. To weaken this internal possession which is of the nature of defilement and defect, it is necessary to limit properly the external possession. Of the things owned by him, if a man keeps some for the use and enjoyment of his own self, his family members and his dependents, he is regarded as having internal possession to the extent and limit of those things alone. But if all other things possessed by him are kept free for the use of others and given to them when they are needed by them, then with regard to these things he is not regarded as having internal possession; on the contrary, he is looked upon as their trustee. It is so because, he has no attachment or delusion for them and keeps them with him simply for the benefit of others; he is like an honest keeper or care-taker.

If a man has a burning desire to amass much wealth so that he can indulge in the enjoyment of worldly pleasures, he has great possession (internal), even though he is penniless. It is to be remembered that if there is in anyone's mind even a trace of attachment for worldly things or even the slightest desire to possess them, then he has internal possession, even though he may live in a forest, naked and destitute of all gross things. Excessive accumulation of riches is a sin and to have such a desire is a sin of equal measure. The attachment or desire for the gross things that answer the ordinary necessities and comforts of life is no doubt internal possession. But as this internal possession is invariably and inevitably associated with the state of a householder and as it involves no unnecessary harm to others, it is not regarded as a vice.

Ordinary necessities and ordinary comforts of life mean those necessities and comforts which a man who is neither too rich nor too poor can peacefully use and enjoy. It is generally observed that it is this middle state where contentment and peace find scope and place, and again it is this middle state which is conducive to self-development and spiritual welfare. If such a contented gentleman happens to earn much wealth as a result of his past wholesome and good acts, he will surely not add it to his possessions, but on the contrary, utilise it in the uplift and welfare of the people.

A man who has sufficient means of his livelihood and hence free from all the troubles of earning, should not remain inactive and idle. Inactivity or idleness is bad and harmful to life. He should engage himself in the work of social welfare according to his ability. Such industrious life will prove beneficial internally and externally as also bring good to him and to others. If he who has wealth sufficient for his livelihood wants to continue his business for sheer joy, he should do so honestly and whatever gains he makes in business he should spend in the acts of social welfare. He should consider himself not as an isolated and independent individual but as a part or unit of the society, and from this standpoint he should perform good acts beneficial to himself as well as to others. When there is decrease in the degree of attachment and feeling of mineness for the possessions, greed is controlled effectively and the interest in the vicious activities, viz. violence, etc., necessarily involved in accumulating wealth becomes weak instead of getting strong. If a man does not set limits to his possessions, then greed and desire will press him greatly to involve himself into all those vicious activities necessary for accumulating wealth. This will degrade and defile his soul as he is carried away by passions. This fact points to the necessity of the observance of this vow. Proper control of desire results in decrease of anxiety and tension invariably associated with wealth and possession.[1] And the less the anxiety and tension, the more is mental peace and the more can one avail of the benefits derivable from benevolent works, study and devotion to God. The practice of religion, that is, observance of this vow brings him spiritual good and welfare.

If this vow of limiting possessions is accepted as a social outlook and as a social philosophical doctrine, all turmoil due to communism and socialism will subside.

Vow of Limiting the Area of one's Unvirtuous Activities (Digvrata)

There are ten directions—the four well-known directions, viz. east, west, north, south; the four intermediary directions, viz. *īśāna, āgneya, nairṛtya,*

1. *asantoṣam aviśvāsam ārambham duḥkhakāraṇam/*
matvā mūrchāphalaṁ kuryāt parigrahaniyantraṇam//—Yogaśāstra, II.106

vāyavya; the upward direction over one's head and the downward direction under one's feet. This is the vow to limit the distance in all the ten directions, up to which and not beyond which the vower will undertake unvirtuous activities. Thus, the purpose of the vow is to limit the area of different activities. The vower limits the area in which and not beyond which he will move, conduct trade and business, give his daughter in marriage or accept in marriage someone's daughter for his son; again, he will use things produced in that much area only. To check the unimpeded spread of desire, to save oneself from the unvirtuous activities that are likely to spread beyond the limited area in the absence of the vow and to give one scope to perform one's duty towards one's neighbours are the objectives of the vow. If the vow is observed, much of the botheration and hubbub will be lessened, tranquillity and peace will be gained and there will be considerable increase in the scope for all-round self-development and spiritual welfare.

Vow of Limiting the Quantity of Things One Will Use (Bhogopabhogaparimāṇa)

There are two types of things, viz. *bhoga* and *upabhoga*. *Bhoga* things are those that can be used only once, viz. eatables, water, etc. *Upabhoga* things are those that can be used repeatedly, viz. clothes, etc. Thus, this vow means to limit their quantity, to refrain from keeping those things more in number than the necessarily required. So, it is a self-imposed restriction as to the number of things to be used. He who practises it knows how much restraint is put on the free play of desire by its observance. This vow covers the prohibition of forbidden food and drink, viz. meat, wine, etc. which are not necessary for living, but, on the contrary, harmful to life and degrading to soul. Similarly, it is also understood that the vower should abandon things of both the types, whose use possibly involves much violence and evil. A householder adopts such renunciation with a view to making progress on the path of peace. So, this vow requires him to abandon even such professions as involve much evil and cruelty to animals. A man who discriminates the good from the evil always chooses lesser evil when he is constrained to choose between two evils.

Man has no control over his desire. This is the reason why India is suffering from acute unemployment, terrible price-hike and unbearable troubles. While on the one side there are mountains of unnecessarily accumulated wealth and useless huge expenditures in the display of one's riches as also in the excessive and even perverse enjoyment of sensual pleasures, there is, on the other hand, a deep dark valley of poverty engulfing the vast population of the country. In this terrible disparity, life forces of the people get dried up and even the independent and free country gets ruined. If all observe proper equanimity and restraint in the use of things, all the struggles for the means of livelihood will end, and strifes and tensions will be removed, all the disparity will disappear and all-encompassing equality will arise. And, as a result, lives of all will be permeated with joy and happiness. The objective of this vow is to make all happy and to divert them to the path of humanity—of course, its leaning towards spiritual welfare is quite evident.

Vow to Abstain from Purposeless Harmful Activities (Anarthadaṇḍaviramaṇa)

In Sanskrit, this vow is called *anarthadaṇḍavirati.* The term '*anartha*' means purposeless, aimless, unnecessary, etc. And the term '*daṇḍa*' means harmful, bad, evil activities. Thus, the term '*anarthadaṇḍa*' means unnecessary and purposeless harmful activities. And refraining from such activities is *anarthadaṇḍavirati.* A householder cannot avoid those acts of violence which are connected with his ordinary daily activities, nor can he avoid violence which is involved in agriculture, business or industry; again, on some special occasion in self-defence or to save others he has to kill the violent attacker. For him it is necessary to undertake proper activities to earn money for the maintenance of his family as also for accumulating some possessions. Thus, his life is full of unvirtuous activities. Yet the observance of the already mentioned five minor-scale vows as also of the other supporting ones constitutes the path of liberation. Taking into account the unvirtuous activities which are invariably and inevitably associated with the householder's life or which have to be performed to fulfil his duties as a householder or which are occasional but necessary, the Jaina thinkers have wisely advised through the present vow that one should not do unnecessary and purposeless harmful activities. This is the essence of the vow. But what are the unvirtuous activities that could be regarded as unnecessary and purposeless? To answer the question is difficult. Is it not easy to prove one's unnecessary and purposeless unvirtuous activity necessary and purposeful? So, how can it be possible to pinpoint certain unvirtuous activities as unnecessary and purposeless when the life itself is full of struggles and passions? Therefore, the Jaina thinkers have attempted to give some idea of unnecessary and purposeless harmful unvirtuous activities, simply by giving broad instructions. They state:

(1) **One should not give harmful advice:** If a man who has gone deep into the vices (*vyasanas*) like drinking wine, taking intoxicating drugs, smoking, gambling and so on advises others to take them, then that advice is purposeless and harmful. Instead of superimposing good qualities on them, he should point out their real defects. To say good words in their praise and carry on their propaganda is the purposeless harmful activity. A householder has to teach others certain things very useful in life. He has to teach how to cultivate land, how to cook food, how to plan a house, how to sew clothes, etc. If he generously teaches these useful subjects to those who really want to learn them, he is not violating the vow. His advice and instruction could not be regarded as purposeless harmful activity. Noble-minded generous persons consider the entire world to be their family.[1] This means that to give advice and instructions with good motive to others for their benefit in such matters as are socially and practically useful is not a purposeless harmful activity. But to give advice to others about evil activities in which they are already engaged, to give vain and needless advice, to give advice merely out of garrulity, to give advice that leads a man astray, to give advice which stimulates others to pursue perverse sensual pleasures, to give advice concerning methods of livelihood involving wrong doings—all these are cases of purposeless harmful activities.

(2) **One should not give means of destroying life to others:** This means that if a man gives a knife to sharpen a pencil and fire to cook food, that is not a purposeless harmful activity. But to give a knife to kill or harm somebody and fire to burn somebody or his property, that is certainly a purposeless harmful activity. It is narrow-mindedness to give these things to one's relatives only with a view to helping them and to refuse to give them to others. It displays harshness of one's heart to refuse to give fire to a stranger to cook food. One should always remember the above-mentioned wise saying that the noble-minded generous persons regard the entire world as their family. The entire world where we live inter-dependently should be the field for our beneficial and good activities. When somebody has violently attacked an innocent man, to give the latter a weapon to defend himself

1. *udāracaritānāṁ tu vasudhaiva kuṭumbakam /*

against the attack or to give it to another person whose sole intention is to save the life of that innocent man is not a purposeless harmful activity. But to give a weapon to the violent attacker to perpetrate violence over others is surely a harmful activity beneficial to none.

(3) **One should not yield to harmful contemplation:** To think continuously of doing harm to others, to yield to evil brooding over unjust means of accumulating wealth, to caress the ideas of sensual pleasures and to think vainly of one's miseries and misfortunes are the purposeless harmful activities. Vain and sorrowful thinking about the contact of the undesirable things, separation of the desirable ones and pains of the diseases comes under the head of purposeless harmful activities. Vain brooding over business worries is no doubt a purposeless harmful activity. But proper thinking about one's business is not a purposeless harmful activity. Similarly, proper thinking about family management is not a purposeless harmful activity. Moreover, our thinking about the victory of the just and righteous persons like Rāma as also about the defeat of the unjust and unrighteous persons like Rāvaṇa is not a purposeless harmful activity. Again, thinking about the ways and means of protecting justice and destroying injustice could not be regarded as purposeless harmful activity, because it is very useful for the uplift and welfare of the society. Similarly, proper thinking as to how to get rid of the contact of the undesirable things as also how to attain the company of the desirable ones could not come under the head of the purposeless harmful activities. Nor can we regard our thinking about the cure of the diseases and recovery of health as a purposeless harmful activity.

(4) **Thoughtless behaviour:** Thoughtless activities like aimlessly digging the ground and igniting fire, ẹtc. are purposeless harmful activities. While walking, to strike a standing animal with a stick is a foolish purposeless harmful activity. One should consciously avoid such purposeless harmful activities. To refrain from killing the immobile, i.e., one-sensed living beings is not included in the minor-scale vow of non-violence, yet their unnecessary and purposeless killing comes under the head of purposeless harmful activities, hence one should avoid it. Lying, etc., of insignificant character are not prohibited in the concerned minor-scale vows, but under the present vow householders are warned against committing them too. This vow prohibits joking which hurts others. It prohibits back-biting and talking ill of others. Watching theatrical representations, dances and other public shows, which arouse sex passion are to be avoided as far as possible. Activities

like going for a walk for fresh air, doing proper bodily exercises which are conducive to health are as useful and good to body and mind as are proper food and drinks; these could not be brought under the head of purposeless harmful activities. To remain clean, to maintain cleanliness, to undergo proper treatment for the cure of a disease and to do any act within proper limit and under decorum for the innocent entertainment and joy could not be regarded as purposeless harmful activities. To remain unclean and to make and keep surroundings dirty is to give way to violence, because by doing so one unnecessarily breeds too many insects.

It will be proper to point out at this juncture that one can maintain one's body well by vegetarian diet. So, to eat meat for relish and bodily growth is surely a purposeless harmful activity. Not only that, but it is also a form of intentional violence (*saṅkalpī hiṁsā*) which a householder should avoid completely and at all cost.

Vow of Remaining Completely Equanimous for a Fixed Period of Time (Sāmāyika)

This vow consists in sitting at one place and on one seat for 48 consecutive minutes in a peaceful mental state, not allowing the passions of attachment and aversion to rise in the mind. For this period of time, the vower contemplates on the nature of self, examines as to how much purity of life he has attained, reads the true religious works showing the path of self-development and spiritual evolution and concentrates on the supreme (i.e., liberated) soul.

Vow of Reducing for a Limited Period of Time the Limits of the Area Set Forth in the Sixth Vow (Deśāvakāśikavrata)

This vow means to reduce for a day or for a fixed period of time the limits of the area set forth by the vower himself in the sixth vow for the unvirtuous activities, and similarly to suppress or contract the concessions he himself has kept while taking other vows. The objective of the present vow is to increase the refrainment from the unvirtuous activities.

Vow of Observing Fast and Living Like a Monk for Certain Days (Poṣadhavrata)

The term '*poṣadha*' is derived from the Sanskrit verbal root '*puṣ*' meaning 'to nourish, to foster, to support, to cause to grow, to develop'. So, the term '*poṣadha*' means that which nourishes, fosters, supports the soul or its natural qualities. In this vow, the vower observes a fast or takes only one meal a day and like a monk remains engaged in the religious rites for 4 or 8 *praharas* (one *prahara* = approximately 3 hours). The objective of this vow is to make the householder relish the nectar of the life of total refrainment from all evil activities, keeping him away from the hubbub, troubles and anxieties of the worldly life. In this vow, the vower observes total abstinence from sex activity before he undertakes religious rites and performs them according to proper procedure. The time left out by these rites is utilised in the study and discussions elevating and ennobling the soul.

Vow of Sharing with Deserving Guests (Atithisaṁvibhāga-vrata)

To offer necessities of life (food, medicine, etc.) to the saintly monks who having renounced the householder's life have adopted the life of renunciation characterised by total refrainment from evil activities and live on begging alms, as also to the benevolent noble persons engaged in the service of the people is the meaning of the present vow. The vow also means to give proper help to the miserable and the poor.

Of the twelve vows, the first five vows are called *aṇuvratas* (atom-scale vows), because compared to the *mahāvratas* (great vows) of the monk they are very small. The next three vows are called *guṇavratas*, because they help, support and strengthen the *aṇuvratas*. The term '*guṇa*' is here used in the sense of help, support. And the four vows enumerated after them are called *śikṣāvratas*. They are so called because they are spiritual exercises of a ritual sort.

If a householder has no strength and energy to take all the twelve vows, he can take as many as are possible for him to observe.

Now let us know about *samyaktva* which is the basic foundation of the final accomplishment of religious practice. It means self-faith purified by discretionary power of thought.

Samyaktva

The literal meaning of the term '*samyaktva*' is rightness or goodness. But in the present context what does rightness or goodness mean? It means integrity or purity. But integrity or purity of what? Of inclination, attitude, outlook. So, here the term '*samyaktva*' conventionally conveys the sense of integrity or purity of inclination, attitude, outlook. That is, integrated or pure inclination, attitude or outlook towards the essence is called '*samyaktva*'. But the essence of what? Essence of spiritual welfare. When the inclination towards the essence of spiritual welfare is integrated, right or pure it is called *samyaktva*. On the attainment of this spiritually beneficent inclination, all fanaticism, strong attachment to one's views, narrow-mindedness and sectarianism are removed; and strong manifestations of passions subside and calm down. Right inclination arouses the pure desire to acquire knowledge and in its light we gain understanding that reality is not absolute but relative, not one-sided but many-sided. As a result of this, synthetic and synoptic outlook is developed. This, in turn, leads to the rise and development of equanimity purified by discretion.

Another term for *samyaktva* is '*samyagdarśana*'. It too has the same meaning. The simple meaning of both these terms is right faith. Right faith is not blind faith, but the faith resulting from the use of discretionary power of thought. Blind faith is thoughtless faith which is without the understanding of the universal law of cause-effect relation, whereas right faith is the faith resulting from the use of discretionary power of thought and accompanied by the understanding of the truth of the universal law of cause-effect relation. In the faith which is purified by logic and which stands to the scrutiny of reason, there can be no such element as can be objected to by the intellect or as cannot stand to the light of the intellect. Such a faith is an inclination or attitude having special strength. This strength is the strength of discretionary faculty, which enables us to discriminate the good from the evil, what is worthy of acceptance from what is worthy of rejection, and what is beneficial from what is harmful. The faith wedded to this strength is the firm faith in the right path leading to liberation or the spiritual good. This is what the Jaina thinkers call *samyagdarśana* or right faith. As soon as right faith makes its appearance, whatever little knowledge — be it little scriptural knowledge, ordinary intellect or limited learning—the soul possesses, turns into right knowledge (*samyagjñāna*). Right faith is of the form of discretionary insight. Its rightness determines the rightness of knowledge. In other words, rightness of knowledge depends on the rightness of faith. By knowledge we know things. But the discretionary insight (right faith) imparts purity to such knowing. On the basis of right faith and right knowledge, conduct (right conduct) is cultivated; and at last, as a result, liberation is attained. This has been expressly stated by Maharṣi Umāsvāti in the first aphorism of his *Tattvārthasūtra*. The aphorism in point is: '*samyagdarśana-jñāna-*

cāritrāṇi mokṣamārgaḥ', that is, 'right faith (inclination, insight), right cognition and right conduct—these three combined are the means of liberation.'

As stated above, right faith (inclination, outlook) is the strong and firm foundation of good conduct. It is so because right or good conduct is cultivated on the basis of right faith. 'As is the faith, so is the world'. However great may be the development of knowledge or intellect, but if the faith (outlook, attitude or inclination) is wrong, evil or perverse, that knowledge or intellect will be misused. And if the faith is right, good or wholesome, whatever little knowledge be there, it will be used rightly. It is faith that directs knowledge this way or that way. So, the question of its rightness or otherwise is of utmost importance.

If the faith is right, both the knowledge and the conduct will become right. And if it is wrong, both the knowledge and the conduct will become wrong. Therefore, it is accorded the first place in the enumeration of the means of liberation and considered supreme among them. This is the reason why Maharṣi Umāsvāti mentions it first in the aphorism which enumerates the three means of liberation. This shows that rightness of knowledge and conduct depends on the rightness of faith.

It is not that right faith (inclination or attitude) is gained only through the study of philosophy or scriptures. Any person belonging to any country, caste or creed, or even if he be dull-witted and illiterate[1], can gain it, provided his soul, i.e., his heart is soft, compassionate and friendly towards all living beings. Some good persons gain it without the help of external conditions like instruction, etc. In other words, in them it manifests itself spontaneously or naturally, i.e., merely on account of internal contemplative thought or spiritual capacity. On the other hand, some require external aids like instruction, etc. for its manifestation.

Some practical matters about right faith (attitude) are given below:

yā deve devatābuddhir gurau ca gurutāmatiḥ/
dharme ca dharmadhī śuddhā samyaktvam idam ucyate//[2]

Translation: To regard, with pure intellect, real God as real God, real teacher as real teacher and true religion as true religion is right faith.

In other words, a person possessed of right faith (attitude) has the

1. Even some fortunate animals can also attain it.
2. *Yogaśāstra*, Ācārya Hemacandra, II.2.

power to discriminate true God from false God, true teacher from false teacher, and true religion from false religion. He can easily identify true God, true teacher and true religion. It is so because he has right standards to determine true God, true teacher and true religion. He has no misconceptions, nor preconceived wrong notions regarding God, teacher and religion.

Let us here recall the essential characteristics of God, teacher and religion.

Essential Characteristics of God

Call him God or Highest Soul, the meaning is the same. The characteristics of God or the Highest Soul have already been shown. The following verse, while describing the nature of God, states:

sarvajño jitarāgādidoṣas trailokyapūjitaḥ /
yathāsthitārthavādī ca devo'rhan parameśvaraḥ //

Translation: That (embodied) soul who is omniscient, free from all defilements like attachment, aversion, etc., worshipped by all the three worlds and preaches reality as it is, is called God.

Essential Characteristics of the teacher

mahāvratadharā dhīrā bhaikṣamātropajīvinaḥ /
sāmāyikasthā dharmopadeśakā guravo matāḥ //[1]

Translation: The saints who observe five great vows, viz., non-violence etc.,[2] are adorned with spiritual quality of calmness and firmly established in equanimity, live on begging alms, and preach religion as it is, are called teachers.

Essence of Religion

pañcaitāni pavitrāṇi sarveṣāṁ dharmacāriṇām/
ahiṁsā satyam asteyaṁ brahmacaryam alobhatā//[3]

Translation: Non-violence, truthfulness, non-stealing, continence and

1. *Ibid.*, II. 4 and 8.
2. Non-violence, truth, non-stealing, continence and non-possession.
3. Ācārya Haribhadra's 13th *Aṣṭaka.*

non-possession—these five are held as pure virtues by the followers of all religions. That is, these five are accepted by all as the basic principles constituting their religions.

The following verse explains the meaning of the term '*dharma*':

durgatiprapatatprāṇidhāraṇād dharma ucyate /
dhatte caitān śubhasthāne tasmād dharma iti smṛtaḥ //

This verse states that that which saves living beings from falling into lower conditions or miserable states is religion. Again, it says that that which lifts their life from the lower state to the higher one is religion. Religion (*dharma*) is the natural quality of soul, which is experienced by all. On account of the removal of traces of the past evil acts, the passions of attachment and aversion become mild, and consequently mental purity is attained; this mental purity is the real religion. This is the lustre of life. Compassion, friendliness, doing good to others, truthfulness, self-control, renunciation—all these good qualities constitute the auspicious light of the internal pure life. Life permeated with such light is called religious life.

Types of Knowledge

When karmic coverings causing delusion are loosened or completely removed, right faith or attitude manifests itself. And as soon as it makes its manifestation, knowledge becomes right. This has been said earlier. Thus, there obtains an invariable relation between right faith and right knowledge. There are five types of knowledge, viz., *mati, śruta, avadhi, manaḥparyāya* and *kevala.* Knowledge obtained through sense-organs in contact with mind is called *matijñāna.* We see with eyes, taste with tongue, smell with nose, hear with ears and touch with skin. All these five knowledges are the cases of *matijñāna.* Memory, recognition, cogitation and inference also come under the head of *matijñāna.* Knowledge gained through words or signs is *śrutajñāna.* Both these types of knowledge being dependent on sense-organs are considered to be indirect. Yet the five knowledges had through five sense-organs, viz., experiences of colour, taste, smell, sound and touch are perceptual from empirical standpoint; so, they are called empirical perceptions. Similarly, experience of pleasure, pain, etc. gained through mind is empirical mental perception. One knows one's internal states through empirical mental perception.

Here the context demands the treatment of sense-organs from the Jaina standpoint.

There are five sense-organs, viz., skin, tongue, nose, eye and ear. Touch, taste, smell, colour and sound are their respective objects. They are different aspects or modes of one and the same physical substance. Again, they reside together in each and every part of the physical substance. In other words, they are copresent in all its different parts. Sense-organs have different special capacities. However efficient one of them might be, it is never in a position to cognise an object that is not its specific object. This is the reason why each of them is restricted to its own special object. That is, no sense-organ taken singly can grasp all the five objects. One sense-organ can grasp one object only, which is its specific object. Eye can grasp colour alone, ear can grasp sound alone and so on.

The object of mind is thought or reflection, just as the objects of five sense-organs are the above-mentioned touch, taste, etc. External sense-organs grasp just physical entities and those too only in parts; on the other hand, mind grasps all entities whatsoever, whether physical or otherwise, and those too with their various modes belonging to all the three divisions of time—past, present and future. This means that the function of mind is to reflect and depending on its level of development—that is, on its capacity—it reflects on all objects whatsoever, whether grasped by the external sense-organs or not. Therefore, the object of mind is reflection or thought. *Matijñāna* alone is generated through five external sense-organs, viz., skin, etc., whereas *matijñāna* and *śrutajñāna* both are generated through mind. The *matijñāna* is of the nature of general grasping, whereas *śrutajñāna* that takes place in its wake is of the nature of reflection, discursion and conception. But of the *mati* and *śruta*, *śruta* is more prominent than *mati*. That is why in the present context, *śruta* has been said to be the object of mind, *śrutam anindriyasya.*[1]

Each of the five external sense-organs is of two types, viz., *dravya* (physical) and *bhāva* (psychical). The *dravyendriya* is again of two sub-types, viz. that of the form of *nirvṛtti* (structure) and that of the form of *upakaraṇa* (capacity). Those shapes of the sense-organs in the body, which are of the form of specific structure made out of physical aggregates are called *nirvṛttīndriya.* Outer structure is outer *nirvṛttīndriya* and the inner structure is inner *nirvṛttīndriya.* If we compare the outer *nirvṛttīndriya* to a sword, we can compare the inner *nirvṛttīndriya* to its edge. And the capacity of this 'edge' to produce cognition is called *upakaraṇendriya.*

The *bhāvendriya* too is of two sub-types, viz., *labdhi* (spiritual capacity)

1. *Tattvārthasūtra* II. 22.

and *upayoga* (resultant knowledge). The soul acquires the capacity to know different objects due to the subsidence-cum-destruction of the respective *karmas* acting as covering of *matijñāna*, etc. This acquisition of capacity is called *labdhīndriya*. And the actual indeterminate or determinate knowledge which takes place in relation to objects like colour, etc. at the time when *labdhi, nirvṛtti* and *upakaraṇa* these three combine together, is *upayogendriya*. Thus, each of the five sense-organs is of four types, viz. *labdhi, nirvṛtti, upakaraṇa* and *upayoga*. That is to say, it is the collective totality of these four types that constitutes a sense-organ taken in its entirety. Thus, precisely to the extent this collective totality is deficient, the corresponding sense-organ too is deficient. Though *upayogendriya* is, in fact, something resulting from the collective totality of *labdhi, nirvṛtti* and *upakaraṇa*, it has been called a sense-organ in a figurative sense, that is, as a result of attributing to an effect a feature which, in fact, belongs to its cause. *Upayoga* means knowledge. *Labdhīndriya* is the inner spiritual capacity instrumental in its generation, while *nirvṛttīndriya* and *upakaraṇendriya* are the two forms of a physical sense-organ which is an external instrument in its generation. The operation (*upayoga*) of the inner spiritual capacity is nothing but knowing or cognising. So, it is quite proper to employ the term '*upayoga*' in the sense of knowledge.

Of the five types of knowledge, we have already dealt with *matijñāna* and *śrutajñāna*. *Avadhijñāna* (clairvoyance) and *manaḥparyāyajñāna* (telepathy) are perceptual really and not merely empirically, because they do not depend on sense-organs for their generation. They are generated directly without the mediation of sense-organs and mind, on account of the power of soul. They arise directly from within the knower's self. *Avadhijñāna* is not of one type, but of innumerable types. It is that knowledge which directly grasps the physical things lying within certain spatial and temporal limits, even if those things are covered or obstructed by some other things like wall, screen, etc. or even if they are spatially and temporally remote. *Manaḥparyāyajñāna* is that knowledge which lucidly perceives the states (modes) of the material mind-substances of others. One having *manaḥparyāyajñāna* can know as to what the other person is thinking. *Kevalajñāna* is the perfect knowledge. It is omniscience.

To attain the highest state of self-isolation or liberation, one should understand the way of ascending the ladder leading to that state, that is, the gradual development of the soul. This being the subject-matter of the Jaina theory of spiritual development, now we propose to deal with it.

STAGES OF SPIRITUAL DEVELOPMENT (GUṆAŚREṆĪ OR GUṆASTHĀNA)

The Jaina thinkers recognise fourteen stages of spiritual development. They are called *guṇasthāna*s. The term '*guṇasthāna*' means a state of spiritual quality. The development of the spiritual quality takes place through the fourteen stages.

In the acquisition of the spiritual quality, the living beings in the second and third stages are more advanced than those in the first and those in the fourth are more advanced than those in the second-third. Thus, living beings in the succeeding stages are more advanced than those in the preceding stages. But there is one exception to this. Initially, all the living beings are in the first stage. Of them some who make spiritual efforts gradually advance and pass through the successive stages; when they attain the twelfth stage, they become free from passions and destroy delusion; when they attain the thirteenth stage, they become liberated-while-living and at death they enter the fourteenth stage and at once attain the disembodied state of liberation. Those whose spiritual efforts are mild have to halt for long at several intermediary stages and to experience rise and fall many times. So, they take much time to reach the twelfth stage or the way leading to it. Some great spiritual practisers whose spiritual efforts are hard, advance very fast not halting at the intermediary stages for long, soon reach the twelfth stage and at once attain the thirteenth stage where they become omniscient.

Though the subject is very subtle, one will find it interesting provided one tries to understand it with due attention. It relates to the spiritual evolution of soul. There is the ladder with steps that helps living beings reach the palace of liberation. They start ascending the ladder from the first step. Some ascend slowly and some ascend fast. All make efforts according to their capacity. Some falter and fall down while ascending, because they are not vigilant and alert. While falling, some go down even to the first step. Even those who have attained the eleventh stage suddenly fall down when delusion strikes them. So, the works on the spiritual science have warned[1] the living beings against being lethargic and negligent while ascending the ladder. Once a person has attained the twelfth

---

1. In the tenth chapter of *Uttarādhyayanasūtra*, Lord Mahāvīra has given good and wholesome advice to all the living beings, though he directly addressed it to Indrabhūti Gautama. He said, "O Gautama! Do not be unmindful and careless even for a moment".

stage, there is no danger whatsoever for him of falling down. After the beginning of destruction of delusion at the eighth-ninth stages, the danger of falling down is totally removed.

[Even one who has attained the eleventh stage falls down because he has caused subsidence of delusion and not its destruction. But if the process of destruction instead of subsidence begins at the eighth-ninth stages, there will remain no possibility of falling down.]

In the term '*guṇasthāna*' the term '*guṇa*' has the meaning 'degrees of spiritual development'. It is believed that the higher the degrees of spiritual development, the higher are the stages of spiritual development. So the stages of spiritual development are innumerable, because they are as many as are the internal changes of the soul. We divide the stream of a river by the imagined measure of mile, etc. But thereby a permanent boundary line does not come into existence in the stream, nor is the stream actually divided into parts, nor is one part actually separated from another. Similarly, the boundary of any one stage is so connected and mingled with those of the immediately preceding and succeeding ones that all the stages form one continuous stream, so to say. But for the sake of convenience of description that stream is divided into fourteen stages of spiritual development.

The names of the fourteen stages are as follows: *Mithyātva, Sāsādana, Miśra, Aviratisamyagdṛṣṭi, Deśavirata, Pramatta, Apramatta, Apūrvakaraṇa, Anivṛttikaraṇa, Sūkṣmasamparāya, Upaśāntamoha, Kṣīṇamoha, Sayogakevalī, Ayogikevalī.*

1. *Mithyātvaguṇasthāna*

When a living being does not have the right faith in or inclination for the path leading to spiritual welfare, or on the contrary has wrong understanding about it and suffers from illusion and ignorance, it is in the first stage. Living beings from the smallest worm to the great pundits, ascetics, kings and sovereigns exist in this stage. It is so because absence of the true spiritual attitude is *mithyātva* and where there is *mithyātva*, all other progress has no value at all. *Mithyātva* means to accept the sinner as the saint, the evil act as the good act, the wrong path as the right path, and *vice versa.* Not only that but to believe in superstitions and harmful customs is also *mithyātva.* In short, in the path of spiritual welfare, the lack of discrimination of what is worthy of action from what is unworthy of it is *mithyātva.*

Ācārya Haribhadra in his *Yogadṛṣṭisamuccaya* traces the spiritual evolution through eight yogic *dṛṣṭi*s (visions). They are—*Mitrā, Tārā, Balā, Dīprā, Sthirā, Kāntā, Prabhā* and *Parā*. That *dṛṣṭi* where the primary good qualities like politeness, compassion, friendliness, absence of the envy of the meritorious, desire for the attainment of spiritual welfare make their appearance is called *Mitrā*. And in attaining this *dṛṣṭi*, one attains the first *guṇasthāna*, says Ācārya Haribhadra. Thus, the first *guṇasthāna* is the primary stage where good qualities manifest themselves. Yet it is given the name '*Mithyātva*', because at this stage right faith or inclination has not manifested itself. In this stage, the good qualities which are the means to the attainment of spiritual development are present, hence here *mithyātva* is not intense. But *mithyātva*, though mild, is no doubt there. So, this stage is given the name '*Mithyātva*'. At the same time, it is characterised by the manifestation of good qualities which lead to spiritual development. So, it is regarded as *guṇasthāna*.

Ācārya Hemacandra in his *Yogaśāstra* (*Vṛtti* on I.16) writes: *guṇasthānatvam etasya bhadrakatvādyapekṣayā*. That is, *Mithyātvaguṇasthāna* is regarded as *guṇasthāna* on the basis of the presence of softness of heart, humility, etc.

All living beings—whether small or great—who have not attained even the first yogic *dṛṣṭi* called *Mitrā* and are still below it are also considered to be in the first *guṇasthāna*. For it three reasons are given in the Jaina philosophical works: (1) Even they know and accept man as man, animal as animal, bird as bird, and so on. Thus, they have valid knowledge about many things. (2) However minute they may be, they do possess sentiency which constitutes the nature of soul. (3) Though they are below the level of *guṇasthāna*, it is possible for them alone to rise to the level of *guṇasthāna*. So, from the standpoint of possibility, they are considered to be in the first *guṇasthāna*.

2. [1]*Sāsādana-guṇasthāna*

This is the stage characterised by the fall from right faith. When at the

1. Passions, viz., anger, etc. of the *anantānubandhī* (the most intense) type are called *āsādana* because they shake and slacken *samyagdarśana* (right faith in or predilection for truth). And *sāsādana* means that which is accompanied by *āsādana*. According to the usages like '*sīdanti mama gātrāṇi*', etc., the verbal root '*sad*' means 'to be loose, to be slack, to be languid'. *Sādana* is a noun formed from the causal of the verbal root '*sad*'. *Sādana* means 'that which loosens or slackens or weakens'. '*Ā*' prefixed to '*sādana*' strengthens this meaning. Thus '*sāsādana*' means 'associated with *āsādana*',

end of the period of the dawn of right faith, there is the rise of the most intense passions, the soul falls down from the right faith to this stage. Thus, this stage is the state of fall from right faith to delusion or wrong faith. Once the process of downfall starts, it does not take much time to land on the first step. So, this stage is of a moments's duration only. The souls climbing up the ladder of subsidence fall down to this stage. But those climbing up the ladder of destruction never fall down to this stage. The souls falling down to this stage necessarily fall back to the first stage. Thus, the souls do not pass on to the second stage from the first, but only halt at it for a moment, while falling down from some higher stage of spiritual development.

3. *Miśra-guṇasthāna*

In this stage, the soul is characterised by a peculiar internal transformation which is of the form of a mixture of right faith and wrong faith. When a soul suddenly for the first time sees truth, it is struck with wonder. Its old tendencies drag it back while the new ones drag it forward. This type of tug of war lasts for some time. Afterwards, it either lapses into *mithyātva* or attains *samyaktva.* This stage is spiritually more advanced than the first two, because here there is an absence of the most intense passions. But here, there is no perfect discrimination of what is right from what is wrong. Here there is a mixture of right faith and wrong faith. That is, the soul in this stage has neither faith nor the absence of faith regarding the right path, but it has the vacillating internal state. Two opposite forces work upon it—one dragging it towards truth and the other dragging it towards untruth. As a result of this, it either falls back to the first stage or rises up to a higher stage of right faith.

4. *Avirati-samyagdṛṣṭi*

The meaning of this term is 'right faith accompanied by non-abstinence'. The soul at this stage acquires the right faith, but is lacking in spiritual efforts, that is, it cannot abstain from the wrong path and evil

---

and '*āsādana*' means 'intense passions, viz., anger, etc. that slacken, weaken or shake the right faith'. The stage called *Sāsādana* is characterised by the rise of intense passions that cause downfall and destroy right faith.

Sāsvādana is also the name of this *guṇasthāna.* It means 'associated with the experience of the taste—the taste of the right faith or inclination which is being "vomitted".'

activities. As soon as it attains right faith, the duration of the period of its transmigratory cycle gets fixed. This stage is the basic ground of the spiritual development. The soul at this stage has steady right faith, but is lacking in the capacity for spiritual self-control in conformity with the right faith.

Let us understand clearly the difference between the two persons—one having wrong faith and the other having right faith. The person possessed of wrong faith does not have any religious feeling. He is destitute of the good mental state which enables one to experience equality and oneness with all living beings. He keeps relation with others with the retaliatory or selfish motive. On the other hand, the person possessed of right faith is saturated with religious feeling and fervour, and has spiritual inclination or attitude. He progresses in the direction of spiritual welfare according to his ability. He has firm conviction that others' souls are like his and therefore he should do to others, as he would be done to by them. If on account of his attachment to worldly objects, he some time performs such bad acts, to achieve his selfish ends, as would do harm to others, his conscience bites him and he repents for his evil acts. He resolves to decrease the defects like anger, etc., and the vicious acts. He lives in conformity with the resolve according to his ability. What is vice and evil from the religious standpoint is not accepted as vice and evil by the one afflicted with wrong faith and inclination (*mithyātva*). As he is after sensual pleasures, he does not make any distinction between good acts and bad acts, while striving for their attainment. He does not accept the evil path as evil path. He adopts the evil path without the slightest hesitation. Even if he does good to others, he does so with selfish motive, partisan spirit or feeling of pride. On the other hand, the person having right faith exudes spiritual lustre of self-dedication and self-sacrifice. He is permeated with the feeling of universal compassion and friendliness.

5. *Deśavirati*

To practise properly the householder's vows with right faith is *deśavirati.* Not complete but partial abstinence from immoral acts is the meaning of the term '*deśavirati*'.

6. *Pramatta-guṇasthāna*

This is the stage of the monks who have taken the great vows. Though, at this stage, there is complete abstinence from unvirtuous acts, there does exist spiritual lethargy or carelessness (*pramāda*). At times, due to idleness the monk neglects the religious acts or acts of duty and thereby shows disrespect towards them; he does not perform them, or performs them carelessly. This is *pramāda*. Negligence, carelessness or unmindfulness causes excessive eating, excessive sleep, etc. So, they are regarded as careless acts. But moderate eating and moderate sleeping are not included in the careless acts. The rise of mild passions is not regarded as a case of *pramāda*. When the passions become intense, they are considered to be a case of *pramāda*. Why is the rise of mild passions not regarded as a case of *pramāda*? It is because the rise of passions is there even in the seventh stage and up to tenth stage too, but their intensity becomes milder and milder. Therefore, the seventh stage, though characterised by the rise of mild passions, is regarded as free from *pramāda*. And though at the stages eighth, ninth and tenth, there is the rise of milder and milder passions, they too are considered to be free from *pramāda*.

7. *Apramatta-guṇasthāna*

This is the stage of a monk who is free from spiritual lethargy (*pramāda*). Even the self-controlled monk fluctuates between the state of spiritual lethargy and that of spiritual vigilance and vigour. Constant zeal for and mindfulness in the performance of what one should perform is the state of spiritual vigilance and vigour (*apramāda*). If the slightest laxity creeps into the state, the monk is sure to lapse into the condition of spiritual lethargy.

In this stage, all careless conducts are stopped and the practice of vows becomes perfect and faultless.

8. *Apūva-karaṇa*[1]

At this stage, the soul attains unprecedented spiritual fervour necessary for effecting suppression or annihilation of the conduct-deluding *karma*. From this stage onwards begins the process of either suppression or annihilation of the conduct-deluding *karma*. (As a matter of fact, having its strong base in this stage, the process actually starts from the next, i.e., ninth *guṇasthāna*).

---

1. '*Karaṇa*' means activity of the soul.

9. *Anivṛttikaraṇa*

Unprecedented spiritual fervour and vigour already attained in the previous stage here becomes uniform in all the souls climbing up the same ladder (ladder of suppression or that of annihilation). This and the previous stage indicate the different degrees of internal purity attained by the soul.[1]

10. *Sūkṣmasamparāya*[2]

While gradually undergoing suppression or annihilation, when all (i.e., with its entire paraphernalia or family) the conduct-deluding *karma* gets suppressed or annihilated and the subtle greed (attachment) alone remains to disturb the soul, this stage is attained. Here the soul is practically free from all the four passions, except a very slight degree of greed.

11. *Upaśāntamoha*

In the case of those who have started in the ninth stage suppressing the conduct-deluding *karma* of the form of four passions, when they completely suppress them, they are in this stage. This is the reason why the stage is given the name '*Upaśāntamoha*'. The subtle greed which was active in the previous stage is also suppressed in this stage. Thus, at this stage there is total suppression of all the four passions. Those who have attained this stage, invariably fall down to some lower stage on the rise of suppressed passions.

12. *Kṣīṇamoha*

But in the case of those who have started in the ninth stage annihilating the conduct-deluding *karmas* of the form of passions, when they completely annihilate them, they are at this stage. The subtle greed which was active in the tenth stage is also destroyed in this stage. That is, the soul which has started climbing up the ladder of destruction in the ninth stage goes up from the tenth directly to this twelfth stage. The eleventh stage

1. *Apūrvakaraṇa* and *anivṛttikaraṇa* operative in the first stage are related to right faith. Similarly, the two operative in the eighth and the ninth stages respectively are related to the highest conduct.
2. '*Samparāya*' means passions in general but in the present context it means a particular passion, viz. greed.

is not for it. The eleventh and the twelfth both the stages are characterised by perfect equanimity, but the only difference between the two is that the former is not permanent whereas the latter is permanent. In other words, the fall from the former is certain, whereas there is no possibility whatsoever of the fall from the latter.

Let us understand the difference between subsidence and destruction. Generally, it is said in explanation that to extinguish fire by pouring water on it is its destruction while to cover it with ashes is its subsidence. Though deluding karmic material particles are totally subsided, they do rise again. Subsidence is a sort of spiritual purity that comes about as a result of complete cessation of the rise of deluding karmic particles, which are still dormantly present in the inmost recesses of the soul, just like the clarity appearing in water in which dirt has gathered at bottom. But how long will this purity last? The subsided deluding karmic particles rise again within a short period of time and soil the soul as soon as it is internally agitated, just as the dirt particles settled down at bottom at once come up and spread throughout the entire water as soon as it is slightly agitated. As a result of this, the soul falls down to the lower stages. The soul who has attained the total subsidence of delusion invariably falls down to the lower stages. On the other hand, the soul who has attained the total destruction of delusion at once gains *kevalajñāna* (omniscience, the pure knowledge). It is so because after its destruction, there is no possibility of the rise of delusion again. At this twelfth stage of spiritual development the soul enters into the pure trance (*śuklasamādhi*), the highest meditation, totally destroys the deluding, knowledge-obscuring, vision-obscuring and obstructive karmic matter, and as a result attains *kevalajñāna* (omniscience).

13. *Sayogakevalī-guṇasthāna*

And on the attainment of omniscience, the spiritual practiser attains this stage. In the name of this stage, there occurs the term '*sayoga*' which means 'possessed of *yoga*'. The term '*yoga*' in the Jaina philosophy has a technical sense. It means 'activity of the mind, the organ of speech and the body'. Even after the attainment of omniscience, a person performs mental, vocal and bodily activities. He walks, speaks, etc. As he is having threefold activity, he is called '*sayoga*'. And as he is possessed of *kevalajñāna* (omniscience), he is called '*kevalī*'. Thus, he is the omniscient with threefold activity (*sayogakevalī*). So, this stage is equivalent of what is known as the *jīvanmukta* (the-liberated-while-living) stage in other systems of Indian philosophy.

Among the eight basic types of *karmas*, the *mohanīya-karma* (the deluding *karma*) is the chief one. As already said, it has two sub-types, viz., *darśana-mohanīya* (faith-deluding) and *cāritra-mohanīya* (conduct-deluding). And as pointed out there, '*darśana*' in this context means right faith in the essentials of spiritual welfare or right spiritual understanding. So, that karmic matter which obstructs it is called *darśana-mohanīya.* And that karmic matter which obstructs good conduct is called *cāritra-mohanīya.* That soul whose all the faith-deluding karmic material particles have stopped rising for an *antarmuhūrta* (a period of up to fortyeight minutes) attains right faith for that much period only, and that right faith is called *upaśamasamyaktva* ('right faith due to the subsidence of faith-deluding karmic matter'). In the light of that right faith, the soul makes efforts to purify the faith-deluding karmic matter which is sure to rise after the *antarmuhūrta.* On account of this process of purification, some portion of the faith-deluding karmic matter becomes pure after the removal of impurities and that portion is called '*samyaktvamohanīya*'; some other portion which becomes semi-pure is called '*miśramohanīya*'; and the third portion which remains as impure as it was before the beginning of the process is called '*mithyātvamohanīya*'.[1] Thus, the entire mass of the faith-deluding karmic matter is divided into three heaps. Of these three heaps, one is pure (that is, it does not obscure the right faith by its rise), the second is semi-pure (that is, it obscures the right faith partially by its rise) and the third is impure (that is, it obscures right faith completely by its rise). On the rise of the pure heap of faith-deluding karmic matter (*samyaktvamohanīya*), the soul acquires the *kṣayopaśamasamyaktva,* because

---

1. The compound '*darśanamohanīya*' is resolved as follows: *darśanaṁ mohayati iti.* The term '*mohanīya*' in the compound means 'that which confuses or obstructs'. Thus, the compound '*darśanamohanīya*' means 'that which obstructs *darśana,* i.e., right faith'. But the names of the sub-types of *darśanamohanīya,* viz., *samyaktvamohanīya, miśramohanīya* and *mithyātvamohanīya* are not to be explained as 'that which obstructs *samyaktva,* i.e., *darśana* (right faith)', 'that which obstructs *miśra,* i.e., mixture of *samyaktva* and *mithyātva*' and 'that which obstructs *mithyātva* (wrong faith)' respectively. Instead, they are to be explained as 'deluding karmic matter of the form of *samyaktva*', 'deluding karmic matter of the form of *miśra,* i.e., mixture of *samyaktva* and *mithyātva*' and 'deluding karmic matter of the form of *mithyātva*' respectively. *Samyaktvam eva mohanīyaṁ samyaktvamohanīyaṁ, miśram eva mohanīyaṁ miśramohanīyaṁ, mithyātvam eva mohanīyaṁ mithyātvamohanīyaṁ /*

the pure faith-deluding karmic matter does not obstruct the right faith just as the pure transparent glass does not obstruct our vision. But if there takes place the rise of the semi-pure heap of faith-deluding karmic matter (*miśramohanīya*), the soul will have mixed state of right and wrong faith, that is, it will fluctuate between the two. And if there takes place the rise of the impure heap of faith-deluding karmic matter (*mithyātvamohanīya*), the soul will again be blinded by wrong faith.

On account of the subsidence of all the three heaps of faith-deluding karmic matter as also of the subsidence of all the four passions of the *anantānubandhī* type, the *upaśamasamyaktva* manifests itself. This type of *samyaktva* is attained by those souls who have taken the course of subsidence in the spiritual ascent.

The difference between *upaśamasamyaktva* and *kṣayopaśamasamyaktva* is that in the former there is neither effective rise[1] nor nominal rise[2] of any faith-deluding karmic matter, whereas in the latter there is destruction of that portion of *mithāytvamohanīya* karmic mater (impure faith-deluding karmic matter) which has nominally manifested itself as also subsidence of its other portion which has not manifested itself. Thus, *kṣayopaśamasamyaktva* is so called, because it is caused by the two processes taking place simultaneously—one, that of subsidence, and the other, that of destruction. Again, it is of the form of the effective manifestation of the *samyaktvamohanīya* karmic matter (pure faith-deluding karmic matter). Thus, *upaśamasamyaktva* being of the nature of pure spiritual state is better than *kṣayopaśamasamyaktva* which depends on the effective rise of *samyaktvamohanīya* karmic matter. But *kṣāyikasamyaktva* is the best because it is the result of the total destruction of the threefold faith-deluding karmic matter, *viz.*, *mithyātvamohanīya*, *miśramohanīya* and *samyaktvamohanīya* and of the four passions of the highest degree. It is called *kṣāyika,* because it is attained through the process of destruction. Thus, *samyaktva* is of three main types.

Now we propose to study the types of conduct-deluding *karma.* They are twenty-five. They are as follows: The sixteen passions (*kaṣāyas*): anger, pride, deceit and greed—these are the four chief types of passions. Each of them has been said to be of four types depending on the degree of its intensity, viz., *anantānubandhī, apratyākhyānāvaraṇa, pratyākhyānāvaraṇa*

---

1. Rise attended with fruit is effective rise (*vipākodaya*).
2. Rise which does not affect the soul is nominal rise (*pradeśodaya*).

and *saṁjvalana*. The previous one is more intense than the succeeding one. Those anger, pride, deceit and greed which make the soul wander about from one worldly state to another for an infinite period of time are of the *anantānubandhī* type. Or, they are so called because they cause infinite misery by causing wrong faith. Those anger, pride, deceit and greed which obstruct partial renunciation of unvirtuous acts, that is, which hamper the proper conduct of a man taking the layman's vows are of the *apratyākhyānāvaraṇa* type. Those anger, pride, deceit and greed which obstruct not partial renunciation but complete renunciation of unvirtuous acts are of the *pratyākhyānāvaraṇa* type. Those anger, pride, deceit and greed which do not obstruct the complete renunciation but do obstruct the pure conduct completely free from attachment are of the *saṁjvalana* type. From this, it follows that when the spiritual practiser gets rid of the passions of the *anantānubandhī* type, he attains right faith which is of the nature of the fourth stage of spiritual development; when he gets rid of the passions of the *apratyākhyānāvaraṇa* type, he attains partial renunciation of unvirtuous acts, that is, now he practises the layman's vows; when he gets rid of the passions of the *pratyākhyānāvaraṇa* type, he attains total renunciation of the unvirtuous acts, that is, now he practises the great vows of the monk; and when he gets rid of the passions of the *saṁjvalana* type, he attains pure conduct free from all sort of attachment. Thus, we have enumerated sixteen types of passions. There are nine quasi-passions (*nokaṣāya*) associated with passions. They are—laughter, liking, disliking, fear, sorrow, disgust, sexual cravings for male, female and hermaphrodite species. Thus, the total number of the types of conduct-deluding *karma* comes to twenty-five. And, as already stated, the total number of the types of right-faith-deluding *karma* is three. So, the total number of the types of the deluding *karma* comes to twenty-eight. The soul who has attained, in the fourth stage of spiritual development, *upaśama* or *kṣāyika samyaktva* by effecting subsidence or destruction of the seven out of twenty-eight types, viz., three types of right-faith-deluding *karma* and the four passions of the *anantānubandhī* type, effects subsidence or destruction of the remaining types except one, viz., greed of the *saṁjvalana* type in the eighth and ninth stages. The soul who has started climbing up the ladder of subsidence suppresses this subtle greed in the tenth stage and ascends to the eleventh stage. And the soul who has started climbing up the ladder of destruction destroys the subtle greed in the tenth stage and ascends from the tenth to the twelfth stage; the eleventh stage is not for him. On the destruction of the subtle greed, the deluding *karma* is totally destroyed. With the destruction of the deluding *karma*, the knowledge-covering, the vision-covering and the obstructive *karmas* are destroyed. And the soul attains omniscience in this twelfth stage. As already stated, wrong faith, non-abstinence, spiritual lethargy, passions and activity are the causes of bondage. On the presence of the previous one, all the succeeding ones are present. But on the presence of the succeeding one, the previous ones may or may not be present. For instance, on the presence of wrong faith, all the other causes of bondage, viz., non-abstinence, etc. are present; but on the presence of non-abstinence, wrong faith may or may not be present. In the first stage of spiritual development, wrong faith and non-abstinence both are present while in the second, third and fourth stages there exists non-abstinence but not wrong faith. Similarly, where there is passion, there is activity; but it is not true that where there is activity, there is passion, because the activity of the omniscient in the embodied state is absolutely free from passions. As the soul advances on the path of spiritual progress, the causes of bondage gradually disappear one by one. For instance, at the fourth stage on the attainment of right faith, the wrong faith disappears; thus at this stage there is the stoppage (*saṁvara*) of the manifestation of wrong faith. Similarly, on the attainment of the spiritual stage of abstinence, non-abstinence disappears; thus at this stage there is the stoppage of non-abstinence. On the attainment of the spiritual stage (seventh) of spiritual vigilance, spiritual lethargy disappears; thus at this stage there is the stoppage of the manifestation of spiritual lethargy. On the attainment of the stage of subsidence or destruction of delusion (eleventh or twelfth stage), passions disappear; thus at this stage, there is the stoppage of the manifestation of passions. And at last at the time of his death the practiser in the fourteenth stage of spiritual development attains the state of non-activity; thus at this stage, there is the stoppage of activity.

On the total and absolute destruction of delusion in the thirteenth stage, no new *karmas* are bound henceforth, that is, there is an end to the process of bondage. This means that there is an absolute stoppage of the inflow of karmic matter into the soul. (The momentary bondage of pleasure-giving *karma* is of no consequence and count.) This is the stage of the liberated-while-living (the omniscient with three-fold activity). And the disembodied state of liberation is attained in the fourteenth stage. Both the processes of *saṁvara* (stoppage of the inflow of karmic matter) and *nirjarā* (dissociation of the bound karmic matter) reach their completion in the thirteenth stage. The process of *nirjarā* reaches its completion when the soul leaves the mortal body at the death in the thirteenth stage.

Before the liberation of the nature of the total destruction of all the *karmas*, there should be gradual increase in the partial destruction of the *karmas*. Here destruction means dissociation. In all the worldly souls, the process of dissociation of the bound *karmas* goes on, but the process of dissociation which is of the nature of spiritual welfare begins only after the soul becomes inclined towards the path of liberation. And the soul's spiritual development reaches its climax when it attains the state of Jinahood. The pilgrim's spiritual progress beginning with the attainment of right inclination (faith) and ending in the attainment of Jinahood is grossly divided into ten stages for the sake of convenience. The greater the internal purity, the more is the karmic matter dissociated from the soul. So, the karmic matter dissociated from the soul in the succeeding stage is innumerable times greater than that dissociated in the immediately preceding one, because the internal purity in the succeeding stage is much more than that in the immediately preceding one. Thus, when the soul attains the state of Jinahood, the quantity of karmic matter dissociated from the soul is highest. The ten stages or states in point are as follows:

1. The state of *samyagdṛṣṭi,* wherein the wrong inclination (faith) is removed and consequently right inclination is attained.
2. The state of *upāsaka,* wherein the partial abstinence from unvirtuous acts manifests itself.
3. The state of *virata,* wherein the total abstinence from unvirtuous acts manifests itself.
4. The state of *anantaviyojaka,* wherein such internal purity as is necessary for the destruction of the most intense passions is attained.
5. The state of *darśanamohakṣapaka,* wherein such internal purity as is necessary for the destruction of the faith-deluding *karma* is attained.
6. The state of *upaśamaka,* wherein the process of subsidence of the conduct-deluding *karma* of various types continues.
7. The state of *upaśānta,* wherein that process of subsidence is completed.

8. The state of *kṣapaka,* wherein the process of destruction of conduct-deluding *karma* of various types continues.
9. The state of *kṣīṇamoha,* wherein that process of destruction is completed.
10. The state of *Jina,* wherein Jinahood (omniscience) manifests itself.

Jina, the highest embodied soul possessed of omniscience, arrests all the activities of the mind, the organ of speech and the body when his life-span comes to an end (i.e., when his death occurs).

14. *Ayogī-kevalī-guṇasthāna*

This is the spiritual stage where the practiser stops all his threefold activity with spiritual efforts. *Ayogī* means one free from all activities or operations. As soon as the omniscient in the embodied state becomes free from all activities, he leaves his mortal body and attains the disembodied state of liberation resplendent with its pure light which is non-corporeal and non-physical.

At this juncture, let us ponder a little over spiritualness.

SPIRITUALNESS (ADHYĀTMA)

The events of the world are incomprehensible and unfathomable. In the world the miserable beings are countless while happy ones are very rare. The entire world is full of sufferings, sorrows, mental distresses, bodily pains, diseases, dangers, humiliations, privations and disappointments. It is like a conflagration in which living beings are burning. All the external means of pleasure and happiness cannot make man happy, calm and peaceful. Acquisition of wealth cannot remove miseries and tensions. Roots of misery lie in the defects of mental perversions like desire, anger, greed, pride, jealousy, hatred, etc. The world afflicted with delusion and attachment to sensual pleasures is the world of misery.

Happiness and misery entirely depend upon mental states. Even a man rolling in riches is unhappy either because he is caught in the whirls of greed or because he is avaricious. On the other hand, a poor man is not agitated because he is under the influence of his mental state of contentedness. This mental state is acquired through the exercise of the power of discrimination. So, he passes his life happily. Streams of experiences of happiness and misery alternate according to the unintelligible rounds of mental states. Roots of miseries lie in the varied agitated mental states.

There is no doubt that we require water and food for the sustenance of our body.[1] Similarly, we require external objects for our livelihood or happiness and peace. But even in the scarcity of these things, the noble and saintly persons can keep their selves calm and composed and do not allow their internal development to be weak. It is so because they have acquired right understanding and the wealth of contentedness gifted by it.

Generally, we can be happy in this life and this world and can live happily, provided we are satisfied with what we have, earn the necessities of life in a just and honest way and with our own labour, cultivate an outlook of taking care of mental peace, and do not hanker after material happiness and sensual pleasure. In short, mental peace and calmness resulting from the contented innocent living constitute the real happiness which anybody can have—be he rich or poor, resident of a village or a city.[2]

Really one who has conquered mind has conquered all. This statement is perfectly true. The victor of mind is the victor of the whole world.

Attachment, aversion and delusion are the mental states. The wheel of

---

1. Reflections of Muni Ṛṣabhadeva before the attainment of omniscience:
pradīpā iva tailena pādapā iva vāriṇā/
āhāreṇaiva vartante śarīrāṇi śarīriṇām //
adyāpi yadi vā"hāram atikrāntadineṣv iva/
na gṛhṇāmy abhigrahāya kintūttiṣṭhe punar yadi//
amī sahasrāś catvāra ivā' bhojanapīḍitā/
tadā bhaṅgaṁ grahīṣyanti bhāvino munayo'pare //
svāmī manasikṛtyaivaṁ bhikṣārthaṁ calitas tataḥ /
—*Triṣaṣṭiśalākāpuruṣacarita,* Ācārya Hemacandra, I.iii. 239-43
"The lamp requires oil and the tree requires water for their existence. Similarly, the embodied souls require food for the sustenance of their bodies. Till to-day for one whole year I lived without food. And if still further I do not take any food and I take the vow to that effect, then the monks in future (in their attempt to follow me) will break their vow on account of the unbearable pain of hunger just as those four thousand monks in the past broke their vow on account of the unbearable pain of hunger." Thinking so, Lord Ṛṣabha started his tour for begging food.
2. A great philosopher Milton writes: "A mind can make heaven of hell and hell of heaven. We may be unhappy even while sitting on a mountain of gold and happy even without a pie in our pocket. I think that true happiness comes when we are neither rich nor poor, but just able to meet our requirements and reasonable comforts of life. The struggle of existence kills the joy of life. Easy life makes life dull and inactive. I think true happiness consists in working for needs but never in becoming greedy."

the worldly existence moves on the pivot of these three. It is only the science of spiritual welfare that can show us how to remove these three defects which cause spiritual disease. But to realise that one is suffering from this disease is very difficult. When the waves of worldly delusion are dashing against the mind and the heart is blinded by the dazzling light of the lightning of sensual pleasures and the self is caught in the strong whirls of desires, it is very difficult to know one's hidden deep-rooted disease. The ignorant souls in such conditions are at the lowest scale of degradation. Those who have risen up from this state of degradation consider themselves to be stricken with those three defects, understand themselves to be burning in the unbearable heat generated by the defects and therefore are eager to find out the remedy of the defects. If the spiritual 'medicine' is brought to light, they will surely be benefited by it.

The term '*adhyātma*' is formed of two words, viz., '*adhi*' and '*ātmā*'. '*Adhi*' means 'with reference to, concerning, on the subject of', and '*ātmā*' means soul. Thus the term '*adhyātma*' means 'concerning soul' and 'concerning spiritual welfare'. To regard the attainment of pure nature of soul as one's ultimate goal and to strive for it is *adhyātma*. Or, to move in the direction of spiritual development is *adhyātma*. In short, *adhyātma* is a spiritual life. In the science of spiritualness, the sentient and insentient reals are treated of, explaining all the essential points. To know the one, the knowledge of the other is necessary. Without knowing the one, the other cannot be known in its entirety.

What is soul? Why does it experience happiness and misery? Is soul's bondage with something else the cause of it? How can the soul be bound with the karmic matter? Has this bondage the beginning? Or, is it beginningless? If beginningless, how can it be destroyed? What is the nature of karmic matter? What are its types and subtypes? What governs the bondage, rise and existence of karmic matter? What is the nature of soul's present state? Is it possible for the soul to attain its pure and pristine state? If yes, how? Treatment of all these points come within the scope of the subject-matter of the science of spiritualness.

Moreover, in its subject-matter is included the vivid description of the emptiness of the worldly cycle and also that of miseries one experiences in one's wanderings in the worldly existence on account of one's defects of attachment, aversion and delusion. By explaining the subject-matter of various meditational reflections in various ways, the science of spiritualness mainly aims at weakening delusion and attachment and its entire teaching flows towards that goal with full force.

Renunciation of obstinacy, freedom from hatred and prejudice, love for listening to truth, liking for the company of saintly persons, their service, listening to truth, predilection for spiritual welfare, removal of wrong faith or inclination, acquisition of right faith or inclination, destruction of passions, viz., anger, pride, deceit and greed, restraint of sense-organs, purity of mind, abandonment of feeling of mineness (attachment), manifestation of equanimity, placidity and calmness of mind, absorption in the pure nature of soul, continuous stream of meditation, manifestation of trance, destruction of the veils of delusion, etc., and at last the attainment of omniscience and liberation—all these which present the gradual spiritual evolution from the initial stage to the final accomplishment according to their order of enumeration are extensively dealt with in the spiritual science.

Terms '*adhyātma*' and '*yoga*' ultimately mean the same thing. The term '*yoga*' is derived from the verbal root '*yuj*' meaning 'to join'. The spiritually beneficial religious practice or the spiritual discipline meant for the attainment of liberation is called *yoga*, because it joins the soul with liberation. It is *adhyātma*, that is, spiritual discipline, spiritual living.

Delusion is the acute spiritual disease. The beginningless stream of karmic bondage and the beginningless wanderings in the worldly existence are due to it. It manifests itself in the forms of anger, pride, deceit and greed. The spiritual means to be employed against them are as follows. Anger is destroyed by forgiveness, pride by humility, deceit by straightforwardness and greed by contentedness. The victory over passions depends on the victory over sense-organs. And control over sense-organs is achieved through purifying mind. Mind becomes pure[1] when the defilements of attachment and aversion are removed. Their removal is effected by the water of equanimity. Equanimity manifests itself when feeling of mineness is renounced. And to renounce it, one should cultivate deep reflections on transitoriness, helplessness, etc. With the growth of strength of the reflections, the darkness of the feeling of mineness is

---

1. *asaṁśayaṁ mahābāho! mano durnigrahaṁ calam/*
abhyāsena ca Kaunteya! vairāgyeṇa ca gṛhyate//

—*Bhagavadgītā* VI. 35

O Strong-armed, the restless mind is certainly difficult to curb, but it can be controlled, O Son of Kunti (Arjuna), by constant practice and non-attachment.

proportionately removed and consequently the light of equanimity is manifested in due proportion. When the highest degree of equanimity is attained, the mental concentration is achieved as its consequence. And on account of mental concentration, the soul rises to the state of meditation or trance. Having attained this state, the spiritual practiser acquires miraculous powers. So, at this stage the danger of being entrapped and entangled in them presents itself and if he develops liking for self-admiration, self-worship, etc., the downfall is certain and immediate. Therefore, the authors of the spiritual works warn the *yogīs* possessed of the miraculous powers of knowledge and meditation against this formidable temptation. They advise them to be ever vigilant and to continue their task of destroying delusion with full perseverance. When the practiser reaches the highest peak of spiritual development, that is, the state of absolute freedom from attachment, he attains his highest cherished goal, the liberation; consequently now there is nothing left for him to attain or to strive for, and the state of the supreme soul is manifested in him. So long as he lives in his body, he is the highest soul having form. But as soon as his body leaves him he becomes the formless highest soul.

The Jaina thinkers describe three different states of the soul and consequently recognise three types of souls, viz., the exterior souls (*bahirātmā*), the interior souls (*antarātmā*), and the transcendental souls (*paramātmā*). The exterior souls are blind to the spiritual welfare. They hanker after sensual pleasures. They have the deluded belief that they are none other than the body. They are extrovert. The souls that clearly distinguish themselves from their bodies and the sense-organs are the interior souls. They turn inward and are attracted towards the inner spiritual wealth. They experience peace and calmness. They are introvert. The pure and perfect souls free from all defilements and limitations are the transcendental souls. They shine with the infinite light of knowledge.

Again, the Jaina theoreticians trace the spiritual evolution through the seven states of soul, viz., the exterior soul (*bahirātmā*), the noble soul (*bhadrātmā*), the interior soul (*antarātmā*)[1], the saintly soul (*sadātmā*)[2], the great soul (*mahātmā*)[3], the *yogī* soul (*yogātmā*) and the transcendental soul (*paramātmā*).

---

1. When the soul attains right faith or attitude, it is called the interior soul.
2. When it lives an active moral life by practising the spiritual discipline prescribed for a householder, it is called the saintly soul.
3. When it leads a life of complete renunciation of all evil acts, it is called the great soul.

The great Patañjali begins his *Yogasūtra* with the aphorism: '*yogaś cittavṛttinirodhaḥ*' ('Control of mental states is *yoga*'). It means: Mental states running outward after the worldly objects and pleasures through the doors of sense-organs should be turned inward and diverted to wholesome reflections and good thoughts; that is *yoga*. This is the first essential lesson of *Yoga*, which everyone should properly understand and constantly remember.

The greater the development of the auspiciousness of mental states, the more are their purity and calmness. Agitation subsides. Consequently mental states attain the stage of concentration. At this stage, a stream of uniform mental states continuously flows for a considerably long period of time. For not allowing the rise of bad thoughts and for keeping mental states uninterruptedly engaged in good thoughts, what is first required is the firm faith in truth; and this firm faith in truth should be followed by firm determination and sincere efforts—both in conformity with the faith. The necessary pre-requisite of the yogic practice is the constant recalling to mind the good qualities of God or the pure and perfect soul, and cultivation of good conduct.

The spiritual discipline meant for the attainment of absolute and total freedom from all karmic matter depends on the two processes[1]—one of stopping the inflow of the karmic matter and the other of dissociating the already bound karmic matter. As we have already seen, the former is called *saṁvara* and the latter *nirjarā*. For the accomplishment of these two processes one is required to undergo the spiritual discipline consist-

---

1. Swāmī Śaṅkarācārya too refers to the same two processes in the following verse of his *Sādhakapañcakastotra*.
   prākkarma pravilāpyatāṁ citibalān nāpy uttaraiḥ ślisyatām /
   prārabdhaṃ tv iha bhujyatām atha parabrahmātmanā sthīyatām //5//
   Translation: Destroy the bound *karmas* by the power of knowledge. Do not bind new *karmas*. And experience the fruits of the fructifying *karmas* (the *karmas* that have risen to give their fruits) with equanimity. This is the way to attain the nature of Supreme Soul.
   In the Jaina philosophy, three states of *karmas* are recognised, viz., that of being bound, that of mere existence and that of rise (fruition), which are called *bandha, sattā* and *udaya* respectively. In the non-Jaina systems of Indian philosophy, for the *karmas* that are being bound the term '*kriyamāṇa*' is used, for those that are merely existent (inoperative) the term '*sañcita*' is used and for those that are rising to give their fruits the term '*prārabdha*' is used.

ing of good thinking, good conduct, equanimity, self-control, austerity, renunciation of desires and passions, spiritual study, and avoidance of bad company or contact. This has been extensively expounded in the Jaina spiritual works.

The soul has infinite powers. By strong spiritual efforts, they can be developed and actualised. They are perfectly manifested when all the karmic coverings are removed. They in their state of perfection are beyond description. The miracles of physical sciences are nothing as compared to those of spiritual powers. The advancement of materialism and the prosperity acquired through it are harmful and destructible and attended with miseries, distresses, afflictions, fears and dangers. But the light of spiritual power is the beneficial, soothing, cool light. And it is the perennial fountain of pure bliss. It is infinite happiness unmixed with misery. Spiritual pilgrimage is the only way to attain it. Learning and science lead to happiness and prosperity, provided they are associated with religiosity and spiritualness; otherwise, they play havoc and cause infinite miseries and calamities.

Soteriological Reflection (Bhāvanā)

As we have just said, the power of reflection weakens delusion and feeling of attachment. The Jaina authors treat of twelve soteriological reflections. These reflections increase man's detachment from the world, protect him from harmful tendencies and spur his efforts towards final emancipation. They are conceived as aids to spiritual progress; they inspire renunciation of desires and promote detachment and dispassion. They are a means of purification of thoughts and incentives to liberation.

(1) *Transitoriness of all worldly objects (anitya)*

To think deeply and continuously that all things are evanescent is the reflection on the momentariness. It is an effective means of the reduction of attachment.

All things are transitory, fleeting, evanescent, in constant flux and transformation. Nothing in this world is eternal, everything is subject to change and decline. Association with loved ones, wealth, prosperity, pleasures, health, body and youth, indeed existence itself—all these are impermanent. The only foundation of embodied beings for achieving their objective is the body; but even this body is destined to destruction like the clouds devastated by strong winds. Life changes like a wave, beauty of youth lasts for a few days, wealth and possessions are transient like thoughts, and enjoyments are like flashes of autumnal lightning; old age frightens men like a tigress, diseases attack men like enemies, and life flows away like water flowing out of a leaky jar. This is contemplation on the transitory nature of things.

The things for the acquisition of which we employ unfair means and do injustice to others are transitory. And life is as short as a flash of lightning. So it is wrong and unwise to lead an unjust, dishonest and irreligious life. We may partially conquer nature, subdue other peoples and states, but we can never vanquish death. Death snatches away all our victories, conquests and gains from us. Life is very short. Why should we defile it with evil thoughts and acts? And if we defile it, there will be no end to miseries. The body is invaded by diseases, it is impermanent and fragile, it turns into ashes when burnt at death. So, why should we indulge in unwholesome acts for the sake of this body and its pleasures? It is foolishness and not wisdom to perform unvirtuous acts of violence, immorality and injustice for this transitory life[1] and as a consequence to fall down to the terrible state of degradation. This type of reflection saves us from going astray and keeps us moving ahead on the path of justice and morality. This is the usefulness of the reflection on impermanence. If we realise that like prosperity or fortune, even adversity or misfortune does not continue for long, we shall not be perturbed and distressed when adversity or misfortune befalls us and we are separated from our beloved ones. This is also the usefulness of the present reflection.

But we should not use this reflection to be inactive and idle. This is

---

1. What the great poet Kālidāsa has said in his *Raghuvaṁśa* (Canto 8, verses 87-90) is very useful in the context. The gist is as follows:
87. Death is the nature of the embodied beings, while life is a passing phase (*maraṇaṁ prakṛtiḥ śarīriṇāṁ vikṛtir jīvitam ucyate budhaiḥ*). It is God's grace that they can have a short momentary life.
88. On the death of the beloved ones, a deluded person feels and thinks that his heart is pierced with an arrow, while a wise man feels and thinks that the arrow has been removed from his heart.
89. If man has to abandon even his own body (at death), then why should he shed tears over the separation of external things that takes place during his life-time?
90. What is the difference between a tree and a mountain, if both were to be shaken by a gust of wind? (A tree is shaken but a mountain remains unshaken and firm). (*druma-sānumatāṁ kim antaraṁ yadi vāyau dvitaye'pi te calāḥ*).

to be regarded as its misuse. Only if we remain engaged in doing good to others according to our ability, it can be said that this reflection of impermanence has rightly permeated our lives. It is so because having known the impermanent as impermanent one desirous of attaining the permanent, that is, the pure nature of the soul should walk steadily on the path of righteousness, which consists of doing good to one's own self as well as to others.

Though the physical things necessary for the sustenance of the body and maintenance of life are impermanent and give pleasure mixed with misery, to secure them regularly till the end of life is inevitable. It is clear that we cannot do without them, life is impossible without them. So, we should secure or earn those things in a just and honest way and use them without any feeling of attachment. To advise us to this effect is also the purpose of this reflection. To commit suicide is prohibited.

Those who see permanence in the realm of impermanence suffer from perverse attitude. Those under delusion consider the persons and objects as permanent. But there is nothing in the world which is permanent except the pure soul with infinite knowledge.

(2) *Reflection on helplessness (aśaraṇa)*

This reflection uproots the passion of pride. Man proudly thinks, "I am a king, a sovereign, a protector of the people, a savior of the whole world, a matchless rich person, a great master, a mighty man, my supporters and followers are many, none can do any harm to me." Such a feeling of pride is improper and wrong, because none is saved from the powerful and inescapable claws of death, nor can anyone save others from them. In the presence of death, the supreme enemy of all embodied souls, everything becomes powerless; all objects of pleasure, vehicles, palaces, women, army, magical charms, medicines, wealth and prowess—all these become useless. The sons are no protection, neither father, nor the relatives, nor friends; for one overcome by death, there is no protection among kinsmen. Man alone has to suffer from the pains of acute diseases, none can share them, even the dearest person cannot mitigate them. Is this small or negligible helplessness? This reflection is to be used to reduce and uproot the feeling of pride. It is not to be used to shun compassion, friendliness and benevolent acts and thus to become utterly selfish and self-centred. Though it is a fact that we cannot cure others of their incurable diseases or protect them from formidable calamities, yet it is also a fact that we can show compassion towards them by trying to help them according to our capacity and can surely be useful to them in their efforts to achieve what is good and beneficial.

The main objective of the reflection on helplessness is to bring home to man that he should become self-dependent without desiring help from others, should take shelter under the religion of the form of good qualities like benevolence, compassion, humility, self-control, etc., he should not be proud in spite of his having good qualities and spiritual powers and benevolent acts to his credit; on the contrary, he should be soft-hearted and humble.

There is no escape from the evil consequences of our evil acts. Such is the grim reality of helplessness. He who is disgusted with the thought of his own complete helplessness, does not seek to identify himself with his body and worldly objects. He seeks to walk on the path of religion shown by the omniscient Lord. For the beings coursing through the round of repeated metempsychosis, there is no other refuge except Faith, Wisdom and Morality which should therefore be honoured with utmost devotion. He who wants to be fearless and deathless must reflect on the omnipotence of Death or Time and adopt ways and means of going beyond the sphere of worldly existence. That is to say, he who wishes to be released from the terrible jaws of Death must immediately embark upon the career of achieving *mokṣa*, the Final Release. The awareness of the fact of helplessness is the initial aim of this reflection; he who has this awareness becomes heedful and seeks only the Ultimate Release, sans fear and danger.

(3) *Reflection on the world of transmigration (saṁsāra)*

In this reflection, one contemplates on the fact that all—whether rich or poor—are miserable. This type of reflection is necessary. It keeps man on the path of righteousness. One should reflect on this fact so that one may not deviate from the path of duty and good actions and may not be a victim of trifling temptations of the world. Others appear happy. But in fact those that appear happy do not consider themselves to be happy. Though man has enough means of happiness, he is not satisfied with them and looking to others' comparatively more wealth his discontentedness flares up and forced by the growing intensity of greed and desire he keeps himself fully engaged in increasing the evils of possessions as also in nourishing other evils connected with possessions. If he realises that in spite of whatever he gets through those so many evil acts he will still remain miserable, nay, will become more miserable, then he will not have an urge to do evil acts.

It is useful to contemplate on the fact that this world is full of miseries, there is no end to natural calamities; howsomany efforts we may put in, it is utterly impossible to remove all of them completely. When such is the situation, is it proper to increase miseries by nurturing mutual indifference through mutual injustice and selfishness? It is necessary to bear in mind that we ourselves create innumerable miseries and add to the already existing ones by our own defects. By developing good humanitarian qualities as also by fostering universal friendliness, we should try to decrease the miseries in the world as far as possible. This is the objective of the present reflection.

In order that craving for the world of transmigration is done away with, a feeling of resignation or indifference has to be cultivated in relation to the things of the world. And with a view to diverting attention from such things one must reflect as follows: "In this beginningless cycle of births and deaths, there is in fact none who is own to me and none who is alien to me. For in the course of so many births, all sorts of relations have been established between me and all the beings that are there. Wandering across the endless cycle of births and deaths, passing through millions of crises in innumerable wombs and families, one assumes different forms of relationship, such as father, son, grandson and so on, or mother, wife, sister, daughter and so on. In this process of endless repetition, the master becomes the servant, and the servant the master, the mother becomes the wife, and the wife the mother; and so on. This is ridiculous and disgusting. Similarly, the beings of the world burning with attachment, aversion and delusion, and entertaining cravings for things sensuous are out to devour one another and suffer unbearable hardships as a result of a behaviour of that sort. Really speaking, this world is a garden nurturing the couples-of-opposites like joy-and-sorrow, pleasure-and-pain, etc., and is truly full of tortures." Thus, one who is disgusted with the ridiculous and terrifying nature of the world of transmigration works for one's deliverance, the Final Release.

(4) *Reflection on aloneness (ekatva)*

In order to attain liberation feeling of aloofness has to be constantly evoked on the occasion of attachment and aversion. For that, the attachment developed in relation to things considered to be one's own and the aversion developed in relation to those considered to be alien to oneself have to be discarded and so one must reflect: "I am born alone, I die alone, and alone do I reap the fruits of the form of pleasure, pain, etc. yielded by the karmic seeds sown by myself." This is called reflection on aloneness. It nourishes self-dependence and non-attachment.

This thought of loneliness should be viewed as enunciating the principle of individual liberty and individual responsibility extending to a person's trans-historical existences. One may prepare oneself to go to hell or to heaven; one may work one's way through the cycle of becoming or one may mobilise one's all resources to effect one's release once for all.

But we should remember that cooperation on which the society and the whole world are sustained is not attacked by the contemplation on aloneness. This means that others desire our help just as we desire others' help; this is an irrefutable fact. We can secure help from others to the extent we have capacity to help them. In securing benefits from our relations with others, what works is our capacity to help them. Wealth goes to him who is deserving. So, it is said, 'Deserve, then desire'. The reflection on aloneness teaches us to be deserving and capable. The aloneness means that the soul alone is useful for the cooperation of many, for the friendship of many and for the service of many. Aloneness does not mean that we should enjoy all the manifest and unmanifest benefits from the world and when we are required to give something in return we should say, 'I belong to nobody, nobody belongs to me, the world is unreal'; it is a case of roguery. The reflection on aloneness is not for strengthening selfishness, but for making us self-dependent and deserving. Again, in the state of helplessness, it saves man from being depressed and miserable and urges him to face difficulties and calamities with his entire energy single-handed. It makes us calm, perseverant and patient.

Looking from another angle, the term '*ekatva*' in the '*ekatvānuprekṣā*' means oneness or unity. Thus, it ultimately means an association of mutually friendly human beings. On the strength of such association, there prevails happiness and peace in the world and the spiritual welfare is also attained. This type of reflection is called *ekatvānuprekṣā*.

(5) *Reflection on difference (anyatva)*

This is the contemplation on the fact that the soul for which 'I' stands is different from body.

Out of an onrush of delusion, man commits the mistake of regarding as his own rise and fall, the rise and fall of his body and of the other things belonging to him; and the result is that he fails to have a realisation of his true duty. In order to forestall a contingency like this, a false imposition of ownership in relation to the alien things like body, etc., has to be done away with. For that the separateness of soul from body is to be reflected over on the basis of their qualities as follows: "This body is gross, possessed of a beginning and an end, and is something inanimate, while I myself am subtle, possessed of no beginning and an end, and am something conscious." On account of this type of reflection, man is not agitated and perturbed by bodily pains and pleasures. Generally, his all energy is used up in thinking about bodily pains and pleasures. If he knows as to who he is, in the light of that pure knowledge, he may not develop attachment for the body, nor will he become a slave of sense-organs, and will be saved from miseries and calamities arising from attachment to body as also from ignorance and delusion. And with the growth of true realisation of 'I', his real happiness increases. He realises that the real happiness does not depend on the external objects, but on the soul itself; its source is the soul or the mind. And the more the purity of soul or mind attained, the higher are the stages of real peace and happiness secured.

(6) *Reflection on the impurity of the body (aśuci)*

One's body being most eminently an object for craving, one must, with a view to reducing attachment for one's body, reflect: "This body is itself impure, it is born out of things impure, it is nourished by things impure, it is a seat of things impure, it is the ultimate cause of a series of things impure." There are two advantages of this reflection: (1) It destroys the pride of family, caste and race, and it removes the hypocrisy of touchability-untouchability. It makes us realise that it is utterly foolish to imagine that bodies of some persons are pure while those of others are impure and consequently to regard the former as touchable and the latter as untouchable. As a matter of fact, all bodies are uniformly impure. (2) It reduces attachment for the body and bodily pleasures. It destroys pride pertaining to our bodies. We should not be proud of the beauty of our body.

But in the name of this reflection on the impurity of the body, one should not be indifferent to cleanliness.

Though the body is impure, we cannot afford to remain indifferent to or careless about it. We should not neglect our body. We should properly maintain it. We should take proper care of it. (In maintaining it and taking its care, proper self-control is not lost sight of.) We should use it in the performance of good and benevolent acts. Instead of employing it in doing even a single evil act, we should employ it in doing good and wholesome acts alone. Its good use brings us happiness, peace and welfare, gradually puts us on the right path leading to liberation, and helps us progress on the path faster. This is the reason why it is regarded as the prime instrument of religion. *Śarīram ādyaṁ khalu dharmasādhanam.*

In view of science, the body is such a 'machine' that separates the useless and unessential substances from what we eat and drink and then discards them and retains the essential and useful ones. Thus, it discards impure substances and retains the proper ones. So, who will say that it is not a useful instrument of living? When forgetting benevolent activity, social welfare and spiritual elevation, one uses it in sensual pleasures, it becomes really impure; none should tolerate such type of impurity and it should be immediately removed. This is the noteworthy point in connection with the reflection on impurity. In other words, the objective of this reflection is to reduce and remove one's attachment for one's body, which causes neglect of soul and spiritual welfare. If one with proper self-control performs good and virtuous acts and remains always engaged in doing good to others, his body no longer remains impure, but on the contrary becomes pure as it leads one on the pure path of spiritual welfare; people desirous of spiritual welfare consider it to be pure to such an extent that they devotionally touch and worship the feet, parts of the body, regarding the touch of the feet as purifying.

(7) *Reflection on āsrava (Inflow of the karmic matter)*

Contemplation on the conditions of the bondage of the karmic matter with soul or on the causes of miseries or on the evil consequences following from attachment to sensual pleasures is called the reflection on *āsrava.*

(8) *Reflection on saṁvara (stoppage of the inflow of the karmic matter)*

Contemplation on the ways and means of the removal of the causes of the inflow of karmic matter as also of the causes of miseries is called the reflection on *saṁvara.* With a view to closing the doors for evil thoughts and evil conduct, to reflect on the merits of good thoughts and good conduct is the reflection on *saṁvara.*

(9) *Reflection on nirjarā (dissociation of karmic matter)*

Contemplation on the ways and means of destroying the causes of miseries, or on how to bear with patience and calmness miseries or on how to destroy attachment causing unending miseries is called reflection on *nirjarā.*

(10) *Reflection on the universe (loka)*

The universe is very vast. We are very small. We are nothing when compared to the stupendous universe. In it we are like an atom. We are insignificant. This makes us humble and dissolves our pride. To contemplate on the vastness of the universe, various worlds situated in it, its firmament and luminaries, etc., is called the reflection on the universe. It causes delight and feeling of wonder in us, generates indifference to our trifling selfish motives and thereby weakens our urge to do evil acts. This is the great advantage of this reflection. It also helps us cultivate many good qualities like humility, etc.

(11) *Reflection on the utter rarity of the attainment of bodhi (enlightenment, vision of truth)*

A human being is specially equipped with potentialities of effecting his Ultimate Release. It is, therefore, important for him to know the difficulties and hazards which beset a spiritual career.

In the first place, one should know that human birth is extremely rare. It is as difficult of attainment as a heap of jewels at street-crossings. After spending an infinitely long time in wanderings in innumerable lower forms of existence, a being is born in human form. Even when one is born in human form, one may still find it very difficult to be born in a favourable country. Even when one is born there, one may still find it very difficult to be born in a good family. Even when one is born in a good family, one may still find it very difficult to have a good teacher. Even when one is fortunate enough to have a good teacher, one may still find it very difficult to have desire to hear the true doctrine from his mouth. Even when one has that desire, one may still find it very difficult to attain vision of truth. One must reflect on these rarities. He who does not know the immense soteriological value of human existence, and wastes it in the pursuit of pleasures or in the acquisition of worldly possessions is like a person who burns precious jewels for ashes. The jewel of right inclination towards, or faith in, or vision of, the truth is the most precious jewel, and it is attained after suffering for innumerable aeons in the course of endless cycle of transmigration.

One cannot easily attain the human birth, good education, good company, etc. Even when one has gained all these, one may still find it very difficult to acquire right attitude or the vision of truth; even after attaining all those former things, if one surrenders to the terrible goblin of pride, one loses all one's gains. In the name of religion and sect, we foster pride and consequently create obstacles in the attainment of *bodhi* (vision of truth). Thus, to contemplate on the rarity of the attainment of vision of pure truth is called *bodhidurlabha-bhāvanā.*

(12) *Reflection on dharmasvākhyātatva*

Dharma means religion, path of purification and spiritual welfare.

Dharma is called *svākhyāta* or 'well expounded', because it is good in the beginning, good in the middle, and good in the end, and because it announces the life of purity that is wholly perfect and immaculate with meaning and with detail. Moreover, it is called *svākhyāta,* because it has been proclaimed for the good of all beings, without any discrimination of class, caste, creed, race, etc. It is described as well expounded, also because it has been well imparted, effecting synthesis of seemingly contradictory interpretations or expositions and making them harmonious and consistent. Again, it is described as well expounded, because while expounding it the large-hearted, open-minded, noble expounder has incorporated all the good points or elements, accepting them from anywhere and anybody. Narrow outlook, sectarianism, etc., have been given no place into it. It is well expounded, because it is effectual for guidance, it is conducive to peace, and also because it has been imparted by one who is supremely Enlightened.

One should contemplate on the greatness and glory of *dharma. Dharma* includes both philosophy and religion, theory and practice of good life, ascetic culture and ethical behaviour. Liberation of the soul from all the impurities is the ultimate aim of *dharma* or religious culture. *Dharma* is that which takes one to the cherished goal of liberation. It destroys *karmas,* rescues beings from the miseries and upholds them in excellent bliss.

Dharma proclaimed by the Jinas is characterised by inoffensiveness and universal love. It is established on truth. It is rooted in humility (*vinaya*), its strength lies in forbearance (*kṣamā*). It is protected by chastity (*brahmacarya*). Its chief feature is quiescence (*upaśama*). Its mark is restraint. And its prop is non-possession and non-attachment (*niṣparigraha*). It is because of their not attaining *dharma* that the beings have been suffering and coursing in endless cycle of births and deaths.

Dharma is well taught by the Jinas for the benefit of the world of beings. Those who are devoted to its practice can easily cross over the ocean of worldly existence. *Dharma* is the kinsman of those without kinsmen, the companion of those without companions, the protector of those without protection; it is indeed the only affectionate one of the whole world. *Dharma* protects one from degradation and downfall. It bestows upon beings that glory of the Omniscient which is incomparable.

Dharma is the means of attaining all the good things and true happiness. One becomes adorable through *dharma*. *Dharma* is the source of good in human life as well as in heaven. In short, *dharma* taught by the Jinas is the destroyer of all sufferings. Contemplation on the powers, attributes, greatness and glories of *dharma* is what is called the reflection on *dharmasvākhyātatva.*

Sectarianism, communalism, narrow-mindedness and vain pride dishonour *dharma* and make one indulge in slandering and cavilling.

So as not to deviate from the path of *dharma* and so as to bring about steadiness in one's practice of it one must reflect: "How highly fortunate it is that *dharma* full of doing good to the entire mass of living beings has been preached by the virtuous personages."

Bhāvanā or *anuprekṣā*[1] means deep reflection. In case a piece of reflection happens to be veracious, wholesome and deep, it prevents the onset of the tendencies like attachment and aversion. Hence, it is that such

---

1. The essence of all the soteriological reflections is found in the following verse:
mano vaco me caritaṁ ca santatam
pavitratāvāhi yadā bhaviṣyati /
tadā bhaviṣyāmi yathārtham unnataḥ
kṛtārthajanmā paramaprasādabhāk // (Author of the present work)
Translation: When all my mental, vocal and bodily activities become absolutely free from passions and thereby eternally pure, I shall attain the highest state of real spiritual welfare; my human birth will achieve the supreme goal and I shall be experiencing the perennial infinite bliss.

reflection has been described as a means of *saṁvara* (the cessation of the inflow of the karmic matter.)

Bondage and Liberation

The well-known statement occurring in the *Maitrī Upaniṣad* declares that the mind alone is the cause of man's bondage as well as liberation. *Mana eva manuṣyāṇāṁ kāraṇaṁ bandhamokṣayoḥ*. The declaration is true. It means that inauspicious mental states cause the bondage of inauspicious karmic matter, and auspicious mental states cause the bondage of auspicious karmic matter. But attachment-free pure mental state cause no bondage whatsoever. In case the activities are caused and guided by the attachment-free mental state or pure (passionless) affection, karmic bondage is not effected by such supremely pure mind; on the contrary, on account of such supremely pure mind the supreme state of Ultimate Release is manifested. This is the reason why in the above quoted half-verse mind is regarded as the cause of liberation also.

From this follows that it is not a rule that activity invariably causes bondage, activity can never cause bondage if it is not urged by the mental states of attachment and aversion. The Omniscient One stands, sits, speaks, walks, etc. like an ordinary man and performs other activities too, yet he does not bind any *karma* (the pleasure-giving *karma* which is bound for a moment being insignificant is to be neglected) because he is free from attachment. One who is really free from attachment is affectionate towards all beings, a friend of the entire world. The Omniscient One can never be inactive; on the contrary, he remains always engaged in the pure passionless activities. His activities are caused by the attachment-free mental state (passionless universal affection) and hence they do not cause bondage of *karmas*.

It is true that to perform activities without attachment and with pure universal affection alone is possible only in a supreme spiritual state. Again, it is also true that even those who have made just an ordinary progress on the path leading to that state find it very difficult to attain it. Yet to attain this difficult goal, one should make gradual progressive attempts in its direction.

The auspicious mental state which causes bondage of auspicious karmic matter is associated with attachment. And attachment invariably goes with aversion. Where there is attachment, there are selfishness, partiality, indifference to the good of others—however little they may be. And hence auspicious mental states do cause bondage according to their natures.

Yet we should remember that auspicious inflow of karmic matter caused by the auspicious activities—good activities beneficial to one's own self as also to others—is spiritually beneficial to the soul. The auspicious karmic matter bound on account of good activities performed with good mental states presents one with the means of spiritual welfare. Therefore, the auspicious karmic matter bound on account of auspicious activities should be regarded as praiseworthy. The auspicious *karmas* bring us auspicious circumstances and good and very good means of religious and spiritual culture, viz. human birth, birth in a favourable country, good family, religious and cultured parents, healthy body, good teacher, good company, etc. How important these auspicious *karmas* are! The auspicious *karma* of the highest type, viz., *tīrthaṅkaranāmakarma* is highly praiseworthy because it is the cause of the attainment of *tīrthaṅkara*hood. In all the high and low states of living except the attachment-free state, the process of karmic bondage incessantly goes on. One should bear in mind one important point that one should assiduously avoid the bondage of evil or inauspicious *karmas*, whereas one should not be afraid of the bondage of good, wholesome or auspicious *karmas*.[1]

Jaina and Non-Jaina Conceptions of Soul

The subject-matter of the spiritual science pertains to soul. So, it mainly discusses the nature of soul. Our study of the various views regarding the nature of soul removes doubts from our mind and generates its true

---

1. Study the following verse by Upādhyāya Yaśovijayaji.
naiva, yat puṇyabandho'pi dharmahetuḥ śubhodayaḥ /
vahner dāhyaṁ vināśya eva naśvaratvāt svato mataḥ // verse 17, First *Dvātriṁśikā*
Explanation: The verse declares that the bondage of auspicious *karmas* has auspicious fruition and is the cause of religious practice. It is not opposed to liberation and dissociation of karmic matter. Auspicious *karmas* destroy themselves after having destroyed the inauspicious *karmas* just as fire itself gets extinguished after having burnt the fuel.
While commenting on the 22nd verse of the same *Dvātriṁśikā*, Upādhyāyajī says that auspicious *karmas* are not an obstruction in our pilgrimage to liberation. On the contrary, they make our pilgrimage easy.
The soul having auspicious or good mental states is not attached to the objects of pleasures which it has attained on the rise of auspicious *karmas*. So, it remains self-controlled, calm, unagitated; it steadily moves on the path of religion; of course, its practice of *yoga* or spiritual discipline is not rigorous. As it is vigilant, ardently desires liberation and has pure intellect, it adopts the great path of liberation when opportunity or occasion arises and gradually advances on it.

knowledge. And on this knowledge, we can base our spiritual practice. Though this is a very vast subject, let us briefly treat of some points related to it.

Firstly, according to some philosophers[1], the soul is not limited or confined to the body, it is all-pervasive, it exists everywhere at the same time, it exists in the body and outside it simultaneously. Each body has a separate soul. Each one of these souls pervades the entire universe. This is what they maintain. Secondly, they contend that cognition is not the nature of soul. It is an accidental and adventitious quality generated in the soul on account of its contact with body, mind and sense-organ. As it is not the nature of soul, in the state of liberation it is absolutely devoid of it.

On these two points, the Jaina philosophers differ from them. Take the first point. The Jaina thinkers too believe in many souls and maintain that each body has a separate soul. But according to them, the soul is not all-pervading, it pervades only the body in which it lives. The qualities of soul, viz., cognition, desire, etc. are experienced in the body alone and not elsewhere. This fact proves that the soul too exists in the body and not outside it.[2]

Now take the second point. Cognition is not an adventitious quality of soul, it is its natural quality, it constitutes its real nature. By nature, soul is cogniser. This is the Jaina view. So, according to the Jaina philosophers, even in the disembodied state of liberation wherein it does not have mind, body and sense-organs and hence their contacts the soul does have its natural quality, viz., cognition. As cognition is its very nature, in its state of liberation it is manifested in its infinity.[3] As opposed to this, those who

---

1. The *Nyāya*, the *Vaiśeṣika* and the *Sāṁkhya* philosophers.
2. The thing exists there alone where its qualities are experienced. All agree that a thing must be there where its quality is found. As for example, a pot exists where its form exists, and not elsewhere. This is what Ācārya Hemacandra has said in his *Anyayogavyavacchedikā Dvātriṁśikā.* His words are: '*yatraiva yo dṛṣṭaguṇaḥ sa tatra kumbhādivan niṣpratipakṣam etat/*' The special qualities of the soul, viz., knowledge, feelings, desire, etc., are experienced in the body alone. Hence the possessor of them should reside in the body alone and not outside it.
3. The sun is covered by clouds. So, its brilliant light becomes dim when it passes through them, and that dim light becomes even more dim when it enters a room through a curtain. But on that account one cannot say that the sun does not naturally possess the brilliant light. Similarly, soul's infinite natural light of knowledge is obstructed by the coverings of karmic matter and on that account manifests itself in different degrees. Its manifestation in the different degrees of dimness does not prove that the soul does not possess the infinite light of knowledge as its nature.

do not consider cognition to be the nature of soul has to maintain that in liberation the soul is devoid of cognition.

The Jaina tenets about soul, which are different from those upheld by others are set out in the following aphorism: '*caitanyasvarūpaḥ pariṇāmī kartā sākṣād bhoktā dehaparimāṇaḥ pratikṣetraṁ*[1] *bhinnaḥ paudgalikādṛṣṭavāṁś cāyam*/' [Vādidevasūri's *Pramāṇanayatattvāloka*, VII.56).

The Jaina thinkers regard the soul as *caitanyasvarūpa*. It means that for them cognition constitutes the real nature of soul. As shown above, on this point they differ from the *Nyāya-Vaiśeṣika* and other philosophers.

Again, the Jaina theoreticians regard the soul as changing (*pariṇāmī*), doer (*kartā*) and direct enjoyer (*sākṣād bhoktā*). It undergoes transformations. It takes births in various species of the four main classes of existence, viz., godly, human, animal and infernal. It passes through different states. It is a doer of actions and it is directly and primarily an enjoyer of the fruits of its actions. On these three points, they differ from the *Sāṁkhya* philosophers, because the latter maintain that the soul is absolutely changeless, performs no action whatsoever and is not the real enjoyer of the fruits of actions.

Moreover, the Jaina philosophers regard the soul as body-sized (*dehaparimāṇa*). The dimension of the soul is equal to that of the body in which it lives. On this point, they differ from the *Naiyāyika*, the *Vaiśeṣika* and the *Sāṁkhya* thinkers who regard the soul as all-pervasive.

The Jaina thinkers think that each body has a separate soul (*pratikṣetraṁ bhinnaḥ*). Thus, they believe in the plurality of souls. On this point, they differ from the *Advaita Vedāntin* who maintains that the soul is one in all bodies.

The Jaina philosophers hold that the soul is associated with the *karmas* which are material (*paudgalikādṛṣṭavāṁś ca*). On this point they differ from the *Nyāya-Vaiśeṣika* philosophers who regard *karma*[2] as one of the nine special qualities of the soul, as also from the *Vedāntin* who do not regard *karmas* as aggregates of material atoms.

It has been declared: '*satyaṁ brahma, mithyā jagat*' (The soul is truth and reality, the world is falsity and appearance). The true import of this sentence is that all the physical objects of the world are ephemeral and evanescent, therefore they should be regarded as essenceless and false.

---

1. The term '*kṣetra*' here means body.
2. They use the term '*adṛṣṭa*' for *karma*.

Only the soul which is of the nature of pure consciousness is the right and proper object of our devotion and worship. One should strive for its attainment, one should devote oneself to its attainment. This import or teaching of the sentence is very important. The ancient great saints thought it absolutely necessary to deliver such teachings in order to destroy the terrible miseries caused by delusion and desire. The sentence does not mean that the objects of the world are absolutely unreal like a hare's horn. That the world is false really means that the objects of the world are impermanent, essenceless and good for nothing. And this meaning is intelligible and not contradicted by our experience. While describing impermanence and essencelessness of all the objects of the world, the Jaina thinkers are not hesitant in calling them unreal (*mithyā*). All the objects and manifold events of the world are impermanent and hence they themselves or our attachment to them are essenceless. To emphasise this truth, the adjective *mithyā* (false, unreal) is given to the world. But on that account we are not entitled to regard the world as absolutely unreal and false like a hare's horn, because its existence is established and proved by our experience. The physical objects which we experience have real existence. Their perception is not false; it is not illusion. A serpent is false and illusory when and where a rope is cognised as a serpent. So, to regard that false serpent as a real serpent is an illusion. But a real serpent is a real serpent. And to regard a real serpent as a real serpent is not an illusion. This is the right understanding.[1]

Speciality of the Jaina Conception of Karma

The spiritual science extensively and deeply discusses the problems relating to the soul and its *karma*. We succinctly presented the various philosophical views about the nature of the soul. Now we propose to say something about *karma*.

Matter (*pudgala*) is an insentient substance. It has infinite energy and powers. *Karma* is a form of matter, which is closely associated with the

1. If the world is as unreal as mirage, all the differences and dualities like bondage-liberation, wickedness-kindness, virtue-vice, good-acts, bad-acts, etc., will not exist, consequently there will not be any necessity of the teachings about the nature of the physical objects, mind and soul as also about the path of purification. If the world is as unreal as mirage, there will be no problem at all, there will be no act of duty. Again, everything being false even the doctrine of the falsity of the world will also be false.

soul. It exerts great influence on the soul. Good or bad actions (thoughts, speeches, overt behaviour) leave behind their traces on the soul. These traces are in the form of aggregates of material atoms. They are *karmas*. Good or bad actions give rise to auspicious or inauspicious *karmas*, which, in turn, give auspicious or inauspicious fruits to the soul. Various differences found among living beings and even among human beings are due to these auspicious and inauspicious *karmas*.

In the world, human beings rather than other living beings attract our attention. As we are closely acquainted with human conditions, our deep reflection on them offers solution to certain philosophical or spiritual problems.

In the world, we find two types of human beings, viz., some living virtuous life and others living vicious life. Again each of these types has two sub-types, viz., the happy and the unhappy. Thus, in all there are four types, viz., 1. those living virtuous life and happy, 2. those living vicious life and happy, 3. those living virtuous life and unhappy, and 4. those living vicious life and unhappy. In the world, we come across these four types of human beings. It is clear that the differences of auspicious *karmas* as also of inauspicious *karmas* cause these different human conditions. And keeping in view the four types of human beings, the Jaina thinkers generally point out that each of the two types of *karmas*, viz., the auspicious and the inauspicious has two sub-types. They are as follows: 1. Auspicious *karmas* related to auspicious activities and resulting in auspicious *karmas*, 2. Auspicious *karmas* related to inauspicious activities and resulting in inauspicious *karmas*, 3. Inauspicious *karmas* related to auspicious activities and resulting in auspicious *karmas*, and 4. Inauspicious *karmas* related to inauspicious activities and resulting in inauspicious *karmas*.

1. *Auspicious karmas related to auspicious activities and resulting in auspicious karmas (puṇyānubandhī puṇya)*

All auspicious *karmas* give man means of happiness on their rise. He acquires wealth, vehicles, bungalows, etc., on account of the fruition of auspicious *karmas*. But some auspicious *karmas* are such as would not wean him away from cherishing right inclination or faith and performing good actions. He does not indulge in sensual pleasures. He spends his wealth in religious and philanthropic activities. He is humble and does not hurt the feelings of others. He likes religious practices, finds pleasure in doing good to others and lives virtuous life. Thus, these auspicious *karmas* are related to auspicious, wholesome and good activities. And as they are related to auspicious activities they cause, through those auspicious activities, the bondage of the auspicious *karmas*. In this way, the auspicious *karmas* of this type make man's life happy, righteous and auspicious. The term '*puṇyānubandhī puṇya*' means that auspicious *karma* which is related to religious practice and good activities leading to good next birth. Auspicious *karmas* of this type are not detrimental to good activities causing good future birth, but on the contrary they are conducive to them. Thus, the auspicious *karmas* of this type cause the bondage of further auspicious *karmas*, through threefold auspicious activities; they are noble.

2. *Auspicious karmas related to inauspicious activities and resulting in inauspicious karmas (pāpānubandhī puṇya)*

As we have already stated, all auspicious *karmas* give man means of happiness on their rise. He acquires wealth, etc., on their fruition. As shown above, of all the auspicious *karmas*, only some are related to auspicious activities. But others are related to inauspicious activities. They are such as would lead man astray. He spends his wealth in luxuries and vicious activities. He indulges in sensual pleasures. He does not like religious and good activities. Auspicious *karmas* of this type are called '*pāpānubandhī puṇya*' because on their rise they give man happiness or pleasures and at the same time degrade his life; they are related to vicious activities which cause low next birth. As auspicious *karmas* of this type are related to inauspicious activities, they cause through them the bondage of inauspicious *karmas*. Thus, the auspicious *karmas* of this type are ignoble.

3. *Inauspicious karmas related to auspicious activities and resulting in auspicious karmas (puṇyānubandhī pāpa)*

All inauspicious *karmas* put man in miserable conditions on their rise. On account of their fruition, he becomes or remains poor, he cannot acquire means of happiness. But some inauspicious *karmas* are such as would not shake man's faith in religion. Even in adverse conditions, he practises religion and helps others according to his capacity. He does not lose his peace of mind. Inauspicious *karmas* of this type are called *puṇyānubandhī,* because they are related to auspicious activities. Though they cause miseries to man, they do not degrade his life. They, through the good and auspicious activities, cause the bondage of auspicious *karmas* as also the good next birth. They do not obstruct wholesome activities which lead to good future birth.

4. *Inauspicious karmas related to inauspicious activities and resulting in inauspicious karmas (pāpānubandhī pāpa)*

As we have already stated, all inauspicious *karmas* cause misery to man on their rise. On account of their fruition, he is deprived of the means of happiness, he cannot acquire wealth in spite of his efforts. As shown above, of all the inauspicious *karmas*, only some are related to auspicious activities. But others are related to inauspicious activities. On account of the fruition of the inauspicious *karmas* of this type, man suffers from poverty and other miseries, but at the same time he does not refrain from indulging in vicious activities; on the contrary, he remains engaged in them. The inauspicious *karmas* of this type are called *pāpānubandhī pāpa,* because on their rise they cause misery to man and at the same time are associated with vicious activities which cause low next birth and bondage of inauspicious *karmas*.[1]

1. Regarding these four types of *karmas*, viz. *puṇyānubandhī puṇya,* etc., what Ācārya Haribhadra has said in his 24th *Aṣṭaka* is as follows:
gehād gehāntaraṁ kañcic chobhanād adhikaṁ naraḥ /
yāti yadvat sudharmeṇa tadvad eva bhavād bhavam //1//
Under the influence of the good religion (religious practice) a living being moves from a good birth to a better one, just as a man moves from a good house to a better one to reside in. (1)
The good religious practice in point is that which a man undertakes while enjoying happiness and wealth as fruits of the accumulated auspicious *karmas*. These auspicious *karmas* (their fruition) are called *puṇyānubandhī,* because they are associated with good and auspicious activities.
gehād gehāntaraṁ kañcic chobhanād itaran naraḥ /
yāti yadvad asaddharmāt tadvad eva bhavād bhavam //2//
Under the influence of vicious activities (irreligious practice) a living being moves from a good birth to a bad one, just as a man moves from a good house to a bad one to reside in. (2)
The vicious and irreligious activities in point are those which a man undertakes while enjoying wealth, etc., as fruits of the strange and incomprehensible accumulated auspicious *karmas*. These auspicious *karmas* (their fruition) are called *pāpānubandhī* because they are associated with the vicious activities.
gehād gehāntaraṁ kañcid aśubhād adhikaṁ naraḥ /
yāti yadvan mahāpāpāt tadvad eva bhavād bhavam //3//

In short, those auspicious *karmas* accumulated through past births, which cause the bondage of new auspicious *karmas* at the time when the soul is enjoying their sweet fruits are called *puṇyānubandhī puṇya.* Those inauspicious *karmas* accumulated through past births, which cause the bondage of the auspicious *karmas* through equanimity, peace, atonement and good activities, at the time when the soul is experiencing their bitter fruits are called *puṇyānubandhī pāpa.* Those auspicious *karmas* accumulated through past births, which cause the bondage of inauspicious *karmas* at the time when the soul is enjoying, with indulgence and infatuation, their sweet fruits are called *pāpānubandhī puṇya.* And those inauspicious *karmas* accumulated through past births, which cause the bondage of new inauspicious *karmas* at the time when the soul is experiencing their bitter fruits are called *pāpānubandhī pāpa.*

In the world, those men and women who are happy and at the same time live righteous and religious life are to be regarded as having *puṇyānubandhī puṇya.* Those who have means of happiness in their pos-

---

On account of his association with the highly vicious, that is, greatly sinful activities a living being moves from a bad birth to a worse one, just as a man moves from a bad house to a worse one to reside in.(3)

The greatly sinful activities in point are those which a person undertakes while experiencing poverty and other miseries as fruits of the accumulated inauspicious *karmas.* These inauspicious *karmas* (their fruition) are called *pāpānubandhī* because they are associated with vicious activities.

gehād gehāntaraṁ kañcid aśubhād itaran naraḥ /
yāti yadvat sudharmeṇa tadvad eva bhavād bhavam//4//

Under the influence of the good and religious activities, a living being moves from a bad birth to a good one, just as a man moves from a bad house to a good one to reside in. (4)

The good and religious activities in point are those which a person undertakes while experiencing poverty and other miseries as fruits of the accumulated inauspicious *karmas.* These inauspicious *karmas* (their fruition) are called *puṇyānubandhī,* because they are associated with the good and religious activities.

After these four verses, in the fifth verse Ācārya Haribhadra advises man to perform good and auspicious activities while enjoying health, wealth, vehicles, bungalows, etc., as fruits of the accumulated auspicious *karmas* so that he can attain inexhaustible infinite wealth. In the sixth verse, he declares that mind free from all passions like attachment etc., is the real jewel, it is the inner spiritual wealth of a living being. One who is robbed of this wealth, gets afflicted with miseries and calamities. In the eighth verse, he observes that cultivation of universal compassion, equanimity, quiescence and good wholesome conduct makes our accumulated auspicious *karmas,* *puṇyānubandhī.*

session and indulge in the vicious activities are to be regarded as having *pāpānubandhī puṇya.* Those who are in miserable condition due to poverty, etc. and yet move on the auspicious path of religion and righteousness are to be regarded as having *puṇyānubandhī pāpa.* And those who are miserable and poor and still indulge in vicious activities are to be regarded as having *pāpānubandhī pāpa.* On noticing men becoming rich and enjoying all the comforts and pleasures of life on the strength of treachery, killing, robbery, beating, theft, cheating, unscrupulous violence, etc., some short-sighted persons say, 'Look, Brother! Miseries and calamities befall the good religious persons, while the wicked rascals roll in riches and enjoy all the pleasures, what is the use of religious practice and good conduct?' But that this statement is made through ignorance is clear from the above discussion about *karma.* A man can enjoy pleasures while indulging in the vicious activities, but he can do so so long as there continues the process of the fruition of the past accumulated auspicious *karmas*. And one should bear in mind that the governance and rule of Nature is not so weak and disorderly that the newly bound inauspicious *karmas* (through those vicious activities) can get destroyed without yielding their bitter fruits. There is a reign of law and order in Nature. Its fine elements and powers are beyond our understanding and comprehension. Groping in the darkness of ignorance, a living being may formulate imaginary hypotheses or theories in order to escape from the real fear of bad consequences of bad acts, but it is certain that from Nature's relentless punishment no culprit can escape. The most intense inauspicious *karmas* demonstrate their inexorable power by yielding their bitter fruits in the very birth in which they are bound through unwholesome activities.[1] This fact too is to be kept in mind.

---

1. '*Satyam atyugrapāpānāṁ phalam atraiva labhyate.* (It is true that the most intense inauspicious *karmas* yield their fruits in the very birth in which they are bound).' Āc. Hemacandra puts this statement in the mouth of Abhayakumāra, an illustrious son of Śreṇika, the king of Magadha. (See the story related in the explanation of the verse 30 of the second chapter of the *Yogaśāstra*). Like the greatly intense inauspicious *karmas*, the greatly intense auspicious *karmas* too yield their fruits in the very birth in which they are bound. Study the following verse:
ja jeṇa kayaṁ kammaṁ annabhave iha bhave a satteṇaṁ /
ta teṇa veiavvaṁ nimittamittaṁ paro hoi //
This verse declares that inevitably one has to experience the fruits of the bound *karmas*—bound in the past births or in the present birth. Other living beings that give pleasure or pain to one are simply an instrumental condition; the real cause of one's pleasure and pain is one's own *karma.* From this verse, we know that the *karmas* can rise to give their fruits in the very birth in which they are bound.

At this juncture in the exposition of the auspicious and the inauspicious *karmas*, it will be proper to clear one important point regarding wealth. Happiness can never be measured by the abundance of wealth. This way of measuring happiness is wrong. The excessive accumulation of wealth is a sin; not only that, but it deprives man of his peace of mind. So, how can it be a measure of happiness? If a man honestly and in a just way acquires just that much wealth as is necessary to buy necessities of life and a residential house, remains satisfied with that only and has good intention to spend the excess honest earnings in the philanthropic works, then he can be regarded as a real happy person, because he does not lose his peace of mind and experiences happiness and bliss through mind. Happiness consists in contentedness. It cannot be denied that wealth is a means of livelihood and hence useful. But it should be earned and acquired honestly and in a just way, it should be spent in buying proper necessities and comforts of life for one's family members and the excess of it should be spent in philanthropic activities. It should be given only this much importance and not more. To give more importance than what it deserves is quite improper and even wrong from the spiritual standpoint. Religious practice or spiritual discipline has connection not with possession but with limited possession or non-possession. Wealth alone should not be understood as a sign of good fortune. Wealth acquired through unfair means is the sign of misfortune. Wealth which is the sign of good fortune and the cause of happiness is not the wealth that is acquired dishonestly and in an unjust way. To view the virtuous more honourable than the wealthy is the right and wholesome outlook and its spread and cultivation in society is absolutely necessary. With the spread and cultivation of the good quality of limiting one's needs and possessions in society, there will be an increase in happiness, peace and morality in society.

For the spiritual practiser, it is necessary to know about the purity of conduct. So, we propose to have a glance at this topic.

JAINA CODE OF CONDUCT

Though earlier we have dealt with, in a general way, the rules of good conduct laid down for laymen as well as monks, we here propose to discuss some important points regarding their conduct. Let us first take up the daily practices of the monks.

Monk's daily practices

The Jaina code of conduct forbids the monks to use vehicles, viz., railways, motorcars, aeroplanes, cycles, trams, steamers, carts drawn by animals, etc.[1] They are commanded to move from place to place on foot[2] and to drink boiled water.[3] They are prohibited to ignite fire and to warm themselves with it[4] and to cook food with its help. There is a command for them to beg cooked food from house to house and to live on it.[5] They should obtain cooked food from different houses in such a manner that the householders experience no inconvenience, diffidence or uneasiness. They should not accept food specially prepared for them. Scriptures do not permit householders to prepare food specially for monks and monks to accept such food. The purpose behind formulating these rules is certainly that the community of monks may not be a burden on the society as also that the monks may not form attachment to delicacies and dainties.

The religious practice of the monk demands that he should not have possessions, he should live in a self-imposed poverty. That is, he should not keep money, he should have no connection whatsoever with wealth, precious metals, etc., he should be free from any connection with them to such an extent that he should not use even metal utensils[6] for begging

---

1. If there is a river on the way and there is no land-route nearby, the monk is permitted to sit in a boat.
2. The Vedic Hindu religious works like the *Mahābhārata, Manusmṛti,* etc., contain this very command for the ascetics.
3. The doctors trained in the Western science of medicine maintain that the boiled water is good for health. They advise the patients suffering from plague, cholera, etc., to use boiled water for drinking. According to the discovery made by the learned scientists, there exist microbes in water, they are so minute that we cannot see them with our eyes, but we can see them through a microscope. Microbes or minute germs generated in water enter our body as soon as we drink that water. And having entered the body, they cause severe diseases. But if the impure and polluted water of a certain place is used as drinking water after boiling it, it causes no harm to the body. Monks do not stay at one place for long. They are constantly on tour. They move from place to place on foot. So, it is inevitable for them to drink different waters of different places. Therefore, the rule that they should drink boiled water is good for their health.
4. *anagnir aniketaḥ syāt* /—*Manusmṛti,* VI. 83
5. *caren mādhukarīṁ vṛttim api mlecchakulād api* /—*Atrismṛti*
6. *ataijasāni pātrāṇi tasya syur nirvraṇāni ca* /
alābu dārupātraṁ ca mṛnmayaṁ vaidalaṁ tathā /

and taking food, the utensils should be made of wood, clay or gourd. He is indifferent towards the world, though he bears no hatred towards it; the worldly ends of power, fame and wealth for which men strive in sweating competition are of no importance to him.

In the rainy season, the monk should stay at one place. He should not even touch women.

In short, the monk should remain totally free from worldly affairs and dealings. He should remain fully engrossed in the spiritual bliss. His religious practice consists of sincere efforts to achieve spiritual welfare[1], to make his life useful and beneficial to others and to guide the people on the right path of purification. His life is a life of a good friend of all living beings. It is pure and luminous on account of the removal of defilements like pride, anger, greed, deceit, attachment, desire for self-worship, etc.

The Sanskrit term *sādhu* is employed to convey the sense of a monk. It means a person who has truly renounced the world. It means a spiritually brilliant and pure person in whom there is good union of right knowledge and wholesome conduct. Not yielding to attachment, he is

---

etāni yatipātrāṇi Manuḥ Svāyambhuvo'bravīt //
His vessels should be non-metallic and free from holes. Manu has declared that the vessels of the ascetic should be a gourd, a vessel of wood or of earthenware, or of splits.

1. Regarding the monk's state of non-attachment, there occurs in *Manusmṛti* (VI. 47-48, 55, 57, 60) excellent teaching:
ativādāṁs titikṣeta nāvamanyeta kañcana /
na cemaṁ deham āśritya vairaṁ kurvīta kenacit //47//
krudhyantaṁ na pratikrudhyed ākruṣṭaḥ kuśalaṁ vadet /48A/
bhaikṣe prasakto hi yatir viṣayeṣv api sajjati //55//
alābhe na viṣādī syād lābhe caiva na harṣayet /
prāṇayātrikamātraḥ syān mātrāsaṅgād vinirgataḥ //57//
indriyāṇāṁ nirodhena rāgadveṣakṣayeṇa ca /
ahiṁsayā ca bhūtānām amṛtatvāya kalpate //60//
The ascetic should patiently bear improper words. He should not insult anyone. He should not make enmity with anyone for the sake of his present body. Towards an angry man he should not retort in anger. When he is cursed, he should pronounce a blessing. The ascetic who becomes addicted to collecting alms becomes attached to sensual objects also. He should not be sorry at not obtaining alms; nor should he rejoice at obtaining it. He should have only what suffices to sustain his life. He should be free from all attachment to his accessories. By the restraining of the senses, by the extermination of attachment and aversion, and by not injuring living beings, he becomes fit for immortality.

satisfied with whatever necessities of life he obtains easily, naturally and without incurring any defilement or defect. He is ever vigilant in his practice of self-control. His spiritual discipline of equanimity, quiescence and austerity is of an advanced stage. His every act is guided by the light of right knowledge. He expects the minimum comforts of life which are inevitably needed to sustain the body and as soon as they are obtained he is contented and happy; and in case he does not obtain them he does not feel sorry and distressed. "I wish I may get food and drink of a particular kind to eat and drink, clothes of a particular type to wear, a residence of a particular type to reside in, or other things of a particular type"—attachment of this type he does not have. He accepts whatever he gets at whatever time naturally and easily and remains satisfied with that. Renunciation of this type is the result of the mental state of real non-attachment. Renunciation without non-attachment is no renunciation, but a mockery of renunciation, because in such cases a person ardently desires the things which he has outwardly renounced. Renunciation does not last long, if it is not the result of non-attachment and is not associated with it.

External ascetic dress or form, on the one side, reminds the monk to live a life in accordance with the path of renunciation willingly accepted by him, while, on the other side, it helps a person pretend to be a monk and cover his impure and unwholesome conduct. If we have blind faith in the external ascetic dress, there may arise a great danger of our being cheated. Similarly, if we do not care to know his life and are simply guided by our feeling of indifference to and disregard for the external dress, there may again arise a great danger of our dishonouring a real saint. So, to arrive at a true decision or judgement, it is necessary to pay attention to both, the external dress and the internal life. And for that, discriminating power and patience are required. There is always a risk in forming our opinion in haste under certain prejudice.

Taking into account their capacity, the monk guides through his preachings and practices householders and monks in their respective fields of religious disciplines. In the religious practice, it is necessary to discriminate the principal matters from the secondary ones. Non-violence, etc., are the five principal matters, while external rites, rituals and ceremonies are the secondary matters. The secondary matters are not so important as the principal ones. That is, the external rites, rituals and ceremonies are not so important as non-violence, etc. So, the monks who propound and preach that these external rites, rituals and ceremonies are all in all and in connection with them raise quarrels or disputes and divide the society, certainly deviate from the true path of religion. They should think as to how peace and amiability prevail in the entire society and strive for them. They should have their soothing and purifying influence on the society. Even their philosophical discussions should be full of sympathy and gentleness and permeated with synthetic and synoptic outlook so that they may not cause any unrest, disturbance or quarrel in the society.

Layman's Conduct

Now we treat of the layman's conduct. The first good quality he should cultivate is that of honesty. He should be honest, straightforward and just in his dealings with others. His activities should be governed by the proper standard of honesty, integrity and truthfulness. At this juncture it is necessary to discuss some specific points about his conduct.

About Non-violence

The first point relates to non-violence. We cannot but do harm and violence to living beings for the sustenance of our body. We cannot live without killing living beings. Even our breathing involves violence. But we should do only that much harm or violence which is absolutely necessary for the sustenance of our body. Instead of making it a rule of our life to do violence to living beings, we should make sincere efforts to find out how we can live with minimum violence, how we can decrease violence as far as possible.

As far as possible one should save the developed living beings (that is, those on the higher scale of evolution and hence having more sense-organs) and kill the undeveloped ones, if it is inevitable to kill living beings for sustaining one's body. Again, one should live in such a manner that killing of even the undeveloped living beings be as minimum as possible. This is the teaching promulgated by the saints. It is from this standpoint that meat-eating, hunting, massacre and killing are forbidden.

Is it bravery to yield to the passion of anger and fury and to enter into fight with one's adversary? Bravery consists in non-violence, that is, in restraining mind from being under the sway of anger and cruelty; it consists in keeping mind cool and calm by using the internal wholesome strength of discretion. The just mentioned mental or spiritual strength which is of the form of non-violence is much superior to the bodily or physical strength which is considered to be an animal strength. Human society achieves progress—religious, spiritual and even material—in proportion to the cultivation of this strength. The strength of non-violence is the light of intellectual discretion and mental purity. And with this strength, the world of human beings can become rich in friendliness, sympathy, love, spiritualness, happiness and bliss.

Non-violence is a spiritual power. Noble bravery or heroism demands self-sacrifice. To sacrifice one's self-interests and even one's life—if the need be—while resisting violence and supporting and fostering non-violence is the bravery of high order. To oppose violence only verbally and to run away out of fear when one is required to face and endure physical sufferings and torture, is really not the practice of non-violence. In spite of his having courage and strength to fight, the person who controls his passion and excitement on the passion-rousing and exciting occasions and does not yield to violence is the true practiser of non-violence. Coward and weak men's claim to the practice of non-violence is wrong. It is because they have no courage and strength to oppose the violent person or mob. So, though outwardly they are not doing any violent overt activity, their weak minds are burning with feelings of violence, rage, wrath and fury. The weak mind of a weak person gets easily overcome by the feeling of violence even at the slightest cause. The saying 'the less the strength, the more is the anger' is quite right. A weak man unnecessarily yields to passion and fury, every now and then. One who wants to practise non-violence properly and rightly should have, in addition to right understanding, mental strength and courage; and for the attainment of mental strength and courage one should cultivate and gain bodily or physical strength also. How great the value of bodily strength is! Bodily strength is very useful. It is needed to save the innocent people from the cruel attacks of tyrants, rioters and the wicked enemies through brave counter-attack and confrontation. It is useful in saving the people from the oppression of the wicked just as it is useful in crushing the wickedness of the wicked. For the internal non-violence of the form of keeping the mind calm and unagitated, this strength is as much needed as for the external non-violence of the form of protecting the people. This is the reason why it is held that strong mind resides in the strong body. It is easy to gain mental strength when one has gained the bodily or physical strength.

It is the kṣatriyas (members of the warrior class/caste) who have taught non-violence, and those who follow their teachings are the brave men of heroic character. Prosperity and all-round development choose and accompany the heroic character. It is this heroic character that attains the worldly or spiritual wealth. Where there is weakness and feeling of fear, the practice of non-violence is utterly impossible. Weakness and feeling of fear are the terrible diseases of life. The saying 'the Earth is ruled and enjoyed by the brave'[1] may or may not be suitable to the ideology of the present age, but that the practice of non-violence can be undertaken by the strong[2] (and not by the weak) is the universal truth never contradicted in all the three divisions of time. It is only the brave endowed with the power of discrimination and discretion, who can practise non-violence. This is possibly the reason why all the *Arhat*s (*tīrthaṅkara*s) belong to the kṣatriya class/caste; and they do have the heroic character of the highest order. And only those who have the heroic character and at the same time possess power of discrimination and discretion can become their followers.

One commits violence by not contributing to the efforts of stopping violence or by simply remaining indifferent to violence, just as one commits violence by indulging in positive violent activity. If one who knows swimming does not rescue a drowning man and simply watches him drowning, it is an act of violence. Not to give food to the hungry in spite of one's ability to give him food is also a case of violence. Violence of such type is the result of callous carelessness of the form: "What concern have I? Why should I invite trouble? I cannot afford to give food, etc., to others". Hard-heartedness is opposed to religion or religious practice. Universal love is the foundation of religion.[3] To remain indifferent to others' happiness, comforts and benefits for the sake of one's own is also a case of violence. To take undue advantage of others' labour is also a form of violence. Though one knows the truth and there is all the possibility of saving an innocent man by one's speaking out the truth in the witness-box in a court, yet if one does not speak out the truth in the court and thus allows the man to be a victim of injustice, then it also is a case of violence as it is a case of untruth. To throw rubbish of our house near our neighbour's, or to leave a scorpion or a plague rat found in our house

1. *vīrabhogyā vasuṁdharā* /
2. *ahiṁsā balavatsādhyā* /
3. *dayā dharma kā mūla hai* /

near our neighbour's and thus to put him in danger or to cause him trouble and harm is also a form of violence.

About Truth

To describe a thing as it is or an event as it happened is generally regarded as the truth, and factually no doubt it is the truth, but from the religious standpoint it may or may not be the truth. If the factual truth is beneficial or at least not harmful to others, it is worthy of being called the truth. But if the factual truth is harmful to others, it is not worthy of being regarded as the truth. So, mere factually truthful statement should not be uttered, if it is harmful to a living being. Let us explain the point by some examples. We know the direction a deer has gone in. But when we are asked the direction the deer has gone in by a hunter, pointing out the right direction endangers its life. So, in such a situation, keeping silence or showing the hunter a wrong direction in order to save the creature is our duty and religion. Again, in spite of our knowing the hiding place of a woman, on being asked as to where she is by the wicked person searching her with evil intention, our keeping silence or misguiding him is a good and religious act. Similarly, rioters ask a householder if a particular man is in his house; now, if he points out them the man whom he has given shelter in his house and a woman's veil to put on, then they will certainly kill him. Under this circumstance, the householder has to lie that the man is not in his house, and to make this factually untrue statement is his duty and religion. If the factual truth is harmful to others, it should not be regarded as truth.[1] It is absolutely necessary to be cautious and to use one's power of discrimination and discretion to decide as to whether or not one should make a statement of fact. If we have to tell the mad, the diseased, etc., a lie for their benefit,

---

1. The etymology of the term '*satya*' is '*sadbhyo hitaṁ satyam*'—that is, that which is beneficial to living beings is the truth.

ukte'nṛte bhaved yatra prāṇināṁ prāṇarakṣaṇam /
anṛtaṁ tatra satyaṁ syāt satyaṃ apy anṛtaṁ bhavet //

The *Mahābhārata, Bahulopākhyāna*

When telling untruth saves or protects living beings, it is not untruth but truth; and at the same time telling the truth is, in fact, telling the untruth.

tusiṇīo uvehejjā jāṇaṁ vā no jāṇaṁ ti vaejjā/

Ācārāṅgasūtra, II *Śrutaskandha,* III *Adhyayana,* III *Uddeśa.*

The statement means that man must simply maintain silence or say that he does not know even if he knows.

it is to be regarded as not untruth but truth, not vice but virtue, not an improper act but a proper act, because it is a lie spoken by us not for our own sake, but for the sake of others.

A man knows a secret. It is necessary for him not to disclose it in the interest of others and at the same time it is not possible for him to keep quiet. Under such a situation, if he speaks a lie, it is not improper.

One does not incur a defect or sin of untruth, if one breaks an unjust and improper vow. For example, a man takes a vow that he will make an offering of a goat to the goddess if his son is cured of a disease. Afterwards when he gains right understanding that killing of an animal is a grave sin and that to perform the killing before the goddess is a highly deplorable, derogatory and despicable act of sin, he should break his vow. To keep and fulfil any evil and sinful vow is bad, while to break it is good.

If one has to speak such exceptional untruths as are illustrated above, then one should undergo some proper atonement and undertake critical self-examination, because both the atonement and critical self-examination enliven and accelerate spiritual progress.

In soft and innocent merriment with children and others, speaking untruth for the moment in such a manner that it causes no harm to anyone is not the untruth of the form of defect. Again, for the sake of formality, the untruth one is required to speak is also pardonable.

Out of hatred and with a view to hurting him if we call the blind a blind one, the one-eyed a one-eyed one, and the fool a fool, we incur the defect of untruth. Out of malice and undue excitement saying bitter words, calling names and cutting cruel jokes are the cases of untruth.

To speak what is factually true but what causes distress to another person is a case of speaking untruth or what is reprehensible.[1]

About Non-theft

A man finds someone stealing things of another person. Yet he does not prevent him from stealing, nor does he draw attention of the owner. On the contrary, he ignores his act of stealing and maintains silence out of

---

1. *Manusmṛti* teaches the good manner of speech as follows:
satyaṁ brūyāt priyaṁ brūyān na brūyāt satyam apriyam /
priyaṁ ca nānṛtaṁ brūyād eṣa dharmaḥ sanātanaḥ //138// *Adhyāya* IV.
One should speak what is true and at the same time pleasing. One should not speak what is true but unpleasant, nor should one speak what is pleasing but untrue. This is the universal and eternal religion.

indifference or fear. The mental state of indifference or fear in this context is very bad. He who himself does not steal, but allows others to steal incurs the sin of theft.

Employing unfair means in business, owning another man's property by fraudulent tricks, deceiving others by misleading them, driving others into losses after having won their confidence, damaging others' interests through cunningness, harassing others unnecessarily and unjustly, distressing the innocent—all these are vicious and sinful acts.

Picking up goods which have been lost or forgotten by their owners, employing thieves to obtain things for oneself, encouraging and prompting others to steal, approving others' acts of stealing, receiving stolen merchandise, using false weights and measures, secretly adulterating commodities or substituting inferior ones for the original, gaining or storing goods without paying taxes, breaking laws formulated by the state for the good of the people, indulging in smuggling, dealing in the prohibited items—all these are acts of theft. Buying goods of much value at a very low price taking advantage of the seller's helplessness or keeping the excess material given by the seller by mistake is also an act of theft. In short, taking anything owned by others, through injustice, dishonesty, fraud and unfair means is an act of theft.

Vices like theft, roguery, dacoity, rascality, etc., come into existence and spread widely as an unwholesome reaction to the undue accumulation of wealth and exploitation of the poor by the industrialists and the rich. So, it is their duty to control their desire for wealth.

Unemployment drives man to stealing. Greed leads him astray and prompts him to do immoral and violent acts of sin. He wrongly thinks that by accumulating wealth and making its display he can attain respectable social status. This is the reason why he becomes ever more greedy and employs all unfair means to accumulate wealth. Indulgence in extravagance and vices like gambling, drinking, etc., leads him to the sinful path of stealing and cheating. Again, he learns stealing and other vices from bad company.

When society achieves moral elevation through the cultivation of good qualities like contentedness in proper limited possession, self-control, simple living and universal brotherhood, then the sins of immorality, theft, roguery and devilry which have spread over the entire society will automatically disappear.

Vicious Professions

Gambling or speculation is neither an honest business nor a profession requiring labour. It fosters idleness and dishonesty. It requires the use of deception and tricks. In it when one gains, so many are ruined. Causing distress to so many and sitting idle, to gain wealth by such vicious profession is deplorable and reprehensible. Afterwards, if one gives donations for religious purposes from the wealth accumulated in this dishonest and unjust manner,[1] can that wash off the sins the donor has incurred by causing distress and sufferings to so many persons and their dependents? That can, provided the donor gives away all his wealth in donation for the philanthropic activities with the firm resolve of renouncing the vicious profession for ever. The reputation one gains in and the honour one receives from the unwise and uncultured society due to one's wealth acquired through unfair and unjust means have no value at all from the spiritual standpoint. And taking pride in such reputation and honour further degrades and lands one on a very low plane.

About Vow of Limiting one's Possessions

Keeping all this in view, the Jaina scriptures propound the vow of limiting one's possessions. The practice of the vow is possible only when one limits one's desire for possessions or one controls one's greed. The vow is preached so that its practice may weaken the attacks of greed, raise the standard of morality and prompt the rich to spend their excess wealth for the good of the society. By utilising their excess wealth in philanthropic activities the rich can properly resist the feeling of hostility directed against them by the unemployed and the poor. Renouncing excessive luxury, inordinate worldly pleasures as also waste of wealth in various ways, and properly limiting their needs, to utilise their excess wealth for the good of the society is beneficial to the rich themselves and the entire society as well.

One can easily understand that sustenance and progress of the society

---

1. The following ancient verse describes as to how the donation of the wealth acquired through unjust means is:
anyāyopāttavittasya dānam atyantadoṣakṛt /
dhenuṁ nihatya tanmāṁsair dhvākṣāṇām iva tarpaṇam //
The donation of the wealth acquired through unjust means causes terrible evils. It is like an act of satisfying crows with the meat of a cow after having killed it.

mainly depend on the facilities for producing and buying-selling things really useful to the society. So, it is necessary to invest money, in one form or the other, in professions and industries which deal in or produce those things. Regarding money invested in various necessary professions and industries, the question arises as to whether or not the investor be regarded as *bhāvaparigrahī* (i.e., one having attachment for the possessions). Pondering over this problem, we feel that the investor should not be regarded as *bhāvaparigrahī* with regard to the money invested in the socially beneficial professions and industries, because *bhāvaparigraha* is related with the determination as to how much and of what kind the *parigraha* (possessions, wealth) be set aside from the net profit in order to meet the necessities of an individual member or the entire family and the future expenses on the good and bad occasions, while the invested money is related with providing the society its necessities through professions and industries. For example, a farmer sows grain-seeds in order that there may grow grains so many times more than what he has sown and thereby members of the society may survive. If the production of grains is less than what is required or the buying-selling business is hampered or arrested, then there will arise grave situation and the society will have to face terrible calamity.

The objective of the vow is to limit one's possessions. The vow should not be used as a means of increasing one's possession or allowing one's desire for wealth to be inordinate and endless. For example, a lower middle class man, while expressing his desire of taking the vow, requests the monk in the following words: "Sire! please, give me the vow of limiting possession, wherein the limits set by me are as follows. I can possess the diamonds up to 20 kg, pearls up to 40 kg, Rupees up to one crore, utensils of the value of Rupees one lakh, and household goods and furnitures of the value of Rupees five lakh." This is really a mockery of the vow and the one who gives such a vow is to be regarded as an indiscreet and thoughtless person, because here the objective of the vower is to foster his desire for the unlimited accumulation of wealth, and not to cultivate the good quality of contentedness or remove the disparity found among the members of the society.

About the Vow of Limiting Quantity of Things We use

The vow of limiting quantity of things we use has concern with:

(1) limiting the things we use once or repeatedly

(2) following professions which produce those things.

Not only that one should not follow or urge others to follow professions wherein violence on a large scale is possibly involved (as for example, manufacturing cloth with the use of machines in mills) but also that one should not use things produced through them, if one wants to remain undefiled by the defect of large scale violence. A man deceives himself if he believes that as he himself does not follow or urge others to follow those professions, he is not defiled by the defect of large scale violence, though he uses things produced through those professions involving large scale violence. Nobody will be convinced by his argument if a meat-eater argues that the animals whose meat he eats are not killed by him nor does he urge others to kill them, therefore the defect of killing animals does not defile him. To strengthen his argument he may further say that if the meat were to contain minute living organisms, the defect of killing them may defile him, but the defect of killing animals will certainly not defile him; and if the meat were to contain no minute living organisms, the defect of killing them will also not defile him. This way of supporting or strengthening his argument is also of no avail. He surely incurs the sin of killing animals. Ācārya Hemacandra declares that one who kills an animal is no doubt its killer, but that those who give permission to kill it and those who sell, buy, cook, serve or eat its meat are also its killers.[1] To support this declaration he further states that when there is the eater of meat, there is the killer of an animal but that in the absence of the meat-eater, there is the absence of the animal-killer too[2]; therefore, the real killer is the meat-eater. Ācārya Hemacandra's words are noteworthy.

If I want to wear clothes manufactured in mills, to enjoy the things of leather which is obtained after killing animals, to use clothes and things made of silk which is produced after having killed the four-sensed silk-

---

1. *hantā palasya vikretā saṁskartā bhakṣakas tathā /*
kretā'numantā dātā ca ghātakā eva yan Manuḥ //—*Yogaśāstra,* III. 20
The verse from *Manusmṛti,* which Ācārya Hemacandra has before him is as follows:
anuyaṁtā viśasitā nihaṁtā krayavikrayī /
saṁskartā sopahartā ca khādakaś ceti ghātakaḥ//
One who indirectly gives permission to kill animals, one who severs limbs from the body, one who actually kills the animal, one who sells meat, one who cooks meat, one who serves meat at the table and one who eats it are all considered killers of the animal.
2. *na vadhako bhakṣakaṁ vinā /*—*Yogaśāstra,* III. 23

worms, to put on ornaments of pearls obtained after having killed the five-sensed fish and similarly to use and enjoy other things whose production involve large scale violence or killing, then for me there is no way out but to register my partnership in that large scale violence.

Before using things, one desirous of spiritual welfare should find out as to whether production of those things involves very little violence or much violence. He should use things whose production involves very little violence. He should scrupulously avoid the use of those things whose production involves large scale violence. It is not possible to observe the vows of non-violence, truthfulness, non-stealing, continence and non-possession without limiting properly the quantity of things one uses. It is so because man (or society) who indulges in the excessive use and enjoyment of things has to take recourse to the large scale violence in the mass-production of those things for satisfying his inordinate and limitless desire for the use and enjoyment of those things. Vices or sins like telling lies, doing injustice to others, exploiting others, etc., are the results of the unbridled desire for enjoying worldly things. And to satisfy this ever growing desire one has to struggle hard to acquire ever more possessions. All sins and vices arise from this dreadful desire. It is the function of strong will-power or mental strength to curb properly the desire for worldly enjoyment. And such a strong-willed or strong-minded man can be saved from many sins and vices and can achieve prosperity and spiritual welfare very easily.

The essence of the vow can be put in one sentence: the vow of limiting the quantity of things one uses consists in renouncing the professions in which large scale violence is involved, scrupulously avoiding food, drink, clothes, ornaments, utensils, etc., whose production involves large scale violence and limiting the quantity, for one's use, of even those things whose production involves very little violence.

Purposeless Evil Activity of the form of Evil Brooding

The Jaina thinkers have recognised two types of evil brooding or inauspicious concentration, viz., one pertaining to pains (*ārta*) and the other pertaining to terribly harmful ideas (*raudra*). The latter is included in the purposeless evil activities. It is a constant reflection related to violence, untruthfulness, theft, protection-of-an-acquisition. It consists in caressing the ideas of vanquishing, imprisoning, beating, torturing, mutilating, lying, despoiling, thieving, doing injustice to others, accumulating wealth by any means, protecting acquired wealth, etc. It includes brooding over the enjoyments of the forbidden sexual and other worldly pleasures. To revel in the constant thoughts of one's achievements in the fields of sinful and vicious activities is also a form of evil brooding of this type.

Purposeless evil activity due to negligence (pramāda)

Though an individual and a society can meet their necessities without any harassment, by things whose production involves very little violence, yet if they use those things whose production involves large scale violence, then they do incur the defect of purposeless evil activity due to negligence.

Purposeless evil inactivity due to idleness (pramāda)

Though one has strength, skill and time to work for one's own comforts and to do one's own personal works, yet if one throws the burden of one's own personal works and comforts on others (that is, on one's servants and dependents) and one remains idle for oneself, then one is defiled by purposeless evil inactivity due to idleness.

Purpose of Sāmāyika

The purpose of *sāmāyika* is the cultivation of equal goodwill (sympathy), equality and evenness, and tranquillity.

I. Equal goodwill (sympathy) (*samabhāva*)
   1. towards all religions
   2. towards all races and castes
   3. towards a man and a woman

II. Equality and evenness (*samatā*)
   1. to regard all living beings equal with one's own self
   2. to maintain evenness (equanimity) of mind on all occasions, favourable and adverse

III. Tranquillity (*śama*)
   to suppress and weaken passions.

About Vows in General

Regarding vows, the Jaina scriptures declare that to become a true vow-practiser first one should be free from the thorns. In brief, the thorns are three in number. They are as follows:

1. False pretension, deception, or a tendency to cheat
2. Greed for worldly enjoyments
3. Not to have faith in what is true, or to insist on what is false.

All the three are of the form of a mental defilement. So long as they are there, they eat up into the vitals of the mind and the body and they do prevent the soul from retaining its balance. Hence, a person possessed of a thorn, even if he formally accepts a vow, cannot concentrate on its observance. When a thorn or some such sharp thing is kept thrust within a bodily part, then the body and the mind of the person concerned are deprived of their balance by this irritant and as a result this person is prevented from concentrating on any task; in a like manner do the mental defilements in question act as a cause of unease—which is why a renunciation of them is the first condition of becoming a true vow-practiser.

Now, we propose to deal with six obligatory daily duties for the Jaina laity.

SIX OBLIGATORY DUTIES (ṢAḌĀVAŚYAKA)

The six obligatory duties for a Jaina layman are as follows: (1) *devapūjā*, worship of the supreme soul; (2) *guru-upāsti*, venerating and serving the elders; (3) *svādhyāya*, study of the spiritually elevating works; (4) *saṃyama*, self-control; (5) *tapa*, austerities; (6) *dāna*, charity. These are the six obligatory duties which a Jaina layman is required to perform everyday.[1]

1. *Devapūjā (Worship of Supreme Soul)*

It means reverential recalling to mind the supreme soul and its spiritual qualities, devotionally praising them and offering prayers to the supreme soul. This is the best way to remove the internal defilements, to purify thoughts, to cultivate good mental states and to rouse and develop spiritual powers.

There are two types of *devapūjā—dravyapūjā* (external worship) and *bhāvapūjā* (internal worship).

Reverential constant recalling to mind the supreme soul and its qualities is *bhāvapūjā*. Thus, *bhāvapūjā* consists in meditation on the supreme soul

---

1. *devapūjā gurūpāstiḥ svādhyāyaḥ saṁyamas tapaḥ /*
dānaṁ ceti gṛhasthānāṁ ṣaṭ karmāṇi dine dine //

and internal efforts for being one with it. External formal ritual of worship is called *dravya-pūjā*. It is considered to be useful in rousing such feelings as may make the path of *bhāvapūjā* easy. In the word *dravyapūjā,* the term '*dravya*' has the sense of assisting cause. The external formal ritual which assists *bhāvapūjā* is *dravyapūjā.* A worshipper who cannot directly reach the state of *bhāvapūjā* is enabled with the assistance of *dravyapūjā* to attain the benefits of *bhāvapūjā. Bhāvapūjā* has power to change the mental attitude from the spiritually unwholesome to the wholesome, to make mind like good qualities and virtuous activities, and to urge it to think over good thoughts and perform virtuous acts. As the spiritual light of *bhāvapūjā* manifests itself more and more, the desire for the good and the spiritual increases. And at last the worshipper attains the highest goal, the supreme spiritual good. Ācārya Haribhadra in his third *Aṣṭaka* writes:

ahiṁsā satyam asteyaṃ brahmacaryam alobhatā /
gurubhaktis tapo jñānaṃ satpuṣpāṇi pracakṣate //
ebhir devādhidevāya bahumānapurassarā /
dīyate pālanād yā tu sā vai śuddhety udāhṛtā //

Gist: Non-violence, truthfulness, non-stealing, continence, non-greed, devotion to and service of the elders, austerity and knowledge—these are the auspicious pure flowers. We offer these flowers to the supreme soul by cultivating these good qualities. Offering of these flowers (this type of flower-worship) is *śuddhapūjā*[1] (pure worship).

And for attaining this *śuddhapūjā, bhāvapūjā* is required as an instrument; and to create the mental state conducive to *bhāvapūjā*, the performance of the formal ritual is required; this formal ritual is *dravyapūjā. Dravyapūjā* being formal ritual is also called *upacārapūjā.*

From the above discussion, it follows that we should not stop at the stage of *dravyapūjā.* We should not consider it to be an end in itself. But we should use it discreetly as an instrument to attain the state of *bhāvapūjā.* It is useful to the extent it helps us to attain the state of *bhāvapūjā.* So, through the instrumentality of *dravyapūjā,* we should make sincere efforts to attain the state of *bhāvapūjā.*

As stated above, *dravyapūjā* is an assisting cause of *bhāvapūjā,* because it creates the atmosphere conducive to *bhāvapūjā.* If it does not achieve

1. *svakarmaṇā tam abhyarcya siddhiṁ vindati mānavaḥ /—Bhagavad-Gītā,* XVIII. 146
By worshipping Him through the performance of his own duty, man attains perfection.

this objective, it is of no use. If it does not lead to *bhāvapūjā*, it cannot be regarded as yielding its proper fruits. The object of *dravyapūjā* is a symbol or an image of the supreme soul, whereas the object of *bhāvapūjā* is the supreme soul itself whereof it is a symbol or an image. *Dravyapūjā* is limited to a specific period of time within which it is completed. On the other hand, *bhāvapūjā* (constant recalling to mind the pure qualities of the supreme soul) has no limitations of space and time, it can be availed of at any place and at any time. While performing worldly activities, the heart of the devotee is constantly set on the supreme soul and its pure qualities, and in this way, he is constantly engrossed in *bhāvapūjā*. When a man vigilantly observes in his worldly dealings non-violence, truthfulness, honesty, etc., he is to be regarded as performing *bhāvapūjā*, rather *śuddhapūjā*. Mind of the true worshipper remains always permeated with the devotion to the supreme soul and its pure qualities and as a result of which his life shines in its eternal purity.

The devotee worships the attachment-free embodied soul who destroyed mountains of *karmas*, attained omniscience, revealed and preached the highest truth and led the living beings on the path of liberation, in order that he may attain similar qualities. Again, so long as he does not attain the state of absolute non-attachment (*vītarāgatā*), he continues to pray: "May I remain in every birth and always devoted to the pure qualities of the attachment-free supreme soul so that I may not give way to bad qualities and fall into the state of degradation." If there is any one in the three worlds and in the three divisions of time who can save a living being from the cycle of births and deaths or from the attacks of miseries, it is only the attachment-free supreme soul or the dependence on its pure quality of non-attachment.

The state of complete non-attachment should be accepted as the ultimate goal and hence as the highest object of our meditation in order that we ourselves may attain that state. On the other hand, if we accept some individual afflicted with attachment as our highest ideal and hence meditate on him, then we nourish attachment and as a result of it make the bondage of worldly existence even stronger.

It is true that in the long journey leading to the ultimate state of non-attachment, many means are required. And it is necessary to accept them as intermediary ends at different stages[1] and to acquire them in an honest

1. Final effect (end) is achieved through stages, if the necessary conditions are available at proper times. The final product (effect) cloth comes into existence only after so

and just manner so that our journey may become easy. But they are to be accepted as means (or intermediary ends) and not as an ultimate end. If a man does not regard the state of non-attachment as an ultimate end and considers the one which is useful as a mere means to be the ultimate end, then he is doomed, he cannot be saved whatever efforts he may make and whatever wealth he may spend.

Bhāvapūjā consists in the meditation on the spiritually wholesome qualities, firm resolve to remove the defiling bad qualities and to cultivate the purifying good qualities, actual sincere efforts to exterminate the former and to develop the latter. Thus, *bhāvapūjā* inspires man to build up good character and to live an honest and just life; it ennobles and elevates his life. This is the objective of *bhāvapūjā*. And in the fulfilment of this objective, *bhāvapūjā* achieves its proper end.

The Jainas are worshippers not of any individual supreme soul, but of his pure qualities.[1] All souls which manifest these pure qualities are equally regarded by the Jainas as supreme souls and hence worthy of man's worship. Thus, these pure qualities themselves constitute the supreme ideal or the highest goal. The first sentence of the most sacred Jaina formula[2] called '*Namokkāra*' ('*Namaskāra*', '*Navakāra*') is '*namo arihaṃtāṇaṃ*' ('I bow before the Destroyer of (internal) enemies'). In it there occurs no mention of a proper name of any individual supreme soul; therein an obeisance is offered to the entire class of the individual supreme souls who have destroyed the internal enemies like attachment, aversion, etc.

---

many intermediary products (effects) like cotton, yarn, etc., have come into existence in due order.

1. There is no doubt that the virtuous individual is also worshipped, not as an individual but through his virtues. It is the virtues that are really worshipped through the worship of the virtuous. The worship of the virtues is heightened through the worship of the virtuous. And the worship-of-the-virtuous in the form of the worship-of-the-virtues enables the worshipper to deeply reflect and meditate on the pure virtues. As a matter of fact, the virtuous is worshipped through virtues, and the virtues are worshipped through the virtuous.
2. In this sacred formula, through the five sacred words, viz., *arihaṁta, siddha, ācārya, upādhyāya* and *sādhu* obeisances are offered to the destroyers of (internal) enemies, the perfected beings, the spiritual leaders and guides, the preceptors and the saints. These five words refer to qualities, they do not refer to any individual. Similarly, even in the two formulas of fourfold refuge (*catuḥ-śaraṇa*) and fourfold auspiciousness or good (*maṅgala-catuṣṭaya*) the four terms viz., *arihaṁta, siddha, sādhu* and *kevalīprajñapta-dharma* (the *dharma*, i.e., Religion propounded by the Omniscient) have reference to qualities and not to any individual.

2. *Guru-upāsti (Venerating and Serving the Elders)*

Guru means an elder. The following verse from Ācārya Haribhadra's *Yogabindu* informs us as to who are to be regarded as *guru.*

mātā pitā kalācārya eteṣām jñātayas tathā /
vṛddhā dharmopadeṣṭāro guruvargaḥ satāṁ mataḥ //110//

In the class of *gurus* Ācārya Haribhadra includes mother, father, teachers of art and sciences, family elders, those advanced in learning and good conduct, and saints who preach religion.

Venerating and serving them is *guru-upāsti.* By our reverence and service we should win their hearts and secure from them the knowledge and culture that ennoble our life.[1] Mother and father are the foremost *gurus.* Scriptures command us to worship them first (*mātā-pitroś ca pūjakaḥ*).[2]

3. *Svādhyāya (Study of the Spiritually Elevating Works)*

The term '*svādhyāya*' is the compound of two members, viz., '*sva*' and '*adhyāya*'. So, it means study of one's own self, that is, one's own life. Reading, listening to and reflecting on the life-elevating teachings are useful in keeping the mind healthy. They inspire man to peep into the innermost recesses of the self. As a result of it, man's journey on the path of progress and enlightenment becomes easy. *Svādhyāya*[3] is a form of austerity. By including it in the species of austerity of high order, the Jaina religion has lent glory to austerity; not only that but it has nicely and convincingly demonstrated the universality of austerity and direct experienceability of its fruits.

4. *Saṁyama (Restraint and Discipline)*

Saṁyama means control over sense-organs, control over mind, control over speech and thoughts, control over desire-anger-greed.[4] How greatly

---

1. *tad viddhi praṇipātena paripraśnena sevayā /*
   upadekṣyanti te jñānaṁ jñāninas tattvadarśinaḥ //34//—Bhagavad-Gītā IV
   Acquire knowledge by humble reverence, by inquiry and by service. The men of wisdom who have seen the truth will instruct you in knowledge.
2. *mātṛdevo bhava / pitṛdevo bhava /—Taittirīya Upaniṣad*
3. *svādhyāyān na pramaditavyam /—Taittirīya Upaniṣad*
4. *trividhaṁ narakasyedaṁ dvāraṁ nāśanam ātmanaḥ /*
   kāmaḥ krodhas tathā lobhas tasmād etat trayaṁ tyajet //—Bhagavad-Gītā XVI.21

we need *saṃyama* to make our life happy, peaceful and blissful![1]

Idleness and spiritual lethargy and weak will-power are the terrible great diseases of life. They cause man's downfall and land him on the most miserable state. *Saṃyama* is the perennial fountain of mental peace and inner happiness. It is, again, *saṃyama* that keeps man fit to experience even the bodily and material happiness. Without *saṁyama*, none can derive true pleasure from the enjoyment of the worldly objects. Study the following verse from the famous Buddhist work *Dhammapada.*

appamādo amatapadaṃ pamādo maccuno padaṃ /
appamattā na mīyanti ye pamattā matā yathā //

It declares that spiritual diligence and wakefulness are the state of immortality, while spiritual lethargy and negligence are an abode of death. The spiritually diligent and wakeful man never dies (—though his physical body leaves him, he is not dead, because he ever lives through his good deeds—), whereas the spiritually lethargic and negligent man, though living, is dead.

Noble ideal is one of the conditions that make man self-controlled and self-disciplined. Though he has some noble ideal, yet if he does not have any field of action where he can gain pleasure of creation,[2] it will be very difficult for him to observe self-control and self-discipline. Again, if he truly understands the value and importance of virtuous conduct and adores it, he can live a self-controlled and self-disciplined life. For the practice of restraint and discipline, proper environment is also required. If the environment is not conducive to restraint and discipline, their practice becomes difficult for both the householder and the monk. In short, true regard for restraint, noble ideal, pleasure of creation, devotion to virtuous conduct and proper environment all together make possible the practice of restraint and discipline.

---

1. *na gaṅgā yamunā cāpi sarayū vā sarasvatī /*
ninnagā vā citravatī mahī cāpi mahānadī //
sakkuṇaṁti visodhetuṁ taṁ malaṁ idha pāṇinaṁ /
visodhayati sattānaṁ yaṁ ve sīla-jala malaṁ //—Visuddhimagga (a Buddhist work)
Meaning: The Ganges, Yamunā, Sarayū, Sarasvatī, etc.,—all these rivers are not able to cleanse the soul and the mind of defilements polluting them. It is only righteous conduct that can cleanse them of their defilements.
2. All joy lies in creation.

5. *Tapa (Austerity)*

The importance and glory of the austerities like fasting (*upavāsa*), etc., depend on the noble purpose behind their observance as also on the purity of mental states. It is only on account of these two elements that fasting, etc., secure the glory of austerity. The noble-minded learned persons practise austerity as a pure spiritual effort to serve the masses and to bring to light the reality and truth covered under the veils of delusion, untruth, injustice and immorality. Thus, as their austerity has pure and auspicious purpose behind it and is associated with pure mental states, it becomes worthy of people's adoration and bestower of spiritual good. If a man gives up all the botheration of food with the purpose of practising *yoga* or meditation, controlling sense-organs, purifying mind, turning inward, attaining spiritual peace, reflecting on good thoughts, studying soul-ennobling works or performing any other good activity, then fasting is a spiritually beneficial austerity. Remaining constantly engaged in acquiring and imparting knowledge and learning, the saintly persons have composed spiritually elevating works; their devoted efforts to acquire knowledge, constant study of the praiseworthy philosophical and religious works, and the painstaking task of writing wholesome works—all this is one of the highest forms of austerity. To undertake a great good work, to think as to how it should be carried out successfully, to collect the required means and assistance, to persuade others to assist, to chalk out the plan, to execute it, and while doing all these, to forget hunger, thirst, bodily pains, exertion and to get completely engrossed in the task—this entire operation or business is also a form of austerity. Devoted and sincere efforts to make available the necessities of life, viz., water, etc., to the masses is again another form of austerity. Thus, all attempts to purify soul and mind of the defilements (passions and vices), and pure zeal for rendering service to others and performing other wholesome activities come under the category of austerity. Truthfulness of the veracious, continence of the continent, service of a servant, yogic practice of a *yogī*, meditation of a meditator, devotion of the devotee, study of the student, devotion to learning of the learned, teaching of the teacher, preaching of the preacher, philanthropic activity of the philanthropist—all these are austerity when done with pure heart. Not only that, but to do the allotted work honestly is also a case of austerity. Devotion to one's duty is also a form of austerity. The pleasure of a special order, which one derives from the practice of austerity is its beauty.

Fast of a right measure observed properly is beneficial to bodily health. For the wise, fasting becomes useful in purifying mind and thereby deriving spiritual benefits. It cultivates endurance. The word '*upavāsa*' is derived from the verbal root *vas* (to be, to exist) with the prefix *upa* (near). Thus, it means an act of being near one's own soul, that is, an act of being in the pure state of one's soul. And fasting becomes austerity to the extent it achieves this objective. By observing '*āṃbela*'[1] we can achieve the purpose of controlling our desire for relishing various sweet juices. Again, its observance is useful in keeping our body healthy. (It controls diabetes and cholesterol). Observance of '*ekāśana*' (taking food only once a day) limits our botheration of food to only one time in a day, keeps our body light and agile, and gives us more time and scope for good activities.

External austerity easily attracts the attention of the people, because it is capable of being seen. Moreover, it does not require any special merit for its practice. Again, its practiser gains fame, praise and honour quickly and easily. This is the reason why it spreads among the people in no time. People do not have any idea of its limitations and uses. Formerly in ancient times, its use was in that the people might take care of their health and repeatedly subject their bodies to various hardships so that they could cultivate power of endurance which on occasions in future might enable them to face hardships and sufferings. Now both these things are not taken into account or kept in view, while practising external austerity; and hence these two objectives are also not achieved. People know Lord Mahāvīra's external austerity, but they do not care to know his internal austerity. That great sage and seer (*ṛṣi*) practised internal austerity more than the external one. We should direct our attention first to his practice of internal austerity.

Lord Mahāvira's external austerity was meant to undergo expiation through finding out and destroying the defiling impressions left behind

1. '*Āṁbela*' is also a vow of taking food only once in a day. But the vower has to refrain from taking milk, curd, butter-milk, oil, ghee, molasses, sugar and spices like chilli powder, etc. Again, he is required not to eat green and dry vegetables as also green and dry fruits. He can take food prepared from grains like wheat, millet, moong, black beans, gram, rice, etc. He can eat *dāla* (semi-liquid preparation made from split pulses), rice, chapatis, etc. He can also eat parched rice, parched jowar, roasted gram. He can take baked salt, dry ginger and black pepper.

on the soul by the evil acts performed in the past births. Again, it was also meant to give concrete form to his strong resolve of rousing righteous indignation among the masses against killings of animals in various Vedic sacrifices, establishing non-violence in place of violence and preaching and propagating the principle of non-violence. Lord Mahāvīra was the compassionate *par excellence.* Again, in those days there was prevalent a debased practice of buying and selling of war prisoners as slaves. To generate disgust among the people against this callous practice so that they may ultimately rise to eradicate it was possibly the altruistic auspicious intention of Lord Mahāvīra, an embodiment of spiritual good, behind his external austerity. All these possibilities come to our mind, if we study the stories of this great saint's past births. When Lord Mahāvīra as a Jaina monk possessed cognitive powers of four types before the attainment of omniscience, he was well-known as *dīrgha-tapasvī* (practiser of austerities of very long duration). We cannot believe that he practised austerities for a long period of time simply for the purpose of causing pains and sufferings to his body. We feel that behind the great austerities of this great friend of all beings was a catholic purpose of achieving universal good. This becomes clear from the study of his biography. Lord Mahāvīra's that 'self-imposed restriction' (*abhigraha*) and its associate special event of setting free Candanabālā from her slavery can very well give us the idea of the catholic altruistic purpose behind his brilliant austerities.

Without internal austerity, the external one is of no value. The main, direct and best austerity is the internal austerity, and the external austerity is useful to the extent it is conducive to the internal one. The austerity which is useful in neither purifying mind, nor elevating life, nor benefiting the bodily health is worthless and purposeless austerity springing from stark ignorance.

Those who practise external austerity should not become a burden to others.

At this juncture, it is advisable to remember that for health what is necessary is the digestion and assimilation of the eaten food accumulated in the stomach. Extinction of the power of digestion entails the gradual destruction of all life-forces and as a result causes various diseases. A disease adversely influences the mind and thereby acts as an obstruction to meditation, study and practice of religion. So the first and foremost requirement is the healthy body. Hence, we should practise external austerities in such a manner that there may not arise any disease due to it and our organs (sense-organs and motor-organs) remain competent to perform their function properly.

Upādhyāya Yaśovijayaji in his *Tapo'ṣṭaka* which forms a part of his work *Jñānasāra* says:

tad evaṃ hi tapaḥ kāryaṁ durdhyānaṁ yatra no bhavet /
yena yogā na hīyante kṣīyante nendriyāṇi ca //

Translation: One should practise austerities in such a manner that there may not be unwholesome brooding, the powers of mind, speech and body may not dwindle and deteriorate, and organs may not become weak.

In this matter, the following verse provides us clear guidance. It declares:

kāyo no kevalam ayaṃ paritāpanīyo /
miṣṭai rasair bahuvidhair na ca lālanīyaḥ //
cittendriyāṇi na caranti yathotpathena /
vaśyāni yena ca tad ācaritaṃ jinānām //

Gist: We should not simply subject the body to hardships, sufferings and tortures, nor should we fondle (pamper, spoil) it with various sweet juices; but we should live in such a manner that mind and organs may not go astray and remain under our control.

Thus the author of this verse, who is a devotee of Jina advises us to abandon two extremes and to adopt the middle path.

Bhagavad-Gītā sets forth in the following verse the universal standard of the right living.

yuktāhāravihārasya yuktaceṣṭasya karmasu /
yuktasvāpāvabodhasya yogo bhavati duḥkhahā //VI.17//

Translation: For the person who is temperate in food and recreation, who is restrained in his activities, whose sleep and waking are well regulated, there ensues spiritual discipline (*yoga*) which destroys all misery.

In short, the external austerities are to be practised for achieving the following auspicious purposes—for preventing diseases, for cultivating power of endurance so that in future one can properly serve others or can face hardships, for averting evil influences of the vicious act committed by a person who loves us, for doing good to others, for getting time for learning, study, teaching, reading, writing, thinking, for purifying mind, so on and so forth.

With a view to developing the spiritual power adequate for reducing passions, whatever means are adopted for placing under burning hardship one's body, organs and mind—they all are called *tapas* or austerity. And it has been very well explained that the importance of the external austerity lies simply in its being conducive to the growth of the internal one. In other words, the Jaina saints teach that the external austerity should assist in our efforts to reach the stage of the internal austerity. Thus the former is merely a means to the latter. In this classification of austerity into external and internal types there are included all the gross and refined rules pertaining to religiosity.

As stated above, according to the Jainas, there are two types of austerity—external and internal.

External Austerity

External austerity is of six types. They are as follows. (1) *Anaśana*—to give up food for one or more days. (2) *Avamaudarya* or *Uṇodarī*—to eat less than what the hunger demands. (3) *Vṛttisaṃkṣepa*—to reduce greed in relation to various sorts of things. (4) *Rasaparityāga*—to give up delicacies like ghee, milk, honey, butter, etc., as also wine, etc. which, when consumed, cause harm to both—the body and the mind. The purpose behind the observance of this external austerity is to gain control over the desire for relishing sweet juices. That we may not long for and hanker after delicacies, that we may get accustomed to tasteless food and that out of our desire for enjoying delicious dishes we may not eat more than what is needed for the nourishment of the body—are the purposes behind the practice of this austerity. Wine is to be given up for all times and places, because it is harmful always at all places. But the harmless, nutritive substances like ghee, milk, etc., could be taken in due proportion with a view to making our life good and developing it. To take them more than they are needed for achieving this purpose is harmful, while to take them in required proportion only is beneficial. (5) *Viviktaśayyāsanasaṃlīnatā*—to reside (for the spiritual benefit) in a lonely place free from all disturbances. (6) *Kāyakleśa*—to place one's body under stress through cold or heat, through adopting diverse postures and the like. The purpose behind this austerity is to cultivate the power of endurance so that in future in adverse times one can endure bodily hardships and maintain mental peace and equanimity. If the mortification of the body is undertaken with a view to simply causing pain and torture to the body, or influencing others, or surprising others, or rousing pity in others to obtain something, then it is an austerity springing from ignorance. This austerity of *kāyakleśa* (mortification of the body) fulfils its spiritual purpose to the extent it is useful in purifying the mind and reducing attachment and passions. So one should reflect as to whether or not a particular form of *kāyakleśa* is conductive to spiritual welfare.

Internal Austerity

Ācārya Hemacandra in his *Yogaśāstra*[1] declares that in effecting dissociation of the karmic matter from soul the internal austerity is superior to the external one.

Internal austerity is also of six types. (1) *Prāyaścitta* (Atonement): That through which it is possible to make clean sweep of the defects born of negligence arisen in connection with a vow (*vrata*) that has been accepted—that is called *Prāyaścitta.* (2) *Vinaya* (Veneration): To hold in great regard the virtuous qualifications like knowledge, etc.—that is called *vinaya.* (3) *Vaiyāvṛttya* (Service): To render service to somebody either through providing him with necessary means or through personally acting for his sake—that is called *Vaiyāvṛttya*[2]. (4) *Svādhyāya* (Study): To undertake various studies and practices with a view to acquiring knowledge—that is called *Svādhyāya* (5) *Vyutsarga* (Renunciation): To renounce the feeling of 'I' and 'my'—that is called *Vyutsarga.* (6) *Dhyāna* (Concentration): Removing the distractions of mind to cultivate its power of concentration—that is called *dhyāna.*

Vinaya (Veneration or Respect) is divided into four categories, viz., *jñānavinaya* (respect for right knowledge), *darśanavinaya* (respect for right faith), *cāritravinaya* (respect for right conduct) and *upacāravinaya* (formal respect). Respect for knowledge consists in acquiring knowledge and in engaging oneself in continuous study. Respect for right faith consists in not swerving from faith in what is real and true as also in attaining doubt-free condition of mind by removing doubts that may arise in its connection according to one's ability. Respect for right conduct consists in keeping one's mind peaceful and unagitated. Formal respect consists in showing respect by overt acts towards persons who are superior to us in virtuous qualities. *Vinaya* suggests renunciation of the mental states of pride and

1. *nirjarākaraṇe bāhyāc chreṣtham ābhyantaraṁ tapaḥ* / IV. 91.
2. The Jaina religion regards even rendering service to others as a form of austerity and includes it in the list of special types of austerity.

contempt. We all should bear in mind the salutary advice of the *Dharmaśāstra* (the science of good conduct) that our behaviour towards all, high and low, should be polite and friendly.

Dhyāna (Mental Concentration)

Dhyāna means mental concentration. It is classified into four types: *ārta* (mournful), *raudra* (cruel), *dharma* (moral) and *śukla* (pure). Of these four, the first two, since they are a cause of an evil rebirth, are evil concentrations and so worthy of rejection. On the other hand, the remaining two, since they are a cause of spiritual good and liberation, are noble concentrations and so worthy of acceptance; hence they find place among the forms of austerity. We describe them in brief.

Ārta-dhyāna

Ārta-dhyāna is that concentration of mind, which is produced owing to some pain or misery either real or imaginary. It is, again, of four varieties. (1) When an undesirable thing comes in one's contact, then one distressed at the pain caused thereby constantly thinks of removing away this thing—of how to get rid of this thing; this constant thinking or concentration constitutes the first variety. (2) When one develops a bodily or mental pain or disease, then one experiences worry caused by a pathetic eagerness to get rid of it; this constant sorrowful thinking constitutes the second variety. (3) When a desirable thing goes out of one's possession, then one constantly thinks of getting it back; this constant thinking is the third variety. (4) The fourth variety is nothing but a concentration of mind on unsatisfied desires. On account of intense hankering after enjoyment of worldly pleasures, one develops a strong volition to get hold of things not yet in one's possession; this constant longing for worldly pleasures or a strong determination to acquire objects of worldly pleasures is the fourth variety. *Ārti* means pain, and mental concentration on one's own pain is *ārta-dhyāna*. The causes that produce pain are four in all—viz., (1) The getting of what is not desired. (2) The losing of what is desired. (3) A disagreeable sensation. (4) A hankering after enjoyment. Depending on the causes the *ārta-dhyāna* is classified into four types, viz. (1) *Aniṣṭasaṃyoga-ārta-dhyāna*, (2) *Iṣṭaviyoga-ārta-dhyāna*, (3) *Rogacintā-ārta-dhyāna*, and (4) *Nidāna-ārta-dhyāna*. *Nidāna* means strong determination to satisfy the unsatisfied desire for enjoyment.

Raudra-dhyāna

Raudra means cruel or callous, and *dhyāna* performed by such a mind or a being is called *raudra-dhyāna.* Cruelty or callousness of heart takes its rise from a tendency to commit violence, to speak untruth, to commit theft and to seek security for the things acquired, and the constant reflections that proceed in connection with them are respectively called *raudra-dhyāna* promoting violence, that promoting untruthfulness, that promoting theft and that promoting protection-of-an-acquisition. These are four types of *raudra-dhyāna.* Thus the four types of *raudra-dhyāna* are: to contemplate to attack and kill others, to tell a lie to deceive others, to take undue possession of someone's property, and to protect one's own property with intense greed. *Raudra-dhyāna* comprises the perverse pleasures of contemplating on evil acts and benefits derived from them. Thus its four varieties can be described as perverse pleasures of violence, untruthfulness, theft and possession. (Perverse pleasure of sexual enjoyment may be included in perverse pleasure of possessions. Or like the fifth great vow of absolute continence, it may be taken as an independent perverse pleasure.)

Dharma-dhyāna

This mental concentration leads to spiritual good. All wholesome and virtuous reflection is *dharma-dhyāna.* It is also of four varieties: (1) What is the commandment of an attachment-free great man? What sort of commandment it ought to be? To apply one's mind to an investigation like this and thus to lay bare the commandment in question—that is called *dharma-dhyāna* devoted to a consideration of *ājñā* or commandment. (2) To apply one's mind to the consideration of the nature of defilements and to the consideration of the question as to how to get rid of them—that is called *dharma-dhyāna* devoted to a consideration of *apāya* or removal (of defilements). (3) To apply one's mind to a consideration of the question as to what consequences that are being experienced are due to what *karmas* as also of the question as to what *karmas* that are being accumulated are to yield what consequences—that is called *dharma-dhyāna* devoted to a consideration of *vipāka* or the consequences-of-*karmas.* (4) To apply one's mind to a consideration of the nature of the universe—that is called *dharma-dhyāna* devoted to a consideration of *saṃsthāna* or structure of the universe.

Śukla-dhyāna (Pure Concentration)

Śukla-dhyāna is a very subtle auspicious mental concentration. It is attained at a very high spiritual stage, where the deluding *karmas* are completely subsided or are subjected to continuous process of destruction. It is so subtle that it is very difficult to understand it merely by reading books or hearing about it from the mouth of the preceptor.[1]

Like the other types of *dhyāna, śukla-dhyāna* too is divided into four subtypes. The four are designated as follows:

(1) *Pṛthaktvavitarkasavicāra* (Constant conceptual thinking applied to various aspects of a substance).

(2) *Ekatvavitarkanirvicāra* (Constant conceptual thinking applied to one aspect only of a substance).

(3) *Sūkṣmakriyā'pratipātin* (Concentration accompanied with subtle physical (bodily) movement and infallible).

(4) *Samucchinnakriyā'nivṛtti* (Concentration accompanied with complete cessation of all activities and infallible).

(1) *Pṛthaktvavitarkasavicāra* (Constant conceptual thinking applied to various aspects of a substance): When a performer of *dhyāna* takes up for consideration an inanimate entity like atom, etc., or a conscious entity like soul and undertakes in relation to its numerous modes like permanence, destruction, tangibility, non-tangibility, etc., and with the help of the various standpoints a reflection dominated by difference—at the same time in the interest of reflection switches over from one mode to another, from

---

1. Regarding *śukla-dhyāna*, Ācārya Hemacandra in his *Yogaśāstra* (XI.3 *Vṛtti*) raises a question: If only those persons who possess the supremely strong bone-structure called *vajra-ṛṣabha-nārāca* are authorised to perform *śukla-dhyāna,* then why do you preach it before the people of this age, who possess only weak bone-structure called *sevārta?*

   In answer to this question he says that though the people of this age are not authorised to perform *śukla-dhyāna*, yet the learned Jaina theoreticians continuously preach and teach it with a view that the tradition of its knowledge may not be broken and it may not fall into oblivion.

   While ending his *Yogaśāstra*, Ācārya Hemacandra writes:
   mokṣo'stu mā'stu yadi vā paramānandas tu vedyate sa khalu /
   yasmin nikhilasukhāni pratibhāsante na kiñcid iva //XII.51//
   There may be or may not be liberation. But it is certain that in the unagitated state of mind we do experience the highest bliss compared to which all the pleasures taken together appear to us trifling and essenceless.

a meaning to a word, from a word to a meaning, or from one *yoga*[1] to another, then the *dhyāna* concerned is called *pṛthaktvavitarkasavicāra.* Let us explain this Sanskrit term. '*Pṛthaktva*' means difference. '*Vitarka*' means conceptual thinking. So, the term '*pṛthaktvavitarka*' means conceptual thinking dominated by difference. And as there is in it transition (*vicāra)* from one type of *yoga* to another, from the word to the meaning, from the meaning to the word, or from one mode to another, it is called '*savicāra*'. Though there is movement of mind in this *dhyāna,* yet it is of the nature of concentration, because the movement is confined to one substance only, that is, its object is one substance only.

(2) *Ekatvavitarkanirvicāra* (Constant conceptual thinking applied to one aspect only of a substance): On the contrary, when a performer of *dhyāna* takes up for concentration some one mode or aspect only and undertakes in relation to it a reflection dominated by oneness or non-difference, again when sticking to some one of the three types of *yoga,*—viz. those pertaining to mind, speech and body—he introduces no change in the form of transition from word to meaning or *vice versa,* or from one type of *yoga* to another, then the *dhyāna* concerned is called *ekatvavitarkanirvicāra.* For in this *dhyāna* there is mainly a reflection of oneness (*ekatva*) and there is introduced in it no change (*vicāra*) as to mode, meaning, word or *yoga.* As for these two types of *śukla-dhyāna,* when one's practice of the first that is dominated by difference has become firm, only then is one enabled to perform the second that is dominated by oneness or non-difference. Thus just as the poison of a snake, etc., circulating throughout the entire body is, by means of a magical chant or the like, concentrated on the spot stung, similarly, one's mind unsteadily wandering about amidst the multifarious objects of the world is, by means of *dhyāna,* made steady by being concentrated on some one object (the minutest mode). When the steadiness of mind thus becomes firm, then just as a burning mass of fire becomes extinct in case all fuel whatsoever is withdrawn away from it, so also does the mind which in the above manner has been made steady by being concentrated on some one object (the minutest mode) ultimately become absolutely calm.[2] That is

1. *Yoga* here means activity. There are three *yogas—manoyoga* (mental activity), *vacanayoga* (vocal activity) and *kāyayoga* (bodily activity).
2. *trijagadviṣayaṁ dhyānād aṇusaṁsthaṁ dhārayet krameṇa manaḥ /*
viṣam iva sarvāṅgagataṁ mantrabalān māntriko daṁśe //
apasāritendhanabharaḥ śeṣastokendhano'nalo jvalitaḥ /
tasmād apanīto vā nirvāti yathā manas tadvat //—Yogaśāstra, XI. 19-20

to say, its fickleness is done away with and it becomes free of all waverings and agitations—with the result that the deluding *karmas* are absolutely dissociated from the soul, which in turn leads to the absolute elimination of knowledge-covering, vision-covering and obstructive *karmas* and ultimately to the manifestation of omniscience. Thus the second type of *śukla-dhyāna* culminates into the manifestation of omniscience.[1]

(3) *Sūkṣmakriyā'pratipāti* (Concentration accompanied with subtle physical (bodily) movement and infallible): When the omniscient Lord, at the time of death, during the course of the process called cessation-of-*yoga*, ultimately takes recourse to just a subtle bodily *yoga*, while putting an end to all the remaining *yogas*, then this act of his is called *sūkṣmakriyā'pratipāti-dhyāna.* This stage of *śukla-dhyāna* is, in fact, not of the nature of mental concentration. So to call it *dhyāna* is merely a convention. Regarding it we are told that just as steadiness of mind is called *dhyāna* so also steadiness of body can also be called *dhyāna.* In this state of *śukla-dhyāna* there proceed only the subtle bodily activities like inbreathing and outbreathing—and there is no possibility of downfall from this state. Therefore it is called *sūkṣmakriyā* (accompanied with subtle bodily activities) and *apratipātī* (infallible).

(4) *Samucchinnakriyā'nivṛtti* (Concentration accompanied with complete cessation of all activities and infallible): When even the subtle bodily activities cease altogether and the constituent-units of the soul concerned become free of all wavering, then the state is called *samucchinnakriyā'-nivṛttidhyāna.* For, in this state there takes place no activity whatsoever—whether gross or subtle and whether pertaining to mind, speech or body; and there is no possibility of downfall from it. Through the instrumentality of this fourth type of *śukla-dhyāna* all karmic inflow and all karmic bondage cease altogether, the soul becomes completely free from all *karmas*, it attains liberation, leaving the mortal body moves upward and within a moment reaches the end of the universe, and remains there motionless. This stage of *śukla-dhyāna* lasts only for a moment.

Thus we complete the exposition of *dhyāna* and with it we complete the exposition of austerity.

---

1. The second variety of *śukla-dhyāna* at the twelfth stage of spiritual development (*guṇasthāna*) is more intense than the same at the eleventh stage. In other words, in the twelfth stage it reaches its culmination. This is the reason why it causes immediate manifestation of omniscience.

Donation (Dāna)

Donation means offering to someone a thing or money come in one's possession through legitimate means. One should offer in donation things or money righteously acquired by oneself. Donation should be offered to the deserving and worthy persons at the proper place and time. The thing offered by way of donation must be such as proves beneficial in the life-journey of the recipient and hence such as proves a cause for the development of his meritorious qualities. One should offer such a thing that suits the concerned place and time and such as proves no obstruction to the righteous development of the donee. The donor should have either respect or compassion or friendly feeling towards the donee, and he should not feel regret for the act of donation—either at the time of offering it or afterwards.

Donation is renunciation to the extent things or money are given in donation. Having renounced all possessions, to devote oneself completely to the service of others is the acme of donation. A man who has renounced all his possessions remains engrossed in the works beneficent to both himself and others, is satisfied with the bare necessities of life, entertains no desire to accumulate anything, and employs all his powers, energies and faculties in achieving the noble and good ends of life. He takes the least from the society and offers the most to it in one form or the other. Such a person is absolved from the duty of offering in donation that which he has not. When he continuously offers the benefits of his spiritual experiences and developing powers and faculties to the masses out of pure affection, then his donation of services is highly superior to the donation of uncountable wealth by the richest of the rich. Mahāvīra, Buddha and other saints who renounced all their possessions are such donors as are greatly superior to those rich men of the world who offered their uncountable wealth in donation.

A wise rich man considers his act of donation to be an act of atonement. He offers his wealth in donation, understanding that employing his wealth in this way is his duty and beneficial to both himself and others. Donation given for the sake of reputation and praise is of no value whatsoever, it is ineffective religiously and spiritually. Just as offering money to the deserving is donation, so also showing the good and righteous path to someone through one's speech, giving wholesome advice to others, doing good to others through one's speech are also forms of donation. Cultured, polite and sweet speech is to be regarded as donation. Similarly, doing good to others by means of one's bodily activities, helping others by employing one's body, or working for others through one's body is again a form of donation. Thus, we can perform the duty of donation in various ways.

Which donation is great? The simple answer to this question is that the donation of that thing which is needed at a particular time is great at that time. For the thirsty donation of water is great, for the hungry donation of food is great, for the one destitute of clothes donation of clothes is great, for the illiterate donation of literacy is great, and for the one who fears danger to one's life donation of safety to one's life is great. Thus donation of that thing which is needed most at a particular time is great at that time.

The donation must prove beneficial both to the person offering donation and to the person receiving it. The benefit accruing to the donor consists in that he is rid of the attachment felt for the thing concerned—as a result of which he comes to develop a feeling of contentment and equanimity. The benefit accruing to the donee consists in that the thing concerned proves helpful to him in his life-journey—as a result of which his virtues receive proper unfolding.

Is it not better to donate directly one's powers and faculties than to employ one's powers and faculties first in earning money and then to donate that money? Direct donation of powers and faculties means living a life imbued with the spirit of selfless service. Such a life becomes a life of renunciation. While treading the path of righteousness and morality and leading a diligent life, to impart pure and useful knowledge to students, to disseminate noble and wholesome ideas among the people, or to exhort others to devote their lives to good activities is superior to the donation of money. Learning and culture occupy the place higher than the one money occupies. Therefore, donation of knowledge is highly superior to that of money. The praiseworthiness of the donation of money lies in its being useful in carrying the benefits of this best donation of knowledge to the masses. It is necessary to bear in mind this gradation.

Service[1] is the best form of donation. '*adveṣaḥ sarvabhūtānām maitraḥ*

1. "The service of the poor is the service of God."
In the *Bhagavatī-sūtra,* Lord Mahāvīra, addressing his principal disciple Gautama Indrabhūti, says, "One who serves the sick and the miserable serves (worships, adores) me through right inclination, faith or vision (*samyak-darśana*); and one who serves (worships, adores) me through right inclination, faith or vision, does serve the sick and the miserable."

karuṇa eva ca'. The mental state free from any ill-will towards any being and full of compassion and friendliness towards all beings itself is the perennial fount of the virtue of donation. Such a mental state keeps constantly flowing the righteous activity of donation through speech and body.

Donation, whether performed through bodily labour or mental labour, whether in the form of imparting knowledge or in the form of compassion, whether of money or of other useful things, is included in renunciation; we have already stated this. There are three possible objectives of renunciation. This will be clear from what follows.

There are three types of renunciation:

(1) *Renunciation rooted in self-control*

Renunciation which helps practice of five vows, the forms of self-control, is renunciation rooted in self-control. Renunciation of unwholesome objects of pleasure which, instead of giving pure bliss, do harm to the body, pervert the mind, lead to the waste of money and increase the feeling of attachment is the renunciation rooted in self-control.

The following are some of the cases of renunciation of this type:

(a) Renunciation of attractive and fine cloth whose production in mills involves large scale violence. One remains satisfied with hand-spun and hand-woven *khaddar* whose production involves very little violence.
(b) Renunciation of silk garments whose production involves killing of the four-sensed silk-worms.
(c) Renunciation of ornaments made of pearls obtained after tearing (splitting) the five-sensed fish.
(d) Renunciation of witnessing dramas, cinemas which rouse sexual passion.
(e) Renunciation of ornaments which are put on for the sake of displaying one's riches or impressing others. Men need no ornaments, and women too need not wear ornaments except those that serve as auspicious marks of their wifehood.
(f) Renunciation of make-up materials like talcum powder, lipstick, etc.

His words are: *Goyamā! je gilāṇaṁ paḍicarai se maṁ daṁsaṇeṇa paḍivajjai, je maṁ daṁsaṇeṇa paḍivajjai se gilāṇaṁ paḍicarai* /
"They asked a great one: How many ways are there to God? He said: There are as many ways as there are atoms in the universe, but the best and shortest is Service."

which are used to decorate one's complexion in order to attract the attention of others and to display one's love for sensual pleasures. As a matter of fact, one should understand that true beauty lies in modesty, virtues and righteous conduct.

(g) Renunciation of drinks which are known as 'cold-drinks' and are taken for the sake of relish.

(2) *Renunciation rooted in love and compassion*

Renouncing, in times of scarcity, those things which one does not have but can have or is offered, in favour of those who really need them for their livelihood, though by doing so one puts oneself into inconvenience and experiences hardship—that act of renunciation is the case of renunciation rooted in love and compassion. For instance, when the people living mainly on wheat give up the ration of rice in order that the people living mainly on rice may get sufficient rice, then that is the case of renunciation rooted in love and compassion.

(3) *Renunciation rooted in donation*

Renunciation of this type is illustrated by the story of a Jaina layman named Pūṇīā. He made slivers of cotton (*pūṇī*) and thereby earned livelihood sufficient for two persons only. In spite of that, everyday he invited one guest and fed him; and Pūṇīā and his wife, by turn, renounced one meal everyday.

If someone tears into pieces a hundred rupee note for the sake of renunciation, could it be regarded as an act of renunciation? No, never. It could be regarded as a sheer act of foolishness or waywardness, because by that act no one is benefited, that money is not spent in meeting the necessities of some needy person but simply destroyed. Similarly, when society is facing crisis due to unemployment and starvation, at that time neglecting that social crisis if someone in the name of religion spends his money simply for the sake of self-advertisement, momentary display and gaining praise, then he will not attain any spiritual benefit which is due to true renunciation. Moreover, money earned through such unjust and dishonest means as black-marketing, gambling, speculation, smuggling, etc., when employed in religious activities, really defile the true religion. Not only that, but it encourages man's passion of greed and his instinct to acquire money in dishonest and unrighteous manner, and creates wrong belief among the people that if one having acquired money through unjust means, employs them in so-called religious activities, one practises true religion. Renunciation is a sort of austerity which is beneficial both to the one who practises and to others.

If those who practise austerities like fasting, etc., do so for the purpose of controlling their desires or for some such other wholesome purposes and understand and follow the moral of the story of Pūṇīā Śrāvaka, then their religion will gain such an esteem in the heart of the masses as can be gained by no other means. Others, especially the masses ignorant of the essence of religion always judge the spiritual efficacy of any religion on the basis of the conduct of its followers. Conduct of religious followers is the measure of the spiritual efficacy of any religion.

As stated above, donation means giving up or spending one's money for the good of others. Giving up wealth, comforts, pleasures which one actually possesses or which one actually does not possess but can possess or is likely to possess or is offered, for the benefit of oneself as well as others is renunciation.

There are four objectives of donation. They are as follows:

(1) To atone for the sins like unjust earning, etc. committed in the past.
(2) To employ in good activities the excess wealth saved after using it for one's comforts.
(3) To accomplish the philanthropic activities like constructing and maintaining educational institutions, hospitals, religious places, etc.
(4) To serve righteous persons, saints, the learned, etc.

As an expression of one's compassion, one should support by donation those who are needy because they have no means of livelihood—whether or not they are one's dependents. It is said that the giving of food embodies all gifts, because the disease of hunger occurs everywhere and also because hunger breeds many vices.

Acquisitiveness (*lobha*) is overcome by donation. There is no place for pride in donation. The donor should not consider himself superior to the donee. If there is any feeling of superiority, it encourages and feeds pride. It is also an expression of pride to offer donations in self-advertisement and self-display.

One who acquires money through honest and righteous means and gives it generously in donation is a good donor. And there is a person who has already renounced all his possession and become an ascetic and lives a simple, pure and self-controlled life; if such a person, according to his state of life, employs his energies, powers and faculties in the service of the people, then he is a great good donor.

With this we finish the brief account of the six obligatory daily duties prescribed for the Jaina layman.

The Jaina works dealing with the rules of conduct devote considerable space to the discussion on what is fit to be eaten and what is not fit to be eaten. Their ban on eating by night is also well-known.

Prohibition of Eating by Night

One can easily understand this ban on eating by night if one recalls the phenomenon of uncountable flying insects that multiply the household—especially Indian—with the advancement of darkness at dusk. At night, innumerable insects are attracted by the light of a lantern or an electric lamp and hover around it and fall dead. Many insects are seen fallen dead in the receptacle for the oil and wick of an earthen lamp. Lighted candles too are no good for them. A cooking fire certainly draws many insects to their death. Apart from it, at night many insects settle on our bodies and move on the different parts including the face or the mouth, thus causing us trouble. Similarly, they must be settling on food too. This possibility cannot be ruled out. And these tiny insects which are barely discernible by day are completely invisible by night even when a lamp is lit. At night almost anything—moths, snakes, mice, ants, small pins, wooden chips, skin, or hairs—may fall into a dish of food, and the person who is eating will not be able to see it. Thus, at night food might be infested with minute invisible organisms, insects may have crawled or fluttered into it, and its contents will in any event be unrecognisable in the dark. To swallow an ant in this way destroys the intelligence, a fly makes one vomit, a louse causes dropsy, a spider leprosy, and a thorn or a wooden chip pain in a throat; and if some poisonous organism is eaten in this way, it will cause death. At night, even the cooks cannot notice the poisonous organisms mixed with cooking materials or boiled with the preparations; as a result those who eat this poisonous food succumb to death; such cases of death happen.[1]

---

1. *medhāṁ pipīlikā hanti yūkā kuryāj jalodaram /*
kurute makṣikā vāntiṁ kuṣṭharogaṁ ca kolikaḥ //
kaṇṭako dārukhaṇḍaś ca vitanoti galavyathām /
vyañjanāntar nipatitas tāluṁ vidhyati vṛścikaḥ //
vilagnaś ca gale bālaḥ svarabhaṅgāya jāyate /
ityādayo dṛṣṭadoṣāḥ sarveṣāṁ niśi bhojane //—Yogaśāstra, III. 50-2

Food eaten before sun-set gets mostly digested through bodily movements and activities conducted during the period before going to bed; and hence it does not cause any uneasiness in sleep. But if we eat by night and go to bed after some time, food eaten do not get digested at all on account of the absence of bodily movements and activities which help digestion; hence stomach remains full and heavy, which causes uneasiness and bad influences in sleep. Indian science of health has formulated a rule that after having taken food one should drink water in small quantity many times (*muhur muhur vāri pībed abhūri*). Those who eat by night cannot observe this rule, because they do not have time to drink water in small quantity many times after taking food. Therefore, they suffer from indigestion. And indigestion is regarded as the root-cause of many diseases (*ajīrṇaprabhavā rogāḥ*).

In short, as shown above, the strongest argument against night-time eating is that it occasions more violence than day-time eating. And from the point of view of health electric light, moon-light or the like might be advantageous, but it is not universal and health-giving like sunlight. Hence where both are available, then from the point of view of health it is sunlight that is more useful and acceptable. Moreover, religion of renunciation lies rooted in contentment—from this point of view too it is proper to finish eating during day-time just like other activities appropriate to day-time and to contentedly give rest to the digestive system during night-time. This facilitates proper sleep and the observance of continence—all this resulting in an augmentation of healthiness. Again, if with a view to contentment either the day-time eating or the night-time eating has to be chosen, then a wakeful, discreet intellect will definitely choose the former. This is the testimony of the life-history of the great saints that have flourished up to this day.

Even common sense understands that one who cannot renounce night-time eating is deprived of its benefits and advantages. But in these days of struggle and competition, men are engaged in such businesses and professions that they cannot renounce night-time eating in spite of their will. Taking into consideration their circumstances, their helplessness in eating food by night is pardonable, as it does not involve intentional violence, nor is it a form of purposeless evil activity.

Discrimination of what to be eaten from what not to be eaten

Till to this age various sciences, viz., science of body and its functioning, that of health, that of medicine and surgery, that of food have made innumerable experiments and brought to light many discoveries. Jainism which is regarded as a scientific religion cannot afford to ignore the beneficial aspect of these discoveries.

Body is the foremost means or instrument of righteous conduct, religious practice and spiritual development and thereby ultimately of liberation. So it is absolutely necessary to see that it maintains its efficiency all right and remains quite healthy. It is better to form such habits of food and drink that the body may remain sound and healthy and gain required strength and energy to resist the attacks of diseases than to form bad habits and subject the body to medical treatment after diseases have already attacked it. Prevention is better than cure. For this purpose, one should reflect as to which food is wholesome and which one is unwholesome, discreetly select the wholesome one that can provide nutritive juices to the body for its health and supplement the loss which the body suffers everyday.

One should assiduously abandon the food and drink which involve killing of mobile creatures, cause intoxication and unconsciousness leading to deviation from duty and to loathsome behaviour, are injurious to health, instead of increasing nutritive juices and helping proper secretion of fluids excite nerves and mental activities relating to them and thereby cause fatigue, weakness and deterioration of the body, are unnecessary and make their users addictive to them, cause no benefit except giving pleasures of taste and relish, and whose properties are not known to us. Similarly, from the religious standpoint, even for the purpose of bodily growth or for that of the cure of a disease, one should not take such medicines or tonics as are prepared from liver, etc., of the mobile creatures after killing them, because their use encourages the business of killing animals. Meat-eating is a very reprehensible and contemptible act, it being a form of intense violence and should be abandoned by all always.

Even though plants do have subtle life, we cannot live without depending on them for our food. Again, vegetable substances form a natural food and do not contain filthy things (like blood, etc.) at all. So by eating this natural and pure food, man is not defiled by the defect of violence, nor is he guilty of it. Nature itself has allowed him to use the immobile one-sensed beings (earth, water, light, air, plants) for his bare necessities of life. His use of them is natural and unsullied. He should not use living beings having more sense-organs than one. The destruction of the higher forms of life from *dvīndriyas* (two-sensed beings) upward is strictly forbidden to all Jainas. Therefore, they should strictly adhere to vegetarianism.

Health

For health proper and moderate food, pure water, fresh unpolluted air, sunlight, cleanliness, sufficient manual labour, sufficient rest and sufficient sleep are essential. Neglecting all or any one of them invites bodily disorders, ailments and diseases.

Reprehensible Vicious Activities (Durvyasanas)

These are those activities which are not necessary for living or livelihood, are worthy of condemnation, and make man such an addict to them that he experiences uneasiness without taking recourse to them. He is obsessed by the debase pleasures of these activities to the point of being unable to concentrate on any work, to perform his duties, or even to sleep.

One should repent or one's conscience should bite one if one enjoys even once the debase pleasure of any one of these activities[1]—so much so that one may remain constantly vigilant lest one may lapse into it again.

Moreover, the Jaina religion commands one to maintain cleanliness and purity. One should not pollute anything. Eating or feeding food eaten or polluted by others is a defect from the religious standpoint; it is injurious to health from the point of view of health. Bacteriology informs us that excreta and urine remaining undisposed for long generate poisonous germs which spread diseases. The Jaina teaching that one should be very careful in performing the excretory functions and that one should perform them in open places in such a manner as would cause no harm or inconvenience to others is very ancient. One should dispose excreta and other things that are of no use at a place free from living beings and after proper inspection. Cleanliness is very important. It is beneficial to health and conducive to mental delight.

At the end, we should remember that righteous conduct and good

---

1. *dyūtaṁ ca māṁsaṁ ca surā ca veśyā pāparddhicaurye paradārasevā /*
etāni sapta vyasanāni loke tatsevitur durgatim āvahanti //
This verse enumerates seven such activities. They are: 1. dicing, gambling (*dyūta*), 2. boozing, drinking alcohol (*madya, surā*), 3. meat-eating (*māṁsa*), 4. whoring (*veśyā*), 5. hunting (*pāparddhi*), 6. thieving (*caurya*), and 7. adultery (*paradārasevā*).

behaviour, self-control and politeness, compassion and love, service and benevolence, brotherhood and friendliness, truthfulness and discreetness, wisdom and prudence, tolerance and humility, diligence and honesty, sincerity and perseverance, bravery and forbearance, liberality and generosity, vigilance and cautiousness, justness and impartiality, fearlessness and courage, power of endurance and moral strength, gratefulness and kindness, uprightness and simplicity, service and self-sacrifice—all these constitute the essence of all religions and religious works and comprise the supreme wealth of human life. Man can build up character by cultivating these good qualities. In it lies the fulfilment of the end of human life. It is the right means to achieve the physical, mental and spiritual progress. It is the life permeated with spiritual good. It is the path of purification leading to liberation.

CHAPTER 3

REFLECTIONS ON SOME PROBLEMS OF METAPHYSICS, ETHICS AND SPIRITUAL DEVELOPMENT

In this chapter, we would like to present some useful stray thoughts on the Jaina religion and philosophy.

Temple of Spiritual Good Open for All

All Jinas, the Jaina prophets, propound and preach essential equality of all living beings. They command us to bear in mind this fundamental truth and conduct our life strictly in accordance with it. Equality is natural to all beings, while differences and distinctions found among them are adventitious. All the differences regarding bodily form, complexion, strength, wealth, status, power, prosperity and intelligence are due to adventitious causes. They are the consequences of auspicious and inauspicious *karmas*. But in their pure and pristine state, all beings are equal. In that state, there is no place whatsoever for any difference and distinction. So if anyone cultivates the feeling of discrimination of high and low, takes pride in his good fortune and despises those who are less fortunate, then by doing so he disrespects and dishonours the supreme spiritual essence equally present in all beings. Those who are born in the so-called low family, caste or conditions are also worthy of our goodwill and compassion, like those who are suffering from diseases and miseries.

The Vedic Hindu religion divided the society into four classes and the individual life into four stages on the basis of qualities and activities so that the society may function smoothly, it may secure essential services easily, it may remain free from the struggle and strife for life as also from mutually harmful competition, and there may be reign of order, accord and harmony in it. Thus in the early Vedic Hindu religion the basis for dividing the society into four classes was not birth; it was qualities, skills and professions. But afterwards when disregarding qualities, skills and activities, birth was recognised as the sole principle of division, then the feeling of discrimination of high and low crept into the hearts of the people and the powerful high caste Hindus began exploiting the weak low caste Hindus. From that very time Lord Mahāvīra, inspired as he was by universal love and infinite compassion, has opened up the doors of religion and spiritual practice for all—including even the sinners and the wicked—irrespective of their birth, caste, creed, race or sex, disregarding all differences and distinctions whatsoever. In spite of this, if anybody prevents someone from practising religion or securing the means to the attainment of religion, then he is surely acting against the noble objective of the teachings of the Jinas, the Jaina prophets. While describing the audience of the Jina, Ācārya Hemacandra in his *Triṣaṣṭiśalākāpuruṣacarita* especially points out that there is no restriction whatsoever to the entry of any person into his lecture-hall. He says: '*nīyantraṇā tatra naiva vikathā na ca kācana*' (I. 3. 474). According to the Jaina philosophy, any human being—be he a householder or an ascetic, an adherent of the Jaina religion or of any other religion, performing rituals according to the Jaina tradition or according to any other tradition—can attain liberation, the only condition being that he should be absolutely free from attachment.

This is the reason why it is said:

seyambaro ya āsambaro ya buddho ya ahava anno vā/
samabhāvabhāviappā lahaī mukkha na sandeho //2//—Sambodhasaptati

'Be he a white-cotton-clad or a sky-clad, a Buddhist or any other, he certainly attains liberation if he is equanimous and passionless.'

The Jaina *Āgamas* do not regard a particular dress,[1] status or state as a necessary condition for the attainment of perfection or liberation. They clearly declare that a worldly soul—be it in the state of a householder or in that of a monk, be it a man or a woman, a follower of the Jaina tradition or of another religious tradition, that is, be it in any state or

---

1. *mokṣaprāptiṁ prati na veṣaprādhānyam, kintu samabhāva eva nirvṛttihetuḥ /*
—Guṇavinaya's Commentary on *Sambodhasaptati,* verse 2.
aha bhave paiṇṇā u mokkhasabbhūasāhaṇo /
nāṇaṁ ca daṁsaṇaṁ ceva carittaṁ ceva nicchae //33//
—Uttarādhyayana, Adhyayana 23
Also study Bhāvavijayagaṇi's commentary on this verse. It is as follows: *jñānādi eva muktisādhanam, na tu liṅgam / śrūyate hi Bharatādīnāṁ liṅgam vinā'pi kevalotpattiḥ/ iti tattvato liṅgasya akiñcitkaratvān na tadbhedo viduṣāṁ vipratyayahetuḥ /*

condition—certainly attains liberation provided it renounces all attachment. They make it crystal-clear that a soul in bondage can attain *siddha*hood (perfection) irrespective of dress, sex, caste, creed, ritual tradition, philosophical affiliation, the only condition being that it should absolutely subdue all passions. The upholder of a particular religion will attain liberation and none else—such a restriction is not found in the Jaina *Agamas*. On the contrary, they expressly state that one can attain liberation even without the acceptance of the dress prescribed and prevalent in the Jaina religion, that one who has not renounced the dress of a lay-votary, that is, who has not accepted the dress of a Jaina monk can attain liberation, and that even a woman can attain it. What a liberal, altruistic and catholic religion Jainism is![1]

Non-attachment or passionlessness is internal or mental characteristic. And when it truely manifests itself in the soul, it is reflected in thought, speech and behaviour. For the cultivation of non-attachment, the path of renunciation or asceticism may be regarded as the royal road or an easy way. Even then it is not the only path without which one can never achieve or attain non-attachment. This is proved by the quotation from the *Āgama* (which expressly states that even a householder can attain *siddha*hood—perfection). And it is not that one can never cultivate non-attachment without the acceptance of the Jaina philosophical views or without the performance of the Jaina rituals. This is also established on the strength of the Āgamic statement (to the effect that one who upholds other philosophical views or performs rituals prevalent in other religious traditions can also attain *siddha*hood). At this juncture, we would like to draw the attention of the readers to the fact that there is nothing in the Jaina philosophical views and rituals, which may prove detrimental to the attainment of non-attachment. On the contrary, they are such as can prove really conducive and strongly helpful to the practice of religion and cultivation of non-attachment, provided the philosophical views are rightly employed in practice and rituals formulated with a view to inspiring righteous conduct are performed with true understanding, aiming at

---

1. *itthīliṁgasiddhā, purisaliṁgasiddhā, saliṁgasiddhā, annaliṁgasiddhā, gihiliṁgasiddhā* / —*Pannavaṇāsūtra*, First Prajñāpanāpada, Siddhaprajñāpanāpada.
Attainment of omniscience is certainly liberation. The omniscient one who lives among the people is called *jīvanmukta*. The embodied state of liberation is called *jīvanmukti*.

fulfilling the said purpose for which they are formulated. One should bear in mind that righteous conduct is the foundation or essence of religion, without which neither philosophical views nor the external rituals are capable of rescuing man from the miseries of worldly existence.

Different religious sects are destined to stay for ever in the world. They are not going to be abolished or destroyed. And it is not necessary to wish their abolition. One belonging to this or that sect can elevate oneself treading on the path of righteousness, even while adhering to one's own sect. Adherence to one's own sect is not wrong; what is wrong is sectarianism. On account of blinding infatuation and attachment for one's own sect to denigrate and depreciate other sects is fanaticism, which is pernicious to the individual and social health. Even while remaining in and adhering to one's own sect, one should keep the doors of his mind open for other wholesome thought-currents. Examining with impartial and judicious intellect, if one finds any system of thought right and beneficial to life, one should be liberal enough to accept it. We should also understand that anyone belonging to any sect certainly attains spiritual good if he, even while remaining in one's own sect, cultivates brotherhood and friendliness with the adherents of other sects and treads on path of righteousness.

God—Spiritual Teacher—Religion

The soul in the body is, essentially in its pristine original nature, the supreme soul—God, but because it is veiled and soiled by the coverings of karmic matter it wanders in the transmigratory existence. Yet it can remove the adventitious impurities and shine in its original pristine light, that is, it can attain non-attachment and thereby divinity. Thus whoever has attained divinity is God; one who is free from attachment is God. God, according to the Jainas, is not eternally free, but has worked out his own freedom or liberation exactly in the same way as the others do.

Our highest goal is to attain this divinity, that is, to manifest the supreme spiritual light. The ascetic saint who has renounced the world, who is self-controlled and without any possessions, and who is rightly engaged in the spiritual efforts of removing the defilements and thereby manifesting the supreme spiritual light, the divinity, is the true spiritual teacher. It is he who can acquaint us with the true spiritual goal, explain us as to what non-attachment means and how to attain it. It is he who can effectively teach us the truth about spiritual matters. In short, it is he who can rightly show us the path of purification, non-attachment and supreme spiritual light.

The path adopting which one can remove defilements and attain the pure state (state of non-attachment) is called religion (*dharma*). Religion, rather practice of religion, means walking on the path of duty, following discipline leading to spiritual development and observing rules of good conduct beneficial to both the individual and the society. It is by means of our relations with other living beings that we can cultivate spiritual qualities, and not in isolation. The ultimate objective of these rules of conduct is the doing of good to other living beings and thereby to oneself.

To understand and recognise these three categories (*tattvas*), viz., God, spiritual teacher and religion in their true nature is called '*samakita*' or '*samyaktva*' (right faith, right attitude, or right conviction). But this *samakita* (right faith or conviction) is empirical. On the other hand, the spiritual state shining with pure faith or conviction that the soul itself in its pure and pristine nature is God and that it can perfectly manifest its pure nature after having removed the veils of karmic matter is the transcendental *samakita* (right faith or conviction).

To recognise unity or equality in diversity or distinctions, that is, to view all living beings as one views oneself is at the root of *samyagdṛṣṭi* (right attitude, faith or inclination). If a man cultivates this attitude, for him the further path of spiritual discipline will be very easy. The four-fold feelings of friendliness, appreciation, compassion and indifference spring from this attitude of viewing others as equal with one's own self. Without the cultivation or manifestation of this attitude, one cannot really become *samyaktvī* (endowed with right attitude, faith or conviction); this is the fundamental truth which everyone should always bear in mind. Where this attitude prevails, there are no defilements like quarrels and disputes, enmity and hostility, fights and attacks, feeling of high and low, egoism and pride. This attitude removes all these defilements and in their place rouses the salutary and noble feelings of friendliness, self-sacrifice, benevolence and service. One who lacks the power of discriminating what is right from what is wrong can never attain this attitude.

Once a man attains the empirical *samakita*, he makes progress in the right direction and achieves the transcendental *samakita*. On the attainment of the transcendental *samakita*, his spiritual attitude or faith or conviction becomes highly pure; at this juncture he is much advanced on the path of spiritual welfare. Now for him there remains to move onward on the excellent path of religion, that is, on the highly elevated path of progressive spiritual discipline and welfare in order to achieve in future the state of absolute non-attachment and thereby to attain Godhood or divinity.

The opposite of *samyaktva* (right attitude, faith or conviction) is *mithyātva* (wrong attitude, faith or conviction). From this, it is clear that on the removal or destruction of *mithyātva, samyaktva* makes its appearance. So it is useful to know, in brief, the types of *mithyātva.*

(1) *Mithyāva about things*

This is illustrated by the wrong conviction or belief that the body itself is soul or by the non-acceptance of their difference.

(2) *Mithyātva about the highest goal*

This is the wrong conviction or belief about the nature of liberation. Instead of regarding liberation or the state of non-attachment or perfect spiritual purity as the highest goal, to regard physical and material happiness as the highest goal is the *mithyātva* about the highest goal.

(3) *Mithyātva about the path (religion)*

This is the wrong conviction or belief about religion. Not to regard as *adharma* (evil path) the performance of evil acts of violence, injustice and immorality, remaining indifferent towards the happiness and comforts of others, with a view to satisfying one's inordinate desire for material pleasures and prosperity is *mithyātva* regarding religion or the path. In other words, not to regard compassion, morality, self-control and righteousness as *dharma* (wholesome path) or to regard the opposite vicious qualities as *dharma* is *mithyātva* regarding *dharma.*

(4) *Mithyātva about spiritual teacher*

To regard an unworthy spiritual teacher as the worthy one is the *mithyātva* about spiritual teacher. He who is attached to worldly things and relations, who hankers after worldly pleasures and fame, who is hypocrite, who is ignorant, and who lacks power of discrimination and judgement is the unworthy spiritual teacher.

(5) *Mithyātva about God*

Wrong understanding about the individual who is the supreme ideal for us to follow is the *mithyātva* about God or Divinity. In other words, instead of regarding the absolutely non-attached supreme being as God, to regard the one who is afflicted with attachment as God is the *mithyātva* about God.

Wrong attitude, belief or conviction of this type is an obstruction to the spiritual development.

Image of God

By uttering the name of God one can recall to mind His pure qualities and supremely spiritual personality. Similarly, by seeing the image of God, one can do the same thing. Generally, seeing of an image or a picture causes the recollection more vivid than the one caused by the mere name. There are persons who feel that for them there is no use of an idol of God. They do not requires its aid. But they should gladly allow others to take recourse to the idol or image, if they feel that they are benefited by such aid; again, they should regard this aid as praiseworthy, because it is sought for achieving a good and wholesome purpose. Similarly, those who take recourse to the image should not indulge in criticising and condemning others who can—or think that they can—recall to mind the pure qualities or supremely spiritual personality of God without the aid of the image. Those who take recourse to the image do so in order to subdue their passions; if they now reprehend and denigrate others who do not take recourse to the image, they give vent to their passions and frustrate the very purpose for which they take recourse to the image. It is no good giving rise to or supporting factionalism, raising a trifling issue as to whether or not one should take recourse to external means. Those who do not take recourse to the image, feeling that they do not require its aid, should take into account and respect the general liking and feeling of masses for the image; they should cherish feelings of esteem for the sacred historical temples—remarkable places of our cultural heritage—built for the purpose of spiritual and devotional practice; and they should adore the image of God just as they adore pictures, photographs and statues of the great men.

Of course, it is true that the image of the attachment-free, passionless, pure God should have the appearance worthy of that supremely spiritual state. We should not impart the appearance unworthy of the attachment-free ascetic and inconsistent with the supremely spiritual state of non-attachment to the image of the absolutely attachment-free God, eternally engrossed in the highest meditation on the pure nature of soul and shining with the lustre of the perfected spiritual qualities like non-attachment, non-aversion, non-violence, self-control, austerity and renunciation.

Reflection on the Scale of Violence for the Sustenance of One's Life

We have to accept the fact that life is impossible without violence or killing. But at the same time, man should strictly follow the rule that one should maintain or sustain one's life with the minimum violence. Here arises a question in the minds of many as to which violence is to be regarded as the minimum, that is, as to how one can decide the scale of violence. Followers of a particular sect maintain that by killing one huge animal, many men can sustain their lives on its flesh for many days, while killing many plant beings even one man cannot sufficiently sustain his life for even one day, therefore killing of one huge animal involves the minimum violence. Their principle of deciding the scale of violence is the number of living beings killed. But they are wrong. The Jaina view decides the scale of violence not on the basis of number of living beings killed, but on the basis of development or evolution of life reached in the being killed. Killing of one being on the higher scale of evolution involves more violence than the killing of many beings on the lower scale of evolution involves. This is what the Jaina religion maintains. This is the reason why it regards plant beings as proper for our food, because they have the lowest number of sense-organs, that is, they possess only one sense-organ. Plant beings are at the lowest scale of evolution. The destruction of the higher forms of life from *dvīndriya* (two-sensed) beings upward is strictly forbidden to all the Jainas. So the Jainas are strict vegetarians. Again, the same is the reason why all the Jainas consider it to be an act of compassion, universal love, virtue and religion to offer water to a thirsty man or an animal to drink, although by doing so they cause killing of so many water-bodied beings. As compared to a man or an animal, the waterbodied beings are at a very low scale of evolution. From this it is clear that to save animal beings at the cost of human beings is not acceptable to the Jaina religion. But so far as it concerns one's own self, there is no objection to developing the virtue of non-violence to the extent of sacrificing one's own life to save the life of a living being at the lower scale of evolution. As for example, Lord Śāntinātha, in his previous birth was ready to sacrifice his own life to save a dove that sought his refuge; similarly, King Dīlīpa was ready to sacrifice his own life to save a cow. But the Jaina religion strictly forbids all types of purposeless violence even though it is as slight as that involved in causing injury to a petal of a flower.

Plant beings are of two types—*pratyeka* and *sādhāraṇa*. *Pratyeka* plant beings are those that have separate plant-bodies—one body for one plant being. *Sādhāraṇa* plant beings are those that have one common plant body. Plant beings which exist together with infinite others in a common plant body are called *sādhāraṇa* plant beings. The bulbous roots, etc., are *sādhāraṇa* (gross *sādhāraṇa*[1]) plant beings. They illustrate the cases of infinite plant beings inhabiting one common plant-body. So this common plant body is called *anantakāya* (= 'a body inhabited by infinite beings or souls'). The life in the *pratyeka* plant beings is much more developed than that in the *sādhāraṇa* plant beings.

Body and its Use

A body is a 'statue' made of bones, flesh, blood, fat, etc. It is filled with impurities like faeces, urine, etc. Such derogatory things are said of the body in order to generate and promote feelings of non-attachment and renunciation towards one's own body. From the scientific standpoint, we should admit that the body is made of those things which are most appropriate for it. It can never be made of things other than bones, etc. Nature is wiser than man. It is necessary to eat food and drink water for the maintenance and sustenance of the body. The food and drink we take contain substances useful as well as useless for the body. The body discharges the useless waste matter in the form of faeces, urine, etc., which are here called impurities. In other words, the body digests the useful and essential part of the food, transforms it into nutritive material, and separates and expels the waste and useless matter from the system. The body is a wonderful 'machine' which continuously keeps itself fit and efficient

1. The entire universe-space is thickly filled with the subtle *sādhāraṇa* plant beings as also with subtle earthbodied, waterbodied, firebodied and airbodied beings. The most subtle beings, that is, the subtle *sādhāraṇa* plant beings exhibit not even the slightest struggle for life, that is, behaviour. *Sādhāraṇa* plant beings are also called *nigoda*. So the subtle (*sūkṣma*) *sādhāraṇa* plant beings are called '*sūkṣma-nigoda*', and the gross (*sthūla*) *sādhāraṇa* plant beings are called *sthūla-nigoda* (*bādara-nigoda*).

by throwing out the useless waste matter called 'impurities' after separating it from the useful one. It is not such a thing that one should renounce it forcibly or destroy it as early as possible. It is essential to properly maintain the body and keep it efficient and healthy because the body affects the mind; if the body is not healthy and suffers from ailments and diseases, then mind remains constantly engaged in brooding over the bodily pains and diseases. If the body is healthy, the mind remains free from the useless brooding and hence can concentrate on the useful and wholesome object or work. In the present context, the most essential and important point one should bear in mind and put into practice is that for bodily enjoyment one should never commit unnecessary purposeless violence, nor should one indulge in untruthful, immoral and unjust activities. Nature has given us a wonderful gift of the body which is the most efficient instrument to achieve the final liberation. It is easily understandable that the soul, while inhabiting the body alone, can operate and employ its cognitive and conative powers and consequently attain liberation. So long as the soul does not attain liberation after having abandoned its last body, this or that physical body is invariably attached to or associated with it. And if one destroys one's body ignorantly under perverse understanding, then it is as good as an act of suicide which is regarded as a sinful or unwholesome act. Wise saints ask us to renounce the attachment to the body and not the body itself, to renounce evil intentions, feelings, thoughts and activities and not the body.

Saṁlekhanā is a well-ordered voluntarily chosen death which is not inspired by any passion and is the result of conscientious gradual withdrawal from the taking of food in such a manner as would never disrupt one's inner peace and dispassionate mindfulness. So there is a fundamental difference between suicide and *saṁlekhanā*. Suicide is the result of the outburst of passions, whereas *saṁlekhanā* is the result of dispassionateness. *Saṁlekhanā* cannot be called suicide, because in it there is complete absence of attachment (*rāga*) which is always present when a person under the sway of passion or hate or delusion poisons or otherwise destroys himself. *Saṁlekhanā* is born of constant practice of the feelings of lack-of-infatuation, lack-of-passion and universal love and compassion, and it attains its completion when these are fully mastered. Thus *saṁlekhanā* is a death while in ultra-pure meditation. It is recommended only when the body is completely disabled by extreme old age or by incurable diseases or when it is rendered hopelessly helpless by the destruction or enfeeblement of the senses and the man becomes conscious of the impending unavoidable death and of the necessity of concentrating on the pure qualities of the soul. When one's body has become utterly weak and useless and hence a burden to others, voluntary renunciation of one's body is an act of compassion towards others. Thus out of this feeling of compassion, one takes recourse to this voluntarily chosen death called *saṁlekhanā*. In the aspirant, there is no dissatisfaction, no sorrow, no fear, no dejection, no turpitude; the mind is cool, calm, composed; the heart is filled with the feeling of universal love and compassion.

Some put an end to their lives by jumping from holy peaks, or by disappearing into the sea, or by some such acts. These forms of suicide are absolutely improper, they are inspired by blind faith. To sacrifice one's life on the altar of duty is the true sacrifice. To lay down one's life while protecting or serving others is the true sacrifice. The belief that meeting death at a particular place or while muttering a particular name makes one attain heaven or liberation is nothing but blind faith. And if inspired by this blind faith one destroys one's life, then it is an absolutely improper act.

Except fasting all other methods of voluntarily chosen death are forbidden in Jainism. This is the praiseworthy improvement. When one is utterly weak or afflicted with incurable diseases and consequently has to depend on the services of others, one is allowed to put an end to one's life by fasting unto death; this is the only proper method. Fasting is not to be severe and short. It is to be gradual. In the beginning, the aspirant subsists on tasteless solid food. This intake of solid food is gradually reduced to nothing. Then he subsists on liquids of a progressively less sustaining nature, for example, from butter-milk to plain pure water. This is a long process drawn out into many days, several months or a few years. The distress which the sudden death causes to the aspirant as well as others is conspicuous by its absence in this long drawn out process. Again, this long process can become the means (*upāya*) not only of death, but also of life. That is, on account of this long drawn out process, it may so happen that a fatal illness undergoes remission or complete cure during the course of the process of progressive fasting. And if the aspirant is cured of the disease during the process, he should discontinue it, now there being no purpose or cause for the voluntarily chosen death called *saṁlekhanā*.

There is a difference between the treatment-by-fasting and *saṁlekhanā*.

In the treatment-by-fasting, the patient has great hope for the cure and long life, so he makes sincere efforts for the cure and saving his life. On the other hand, the person undertakes *saṁlekhanā,* when there is no hope whatsoever for the cure and hence no efforts for the cure. If during the process of *saṁlekhanā* and on account of gradual fasting, the aspirant is cured of the disease, there is no necessity of forcibly surrendering his body to death, because *saṁlekhanā* is not suicide but an act of 'self-offering' to the imminent death fearlessly and bravely. So in *saṁlekhanā,* the man ends his life peacefully and blissfully; he does what he should do before death. If the disease is cured and imminent death is averted, then one should not forcibly and unnecessarily invite death.

Compassion and Donation

Compassion is the foundation of religion. And proper offering of donation is nothing but putting into practice this religion of compassion—may the donation be of our bodily, mental or vocal powers or of our wealth.

It is a grave sin to dry up the stream of the feeling of compassion in the hearts of masses by generating in their minds a wrong belief that the donor is responsible for all the vices the donee indulges in during the remaining course of his life if the latter survives or continues to live on account of the compassion of the former. Human behaviour is unpredictable. We can never know as to how a particular individual will behave in future. Yet, in the absence of such knowledge, if we entertain prejudice that the concerned person will not behave rightly but will certainly behave wrongly, and on that account prevent ourselves from doing an act of compassion, then this entire act of ours is improper and wrong because it springs from ignorance. Every individual is free to choose a course of his action or behaviour. And if a man whose life is saved on account of another man's compassion and service acts or behaves wrongly or badly in future, then we can say this much only that he then misuses his freedom of choice or will, and so we should not blame the other man who, out of compassion, helped him in his miseries or lengthening his life-span, or saved or rescued him. The person who shows compassion has nothing to do with as to how the beneficiary behaves after having gained peace and benefits by the act of donation inspired by pure compassion. He certainly reaps the fruits of his act of pure compassion. Of course, in spite of our knowledge that the person who has come to our house is a robber and is on his way to some place where he is going to perform his act of robbery, if we give him shelter and offer him food, then we are no doubt a party to his sinful act or share the sin committed by him through his act of robbery.

Cultivation of Four attitudes or feelings (Bhāvanā)

Friendship flourish among men of similar conduct and character, habits and hobbies. (*Samānaśīlavyasaneṣu sakhyam*). All worldly embodied souls—from those at the lowest scale of evolution to those at the highest one—are uniform in nature; in other words, all worldly beings are identical when viewed from the standpoint of their original pure state. And keeping in view this uniform and perfectly identical nature of these beings, there may arise in one's mind a delighting conception of their mutual friendship. Animal beings are without any power of discrimination, discretion and judgement; and blinded as they are by ignorance there cannot flourish friendship among them; we can easily understand this. But human beings are endowed with understanding and special power of discrimination. Hence, there is high possibility of friendship thriving among them. Yet instead of seeing them behaving friendly, when we see them caught in the violent hurricane of jealousy, cruelty, enmity, blind selfishness—all of which proper in animals—, we naturally deduce that they have not risen breaking open the various hard shells of perverse desires and inclinations proper for animals. But power of discrimination and judgement being the very nature of human mind, if man coolly and placidly uses this power and thinks rightly, then he can at once realise the unity of all beings and consequently in consonance with this realisation certainly there arises in his heart the feeling of friendship towards all beings; this is quite possible. The *Vedānta* philosophy views all beings as sparks of the Supreme Soul called *Brahman.* Thinkers of the Jaina, the *Vaiśeṣika*, the *Sāṁkhya* and the *Yoga* philosophies maintain that all beings are independent impartite primary substances and at the same time hold that they are uniform in their pure original nature. Thus all Indian philosophers propound that all beings are uniformly of the nature of light and consequently declare that one should not bear any ill-will towards any being, instead should cultivate a feeling of friendliness towards all beings and be compassionate towards the miserable and the poor.[1] We should consider all living beings as our friends and not as our enemies

1. *adveṣṭā sarvabhūtānāṁ maitraḥ karuṇa eva ca* /

at all. When we injure others, we injure ourselves, that is, our spiritual nature. Vices like jealousy, envy, hatred, enmity, etc., harm others and generate social unrest and disturbances and perpetrate violence on one's ownself. So all Indian saints strongly teach man to shun all these defects and defilements.[1] The Jaina and the *Pātañjala Yoga* philosophies recommend man to cultivate four good qualities (feelings) of heart on the basis and for the promotion of the fundamentally wholesome attitude of viewing all beings as equal with one's own self. And on account of the constant practice of these four feelings, it becomes very easy for one to gradually ascend the higher and higher stages of spiritual evolution. The four feelings in point are as follows:

Feeling of Friendliness (Maitrī-bhāvanā)

To cultivate and nourish feeling of friendliness towards all beings is called *maitrī-bhāvanā.* When the feeling of friendliness is cultivated and practised in regard to all living beings whatsoever, then alone is it possible for one to be non-violent, truthful, etc., towards all living beings. Friendliness means to view others as one views oneself and hence the tendency or desire not to cause pain or injury to others just as one does not cause pain or injury to oneself; not only that, but it also means positive tendency or desire to do good to others. The specific referential object of friendliness is all living beings.

Feeling of Gladness (Pramoda-bhāvanā)

Often it so happens that one develops a feeling of jealousy on seeing someone superior to oneself in respect of material wealth and prosperity. If this superiority of that person is the result of his good qualities or of the merit acquired through past good actions and if he employs it again in good activities, then instead of being jealous of him one should praise his good activities and spiritual qualities and feel pleased to see him advancing on the path of righteousness and nobleness. Of course, it is quite proper if one feels righteous indignation towards immoral and vicious conduct of others. But it is absolutely wrong for us to entertain

1. *kāma eṣa krodha eṣa rajoguṇasamudbhavaḥ/*
mahāśano mahāpāpmā viddhy enam iha vairiṇam //37//—Bhagavad-Gītā, III.
This is craving, this is anger, born of passion, all-consuming and most evil. Know this to be the foe here.

a feeling of jealousy or hatred towards someone, simply because he is superior to us. A jealous man becomes doubly miserable. He is already miserable on account of his own misfortune. And he makes himself still more miserable by envying others of their happiness. He unnecessarily burns himself with the fire of jealousy. Now so long as this tendency of jealousy is not exterminated, it is not possible for non-violence, truthfulness, etc., to find firm standing. Hence as against jealousy, one is instructed to cultivate and practise the feeling or tendency of the virtuous gladness. Gladness means to evince respect for one superior to us in merit and to feel pleased on seeing him flourishing. The referential object of this feeling or tendency is a person superior to oneself in merit, for evil tendencies like jealousy, envy, etc., are possible only in relation to such a person. Just as one becomes glad on seeing dear ones surpassing oneself in good qualities even so one can also become glad on seeing any living being surpassing oneself in good qualities, if one has cultivated a feeling of mineness with respect to all beings or a feeling of one's identity with all beings. Thus at the root of this feeling of gladness is the attitude of one's identity with all beings, that is, the attitude of universal love and friendliness.

Generally, to be glad and pleased on seeing the flourishing spiritual qualities of the meritorious is *pramoda-bhāvanā.* The path of becoming meritorious is to cultivate, entertain and practise a feeling of devotion, respect and reverence towards the meritorious.

Let us reflect somewhat more deeply on the respective specific objects of these two *bhāvanās*. On seeing someone happy, or more happy than oneself, one develops a feeling of jealousy and burns with it. If there springs in one's heart the universal friendliness, then on seeing happiness of others, one regards it as belonging to one's own friends or beloved persons and consequently instead of one's mind being disturbed or agitated with the feeling of jealousy and envy towards them, it remains placid, peaceful, calm, composed and unruffled. This is the reason why even happiness of others is regarded as the referential object of the feeling of friendliness.[1] That is, a feeling of mineness or love with respect to happy beings is friendliness.

---

1. *maitrī-karuṇā-muditopekṣāṇāṁ sukha-duḥkha-puṇyāpuṇyaviṣayāṇāṁ bhāvanātaś cittaprasādanam* /—*Yogasūtra* by Patañjali I.33.
Meaning of this aphorism is as follows: Happiness, misery, merit and demerit are the respective objects of the feelings of friendliness, compassion, gladness and neutrality

Regarding the feeling of gladness (*pramoda-bhāvanā),* we do not intend to say that one should be glad simply because someone is rich, strong, powerful or materially happy. But we intend to say that if he makes good use of his riches, strength, power and material means by employing them in giving relief and comforts to the miserable and the poor and in removing their miseries and distresses, then it is proper for one to be glad at his good qualities. If a man, though poor, earns his livelihood honestly doing manual labour or engaging himself in some industry or craft and remains satisfied with his lot, then on seeing such good qualities in him it is proper for one to be glad. The referential object of the feeling of gladness is stated to be the acquisition of good fortune as a result of past good actions, but that does not mean that even if a man makes bad use of his good fortune, we should be glad on his acquisition of good fortune. When it is stated that the referential object of the feeling of gladness is the acquisition of good fortune, what it really means is that it is not good fortune itself but the good activities conducted with its help is the referential object of the feeling of gladness.

Feeling of Compassion (Karuṇā-bhāvanā)

Now let us deal with the feeling of compassion. If on seeing someone suffering from pain a feeling of compassion is not roused in man, then it is impossible for him to observe the vows like non-violence, etc. So the feeling of compassion has been deemed necessary. Its referential object is a miserable person suffering from pain; for it is a miserable, poor, helpless person who stands in need of considerate regard and assistance. If one has cultivated the feeling of mineness towards all beings, or the feeling of one's identity with all beings, then alone one is overcome by the feeling of compassion on seeing someone suffering from pain, just as one is overcome by the same feeling on seeing one's own beloved

---

(indifference). By the constant practice and nourishment of these four feelings, one can attain mental purity.

The sixth aphorism of the seventh chapter of Maharṣi Umāsvāti's *Tattvārthasūtra* relates to this subject-matter. It is as follows: '*maitrī-pramoda-kāruṇya-mādhyasthyāni sattva-guṇādhikya-kliśyamānāvineyeṣu*'. It means: One should develop a feeling of friendliness in relation to beings in general, a feeling of gladness in relation to those superior to oneself in merits, a feeling of compassion for those in misery, a feeling of neutrality in relation to those who in an idiot-like fashion are unworthy of instruction.

person suffering from pain. Thus at the root of the feeling of compassion is the attitude of mineness towards all beings or the attitude of one's identity with all beings. Awakening of the desire in the heart of some saint to rescue living beings from the miseries of worldly existence is also a case of compassion. The enlightened great saints and the omniscient pure perfected men are permeated through and through with compassion encompassing in its fold all living beings. This is the reason why they are described as the Compassionate *par excellence.*

Feeling of Neutrality (Mādhyasthya-bhāvanā)

It is not on every occasion and at every place that positive feeling or attitude prove effective; for only too often the maintenance of an attitude of mere neutrality or indifference is of use in rendering steady the vows like non-violence, etc. So one is instructed to practise the feeling or attitude of neutrality. Neutrality means indifference or standing aloof. Thus when one comes across a person with an utterly idiotic mental background or a person who is incapable of receiving into his head even a single salutary subject-matter—moreover, when all attempts at reforming him ultimately comes to utter nought—then it is only worthwhile that an attitude of neutrality be maintained by one in relation to such a person. Hence the referential object of the attitude of neutrality is a person unworthy of instruction—that is, an incapable person. If one has cultivated the attitude of mineness towards all beings or of oneness with all beings, then alone one can remain purely neutral towards an unworthy (intellectually perverse, wicked and idiotic) person, not entertaining any feeling of cruelty, hatred or ill-will, just as one remains purely neutral towards one's beloved person even though he is unworthy.

Just as a miserable person is the referential object of compassion, even so an intellectually perverse and idiotic person is also the referential object of compassion—hidden compassion. The feeling of neutrality that rouses in one's mind towards an unworthy, intellectually perverse and idiotic person is nothing but the hidden feeling of compassion. At this juncture we should bear in mind that just as we do not feel hurt when a child, a friend or beloved person disrespects or insults us even so a wise man endowed with mind purified and enlightened by the constant practice of the feelings of friendliness, etc., never feels insulted even when he is insulted by others. For a saintly person whose heart is saturated thoroughly with the feeling of universal brotherhood, a meritorious person is an object of his feeling of gladness while an intellectually perverse and wicked person is an object of his feeling of neutrality which is nothing but hidden compassion. Ācārya Hemacandra says:

> *kṛtāparādhe'pi jane kṛpāmantharatārayoḥ /*
> *īṣadbāṣpārdrayor bhadraṁ śrīvīrajinanetrayoḥ //3//*
>
> —Benedictory verses, *Yogaśāstra.*
>
> Meaning: Eyes of Lord Mahāvīra, which are set on the guilty person, have their pupils slightly lowered in pity and are somewhat wet with tears springing from compassion.

Universal Love and Purification of Mind

A virtuous feeling of pure love (universal friendliness) converts itself into wholesome activities, keeping in view the welfare of all beings. In other words, one impelled by pure love performs such activities as are beneficial to all beings. And such an affectionate person achieves his own welfare, considering himself to be a member of the universal family of all beings. His individual welfare is not opposed to universal welfare. (Here by 'welfare', we are to understand the threefold welfare, viz., the physical, the mental and the spiritual.) One's activities inspired by pure love are always such as would do good to both oneself and others.

There are two forms of pure love (non-violence)—negative and positive. Or, we may say that it has two aspects—one positive and another negative. Pure love in its negative form achieves its objective by simply abstaining from causing injury or harm of any sort to any living being. Pure love of this form encompasses in its fold all beings of the entire universe. On the other hand, pure love in its positive form transforms itself into positive virtuous activities like serving or helping others and doing good to them. So pure love in its positive form can in practice fulfil its objective within limits set out by one's energy and strength. Even though love of a saint is universal, in practice it can translate itself into positive virtuous activities with reference to a limited number of beings—limited in proportion to his energy and capacity. But on that account it does not cease to be universal. Though in practice he is not able to serve and help all beings, in his heart there constantly burns the flame of wholesome desire for the welfare of all beings. And so he always prays for their well-being and welfare.

Regarding priorities to be followed in the implementation of pure or universal love, generally it is said that while putting it into practice or converting it into good activities one should start with one's own family; and this is quite proper and desirable. If one has more energy and strength, one should not stop there only. One's love in the form of positive activities should expand more and more with the increase in one's energy and strength. 'Charity begins at home but it does not end there'. Generally one should not do good to others at the cost of one's family or dependents. One should not neglect one's family, while putting into practice one's love for all beings. One's love should gradually expand, first taking in its fold one's own family, then one's own village, then one's own state, then one's own nation, so on and so forth. But sometimes there may arise exceptional occasions when we are required to work for our country at the cost of even our family. Such exceptional occasions are very rare, and they arise in the lives of uncommon men and women in uncommon circumstances.

Here one thing specially to be borne in mind is that if on account of one's love for one's family, etc., one causes any harm to another family, village, state or nation, or exploits them, then one's pure love ceases to be pure and becomes defiling attachment that one should renounce.

Some remain satisfied with mere negative aspect of love and neglect its positive aspect. They think that by following the negative aspect alone they can achieve the entire objective of pure love, and consequently they become inactive. But their love of such type is imperfect. Love attains its perfection when its both the aspects—negative and positive—supplement each other. Love in its negative aspect takes the form of refrainment from doing any harm to any being while in its positive aspect takes the form of positive activities of service, help, donation, etc. The negative aspect implies the positive one, and *vice versa.*

In our life, we depend on various animals. We receive so many benefits from animal kingdom. We are very much indebted to them. So we should be grateful to them and pay off the debt by being kind to them, by protecting, feeding and taking care, and by attending those that are suffering.

There are inwardly enlightened saints who live in solitude, constantly engrossed in the practice of higher spiritual discipline. They send spiritually elevating soul-vibrations and yogic light-waves in all the directions throughout the universe (in an unintelligible and mystic way) and thereby contribute much to the welfare of all beings.

Real saints give the society much more than what they receive. So the society remains always indebted to them. And such persons have the moral right to demand from it the proper necessities of life. Whatever and to whatever extent the society may give to them, it will always remain less than what the society has gained from them.

Universal love can be called spiritual love. It depends on the development of spiritual life. The attitude of one's identity with others goes on expanding and the affection for others becomes more and more free from defilements as the mind attains more and more purity. Removal of enmity, pride, attachment, hatred, anger, etc., means the purification of mind. Mind attains purity on the removal of all these defilements. Process of reducing attachment and other passions is the process of purifying mind. As passions continuously become milder and milder, the unwholesome and evil thinking gradually wanes and wholesome and good thinking gradually waxes. When in the favourable and adverse circumstances, the mind does not get agitated, does not lose its balance and does not come under the sway of attachment and aversion, then alone it can be said that the practice of purifying mind is advancing in the right direction. When this practice is continuous and conducted with vigilance and attains firm standing, then at last the state of absolute non-attachment and steadfast intellect is attained. On the occasions of tempting and distressing worldly events, one should reflect on their fleeting nature, contemplate on the momentariness of the pleasures derived from worldly objects, and understand that joy generated by infatuation ends in misery as also that association and separation, birth and death, pleasure and pain, etc., are invariably and inevitably associated with worldly existence. Conducting reflection on this line and cultivating understanding of this sort, one should keep one's mind placid and peaceful.

Purity of mind is attained gradually. Path of mental purification becomes easily treadable, if one properly controls one's sense-organs. Agitation of mind gets almost removed after long time long 'journey'. So one should not be depressed on account of the occasional manifestation of mental agitation, instead one should always keep one's sense-organs under control and be ever vigilant.[1] As soon as one gains firm victory over one's

1. *tāni sarvāṇi saṁyamya yukta āsīta matparaḥ /*
vaśe hi yasyendriyāṇi tasya prajñā pratiṣṭhitā //—Bhagavad-Gītā, II.61
Having curbed all the senses, he should remain unagitated and calm and completely surrender to God. For, when he brings his senses under control, his intelligence is firmly set and steady.

sense-organs, one's mind manifests full restraint and consequently reveals purity and divine light.

Internal Battle

What to talk of mental weakness! Many persons are so weak-minded that they constantly dream of the association of tempting and degrading objects and hanker after them.

External circumstances constitute only one of the conditions of the fall of man. In fact, man himself is the cause of his fall. The germs of diseases are in the environment, but they affect those who have no strength to resist them and not those who have enough resisting power. Similarly, external temptations cause the fall of those whose minds are weak and filled with perverse desires and inclinations, and not of those whose minds are strong and pure.

Man blames external circumstances for his own weaknesses and says in his defence, 'What can I do? Tempting circumstances arose before me, so I could not withstand them.' But to blame one's own weakness is more proper and just than to blame circumstances. In fact, one should hold oneself responsible for one's fall, and not the circumstances. Man's mind looks for tempting objects, hankers after them and entertains strong attachment for them. Hence, when they make their appearance before him, then he receives them with pleasure, comes under the sway of infatuation, is enticed and degraded. One desirous of moral and spiritual upliftment should know one's weaknesses, consider oneself to be responsible for them and gird up one's loins to remove them. Physical power is nothing before strong and pure mental power (will-power).

Generally, it is safe to remain aloof from the tempting circumstances. But even that certainly requires mental power. If one lacks even that much mental power, one will surely go on dying every moment. Royal road to the cultivation of power of resistance against temptations is to avoid the tempting circumstances as far as possible. This power of resistance is to be cultivated first against one's perverse thoughts; it is safe to begin with this. One should resist evil thoughts with determination. One who is under training should not consider oneself to be an accomplished man. Otherwise, one's fall is certain. Trainee should not be proud of his achievements, he should be humble and cautious. There is always danger in being rash. So one should not be rash and jump into tempting situations. Again, one should see that the achievement attained through remaining aloof from tempting objects is not mere deception or illusion. Its real test is the unagitated state of mind in the presence of even the tempting objects and situations. So it is not good for man to ignore the importance of close and severe repeated self-examination. Such self-examination enables him to know as to how far he has advanced in curbing and exterminating his attachment and aversion.

One should never be indifferent to external environment or circumstances. Knowingly one does never eat food contaminated with germs of diseases, nor does one stay in the place which is infected with such germs. But man has little control over external circumstances and he never knows when and where he will confront particular circumstances or situations. So he should be always vigilant, alert, determined and strong. The right means of saving oneself from degradation and fall is always to keep one's mind pure, fortified with courage and patience, and unsullied by passions and perverse desires so that one may not be defeated and degraded and may remain peaceful, unagitated and dignified.

Minds of even good men agitate and become unsteady when confronted with the disturbing and tempting objects or situations. On such occasions, the wise man has to fight with his own mind (lower self). Through this war—internal battle—great men develop spiritual strength, and their power of self-restraint develops to such an extent that they can experience joy of a victor standing firm and straight against any temptation.

Attachment and Non-attachment

In reality, worldly beings are in very tight and hard bondages of attachment and aversion. Between the two, attachment is principal. It is at the root of aversion. In fact, it is attachment that gives rise to all mental defects and defilements. Again, attachment has both the sentient and the insentient for its object. Just as one has attachment for living beings like men, women, dogs, etc., even so one does have attachment for attractive insentient things like watches, pens, stationary, furniture, clothes, ornaments, etc. On the other hand, aversion has for its object generally the sentient beings alone. It does not have insentient things for its object.[1] If we are hurt by colliding with a post, then there does arise in us a

1. For this point, study Jineśvarasūri's commentary on '*na ca dveṣo'pi sattveṣu*' (1c, First *Aṣṭaka, Aṣṭakagrantha* by Ācārya Haribhadra).

passion similar to aversion, but it is not aversion proper, it is simply mad exuberance of infatuation (ignorance, foolishness).

Attachment is nothing but infatuation in its strongest form. It is the paramount ruler of the entire worldly existence. All mental defects and defilements depend on it for their existence. So on its removal they are removed. This is the reason why the supremely pure being is simply called '*vītarāga*' (one free from attachment).

Attachment whose objects are living beings is of three types, viz., religious, sectarian and worldly. Attachment of the form of self-elevating devotion to an enlightened great saint or a spiritual teacher is the religious attachment. Again, pure attachment for virtuous qualities is also a case of the religious attachment. As it is of the nature of devotion, it is spiritually beneficial. (Great sage Gautama Indrabhūti had this devotional attachment for Lord Mahāvīra).

Bigotry attachment for the followers and the views of one's own sect is the sectarian attachment[1] which one should renounce. Attachment for one's own family, relatives, friends, etc., is the worldly attachment. It is of two types—one affection and the other erotic love. Attachment of the form of affection is respectable and praiseworthy if it is pure, that is, not sullied by mental impurities or defilements. Attachment of the form of erotic love has two sub-types viz., the forbidden and the permissible. The proper, decent and moderate erotic love for one's own wife or husband is the permissible erotic love. And the erotic love for the forbidden men or women is the forbidden erotic love.

One should know that attachment for the virtuous qualities is superior to the attachment for an individual having those qualities, even if the attachment for the individual is due to those qualities. Attachment for such a person certainly helps in one's spiritual progress. Nevertheless it

---

1. *kāmarāgasneharāgāv īṣatkaranīvāraṇau/*
dṛṣṭirāgas tu pāpīyān durucchedaḥ satām api //—*Vītarāgastotra* by Ācārya Hemacandra. It is easy to renounce the attachment of the form of erotic love (*kāmarāga*) as also the attachment of the form of affection (*sneharāga*). But it is very difficult even for the learned and the saints to destroy attachment to one's views (*dṛṣṭirāga*), which is of a very evil nature. [Attachment to one's views is the sectarian attachment.] The verse enumerates three attachments, viz., attachment of the form of erotic love, attachment of the form of affection and attachment to one's views. Attachment of the form of devotion, that is, religious attachment is included in the highly pure and spiritually wholesome affection—one of the divisions of affection.

causes feeling of helplessness, leads to depression and lamentation, and ultimately acts as an obstruction in the path of spiritual progress, when one is separated from such an individual. A case of Gautama Indrabhūti, a great sage, is an instance in point.

Non-attachment means absolute absence of attachment and aversion. This suggests absence of all mental states generated by attachment and aversion. Non-attachment is not opposed to universal brotherhood, universal love and universal affection. Affection for living beings develops and expands to the extent attachment and aversion are subdued. And when non-attachment attains its perfection and manifests itself fully, affection too reaches its consummation and encompasses in its fold all beings of the entire universe. Non-attachment is there where perfectly pure non-illusory knowledge shines, where there is no longing for material pleasures and no selfishness, where there are no defiling passions and perverse tendencies, where there is no pride for the special faculties or good fortune attained on account of auspicious *karmas*, where there is neither partiality nor injustice, where there is no invidious feeling of discrimination of high and low, and where there are evenmindedness and supreme devotion to the good of all beings. Thus non-attachment is the other name of universally beneficial, perfectly pure and supremely luminous life.

That attachment which is associated with mental defilements like aversion, selfishness, partiality, etc., or which is connected directly or indirectly with these defilements is impure attachment. The world is harassed and distressed on account of the atrocities of this impure attachment. Impure attachment becomes pure to the extent the impurities of the form of aversion, selfishness, infatuation, etc., are removed from it. And then on account of its purity it is described as 'pure affection', 'pure love'. Soul achieves spiritual progress to the extent this pure affection encompasses more and more beings in its fold. When even the pure karmic matter that allows the manifestation of pure attachment is totally dissociated from soul, the manifestation of pure attachment attains its consummation, just as when the pure karmic matter of the inclination-deluding *karma*, which allows the manifestation of soul's natural inclination for truth, is totally dissociated from soul, the manifestation of the inclination for truth—a natural quality of soul—reaches its perfection. And when soul attains the acme of spiritual evolution, this pure karmic matter allowing the manifestation of pure attachment is totally removed and consequently soul attains the state of absolute non-attachment; at that time absolutely pure and divine (spiritual) love—which is the supreme light of non-violence—embraces all beings; and so long as the absolutely non-attached Lord lives among the people (in his embodied state), he makes the best use of it in allaying miseries of worldly beings and in imparting soothing and soul-purifying knowledge to them. This is the reason why he is praised as a brother, friend and lover of all beings.

Grace of God

'It is all God's grace that we are healthy, our intellect functions rightly, we think good thoughts, we perform virtuous activities, and we are happy and peaceful'. This is what people say. Even the Jainas say so. And there is nothing wrong in it. Good speech of this type evinces great humility. Such words uttered sincerely and consciously free us from pride. This attitude nourishes our humility towards God and our devotion to Him and rouses in our heart devotional love so much so that we intensely desire to be His true devotee and to sit at His feet in great reverence.

On the other hand, from the rational standpoint we feel that supremely beneficial and good God is so non-attached and equanimous, so unstained and neutral that He can never indulge in the diplomacy of doing good to some and causing harm to others. Man attains good or evil according to his own merits and demerits acquired through his past actions. It is he who has to achieve welfare and well-being by his own efforts. It is he who has to carve out his own future or destiny. It is he who has to work out his own salvation. It is an established and self-evident truth that certainly God's grace is always there for all without any discrimination; He always wishes that without any exception let all be healthy and happy and have good intellect, good thoughts and good conduct. So if man were to attain happiness and peace and become righteous simply on account of God's grace, then as He bestows His grace equally on all, all should at once simultaneously become righteous and happy. But in reality this does not happen. Even though God's natural grace is all-embracing and equally showered on all, some are happy while others are unhappy, some are righteous while others are wicked, some are progressive while others are retrogressive, some are attended with good fortune while others are attended with misfortune, so on and so forth; so we should understand that one's happiness or misery, good fortune or misfortune, righteousness or wickedness, rise or fall, etc., depend on one's own activities. Man's vicious conduct causes his fall and degradation, while his virtuous conduct causes his rise and progress. His righteous conduct is his saviour. There is no other saviour. And for becoming righteous he has not to wait for the descent of God's grace on him. It is certainly always there for him. Undoubtedly, he becomes happy as soon as he becomes righteous. It may so happen that due to the force of past evil activities there befalls him miseries and calamities during his present practice of righteousness. But if he remains firm and steadfast in the eternal path of righteousness, then he no doubt gradually develops into a perfect soul, attains liberation from all miseries and achieves perfect peace.

In the world, the wicked persons indulge in evil activities. Why? Is it because God's grace has not descended on them? No, not at all. As stated above, His grace is always there for all and He wishes that all may become good and happy. In spite of that, how defiled the world is! In this world the number of the wicked, the ignorant and the unhappy exceeds by far that of the good, the wise and the happy respectively. As a matter of fact, in the worldly affairs there is nothing like His grace or ungrace. He is engrossed in His pure self, He is non-attached and neutral. Our devotion to Him and our practice of righteousness inspired by this divine devotion should be understood as His grace. Even our intellect or reason cannot raise any objection against this understanding. And this is the viewpoint which is beneficial to one's progress in the right direction.

Whatever good happens to us is due to good impressions or forces (*puṇya*) and whatever evil or bad happens to us is due to bad impressions or forces (*pāpa*). This is a well-known philosophical doctrine upheld by all Indian philosophers. Now, acquisition of the means of happiness and comforts, happening of desirable good events, escape from an accident, etc., are the results of the workings or rise of good impressions or forces. On the other hand, befalling of calamities, cropping up of difficulties, falling on evil times, etc., are the results of the workings or rise of bad impressions or forces. This is what all Indian thinkers accept without any hesitation. But what is the cause of these good or bad impressions (forces)? In answer, we should say that good impressions or forces are generated by one's good activities or righteous conduct, while bad impressions or forces are generated by one's evil activities or vicious conduct. But originally from where has this understanding of the good and evil activities and of their generating good and bad impressions (forces) entailing good and bad fruits (results) respectively descended in this world? The only answer to this question is that this understanding has traditionally come down to us through a long beginningless line of the great enlightened saints. As one can generate good impressions or forces by living according to the teachings of the enlightened saint and attain happiness through the working or rise of these impressions or forces, the enlightened saint could very well be regarded as the bestower of happiness. Similarly, as one can generate bad impressions or forces by living against the teachings of the enlightened saint and attain miseries and misfortune through the working or rise of these bad impressions or forces, the enlightened saint could very well be regarded as the giver of miseries. In the world, we see that the person following whose advice one attains happiness is regarded by the latter as the bestower of happiness. Similarly, the enlightened saint following whose teachings the people attain happiness is regarded by them as the bestower of happiness. It is in this sense only that the Supreme Soul or God could be held as the bestower of happiness or liberation. Not only that but we can also justify the agenthood or creatorship of God from this standpoint, to this extent and in this sense only.

So if one expresses one's gratefulness to God and praises his grace when one is saved from calamities or attains some benefits, then one is certainly quite right and well justified in doing so.

About the Vower of Anaśana (Complete Giving up of Food)

In the Jaina religion as also in some other sects, while undertaking the austerity called *anaśana* (complete giving up of food) some renounce water also. Rarely it so happens that one who has taken the vow of giving up all types of food and drinks including even water, suffers from intense thirst and consequently experiences much unrest and mental distress. And in spite of our reminding him of his vow, he persists in his strong desire for water. On such an occasion when he eagerly asks for water, it is our duty and religion to satisfy his thirst by offering him water because thereby we save the vower from evil brooding and consequently from bad death. On the contrary, not to offer him water and thus torture him is an unpardonable grave sin and crime of man-killing (murder). The Jaina religion commands us to take into account the substance, the place, the time and the state (situation and circumstances), before performing any activity.

Someone may raise a question as to what about the violation of the vow. An answer to the question is that it is only the vower who has to think about it. We have no right to command him to carry out the vow or to force him to practise it. We can at the most remind him of his vow, then he is free to act as he likes. We must understand that one who offers water offers it not to the vower but to him who has already fallen from the vow and is struggling for water, and that too on his demand—who, not obtaining water to drink is constantly engaged in evil brooding. So one who offers him water has nothing to do with the violation of the vow. On the contrary, to offer water to a person who wants it to drink is his religion of compassion and in doing so he performs a virtuous act. For, one who continuously utters 'give me water' and without water tosses about with pain and restlessness is saved from evil brooding and mental distress as soon as he is offered water to drink. And thus he is saved from bad death. Peaceful death while in religious meditation (*samādhi-maraṇa*) is good death. On the other hand, death in intense attachment and distress is a bad death. Good death favourably affects one's next birth, while bad death adversely affects it. There is no reason to believe that offering of water occasions a grave situation of the violation of the vow. On the contrary, a grave and dreadful situation occurs if we do not offer him water. For, in that case he indulges in sorrowful brooding (*ārta-dhyāna*) and cruel brooding (*raudra-dhyāna*)—two forms of evil brooding. If he is offered water or food according to his request, he experiences mental peace. And possibly this peace may again awaken in him a religious fervour and provide him an opportunity to cultivate more and more restraint and to advance steadily on the path of religious practice and spiritual discipline.

It is obligatory for the vower to continue the practice not only of the vow of *anaśana* but also of all other vows so long as his mind remains peaceful and engaged in virtuous meditation. But on the destruction of mental peace and virtuous meditation, he is automatically absolved from his obligation. This is the reason why in all the formulas the vower is required to utter while taking the vows like *anaśana,* etc., are included the words '*savva-samāhi-vatti-āgāreṇaṃ vosirāmi*' ('except in order to attain full tranquillity of mind I abandon them'). Thus when the vower is afflicted with an acute pain provoking *ārta-dhyāna* and *raudra-dhyāna,* it is legitimate for him to break the vow in order to attain full tranquillity of mind.

Wholesome Desire for Universal Welfare

Man is a social animal. He cannot live alone. He lives in a society, in the company of his fellow-men. His career is a life of mutual assistance and cooperation. Industry, labour, service and sacrifice of innumerable living beings are there behind the sustenance and growth of an individual. Thus every individual is indebted to the universal society of all beings. So he should not think of his own welfare alone. He should think of the welfare of all beings. He should always see to it that no activity of his obstructs the progress or welfare of others, nor does it harm or injure others. His heart should be full of pure universal brotherhood. If he believes that he is quite independent of and aloof from the society and behaves in accordance with this belief, then he is morally and intellectually bankrupt because he does not recognise his obviously evident indebtedness to the society. He should understand that he is simply a member, a unit of the society and hence there cannot be his own welfare which is opposed to the social welfare. So in his heart there should be flowing the unbounded perennial fount of the wholesome feeling of social welfare.

Religion can never be separated from day-to-day living. It should permeate one's day-to-day living and one's dealings with others. If it is separated from one's day-to-day living and practical conduct, then it ceases to be religion and turns into the subject-matter of senseless idle talk. Fixing the attention on the definitive standpoint (that is, ultimate ideal) to practise righteous conduct which is not pernicious to it but conducive to it is really the practice of religion. Where there is neglect of morality, rectitude and justice in dealings with others, there is no firm stand of religion. Universal brotherhood is the light of non-violence and hence the heart of religion. The supreme beauty of living manifests itself in the active universal brotherhood.

The Straight and Simple Path

The world is afflicted with uncountable miseries. These miseries are the results of wrongs committed by man. And man commits wrong by not following the path of duty, righteousness and religion. Consequently, he becomes miserable. The philosopher saints have shown the path of duty and religion by expounding and teaching restraint (*yama*) and culture (*niyama*). Restraint consists in abstinence from injury to life, from falsehood, theft, incontinence and avarice. And culture consists in the cultivation of positive virtues like forbearance, humility, contentedness, etc. Treading on this path of religion and righteousness one attains welfare, peace and happiness. The purpose of practising vows is to make one's life peaceful and happy by reducing the passion of greed, by contracting selfish worldly activities and by steadily advancing on the path of self-restraint and self-culture. That in society fellow-beings may live together amicably and peacefully and that their life may constantly develop towards perfection is the sole objective of the practice of religion and righteousness. And the only path of every man's religion consists in the cultivation of virtuous qualities like truthfulness, non-violence, contentedness, friendliness, service, etc.

There is no harm in enjoying the acceptable and permissible things which we obtain honestly; and we should be contented with what we obtain. But to entertain inordinate desire for attaining and enjoying those things very often on account of our having developed strong liking for them and to experience restlessness in their absence or non-attainment is the passion of attachment which makes our whole life miserable and disturbed. And the path of non-attachment consists in the patient and peaceful efforts to subdue this passion of attachment. Generally man is allowed to enjoy the permissible proper food obtained honestly. But he should enjoy it without being a slave of the palate and in such a manner as there would be no harm whatsoever to his health and mental purity. Such a wise and virtuous person will never be a slave of the organ of taste and following the middle path of self-development will easily and steadily move on towards the final destination of liberation.

Philosophical Exposition of the Nature of Soul

The defining characteristic of soul is consciousness (*cetanā*) which means cognitive power. Such a power does not characterise any other substance—physical or non-physical. Soul cognises or can cognise external objects by its cognitive power. It can cognise not only the external objects but itself also. So it is called self-revelatory-cum-other-revelatory (*sva-paraprakāśaka*). All cognition—valid or invalid—always cognises itself, that is, it always reveals itself.[1] But valid cognition cognises itself as well as an external object. So it is regarded as self-revelatory-cum-other-revelatory. Like a lamp[2] it being of the nature of light reveals the external object while

1. *svanirṇayas tu apramāṇe'pi saṁśayādau vartate / na hi kācit jñānamātrā sāsti yā na svasaṁviditā nāma/* Ācārya Hemacandra's *Pramāṇamīmāṁsā-vṛtti* on the third aphorism.
2. *jñānaṁ prakāśamānam eva arthaṁ prakāśayati prakāśakatvāt pradīpavat /* Preface to the above aphorism.

Meaning: A lamp does never depend on any other thing to reveal itself. It is itself revealing itself. The invalid cognition (doubt, illusory cognition) can never reveal the external object; this is quite obvious.

All objects in the world have general as well as specific characteristics. Not directing its attention to the specific characteristics of a thing, when consciousness directs its attention mainly to the general characteristics of the thing, the form that the consciousness assumes is called *darśana*. On the other hand, not directing its attention to the general characteristics of a thing, when consciousness directs its attention mainly to the specific characteristics of the thing, the form that the consciousness assumes is called *jñāna*. The transformation of pure consciousness into cognitive operation or cognition (*upayoga*) is generally divided into two types—general cognition and specific cognition. The cognition which cognises an object in its general form is general cognition. And the cognition which cognises an object in its specific form is specific cognition. Specific cognition is described as *sākāra*, while general cognition is described as *nirākāra*. In this context, by the term *'ākāra'* we are to understand specific characteristics or form. So *nirākāra* means that which does not have specific characters or form as its content. Therefore, *nirākāra* cognition means that cognition which does not grasp the specific characteristics or form. Thus the general cognition is *nirākāra*, while the specific cognition is *sākāra*. The former is *darśana*, while the latter is *jñāna*.

General cognition concentrates on the general characteristics. So at this stage, there arises the consciousness of identity or similarity. Specific cognition concentrates on the specific characteristics. So at this stage, there arises the consciousness of difference or particularity. First there takes place general cognition and specific cognition follows it. This is generally the order of their occurrence. Before we cognise a thing in a detailed way, there is the stage where we cognise it in a general way. First we simply cognise a thing as belonging to a class. If this stage is not experienced, there can be no specific—detailed—cognition of the thing. How can there arise the specific cognition without first there being the general—detail-less cognition? Let us understand the difference between

---

of the nature of light. This is the only reason why it reveals the external objects. Similarly, cognition reveals external objects, only because it reveals itself. That which itself is not of the nature of light—that is, which does not reveal itself—can never reveal other things. A particular cognition (say, pot-cognition) cognises an external object (pot); therefore, it must be self-revelatory. Thus it is proved that cognition is self-revelatory (self-cognitive).

the two with the help of a gross illustration. When we see a group of cows from a distance, we first have a general cognition of the form 'They are all cows'. At this stage we direct our attention to the general features or the common nature of the cows. When the group approaches us, then if we pay attention to the specific features of the cows, viz., their colours, horns, shapes, sizes, etc., we grasp the differences obtaining among them. At this stage, we direct our attention mainly to the specific features of different cows.

Essentially, there is no difference between general cognition (*darśana*) and specific cognition (*jñāna*). Both are of the nature of cognition (*bodha*). Whatever difference obtains there between them is due to the difference in their respective objects. Hence, if we take *jñāna* in a broad sense, that is, in the sense of cognition (*bodha*), then it will cover *darśana*[1] also.

Almost all systems of Indian philosophy maintain that in the genesis of knowledge, at first there necessarily arises a type of cognition which reveals bare existence of a thing, without any particular. In other words, thinkers of all systems of Indian philosophy agree in maintaining that all cognitive process invariably takes its rise in a cognition which grasps the bare existence but where nothing is revealed in the form of a qualifier or a qualificand.

All our worldly dealings depend on the specific cognition (*jñāna* = knowledge). This is the reason why while enumerating the eight main types of *karmas* already referred to by us, knowledge-covering *karma* is mentioned first. We have briefly dealt with the topic of *jñāna* (knowledge or specific cognition). Therein we have mentioned five types of knowledge, viz., *mati*, etc. Here let us go somewhat deep into the topic.

Matijñāna and *śrutajñāna* (specific verbal cognition = verbal knowledge) originate through the instrumentality of sense-organs and mind. In other words, as in the production of *matijñāna* so also in that of *śrutajñāna*, the assistance of the sense-organs and mind is needed. The specific cognition of the external objects like colour, taste, smell, etc., generated by sense-organs in contact with mind is a *matijñāna* of the form of empirical perception (*sāṁvyavahārika pratyakṣa*). And the experience

1. *Darśana* is called *sāmānya avabodha* (general cognition), *sāmānya upayoga* (general cognition), *nirākāra upayoga* (detail-less cognition) or *nirvikalpaka jñāna* (indeterminate cognition = non-conceptual cognition = cognition free from thought), while *jñāna* is called *viśeṣa avabodha* (specific cognition), *viśeṣa upayoga* (specific cognition), *sākāra upayoga* (detailed cognition) or *savikalpaka jñāna* (determinate cognition = conceptual cognition = cognition involving thought).

of the internal objects like pleasure, pain, etc., had through mind alone is also a *matijñāna* of the form of empirical perception. But empirical perception of external objects which is generated by sense-organs assisted by mind is sense-perception, while empirical perception of internal objects which is generated by mind alone is mental perception. This means that empirical perception is either sense-perception or mental perception. Thus one division of *matijñāna* is empirical perception. Another division of it is indirect knowledge. Cogitation, thinking, memory, recognition, inference, anticipation, which originate through the instrumentality of mind alone are *matijñāna* of the form of indirect knowledge; it means that even empirically they are not perceptual. Thus *matijñāna* is divided into two main types—one is empirically perceptual but transcendentally non-perceptual, and the other is empirically as well as transcendentally non-perceptual.

Matijñāna of the type of empirical perception has been analysed into four stages, viz., *avagraha, īhā, avāya* and *dhāraṇā*. As we have seen, *darśana* cognises the general features, rather bare existence. And the cognition that follows in the wake of *darśana* is called *avagraha.* It generally grasps colour, touch, etc. After *avagraha,* there arises a doubt as to the specific characteristic of the object, and the mind conducts enquiry or cogitation bent on determining it. This type of cogitation is called *īhā.* After general grasping (*avagraha*) of some visible form through eyes, of some sound through ears, of some touch through an organ of touch, and on knowing some specific signs, there arises, judgement-leading cogitation of the form 'This must be a tree, and not a man', 'This man must be a Bengali, and not a Punjabi', 'This sound must be of a conch, and not of a horn', 'This touch must be of a rope, and not of a serpent', this is *īhā.* After *īhā,* there comes the stage called *avāya. Avāya* means the ascertainment of the specific features of the object. It takes the form of judgements like 'This is certainly a tree', 'This is certainly a Bengali'[1], 'This is certainly a sound of a conch'[2], 'This is certainly a touch of a rope'. Thus *avāya* is a deter-

---

1. *avagraheṇa viṣayīkṛto yo'rtho'vāntaramanuṣyatvādijātiviśeṣalakṣaṇaḥ, tasya 'viśeṣaḥ' karṇāṭalāṭādibhedaḥ, tasya 'ākāṅkṣaṇaṁ' bhavitavyatāpratyayarūpatayā grahaṇābhimukhyam īhā /—Ratnākarāvatārikā* II. 8
yathā puruṣa ity avagṛhīte tasya bhāṣāvayorūpādiviśeṣair ākāṅkṣaṇam īhā /—Tattvārtha Rājavārtika I. 15
2. *avagrahagṛhītasya śabdāder arthasya 'kim ayaṁ śabdaḥ śāṅkhaḥ śārṅgo vā' iti saṁśaye sati 'mādhuryādayaḥ śāṅkhadharmā evopalabhyante, na kārkaśyādayaḥ śārṅgadharmāḥ' ity anvayavyatirekarūpaviśeṣaparyālocanarūpā mateś ceṣṭā īhā/—Pramāṇamīmāṁsā* I. i. 27

minate cognition of the object. The determinate cognition of the form of *avāya* leaves behind its traces (*saṁskāra*). When these traces are revived in future, they give rise to the memory of the thing determinately cognised in the past. These traces and the memory are called *dhāraṇā.* Retention of the determinate cognition in the form of traces, revival of these traces and memory of the thing determinately cognised in *avāya*—all this operation of *matijñāna* is designated by the term *dhāraṇā.*

Here we close the topic of the four gradual stages of empirical perception.

The scriptures recognise four types of intellect, viz., *autpattikī, vainayikī, karmajā* and *pāriṇāmikī* and regard them as forms of *matijñāna.* The intellect that can instantaneously and spontaneously solve the difficult problem is called *autpattikī* intellect. So the *autpattikī* intellect can be called 'the instantaneous intellect'. The intellect born of humility, service and culture is called *vainayikī* intellect. The intellect developed due to skill in arts and crafts as also due to practical experience is called *karmajā* intellect. The intellect that develops and becomes mature with the maturity of age is called *pāriṇāmikī* intellect.

The *Nandīsūtra* mentions these four intellects and points out the well-known illustrations of each of them by giving their short names or titles. And Ācārya Malayagiri has narrated those illustrative stories in brief in his commentary on the concerned portion of the *Nandīsūtra.* Some of them are very interesting. Depending on this commentary, we narrate here one or two of them in order to give some idea of the subject-matter.

To illustrate the *autpattikī* intellect, the commentator has given an illustrative story well-known even to-day among the people. It is as follows: There were two widows of the same husband. Either of them claimed to be the mother of the same male child. The judge, after listening to the quarrels for a long time, ordered to divide the living child into two, and give half to one, and half to the other. The pseudo-mother kept quiet on hearing the judgement. But the real mother experienced shudder, broke down and with overwhelming affection said, "Sir, the child is not mine. Please, give it to her." On hearing these words, the judge at once decided as to who was the real mother. That settled the question. The intellect of the judge was the *autpattikī* intellect.

To illustrate the *vainayikī* intellect, the following story is narrated. There were two astrologers. An old woman with a pot on her head met them on her way back home. She asked them as to when her son would come home from a distant country. When she put the question to them, the pot on her head fell down on the ground and broke into small pieces. On seeing this, one astrologer said, "O Mother, your son has already been destroyed (dead), just as the pot is just now destroyed." The other astrologer stopped her and said, "O Mother, your son has already arrived. Please, go home to see him there." The old woman hurriedly went home and was very much pleased to see her beloved son there after a long time. This illustrates the *vainayikī* intellect. The prediction was based on the reasoning that just as the pot met its mother—the earth, even so the son too should meet his mother just then.

The illustrative stories narrated in order to explain the *karmajā* intellect demonstrate the skill in arts and crafts. An experienced goldsmith can easily differentiate between pure gold and an alloy, while a layman is easily deceived.

One of the illustrative stories told to illustrate the *pārināmikī* intellect is as follows. There was a Jaina layman. He was observing a vow of abstinence from sexual intercourse with the wives of others. Once he was enamoured of his wife's female friend. The wife understood the whole situation. On seeing her husband infatuated with lust and pining for the sexual intercourse with her female friend, she said to him, "Don't be sorry and miserable. I shall get your desire satisfied." At night she dressed as her female friend dressed herself. Moreover, she put on ornaments exactly similar to those which her female friend put on. And in the guise of her female friend, she met her husband in a solitary place. After having sexual intercourse with her, the man became very sorry for the transgression or violation of the vow. When his wife told him the truth, his sorrow was allayed. He approached the spiritual teacher and requested him to show the proper atonement for the violation of the vow. The intellect of his wife was the *pāriṇāmikī* intellect.

Thus with the explanation of the four intellects, we complete the treatment of *matijñāna.*

Now we take up the topic of *śrutajñāna* (verbal knowledge). *Śrutajñāna* means knowledge obtained from what is heard from others. In one sense, it is a scriptural knowledge. Generally that knowledge which is generated through systematic treatises relating to various sciences and arts is *śrutajñāna.* Any treatise or knowledge can be put to good or bad use. To be or not to be of use for the attainment of liberation (*mokṣa*) is not the fixed nature of a systematic treatise, for that depends on the worthiness or capacity of the connoisseur concerned. If the connoisseur concerned is competent and is desirous of attaining liberation, then he can make use of even secular treatises for attaining liberation; on the other hand, if he is not a fit person then he will downgrade himself even with the help of the treatises that are generally considered spiritual. Nevertheless, the super-ordinary spiritual treatises hold a special position on account of their subject-matter as also on account of the competence of their author.

Broadly thinking, any knowledge that is generated through the instrumentality of words, signs or gestures is verbal knowledge. It is needless to say that knowledge generated in the hearers or readers after having heard or read words is verbal knowledge. But knowledge generated through gestures is also regarded as verbal knowledge. As for example, whatever knowledge one has through the gestures of hands or through the gurgling sounds of a throat is also verbal knowledge. When a beggar puts his one hand on his stomach and lifts the other towards his mouth, we at once understand that he is hungry and wants something to eat. This knowledge is also verbal knowledge. By moving fingers on the embossed letters whatever knowledge the blind obtains is also verbal knowledge. By hearing the 'tik tik' sound signals of coming telegram whatever knowledge the man trained in that branch gains is also verbal knowledge. Whatever knowledge the two persons standing face to face have through the signs or gestures that one makes to the other is also verbal knowledge. The deaf understands what another person conveys through hand-gestures. And the dumb conveys the meaning to another person through hand-gestures. Sometimes even men whose all the five sense-organs are efficient take recourse to various gestures and signs to convey the meaning, rather than taking recourse to words. And the knowledge through them is also regarded as verbal knowledge.

We grasp the meaning after having heard words. Similarly, we grasp the meaning after having seen signs or gestures. Again, the process through which we obtain knowledge through signs or gestures is the same as the one through which we obtain knowledge through words. So knowledge through signs and gestures is also regarded as verbal knowledge.

Grasping through ears, of mere sounds of spoken letters constituting words is simply an auditory perception which, as we have already seen, develops through four stages, viz., *avagraha*, etc. But the understanding of the meaning of these spoken words is the verbal knowledge. Similarly, seeing or grasping, through eyes, of merely signs or gestures is simply a visual perception having its four gradual stages. But the understanding of the meaning for which they stand is verbal knowledge. In the same way, grasping of sound signals through ears is simply an auditory perception; and the understanding of the meaning for which they stand is verbal knowledge. This is the reason why *matijñāna* of the form of sense-perception is regarded as a cause of *śrutajñāna* (verbal knowledge). *Śrutajñāna* is invariably preceded by *matijñāna* (of the form of sense-perception).

All persons who have heard or seen words, signs, gestures or signals do not understand their meaning, but only those who have acquired knowledge of convention can understand their meaning. Convention means the man-made rule that this word denotes this thing or that a particular sign, gesture or signal stands for a particular meaning. Just as smoke could not enable a man who does not know that smoke is an invariable mark of fire, to infer fire, even so a word, sign, gesture or signal could not enable a man who has not learnt the relevant convention, to know the corresponding meaning.

What is the difference between *matijñāna* and *śrutajñāna*? Answer given by the author of the *Viśeṣāvaśyakabhāṣya* is noteworthy. It is as follows: All knowledge generated through sense-organs and mind is *matijñāna*. That very *matijñāna* is called *śrutajñāna*, when to its causal conditions is added the instruction of others or the study of scriptures. Thus *śrutajñāna* is nothing but a special type of *matijñāna*.[1]

Generally we can identify *matijñāna* with intelligence, and *śrutajñāna* with scholarship. Thus, whatever difference obtains between intelligence and scholarship is the difference obtaining between *matijñāna* and *śrutajñāna*.. We can regard a person possessed of *matijñāna* as an intelligent person, while we can call an individual possessed of *śrutajñāna* a scholar. The *matijñāna* of a scholar is always coloured with *śrutajñāna*. In him, they get merged with one another.

Matijñāna does not require the aid of instruction for its origination, while *śrutajñāna* does require it. Again, as stated earlier, knowledge of convention is also a necessary condition for the generation of *śrutajñāna*.

---

1. *indriyānindriyanimittadvāreṇa upajāyamānaṁ sarvaṁ matijñānam eva, kevalaṁ paropadeśād āgamavacanād yaḥ bhavan viśiṣṭah kaścin matibheda eva śrutaṁ, nānyat/*—Maladhārī's commentary on verse 86 of *Viśeṣāvaśyakabhāṣya* (Beginning).

When we transform in our mind our empirical perceptual knowledge (*matijñāna*) into the form of language in order to impart it to others, then it does not turn into verbal knowledge (*śrutajñāna*), simply because it is transformed into the form of language; it still remains empirical perceptual knowledge (*matijñāna*). Verbal knowledge is verbal knowledge by virtue of being generated by language or words. So long as empirical perceptual knowledge is there in the mind of a speaker, it remains to be simply empirical perceptual knowledge even though it is associated with words in his mind. But when the speaker's spoken words generate knowledge in the mind of a hearer, then this knowledge generated in the mind of the hearer through words is verbal knowledge. Whatever is known through empirical perception can be presented in language. And whatever is known through verbal knowledge can also be presented in language. Special reflection or pondering on what is known through verbal knowledge is of the nature of intellect. And as we have already seen, intellect is a form of *matijñāna. Vainayikī* intellect which we have described earlier is of the nature of special reflection; hence it is a form of *matijñāna.*

Though *matijñāna* of the form of empirical perception is extensive and basic, its clarity, growth and strength depend on *śrutajñāna* (verbal knowledge). It is *śrutajñāna* that puts and leads us on the path of progress. If man were deprived of the benefits of the experiences of his fore-fathers and companions, his condition would have been even lower than that of a beast. Man cannot progress if he were to depend on his own personal experience for the knowledge of the world and were not to accept the findings of his predecessors. In that case, he would have to start anew in every generation. Again, were he to know things depending exclusively upon his own experience, his stock of knowledge would be very meagre, his mental outlook would be narrow and he could neither impart to others the results of his own experiences nor become acquainted with the achievements of others. This is the reason why *śrutajñāna* is regarded as very much important for the progress of man and its field considered to be very vast. Though *śrutajñāna* cannot arise without the rise of *matijñāna*, *matijñāna* without *śrutajñāna* cannot raise us to the plane higher than that of a beast. Thus, though *matijñāna* and *śrutajñāna* are interdependent, we can very well understand their difference.

All beings, from the most subtle microbes to the five-sensed, possess *matijñāna* and *śrutajñāna* both. According to scriptures, *matijñāna* and *śrutajñāna* have for their objects all substances—physical as well as non-physical. In other words, through *matijñāna* and *śrutajñāna*, we can reflect on, think of or know all substances, physical and non-physical. But through them we can know only limited number of modes of those substances. In short, though *matijñāna* and *śrutajñāna* can grasp all substances, they cannot grasp all the modes of even one substance. Here we should note that *śrutajñāna* can grasp greater number of modes than those *matijñāna* can grasp.

As we have already seen, there are forms of *matijñāna* that are generated through mind alone. Mind reflects on all substances—physical as well as non-physical—known through one's own experience or through scriptures and scientific treatises. So, from the standpoint of these forms of *matijñāna*, it can be said that *matijñāna* has for its object all substances. When mental reflection is accompanied by the employment of words,[1] it is *śrutajñāna*. But, when it is not accompanied by the employment of words it is *matijñāna*.

From the scriptural standpoint, *matijñāna* and *śrutajñāna* are called *parokṣa* (indirect or non-perceptual) because they depend on sense-organs and mind for their origination. *Matijñāna* includes those cognitions that are generated through the instrumentality of sense-organs and have for their objects colour, etc. In practice, these cognitions generated through sense-organs and mind and having colour, etc. for their objects are regarded as perceptual (*pratyakṣa*). So, even Jaina scriptures have to take into account this common practice and recognise them as perceptual. Though from the transcendental standpoint, those cognitions are not perceptual, from the empirical standpoint they have to be regarded as perceptual. Hence, they are designated as 'empirical perception' (*sāṁvyavahārika pratyakṣa*). The Jaina scriptures regard all forms of *matijñāna* (including even sense cognitions) and *śrutajñāna* (verbal cognition) as *parokṣa* (indirect or non-perceptual) as they are born with the

1. 'Being accompanied by the employment of words' means 'being in practice (at the time of communication) produced as a result of grasping the connotative potency of the words concerned'. That is to say, at the time of the production of *śrutajñāna*, it is required that the conventional meaning of the words concerned be remembered and the text concerned that is heard be followed. On the other hand, at the time of the production of the forms of *matijñāna*, *īhā*, etc. nothing like that is required. So *matijñāna* is described as 'being not accompanied by an employment of words' even when it is associated with the occurrence of words to mind.

help of sense-organs and mind, which are external instruments different from self. But in deference to common practice and common sense, the Jaina thinkers have accorded the status of empirical perception to those forms of *matijñāna,* which are generated through the instrumentality of sense-organs and recognised as perceptual in practice as also in the science of logic.

According to the Jaina scriptures, the transcendental perceptions are of three types, viz., *avadhijñāna, manaḥparyāyajñāna* and *kevalajñāna.* They are transcendental perceptions, because they originate without the aid of sense-organs and mind, and on the basis of the capacity of soul alone. So they are extra-sensory perceptions.

Avadhijñāna directly cognises physical objects irrespective of temporal and spatial distance. It has for its object the physical substances alone.

There are innumerable types of *avadhijñāna.* There can be such an advanced type of *avadhijñāna* that can cognise material mind-substance and even karmic material particles.

Manaḥparyāyajñāna too directly cognises the physical substances alone but not all physical substances. It cognises only those physical substances that are transformed into mind-substance. In other words, it can perceive nothing but the constituent stuff of the material mind substance. This means that it cognises the material mind-substances of the five-sensed living beings who possess the faculty of discrimination (*sañjñā*) and inhabit the human region. This is the reason why it is said that *manaḥparyāyajñāna* knows only an infinitesimal part of the objects of *avadhijñana.*

Manaḥparyāyajñāna does not directly cognise the external objects thought of by the minds of other persons. But, when the minds of other persons think of external objects, they assume modes i.e., forms appropriate to the objects thought of. And *manaḥparyāyajñāna* directly cognises these modes of the mind-substances of other persons. And the objects thought of by the mind-substances are afterwards inferred from these modes which *manaḥparyāyajñāna* has already directly cognised. Just as visual sense perception perceives the form of the written or carved script, even so *manaḥparyāyajñāna* perceives the specific modes of a mind-substance. Thus the perception of the modes of the mind-substance of another person is *manaḥparyāyajñāna.* But just as the knowledge which follows the visual sense perception of the script is itself not perception, but simply verbal knowledge, even so the knowledge (of the object thought of by the mind-substance of another person) which follows the perception of the modes of the mind-substance is itself is not perception, but simply inference; hence it falls outside the purview of *manaḥparyāyajñāna.*

Mind, according to the Jainas, is a material substance. Its modes are its different changing states running parallel to the acts of thought. Every state of our mind is a particular mode of the mind-substance. As our thoughts change, the mind also changes correspondingly. Thus every mode of thought is appropriately reflected in the mind-substance. The direct cognition of the modes of mind-substance is called *manaḥparyāyajñāna.* All this means that *manaḥparyāyajñāna* is the perception of the modes of the stuff of which the mind is fashioned.

The Jaina thinkers reject the possibility of a direct cognition of the external objects thought of by another person. They are of the view that they are cognised through inference. Only the modes of the mind-substance are here directly cognised.

Avadhijñāna and *manaḥparyāyajñāna* differ in respect of purity, spatial extent, person authorised and object.

Manaḥparyāyajñāna perceives its object much more clearly than does *avadhijñāna,* hence the former is purer than the latter. This is their difference in respect of purity. The lowest type of *avadhijñāna* can extend to one of the innumerable parts of a finger-measure. And its highest type can extend up to the entire universe. This means that it can directly cognise any physical object present anywhere in the entire universe. The Jaina thinkers conceive universe-space as having innumerable ultimate indivisible space-units. On this account, *avadhijñāna* comes to have innumerable divisions on the basis of its extending to more or less space. Thus the spatial extent of *avadhijñāna* stretches from a fraction of a finger-measure up to the entire universe-space. On the other hand, the spatial extent of *manaḥparyāyajñāna* is the region inhabited by human beings. This is the difference pertaining to spatial extent. Beings belonging to all the four classes (of hellish beings, celestial beings, animal beings and human beings) are authorised to acquire *avadhijñāna,* but only human beings possessed of total abstinence from violence, etc., are authorised to acquire *manaḥparyāyajñāna.* This is their difference in respect of person authorised. The highest form of *avadhijñāna* can directly cognise all the physical substances. On the other hand, *manaḥparyāyajñāna* can directly cognise only one out of infinite of them—that is to say, only those physical substances which are in the form of mind.

Thus, *manaḥparyāyajñāna* has got a less extensive sphere of objects than *avadhijñāna.* Yet, it is considered to be purer than the latter. It is because the ground of purity is not a lesser or greater extent of the sphere of objects, but the knowledge of a lesser or greater number of subtle features of the objects concerned. Thus among two persons, one is conversant with a number of disciplines and the other with only one but if the latter is better conversant with the subtleties of his discipline than the former is with those of his, then it is the latter's knowledge that is considered to be purer; similarly, *manaḥparyāyajñāna* is considered to be purer than *avadhijñāna* because though its sphere of objects is less extensive than that of the latter, it is better conversant with the subtleties of the objects concerned.

Avadhijñāna, manaḥparyāyajñāna and *kevalajñāna*—only these three are transcendental perceptions. Among them *kevalajñāna* directly cognises all substances—physical as well as non-physical—with all their modes. So it is called perfect (*sakala*) transcendental perception, while the other two are regarded as imperfect (*vikala*) transcendental perceptions.

Thus, *kevalajñāna* is omniscience. It means simultaneous knowledge of all the substances and all their modes, that is, their modes whether belonging to the past, present or future.

The possibility of omniscience is implied in the Jaina conception of soul. A soul in its pure state possesses infinite knowledge. It is omniscient. But this faculty of it is obscured by the veil of knowledge-covering *karma.* This veil can be removed totally by the practice of meditation and self-control, just as the obscuration of the sun or the moon caused by clouds can be removed by a blast of wind. And when this veil is removed totally, then omniscience dawns.

Now let us say something about the general cognition (*darśana*) which flashes into existence before the occurrence of the specific cognition (*jñāna*). There are four types of the general cognition. And the following is the account of their nature. (1) That general cognition which is had through the visual sense-organ is *cakṣurdarśana.* (2) That general cognition which is gained through a non-visual sense-organ is *acakṣurdarśana.* (3) That general cognition pertaining to physical things, which is generated through the super-ordinary power of *avadhi* is *avadhidarśana.* (4) That general cognition pertaining to all things—belonging to all the three divisions of time, which is gained through the super-ordinary power of *kevala* or omniscience is *kevaladarśana.* The Jaina thinkers do not recognise *darśana* in the case of *manaḥparyāya*[1], inasmuch as the *manaḥparyāya* cognises only particular features of the mind-substance of others, and not its generic form. And further, it is maintained that the type of *avadhijñāna* which cognises matter transformed into mind-substances is itself *manaḥparyāyajñāna*. Thus *manaḥparyāyajñāna* is simply an advanced *avadhijñāna*. So it can be said that it is *avadhijñāna* that develops into *manaḥparyāyajñāna*. Thus there is no *manaḥparyāyadarśana* immediately preceding *manaḥparyāyajñāna*. Only *avadhidarśana* can be regarded as preceding *manaḥparyāyajñāna*, because *manaḥparyāyajñāna* is nothing but a special type of *avadhijñāna*. A great Ācārya Siddhasena considers *manaḥparyāyajñāna* to be a division of *avadhijñāna*, because *avadhijñāna* has innumerable divisions. (Refer to his *Niścayadvātriṁśikā*). Thus he maintains that *manaḥparyāyajñāna* is not anything over and above *avadhijñāna*.

The general cognition had through *darśana* is so generic that there is no difference between the two general cognitions (*darśana*s) of the same type (say, visual) even though they are possessed by two different persons having contradictory attitudes, right and perverse. In other words, as *darśana* (say, *cakṣurdarśana*) is a form of cognition that grasps something merely generic, no difference can be pointed out between *darśana* (say, *cakṣurdarśana*) had by one possessed of *samyaktva* (right attitude) and the same (i.e., *cakṣurdarśana*) had by one devoid of the same.

Matijñāna, śrutajñāna and *avadhijñāna* are regarded as right-cognitions when they are generated in persons having right attitude (*samyaktva*). But the same are regarded as wrong cognitions when they are generated in persons having wrong or perverse attitude (*mithyātva*). Let us consider this point briefly.

In the science of logic, only that cognition is called right-cognition or valid-cognition (*pramāṇa*) whose object is true to the concerned factual situation, while that cognition is called wrong cognition or invalid-cognition (*apramāṇa*) whose object is false to the same. The division of right and wrong cognitions, based on the correspondence and non-correspondence of cognitions with the nature of their concerned objects or with the concerned factual situations is certainly recognised in the Jaina spiritual treatises. But such treatises do not attach much importance to it. In

---

1. *manaḥparyāyajñānaṁ paṭukṣayopaśamaprabhavatvād viśeṣam eva gṛhṇad utpadyate, na sāmānyam, ato jñānarūpam evedam, na punar iha darśanam asti/*—Maladhārī's commentary on *Viśeṣāvaśyakabhāṣya, gāthā* 814.

other words, in spiritual treatises, the distinction between right-cognition and wrong-cognition that is proposed by the science of logic is no doubt admitted but is treated as secondary. For them that distinction is primary according to which right-cognition is the cognition that is conducive to spiritual upgrading or development, while wrong-cognition is the cognition that is conducive to an increment in worldly entanglement or spiritual degradation. This means that the discrimination between right-cognition and wrong-cognition is made from an objective standpoint in the science of logic, while the same is made from a spiritual standpoint in the treatises concerned with matters spiritual. Thus it is just possible that owing to a lack of necessary means a person who is possessed of right attitude (*samyaktva*) might perchance be in doubt concerning the nature of an object or be under illusion concerning it or be having indistinct cognition concerning it, but inasmuch as he is a seeker after truth and one free from pre-possessions, he is always eager to correct himself—and does correct himself—with the help of an expert personage who is superior to and more authoritative than himself; besides, he chiefly employs his knowledge not for a satisfaction of his carnal desires but in the interest of his spiritual development. In contrast, the nature of a person afflicted with wrong and perverse attitude (*mithyātva*) is just the opposite of it. Thus owing to the availability of all necessary means such a person might have cognition that is definitive, more extensive and distinct but being under the grip of prepossessions, egoism and pride he is not ready to correct himself even when he realises that he is wrong. He tries to prove what is wrong to be right. Though he finds that his views or actions are wrong, he hesitates to confess to that effect on account of pride. His pride prevents him from abandoning his wrong views, notions and doctrines. Again, he is so attached to them that he cannot renounce them. Under the sway of pride, egoism and attachment to his views, he assumes arrogance and belittles the ideas of an expert and wise personage. This being so, he employs his knowledge not in the interest of his spiritual progress, but for the satisfaction of his worldly ambitions and desires.

All this means that those desirous of spiritual welfare and liberation never swerve from equanimity and always discriminate what is good from what is evil. So they employ their knowledge in the growth of equanimity and not in the increase of worldly desires. On this account, howsoever meagre their knowledge may be, it is regarded as right knowledge because it leads them on the right path of spiritual welfare. On the contrary, the knowledge of those who hanker after sensual pleasures and worldly ambitions is regarded as wrong knowledge, however extensive and definitive it may be, because it fosters inordinate and perverse desires and no equanimity; it leads them astray. How can that knowledge which nourishes perverse desires be the means to liberation? It can only place man on the evil path. So the reason why it is regarded as wrong knowledge is quite obvious.

The acquired knowledge may be put to good or bad use. A person possessed of right attitude and a person possessed of wrong attitude adopt diametrically opposite standpoints with regard to the acquired knowledge. The former is always inclined to use it rightly; when under the sway of passions and selfishness, he occasionally makes its bad use, his conscience bites him. On the other hand, the latter being a slave of sensual pleasures and inordinate desires, he uses his knowledge indiscriminately for achieving his selfish ends. He does not feel sorry when he employs his knowledge in accomplishing evil acts; on the contrary, he finds pleasure in doing so. A person having right attitude knows what is right to be right and what is wrong to be wrong; so if at all he inadvertently performs an evil act, he feels very sorry and repents for it. As his intellect is discreet and good, and his soul aspires after spiritual welfare and liberation, he steadily advances on the path of spiritual progress. On the other hand, a person afflicted with wrong attitude does not recognise the difference between good and evil, his mental state is defiled by evil thoughts and desires even when he pretends to be a good man, and so long as this is the state of affairs there is no possibility of his release and rescue.

Thus the Jaina philosophy discriminates between right cognition and wrong cognition from the spiritual standpoint.

The Jaina philosophers recognise five different states (*bhāva*) of soul. Of them one is essential (natural — *svābhāvika*) and others are adventitious. In other words, the former does not depend on the presence of material particles of the *karma*, while the latter depend on it. The five states are as follows: *aupaśamika-bhāva, kṣāyika-bhāva, kṣāyopaśamika-bhāva, audayika-bhāva* and *pāriṇāmika-bhāva.* (1) The *aupaśamika-bhāva* is that state which is born of *upaśama* (subsidence) of the material karmic particles associated with soul. *Upaśama* is a sort of spiritual purification that comes about as a result of complete cessation of the manifestation of material particles of the concerned *karma* which is yet in existence—just like the clarity appearing in water in which dirt has gathered at bottom. (2) The *kṣāyika-bhāva* is that state which is born of *kṣaya* (destruction) of the material particles of the concerned *karma*. *Kṣaya* is the supreme sort of spiritual purification that comes about as a result of soul's complete dissociation from the material particles of the concerned *karma*—just like the clarity appearing in water that has been rendered absolutely free of dirt. (3) The *kṣāyopaśamika-bhāva* is that state which is born of both *kṣaya* and *upaśama*. This state comes into being when the efficacy of the material particles of the concerned *karma* which are manifesting themselves is destroyed or rendered void and the manifestation of the material particles of the same *karma* which exist in potentia is suppressed. Thus *kṣayopaśama* is a sort of spiritual purification that comes about as a result of destruction of the efficacy of the manifesting particles of the concerned *karma* and the suppression of the manifestation of the particles of the same *karma* existing in potentia. This purification is a mixed sort—just like the water-washed rice *kodrava* whose intoxicating power partly vanishes and partly remains. (4) The *audayika-bhāva* is that state which is born of *udaya* or effective manifestation of the material particles of the concerned *karma*. *Udaya* is a sort of spiritual blemish or pollution that comes about at the time of an effective manifestation of the particles of the concerned *karma*—just as dirtiness appears in water in which dirt has been mixed. (5) The *pāriṇāmika-bhāva* is that state or transformation of a substance, which is automatically called forth by a mere existence of this substance. That is to say, the natural self-transformation undergone by a substance is called its *pāriṇāmika-bhāva*.

We have already referred to the eight basic *karma*-types: *jñānāvaraṇīya-karma* (knowledge-covering *karma*), *darśanāvaraṇīya-karma* (vision-covering *karma*), *vedanīya-karma* (feeling-producing *karma*), *mohanīya-karma* (deluding *karma*), *āyu-karma* (longevity-determining *karma*), *nāma-karma* (personality-determining *karma*), *gotra-karma* (status-determining *karma*) and *antarāya-karma* (obstructive *karma*).

Let us recapitulate what we have already said about the nature of these *karma*-types.

As we have already stated, there are five types of *jñānas* (knowledges), viz., *matijñāna, śrutajñāna, avadhijñāna, manaḥparyāyajñāna* and *kevalajñāna*. So correspondingly there are five types of *jñānāvaraṇīya-karma,* viz., *matijñānāvaraṇīya-karma, śrutajñānāvaraṇīya-karma, avadhijñānāvaraṇīya-karma, manaḥparyāyajñānāvaraṇīya-karma* and *kevalajñānāvaraṇīya-karma.* The different degrees of intellectual development, which we find in different men (or beings) are due to the different degrees of *kṣayopaśama* (weakening) of the *jñānāvaraṇīya-karma.* As there are four types of *darśana* (vision or general cognition), viz., *cakṣurdarśana, acakṣurdarśana, avadhidarśana* and *kevaladarśana,* correspondingly there are also four types of *darśanāvaraṇīya karma,* viz., *cakṣurdarśanāvaraṇīya-karma, acakṣurdarśanāvaraṇīya-karma, avadhidarśanāvaraṇīya-karma* and *kevaladarśanāvaraṇīya-karma.* Besides these four, there are five more types of *darśanāvaraṇīya-karma;* they are as follows: (1) The *karma* whose manifestation brings about the type of sleep from which one can be easily awakened is called *nidrāvedanīya.* (2) The *karma* whose manifestation brings about the type of sleep from which one can be awakened with difficulty is called *nidrānidrāvedanīya.* (3) The *karma* whose manifestation brings about the type of sleep which overtakes one while sitting or standing is called *pracalāvedanīya.* (4) The *karma* whose manifestation brings about the type of sleep which overtakes one while walking is called *pracalāpracalāvedanīya.* (5) And the *karma* whose manifestation brings about the type of sleep when one comes to possess the energy enabling one to accomplish a task thought of during the waking state is called *styānagṛddhi.*[1] There are two types of *vedanīya-karma,* viz., *sātavedanīya* and *asātavedanīya.* The *karma* whose manifestation makes a being experience pleasure is called *sātavedanīya.* And the *karma* whose manifestation makes a being experience pain is called *asātavedanīya.* There are two main types of *mohanīya-karma,* viz., *darśanamohanīya-karma* (right-attitude-deluding *karma*) and *cāritramohanīya-karma* (right-conduct-deluding *karma*). We have already described *āyuṣya-karma, nāma-karma, gotra-karma,* and *antarāya-karma.* There are five types of *antarāya-karma,* viz., *dānāntarāya, lābhāntarāya, bhogāntarāya, upabhogāntarāya* and *vīryāntarāya. Dānāntarāya-karma* places obstacles in the way of offering something. *Lābhāntarāya-karma* acts as an obstacle to gain or profit. *Bhogāntarāya-karma* prevents the enjoying of objects or things which can be enjoyed more than once. *Upabhogāntarāya-karma* prevents the enjoying of things which can be enjoyed only once. *Vīryāntarāya-karma* acts as an obstacle to the will-power; you would like to do an act but still you cannot; you know that it is right yet you cannot do it. The different degrees of efficiency or energy, which are seen in different men (or beings) are due to the different degrees of *kṣayopaśama*

1. Thus there are five types of sleep, viz. *nidrā, nidrā-nidrā, pracalā, pracalā-pracalā* and *styānagṛddhi.* These divisions of sleep are based on the different degrees of the intensity of sleep.

(weakening) of the *antarāya-karma.* In the world, we do notice the efficacy of *dānāntarāya-karma,* etc.; and the achievements in respect of donation, profit, non-recurrent enjoyment, recurrent enjoyment and will-power, which we observe are on account of the *kṣayopaśama* of the respective *antarāya-karmas.*

Now we propose to say something more about the five states (*bhāva*).

Aupaśamika-bhāva: The state which is due to the *upaśama* (subsidence, suppression) of the *mohanīya-karma* is called *aupaśamika-bhāva.* The type of right attitude which the soul attains on account of the *upaśama* of the *darśanamohanīya-karma,* and the type of right conduct which the soul attains on account of the *upaśama* of the *cāritramohanīya-karma,* the other type of *mohanīya-karma,* belong to the *aupaśamika-bhāva.* The right attitude and the right conduct that manifest themselves on account of the *upaśama* of the respective *karmas* are respectively called *aupaśamika* right attitude and *aupaśamika* right conduct. Hence the *aupaśamika* state is possible in the case of two modes of the soul, viz., right attitude and right conduct alone. Thus there are two *aupaśamika-bhāvas.*

Kṣāyika-bhāva : That state which is due to the *kṣaya* of the *karmas* is called *kṣāyika-bhāva. Kevalajñāna* or all-comprehensive determinate cognition results from the destruction of the *kevalajñānāvaraṇīya-karma, kevaladarśana* or all-comprehensive indeterminate cognition from that of *kevaladarśanāvaraṇīya-karma.* Again, the five fortunes, viz., donation, gain, non-recurrent enjoyment, recurrent enjoyment and endeavour result from the destruction of the five respective types of *antarāya-karma,* right attitude from that of the *darśanamohanīya-karma,* right conduct from that of the *cāritramohanīya-karma.* Hence, these nine modes of the soul, viz., *kevalajñāna,* etc., are to be treated as characterised by *kṣāyika-bhāva.* Here only those modes of the soul are taken into account which manifest themselves on account of the destruction of the respective *ghātī-karmas*[1] alone, even though other modes too manifest themselves on account of the destruction of other *karmas*; all *karmas* get destroyed when one attains disembodied state of liberation. It is because here the exposition is conducted keeping in view the embodied state alone. Thus there are only nine *kṣāyika-bhāvas,* viz., *kevalajñāna, kevaladarśana, samyaktva, cāritra* and five fortunes donation, etc.

---

1. *Ghātī karmas* are those that have a vitiating effect on the natural qualities of soul, viz., *jñāna, darśana, cāritra* and *vīrya.*

Kṣāyopaśamika-bhāva: That state which is due to the *kṣayopaśama* (a type of weakening) of the *ghātī-karmas* is called *kṣāyopaśamika-bhāva. Matijñāna, śrutajñāna, avadhijñāna* and *manaḥparyāyajñāna* result from the *kṣayopaśama* of *matijñānāvaraṇīya-karma, śrutajñānāvaraṇīya-karma, avadhijñānāvaraṇīya-karma* and *manaḥparyāyajñānāvaraṇīya-karma* respectively; false *matijñāna*, false *śrutajñāna* and false *avadhijñāna* (also called *vibhaṅgajñāna*) from that of the *matijñānāvaraṇīya-karma, śrutajñānāvaraṇīya-karma* and *avadhijñānāvaraṇīya-karma* respectively; visual indeterminate cognition (*cakṣurdarśana*), non-visual indeterminate cognition (*acakṣurdarśana*), *avadhi*-type of indeterminate cognition (*avadhidarśana*) from that of *cakṣurdarśanāvaraṇīya-karma, acakṣurdarśanāvaraṇīya-karma* and *avadhidarśanāvaraṇīya-karma* respectively; the five fortunes—donation, etc., from that of the five types of *antarāya-karma.* Again, right inclination (*samyaktva*) results from the *kṣayopaśama* of *darśanamohanīya-karma*; right conduct of the nature of complete restraint (*sarvavirati*) and right conduct of the nature of partial restraint (*deśavirati*) result from that of *cāritramohanīya-karma.* Hence, the eighteen modes *matijñāna*, etc., are alone to be treated as characterised by *kṣāyopaśamika-bhāva.* Thus there are in all eighteen *kṣāyopaśamika bhāvas.*

From what we said above one can easily understand that both right attitude (*samyaktva*) and right conduct (*samyakcāritra*) are of three types, viz., *kṣāyopaśamika, aupaśamika* and *kṣāyika.* It is because *mohanīya-karma* can undergo the processes of *kṣayopaśama, upaśama* and *kṣaya.* So right attitude and right conduct which result from the *kṣayopaśama, upaśama* and *kṣaya* of *darśanamohanīya* and *cāritramohanīya* are each threefold. *Antarāya-karma* can undergo only two processes, viz., *kṣayopaśama* and *kṣaya.* Hence five fortunes which result from *kṣayopaśama* and *kṣaya* of *dānāntarāya*, etc., are characterised by two *bhāvas* only, viz., *kṣāyopaśamika* and *kṣāyika.* Again, *jñānāvaraṇīya-karma* and *darśanāvaraṇīya-karma* also can undergo two processes alone, viz., *kṣayopaśama* and *kṣaya.* Hence right determinate knowledge (*samyagjñāna*) and indeterminate knowledge (*darśana*) result from *kṣayopaśama* and *kṣaya* of *jñānāvaraniya-karma* and *darśanāvaraṇīya-karma* respectively. So right determinate knowledge and indeterminate knowledge can have two *bhāvas* only, viz., *kṣāyopaśamika-bhāva* and *kṣāyika-bhāva.* And wrong knowledge (of the form of false *matijñāna*, false *śrutajñāna* and false *avadhijñāna*) results from the *kṣayopaśama* alone of the *jñānāvaraṇīya-karma.* So wrong knowledge is characterised by *kṣāyopaśamika-bhāva* alone.

(1) *Matijñāna,* (2) *śrutajñāna,* (3) *avadhijñāna,* (4) *manaḥparyāyajñāna,* (5) *matiajñāna,* (6) *śrutaajñāna,* (7) *vibhaṅgajñāna,* (8) *cakṣurdarśana,* (9) *acakṣurdarśana,* (10) *avadhidarśana,* (11) *samyaktva,* (12) *deśavirati* (partial abstinence from violence, etc.), (13) *sarvavirati* (total abstinence from violence, etc.), (14) donation, (15) gain, (16) non-recurrent enjoyment, (17) recurrent enjoyment and (18) will-power (endeavour or energy)—these eighteen are *kṣāyopaśamika-bhāvas.*

Audayika-bhāva : That state which is due to the *udaya* (effective manifestation or rise) of the *karmas* is called *audayika-bhāva.* All the states or modes which all the worldly beings experience or attain on account of the effective manifestation or rise of *karmas* are characterised by *audayika-bhāva.* Yet taking into account only the main modes, twenty-one divisions of *audayika-bhāva* are enumerated. They are as follows: *ajñāna* (false knowledge or dullness of intellect), *asiddhatva* (embodied state), *asaṁyama* (lack of self-control), six types of *leśyā* (spiritual colouration—black, blue, grey, yellow, lotus-pink and white), four *kaṣāyas* (passions, viz., anger, pride, deceitfulness and greed), four *gatis* (birth-species, viz., heavenly, human, animal and hellish), three *vedas* (feminine, masculine and neuter sex-feelings) and *mithyātva* (wrong attitude).

Now let us note as to which of these 21 enumerated states is due to the active manifestation of which *karma. Ajñāna* (wrong knowledge or dullness of intellect) results from the active manifestation of *jñānāvaraṇīya-karma. Asiddhatva* (embodied state) results from the active manifestation of all the eight types of *karmas. Asaṁyama* (lack of self-control or non-abstinence from violence, etc.) results from the active manifestation of *apratyākhyānāvaraṇa-karma. Leśyā* is nothing but mental transformation or activity. And mental activities depend on the mental capacity (*manaḥparyāpti*) which is a type of *nāma-karma.* Thus ultimately *leśyā* is connected with *nāma-karma.* So six types of *leśyā* result from the active manifestation of the concerned type of *nāma-karma.* The four *kaṣāyas* or passions result from the active manifestation of the *cāritramohanīya-karma.* The four types of *gati* or birth-species, viz., hellish, animal-type, human and heavenly result from the active manifestation of the *gatināma-karma.* The feminine, masculine and neuter sex-feelings result from the active manifestation of *vedamohanīya-karma.* And *mithyātva* (wrong attitude or inclination) results from the active manifestation of *mithyātvamohanīya-karma.*

In addition to these twenty-one modes listed here, five types of sleep resulting from the rise or manifestation of *darśanāvaraṇīya-karma*, six quasi-passions laughter, etc. (i.e., laughter, liking, dislike, fearing disposition, sorrowing disposition and despising disposition) from that of *mohanīya-karma*, four types of life-span (heavenly, human, animal and hellish) from that of *āyuṣya-karma*, all bodily traits from that of *nāma-karma*, high and low status from that of *gotra-karma*—all these modes are to be understood as characterised by *audayika-bhāva*, because any effect that results from the rise or manifestation of any *karma* is always characterised by *audayika-bhāva*. Scriptures show as to how these modes like five types of sleep, etc., are included in those twenty-one modes characterised by *audayika-bhāva*. In various ways they are included in them.

Twenty-one *audayika-bhāvas* are—1. *ajñāna* (wrong-knowledge or dullness of intellect), 2. *asiddhatva* (embodied state), 3. *asaṁyama* (lack of self-control, 4-9. *leśyā* (6 spiritual colouration), 10-13. *kaṣāya* (4 passions), 14-17. *gatis* (4 birth-species), 18-20. *vedas* (3 sex-feelings), 21. *mithyātva* (wrong attitude or inclination).

Pāriṇāmika-bhāva: That state which is natural to the soul is called *pāriṇāmika-bhāva*. *Jīvatva* or being a soul—i.e., being conscious (rather sentient), *bhavyatva* or being worthy of liberation, and *abhavyatva* or being unworthy of liberation—these three modes are natural; that is to say, these modes result neither from subsidence (*upaśama*) nor from destruction (*kṣaya*), nor from subsidence-cum-destruction (*kṣayopaśama*) nor from rise (*udaya*) of *karma*, but are present there merely on account of the nature of the soul.

Thus there are only three *pāriṇāmika-bhāvas*, viz., *jīvatva*, *bhavyatva* and *abhavyatva*.

The total number of the types of each of five *bhāvas* are as follows:

The total number of the types of	*aupaśamika-bhāva*	02
" " " "	*kṣāyika-bhāva*	09
" " " "	*kṣāyopaśamika-bhāva*	18
" " " "	*audayika-bhāva*	21
" " " "	*pāriṇāmika-bhāva*	03
	Grand total	53

Now we propose to describe as to how many of these main states or modes are possible in which souls.

Only two types of *bhāvas*, viz., *kṣāyika* and *pāriṇāmika* are found in the liberated souls. All the nine *kṣāyika-bhāvas*, viz., *kevalajñāna*, etc., and one *pāriṇāmika-bhāva*, viz., *jīvatva* are found in them.

Only three types of *bhāvas*, viz., *kṣāyika, audayika* and *pāriṇāmika* are available in the omniscient being in an embodied state. They are as follows: all the nine *kṣāyika-bhāvas*, viz., *kevalajñāna,* etc., two *audayika-bhāvas*, viz., *manuṣyagati* and *śuklaleśyā* (white spiritual colouration), and one *pāriṇāmika-bhāva,* viz., *jīvatva.*

Only three types of *bhāvas*, viz., *kṣāyopaśamika, audayika* and *pāriṇāmika* are found in all the non-omniscient beings. It is because all the non-omniscient beings without exception do possess *kṣāyopaśamika* and *audayika bhāvas. Kṣāyopaśamika-bhāvas*, viz., *matijñāna* or *matiajñāna, śrutajñāna* or *śrutaajñāna* and *audayika-bhāvas*, viz., this or that *gati* (birth-species) and this or that *leśyā* (except white), etc., are there in all the non-omniscient beings. Just as these three types of *bhāvas* are there in all the *mithyātvī* beings (i.e., beings afflicted with perverse attitude or inclination) of all the four *gatis* (birth-species) even so they are there in all the beings of all the four *gatis* who possess *kṣāyopaśamika samyaktva* (right attitude or inclination). Again, even those animal beings[1] and those human beings who possess both the *kṣāyopaśamika samyaktva* and the *kṣāyopaśamika cāritra* have these three types of *bhāvas*.

Some non-omniscient beings may possess one or two more types of *bhāvas* in addition to the above-mentioned three types of *bhāvas*. As for example, the non-omniscient beings possessed of *aupaśamika samyaktva* with or without *aupaśamika-cāritra* do have *aupaśamika-bhāva* in addition to the above three *bhāvas*, i.e., they have four *bhāvas* viz., *aupaśamika-bhāva, kṣāyopaśamika-bhāva, audayika-bhāva* and *pāriṇāmika-bhāva.* And the non-omniscient beings, who are not ascending the ladder of subsidence (*upaśamaśreṇī*) and who possess *kṣāyika samyaktva* with or without *kṣāyika cāritra* do possess *kṣāyika-bhāva* in addition to the trio of *kṣāyopaśamika-bhāva, audayika-bhāva* and *pāriṇāmika-bhāva.* Again, *aupaśamika samyaktva* without *aupaśamika cāritra* is possible in all the four *gatis* (birth-species—viz., heavenly, human, animal and hellish), but the same with *aupaśamika cāritra* is possible in human beings alone. So beings of both the groups suggested here have the following four *bhāvas* alone, viz., *aupaśamika-bhāva, kṣāyopaśamika-bhāva, audayika-bhāva* and *pāriṇāmika-bhāva. Kṣāyika*

---

1. The five-sensed animal beings having mind can rise up to the fifth stage of spiritual evolution called *deśavirati-guṇasthāna* (the spiritual stage characterised by partial abstinence from violence, etc.). Gods and hellish beings can rise up to the fourth stage of spiritual evolution.

samyaktva is also possible in all the four *gatis*. So the four *bhāvas* viz., *kṣāyika-bhāva, kṣāyopaśamika-bhāva, audayika-bhāva* and *pāriṇāmika-bhāva* are present in those gods, hellish beings or animals, who possess *kṣāyika samyaktva* without *kṣāyika cāritra,* in those non-omniscient human beings who possess *kṣāyika samyaktva* without *kṣāyika cāritra,* and are not on the ladder of subsidence or in the eleventh[1] stage of spiritual evolution, and also in those non-omniscient human beings who possess *kṣāyika samyaktva* with *kṣāyika cāritra.*

Aupaśamika, kṣāyika, kṣāyopaśamika, audayika and *pāriṇāmika*—all these five *bhāvas* are possible in one soul or being. Which type of soul or being? That soul or being who possesses *kṣāyika samyaktva* and at the same time is on the ladder of subsidence (i.e., and at the same time who has attained the eleventh[2] stage of spiritual evolution by the ladder of subsidence).

The possible *udaya* (rise or manifestation), *kṣaya* (destruction), *upaśama* (subsidence) and *kṣayopaśama* (destruction-cum-subsidence) of the concerned *karmas* take place depending on the substance (*dravya*), place (*kṣetra*), time (*kāla*), state (*bhāva*) and birth (*bhava*).

In this connection, let us think about the *udaya* (rise or manifestation) of the *asātavedanīya* (pain-giving *karma*), a type of *vedanīya-karma* (feeling-producing *karma*). The manifestation of this *karma* depends on the substances like a serpent, poison, a thorn, bad food and drink, etc., on the places like an unfortunate house, bad building, sandy or gritty or uneven ground and jail, on times like disturbing period or viral seasons, on states like bad temperament, worried nature, old age, diseased condition, and on births like animal birth, birth in a poor family, etc.

Now we think about the destruction of the same *karma.* It depends on the substances like the true spiritual teacher, etc., on the places of pilgrimage and other holy places, on the favourable times, on the states of the form of right knowledge and right conduct, and on the proper human birth.

Let us take up *mithyātva-mohanīya karma.* The manifestation of this *karma* depends on the substance of the form of wicked person of perverse convictions and wrong knowledge, on the uncultured places or countries,

1. It is because the possibility of *aupaśamika cāritra* is not accepted in the ninth and the tenth stages of spiritual evolution.
2. It is because it is only that human being who has attained the eleventh spiritual stage can gain *aupaśamika cāritra.*

on bad times defiled by vicious atmosphere, on the state of inclination for unwholesome teachings and bad company, and on the birth in the uncultured class.

And the destruction, destruction-cum-subsidence and subsidence of the same *karma* depend on the substances like a saintly spiritual teacher, etc., on the cultured countries or places, on the favourable times, on the states of the form of right knowledge and right conduct, and on the proper birth.

The following point is noteworthy. All types of *karmas* undergo *udaya* and *kṣaya.* But it is only *ghātī karmas* that undergo *kṣayopaśama.*[1] Again, it is only *mohanīya-karma* that undergoes *upaśama.*

The results of the manifestation (*udaya*) of each of the eight types of *karmas* have been described. Now we propose to describe the results of subsidence (*upaśama*) as well as destruction-cum-subsidence (*kṣayopaśama*).

The state of total non-manifestation of *karmas* (non-manifestation of even mere karmic particles) for a fixed duration of time, which is like that of burning coal covered with a heap of ashes, is called *upaśama. Upaśama* is possible only of the two types of *mohanīya-karma,* viz., *darśanamohanīya-karma* and *cāritramohanīya-karma.* And from the *upaśama* of the former results *aupaśamika samyaktva,* and from that of the latter *aupaśamika cāritra.*

Of the four *ghātī karmas,* when *jñānāvaraṇīya-karma* and *darśanāvaraṇīya-karma* undergo *kṣayopaśama*[2], right or wrong determinate cognition (*jñāna*

1. As already pointed out, the *karmas* that have vitiating effect on the natural qualities of the soul are called *ghātī karmas.* They are four viz., *jñānāvaraṇīya-karma, darśanāvaraṇīya-karma, mohanīya-karma* and *antarāya-karma.* On account of the *kṣayopaśama* of the *ghātī karmas,* the corresponding natural qualities of the soul manifest themselves in the direct proportion of the *kṣayopaśama* of the concerned *ghātī karmas.* As the *aghātī karmas* do not vitiate the natural qualities of the soul, they never undergo *kṣayopaśama.*
2. The compound word '*kṣayopaśama*' contains two simple words '*kṣaya*' and '*upaśama*'. *Kṣaya* means destruction of the karmic particles that have just manifested themselves; it is present in all *kṣayopaśama.* But *upaśama* that goes with *kṣaya* in *kṣayopaśama* is of two types. One type of *upaśama* is that which takes place when the *ghātī karmas* of *sarvaghātī*[3] (completely obscuring) type, viz. *mithyātvamohanīya karma* and twelve *kaṣāyas* (passions) beginning with the *anantānubandhī krodha* (the most intense anger) undergo *kṣayopaśama.* And the other type of *upaśama* is that which takes place when the *ghātī karmas* of *deśaghātī* (partially obscuring) type, viz. *matijñānāvaraṇīya karma,* etc. undergo *kṣayopaśama.*

3. Four *kaṣāyas* (passions, viz. anger, pride, deceitfulness and greed) of *anantānubandhī* type completely obscure *samyaktva* (right inclination, right attitude or love for truth),

or *ajñāna*) and indeterminate cognition (*darśana*) manifest themselves in direct proportion to the *kṣāyopaśama* of the respective *karmas*. The *kṣayopaśama* of these two *karmas* is present there even in the most subtle living being. It is because even that being does possess less, lesser or the least degree of knowledge. Consciousness is the nature of soul. So no soul can be absolutely devoid of knowledge. Even the most dense knowledge-covering *karma* of the most subtle living being does have some opening, however small it may be.

The former type of *upaśama* is of the form of suppression of the effectiveness (*vipāka*) of the concerned *karmas* that have just manifested themselves. The *karmas* were made so weak when they were in the state of mere existence (*sattā*) that they cannot manifest their effectiveness when they manifest themselves. This means that in this type of *upaśama* there is manifestation of karmic particles (*pradeśodaya*) alone and not that of their flavour or effectiveness (*vipākodaya*). That is, there is nominal manifestation and not effective manifestation. In other words, the *kṣayopaśama* of the *karmas* of *sarvaghātī* type is possible when there takes place manifestation of karmic particles whose effectiveness or flavour has already been rendered void.

In the latter type of *upaśama,* along with the manifestation of karmic particles of the concerned *karmas,* there is also the manifestation of their effectiveness which has already been rendered mild. The karmic particles that are having manifestation of their effectiveness do not completely obscure the qualities obscurable by them because they are having mild flavour or efectiveness. In other words, when the *karmas* of *deśaghātī* type undergo *kṣayopaśama,* then along with the manifestation of karmic particles of the concerned *karma,* there takes place the manifestation of their effectiveness whose intensity has already been reduced. We may put it in still a different way and say that those *ghātī karmas* whose *kṣayopaśama* is possible even when they have manifestation of their effectiveness (*vipākodaya*) are *deśaghātī* (partially obscuring) *karmas*. The qualities *matijñāna,* etc. manifest themselves in direct proportion to the reduction of the intensity of the effectiveness of the just manifested karmic particles of the respective *karmas*.

Matijñāna, śrutajñāna, etc. are the qualities that the soul has been having from the beginningless time. And the stream of the *kṣayopaśama* of the *karmas* covering or obscuring them has also been flowing from the beginningless time. And in the *kṣayopaśama* of those *deśaghātī karmas* there is the manifestation of effectiveness which can only partially obscure the concerned qualtiy; there can never be the manifestation of effectiveness which completely obscures the concerned quality. It is because

---

those of *apratyākhyānāvaraṇa* type completely obscure the partial abstinence from violence, etc. and those of *pratyākhyānāvaraṇa* type completely obscure the total abstinence from violence, etc. And *mithyātva* completely obscures *samyaktva.* So these twelve *kaṣāyas* and *mithyātva* are *sarvaghātī.* Four *kaṣāyas* of the *saṁjvalana* type only partially obsure the perfect right conduct. So they are *deśaghātī. Kevalajñānāvaraṇīya-karma* and *kevaladarśanāvaraṇīya karma* are *sarvaghātī,* but they can undergo *kṣaya* alone; in their case there is no possibility of *kṣayopaśama.*

On account of the *kṣayopaśama* (destruction-cum-subsidence) of *antarāya-karma* (obstructive *karma*), five fortunes, viz., charity-making, etc., are attained. As already stated, *antarāya-karma* is divided into five types according as it obstructs charity (*dāna*), gain (*lābha*), non-recurrent enjoyment (*bhoga*), recurrent enjoyment (*upabhoga*) and will-power (*vīrya*). Hence the five types are named as *dānāntarāya, lābhāntarāya, bhogāntarāya,*

---

at the time of *kṣayopaśama* accompanied by the manifestation of effectiveness of the karmic particles of the concerned *deśaghātī*[1] *karmas*, not a single karmic particle of those just mentioned ones is of the effectiveness that can completely obscure the concerned quality. But the karmic veils like *cakṣurdarśanāvaraṇīya-karma, avadhidarśanāvaraṇīya-karma* cannot undergo *kṣayopaśama* and the concerned qualities obscured by such karmic veil (*āvaraṇa*) cannot manifest themselves, so long as those *karmas* are manifested with effectiveness that completely obscures the concerned qualities. But when the *sarvaghātī* (completely obscuring) effectiveness of those karmic veils is transformed into *deśaghātī* (partially obscuring) effectiveness, then alone those *karmas* can undergo *kṣayopaśama.* As stated above, the *kṣayopaśama* of *deśaghātī karmas* is associated with the manifestation of effectiveness of the just manifested karmic particles having only *deśaghātī* (partially obscuring) effectiveness. Here the karmic particles manifested with effectiveness cannot completely obscure the concerned qualities because the effectiveness is mild.

The meaning of the basic term '*upaśama*' in the technical term '*aupaśamika*' is much wider than that we noted of the same term '*upaśama*' occurring in the compound '*kṣayopaśama*'. The meaning of '*upaśama*' occurring in '*kṣayopaśama*' is either absence of capacity to manifest effectiveness (flavour) or transformation of intense effectiveness into mild one, that is, manifestation of mild effectiveness. On the other hand, the basic word '*upaśama*' in the technical term '*aupaśamika*' means absence of the manifestation of karmic particles (that is, absence of nominal manifestation) as also absence of the manifestation of effectiveness (that is, absence of effective manifestation). It is because in *kṣayopaśama* there is *kṣaya* of *karma,* which can never take place without the manifestation of at least the karmic particles, while in simple *upaśama* this is not the case (that is, there is not manifestation of even karmic particles). When the *karma* starts undergoing simple *upaśama,* its *kṣaya* is arrested for the entire period from the start to the end of *upaśama.*

---

1. *Jñānāvaraṇa-karma* except *kevalajñānāvaraṇa-karma, darśanāvaraṇa-karma* except *kevaladarśanāvaraṇa-karma, kaṣāyas* (passions) of the *saṁjvalana* type (smoldering or very mild type) and *no-kaṣāyas* (quasi-passions) of the *mohanīya-karma,* and five types of *antarāya-karma*—these are *deśaghātī karmas. Nidrā* (sleep) is included in the group of *sarvaghātī karmas.*

The 'flavour' (effectiveness) is the capacity of *karma* to yield its fruit. Its intensity or mildness is varied. The types of *karmas* that completely obscure the concerned qualities obscurable by them are called *sarvaghātī.* And the types of *karmas* that partially obscure the concerned qualities obscurable by them are called *deśaghātī.* The flavour or effectiveness of the *sarvaghātī karma* is always *sarvaghātī.* On the other hand, the flavour or effectiveness of the *deśaghātī karma* may be *sarvaghātī* or *deśaghātī.*

upabhogāntarāya and *vīryāntarāya* respectively. So on account of the *kṣayopaśama* of *dānāntarāya*, etc., the respective qualities *dāna* (charity), etc., obstructed by them get manifested. And the greater the *kṣayopaśama* of a particular *antarāya-karma*, more is the manifestation of the quality obstructed by it.

As stated earlier, there are two types of *mohanīya karma* (deluding *karma*), viz., *darśanamohanīya* (what deludes natural love of truth) and *cāritramohanīya* (which deludes spiritually wholesome conduct). On account of the *kṣayopaśama* of *darśanamohanīya* and *cāritramohanīya* one attains *kṣāyopaśamika samyaktva* and *kṣāyopaśamika cāritra* respectively.

Opposite of *samyaktva* is *mithyātva*. *Samyaktva* means natural predilection for what is true and spiritually wholesome. So *mithyātva* means spiritually perverse attitude, dislike for spiritual truths and attraction for wrong views. The Jaina thinkers have noted its five varieties. They are as follows.

(1) *Ābhigrahika mithyātva* (uncritical and obstinate acceptance of views)

Acceptance of a particular view without critical examination, accompanied with contempt for all other views is *ābhigrahika mithyātva*.

A person possessed of *samyaktva* never accepts any doctrine without critical examination. So, if a man critically examines a doctrine, finds it true, accepts it and refutes others, then he is not considered to be a person afflicted with *ābhigrahika mithyātva*. If a man does not examine the views into which he is born, but accepts them without critical examination as to their merits and demerits, then he is surely afflicted with it. A person who considers himself to be a Jaina (*samyaktvī*, a person possessed of spiritually right attitude and views) on account of his birth in a Jaina family and tradition, who has inherited Jaina traditional views, who does not examine them and does not know their merits and truth, who have uncritically accepted them, who lacks the power of discriminating what is right and wholesome from what is wrong and unwholesome is Jaina by name only, but in reality afflicted with *ābhigrahika mithyātva*. Thus *ābhigrahika mithyātva* is obstinate and uncritical clinging to preconceived notions and inherited views.

The persons themselves unable to examine the views about truth and reality are not afflicted with *mithyātva* provided they are under the shelter and guidance of saint scholars well versed in spiritual science and endowed with critical acumen. This is so because there is no possibility in them of the wrong and perverse inclination as they are under the shelter of the spiritually advanced saint-scholars of acute power of discrimination. An instance in point is that of Māṣatuṣa Muni.

(2) *Anābhigrahika mithyātva* (Indiscriminate acceptance of all views)

It means acceptance of all views as true without the examination as to their merits and demerits. In other words, it is nothing but indiscriminate faith in the truth of each and every view.

This type of *mithyātva* is found in all the dull-witted persons who are unable to examine and evaluate the views. Mostly without any understanding such persons say, "Well, this is true, also that is true, or all views are true".

(3) *Ābhiniveśika mithyātva* (Intentional clinging to a wrong view due to attachment)

It means obstinate attempts to establish one's view which one knows to be wrong. In other words, it is one's attachment to a wrong view in spite of one's knowledge that it is wrong.

Even the faith or conviction of one who is not obstinate and is desirous of knowing truth and attaining spiritual good may be wrong on account of the lack of critical power of thought and discrimination or on account of the wrong teachings of one's spiritual guide and teacher. Yet, he should not be regarded as afflicted with *ābhiniveśika mithyātva*, because he is not obstinate, is ready to correct himself and his views and sincerely desires spiritual welfare. He is an honest truth-seeker. On account of these qualities, his faith or conviction turned wrong cannot obscure his innate inclination for and love of truth.[1] And hence as soon as he happens to meet

1. This has been clearly stated in the latter half of the 24th verse of *Upaśamanādhikāra* of the *Kammapayaḍī*. The line in point is: '*saddahai asabbhāvaṁ ajāṇamāṇo guruniyogā*'/ In his commentary on the same Upādhyāya Yaśovijayajī writes as follows: If a man is free from obstinate attachment and he is to have faith in or conviction of wrong views simply on account of his association with the propounder of wrong views, then his wrong faith or conviction does not obstruct his natural inclination for or love of the path shown by the great sages, that is, his innate inclination for spiritual good is not hampered. On the other hand, a man afflicted with obstinacy and attachment is always afflicted with *mithyātva*, be he the upholder of this or that view.

a proper spiritual guide, his wrong faith or conviction gets transformed into right one.

Ācāryas like Śrī Siddhasena Divākara, Śrī Jinabhadragaṇi Kṣamāśramaṇa, etc., have strongly established their views. And much has been said by them in support of their views. In spite of this, they could not be regarded as afflicted with *ābhiniveśika mithyātva.* It is because they have strongly supported their views not out of their attachment to them, but on the basis of the uninterrupted tradition of the preachings of the Non-attached One and after having understood the purport of the scriptures to be in consonance with them. On the other hand, Jamāli, etc., supported their views in spite of knowing that they are opposed to the purport of the scriptures; therefore, they are regarded as afflicted with *ābhiniveśika mithyātva.*

(4) *Sāṁśayika mithyātva* (the attitude of uncertainty and doubt about the spiritual truths)

It means sceptic attitude even towards what is spiritually beneficial, viz., the supreme divinity, etc. It is the state of doubt as to whether the path shown by the supreme souls (*Jinas*) is or is not conducive to spiritual good.

There may arise doubts in the minds of great saints about the intricate subjects. But their state cannot be regarded as that of *sāṁśayika mithyātva.* It is because they consider the greatly learned saints to be the final authority on such questions, leave the questions to them for answers, and do not allow their faith in the spiritual path to be shaken and their spiritual peace to be disturbed.

(5) *Anābhoga mithyātva* (sticking to the false beliefs and views due to lack of development)

Anābhoga mithyātva means incapacity of the mind to think and lack of special knowledge. In other words, it is the state of intense ignorance or nescience. This state is found in living organisms which have not attained to a higher stage of development, that is, in the one-sensed beings, etc. It is also found in beings under intense influence of delusion or nescience.

Samyaktva which is attained on the removal of *mithyātva* of these five varieties is either *aupaśamika* or *kṣāyopaśamika* or *kṣāyika.* Of these three, the *aupaśamika samyaktva* is of a very short duration of an *antarmuhūrta* (a period of up to fortyeight minutes). A soul capable of attaining liberation can attain this type of *samyaktva* at the most five times before the attainment of liberation. For the first time, on account of the subsidence of four passions of *anantānubandhi* type as also on account the subsidence of *darśanamohanīya-karma,* it is attained by a soul afflicted with beginningless *mithyātva.* After that, it can be attained at the most four times, because before the attainment of liberation one can ascend the ladder of subsidence at the most four times. [The ascent on the ladder of subsidence consists in the process of subsidence of four passions of *anantānubandhī* type as also of subsidence of three types of *darśanamohanīya-karma.*]

A living being can attain *kṣāyopaśamika samyaktva* innumerable times. The minimum duration of this type of *samyaktva* is an *antarmuhūrta,* while its maximum duration is a period measuring somewhat more than sixty-six *sāgaropama*[1] years.

Kṣāyika samyaktva once attained never disappears. From the standpoint of an embodied state of the soul possessed of this *samyaktva,* its minimum duration is an *antarmuhūrta* and its maximum duration is a period somewhat more than thirtythree *sāgaropama* years.

In *kṣāyopaśamika samyaktva,* there is vision of truth, that is, there is firm faith in truth or in spiritually beneficial fundamental categories. But it is associated with slight impurity of the form of attachment for one's name or for what one regards as one's own. As for example, he is attached more to the deity of the temple built by him than to one of another built by someone else.[2] And of many supreme deities, he is devoted more to one than to others.[3] Again, he has attachment for the external means, forms and rituals of true religion and mistakes true religion for them; not only that but for them he gives vent to his passions. He has attachment for his name and fame, for antiquity, for a particular spiritual teacher, for a particular chapter of monks, etc. And equanimity, easily attainable

1. A *sāgaropama* is one thousand billion *palyopamas.* A *palyopama* is an innumerable (not infinite, but having a limit) quantity of years, so great that it cannot be numbered. An innumerable quantity is a limited quantity and will in time be exhausted. An infinite quanity will never be exhausted. So *sāgaropama* is also a type of *asaṁkhyāta* (innumerable) number.

1. *svakārite'rhaccaityādau devo'yaṁ me'nyakārite /*
anyasyāyam iti bhrāmyan mohāc chrāddho'pi ceṣṭate //—Gommaṭasāra, Jīvakāṇḍa-ṭīkā.

2. *same'py anantaśaktitve sarveṣām arhatām ayam /*
devo'smai prabhur eṣo'smā ity āsthā sudṛśām api /—Gommaṭasāra, Jīvakāṇḍa-ṭīkā.

through *samyaktva*, gets somewhat impaired by all this attachment; as a result, *samyaktva* itself is slightly soiled. When this *samyaktva* is associated with doubts about subtle subjects, it is distracted by or confounded with dilemmas. *Aupaśamika* or *kṣāyika samyaktva* is free from such impurities. *Aupaśamika samyaktva* is temporary and lasts for a very short duration of time. On the other hand, *kṣāyika samyaktva* is permanent and endless. Though these two *samyaktva*s are of the nature of pure state of soul, there is a great difference between the two with regard to their duration of time. Of course, as there is a difference between the influence of *upaśama* and that of *kṣaya*, there must be some difference between the visions of or faith in truth, which one attains in *aupaśamika samyaktva* and *kṣāyika samyaktva*.

When the soul in the state of *kṣāyopaśamika samyaktva* destroys the impure and semi-pure heaps of the karmic particles of *mithyātvamohanīya-karma*[1] and *miśramohanīya-karma* respectively and experiences the manifestation of the pure heap of karmic particles of *samyaktvamohanīya-karma*, then that is the last stage of the termination of *kṣāyopaśamika samyaktva*. And it is given the name '*vedaka*' ('that which experiences'). As soon as there ends the process of experiencing these pure particles, there manifests the *kṣāyika samyaktva* on account of the destruction of all the three heaps, viz., impure, semi-pure and pure. Manifestation of *kṣāyika samyaktva* is regarded as the ladder of destruction. Similarly, total subsidence of the *karma* which deludes or obscures predilection for or vision of truth results in the manifestation of *aupaśamika samyaktva*; and the manifestation of *aupaśamika samyaktva* is regarded as the ladder of subsidence. In the eighth stage of spiritual development, the soul makes full preparation either for the ascent on the ladder-of-subsidence of the form of the continuous process of subsidence of conduct-deluding *karma* or for the ascent on the ladder-of-destruction of the form of the continuous process of destruction of conduct-deluding *karma*. And in the ninth stage it starts the process of subsidence or destruction of the same *karma*; it means that in this stage there begins the subsidence or destruction of the four passions (anger,

1. There are three types of *darśanamohanīya-karma*, viz., *mithyātvamohanīya-karma*, *miśramohanīya-karma* and *samyaktvamohanīya-karma*. *Mithyātvamohanīya-karma* is that *karma* which obscures predilection for or vision of truth completely. *Miśramohanīya-karma* is that *karma* which obscures the same partially. And *samyaktvamohanīya-karma* is that *karma* which does not obscure the same by its rise or manifestation.

etc.) and nine quasi-passions (laughter, etc.); the quasi-passions co-exist with and strengthen the passions; these passions and quasi-passions delude the wholesome conduct. In the ninth and tenth stages, the suppresser continues the act of suppressing the conduct-deluding *karma,* while the destroyer continues the act of destroying the same. When they are about to complete their respective processes, their paths branch off and take different directions. The stage the suppresser moves towards and reaches is the eleventh one called *upaśāntamoha* (the stage of total subsidence of deluding *karma*). And the stage the destroyer moves towards and reaches is the twelfth one called *kṣīṇamoha* (the stage of total destruction of deluding *karma*). He who has totally destroyed the deluding *karma* neither falters nor falls down, but without fail attains the final goal, that is, liberation. The nature of suppression being what it is, he who has totally suppressed the deluding *karma* invariably falls down on its rise. While falling if he controls himself and becomes steady at some proper stage and employs his irrepressible spiritual energy for ascending the ladder-of-destruction leading to perfection, then he attains omniscience in that very birth. Otherwise, that is, if his spiritual lethargy increases, then he 'vomits' even *samyaktva* and falls back on the first stage called *mithyātva.*

Of the eight *karmas*, the four which obscure the natural qualities of soul are destroyed simultaneously. And the remaining four *karmas*, which do not obscure the natural qualities of soul are also destroyed simultaneously. But the former group is destroyed first and the latter one is destroyed afterwards. The results of the destruction of each of the eight *karmas* is mentioned below.

The result of the destruction of knowledge-covering *karma* is infinite knowledge, that of the destruction of *darśana*-covering *karma* is infinite *darśana* (vision or general cognition), and that of the destruction of feeling-producing *karma* is infinite bliss. Of the two divisions of deluding *karma,* viz., *karma*-that-deludes-the-predilection-for-truth and conduct-deluding *karma,* the destruction of the former results in perfect love of truth and that of the latter in perfect conduct. The result of the destruction of life-span-determining *karma* is everlasting life. The joint result of the destruction of personality-determining (i.e., body-making) *karma* and status-determining *karma* is occupation of the same space by the non-physical infinite souls. And the result of the destruction of the obstructive *karma* is infinite energy.

The essence of all this exposition is that the attainment of the spiritual good depends solely on the right understanding and good conduct. Of these two stages, the former is called *samyaktva* or *samyag-dṛṣṭi,* while the latter is called *cāritra* (*samyak cāritra*). Again, the former is manifested on the subsidence or destruction of *karma*-that-deludes-the-predilection-for-truth (*darśanamohanīya-karma*), a division of deluding *karma*; and the latter is manifested on the subsidence or destruction of conduct-deluding *karma,* the other division of deluding *karma.* Thus, right (spiritually wholesome) understanding and conduct, the two fundamental elements of life, depend on the subdual of deluding *karma.* As already stated, that division of deluding *karma,* which obscures the natural predilection for truth is called *darśanamohanīya-karma.* The greater the removal of *darśanamohanīya-karma,* the greater is the manifestation of the natural predilection for truth. And when *darśanamohanīya-karma* is totally removed, there is the full manifestation of the natural predilection for truth. Even after the manifestation of the natural predilection for truth, a very difficult task of removing the obstructions in the attainment of good conduct remains to be accomplished; it can be carried through successfully only with great efforts. But after the manifestation of the natural predilection for truth one will surely accomplish the task sooner or later. Again, that division of deluding *karma,* which obscures good conduct is called *cāritramohanīya-karma.* The greater the removal of *cāritramohanīya-karma,* the greater is the manifestation of good conduct. And when the *cāritramohanīya-karma* is totally removed, there is the full manifestation of good conduct. Thus after the removal of *darśanamohanīya-karma, cāritramohanīya-karma* is removed and on the removal of the latter, there takes place the total removal of all deluding *karma.* On the removal (i.e., destruction) of deluding *karma,* there occurs the destruction of its associate *karmas* which obscure the natural qualities of soul. And as a result of it, the soul attains liberation—if it is still in an embodied state, then it is liberated-while-living (*jīvanmukta*); after that state it attains the disembodied state of liberation (*videhamukti*).

When there arises right understanding about soul, the veil of *darśanamohanīya-karma* is removed and *samyaktva* or *samyag-dṛṣṭi* is attained. On the attainment of *samyag-dṛṣṭi* (right spiritual inclination or predilection for truth), whatever knowledge the soul possesses is automatically turned into right (spiritually wholesome) knowledge. And when on the advanced stage of spiritual progress non-restraint, attachment and passions are destroyed, then *cāritramohanīya-karma* gets eliminated. With its elimination, right conduct manifests itself. Thus right inclination, right knowledge and right conduct which is in consonance with the former two—all these three combined are the means of liberation.

Spiritual-Mental-Colouration (Leśyā)

Now, we propose to deal with the topic of spiritual-mental-colouration (*leśyā*), depending on the Jaina scriptures.

Bondage and liberation mainly depend on mental states. So, it is necessary to pay attention to the consideration as to what type of mental states are associated with the activities we undertake.

Mental states are never uniform. They never remain uniform, but go on changing. Sometimes, they are intensely black, highly defiled, excessively evil; sometimes black, defiled, evil; sometimes grey, less defiled, less evil; sometimes evil-cum-good, impure-cum-pure; sometimes good or pure; sometimes better, purer; and sometimes best, purest, highly luminous. This is what we all experience. These mental states or transformations are called *leśyā.* A crystal assumes the colour of a thing placed in its vicinity. Similarly, mental states change according as the mind comes in contact with different substances, that is, aggregates of atoms. When man is angry, we all notice as to how the influence of his mental state of anger is seen on his face. At that time, his face turns red with anger and becomes deformed and distorted. This is the outward appearance of the agitation reflected in mind, of the aggregate of atoms of anger; it spreads over the face. On account of its association with various types of aggregates of atoms, mind undergoes different transformations or experiences varied influences. They are called *leśyā.* Such aggregates of atoms or physical substances are classified into six divisions, viz., those of black colour, those of blue colour, those of grey colour (which is like the colour of the brinjal flowers), those of yellow colour (which is like the colour of the rising sun), those of the lotus-colour (resembling the colour of gold) and those of luminous white colour. Of these six types of substances, the mental state assumes the colour of that type of substance in whose vicinity the mind happens to be. This colouration of mental states is called *leśyā.* So it is said:

kṛṣṇādidravyasācivyāt pariṇāmo ya ātmanaḥ /
sphaṭikasyeva tatrāyaṁ 'leśyā' śabdaḥ pravartate //

The meaning is: Just as a pure crystal assumes different states in the vicinity of things of different colours placed successively before it, even so the soul undergoes different states or transformations in the vicinity of physical substances of different colours; they are called *leśyā*.

Physical substances of black, blue and grey colours are evil, unwholesome, while those of yellow, golden and white colours are good or wholesome. Black physical substances are intensely evil, the blue ones are moderately evil and the grey ones are mildly evil. And the yellow substances are mildly good, the golden ones are moderately good and the white ones are intensely good. The good mental state that arises on account of the association of mind with good substances is good *leśyā*. On the other hand, the evil mental state that arises on account of the association of mind with evil substances is evil *leśyā*. The black—the intensely impure—mental or spiritual state which originates on account of the association of mind or soul with the black material particles is the black (*kṛṣṇa*) *leśyā*. The blue—the moderately impure—mental state which originates on account of the association of mind with the blue material particles is the blue (*nīla*) *leśyā*. The grey—the mildly impure—mental state, which originates on account of the association of mind with the grey (brinjal-flower-colour) material particles is the grey (*kāpota*) *leśyā*. The yellow (rising-sun-colour)—mildly pure—mental state which originates on account of the association of mind with the yellow material particles is the yellow (*pīta*) *leśyā*, also called *tejo-leśyā*. The lotus-colour (*kareṇa*-flower-colour or *campaka*-flower-colour)—moderately pure—mental state which originates on account of the association of mind with the material particles of the same colour is *padma-leśyā*. And white—intensely pure—mental state, which arises on account of the association of mind with the white material particles is the white (*śukla*) *leśyā*.[1]

---

1. In the modern scientific experiments, it has been found that even thought vibrations ensuing from mind have colours. The theory of six *leśyās* indicating different degrees of soul's internal purity or impurity, as shown above, is enunciated in the Jaina scriptures. And Maṅkhaliputta Gośālaka, a leader of the *Ājīvika* sect, has described six psychic colours (*abhijāti*), viz., black (*kṛṣṇa*), blue (*nīla*), red (*lohita*), yellow (*hāridra*), white (*śukla*) and supremely white (*parama śukla*), classified on the basis of purity-impurity of activities. (This has been noted in the Buddhist *Piṭaka Aṁguttaranikāya*).
   (This Gośālaka had spent six years with Lord Mahāvīra as his pupil when Mahāvīra had not still attained omniscience).
   The *Mahābhārata Śāntiparva* 12. 286 *Adhyāya* contains the following verse:
   ṣaḍ jīvavarṇāḥ paramaṁ pramāṇaṁ kṛṣṇo dhūmro nīlam athāsya madhyam/
   raktaṁ punaḥ sahyataraṁ sukhaṁ tu hāridravarṇaṁ susukhaṁ ca śuklam //33//

The material substances that reflect their colours in the mental or spiritual states are called *leśyā*-substances. The *leśyā*-substances are included in activities (*yoga*) of mind, speech and body. Just as bile in the body excites anger, substances like wine, etc. cause rise of the knowledge-obscuring *karma* (i.e., cause dullness of intellect) and substances like *brāhmī* ghee cause subsidence-cum-destruction of the same *karma* (i.e., cause development of intellect)—that is, just as substances included in activities (*yoga*) and the external substances cause rise, etc. of the *karmas*—even so *leśyā*-substances included in activities (*yoga*) assist and nourish passions so long as passions exist and are not destroyed. Thus, though a *leśyā* excites passions, it is not itself of the nature of passions, because even an omniscient who is absolutely free from passions does have a *leśyā*—the supremely white *leśyā* alone. A *leśyā* being of the nature of transformation of activities (*yoga*), it lasts so long as activities last. So even an omniscient person performing activities does have a *leśyā*[1]—the supremely white one—, and when there ceases all activity absolutely, that is, only in the

---

paraṁ tu śuklaṁ vimalaṁ viśokaṃ /

This statement enumerates six psychic colours of living beings, viz. black, blue, red, yellow, white and supremely white. The six psychic colours enumerated here are the same as those accepted in the *Ājīvika* sect of Gośālaka.

Patañjali in his *Yogasūtra* (4.7) classifies *karmas* into four divisions, viz. black, white-cum-black, white and neither-white-nor-black, and thus presents the analysis of purity-impurity of the internal states of living beings.

1. An omniscient person in the embodied state does have *leśyā* (spiritual-mental-colouration). And as he has *leśyā*, he has activities (*yoga*) of mind, speech and body. Of course, his activities promote religion and achieve spiritual good of the people. His life is full of pure and luminous activities. From this we can have an idea of the daily activities of the omniscient Lord living among the common people. He is delighted to see the virtuous but remains indifferent towards those who are wicked and behave wickedly. He holds dialogues with others to explain this or that spiritual point, shows the people the path of peace to pacify quarrels and disputes, sends blessings to some, consoles and inspires others, enters into discussions with those who are opposed to the good of the people or who hold different views. Thus outwardly, he appears like a worldly man. So monks, saints and the honourable elder ascetics too, who do not know him, cannot recognise him as an omniscient person. It is because he does not possess any special outward sign that can declare his internal state of omniscience or Jinahood, nor does such a sign manifest in him when he attains omniscience or Arhathood. But when they get acquainted with his supreme wealth of pure knowledge, then only they recognise him as Arhat or Jina. The common people talk among them: 'In the city two Jinas—two omniscient persons have arrived.' As for example, such a talk spreads among the people when both Lord Mahāvīra and Maṅkhaliputta Gośālaka—Gośālaka, the self-styled *Jina Tīrthaṅkara* and

14th stage of spiritual development, wherein all activity ceases (at the time of death), *leśyā* too ceases to exist, that is, soul becomes totally free from any colouration whatsoever.

According to the evidence of scriptures, activity (*yoga*) (of mind, speech and body) is the determinant condition of type-bondage (*prakṛti-bandha*) and quantity-bondage (*pradeśa-bandha*), while passion (*kaṣāya*) is the determinant condition of intensity-bondage (*anubhāva-bandha*) and duration-bondage (*sthiti-bandha*). Though *leśyā* is of the nature of transformation of activities, it becomes one with passion to such an extent that it too comes to be regarded as the condition of intensity-bondage; not only that but it comes to be regarded as of the nature of passion—of course, metaphorically or secondarily.

To explain the concept of *leśyā* (mental or spiritual colouration) which is nothing but colour-index to mental state or temperament, the following illustration is given in the scriptures.

There were six friends. They approached a *jambū*-tree to eat *jambū* fruits. One of them said, "O friends! cut down the tree from its very roots, then we shall enjoy leisurely eating of the fruits." This mental state is the black (*kṛṣṇa*) *leśyā*. The second said, "No! Brothers! Why should we cut the whole tree? Let us cut only the principal branch." This mental state is the blue (*nīla*) *leśyā*. The third said, "Why should we cut the principal branch? *Jambū* fruits are on the small branches. So let us cut them." This mental state is the grey (*kāpota*) *leśyā*. The fourth said, "This is a wrong method. Let us break only those twigs which have bunches of fruits." This mental state is the yellow (*pīta*) *leśyā*, also called *tejoleśyā*. The fifth said, "Your suggestion is also not proper. We want to eat fruits. So we should

---

founder-leader of the *Ājīvika* sect—make their stay in the city of Sāvatthī. The mendicants of the tradition of Lord Pārśva approach Lord Mahāvīra, do not salute him, and keeping some distance from him, ask him some questions. But when he gives satisfactory answers to their questions, they recognise him as an omniscient person; and having recognised him as such they devotionally salute him according to the prescribed procedure. This information is available in the *Bhagavatīsūtra* (5th *Śataka*, 9th *Uddeśa*). Similarly, in the 32nd *Uddeśa* of the 9th *Śataka* of the same *Sūtra*, there occurs a story of the elder monk Gāṅgeya, a follower of the tradition of Lord Pārśva.

The text (5th *Śataka* 9th *Uddeśa*) in point is as follows: *teṇaṁ kāleṇaṁ teṇaṁ samayeṇaṁ pāsāvaccijjā therā bhagavaṁto jeṇeva samaṇe bhagavaṁ Mahāvīre teṇeva uvāgacchanti, samaṇassa bhagavao Mahāvīrassa adūrasāmaṁte ṭhiccā evaṁ vayāsī. . . ./ tappamiti te pāsāvccījjā therā bhagavaṁtā samaṇaṁ bhagavaṁ Mahāvīraṁ paccabhijāṇaṁti—savvannū savvadarisi, . . . vaṁdaṁti namaṁsaṁti /*

pluck the fruits alone." This mental state is lotus-colour (*padma*) *leśyā*. The last said, "Brothers! Why bother? There are so many ripe fruits fallen to the ground. Let us pick them up and eat." This mental state is the white (*śukla*) *leśyā*.

The objective they want to achieve is one and the same. All want to eat *jambū* fruits. But the methods they suggest for achieving the objective differ widely. The methods suggested by them are the expressions of their internal mental states or *leśyās*.

Leśyā is of two types—*dravya-leśyā* and *bhāva-leśyā*. *Dravya-leśyā* is the material *leśyā* and *bhāva-leśyā* is its spiritual counterpart. *Dravya-leśyā*, as stated above, is of the nature of special material atoms. And *bhāva-leśyā* is the special state or transformation of soul due to passions and activities. The soul has infinitefold transformations due to the infinitefold degrees of passions. But in the scriptures, these transformations are classified, for the sake of convenience, into six main types, as shown above.

In the first three *leśyās*, there is indiscretion (*aviveka*). On the other hand, in the last three, there is discretion (*viveka*). In the first *leśyā*, indiscretion is at its highest degree. And in the last *leśyā*, discretion is at its highest degree. The intensity of indiscretion decreases more and more in the first three *leśyās* in accordance with their order of enumeration, while the intensity of discretion increases in the last three in accordance with their order of enumeration. The dense bondage of inauspicious or unwholesome *karmas* gradually decreases in the first three, while the bondage of auspicious or wholesome *karmas* gradually increases in the last three. Again, auspicious dissociation of *karmas* gradually increases in the last three *leśyās*.

Cause-Effect Relationship

Cause-effect relationship means relation of the production of an effect with its cause. Let us take an illustration to understand it.

It is a rule of the science of logic that man first knows (conceives), then desires and after that performs volitional activity.[1] Accordingly, in a potter who knows how to produce a pot, first there arises a desire to produce it, and after the desire, there takes place volitional activity. The potter who is ready to produce the pot must first conceive in his mind the form of the pot, of his choice, know how to produce it, the effect which he wants to produce, and keep constantly before his mind's eye the concep-

---

1. *jānāti, icchati, tato yatate* /

tual or ideal pot. Otherwise, he will produce something altogether different from the intended effect, that is, a bowl instead of the pot.

In the production of the effect, the pot, the agent (*kartā*) is the potter, because he, voluntarily depending upon causes and performing activity through (self-attained) sense-organs and motor-organs, produces the effect.

To produce the effect, the pot, the potter has to collect causes, because 'no effect can be produced without causes'. When we see an effect, we desire to find out and understand as to how it has come into being. And when on account of our limited experience we are not able to find out its cause, we remain contented by calling it a miracle or assigning an 'unseen' cause to it. We do not know as to what this 'unseen' is and how it works. We observe silence on these points, because we are unable to enter deep into their investigation and search. At this juncture, it is necessary to draw attention to the fact that modern science has succeeded in rationally explaining events which were wrongly regarded as miracles; it has experimentally discovered their proper causes. And it is possible that with the advancement of modern science more and more so-called miracles will be stripped of their superimposed miraculous nature and turned into ordinary events with their causes made known. When man in his search for a cause of a particular effect or event does not find satisfactory answer and fails, he regards it as a miracle and is tempted to associate it with the so-called extraordinary power (*siddhi*) of some saint or with the so-called supernatural power of some idol. In this, there predominates the element of superstition. And we cannot but accept that among people various such superstitions are current. When science will pay special attention to its branches dealing with mind and spirit as it does to those dealing with body and matter, satisfactory answers to many such unaccounted-for 'miraculous' events will be found. Almost the entire world of superstitions fades away of itself with the extension of our knowledge of the laws of nature and psyche, as surely as the mists melt before the rays of the morning sun. We should bear in mind that progress in science is not possible so long as our minds are saturated with superstitions and perverse beliefs or attitudes. It is good and proper to acknowledge our intellectual inability to find out the cause of a particular effect or event. But it is quite wrong and degrading to imagine some supernatural or miraculous power and connect the event with it, it is from such perverse practice that an unending series of superstitions originates and continues.

A potter knows that a pot can be made of clay dug out from a mine. So he brings clay, separates it from small pieces of stones, etc., mixes water with it, kneads it, and makes soft and smooth lump of it. This clay-lump itself gets transformed into the pot at the end of the activity. Hence clay is called the material cause (*upādāna-kāraṇa*) of the pot. It is also known as 'the transforming cause' (*pariṇāmi-kāraṇa*) because clay itself is transformed into the pot. Initial perceptual grasping (*avagraha*) transforms itself into perceptual cogitation (*īhā*), perceptual cogitation into perceptual judgement (*avāya*), perceptual judgement into retention or mental traces (*dhāraṇā*), and retention or metal traces into memory (*smṛti*). Thus in the series, each predecessor is the material or transforming cause of its respective immediate successor.

The potter requires means or instruments also in his activity of producing the pot. So he obtains a wheel, a staff, etc. It is because he knows that if the activity is performed by revolving the wheel with the help of the staff, it will be very easy for him to produce the pot. So he employs them. Thus the external means or instruments (as for example, a wheel, a staff, etc., in the production of a pot) that are useful in the production of an effect are called instrumental causes (*nimitta-kāraṇa*).

That which wholly enters (transforms itself into) the other is called the material cause (*upādāna-kāraṇa*) of the latter. Clay entirely enters (transforms itself into) the pot. So clay is the material cause of the pot. Threads entirely enter (transform themselves into) a piece of cloth. Therefore, threads are regarded as the material cause of the piece of cloth. Gold entirely enters (transforms itself into) a bracelet, a bangle, an ear-ring, etc. Hence gold is their material cause. And the means that are universally necessary for transforming the material cause into the effect as also directly and actively associated with the activity of producing the effect are called instrumental causes.

Thus in the production of the pot, the potter is the agent, clay is the material cause, and a staff, etc., are the instrumental causes. These three types of causes are mainly required in the production of an effect.

For the performance of the activity of producing an effect, the agent expects the ground and the open sky to sit and act with his instruments. So the ground and the sky could be regarded as the expected causes (*apekṣā-kāraṇa*). Has anybody to go somewhere to obtain the sky? No, not at all. It is present everywhere. It is true that no effect can be produced in its absence. But it is impossible for it not to exist at any place and at any time. It is omnipresent and eternal. It is present always and at all places. As its mere passive presence is expected in the activity of producing an effect, it is regarded as the expected cause. The land is not present everywhere as the sky is. Again, it is more comfort-giving than the sky. Yet from the standpoint of its easy availability and the degree of its usefulness in the activity of producing an effect, it too is regarded as the expected cause. The thing which is naturally and universally present in the activity of producing all effects and hence offers general assistance in the activity of producing all effects is called the expected cause. It is the universal common cause of all effects. It is the naturally and universally available causal condition, or is the expected external convenience naturally and universally available to the agent, etc.

The expected or common cause could also be regarded as the instrumental cause, because instrumental causes are of two types, viz., common (universal) and special. Those instrumental causes which are common causes of all effects, which serve as their causes by their mere passive presence or offer convenience to the agent, etc., by their mere passive presence are the common (universal) or expected instrumental causes. And those instrumental causes which are universally necessary in the production of a special effect and which are directly and actively associated with the activity of producing the effect are the special instrumental causes. Again, the cause without which the agent can do but which, if employed, can more or less help the activity of producing an effect is called the adventitious instrumental cause (*āgantuka nimitta-kāraṇa*).

Even an ass is useful to the potter for bringing clay. Yet, it cannot be regarded as a cause (an instrumental cause) of the order of a wheel and a staff. Such things, though useful in producing an effect, could be regarded as *anyathāsiddha*[1] (remote causes) or adventitious instrumental causes.

---

1. According to the *Nyāya-Vaiśeṣika* system of Indian philosophy, an ass, etc., are regarded as *anyathāsiddhas* (remote causes). The word '*anyathā-siddha*' really means 'a thing which is proved to be antecedent (cause) to the effect, through another (the primary or real cause) or because it accompanies another (the primary or real cause)', that is, 'a remote cause'. According to the *Nyāya-Vaiśeṣika* position, only those things which are universally necessary in the production of a particular effect and which actively and directly help complete the activity the moment immediately antecedent to the production of an effect fall under the category of the primary or real cause (the instrumental cause). All other things which are antecedent to the effect are regarded as *anyathāsiddhas* (remote causes).

When the potter undertakes an activity of producing the pot out of the material cause clay with the instruments like a wheel, a staff, etc., clay does not at once become the pot. But in this long activity, it assumes one after another different forms or transformations and it is only after passing through many different states or forms that clay becomes the pot at the end. In the different states or forms which clay assumes before the production of the pot, each preceding state is the material cause of the respective immediately succeeding state. From this long chain of causes and effects, we can understand that the development or evolution is gradual. Clay becomes the pot after having passed through many gradual states flowing towards the final effect, the pot. A flower or a fruit is the final effect of a series of effects, one leading to another in a determined order of succession. Similarly, life develops passing through various states leading to development. In the successive states which clay undergoes before the emergence of the pot, the latter one is nearer to the form of the pot than the former. And when in the last state, the minimum deficiency withholding the emergence of the pot is made good or removed, the pot at once manifests itself. Thus a series of different gradual successive forms, states or transformations of clay is absolutely necessary before and also for the production of the pot. Its contribution in the production of the effect being uncommon or unique (*asādhāraṇa*), it is called the uncommon cause (*asādhārana-kāraṇa*). Thus the uncommon cause gives us an idea of successive or gradual activity leading to the production of the final effect.

A stream of different states, gradually developing into the final effect, is nothing but a stream of successive transformations of the material cause. The final ripe fruit of the stream of the successive transformations of the material cause is the effect. So the final ripe fruit of the stream of the successive transformations of the clay-lump is the pot.

From the above exposition, it follows that if man wants to produce a particular effect, he should have the true knowledge of the effect and its means (causes)—as also he should properly know how to employ the means in the production of the effect.

Now let us think about the spiritual development of man. All good men desire to achieve spiritual progress. They know that it is only man who possesses the best ability to achieve it. And their goal is perfect non-attachment which means total extermination of all defects like attachment, etc. The soul is of the nature of knowledge. So perfect knowledge always exists there in the soul. But it is covered with the karmic veils. Hence, the great problem is as to how to remove these veils. Their removal requires great efforts. Only those persons who are desirous of liberation, have natural predilection for truth, possess knowledge conducive to spiritual progress and make vigorous spiritual efforts, achieve the goal of non-attachment. Soul becomes the supreme soul, i.e., God as soon as non-attachment is firmly established in it. Thinkers of almost all the systems of Indian philosophy recognise non-attachment as the supreme goal. The *Naiyāyika*, the *Vaiśeṣika*, the *Sāṁkhya*, the *Yoga*, the Buddhist and the Vedāntist—all declare that the supreme purpose of propounding their systems of philosophy is the attainment of the supreme spiritual goal. Though they differ on the nature of the supreme spiritual goal, that is, on the nature of the state of the non-attached supreme soul—the state which lies beyond the cycle of births and deaths and which is called final liberation (*mokṣa*)—, they all agree on the point that attainment of non-attachment is the absolutely necessary pre-condition for the attainment of the supreme spiritual good, i.e., final liberation. Again, they all maintain that the true nature of final liberation is non-attachment.

The activity which is useful as a means to the attainment of the goal of non-attachment is that of self-restraint. Self-restraint means constant efforts to remove defects like violence, etc. and to cultivate spiritual qualities like non-violence, truthfulness, etc., to remove evil mental states of anger, deceitfulness, pride, greed, etc., and to develop pure and wholesome mental states of equanimity, contentedness, kindness, friendliness, etc. All this is called good conduct.

The spiritual aspirant employs his sense-organs, motor-organs and mind in wholesome activities. He attains higher and higher stages of spiritual evolution as he cultivates more and more self-control.

The pot potentially exists in clay. Similarly, each and every soul is the Supreme Soul or God potentially. Every soul in its original nature (that is, in potentiality) is the Supreme Soul. By the employment of instruments or means, one can transform clay into the pot. Similarly, by the practice of self-control the spiritual aspirant transforms his soul into the Supreme Soul or God. For attaining the state of Godhood or Supreme Soul, what is needed is the constant progressive efforts leading to the spiritual development. Thus progressive wholesome efforts cause progressive spiritual development. The progressive spiritual development is called *guṇasthānakramāroha* in the Jaina philosophical works. We have already dealt with the fourteen stages of spiritual development. In short, the attainment of the spiritually beneficial attitude or the predilection for truth on the removal of spiritually harmful attitude or aversion to truth is the first and fundamental stage of spiritual development. After that the aspirant attains the stage of partial abstinence from violence, etc., then that of total abstinence from the same, then that of pure elevated living with great spiritual vigilance and at last that of a spiritually advanced yogic life—thus he gradually progresses on the path of spiritual development, secures higher and higher stages of spiritual development. At last this series of gradual progressive stages results in the manifestation of spiritual perfection, that is, Godhood or the state of the Supreme Soul. As all the intermediary progressive states of spiritual development result in the final attainment of spiritual perfection, they could be regarded as its uncommon (*asādhāraṇa*) cause.

In the production of an effect, the assistance of the instrumental cause is invariably required. What are the instrumental causes of the manifestation of spiritual perfection? They are right deity, right spiritual teacher and right external activity (i.e., righteous conduct). So one has to necessarily depend on them for the attainment of spiritual perfection.

The person who is absolutely free from attachment and hence has attained Godhood or the state of the Supreme Soul is right deity. He is the highest ideal worthy of being followed by all of us. We should constantly keep it before our mind with the objective that we may also ultimately become like him. By thinking about and reflecting deeply on his non-attachment, we too can attain non-attachment. This is what we feel, and there arises in us firm conviction to that effect. By keeping the company of a person full of attachment, one soils one's soul with attachment. Similarly, by keeping the company of (that is, by deeply reflecting and meditating on) the person free of attachment, one gets purified of the defilement of attachment. When in reflection or meditation we get acquainted with the nature of right deity, we realise at once that our original pure nature is also the same as that of right deity. A cub brought up among sheep realises at once its true nature of lionhood, when it sees a lion and hears its thundering roar. Similarly, man realises his original pure nature when he meditates on the nature of deity.

The right spiritual teacher has acquired spiritually right knowledge through the study of scriptures as also through his own experience. Possessed as he is of the spiritual knowledge, he acquaints us with our highest goal and takes into account our present capacity and grade while showing the path leading to that goal so that we can make gradual progress from the stage where we are. It is quite obvious that the person who is hypocrite, ostentatious, destitute of knowledge, who lacks power of discrimination and discretion, and who hankers after fame can never be the right spiritual teacher. On the other hand, one who is calm and resolute, unruffled and unagitated, peaceful and equanimous, impartial and even-minded, wise and learned, great seer and noble expounder of spiritual truths, endowed with auspicious and wholesome desire for universal welfare, saintly and friendly, an embodiment of purity and righteousness, is the right spiritual teacher. Only that person who has crossed the ocean of passions can rescue others by properly instructing as to how to cross it.[1] Such a spiritual teacher does not prescribe disciplinary practices beyond aspirant's capacity. He guides him properly on the path of spiritual progress. He does never advise us to take undue long strides or jump over several steps. On the contrary, he rightly and properly inspires us to advance steadily but firmly on the path of purification.

No man can live without activity, mental or bodily. All religious sects have devised in their own way religious activities or rituals in order to awaken in man religious sentiment or fervour. Thus the objective of rituals is to make man's life righteous. If rituals considered to be religious turn and lead man in the direction and on the path of righteousness, then they fulfil their objectives for which they are devised and meant; this is a very important point everyone should always bear in mind. We should know that to quarrel on and not to tolerate different kinds of rituals prevalent among peoples of various religious sects is the sign of ignorance. We should firmly understand that any religious activity or ritual (of any sect or religion), which includes recalling to mind and praising of good qualities of the Supreme Divinity, confession and repentance of one's faults and sins, and manifestation of the noble desire for spiritual welfare is self-purifying and self-elevating.

Human birth, cultured family and country, strong bodily structure and constitution—all these are commonly expected to achieve spiritual progress; hence they could be regarded as its expected causes. If man, though blessed with these factors making his efforts easy to achieve spiritual progress, does not employ them in achieving that objective, then he will

---

1. *svayaṁ taras tārayituṁ kṣamaḥ parān /*

wander in darkness and experience miseries. They are greatly helpful to those who sincerely desire spiritual development and make honest efforts for that. When we classify the instrumental causes into two types—primary instrumental causes and secondary instrumental causes, then the company of saints, practice of the religious activities or rituals, etc., belong to the former type, while human birth, etc., belong to the latter type.

Let me tell you an instructive story. There lived two strong and stout brāhmaṇas in the city of Mathura. They wanted to go to the town of Gokula. They decided to travel by a boat. Early night they boarded the boat. Throughout the whole night, they rowed vigorously. But at dawn, they found that the boat had not moved; it had remained there only where it had been. They wondered as to how that happened in spite of their great efforts. There arrived a wise man. He drew their attention to the fact that they had not untied the rope with which the boat was fastened to the trunk of a tree on the bank of a river.

Similarly, we are bound to this miserable worldly existence with the strong bonds of passions like anger, greed, etc. Without cutting or loosening them, we cannot free ourselves from the miserable worldly existence. There is no other way. This is the eternal truth.

Now let us recall and enumerate in brief the different types of causes required for the production of an effect.

Regarding a pot:

Agent or doer	- A potter
Effect	- A pot
Activity	- Activity performed by the potter with his skilled hands.
Material Cause	- Clay
Instrumental Cause	- A wheel, a staff, etc.
Uncommon Cause	- All the intermediary states, forms or transformations clay assumes before the emergence of a pot.
Expected Cause	- The sky, land, etc.

Regarding spiritual development:

Agent or doer	- Soul
Effect	- Godhood or the state of the Supreme Soul
Activity	- Righteous conduct
Material Cause	- Soul itself

Instrumental Cause	-	Dependence on right deity, right spiritual teacher and right activity.
Uncommon Cause	-	A series of gradually progressing intermediary states.
Expected Cause	-	Human birth, bodily strength and capacity, etc.

Time (Kāla)

Time is one of the six substances recognised in the Jaina philosophy.

The following aphorism of the *Tattvārthasūtra* mentions the functions of Time.

vartanā pāriṇāmaḥ kriyā paratvāparatve ca kālasya/ V.22

It means: Incessant minute imperceptible change, perceptible transformation, activity, anteriority-posteriority—these are functions of time.

Time assists substances to undergo by their own nature incessant minute imperceptible changes constituting their own modes, that is, to exist in this manner, to assume transformations or modes like oldness, newness etc., to undertake movements from one place to another or activities of limbs, and to become younger or older.

When rice is cooked on fire, it becomes cooked rice after a long process. Rice does not at once become cooked rice. But every moment rice undergoes minute imperceptible changes which ultimately result in the perceptible gross change or transformation. Without the incessant minute imperceptible changes, there cannot take place the perceptible gross change. The incessant minute imperceptible changes that continuously go on in rice take place with the assistance of time. Thus time is the auxiliary or occasioning cause of all the changes that substances undergo.

Incessant imperceptible minute change, etc., are the functions of the substances themselves, but Time is only the auxiliary cause which helps substances to perform them.

Among ancient Jaina philosophers there was a difference of opinion regarding Time substance. According to one view, Time is not an independent substance. Time is nothing but modes or changes of substances. In other words, Time is identical with change and nothing over and above change. The minute changes and gross changes are merely the modes of substances.

Upādhyāya Vinayavijayajī in the third part of his voluminous work

Lokaprakāśa presents this view in the following verses.

evaṁ ca dravyaparyāyā evāmī vartanādayaḥ /
sampannāḥ 'kāla'śabdena vyapadeśyā bhavanti ye //
paryāyāś ca kathañcit syur dravyābhinnās tataś ca te /
'dravya'nāmnāpi kathyante jātu proktaṁ yad āgame //

Verses 9-10 occurring in the beginning.

The verses state: The incessant minute imperceptible change, perceptible gross change, etc. (enumerated in the above-mentioned aphorism of the *Tattvārthasūtra*) which are designated 'Time' are nothing but modes of sentient and insentient substances. And as there obtains a relation of identity between a substance and its modes from a certain standpoint, these modes are given the name 'substance' ('sentient substance' and 'insentient substance'). The *Āgama* text declares to this effect. The following is the passage in point.

"kim idaṁ bhaṁte! kālo tti pavuccai?"
"Goyamā! jīvā ceva ajīvā ceva tti."—Bhagavatī-Sūtra
"O Lord! What is it that is called Time?"
"O Gautama! Time is nothing but *jīva-dravyas* (sentient substances) and *ajīva-dravyas* (insentient substances)."

Let us elucidate the point. As already stated, according to the present view, Time is identical with changes or modes of substances. And the Jainas being upholders of the theory of non-absolutism (*syādvāda*), believe that there obtains a relation of identity-cum-difference between a substance and its modes. In other words, according to them modes are in a way identical with the substance. Hence, the name 'substance' (*'dravya'*) is secondarily applied to them also. As a result, Time which is nothing but modes of substances is also called substance. The statement, occurring in the *Bhagavatīsūtra*, that *jīva* and *ajīva* substances themselves are called Time means that modes of these substances are called Time; Time is nothing over and above these modes.

Conventional divisions of Time like *samaya, āvalikā, muhūrta*, a day, etc., as also states like oldness-newness, anteriority-posteriority, etc., which are shown as functions or effects of Time are all modes or changes of substances. An ultimate indivisible—even mentally indivisible—mode of a sentient or an insentient substance is called '*samaya*'. It is the most subtle mode of a substance. Innumerable *samayas* form an *āvalikā*. 16,777,216 *āvalikās* make a *muhūrta*, which is of forty-eight minutes of modern time. Thirty *muhūrtas* make a day (i.e., one day-and-night). Thirty days form a month and twelve months a year, so on and so forth. Of two things, that one which is produced earlier is old and the other is new. Similarly, of two living beings, one who is born earlier is old and the other is young. All the conventional divisions of time like *samaya, āvalikā, muhūrta, ahorātra, pakṣa* (fortnight), *māsa* (month), *varṣa* (year), etc., as also states like old-new, young-old, etc., are nothing but modes of things (i.e., sentient and insentient substances). A mode of a substance is change. A substance incessantly goes on changing into its proper modes—subtle or gross transformations. Thus a series of modes of a substance is Time. So the upholders of this view do not see any necessity for the acceptance of an independent Time-substance.

There is another view. According to it, Time is an independent substance. Upholders of this view argue as follows: The Jainas should accept Time as an independent substance. Though the sentient and insentient substances are regarded capable by nature to move and to rest, yet the Jainas have posited two independent substances, viz., *dharma* and *adharma* serving as the media or auxiliary causes of motion and inertia respectively. Similarly, though the five substances are by nature capable of transforming themselves into their proper modes, some auxiliary or general cause like Time should be posited to help them in their transformations. If they reject Time as an independent substance, they have no right to posit *dharma* and *adharma*. The case of Time is on par with that of *dharma* and *adharma*.

Moreover, according to this view Time discharges its functions with the help of the movements of heavenly luminaries, viz., the sun, the moon, constellations, etc. As the movements of heavenly luminaries are not available outside human region (i.e., the region inhabited by human beings), Time is confined to this portion of the cosmic space. Study the following verse from the *Jyotiṣkaraṇḍaka*.

logāṇubhāvajaṇiya joisacakka bhaṇati arihaṃtā /
savve kālavisesā jassa gaivisesanippannā //

The verse means that all the divisions of time like solar month, lunar month, etc., arise on account of particular movements of the heavenly luminaries, viz., the sun, the moon, the constellations, etc.

The *Viśeṣāvaśyaka-bhāṣya* in its verses 2027, 2032, 2033 and 2035 says: "Existence through the states of newness-oldness, etc., that is, eternal existence through constant change (*vartanāpariṇāma*), movement from one place to another (*kriyā*), anteriority-posteriority of the form of being old and young (*paratvāparatva*)—these are the logical reasons to prove the existence of Time, because they are the effects of Time. Time is nothing but these modes of the form of *vartanā*, etc., which substances assume or undergo. And from the standpoint of mutual identity of substance and its modes, the substance whose modes they are is also called Time. It is because in the scriptures the sentient and insentient substances themselves are called *samaya, āvallkā,* etc. These *samaya,* etc., are not different from substances.

That Time which is manifested as *samaya, āvalikā, muhūrta, ahorātra* (a day-and-night), *pakṣa* (a fortnight), *māsa* (a month), *varṣa* (a year), etc., in the human region through the movements of heavenly luminaries like the sun, the moon, planets, stars and constellations is called '*addhāsamaya*'. That much region which is lighted by the rays of the moving sun is called day. The opposite is called night. The indivisible unit of a day is called *samaya.* Innumerable such *samaya*s make an *āvalikā*, and so many *āvalikā*s make a *muhūrta,* so on and so forth."

The arguments put forward to establish Time as an independent substance are as follows: In the absence of Time as the condition governing sequence of serial effects, a sprout, a bud, a flower and a fruit—all would emerge and exist simultaneously. Thus but for Time-substance, there would result chaos, all actions and effects being simultaneous. How can there be different bodily states, viz., childhood, youth and old age, without Time substance? How can different manifestations which we notice in six different seasons be possible without Time substance? The fact that a mango tree does not bear mango fruits in other seasons even though all the causal conditions except the proper season are present proves the existence of an independent Time substance. Without Time substance, how can we have divisions of Time, viz., past, present and future? Divisions imply something of which they are divisions. Early, late, simultaneous, to-day, tomorrow, yesterday, month, year, age (*yuga*)—all this establishes the existence of Time substance. Scriptures too mention Time as the sixth substance. The text in point is as follows: "*kai ṇaṃ bhaṁte! davvā pannattā? Goyamā! ccha davvā pannattā / taṁ jahā—dhammatthikāe, adhammatthikāe, āgāsatthikāe, puggalatthikāe, jīvatthikāe, addhāsamaye ya /*"

"How many, O Lord, are the substances propounded?"

"Six substances, O Gautama, are propounded. They are as follows: *dharmāstikāya* (Medium of motion), *adharmāstikāya* (Medium of rest), *ākāśāstikāya* (Space) *pudgalāstikāya* (Matter), *jīvāstikāya* (Soul) and *addhāsamaya* (Time)..

In this scriptural passage at the end, the term '*addhāsamaya*' is used for Time. May be this term does not denote the real Time. On the contrary, it is quite possible that it denotes merely the conventional time of the form of *samaya, āvalikā,* etc. This is suggested by the description of time, we meet with in the *Viśeṣāvaśyaka-bhāṣya.* Its verses 2027, 2032 and 2033 describe time of the form of modes or changes of various types (*vartanā,* etc.) and declare that it is manifested through the movements of the sun, the moon, etc. Even those who do not accept time as an independent substance regard *addhāsamaya* of the above description as conventional time; in reality, for them time is essentially mere modes or changes of the sentient and insentient substances.

There is yet another view which accepts Time as an independent substance and yet is different from the one just dealt with. According to this view, time is atomic. There are innumerable time-atoms. They are confined to cosmic space only. They are not present in the space beyond cosmos. They are motionless. Hence they eternally remain there only where they are. So each time atom eternally occupies the same space-point of the cosmic space. Each time-atom occupies a separate space-point. This is the reason why they do not combine to form molecules as the material atoms do. Hence they have no spatial extension. Only those substances that have spatial extension are called *astikāya.* So Time is not counted among *astikāyas*. Time-atoms go on assuming different modes all the while without any interruption. The smallest measurable mode of time-atom is called *samaya.* Each time-atom has infinite such modes. These modes of time-atoms serve as an auxiliary cause of the modes of other substances. And all the states like oldness-newness, anteriority-posteriority, etc., arise depending upon the *samaya*[1]-modes of time-atoms.

---

1. *Samaya* is defined as the time taken by a material atom to traverse one space-point by slow movement.
Compare this Jaina conception of *samaya* with the Yoga conception of *kṣaṇa.* Study the following passage from the *Vyāsabhāṣya* on the 52nd aphorism of the third chapter of the *Yogasūtra* of Patañjali: *yathā'pakarṣaparyantaṁ dravyaṁ paramāṇuḥ, evaṁ paramāpakarṣaparyantaḥ kālaḥ kṣaṇaḥ / yāvatā vā samayena calitaḥ paramāṇuḥ pūrvadeśaṁ jahyād uttaradeśam upasampadyeta sa kālaḥ kṣaṇaḥ /* Meaning: Just as an atom is the ultimate minutest unit of a substance even so a *kṣaṇa* is the ultimate minutest unit of time. Or, *kṣaṇa* is that much time which is taken by a moving atom to reach the space-point immediately next to the one it leaves.

According to this view, *pariṇāma*, etc., which are enumerated after *vartanā* in the above-mentioned aphorism of the *Tattvārthasūtra* are nothing but special forms of *vartanā* itself. So they can easily be included in *vartanā*. Yet they are separately mentioned in the aphorism. Why? It is because the author wants to show that there are two types of time—real time and conventional time. Real time is of the form of *vartanā*, while conventional time is of the form of *pariṇāma, kriyā, paratvāparatva*. Again, '*samaya*', '*āvalikā*', etc., which are used in our everyday dealings and arise depending upon the movements of the sun, etc., are also forms of conventional time.

This view of atomic time substance is found in the Digambara works. It is not acceptable to the Śvetāmbara thinkers. But Ācārya Hemacandra, an eminent Śvetāmbara master, accepts this view. In his *Yogaśāstra*, he writes:

lokākāśapradeśasthā bhinnāḥ kālāṇavas tu ye /
bhāvānāṁ parivartāya mukhyaḥ kālaḥ sa ucyate //52//
jyotiḥśāstre yasya mānam ucyate samayādikam /
sa vyāvahārikaḥ kālaḥ kālavedibhir abhimataḥ //53//

The meaning of the verses is: Time-atoms are present on different space-points of cosmic space. They serve as an auxiliary cause in the production of changes in substances. They are real time. And *samaya, āvalikā*, etc. whose measures are given in Astronomy are forms of conventional time.

Regarding these differences of opinion, Pt. Śrī Sukhlālji, an erudite and eminent scholar, thinks that from the definitive standpoint the view which regards time as nothing but modes of substances seems to be logically sound and essentially right. Even in cosmic space outside human region the states or modes like newness, oldness do arise in substances, but it is maintained that those states or modes do not require time substance as an auxiliary cause for their production. Similarly, we can do without the conception of the independent time substance even in the human region. Thus it is obvious that the view of the independent time substance is based simply on worldly convention. And reflecting on the atomic nature of time substance, we feel that if each and every material atom is viewed as time-atom, then there is no need of positing an independent atomic time substance. Moreover, if an independent atomic time substance is accepted, then there arises a question as to why its molecular form is not accepted; time-atoms also should form molecules as the material atoms do. Again, time substance is posited to account for changes in other substances; but what would account for changes in time substance itself? If it be said that modifications of time substance are natural and hence require no causal condition, then the same logic should be applied to explain modifications of other substances. If some other auxiliary cause is posited to explain changes in time substance, then it will involve infinite regress. So it should be maintained that changes or modifications of substances are natural and hence do not require independent time substance as an auxiliary cause to generate them.

Regarding time, two main views are found in the Vedic systems of Indian philosophy. Time in the *Nyāya-Vaiśeṣika* system is regarded as an independent all-pervading substance existing by itself. The *Bhāṣya* on the *Yogasūtra* (III. 52) of Patañjali deals with time. The author of the *Bhāṣya* maintains that time is not an independent entity. As already seen, the unit of time (*kṣaṇa*) is regarded as time taken by a material atom to traverse its own unit of space, it has no existence separate from material atoms and their movements. A minute, an hour, etc., are nothing but mentally constructed short or long series of *kṣaṇas*. *Sāṁkhya* and *Yoga* are companion systems. So the *Sāṁkhya* view of time cannot be different from the *Yoga* view of the same. The tendency of the *Vedānta* being what it is, it can never regard time as real.

The view upheld by the systems like *Nyāya, Vaiśeṣika* is based on empirical standpoint, while the view upheld by the systems like *Yoga* is based on definitive or transcendental standpoint.

Determinism (Niyativāda)

Determinism is also called fatalism or doctrine of Destiny. Ignorant, coward and weak men believe that nothing is in the hands of man. Whatever is ordained or predetermined by Fate is sure to happen. Teachings of human efforts, moral responsibility and freedom of will are false. The rich who indulge in evil activities and employ unfair means to accumulate wealth become impudent and shameless, taking shelter under predeterminism. They say that they are not free to do what they do. They are not at fault. They are not responsible for what they do. Whatever is destined or determined can never be altered or averted. Man cannot be an effective agent. What man does or experiences is predetermined.

Determinism is an enemy of self-reform and self-development. It is a silken robe under which the wicked conceal their sins, the rich their legally and morally forbidden loot and the coward their cowardice. It is said that fatalism gives man peace. But, in fact, it is no peace; it is dullness, idleness, degradation and degeneration of life. If a man's soul after death transmigrates to the vegetable kingdom, its sensitivity will greatly decrease, it will not be sensitive to the questions of its life and death as also to the moral problems, namely, what is to be done and what is not to be done. Can we, on that account, say that man attains peace, if he is born as a tree in the next birth? Can this dullness or insensitivity be called peace? A man loses his sensitivity and power of discretion by drinking liquor; can we describe his loss of sensitivity and of power of discretion as peace? Is it good for man to forget his responsibilities and to experience satisfaction and peace even in his evil and degraded life? No, not at all. It is his fall and degeneration. It is quite obvious that the preaching of fatalism or determinism leads masses astray; it is unwholesome, harmful and degrading.

In the days of Lord Mahāvīra, there was a rich potter named Saddālaputta.[1] He believed in the doctrine of determinism, propounded by Maṅkhaliputta Gośālaka, a leader of the *Ājīvika* sect. Lord Mahāvīra wanted to persuade him that the doctrine of determinism is false. With this object in view, Lord Mahāvīra held a dialogue with him. It is as follows:

> Mahāvīra: "O Saddālaputta! Are the potter's wares made by dint of exertion or not?"
>
> Saddālaputta: "They are made by force of Fate. All things are predetermined. Their states are fixed. Their production and destruction require neither human efforts nor the operation of causes."
>
> Mahāvīra: "O Saddālaputta! Suppose someone breaks your pots or makes overtures to your wife. Will you hold him responsible for his misdeeds? Or, will you consider them to be ordained by Fate and hence remain calm?"
>
> Saddālaputta: "I shall berate and strike the culprit, or even kill him. How can I remain calm?"
>
> Mahāvīra: "This means that you hold that man responsible for his acts. If the acts are fixed by Fate or Destiny, then why should you hold him

1. There occurs in the *Uvāsagadasāo-sutta* life-stories of Lord Mahāvīra's ten lay-devotees. Among them there is a story of a potter named Saddālaputta. The account given here is from it.

responsible for the acts? Is it so that man accepts determinism solely to disown his responsibility for his evil deeds and rejects it solely to revenge upon others for their offences? O Saddālaputta! Is the doctrine of determinism conducive to progress? Can it bring and establish order in the world?"

Lord Mahāvīra's persuasion and explanation enlightened Saddālaputta who declared: "O Lord! by your grace I realised the truth. Now I clearly see that determinism leads to idleness, dullness and hypocrisy; it is escapism; it is an excuse for escaping from the responsibility of one's own sinful and degenerated life. By accepting it one deceives oneself and others."

Mahāvīra: O Saddālaputta! One may deceive oneself. One may deceive even others. But one can never deceive the well-established order based on causation."

Determinism has its own place. The objection is to the view which holds determinism as the only cause, rejecting all other causal factors. As a matter of fact, Time, Nature, Fate, Past Action and Human Effort—all these factors contribute more or less according to their capacity to the production of an effect. So all of them should be accepted as the necessary causal factors in the production of an effect, giving them their proper place in the production.[1] This is the cogent and logical position. Ācārya Siddhasena in his *Sanmati* says:

kālo sahāvo niyaī puvvakayaṁ purisaṁ kāraṇegaṁtā /
micchattaṁ te ceva ya samāsao honti sammattaṁ // III. 53

Meaning: Of the five, viz., Time, Nature, Fate, Past Action and Human Effort to favour one alone is the wrong view, but to accept all of them giving them their due place is the right view.

Let us reflect further on the subject.

All substances have their intrinsic original capacities fixed. A soul can never be without consciousness. And it can never have physical qualities like colour, etc. Similarly, matter can never be without physical qualities, and it can never have consciousness. Thus a soul can never transform itself into matter, nor can matter ever transform itself into soul. This is fixed and absolutely unalterable. Conscious or human effort can do

1. A detailed exposition is there in the fifth chapter on *Syādvāda*.

nothing in this matter. It càn never turn a man into a stone, nor a stone into a man. Matter can assume physical modes or transformations alone. And soul can assume spiritual modes or transformations alone. Each substance undergoes incessant change. It has its own continuum of instantaneous changes or modes, some perceptible and others imperceptible. Here we shall talk of perceptible modes. Though possible modes which matter can assume are fixed, it is not fixed as to which mode it will assume at a particular time. It depends on the availability of the required totality of causal factors. A lump of clay has the capacity to manifest many modes, viz., a bowl, a pot, a cup, a pan, a plate, etc. But it cannot manifest all these modes simultaneously. It manifests that mode alone, whose necessary instrumental causes are available. This means that the totality of causal factors for the production of a particular mode (effect) is also fixed. Human effort is required to bring together the necessary instrumental causes of the totality. We cannot say that it is fixed for a lump of clay to transform itself into a pot at a particular time. It is not fixed. What is fixed is that a lump of clay necessarily transforms itself into a pot, when all the necessary instrumental causes are present. If the instrumetal causes necessary for the production of a bowl were present, then the bowl would have been produced from a lump of clay. Thus the cause-effect relation is fixed. The nature of the present totality of causal conditions determines the nature of the mode to be produced the next moment. Some effects require human effort, others do not. In other words, causation is of two types, one natural and the other involving human agency. The circumstances or instrumental causes determine the nature of the mode or transformation of a substance. Again, material atoms can transform themselves into a pot, but not all at once. When they get favourable totality of causal conditions, they first transform themselves into molecules, then into clay, then into a lump of clay; and when this lump of clay gets favourable totality of causal conditions, it transforms itself into a pot. There are so many capacities in matter. It has a capacity to transform itself into a pot, it has a capacity to transform itself into a diamond, it has a capacity to transform itself into gold, so on and so forth. But that capacity which is proximate to actual manifestation, manifests itself on the presence of the favourable totality of causal conditions. The proximate capacity in sand is to get transformed into glass, that in coal is to get transformed into a diamond; so sand becomes glass on the presence of the necessary totality of causal conditions, coal becomes a diamond on the presence of the necessary totality of causal conditions. The totality of causal conditions that produces glass is different from the one that produces diamond. We all know that filthy manure assumes an attractive mode, when it comes in contact with appropriate instrumental causes. Even poison turns into nectar when it comes in contact with appropriate instrumental causes. And even nectar turns into poison when it comes in contact with appropriate instumental causes. Though a substance has capacity to transform itself into many modes, it transforms itself into that mode alone for which the instrumental causes are available to it. If a teacher makes good efforts for a dull pupil the latter's intellect and cognitive faculty can develop. Poisonhood is potentially present in nectar, and nectarhood is potentially present in poison. It is only proper instrumental causes that make them actual or bring them out. Even a dull student has knowledge, but it is lying dormant in him. When proper instrumental causes operate on him it manifests itself. A substance manifests that mode alone which it has capacity to manifest on the presence of proper instrumental causes. Sand is matter. Oil too is matter. But sand cannot manifest or yield oil. The substance which does not have the proximate capacity to manifest a particular mode cannot manifest it, in spite of the presence of necessary instrumental causes. Atoms constituting sand must first get disintegrated and be free, and then form molecules of a special kind, then only they yield or manifest oil. The number of modes potentially present in a substance is fixed. They do not become actual or manifest simultaneously, because for manifestation they require different sets of instrumental causes. The substance manifests that mode alone, which is proper to be produced by the present necessary instrumental causes. Thus the possible modes of a substance are fixed. Of them, which will be manifested when is not fixed. The manifestation of modes depends on the presence of their respective sets of instrumental causes.

If all events, all mental states and all activities are predetermined, then there is no need of paying any heed to human efforts, activities, self-discipline, good works, etc. In that case, all differences of vitrue and vice, merit and demerit, good and evil, violence and non-violence, etc., have no meaning whatsoever; they stand rejected and refuted; all human efforts and activities turn out to be absolutely ineffectual; all moral responsibility is proved to be illusory; man is not free; he does what is destined for him to do. One who kills a man by stabbing him with a dagger does not incur the sin or demerit of violence, because the entire event with all its characters and details was predetermined. It was predetermined as to who was to kill whom, how and when. Again, it was also fixed that such and such mental states would arise in the mind of the murderer at that destined time. This being the case, what is the fault or sin of the murderer? He is not responsible for the act. A man saves a saint caught in the flames of fire by extinguishing fire and giving proper treatment. Another person saves a saint dying of hunger by giving him food. What merit do they earn by their good activities? They earn neither merit nor demerit. They cannot take credit of their good works. It is because they are predetermined. It was predetermined that the former would go there, extinguish fire, save the saint and the latter would approach the hungry, give him food, etc. Each and every event is predetermined to happen when it happens. What did the saviour do? As a matter of fact he did nothing. He is simply the instrument of Fate or Destiny. Alas! what a terrible doctrine!

In the doctrine of determinism, is there anything like carving out of one's own future? If man's future is fixed, there will remain no scope for him to plan for his future and it will be futile to talk of effectual human efforts. From determinism follows that nothing is achieved by human effort. The doctrine of determinism tramples to death under its hard heel ideas of efficacious human efforts, free-will, morality, self-development, spiritual discipline, etc. In it, there is no possibility of improving one's destiny by good works, self-control, righteous conduct, etc. For mankind, doctrine of determinism is unending pithy ghastly darkness; it is a terrific curse.

We should understand that instrumental causes are efficient in their own way and field. Even before its production or manifestation, an effect exists in its substance—material cause—in a potential form. Oil exists in the sesamum, a statue in a stone, curd in milk. The operation of instrumental causes renders that manifest which was formerly in an unmanifested condition. Substance or material cause requires the help of instrumental causes to manifest its proper modes existing in it potentially. This brings out the utmost importance and necessity of the instrumental causes in the production or manifestation of an effect. Worshipping images of God, studying scriptures, approaching a spiritual teacher and listening to his discourses, residing in a pure, holy and peaceful place, taking wholesome food and drink—who does not recognise the usefulness of all these factors in making life more and more elevated, noble and righteous? If anyone who accepts all these factors as useful and also puts them into practice does not recognise the proper efficiency of instrumental causes, then his belief or speech is to be regarded as contradictory to his practice.

Pride of Caste and Family

Ācārya Hemacandra in his *Yogaśāstra* declares: A person who prides himself upon his caste, family, gain, wealth, power, figure, austerity and knowledge gets, as a result of his pride, these things of inferior kind or grade in the next birth.[1] As for example, a man who prides himself as belonging to a high family should invariably enter into lower existence in his next birth.

Material wealth is fickle and ephemeral. To take pride in it, betrays lack of wisdom and understanding. One should not be proud of one's wealth of knowledge. Its fulfilment consists in the cultivation of love and compassion for the ignorant as also in the spread of knowledge to make their lives enlightened and noble. Greatness of caste and family, or highness of those regarded as high consists in having good human qualities as also in behaving affectionately with others regarded as low, and not in priding oneself on one's 'greatness' or in behaving rudely and meanly with others considering them to be low concerning their caste and family. Highness or lowness, greatness or otherwise does not depend on birth, but it depends on merit or demerit. Real greatness depends on good qualities and good works. Where there is real greatness, there is no scope whatsoever for the mental defects like pride. Pride of good qualities dulls and darkens them. It obstructs progress and robs life of its natural joy and sweetness. There is not a single thing which we should be proud of. One who behaves rudely and arrogantly considering oneself to be 'high' causes one's steep fall from great heights. Highness consists in the cultivation of good qualities. There can never be greatness without culture. Where there is light of culture, there does not arise feeling of discrimination of high and low; on the contrary, there prevails compassion, friendliness and love in the behaviour with persons regarded as belonging to the low stratum of society. Right attitude or view consists in understanding that highness depends on good qualities and good works and lowness on bad qualities and bad works. On the other hand, it is wrong attitude or view

---

1. *jāti-lābha-kulaiśvarya-bala-rūpa-tapaḥ-śrutaiḥ /*
kurvan madaṁ punas tāni hīnāni labhate janaḥ // IV. 13

to regard man as high or low on the basis of his birth.

For the sustenance and maintenance of the society, its members are required to undertake different professions or occupations. The professional activities were broadly classified into four divisions and the members who undertook them formed four classes accordingly. These four classes were given the names brāhmaṇa, kṣatriya, vaiśya and śūdra.

The brāhmaṇa class corresponded to the intellectual class, the kṣatriya class to the warrior class, the vaiśya class to the mercantile class and the śūdra class to the labour class. Those who devoted themselves to teaching and learning were called brāhmaṇas. They spread knowledge among the people, preserved and maintained the cultural and intellectual heritage come down to them through tradition, guided the people in matters religious and spiritual and the rulers in the state policies. They were also the repository of scriptural knowledge. Those who took to the profession of protecting the country were called kṣatriyas. It was their business to fight in defence of the country. It was also their duty to curb evil activities harmful to society and thereby to maintain its health. The kṣatriya class included rulers and warriors. Those who mainly engaged themselves in agriculture, trade and business were called vaiśyas. Their duty was to produce and supply necessities of life. Thus the vaiśya class included the cultivators of soil, merchants and artisans. And those who served the society in some other way by manual labour were called śūdras.

This was the original caste system. There was the functional basis underlying it. The groups or castes were almost always functional. There was considerable freedom to people to choose their professions and occupations according to their aptitude, liking and capacity, and thereby to choose their caste or class. Thus the system was very flexible. Capacity, character and occupation were the determinants of castes. Birth was not the determinant factor. When birth came to be regarded as the sole determinant factor to the disregard of capacity, character and occupation, the system became rigid and perverted, and the society degenerate, weak and degraded. Caste should not depend on birth. It should depend on merit.

All the four types of activities are necessary for happiness, comforts and progress of society. In the absence of any of them, society cannot sustain itself, nor can it make any progress. So we should not regard one man high and another low on the basis of their professions. Profession is not the measure of man and does not determine him as high or low. For determining highness or lowness of man, we should use another standard. It is character. Whoever a person may be or whatever profession he may follow, he should be regarded as high or low on the basis of his good or bad qualities. Again, his highness or lowness depends on the mind with which he performs his activities. If he performs his special professional activities honestly and wholeheartedly, he is high or great. On the other hand, if he performs them without sincerity, he is low. If a person who has accepted the profession of a brāhmaṇa (i.e., teacher) is of bad character or is not sincere and honest in the performance of his duties, he is low. On the other hand, if a person who follows the profession of a śūdra (a labourer) is of good character and performs the work alloted to him honestly and sincerely, he is high. One's being high or low depends neither on birth nor on occupation, but on character.

As a matter of fact, in man there should be confluence of all the four elements, viz., brāhmaṇahood, kṣatriyahood, vaiśyahood and śūdrahood. It is because in his daily life four things, viz., study or devotion to learning, valour or bravery, mind to develop business or agriculture, etc., and desire to serve others are more or less necessary. When all the four are present in him in considerable degree and proportion, he attains real manhood. For the all-round development of man, all these four elements are necessary.

Head, hands, belly and feet are parts of the body. Of them, which is high and which is low? Are feet less useful? How can we rate śūdras who are compared to feet low? How can we regard them as less important? If all limbs cooperate with each other, they can remain alive and be happy. And if they quarrel with each other, are jealous of each other and get offended with each other, then they are doomed to death. Similarly, if the four castes, viz., the brāhmaṇa, etc., live together amiably and affectionately, they will progress and prosper. But if they become arrogant and as a result despise, hate and run down each other, then their fall and degeneration are certain.

Let us reflect further on the subject.

Highness and lowness are of two types, viz., natural and imagined by the human society. First, we shall deal with highness and lowness imagined by the human society.

It is quite understandable that birth in the miserable circumstances and environment is the result of the rise of the unwholesome *karmas*, while birth in the pleasant circumstances and environment is the result of the rise of the wholesome *karmas*. Thus birth in the diseased house and in the intellectually perverse and dull, or financially poor and destitute family is the result of the rise of unwholesome *karmas*. Similarly, birth in the country ruled by bad government can also be regarded as the result of the rise of the unwholesome *karmas*. Again, birth in the degenerate society with harmul social structure can also be considered to be the result of the rise of the unwhoesome *karmas*. After having born in the diseased condition of the house, when man grows up he may improve and make it conducive to health; but if at all it happens so, it happens after a long time. Similarly, after having born in a poor and destitute family, when man grows up he may improve its financial position; but if at all it happens so, it happens after a long time. Thus to be born in miserable circumstances and environment and to experience pains and miseries on that account in spite of one's sincere efforts, till the circumstances improve and become favourable, is the result of the rise of the unwholesome *karmas*.

Here our question pertains to the social structure. Of several defective social structures, one is the degenerate caste system in which a person is held high or low on the basis of his birth and occupation. One who is born in the caste imagined to be low by society ridden with such a debase social structure has to be the victim of the degenerate social structure and has to endure the tortures of contempt and insulting and hurting looks from persons considering their caste to be high. This type of unjust humiliations and sufferings are due to the social structure not natural but imagined by society. The revolutionary and reformist brave men may try to reform and improve society; and due to their continuous persistent efforts through ages, there may take place reforms in the social structure and there may come about change in the rigid attitude of men, which views a person as high or low on the basis of his birth and occupation; and as a result of this, men may not have to experience humiliations and insults which are due to discrimination of high and low concerning castes—the discrimination imagined by the society. But so long as there is no proper spread and acceptance of such reforms, those who are born in the so-called 'low' caste have to suffer humiliation and insult in spite of their best efforts, and the *karma* which causes this experience of humiliations and insults is called '*nīcagotra-karma*' (= low status determining *karma*).

As stated above, there may dawn an age when the social structure may get reformed and improved, the differences of high and low imagined on the basis of birth and occupation may totally disappear. At that time also, the *gotra-karma* (the status determining *karma*) will have its place. In other words, even in those days the *gotra-karma* will function and give its proper fruits. Then it will account for the difference of high and low status governed by other factors. At that time we shall have to posit some *karma* to account for one's birth in cultured, civilised and noble family or in uncultured, uncivilised and wicked family. These conditions or circumstances are the result of *uccagotra* (high status) and *nīcagotra* (low status) *karmas* respectively. This type of highness or lowness is natural.

The Jaina scriptures declare that even in a person born in a low family in the present age, there is, in fact, rise of high status determining *karma* (*uccagotra-karma*), if he is endowed with right attitude or love for truth, follows rules of conduct and observes vows. In other words, the Jaina scriptures teach that whatever caste, family or lineage man may belong to, he does have the rise of *uccagotra-karma*—and not of *nīcagotra-karma*—if he is endowed with good qualities of attitude and character. The Jaina scriptures have described with highly respectful terms and thereby honoured those who, though belonging to the lowest caste called cāṇḍāla, were possessed of excellent character or conduct.

Knowledge-Devotion-Action

We see that theism or doctrine of God is useful in achieving purity of mind, in building good character, in gaining self-developing inspiration and in making progress on the path of righteousness. Similarly, it is established by experience that the doctrine of *karma* (moral causation) is useful in keeping mental equanimity in good and bad times and in receiving urge from within for performing good acts. True devotee of God develops pure devotion to God and thereby elevates his character. Similarly, a convinced believer in the law of moral causation (*karma*) does never become arrogant in the days of his happiness and good fortune, nor does he become downcast and depressed in the days of his miseries and misfortune. But he remains calm and composed and maintains balance of mind at all times—favourable and adverse, because he knows that all the circumstances and situations that arise in man's life are but plays of *karma*. He is convinced that by force of good works, man can overcome difficulties and remove miseries as also that he can make his life more and more happy by advancing on the path of righteousness. This inspires him to make sincere efforts for making his life lofty. In short, doctrine of moral causation inspires optimism and makes man the master of his own destiny. Theism and doctrine of moral causation are great doctrines. They are not in any way connected with inactivity. Certainly, they do not teach lessons of inactivity. But on the contrary, they teach man to remain always engaged in good works and to perform his duties well. Not only that but they provide man with all the idea-l ingredients necessary for making him active in true sense. Those who work with altruistic and sublime motives, without being swayed by the ordinary passions and impulses, are active in true sense. Doctrine of *karma* has the message for man that he can attain fortune—great fortune—by good works. And theism has the message for him that he can become a man of good character depending on God or that through righteous good conduct he can attain God. Both these doctrines are efficient to remove gloom and depression and pessimism from man's life, to give him solace, to make him contented and unagitated, and to inspire him to live a lofty, noble and righteous life.

Fate or destiny is nothing but the collective force (*karma*) generated by one's own actions performed in past lives. By his own efforts, man creates his own destiny or *karma.* He is the master of his own destiny or *karma.* By his good actions in the present life, he creates his good destiny or *karmas*, while by his evil actions in the present life, he creates his bad destiny or *karma.* It is in his own hands to shape his own good or bad destiny and consequently to experience their good or bad fruits. Man is the architect of his fortune. This is the only reason why good men desirous of happiness and prosperity tread the path of righteousness and purity with zeal. If a person while enjoying riches attained on account of his good *karma* (destiny) becomes depraved, arrogant, infatuated and thoughtless, then he binds new bad *karmas* for the future—that is, creates bad destiny—and his present enjoyment of happiness remains confined only to the period which ends with the end of the present rise of the concerned *karmas*. So the doctrine of *karma* rightly teaches us that just as one should experience the bad fruits of bad *karmas* with equanimity and placidity, even so one should experience the good fruits of good *karmas* with the same equanimity and placidity.

As stated above, doctrine of *karma* inspires man to live righteously; and tendency to live righteously develops and is nourished by surrender and devotion to God. There is not such God as would directly alter, create or destroy man's *karma* (destiny). But it is certain that his surrender and devotion to God do foster his love and practice of religion, they (=love and practice of religion) influence his *karma* (destiny) in accordance with their intensity and thereby can alter his *karma*, transform the bad into the good and almost destroy it. No *karma* (destiny) lasts for ever. On the expiry of its time-limit it is destroyed and with its end ends its fruition. This is the reason why the wise remain continuously engaged in the activity of creating good destiny in order to perpetuate for ever their good state. (And activity of creating good destiny is nothing but righteous living.) By doing so man makes himself permanently happy and at the same time attains higher and higher stages of spiritual development and becomes more and more spiritually sublime and elevated. In the auspicious stream of life becoming spiritually richer and richer, there arises an unprecedented great opportune moment when man attains a state leading to the highest peak of spiritual evolution and consequently attains liberation lying beyond the duality of good and evil.

Those who practise spiritual discipline to attain liberation, make use of the good teachings of the doctrine of *karma* in cultivating the good quality of forgiveness towards others who have done harm to them. And those who take recourse to the court of law to resist the wickedness of others who have harmed them, make use of the good teachings of the doctrine of *karma* in adopting mental attitude of forgiveness, not yielding to the feeling of enmity. "Whatever harm my opponent or adversary does to me, does on the strength of my own *karma*, my *karma* uses him as its instrument and causes him to act the way he does, so it is wrong to be furious with him, in fact I should be furious with my own *karma*"—adoption of this line of thinking helps man to cultivate the good quality of forgiveness and to keep away his mind from the filthy and defiling states of anger, passions and quarrels causing bondage of unwholesome *karmas*.

Wickedness of the wicked is the result of the disease of ignorance and passions. This disease urges men to act wickedly. Their condition is like that of ordinary patients afflicted with high fever and other diseases. So like ordinary patients, they too deserve our sympathy and forgiveness. One who knows and understands the essence of the doctrine of *karma* thinks on this line.

One who understands the doctrine of *karma* is not proud of the good fruits of his good *karma*, nor is he unhappy and sorry for the bad fruits of his bad *karma*, because he knows that they are not to last for ever, that they have fixed duration. He endures miseries and calamities with tranquillity and equanimity, understanding that they are the results of his own *karma.* Thus the strength of enduring them with tranquillity as also of keeping his life free from pride and gloom, he derives from the philosophy of moral causation. And surrender and devotion to God instils in the strength much peace, solace, consolation and inspiration.

If God were pleased by His praise and all formalities of devotion to Him, then He would surely be displeased with those who do not sing His praise and do not perform all formalities of devotion to Him. But God can never have such nature. He is totally free from attachment and aversion. He is perfect. He is of the nature of perfect bliss. He is called Viśvambhara (One who pervades and sustains the whole world). Our belief that God is pleased by our devotional songs and music, or by our gifts of ornaments or by our offerings of plates full of sweets, springs from our ignorance of His true nature. If man's mind is desirous of spiritual welfare, is disposed and devoted to God, is solely under His shelter and is becoming ever more pure by recalling His good qualities, then the brilliance and purity which the soul or mind attains is the natural gift earned by his own spiritual strength and merit—and not given by somebody. Recalling to our mind good qualities of God is not an ordinary means but a very strong and effective one. The rising strength of meditation on the supremely pure, brilliant and bright Supreme Soul opens the closed doors of the heart of the meditator and makes such a powerful impact on him that his passions and infatuation suffer a great blow, entailing the spread into his heart of the light of purity of the object of meditation. Meditation on the pure and sublime object causes transmission of pure and sublime light waves from the object to the mind of the meditator. Similarly, meditation on the impure and evil object causes transmission of impure and evil light waves from the object to the mind of the meditator The kind of influence the mind is subjected to depends on the kind of the object meditated on. Meditation on, remembering of and devotion to attachment-free Supreme Soul are very effective in washing off the mental defilements of infatuation and delusion. Thus the benefit or gain which we secure of the mental purity, mental development and mental bliss through devotion to God can be regarded as God-given, but only secondarily or metaphorically. If it were in the hands of God to give light directly and primarily, then He would not allow darkness (ignorance) to persist in the mind of any being, He would turn the wicked and evil-intellect into the righteous and good-intellect, He would lift each and every being from the lowest or lower plane to the highest one, and He would endow all souls of the world with perfect light (knowledge) and perfect bliss. Perfection is to be attained by man himself by his own efforts. No one else (not even God) can make man a perfect soul, or can bring that perfection or liberation, the ultimate goal, to him.

If at all God is pleased, He is pleased with our good qualities and good works alone, with our good character and conduct alone. There is no other way to please Him. *Nā'nyaḥ panthā vidyate śivāya.*

The sun shines with all its light. But it depeds on the will of man to receive or not to receive its light. And it is certain that those who receive its light remain healthy, while others who do not receive it suffer from deterioration of health. Similarly, those who accept and follow the light of the wholesome teachings of the saints and great souls gain spiritual welfare and cross the ocean of worldly existence while others who reject and do not follow it wander in the dark.

The Supreme Soul or God is not seen at all. But having rightly visualised His nature with his pure mind, if man keeps His idea-l company, then his outlook or attitude gets purified and he derives holy inspiration and strength from it. And the closer and longer the company, greater is the devotion, joy and purification of mind. In this manner, the veil of infatuation and delusion is gradually removed, perverse desires are gradually extinguished, and the soul gradually gains spiritual excellence. (In other words, the soul gains greater and greater degrees of spiritually right attitude, right knowledge and right conduct). Thus having attained the great spiritual state, the soul advances further from the state of a great soul and enters that of the Supreme Soul. Devotion to God is very useful in adopting the path of self-development as also in progressing on it. Here by knowledge is meant the true knowledge about the nature of God and about the way to attain spiritual welfare and final liberation. Having sought the shelter of God, to worship and adore the spiritual path shown by Him is devotion. And to follow that path is action. In this way knowledge, devotion and action are closely interrelated.

If we reflect somewhat deeply, we find that devotion is invariably associated with knowledge; devotion necessarily depends on knowledge. Without the knowledge of the object of devotion, how can there arise feeling of devotion towards it? As a result of our knowledge and understanding of the special nature of the object of devotion, there is generated in us auspicious spiritual attraction towards it; this attraction is called devotion. Thus devotion necessarily implies the knowledge of the special nature of the object of devotion as also the knowledge or conviction: 'My company of or association with it will cause my uplift and progress'. Knowledge constitutes the basis of devotion. What is devotion without knowledge? Devotion originates depending on knowledge. The place of devotion in knowledge is on par with that of sugar in milk. As soon as sugar is mixed with milk, the latter becomes a sweet substance. Similarly, as soon as devotion is associated with knowledge, the latter becomes an extraordinary thing. When, on account of the knowledge of the speciality of the object of devotion, there arises spiritually wholesome attraction or auspicious feeling of devotion towards it, then it can be said that devotion is associated with knowledge. Thus when knowledge is associated with devotion, it becomes a spiritually wholesome mixture.

It is easily understandable that man follows the person whom he is greatly devoted to. Not only that but he gets absorbed in him, obeys his commands, walks on his path and wholeheartedly surrenders himself to him. It is quite natural that a devotee earnestly desires and tries to become like him whom he is devoted to. He strictly follows in his foot-steps. He makes great efforts to become as good as he is in qualities, character and actions. Self-surrender to him is not the result of knowledge alone; it is the result of devotion conjoined with knowledge. Thus devotion associated with knowledge or knowledge embellished with devotion moulds our actions (character or conduct).

In this way, knowledge (*jñāna*), devotion (*bhakti)* and action (*karma*)—all the three[1] together, fused with one another, form the uncommon and exclusive path of Highest Good and Supreme Welfare.

In the world, the mother is regarded as the most affectionate person. In her presence, the child babbles, and indulging in babblings it experiences the matchless joy of the mother's affection. Similarly, before God a devotee prattles and acts like a simple, innocent child, and thereby enjoys the pure, dovotional, spiritual sentiment of love. Thus he makes the path of purifying his life and conduct very easy. How can his impure

1. The trio of *jñāna* (knowledge), *darśana* (faith in or love of truth) and *cāritra* (conduct), well-known in the Jaina philosophy, is identical with that of *jñāna, bhakti* and *karma. Darśana* and *bhakti* are interchangeable terms. And *cāritra* and *karma* mean the same thing.

or defiled conduct go well with his devotion to God, the pure *par excellence*? How can there be the company, union or alliance of the impure soul with the absolutely pure one? There can never be the union of the impure devotee and the pure Lord. A devotee must purify his mind and conduct by means of devotion; then and then only he can unite with God. Devotion must result in the purity of conduct and character. In it alone lies the success and fulfilment of devotion.

And I even go to the extent of saying that if theism does not stand to reason and logic and remains unproved and unestablished, we should have ideal God installed in our heart and we should have faith in God. Idea-l God or faith in God is necessary to give solace to human heart and to make human life dynamic. If God does not exist in the outer world, we should invent Him. Idea of God is powerful, it works for the betterment of mankind, it elevates man to greater and greater spiritual planes. On the basis of experience, we can confidently declare that one who surrenders to God and takes shelter in Him finds great solace, inspiration and peace. We need Him as an object of our devotion.

Faith (Śraddhā)

To attain success in any work or undertaking three things are necessary, viz., *śraddhā* (faith), *jñāna* (knowledge) and *kriyā* (activity).[1] These three together constitute the path of liberation or success in any undertaking.

Śraddhā means firm faith backed by and associated with discretion. *Jñāna* means knowledge. And to act in accordance with knowledge is *cāritra* (conduct).

If a patient has faith in the efficacy of medicines, knows as to which medicine works effectively on the disease he is suffering from, and takes that medicine properly, then he can cure himself of the disease. Similarly, to be free from all miseries, or to attain eternal bliss or liberation, one should have faith that there must be the path leading to liberation or to the end of all miseries, should know the path and follow it. All the three are necessary. Bliss or liberation or freedom from all miseries can be

1. "The unity of heart, head and hand leads to liberation." This English saying too teaches us that we can attain liberation with the help of the three, viz. *darśana* (*śraddhāna*—faith), *jñāna* (knowledge) and *cāritra* (conduct). Thus it presents the same idea as is embodied in the aphorism '*samyagdarśana-jñāna-cāritrāṇi mokṣamārgaḥ*' (I.1, *Tattvārthasūtra* by Umāsvāti).

attained only when the three combine with one another. The means to the desired goal by itself cannot lead to the attainment of the goal. Faith in the existence and efficacy of the means, knowledge about the means and the proper employment of the means—all the three together are required for the attainment of the desired goal.

We have given above an illustration of a medicine. Regarding it one may argue that the patient's knowledge of the medicine and his taking it properly—these two are sufficient for the cure of the disease. Is there any scope for faith? In answer, it can be said that even in this case faith is necessary. When the patient does not see any immediate improvement on taking the medicine, he loses his patience and discontinues the medicine. It is only faith in the efficacy of the medicine that can prevent him from discontinuing it. And if he continues it for the required period of time, he will be cured of the disease.

"Poison kills man even if it is taken unknowingly. Its working has nothing to do with our faith or no-faith in its efficacy. Similarly, the right medicine certainly improves our health; its working has nothing to do with our faith or no-faith in its efficacy." Even if we agree with this view, we uphold that in the field of spiritualness, faith is absolutely necessary. The whole edifice of spiritual progress stands on the foundation of faith. Without faith, there cannot be the spiritual evolution of a soul. One who wants to attain Highest Good or liberation must have faith in truthfulness and self-control as means to liberation. Such faith keeps us firm in our observance of truthfulness and self-control. When truthfulness and self-control become the objects of our faith, knowledge and conduct—all the three—, then and then only they (truthfulness and self-control) bring us the Highest Good and Perfect Bliss.

Scientists undertake research activities. They start with hypothesis. They conduct experiments. As the experiments reveal to them more and more truth of the hypothesis, their faith in the truth (correctness) of the hypothesis increases. This shows that knowledge always precedes faith. As faith follows knowledge and is based on knowledge, it is always firm and it can be called faith in the true sense of the term. In other words, knowledge is the foundation of faith. Faith is nothing without knowledge.

Thus faith is always based on knowledge. It is never blind. Knowledge develops and its horizon widens as we employ it in experiments and activities with faith. And with the development of knowledge, faith too develops. In this way, both nourish each other.

Faith and knowledge constitute the basis of conduct or activities. The strength or force of activity is determined by the strength of faith and knowledge. In other words, activity derives its strength from faith and knowledge.

Faith generates and increases enthusiasm for accomplishing the undertaken work. On the basis of knowledge, we start activity; knowledge is the ground of our activity. But activity gains force and vigour when it is impelled by faith. Of course, skill or proficiency depends on knowledge. More the knowledge, better is the work done. But in the absence of faith, activity does not gather strength, vigour and momentum. Faith in the attainment of the goal, however remote the attainment may be, instils vigour in the activity performed for the attainment. Faith causes us to take interest in the activity; and on its account, our devotion to or absorption in activity becomes concentrated and brilliant.

In the Jaina scriptures, the term '*samyagdarśana*' is employed for *śraddhā* (faith).

The function of knowledge is to grasp, cognise or know the object to a considerable extent. But the faculty which is responsible for the rise of discrimination as to the spiritual wholesomeness or otherwise of the object known as also for predilection or love for the former is *samyagdarśana.* Thus *samyagdarśana* is nothing but predisposition or inclination rooted in the faculty of discrimination and discretion and permeated with faith.

There is a vast difference between faith (*śraddhā*) and blind belief. Faith is invariably accompanied by discrimination and discretion. On the other hand, blind belief is always destitute of discrimination and discretion, as is suggested by the adjective 'blind' given to belief. When belief is generated by the faculty of discrimination, it is given the good name 'faith' ('*śraddhā*'). We determine as to the wholesomeness or otherwise, etc., of an object or an act with the instrumentality of the faculty of discrimination. And faith is required to impel us to act accordingly. In this way, there obtains a very close relation between faith and faculty of discrimination.

Knowledge, when infused with faith, turns into a unique tonic of spiritual life. Such knowledge is the main ground of spiritual welfare.[1] It is *samyagdarśana* alone and it alone is *samyagdarśana.*

As already stated, *darśana* (faith), *jñāna* (knowledge) and *cāritra* (con-

---

1. 'Knowledge is the wing with which we fly to heaven.'—Shakespeare

duct)—all the three together constitute the path of liberation. Similarly, it is declared by the ancient seers that *jñāna* (knowledge) and *kriyā* (activity = conduct)—these two together constitute the path of liberation.[1] When they say so, they include faith (*darśana* = *śraddhā*) in knowledge. The sages of olden times, well versed in the Jaina scriptures, have stated that faith (*samyaktva=darśana*) is nothing but knowledge of a special type.[2]

By faith we are to understand here that faith alone which is spiritually beneficial. And that faith which brings about wholesome change in our attitude and turns the entire course of our life towards the final goal of spiritual perfection is the spiritually beneficial faith. The soul, its merit and demerit, rebirth, liberation and its path—these reals are its objects. Faith in them with right understanding and firm conviction is very useful in the spiritual life, and it is this faith that is called *samyagdarśana* or *samyaktva.* It is not necessary for a man possessed of this faith or *samyaktva* to have faith in the various mythological descriptions of heavens and hells, that are there in the Vedic, Buddhist and Jaina literature. One who has faith in the existence of soul, in its good and bad states or births, as also in the possibility of its attaining spiritual perfection is to be regarded as possessed of *samyaktva* or faith. Such faith alone is an elixir of life. It is the indispensable provender to the pilgrim on the path of spiritual perfection or liberation.

The belief in the six substances is not an essential condition of faith or *samyaktva.* Even a person who knows nothing about the six substances, viz., *dharmāstikāya* (the substance serving as a medium of motion), etc., can be or become possessed of faith or *samyaktva* on the strength of his having spiritually beneficial attitude. Those who belong to non-Jaina sects have no knowledge of the substances like *dharmāstikāya,* etc., accepted in the Jaina philosophy. Yet, on account of their faith in the existence and energies of the soul, they become noble in character, make advancement on the path of non-attachment, and ultimately attain perfection, liberation and omniscience. This has been accepted by the Jaina tradition.[3]

---

1. *nāṇa-kiriyāhi mokkho /—Viśeṣāvaśyaka-bhāṣya, gāthā* 2.
2. *jñānaviśeṣa eva samyaktvam /—Vṛtti* on *Viśeṣāvaśyaka-bhāṣya, gāthā* 1174.
3. '*anyaliṅge siddhāḥ*'
Upādhyāya Yaśovijayajī writes:
anyaliṅgādisiddhānām ādhāraḥ samataiva hi /
ratnatrayaphalaprāpter yayā syād bhāvajainatā //—Samatādhikāra, Adhyātmasāra.
The verse means: The ground for souls attaining liberation even in conditions like

One who has not even heard the words '*saṁvara*', '*āsrava*', '*nirjarā*', etc., is *samyagdṛṣṭi* (possessed of right faith), if he is convinced that by following the path of violence, etc., man harms his soul, while by following the path of non-violence, etc., he spiritually elevates and ennobles his soul. Thus faith or *samyagdarśana* invariably has conviction of a special sort as its essential ingredient.

The firm belief that the soul, though residing in body, is different from body and possesses special qualities not found in the body, and by means of the practice of the proper spiritual discipline can become free from the cycle of births and deaths is called *samyaktva.* It is not that such belief or faith is cherished by followers of a particular religious sect alone to the exclusion of all other sects. In fact, followers of any religious sect that accepts soul can entertain it. And whosoever lives strictly in accordance with it and thereby frees himself from the feeling of attachment as also from passions attains liberation.

The philosophy of soul is very deep and serene. Even a person who has no philosophical knowledge of the soul can have *samyaktva,* if he follows the righteous path of non-violence and truth. As a matter of fact, faith in the path of non-violence and truth is identical with faith in soul; or the former is closely related to the latter, one entails the other. And faith in the path of non-violence and truth is the essence of the faith in seven or nine reals accepted in the Jaina philosophy.

Each and every living being tries to be free from miseries and desires to be happy. 'May I be happy'—this desire is universal, it is found in all beings. The entity 'I' experienced in this act of desiring is accepted even by the hard-core materialist.

In the scriptures, we are asked to experience the soul and body as different and distinct. In other words, we are asked to have knowledge of the difference between self and not-self. Even understanding and wise materialists do have this knowledge. They acquire it in the following manner. They regard the entity referred to by 'I' as self, and the body and all external objects as not-self. Thus having established I-entity as the main base or foundation and having understood feelings of misery and happiness of other beings in the light of direct experience of their own desirable and undesirable feelings of happiness and misery, they think it

---

that of belonging to non-Jaina sects, etc., is nothing but equanimity. On the strength of equanimity, they possess three jewels (right attitude—faith, right knowledge and right conduct) and consequently attain the internal state of a true Jaina.

their duty to give happiness and satisfaction to others and consider it an evil act to cause harm and injury to others by treating them harshly and unjustly. This path of good conduct is a blessing to one's own self as also to others. And one who follows this path of universal Good makes one's life blessed and praiseworthy.

Religion is as much necessary and useful to those whose mind refuses to accept life after death as it is to those who firmly believe in it. It is because religion is something whose results we experience in the present life itself. Just as water, food, etc., have clear perceptible effects on our body, even so the practice of religion does have clear perceptible effects on our mind. In reality, religion is nothing but removing defilements and perversions from mind and making life pure and noble by cultivating lofty qualities like compassion, truthfulness and self-control. It is the essence of life. It is the natural state of life. It does not depend on the discursive philosophy of life after death, heavens and hells, etc. The key to happiness lies in that real and pure state of life. Without that pure and natural state of life all our efforts in the quest of happiness will be futile and result in miseries.

Where there is hunger for religion, the question of the school or place of religion becomes secondary. A person hungry for religion makes sincere efforts to satisfy that hunger. He understands and knows that he can satisfy his hunger in any school or place of religion; there is no use of boasting of greatness of a particular school or place. But when man is ensnared in the pride about his school or place of religion as he is in the pride about his family, etc., he forgets the main objective of the school or place, which is nothing but to foster devotion to and practice of religion, ceases to devote himself to religion itself and becomes a devotee of school and place alone. Different religious sects are neighbours. And if we understand and perform our duties toward our neighbours, harmony and love will prevail all around. If somebody's school or place of religion has some specialities and more soothing elements, he may no doubt relate them to his neighbours, but that too he should do politely and affectionately. Not only that, but he may suggest them lovingly to take advantage of them. Howsoever great is held the school or place due to its speciality, it will not benefit man merely on account of his image of himself as its upholder or as a fighter for its cause, if he has no 'hunger' at all or is careless and lethargic in satisfying his 'hunger'. On the other hand, an upholder of even a small or insignificant school will get necessary nourishment for spiritual life and attain spiritual welfare, if he makes sincere efforts to satisfy his 'hunger'.

True religion or the path of purification and spiritual welfare is good conduct. To understand rightly that unfailing means of spiritual welfare is right knowledge. To have unflinching faith in that means is right faith. And to employ that means into practice is good conduct. Thus right faith, right knowledge and right conduct—all the three have good conduct for their object. [When it is said that the object of right conduct is good conduct, it means that good conduct is the object of practice and observance.] Thus we should have faith in good conduct, we should know as to what constitutes good conduct, and we should practise good conduct in accordance with our faith and knowledge.

In his *Yogaśāstra* (*Vṛtti* on iv. 109) Ācārya Hemacandra states that faith means desire for religion.[1] Religion is nothing but path of duty and righteousness. So desire for religion ultimately means desire to follow that path. Faith or *samyagdarśana,* being desire-for-religion having this sense alone, can never be confined to a particular religious sect alone.

We should know that the fruit of religion is not other-worldly alone. In other words, it is not that the results of the practice of religion are not gained in the present birth but in the future births alone. Even a wise man who has faith neither in soul nor in life after death (i.e., rebirth), or who has doubts about them, follows the path of religion, that is, the path of justice and righteousness with pleasure and delight. Why? It is because he is convinced that if man follows the path of friendliness and justice, his present life will be happy and peaceful and his life after death, if at all it exists, will also be full of happiness on account of the influence of the continuously flowing wholesome stream of the present life. He firmly believes that love breeds love, goodness breeds goodness. The understanding that the practice of religion gives its fruit to practiser in this very birth is not only right but necessary also. If a man leads godly life here, then only he will be born as a god in his next birth. It is wholly on account of his leading beastly or hellishly evil life that he is born as a beast or an infernal being in the next birth. And if he develops humane qualities in the present life, he will be born again as a human being. It is natural that a man performing actions befitting hellish life goes to hell after death; and if he performs acts that fit in with the life of an animal

1. *śraddhā dharmābhilāṣaḥ /*

or vegetable kingdom, he has no choice but to take birth in that state of existence. Men who possess good conduct here will attain good birth after death. And men who are of bad conduct here will attain bad birth after death. The kind of life man lives in the present birth determines the class in which he will be born after death.

The essential point that emerges from the above discussion is that right faith (*samyagdarśana* or *samyaktva*) is nothing but understanding or conviction that one should avoid bad conduct of immorality, injustice, incontinence and greed, and practise good conduct of morality, justice, continence, self-control and contentedness. The extensive spread of this right faith among masses cures the society of the terrific fatal diseases of immorality, injustice, inequality, cruelty and exploitation which originate from and thrive on lust, gross hedonism, capitalism, imperialism, despotism and superstitions. As a result, there emerges and spreads in the world the health-giving light of all-elevating good qualities of non-violence, truthfulness, contentedness, evenmindedness, equanimity and universal friendliness. Thus even this miserable world can be turned into Heaven of heavens.

The five signs or characteristics of *samyaktva* (right faith) are mentioned in the Jaina philosophical works.[1] They are—*śama* (tranquillity), *saṁvega* (spiritual craving), *nirveda* (disgust), *anukampā* (compassion) and *āstikya* (conviction).

Śama (tranquillity)—This is the mental state when the passions like anger, greed, etc., are suppressed or controlled and desires for worldly pleasures are properly curbed.

Saṃvega (spiritual craving)—This is the intense desire to attain liberation or the highest spiritual Good.

Nirveda (disgust)—This is disgust with unwholesome, sinful and evil activities.

Anukampā (compassion)—This is the desire to eliminate sufferings of living beings without any partiality. This desire expresses itself in tenderness of heart. And when put into practice, it takes the form of practical steps to remedy sufferings of beings.

Āstikya (conviction)—It is the conviction that good conduct leads to spiritual welfare while bad conduct to degradation and misery.

---

1. *śama-saṁvega-nirvedānukampāstikyalakṣaṇaiḥ* /
lakṣaṇaiḥ pañcabhiḥ samyak samyaktvam upalakṣyate //
—Ācārya Hemacandra's *Yogaśāstra,* II.15

Scriptures (Śāstra)

It is necessary to know that scriptures are originated from experience. They do not generate the experience directly. After proper study of the preachings contained in them, when man desirous of spiritual welfare and liberation takes to the path of internal yogic practice and makes considerable progress on that path, then and then only he gains such experience as could not be gained from the mere study of scriptures. From this experience are created the sacred scriptures that serve as guiding light to the entire world. Thus the place of experience is higher than that of scriptures. Experience is superior to scriptures.

In the world we find so many diverse streams of thought flowing from scriptures. All the sages who composed them were not on the same plane of spiritual development. Their internal purity and equanimity were not of the same degree. How strong and how numerous the differences of opinion among the great teachers, the repositories of spiritual learning, are! Unable to keep the balance of mind or impartiality about their own view, they display obstinacy and are seen possessed with passions and subdued by infatuation. In most of the scriptures, we find their sage-authors or preceptor-authors refuting the views of their opponents and establishing their own views with vehemence and passion. They are full of attacks and counter-attacks. Being puzzled by the frightful whirlwind of attacks and counter-attacks, a Gujarātī saint-poet Akho Bhagat spontaneously utters: '*akho kahe e aṃdhāro kūvo, jhaghaḍo cukāvi koī na mūo.*' (Akho tells that this is a dark deep well; none has settled the quarrel or dispute before death).

The purport is that man should not be a blind devotee of scriptures under the influence of infatuation. He should move in the garden of scriptures, keeping the lamp of reason and wisdom with him. Therein lies his happiness and peace. A wise and understanding person should drink water of scriptural teaching after having filtered or purified it with a filter-cloth of his own calm and composed intellect. Revered saint Haribhadrācārya has also advised us to this effect. We have to become brave and fearless divers to collect pearls from the bottom of the sea of scriptures. We are to use scriptures as a means to cross the ocean of transmigratory cycle. We are not to transform any scripture into a well to drown ourselves to death. Holy, supremely divine scriptures contain the invaluable treasures of knowledge and pure thoughts. But they have come down to us after having passed through innumerable tempests during the long past. This suggests us the necessity of the use of our impartial natural reason or wisdom in studying scriptures. Statements of the former saints or elders should not be regarded valid so long as they are not supported by reason. Again, we should not be startled on finding the thoughts of the modern masters endowed with genius, going against the scriptural tradition. In such a situation, we should impartially and calmly reflect on the new thoughts and ideas. And if they are found right and wholesome, we as seekers after truth should accept and honour them and thereby enrich our treasure of knowledge and thoughts. We should appreciate the ideas and thoughts of others to the extent they are reasonable, right, cogent and wholesome. This is the good and praiseworthy feature of the devotion to truth and knowledge.

Scriptures are for the sake of truth. But truth is not for the sake of scriptures. Scriptures are to be set aside if they go against truth. But truth is not to be set aside if it goes against scriptures. That which is true and right, rational and cogent, purified by thought and reflection, and established by intellect and logic can never be toppled down, rejected or shaken by scriptures. If scriptures try to do so, they themselves will be shaken and effaced. Where is the possibility of intellect or reason opposing that which is not amenable to it and beyond its reach? We have no other go, but to keep mum with regard to such cases. But that which is opposed to reason and detrimental to public weal should never be believed in on the authority of scriptures. *Bṛhaspati-smṛti* declares: "One should not depend solely on scriptures to come to decision as to the rightness or wrongness of an act. It is because if we follow the idea or thought opposed to reason or intellect, then we do great harm to religion, rectitude or righteousness."[1]

What Indian philosophers said[2] regarding testing of scriptures, is noteworthy. It is as follows: Gold is tested in four ways, viz., rubbing (on the touch-stone), cutting, heating and hammering. Similarly, scriptures are tested on the basis of four qualities, viz., knowledge, good conduct, austerity and compassion. That scripture which embodies knowledge or philosophy not going against the findings of perception and reason, gives utmost importance to righteous conduct, prescribes austerities conducive to the

1. *kevalaṁ śāstram āśritya na kartavyo vinirṇayaḥ /*
yuktihīnavicāre tu dharmahāniḥ prajāyate //
2. *yathā caturbhiḥ kanakaṁ parīkṣyate nigharṣaṇa-cchedana-tāpa-tāḍanaiḥ /*
tathaiva śāstraṁ viduṣā parīkṣyate śrutena śīlena tapo-dayāguṇaiḥ //

sublimation of life, and discreetly explains as to how it is our duty or religion to practise non-violence—compassion, is respectable and acceptable. The right path—preached and taught by such scriptures—of spiritual study, righteous conduct, wholesome austerity and all-embracing love or friendliness is religion, the path of spiritual welfare.

Incidentally, we should note that good acts performed on account of family tradition are laudable. But when they are performed with understanding, they give us indescribable internal pleasure and satisfaction. Those who are Jaina, Bauddha or Vaiṣṇava by birth or family tradition are not so great as are those who are Jaina, Bauddha or Vaiṣṇava with full understanding and knowledge as to what constitutes Jainahood, Bauddhahood and Vaiṣṇavahood. In other words, those who are Jaina, Bauddha or Vaiṣṇava on account of their following the self-purifying, lofty, altruistic ideals that constitute the essence of Jainahood, Bauddhahood and Vaiṣṇavahood are the true Jainas, Bauddhas or Vaiṣṇavas. It is because those who accept and follow this path of righteousness, known by the name of Jainism, Buddhism or Vaiṣṇavism, with full knowledge and understanding, use their power of discretion and judgement to remove dust, dirt and impurities that have crept into the long tradition of the path. With their power of discretion and judgement, they remove the perverse and degenerate elements, and thereby achieve spiritual development and present before the people the pure path of righteous living and spiritual knowledge.

If the Jaina, Bauddha, Vaiṣṇava, etc., are narrow-minded and sectarian, then and then only their paths are divergent. But if they are endowed with faculty of discretion and judgement and really desire the spiritual good, then they are followers of the same path of spiritual welfare, though they bear the different labels of sects and cults. Such good men who are even-minded, equanimous, charitable, purely devoted to knowledge, and worshippers of good spiritual qualities are the co-travellers of the same path.

'*Vaiṣṇavajana to tene kahīe, je pīḍa parāī jāṇe re*'[1]—this devotional song is well-known throughout India. The good moral qualities enumerated in it are as much necessary for being Jaina or Bauddha as they are for being Vaiṣṇava. If to possess these good qualities is the only condition

1. The meaning of the line is: 'Those men who are pained to see the sufferings of others are called the Vaiṣṇavas.'

of one's being Vaiṣṇava, Bauddha and Jaina, then Vaiṣṇavahood, Bauddhahood and Jainahood are not different things, but one and the same thing. It is because just as words '*jala*', '*pāṇī*', '*vāri*', '*water*', '*nīra*', etc., mean one and the same thing, even so Vaiṣṇavahood, Bauddhahood and Jainahood mean one and the same thing, viz., to possess those good qualities. So the Jaina, the Bauddha and the Vaiṣṇava are one.[1] [The same can be said in connection with the followers of other religious sects.]

In the world, there will always exist diverse philosophical views and varied traditions of rituals.

Philosophical thoughts of the learned thinkers differ from one another on account of the difference in the purity of their intellect. Of them, some may be right, some may be wrong, and some may be partly right and partly wrong. But the case with rituals is quite different. The external form of the worship of God as also of the act of spiritual reflection or concentration is related to the limbs of the body, to the external paraphernalia and to the chosen periods of time—particular hours of day or night, week, fortnight, month and year. So according to the different appearances of different places and times, as also according to the diverse tastes of the different peoples, the rituals will be always naturally different and their method of performance will also be different. Difference or diversity is natural to external rituals. This fact is very simple and quite understandable. Yet, those who lose their temper and become ready to fight on the difference in rituals are unwise. Those who despise the difference in rituals really lack understanding and tolerance.

It is necessary to understand and know that diversity of philosophical views and rituals can never cause the diversity of religion. Although men uphold different philosophical views and perform different rituals, their religion may be one provided they believe in the religion of truth and non-violence.

It is crystal-clear that religiosity is measured by the practice of religion or righteousness, and not by sharpness of philosophical thinking, nor by ritualistic performance. And it is also clear that the only means to the spiritual elevation of life is religion (i.e., practice of the true religion of

1. The etymological meanings of the words 'Jaina', 'Bauddha' and 'Vaiṣṇava' point to the same significance. 'Jaina' etymologically means 'one who practises the discipline of controlling and subduing sense organs'. 'Bauddha' etymologically means 'one who delightfully walks on the path of pure and right intellect.' And 'Vaiṣṇava' means 'one who pervades, i.e., embraces all living beings with spiritual friendliness'.

non-violence and truth); spiritual elevation of life can never be attained by mere performance of rituals. Yet, if any philosophical system helps man practise true religion and if any ritualistic system instils in him joy and zeal to practise religion, then both the philosophical system and the ritualistic system become spiritually beneficial to him.

Thus religion is the most important thing. And the beauty of a philosophical or a ritualistic system lies only in its becoming useful and helpful to man in his practice of religion. That philosophical or ritualisic system which helps man practise religion proves itself to be spiritual ambrosia for him. So, the attitude which considers religion to be different with different philosophical or ritualistic systems is wrong and hence it should be given up. All those who follow the right path of non-violence and truth—let them be in lakh or crore—should be regarded as followers of one and the same religion, the co-religionists (*sādharmika*).

Spiritual good depends not on one's acquisition of vast scriptural knowledge, but on putting into practice the principles that one's understanding and intellect find wholesome. Even dull persons have crossed the ocean of transmigratory cycle, putting into practice the teaching that one should abandon immoral and unjust conduct as also attachment and aversion. Though they are dull in intellect, they are naturally inclined to what is spiritually true and wholesome. On the other hand, great pundits, scholars and philosophers lack this inclination and understanding; as a result of it, they remain submerged in the ocean of transmigratory existence.

No doubt that many display their cleverness in saying, 'Not that whatever is mine is true; but whatever is true is mine'. But in practice, they are too much attached to their own views, parties or sects and do not halt even for a while to reflect as to what truth is, wherein it lies, etc.; they are guided by the strong prejudice that their own views are right and those of others are wrong. As a result, they denigrate others calling them atheists, infidels, irreligious, upholders of wrong views, etc. They lack power of discretion and judgement.

It is natural that we put faith in those persons whom we regard as authority. But faith should not be blind. Faith, though placed in right authority, is not enlightened and unshakable, if it is not based on the foundation of reason and discretion. When it is backed by reason and discretion, it becomes right and spiritually beneficial.

It is easy to utter statements like 'one should accept him as authority whose statements stand to reason' (*yuktimad vacanaṁ yasya tasya kāryaḥ parigrahaḥ*—Ācārya Haribhadra). But when somebody calls our view irrational, then we become furious with him, do not pause to reflect on our views impartially and calmly, and hesitate to accept the rational views of others or other traditions. If this is our mental state, then how can we claim that we follow and respect the above quoted liberal and noble dictum of Ācārya Haribhadra?

Ācārya Haribhadra was a learned brāhmaṇa. He was a great erudite scholar of the systems of Indian philosophy. He accepted the Jaina religion and became an illustrious Jaina monk who greatly promoted and propagated the noble principles of the Jaina religion and philosophy. In his *Lokatattvanirṇaya* (38) he rightly and openly declares "I have no partiality for Lord Mahāvīra (though I am his follower), nor have I any hatred for the great sages Kapila, etc., (who propounded other religious sects or systems). I should accept him as an authority whose statements are rational.[1] I do not advise you to accept a particular statement simply because it is from the mouth of Mahāvīra, nor do I advise you to reject it simply because it is from the mouth of the great sages like Kapila, etc. Forget as to who has uttered it. But reflect on it, test it on the touchstone of reason. Then if you find it right and cogent, accept it without any hesitation and without paying any heed to the fact of its authorship." Man should not accept a view or a doctrine on authority. He should neither accept nor reject it on the basis of the consideration as to its author. He should test and verify it by reason. This is the reason why our *ācāryas* appeal to us not to accept their statements on authority; they ask us to examine them, and to accept them if they are found true and to reject them if they are found false.

The purport of Ācārya Haribhadra's statement is as follows: We should abandon partiality and prejudice. We should not be obstinate. We should not go on saying that whatever is mine is good and true. We should cultivate neutral or impartial intellect and accept whatever is found wholesome and true. In order to exterminate dogmatism from our mind, we should cultivate broad-mindedness, liberality and nobility. As a result, our heart becomes soft, equanimous, impartial and devoted to truth alone; narrow-mindedness, sectarianism, communalism and obstinacy find no place in it.

---

1. *pakṣapāto na me Vīre na dveṣaḥ Kapilādiṣu /*
yuktimad vacanaṁ yasya tasya kāryaḥ parigrahaḥ //

At this juncture, it is useful to note that for all-round development of man, balancing of head (reason, intellect) and heart (faith) is necessary and essential. They are complementary to each other. Intellect shows us the path of purification and goodness, and faith inspires us to walk on that path. Futile indeed is intellect without faith. Even so is faith futile without intellect. Without faith intellect is inactive; and without intellect faith is blind, and mistakes the wrong path for the right one and *vice versa.* A chariot of life moves on the two wheels of faith and intellect. For human progress their mutual cooperation is extremely necessary.

Man can progress on the path of purification by supplementing faith to knowledge to remedy the deficiency of the latter. As the field of experience expands more and more, the field of faith becomes narrower and narrower; of course, the intensity of faith increases. And when the experiential knowledge attains its perfection, faith loses its independent identity and gets merged in the experiential knowledge.

If there is any scope for doubt regarding the existence of anything or regarding the cause-effect relation between any two things or events, then there arises the question as to whether or not we should have faith in the existence of that thing or in the cause-effect relation between those two things or events. But when there is the experiential knowledge of those matters experimentally and directly, then there arises no question at all of having faith in them.

Feeling of non-attachment (Vairāgya)

Worldly existence (*saṁsāra*) is not a house made up of bricks and chunam; nor is it father, mother, brother or friend; nor is it gardens, orchards or fields; nor is it wealth; nor is it industry or business; it is not constituted of any one or all of them. So renunciation of them is not to be understood as the true renunciation of worldly existence. The true worldly existence is there in the mind of man. Man with such mind—be he in the city or in the jungle—is in the worldly existence. Desire for worldly pleasures (which is due to *moha,* i.e., ignorance, delusion, nescience; or due to attachment and aversion) is worldly existence. So long as man is under its sway, he remains caught up in the transmigratory cycle—be he in the state of a layman or a monk. He can renounce the gross objects and run away from them; but how can he run away from his own mind fraught with desires? He remains entangled in the worldly existence as long as his mind is afflicted with desires. Real play of worldly existence is enacted in the inner heart of man. What we see outward is but mere gross manifestations of the inner states.

Attachment is the repository of defects like immorality, injustice and selfishness. So non-attachment (*vairāgya*) attained owing to the removal of attachment makes man noble, truthful, discreet and affectionate. A pure state is developed to the extent attachment is reduced. And man becomes self-sacrificing, benevolent, indifferent to worldly pleasures, charitable, and develops the feeling of universal brotherhood to the extent this pure state is developed. Charity, self-sacrifice, generosity and renunciation constitute his nature in which he constantly revels.

Non-attachment literally and meaningfully means the extermination and extinction of attachment. It is achieved by very hard and sincere efforts. It equally depends on firm, dispassionate (pure) and brilliant attitude, outlook or faith. Non-attachment gets spoiled like milk as soon as pure faith is shaken or dispassionate outlook or attitude becomes perverse. Even though a person resides in a house, takes food and drink, and lives among the people, non-attachment ingrained in him remains unimpaired, if it is based on discretionary and discriminative attitude, outlook or faith. On the other hand, even though a person lives in woods and moves as a recluse and thus outwardly seems to be possessed of high renunciation, he is not free from attachment if he is overcome by delusion and crushed under the pressure of inordinate desires.[1]

To be caught up in and bound by attachment, and as a result to cling to a thing or place or to get stuck up in them on account of infatuation and ignorance instead of advancing on the path of spiritual development according to the great law of Nature is the state quite opposite to the state of non-attachment. Non-attachment consists in rising above attachment after having removed infatuation and ignorance. To make the atmosphere of the world poisonous or nectareous is in the hands of man; it depends on his attitude or outlook. Poison is in his mind. So he experiences and spreads poison all around him. Pure and blissful mind experiences and diffuses nectar everywhere. Bliss and joy are abundant at every step on the path of spiritual good. Rising to the higher and higher stages of spiritual development the soul continuously experiences bliss and joy and at last attains Ultimate Release.

---

1. *vane'pi doṣāḥ prabhavanti rāgiṇāṁ gṛheṣu pañcendriyanigrahas tapaḥ / akutsite vartmani yaḥ pravartate nivṛttarāgasya gṛhaṁ tapovanam //*

It is wretchedness to get bound by attachment for the sake of joy and happiness. But one who is the master of joy and happiness enjoys them without any impediment and obstruction. And one who is fond of that joy or bliss experienceable only on the path of spiritual progress and belonging to the type higher than that of physical joy or happiness is the true man, true hero; he soars very high beyond earthly world, remains eternally engrossed in the pure matchless bliss or joy and becomes a guiding spiritual light to the worldly men.

Above exposition shows that non-attachment or its teaching does not make man lazy, idle or inactive. Nor does it instruct him to be inactive. On the contrary, it teaches him lessons of non-violence and truthfulness. Through such education or instruction it makes him honest, truthful, benevolent, generous, charitable and imbued with the spirit of service and self-sacrifice. Mere lip-service is not enough. Even ascetics and saints are always eager to enjoy the pleasures of helping and serving others through their actual bodily activities. When man develops the right, wholesome attitude or outlook, he understands that all beings are one[1], that is, uniform in nature. When this divine understanding dawns upon him, he becomes elated on seeing others happy and his heart melts with the feeling of compassion on seeing the sufferings of others. Thus he experiences his identity with all beings. When this experience of identity reaches its climax, then the soul attains the acme of spiritual development, its true original nature manifests itself in its perfection, and it becomes a supreme soul absolutely pure and pristine.

Liberation (Mukti)

So long as the transmigratory soul (that is, the soul covered with and obscured by karmic veils) is in the state of worldly existence (that is, in the state of karmic coveration and obscuration), it is not alone but always conjoined with body, sense-organs, mind, intellect and their associates. Hence, it is clear that development of the soul or its life depends on the development of these parts. Health of life consists in their health. If they are defective, then life is also defective and consequently the state is miserable. So it is of prime importance for us to remove all the defects pertaining to them. In other words, we should be free from bad habits,

1. *ege āyā* /—*Ṭhāṇaṁgasutta, Sūtra* 2

vicious tendencies, evil thoughts, diseases, weakness, cowardice, idleness, hard-heartedness, perverse feelings, sensuality, miserliness, pride, greed, inclination to temptations, hypocrisy, suspiciousness, superstitiousness, crookedness, slavishness, etc. This is the first necessary qualification required of one who embarks upon the spiritual discipline for liberation. Vigorous and sincere efforts to free body, heart, mind, intellect and sense-organs from their respective defects are really efforts for the attainment of liberation. Such efforts are absolutely necessary for one desirous of liberation. One can remove defects of body, mind, etc. with the instrumentality of true knowledge, education or training. Or, it is only that knowledge, education or training which is useful in attaining freedom from the defects is the right knowledge, right education or right training. The ancient maxim '*sā vidyā yā vimuktaye*' rightly declares that the true learning is that which frees man from bondages, that is, from economic, social, political and intellectual slavery, and makes him strong, energetic, discreet, dynamic, benevolent, charitable, kind and virtuous. This freedom is closely related with the ultimate spiritual freedom, that is, liberation. The education or training which does not help man to improve his thoughts, does not teach him how to control his mind and sense-organs, does not generate in him qualities of fearlessness and self-reliance, does not show him the right way of earning livelihood, and does not awaken and keep burning the feeling of freedom is not true, wholesome and capable of achieving the right objective, however much it may sharpen our intellect, intensify and broaden our knowledge of language, and impart us varied informations. That education or training which brings the material (external) and spiritual (internal) freedom is the best and true education or training.

The path of spiritual good or liberation is neither absolute inactivity nor absolute activity. At right time, inactivity is automatically attained. Mutual amiable cooperation of activity and inactivity is real life. Inactivity is necessary to enliven and vitalise activity. A traveller takes rest in order to gather strength to walk further. After having taken rest, he again starts his journey. Similarly, remaining inactive for some time at regular intervals one can make one's activity energetic, lively and brilliant. If we want to construct a high-rise building, then we are required to excavate deep foundation. Similarly, to prepare ourselves for activity, we have to accept inactivity for some time. In a way inactivity fosters activity. Thus activity properly nourished by inactivity is a source of sweet, wholesome, eternal bliss. Inactivity (purposeless inactivity) can never be such a source, however lofty be the conception or ideal on which it is based. Activity should not be impelled by passions and attachment. It should be impelled by universal compassion and friendliness. Such pure activity is the cause of liberation.

As stated earlier, the meaning of *ahiṁsā* (non-violence) is not only negative but positive also. *Ahiṁsā* (non-violence) means not only refrainment from violence but also compassion, affection, benevolence, and virtuous conduct. Like two sides of the same coin, refrainment and positive activity are also two aspects of good conduct or religion. Good conduct or religion consists in refrainment from evil activities as also in engagement in good activities. Thus religion is of the nature of both activity (engagement in good activity) and inactivity (refrainment from bad activity).

We should know that there are two aspects of good conduct, viz., removal of defects and cultivation of good qualities. The second aspect is impossible in the absence of the first. And the first aspect becomes aimless without the second one. Both these aspects are inseparably associated with one another. We should not neglect either of them.

Refrainment and positive activity—these are two aspects of good conduct or religion. When both these aspects are present there, then alone is good conduct or religion complete. To be engaged in a virtuous activity means a prior refrainment from evil activities that are its opposite. Similarly, refrainment from an evil activity means engagement in virtuous activities that are its opposite. Engagement in virtuous activities implies refrainment from evil activities, and *vice versa.*

Thus in the cooperation of refrainment and positive activity lies the attainment of prosperity and spiritual welfare.

CHAPTER 4

KARMA PHILOSOPHY

(LAW OF MORAL CAUSATION)

(1)

Each individual is responsible for his or her own actions. But the whole society is responsible for its 'joint, corporate or collective actions'. So the entire society—all its members and all future generations—has to experience the fruits of the joint actions which the society as a whole might have performed. We, the people of India, had to experience hardships and humiliations of dependence and slavery to which India was subjected owing to internal dissension and mutual fighting in which our fore-fathers indulged. And even after the attainment of political freedom India is still steeped in the traitorous activities of smuggling, black-marketing, corruption, bribery, etc. As a result, the innocent common people of India suffer hardships and harassments under the crushing pressure of poverty and privation.

'As man sows, so does he reap.' Our actions are the cause that produce proper effects at proper times. This is the eternal and universal law of *karma.* Man should make good use of his knowledge of this law at the time of undertaking any activity. If he bears in mind this law that good actions generate good fruits and bad actions generate bad fruits, he will shiver and hesitate to perform bad actions and feel elated to perform good actions. It is of no use to lament and indulge in evil contemplations while experiencing bad fruits of one's own past evil actions. It is like shedding tears over split milk. If at the time of experiencing bitter or unpleasant fruits of one's past evil actions, one repents for what one did in the past, learns a good lesson and resolves not to indulge in such actions in future, then one will surely be benefited.

We can consider ourselves to be really convinced of the truth of the law of *karma*, only when we are convinced of the misery-causing dreadful nature of our evil actions, just as we are convinced of the misery-causing dreadful nature of poison, cobras, etc. We cannot deny this. This is the truth.

To say that the law of *karma* is right or true and at the same time to intentionally disregard it in practice mean that we have really no faith in the law or that we prefer immediate material gain to the prevention of the future bitter results or consequences. At times, under certain circumstances, we are constrained to disregard the law of *karma* and forced to do evil actions against our will. On such occasions too, we do bind *karmas* and as a result of it we have to experience their bitter fruits at the time of their fruition, but the duration of such *karmas* is short and the bitterness of their fruits is less intense.

(2)

It is wise to experience the fruits of *karmas* with equanimity, when the *karmas* rise to give their fruits. *Karmas* do not generate new *karmas*, when their fruits are experienced with equanimity. If man enjoys the pleasant fruits with attachment and experiences the painful ones with evil contemplations, then this way of experiencing the fruits of *karmas* causes the bondage of new *karmas*. Therefore, when the *karmas* rise to give their fruits, man should not be engrossed in or infatuated with the enjoyment of their pleasant fruits, that is, he should experience the pleasant fruits of *karmas* without attachment and with equanimity, and in his miserable state, he should experience the painful fruits of the risen *karmas* with courage, keeping the mind calm and unagitated; as a result of this, the risen *karmas* get dissociated from the soul in such a way that they could not cause the bondage of new *karmas* in their trail.

On account of its *karmas*, the objects of sense-pleasures are presented to the soul. But it is left to the will of the concerned soul as to whether or not to be overpowered and subdued by them. Only those persons whose minds are not disturbed or agitated even in the presence of the causes of mental disturbances, (that is, in the presence of the objects of sense-pleasures), are really wise and steady.[1] The delicious food (of six

1. *vikārahetau sati vikriyante yeṣāṃ na cetāṃsi ta eva dhīrāḥ* / —*Kumārasambhava* by Kālidāsa, I Canto, the last but one verse, second half.

flavours[1]) does not enter man's mouth per force and come in contact with his tongue; attractive tunes do not enter his ears per force to infatuate him. Similarly, the objects of senses do not forcibly yoke him to the enjoyment of sense-pleasures against his will. Though it is a fact that objects of senses do not forcibly cling to man, it is also a fact that their gross experience is inevitable so long as he is living. His life is impossible without their gross experience. But the point to be ever remembered is that in this gross experience, it all depends entirely on his will as to whether or not to give way to the rise of passion for sense-pleasures, to indulge in their inordinate enjoyment and to be infatuated with them. The only means for keeping one's mind calm and composed even in the midst of sense-objects presented to one by the fruition of one's *karmas* is the extermination of the longing for sense-pleasures by means of the fire of knowledge.

The objects of sense-pleasures are present before a man; even then if he remains firm, steady and calm on the strength of his internal spiritual power and does not move from his seat, will those objects move towards him and embrace him? This means that he can refrain from joining the enjoyment of sense-pleasures and remain aloof from the objects of sense-pleasures by his strong will. But if he loses patience, courage and self-confidence, he will surely slip into the deep valley of degeneration. It is, therefore, more proper and meaningful to blame one's own spiritual weakness than to put a blame on one's *karma.*

Although a wise man may eat sweets, etc., drink fruit-juices, etc., he would not bind harmful *karmas* (i.e., inauspicious *karmas*), because he is ever vigilant, not overpowered or agitated by them and experiences them without any attachment. This is illustrated by the lives of the learned wise men of the past and the present. One has nothing to fear if one utilises the objects of senses with equanimity, sense of justice and that of propriety.

---

1. In the first chapter of this work, while treating of *pudgala* (matter), five (basic) flavours are enumerated according to scriptures. They are: bitter (*kaḍavo*), pungent (*tīkho*), astringent (*tūro*), sour (*khāṭo*) and sweet (*mīṭho*). Then what about saltish flavour (*lavaṇa rasa*)? In answer to this question, Guṇaratnasūri writes in his commentary on Ācārya Haribhadrasūri's *Ṣaḍdarśanasamuccaya* as follows: *lavaṇo madhurāntargata ity eke / saṃsargaja ity apare* / That is, some include it in sweet flavour, while others regard it as a mixture of two particular basic flavours.

(3)

Each and every member of the society should be free to strive for the attainment of the material, mental and spiritual good. But at the same time, he should accept the restrictions imposed by the rules of social ethics and justice. The observance of those social customs and conventions that are in consonance with and conducive to justice and morality is necessary for the stability and order of the society. There are other customs which are positively harmful to the society; they are the product of ignorance; they are destitute of discretion; they might have been relevant in the days of their origination, but are now irrelevant and pernicious; their removal surely causes increase in the happiness of the members of the society or causes decrease in their misery. If the society sticks to such harmful customs out of ignorance or obstinacy, its members will have to suffer miseries. To tell the sufferers that their miseries are not due to bad customs but due to their past *karma* and they should, therefore, bear them meekly is like giving opium to a person to deprive him of his consciousness. Here the fault lies directly and perceptibly with harmful customs or superstitions. Miseries found as resulting from harmful customs are no doubt due to them, just as pain seen or experienced as resulting from piercing of the heel by a thorn is no doubt due to the thorn. And it is those who spread and nourish harmful customs that should be held responsible for the miseries. Those who suffer miseries ought to oppose the harmful customs with properly organised agitation and thereby should eradicate the miserable and degenerating environment of harmful customs and superstitions. This will certainly destroy the dreadful power of the weapon of harmful customs and superstitions—the weapon wielded by the past *karma*. What applies to harmful customs and superstitions applies also to capitalism that exploits the poor and to imperialism that makes weak nations slave and sucks their blood.

(4)

Behind any event taking place in the life of a mundane soul, there is certainly the force of its past *karma*. Thus, when a physical (natural), bodily or financial calamity befalls a person, that force is indubitably working behind it. In spite of this fact, if a person intentionally invites the calamity, he cannot escape from the crime of inviting it. The worldly laws may or may not punish him for this crime, but the Law of Nature (*karma*) will certainly punish him.

When a man is murdered or robbed of, his past *karma* is one of the causal conditions of his murder or his being looted. But a person who has committed a murder or an act of robbery is no doubt guilty of that crime and will be punished by the Law of Nature (*karma*) just as he is justly punished by the worldly rule of justice. The murderer or robber cannot argue in his defence that it is the destiny of the man, which is the cause of his murder or of his being looted. He cannot defend himself in this manner even according to the law of religion or philosophical jurisprudence. The murderer's or robber's presenting the destiny of the victim as the cause of the murder or robbery, though howsoever true or right in the ultimate analysis, is nothing but blatant rudeness or shamelessness on the part of the murderer or robber. This rudeness or shamelessness is of no help to him and he has to reap the fruits of his heinous acts without fail.

At this juncture, let us note that all crimes are not equal. When we are the victims of the crimes that are ordinary or that cannot be properly countered or against which there is no effective remedy, then it is of no use to harbour rancour in the mind and to entertain vain revengefulness. It is no good to remember in vain the past cases of somebody's doing bad to us and to again generate the poison of enmity or passions in our mind. So, on such occasions it is proper for us to use our faculty of discretion and to reflect on the force of karmic traces or on the inexorable law of *karma*. But it is never beneficial to us to entertain feeling of revengefulness or retaliation towards the culprit. It is really useful and beneficial to take recourse to the reflections such as referred to above in order to keep one's mind calm and cool and to establish it firmly in equanimity.

But if somebody attacks you and you counter his attack, nobody will say that you entertain enmity towards him. If you have lent your money and he is not returning it and you file a suit against him for getting your money back, then nobody will accuse you of revengefulness. If somebody forcibly takes away your things and you try to protect and retain them, then nobody will accuse you of returning evil. There is nothing wrong if one properly opposes, confronts or counteracts a rogue, a thief, a cheat, a liar or a rascal. According to the rule of religious law, it is rightful and fair. And even the science of moral causation (*Karmaśāstra*) concedes the scope and role of proper human effort in hastening or weakening the fructification of *karma*. It rightly recognises and emphatically supports the point that proper effort, industry or endeavour has important place in life. Effort is useful and necessary for regaining the lost things. Do we not take medicine to regain health when we are sick? Man always tries to attain happiness and its means, to ward off future miseries and their causes, and to remove the present miseries already befallen him. All worldly beings undertake such activities. None can say that proper counter-attacks undertaken with a views to defending one's own self and others, or to protecting the glory of justice, spring from the feelings of revengefulness, retaliation or enmity. Rāma's attack on Rāvaṇa was just and rightful. If a robber robs you of your possessions and you, though inwardly burning with rage, meekly and impotently gaze at him, it is an act of cowardliness. Of course, it is necessary to weigh the situation before taking any step. One should not be rash. One should undertake only proper measures in accordance with one's estimate of the situation. It is true that one's measures should be commensurate with the situation. It is because in the world one who seeks to lose a lot in order to save a bit is a thoughtless person.[1]

(5)

Destiny is incomprehensible. Man is, therefore, free just to make efforts. If we dig the ground, we shall get water, provided it is there. Similarly, if the good fortune is in store for man, it is manifested or brought about through efforts only. Human effort accompanied with pure light of right knowledge destroys man's present miserable state and opens up the doors of happiness, as also strongly counters the future onslaughts of inauspicious *karmas*. That is to say, under the pretext of *karma* theory, man should not be lazy, depressed and downcast, but should become industrious and brave, taking into account the supreme importance of the spiritual power. If it is not possible for him to remove or allay suffering already befallen on him and hence he has no alternative but to experience it, then, instead of experiencing it with cowardliness and as a result binding new inauspicious *karmas*, he should experience it with

1. *alpasya hetor bahu hātum icchan vicāramūḍhaḥ pratibhāti loke /*
—*Raghuvaṁśa* by Kālidāsa, II Canto, second half of verse 47 (with the change of last three letters).

praiseworthy equanimity and peace, which evinces true understanding and heroic spirit; and at that time *karma* theory gives him required strength to keep the mind cool, composed and unagitated. The *karma* theory points out that inevitable *karma* never allows man to escape from the consequences of his past actions; it compels him to experience its fruits completely. Even great men could not escape the consequences of their *karmas*. We must realise that sufferings and calamities do not befall us of their own accord; those that are sown, sprout up. So even while taking proper measures for their removal, one should experience bravely the portion thereof which one has to experience inevitably. If one experiences the sufferings in this manner, one does not bind new misery-causing *karmas* but on the contrary allays the burden to that extent. If we keep the stream of life auspicious, that is, free of sins and evils, no new inauspicious *karmas* are bound to us and as a result the stream of life gradually becomes more and more blissful and more and more spiritually bright. The *karma* theory enunciates that the practice of immorality, injustice and treachery causes the bondage of inauspicious *karmas*, while the practice of virtues like truthfulness, self-control, service causes the bondage of auspicious *karmas*.[1] In this way, the law of *karma* obviously inspires man to become virtuous and righteous and thereby elevates the whole society.

(6)

When man is afflicted with a disease, or incurs losses, or suffers any other calamity, he blames his *karma*. Now, if the situation or condition is the *direct* result of his past *karma*, then it would be proper to do so. But even in that case, he should make proper efforts to remove such calamity or misery. And if, in spite of his efforts, it is not removed, then without indulging in evil broodings he should experience it with courage;

1. The actions performed in the previous birth give their fruits in the present birth, and even the actions performed in the present birth give their fruits in this very present birth. This is stated in the *Bhagavatīsūtra*. The statement in point is as follows:
paraloakaḍā kammā ihaloe veijjaṁti,
ihaloakaḍā kammā ihaloe veijjaṁti /
And the *Yogasūtra* (II. 12) too says the same thing. The aphorism is as follows: '*kleśamūlaḥ karmāśayo dṛṣṭādṛṣṭajanmavedanīyaḥ /*'

this becomes his duty. On such occasions, if he fails to put forth proper efforts to remove the calamity or suffering befallen on him, then in the absence of such efforts his lethargy or inactivity is responsible for whatever misery or calamity he suffers. It is, therefore, not wise to remain idle and inactive and blame only one's past *karma* for one's miseries and calamities. When bodily, financial or any other calamity befalls us on account of our own actions performed in the present birth itself, we all conveniently blame our past *karma* in order to shirk from the responsibility. But in such cases it would be proper to blame our own known activities or behaviour on account of which we have been put into the miserable state; at the same time, we should resolve not to do such acts again in future and repent for what we did. To lose health and become weak by living careless and irregular life, by taking unwholesome and harmful food, by subjecting the body to prolonged hunger[1], or by not supplying the required nutritive elements to the body through food; to invite poverty by losing money in habitual gambling or speculation; to become debtor by expending more money than one's income affords, by indulging in worldly pleasures, or by submitting to harmful customs; to fail in examination by neglecting study and by indulging in sense-pleasures; to put the life of a sick man in danger by not taking him to the expert doctor for treatment and instead by taking recourse to superstitions of evil spirits and of possession of men and women by them; and to put the blame for all this on the past *karma* is nothing but bankruptcy of human reason. One should blame one's foolish and thoughtless behaviour or activities and should learn proper lesson from such behaviour or activities.

The working of *karma* is well concealed and beyond the ken of our comprehension and understanding. So it is only human effort with discretion and thought that is left in the hands of man. This effort is aimed at removing the calamity befallen on one's own self or on others, or it is aimed at achieving individual or social upliftment and progress. But when man attains the desired fruit through his efforts, he should not be elated and puffed up. And when he does not attain the desired fruit in

---

1. It is a different matter, if one cheerfully observes fast, a form of austerity, in order to achieve some noble goal or if one gives up food for a certain period of time according to the advice of an expert doctor in order to cure oneself of a severe disease.

spite of his efforts, he should not be disappointed and dejected. In making efforts, it is not that we transgress the law of *karma* but on the contrary respecting the law we desire to achieve progress and to remove calamity. Human effort does not contradict the law of *karma.* As a matter of fact, human effort goes well with the law of *karma.* We do not violate the Law of Nature by planning to dig out channels for diverting rushing waters of the flood, which would otherwise inundate many villages, but on the contrary we make use of the Law of Nature by making efforts to save the villages. Similarly, we should also make use of the law of *karma* as far as possible by making efforts to remove calamity or to achieve upliftment. The fact that every effort bears its proper fruit is the foundation of the law of *karma.*

When some helpless person is suffering from miseries or is unjustly tortured, we should not blame his past *karma* but should at once rush to his help; it is our duty. It is a sin to leave the miserable person to his destiny or *karma* and not to attempt to relieve him of the misery. Both the science of Religion and the science of *karma* advise us to make sincere efforts to dissipate and destroy the influence of *karma* and not in the least to sit idle, blaming our *karma.* From the moment of man's descent in embryo to that of the end of his life, he depends on others, he seeks and receives cooperation and help from others. Thus entire humanity is like one family, and its happiness and peace, upliftment and progress depend on mutual cooperation and affection and amicable living. It is a crime in the regime of spirituality to be selfish, to remain always clung to one's possessions with strong attachment, to neglect other's interests thinking constantly of one's own, and to be hard-hearted.

Doctrine of rebirth or that of *karma* is not the doctrine nourishing and encouraging inactivity or idleness. On the contrary, it is the doctrine that inspires man to make proper efforts and to undertake good works leading to progress. So it is a very useful doctrine conducive to all progress. It advises man to put forth proper efforts to destroy veils of *karmas*, to advance on the path of liberation and ultimately to attain liberation. It is the function of the doctrine of *karma* to connect the present birth with the past and the future births in the cause-effect chain. If the future birth is not good, then it is in the hands of man to make efforts to improve it as also to effect changes in inauspicious *karmas* and in their fruition. This is what the doctrine of *karma* teaches. So the doctrine of *karma* is not in any sense the doctrine of fatalism.

We should bear in mind that by its own activities the soul binds *karmas* and can also dissociate the bound *karmas* from it by its own activities. All *karmas* are not unalterable. Many of them are such as can be altered by proper spiritual efforts. The *karma* philosophy goes to the extent of declaring that even the unalterable (*nikācita*) *karmas* can be altered and even destroyed[1], but it can be done only by highly pure and intense spiritual discipline. What is meant is that we should not become inactive and lazy depending on *karma.* It is neither proper nor good for us. Of course, when the continuous efforts do not bring us success or when one does not find the proper ground for putting forth such efforts, then in such a situation one should consider the concerned *karma* to be of the unalterable (*nikācita*) type, should keep the mind cool and placid, and should patiently endure the favourable and unfavourable circumstances. If, without thinking as to what would be the influence of one's act on one's body, on one's mind or on others, that is, without paying any heed to the well established or possible cause-effect relationship, one performs an act following others blindly, or impelled by blind faith, ignorance, greed or temptation, then the act will not produce the desired effect. And in that case, one should blame one's own ignorance, thoughtlessness and miserliness for the failure of one's efforts. Power of discretion is that aspect of intellect which enables us to visualise the possible and impossible, the good and bad consequences of a particular act. We should use our power of discretion and should do nothing without first giving thought to cause-effect relationship. In the absence of the utilisation of this faculty, blind faith, blind following and imitation, ignorance, greed and temptation thrive. In spite of his knowledge that greed, etc., are defects, man yields to them and under their sway he performs wrong and evil activities, and as a result falls a victim to their evil consequences.

---

1. Upādhyāya Yaśovijayajī shows as to how one can destroy even the unalterable (*nikācita*) *karmas* in the following verse of his 27th *Dvātriṁśikā*:
nikācitānām api yaḥ karmaṇām tapasā kṣayaḥ /
so'bhipretyottamaṁ yogam apūrvakaraṇodayam // 24//
The *nikācita karmas* can be destroyed by *tapas* (austerity). But by *tapas* is here meant not external austerities or any such austerities, but only those highly spiritual and yogic practices that characterise the far advanced stage of spiritual development.

(7)

People say that by undertaking activities like donation, worship, service, etc., man earns merit (*puṇya*) or binds auspicious *karmas* and by torturing others or by doing something to them against their will he accumulates demerit (*pāpa*) or binds inauspicious *karmas*. But this external activity is not the main factor determinant of merit and demerit, or of auspicious *karma* and inauspicious *karma*. It is so because in spite of even causing pain to others or doing something to them against their will, man can earn merit, and in spite of performing activities of donation, worship, service, etc., he earns demerit. When a benevolent and kind surgeon performs surgical operation on the patient, the latter no doubt suffers pain. Similarly, when well-wisher parents try to send their playful and immature son to school against his will, the latter cries and feels unhappy. But merely on that account no one regards the surgeon as the doer of improper or vicious activity, nor does anybody blame the parents for causing pain to their son. On the contrary, when somebody performs activities of donation, service, worship, etc., in order to cheat the simple people or in order to achieve some trifling selfish end, he binds inauspicious *karmas* instead of auspicious *karmas*. So the real test of one's earning merit or demerit (that is, binding auspicious *karmas* or inauspicious *karmas*) is not the visible bodily or vocal activity (overt behaviour), but the performer's intention behind that activity. Whatever is done with good intention is the cause of the bondage of auspicious *karma* (*puṇya*). And whatever is done with bad intentions is the cause of the bondage of inauspicious *karma* (*pāpa*). All accept this test of auspicious *karma* and inauspicious *karma*. It is because all accept the rule that the kind of gain is determined by the kind of feeling or intention. In other words, as is the feeling or desire or intention, so is the gain.[1] But it is also possible that the activity of a thoughtless person, though performed with good intention, is idiotic, evil and hence the cause of the bondage of inauspicious *karma*. Therefore, even in the case of activity performed with good intention, one should be vigilant and discreet. *Dharma* (religion or good conduct) consists in vigilance and carefulness. And it is said that *viveka* (power of discretion) is the tenth treasure. If one lacks it, it is possible that one will cause harm or loss instead of benefit or gain.

---

1. *yādṛśī bhāvanā yasya, siddhir bhavati tādṛśī* /

(8)

Ordinary people believe that if one renounces all activities, then one remains untouched by *puṇya* (auspicious *karmas*) or *pāpa* (inauspicious *karmas*). They think that auspicious (wholesome) activities cause the bondage of auspicious *karmas* which are likened to a golden chain, and inauspicious (unwholesome) activities cause the bondage of inauspicious *karmas* which are likened to an iron chain. That is, whatever be the type of activity—auspicious or inauspicious—it certainly causes bondages. And the soul can attain liberation only by effecting release from the chain of karmic bondage and not in any other manner. With such thought or philosophy, they renounce all activities except those absolutely necessary for obtaining the necessaries, become inactive and sit idle waiting for the liberation. Idle living opens up the doors for the entry of Satan. Idle mind is Devil's workshop. As a matter of fact, every man is always engaged in some sort of activity.He cannot live without activity. Some time he appears to be outwardly inactive, but his mind is surely active even at that time. It is the nature of unsteady mind. So, outward display of renunciation of all activity is nothing but mere hypocrisy.

One should ever give up all evil activities; there is no question about it. But when can one give up all evil activities? One can give up all evil activities, when one employs one's mind fully in good activities. A thorn stuck deep into the heel is extracted with the instrumentality of a needle. Similarly, to make oneself free from evil activities one should use the good activities as an instrument. It is necessary. We throw away a thorn after we have extracted it, but we keep the needle with us for future use. Similarly, we should not renounce good activities so long as our tendency to do evil activity is not totally exterminated.

To be free from the bondage of auspicious activities, what is needed is the transformation of auspicious intention into pure intention, and not the renunciation of auspicious activities. Of course, this is a very difficult spiritual process. But the means to attain the difficult liberation can never be easy.

The crux of the above discussion is that we cannot renounce activity on our own. But when it gets useless and unnecessary, it stops by itself naturally. Man should renounce the evil activities alone and remain engrossed in good and wholesome activities, so long as the state of life is naturally prone to activity. Untimely renunciation of activity means the deviation from the natural and right path of duty. It is not conducive to spiritual development. It is rather a mockery of life; it is ridiculous.

Transition from one type of activity to another type of activity serves also one's need of inactivity (*nivṛtti*). In this way, the uninterrupted flow of activities can keep one's life cheerful and happy.

Of course, the field of activity is different for different individuals according to their different capacities. It is needless to say that to make the activity brilliant and vigorous, it is quite necessary to take proper rest and to have peace at regular intervals.

The question as to how far the activity is concerned with the bondage of *karma* has been discussed in Chapter III (pages 104-7).

In Chapter III under **Liberation,** we have treated of the problem of activity-inactivity (*pravṛtti-nivṛtti*).

(9)

Generally the term '*karma*' has two meanings—one is 'any activity' and the other is 'fine material particles that get attracted towards and stick to the soul on account of its activity'. 'That which is being done is *karma*' is the etymology of the term *karma*. Both these meanings are appropriate in the context. The whole universe is packed with the fine karmic material particles. But when they get attracted towards the soul and stick to it and bind it through its activity, then only they are designated by the term '*karma*'. Thus the material particles bound with the soul (i.e., transformed into *karma*) are called *karma*. The karmic material particles bound with the soul are called '*dravya-karma*' (physical *karma*), while internal mental states of attachment, aversion, etc., are called '*bhāva-karma*' (mental *karma*). In other words, the Jainas distinguish between the material *karma* called *dravya-karma* and its spiritual counterpart called *bhāva-karma*. The soul (in its impure or perverse states) is the doer of *bhāva-karma* as also of *dravya-karma*. *Bhāva-karma* causes *dravya-karma*, and *dravya-karma* causes *bhāva-karma*. They are mutually related as cause and effect, each of the other, just as a seed and a sprout are.[1]

---

1. In the non-Jaina systems of Indian philosophy, the following terms are employed for *karma*: *māyā, avidyā, prakṛti, apūrva, vāsanā, āśaya, dharmādharma, adṛṣṭa, saṁskāra, daiva, bhāgya,* etc. In the *Vedānta* philosophy, we come across the three terms, viz., *māyā, avidyā, prakṛti* . The term '*apūrva*' is found in the *Mīmāṁsā* philosophy. The term '*vāsanā*' is current in the Buddhist philosophy. (Even *Yoga* philosophy employs it.) The term '*āśaya*' is generally used in the *Sāṁkhya* and *Yoga* philosophy. The *Nyāya* and the *Vaiśeṣika* systems employ the terms '*dharmādharma*', '*adṛṣṭa*' and

(10)

The karmic material particles are first attracted to the soul and then bound with it. The function of attracting them to a soul is performed by the activity (the activity of mind, speech and body). So the activity is called *āsrava* (influx), rather cause of the influx. And the function of binding the karmic material particles with the soul is performed by *mithyātva* (unwholesome inclination or faith or conviction), *avirati* (non-restraint), *pramāda* (lethargy) and *kaṣāya* (passion). So they are called the causes-of-bondage. Even activity is there with these four, viz., *mithyātva,* etc., to act as a cause of bondage. This is the reason why the *Tattvārthasūtra* VIII.1 declares all these five as the causes of bondage. But in the *Tattvārthasūtra* VI. I *yoga* (activity) alone is called *āsrava,* the remaining four, viz., *mithyātva,* etc., are not called *āsrava* (influx), rather causes-of-*āsrava.*

From this we can understand that *yoga* (activity) is the cause of both the influx and the bondage. Similarly, *mithyātva,* etc., which are the causes of bondage can also be regarded as *āsrava* (influx), rather causes of *āsrava* (influx). This can be explained as follows.

In scriptures, the separate causes of influxes of eight basic *karma*-types and their sub-divisions are mentioned. Therein the different tendencies and mental dispositions of the form of defects like *mithyātva, avirati, pramāda* and *kaṣāya* are mentioned as the causes of influxes of those different *karmas*. As the activity (*yoga*) causes the influx when it is vitiated by *mithyātva* etc., the latter can also be regarded as causes of influx.

The above observation shows that activity is known as *āsrava* (influx), rather *āsravahetu* (cause of influx). And as the scriptures include it in the list of the causes of bondage, it is also a cause of bondage. Again, as *mithyātva,* etc., are attached to *yoga* (activity), the cause of influx, they too are the causes of influx. And they are surely the causes of bondage. In other words, activity is a cause of influx and a cause of bondage as well; and *mithyātva,* etc., which are causes of bondage are causes of influx as well. From this we can notice that the functions of attracting (influxing) and binding are done by almost this one 'gang' alone—the gang of the

---

'saṁskāra'. The terms *'daiva'*, *'bhāgya'* *'puṇya-pāpa'* are such as are generally used in all the systems and religious sects and by the masses. All the systems that accept soul and rebirth accept also *karma.* And rebirth is the result of *karma.*

five. In this way, the identity of influx and bondage is shown to us.[1]

Now let us see as to what type of activity causes the bondage of a particular *karma.*

Insulting the learned, harassing him, being ungrateful to him, entertaining hatred towards him, neglecting and disrespecting the means of knowledge, obstructing others in their endeavour to acquire knowledge, refusing to impart knowledge or means of knowledge in spite of one's having them on account of one's mental impurities and defects, imparting unwholesome teaching, remaining idle—these are the causes of the bondage of knowledge-obscuring (*jñānāvaraṇīya*) *karma.*

When the above-enumerated features pertain to *darśana* (vision or indeterminate cognition), to a possessor of *darśana,* or to a means of *darśana,* they cause the bondage of *darśana*-obscuring (*darśanāvaraṇīya*) *karma.*

Compassion, service, forgiveness, love, forbearance, donation, self-control—these are the causes of the bondage of *sātavedanīya karma.* Even childish austerity (*bāla-tapa,* austerity not associated with genuine under-

---

1. Study the following verse (IV. 78) from Ācārya Hemacandra's *Yogaśāstra:*
kaṣāyā viṣayā yogāḥ pramādāviratī tathā/
mithyātvam ārtaraudre cety aśubhaṃ prati hetavaḥ//
Translation: *kaṣāyāḥ* (passions), *viṣayāḥ* (objects of sense-pleasure), *yogāḥ* (activities), *pramāda* (spiritual lethargy), *avirati* (non-restraint), *mithyātvam* (unwholesome inclination or conviction), *ārtadhyāna* (painful concentration) and *raudradhyāna* (cruel concentration) are the causes of the influx of inauspicious *karmas.*
In the auto-commentary on this verse Ācārya Hemacandra discusses the topic of *āsrava-bandha* in the question-answer style. He raises a question—The *kaṣāya,* etc., are called the causes-of-bondage, then why are they enumerated in the *bhāvanā* of *āsrava?* Let me reproduce the original text discussing this question and its answer. It is as follows:
"*nanv ete bandhaṃ prati hetutvenoktāḥ, yad vācakamukhyāḥ "mithyādarśanāvirati-pramāda-kaṣāya-yogā bandhahetavaḥ" iti/ tat kim āśravabhāvanāyāṃ bandhahetūnām eteṣām abhidhānam? satyam, āśravabhāvaneva bandhabhāvanā'pi na mahadbhir bhāvanātvenoktā, āśravabhāvanayaiva gatārthatvāt/ āśraveṇa hy upāttāḥ karmapudgalā ātmanā sambadhyamānā bandha ity abhidhīyate/ yad āha "sakaṣāyatvāj jīvaḥ karmaṇo yogyān pudgalān ādatte, sa bandhaḥ" iti/ tataś ca bandhāśravayor bhedo na vivakṣitaḥ/ nanu karmapudgalaiḥ saha kṣīranīranyāyenā"tmanaḥ sambandho bandha ucyate, tat katham āśrava eva bandhaḥ? yuktam etat, tathāpy āśraveṇānupāttānāṃ karmapudgalānāṁ kathaṁ bandhaḥ syāt? ity ato'pi karmapudgalādānahetav āśrave bandhahetūnām abhidhānam aduṣṭam/ nanu tathāpi bandhahetūnāṃ pāṭho nirarthakaḥ/ naivam, bandhāśravayor ekatvenoktatvād āśravahetūnām evāyaṃ pāṭha iti sarvam avadātam/*"

standing and knowledge) causes the bondage of *sātavedanīya karma. Sātavedanīya karma* is that *karma* the result of which is the pleasant experience or feeling.

Pain, sorrow, heart-burning, crying, killing, bewailing, each caused to oneself, to someone else or both—these are the causes of the bondage of *asātavedanīya karma. Asātavedanīya karma* is that *karma* the result of which is the painful experience or feeling.

Preaching and propagating unwholesome path, denigrating the wholesome one, ill-treating the saints and good persons, and adopting adverse attitude and behavior towards the means of spiritual welfare—these are the causes of the bondage of *darśana-mohanīya karma* (the *karma* which deludes our love for truth or our inclination towards truth).

The acutely unwholesome mental state resulting from the manifestation of passions causes the bondage of conduct-deluding (*cāritra-mohanīya*) *karma.*

Too much inclination for hurting, too much accumulation of possessions, killing of the five-sensed beings, cruel mental states—these are the causes of the bondage of *narakāyuṣ-karma* (infernal-lifespan-determining *karma*).

Deceit is the cause of the bondage of *tiryagāyuṣ-karma* (animal-lifespan-determining *karma*).

Minimum infliction of injury, minimum accumulation of possessions, softness and simplicity of nature—these are the causes of the bondage of *manuṣyāyuṣ-karma* (human-lifespan-determining *karma*).

Self-control of moderate degree, self-control accompanied with attachment, childish austerity, refraining from evil acts out of compulsion—these are the causes of the bondage of *devāyuṣ-karma* (celestial-lifespan-determining *karma*).

Straightforwardness, softness, truthfulness, healing dissensions—these are the causes of the bondage of auspicious personality-determining *karma* (*śubha-nāma-karma*).

The opposite of the just-mentioned features—that is, crookedness, hard-heartedness, untruthfulness, creating and fostering dissensions, roguery, cunningness and treachery—these are the causes of the bondage of inauspicious personality-determining *karma* (*aśubha-nāma-karma*).

Condemning oneself, praising others, turning a blind eye towards one's own merits, displaying one's own shortcomings, humility and non-arrogance—these are the causes of the bondage of the high-status-determining *karma* (*ucca-gotra-karma*).

Condemning others, praising oneself, turning a blind eye towards even the existing merits of others, displaying even the non-existing merits in oneself, pride of family—these are the causes of the bondage of the low-status-determining *karma* (*nīca-gotra-karma*).

To cause obstruction to others engaged in the task of donation, reception, enjoyment, etc., is the cause of the bondage of obstructive *karma* (*antarāya-karma*).

This enumeration of the causes of the bondage of the different *karma*-types is not exhaustive, but only suggestive or indicatory.

At this juncture, there arises the following question: In the case of each type of *karma,* a different set of causes-of-bondage has been mentioned. Hence the question arises: Causes-of-bondage like jealousy in respect of knowledge have been enumerated in connection with the *karma*-type like knowledge-obscuring *karma.* Does such a cause-of-bondage binds down just one *karma*-type like knowledge-obscuring *karma* or is it able to bind down other *karma*-types as well? If a cause-of-bondage enumerated in connection with one *karma*-type can bind down other *karma*-types as well, then it is futile to mention different causes-of-bondage for the different *karma*-types; for now it turns out that a cause-of-bondage already appropriate to one *karma*-type is operative in connection with another *karma*-type as well. And if a cause-of-bondage enumerated in connection with one *karma*-type binds down just this *karma*-type and no other, then there ensues conflict with a particular scriptural rule. For there is a scriptural rule to the effect that generally speaking all the *karma*-types minus the *āyuṣ-karma*—that is seven *karma*-types in all—are bound down simultaneously. Following this rule one must admit that at the time when there is a bondage of the knowledge-obscuring *karma,* there is also a simultaneous bondage of the six *karma*-types *vedanīya,* etc. Thus so far as cause-of-bondage is concerned there is available at one time just that which is appropriate to one particular *karma*-type; but on the other hand, there is bondage at this particular time also of the other *karma*-types not standing in conflict with this particular one. That is to say, the alternative that a particular cause-of-bondage causes the bondage of just one particular *karma*-type stands cancelled by the scriptural rule in question. What, then, is the purpose behind enumerating separate causes-of-bondage for the separate *karma*-types?

The answer is as follows: The separate mention of causes-of-bondage that we find here must be understood as referring to bondage in respect of flavour. The idea is that the scriptural rule to the effect that at the time of experiencing the cause-of-bondage appropriate to one *karma*-type there is also a bondage of the other *karma*-types should be understood as referring to bondage in respect of karmic particles, and not to that in respect of flavour. So, the net conclusion is that the separate mention of cause-of-bondage refers not to the bondage in respect of karmic particles but to that in respect of flavour. So, on conceding that experiencing bondage in respect of karmic particles is simultaneously possible for a number of *karma*-types, there remains no difficulty about the just quoted scriptural rule. On the other hand, the different causes-of-bondage enumerated in connection with the different *karma*-types are responsible only for the bondage-in-respect-of-flavour pertaining to those *karma*-types; so the separate mention of causes-of-bondage that we find here remains equally free from difficulty.

When things are thus specified, the just quoted scriptural rule and the separate mention of causes-of-bondage that we find here remain equally free from difficulty. Even so, it has been further understood that when the separate mention of the causes-of-bondage is defended by suggesting that the mention refers to bondage-in-respect-of-flavour, then this defence too has in view just the equality of bondage. That is to say, at the time of experiencing a cause-of-bondage like jealousy-in-respect-of-knowledge, there is chiefly bondage-in-respect-of-flavour of a *karma*-type like knowledge-obscuring *karma*; as for the other *karma*-types that are simultaneously bound down, there is bondage-in-respect-of-flavour in their case too, but it obtains in a subordinate measure. For, it is impossible to maintain that bondage-in-respect-of-flavour obtains for just one *karma*-type and not for the others that are simultaneously bound down. The reason is that whatever *karma*-types experience on account of *yoga* (activity) bondage-in-respect-of-*karma*-particles, the same simultaneously experience on account of passions (*kaṣāya*) bondage-in-respect-of-flavour. Hence the separate mention of causes-of-bondage we find here can be defended by suggesting that it refers to bondage-in-respect-of-flavour and that obtaining chiefly and primarily.

Again, the separate mention of the causes of bondage of the auspicious and inauspicious sub-types of each *karma*-type clearly helps man understand as to which set of good activities leads to the bondage of a particular auspicious *karma*-type as also which set of evil activities leads to the bondage of a particular inauspicious *karma*-type. This urges him to undertake good activities and to refrain from evil activities. This is the obvious purpose behind the separate mention of the causes-of-bondage of different *karma*-types.

(11)

(About Life-span)

We have already mentioned four sub-divisions of the life-span-determining *karma*, viz., human-life-span-determining *karma*, animal-life-span-determining *karma*, celestial-life-span-determining *karma* and infernal-life-span-determining *karma*.

The clock which has been wound moves for a definite period of time and after that it automatically stops. And if it is obstructed by something during the period, it stops even before the end of that period. Similarly, soul's association with a physical body in human, animal, celestial or infernal existence continues till the end of the fixed duration of time, provided it is not confronted with any obstruction. And the soul does not inhabit the physical body even for a moment more than the fixed duration. But when this clock of the form of body stops even before the completion of the fixed duration on account of some obstructive causes like poison, fear, attack of weapon, unbearable pain, etc., the cessation or death occurring on account of these causes is known as 'untimely death'.

A long rope spread out takes long time to burn out, when it is set to fire at one end only and gradually burns. But the same rope, coiled and folded, burns to ashes at once, when it is set to fire. Similarly, if the material karmic particles of the life-span-determining *karma* are experienced gradually, then they are worked out at the end of the fixed duration; but, if they are experienced all together at once on account of the calamities like weapon, water (flood), poison, fire, etc., then they are worked out before the completion of the fixed duration and 'untimely death' occurs. When the quantum of karmic particles of a life-span of seventy years is experienced gradually, death occurs at the end of seventy years. But, instead of experiencing them gradually, if at the age of twenty-five years, some deadly accident takes place or some destructive attempt is made on one's life, and as a result all the remaining karmic particles of forty five years are experienced together all at once in a moment or two, or in two or four hours, then death will take place at that very time.

If a person has one thousand rupees and he spends a rupee a day, then it will take one thousand days for him to spend all the one thousand rupees. But if he spends one thousand rupees or the remaining part of the capital in a day, then destitution or poverty befalls him at once.

The life-quantum is of two types—viz., *apavartanīya* (i.e., one whose temporal duration is reducible) and *anapavartanīya* (i.e., one whose temporal duration is irreducible). Thus the *apavartanīya* life-quantum can possibly be enjoyed away even before that period is over which was its due period at the time when it was earned by way of karmic bondage, while *anapavartanīya* life-quantum cannot be thus enjoyed away. That is to say, *apavartanīya* life-quantum is that life-quantum whose period of enjoyment is less than the period that was due at the time of the concerned karmic bondage, while *anapavartanīya* life-quantum is that life-quantum whose period of enjoyment is equivalent to this latter period.

Whether the life-quantum earned by way of karmic bondage will be earned in an *apavartanīya* or an *anapavartanīya* form is not something that happens automatically, but it depends on the intensity or mildness of the mental perturbation of the time concerned. Thus life-quantum for the immediately next birth is earned by way of a karmic bondage some time during this birth. And if at this time, the prevailing mental perturbation happens to be mild, the resulting bondage of life-quantum is loose—so that when an occasion is available, the period that was its due at the time of bondage can well be reduced. On the contrary, if at that time the prevailing mental perturbation happens to be intense, the resulting bondage of life-quantum is tight—so that even when an occasion is available, the period that was its due at the time of bondage is never reduced, nor is it possible to enjoy it away at one go. The life-quantum that was subject to tight bondage on account of the intensity of the then prevailing mental perturbation is not exhausted before its due period is over, however much one might employ weapon, poison, etc., against the person concerned, while on the other hand the life-quantum that was subject to loose bondage on account of the mildness of the then prevailing mental perturbation can well be enjoyed away even before its due period is over but as soon as one happens to employ weapon, etc., against the person concerned. It is this sudden enjoying away of life-quantum which is called *apavartana*—i.e., time-reduction—or *akāla-mṛtyu*, that is, untimely death; on the other hand, the enjoyment of life-quantum for a period that was its fixed due is called *anapavartana*—that is, impossibility of time-reduction—or *kāla-mṛtyu*—that is, timely death. The idea is that the beings possessed of the life-quantum open to time-reduction do happen to encounter some means or other like a weapon, etc., that hastens death—with the result that they meet an untimely death. On the other hand, the beings possessed of the life-quantum not open to time-reduction never meet untimely death however powerful might be the means of hastening death that they might possibly encounter.

Soul is an eternal, indestructible substance. In its pure state, it is beyond birth and death. But in its impure mundane state, it manifests itself in any of the life-species (*yoni*) by assuming a physical body; this manifestation of soul through a physical body is called 'birth'. Thus its every new association with a new body is its new birth. And its separation from a physical body is called 'death'.

As already stated, the fixed due duration of life can be reduced by untimely death. But the fixed due duration of life can never be increased even by one moment in any way by any attempt. Under the chief influence of the deluding *karma* life-quantum of the immediately next birth is bound in the present birth. Therefore, the series of successive births and consequently the wandering in the transmigratory existence continue so long as the soul is under the influence of the deluding *karma*.

(12)

In the Jaina philosophy '*karma*' is not a mere trace or an impression of activity, but it is also a real thing, a real substance. As we have already said more than once, through the activity (of mind, speech and body) which is technically called '*yoga*' the material karmic particles[1] are attracted to soul, touch it and through the force of passions (attachment and aversion, i.e., *kaṣāyas*) stick to it. The passions (attachment and aversion) have been soiling the soul from the time immemorial, and the soul has been assuming different physical bodies from the beginningless time, so it has been caught in the cycle of influx and bondage from the beginningless time. This cycle is called *saṃsāra*—a transmigratory cycle. Thus on account of its association with material karmic particles, the soul wanders (takes births) in the various life-species (*yonis*). When it is ab-

1. The whole universe is packed with different groups of material particles. Of them, one group is of the type of '*karma*'. When the material particles of this group are bound to soul, they are called '*karma*'.

solutely separated or dissociated from all the material karmic particles, it is called 'a liberated soul'. And liberation of this kind is called perfect or ultimate liberation. Delusion, or a trio of attachment, aversion and delusion, or a gang of desire, anger, pride, deceitfulness and greed has the chief and prime power over all the *karmas*. They constitute the pivot on which moves the wheel of transmigration. They are chief amongst all defects. They control and rule over the entire karmic system. Once one frees oneself from them, one automatically frees oneself from the entire karmic cycle. Therefore, it is said that Ultimate Liberation is nothing but liberation from passions. In other words, Ultimate Liberation consists only in one's being free from passions. *Kaṣāyamuktiḥ kila muktir eva.*

Human being is superior to all other beings. He is endowed with the power of discretion and intelligence. When he makes the right use of his power of intelligence and treads the path of righteousness and good conduct, the bitterness of the forces of karmic bondages decreases and their sweetness increases. And when he makes great spiritual efforts and manifests his special spiritual power, then the karmic material particles stop sticking to his soul and soiling it and at the same time the already stuck karmic material particles fall off from it. This condition of the soul is considered to be its advancement towards the final goal of liberation.

The mundane living being can never be without activity. It does have at least mental activity. So it binds *karmas* on account of some activity. But one who follows the noble path of righteouness and rectitude should not be afraid of the karmic bondage effected by activity. It is because during its spiritually progressive living whatever *karmas* are bound will never give bitter fruits, during its auspicious living chiefly auspicious *karmas* are accumulated, and along with accumulation of auspicious *karmas* there goes on the continuous process of spiritually beneficial dissociation of the bound *karmas*. This course of life causes happiness and becomes very useful in the attainment of spiritual good.

Man should keep his intellect pure, he should not swerve from the path of spiritual welfare, and he should remain engaged in good activities. It is enough for him, if he bears this in mind. All the remedies of all miseries and misery-causing *karmas* are covered in it.

Dust particles move towards and enter the room or any other place on account of the wind blowing in that direction, and stick to the unctuous thing that is there. Similarly, karmic material particles move towards and fall on the soul on account of the blowing wind in the form of threefold activities of mind, speech and body, and they stick to it on account of the unctuousness of passions. When passions are destroyed, the material karmic particles are no doubt attracted to the soul, so long as the soul performs activities but they do not remain stuck to it, they get immediately dissociated from it after having simply touched it. Naturally one can raise a question: How can the material karmic particles get bound to or associated with the soul which itself is immaterial? Though the soul in its original nature is not material, it looks like a material thing, because it has been soiled by the impurities of attachment, aversion and delusion from time immemorial, and consequently it has been receiving into itself and binding with itself karmic material particles from the beginingless time. That is to say, even though immaterial by nature the soul has become akin to something material, since it has been associated with material karmic particles from the beginningless time; and it is as such that it receives into itself the material karmic particles. It is the soul that assumes different physical bodies, wanders in the transmigratory existence, suffers miseries, experiences pleasures and lives the life soiled with passions. How can all this trouble be without any cause? So, it is easy to understand that the cause of this mundane condition of the soul should also be there with the soul itself. And as this condition obtains from the beginningless time, its cause should also be there with the soul from the beginningless time. The cause—*moha* (delusion), *avidyā* (nescience), *māyā, vāsanā, karma,* whatever name you may like to give—is associated with the soul from the beginningless time. This is the reason why the soul looks like a material thing, though it is not really material; and it is on account of this that the soul is entangled in the karmic bondage, karmic fruition, etc., and is caught in the cycle of birth and death.

Just as the faculty of knowledge is not material, yet it is veiled by liquor, etc., similarly, though the soul is not material, its mundane condition with karmic coverings can well be explained in the same manner.

The seed sown does not develop into a sprout instantly, but it takes time and develops into the sprout in due course. Liquor does not produce intoxicating influence as soon as it is drunk; it does so only after having entered into the blood-stream. Similarly, whatsoever material *karmas* are bound with soul through its activities, give their proper fruits to the soul at the end of particular fixed duration of time after the bondage has been effected. They remain dormant there in the soul so long as their time of fruition does not mature. To say that *karma* has risen means that it has matured to give its fruit to the concerned soul. Every *karma* is called '*karma*' on account of its bondage with the soul. And once it is bound with the soul, it must get dissociated from it at some time. This is certain. Having risen to give its fruit, the *karma* makes the soul experience its fruit fully, and then gets automatically dissociated from the soul. This is a case of effective rise (*vipākodaya*) . But there is also such a state of *karma,* where even though *karma* rises, it does not cause the soul to experience its fruit and even without causing this experience, it gets dissociated from the soul. Such a rise of *karma,* as characterized by the absence of the experience of its fruit, is called nominal rise—that is, rise only of the karmic particles (*pradeśodaya*). If the soul were to experience the greatly accumulated *karmas* through the effective rise (*vipākodaya*) alone, then the attainment of liberation would become impossible. By the force of great spiritual efforts and austerities, many aggregates of *karmas* get dissociated from the soul in this way, that is, by mere nominal rise. And at last, when the huge store-house of the accumulated *karmas* becomes empty, the liberation is attained.[1]

1. Each *karma* is experienced without fail. This rule is rightly inexorable. But this rule is posited from the standpoint of the experience of karmic particles, and not from the standpoint of the experience of the flavour. It is not a rule that the flavour of each and every *karma* is invariably experienced by the soul. It is possible that karmic particles get dissociated from the soul through the experience of the karmic particles alone without the experience of flavour. Prasannacandra and others had bound *karmas,* the fruits of which were infernal existence and infernal miseries. But by the force of auspicious mental states, they destroyed their flavour and experienced simply the flavourless material karmic particles of those *karmas*. This is the only reason why they had not to experience the tortures of hell, even though they had bound the *karmas* whose fruits were infernal existence and infernal tortures. It is because the experience of pleasure and pain is caused only by the effective rise, that is, by the rise of flavour (*vipākodaya*). (See *Viśeṣāvaśyakabhāṣya-vṛtti* on *gāthā* 2049) .

If it is a rule that bound karmic particles get dissociated from the soul by effective rise alone and not by any other method, then no soul can attain liberation. It is so because the soul that attains liberation in that very birth does have *karmas*—in their dormant state—accumulated through innumerable births, and as they are bound on account of various mental states, they are the causes of future births in innumerable life-species like infernal being, human being, etc. So, if these *karmas* are to be dissociated from the soul by effective rise alone, then in the last birth the soul should experience various births. But that is impossible, because in the human birth, the soul cannot experience many births like a hellish birth, a celestial birth, etc. And if the different *karmas* which are the causes of births in different life-species cause the soul to experience their fruits in proper births taken one by one, then the soul

At the very time when the soul receives karmic material particles four aspects are generated in them, viz., their nature, their duration, their flavour and their quantity. The generation of any one of the different natures in the karmic particles is called the bondage in respect of nature. These natures are: knowledge-obscuring nature, vision(*darśana*)-obscuring nature, pleasant-painful-feeling-producing nature, etc. With the generation of nature is generated or is rather fixed the duration of time for which the karmic particles remain stuck to the soul. This fixation of duration of time is called the bondage in respect of duration. The capacity to give good or bad fruits of different degrees of intensity is also generated at that very time in those karmic particles; this is called the bondage in respect of flavour. The quantity of karmic particles is also fixed at that very time. This fixation is called the bondage in respect of the quantity. As soon as the karmic particles are received by the soul, they get transformed into different natures, form different groups according to their natures and their quantity in different groups too is different.

To explain these four types of bondage, an illustration of a sweet ball (*modaka*) is given. A sweet ball prepared from gas-destroying ingredients causes subsidence of gas; the one prepared from bile-destroying ingredients causes subsidence of bile; and the one prepared from phlegm-destroying ingredients causes subsidence of phlegm. Again, one sweet ball does not become rancid for four days, another for eight days, and a third one for a fortnight. Moreover, one sweet ball is more sweet and another less sweet, one more bitter and another less bitter. Further, one sweet ball contains two hundred grams of ingredients, another five hundred grams of ingredients; that is, different sweet balls contain different quantities of ingredients. Similarly, some karmic particles by their nature obscure the faculty of knowledge, some obscure the faculty of vision, some cause the experience of pleasure or pain, and so on. Again, different groups of karmic particles remain stuck to the soul for different durations of time and they have different capacities to give auspicious (sweet) or inauspi-

---

in those births will again bind new *karmas* which are the causes of births in different life-species, and these newly bound *karmas* will in turn cause the soul wander in different births and these births will again cause bondage of still new *karmas* causing births in different life-species, and this will go on *ad infinitum*. Thus liberation will become impossible. (See *Viśeṣāvaśyakabhāṣya-vṛtti gāthās* 2052-2053).

cious (bitter) fruits of different degrees of intensity. Moreover, different groups of karmic particles contain different quantities of karmic particles.

Of these four types of bondage, the first and the last depend on activity (*yoga*), because the bondage in respect of nature depends on the type of activity and the bondage in respect of quantity depends on the quantum of activity. In the karmic particles that are being attracted to soul, the different natures are generated according to the different natures of activity and the quantity of the particles is determined in accordance with the quantum of activity. Disrespecting and insulting the learned, destroying the means of knowledge, obstructing others' efforts to acquire knowledge, etc.—this type of activity generates the knowledge-obscuring nature in the karmic particles that are attracted to soul owing to its activity. And the more the activity, the greater is the quantity of those karmic particles. The bondage in respect of duration and the bondage in respect of flavour depend on passions (*kaṣāya*). We shall make this point clear in the following pages.

The bondage in respect of flavour is called in Sanskrit '*anubhāva-bandha*' or '*rasa-bandha*'. The term '*anubhāga*' in place of '*anubhāva*' is also in usage. Flavour (*rasa*) is of two kinds, viz., intense and mild. So the bondage of flavour is also of two types, viz., bondage of intense flavour and bondage of mild flavour. Both these kinds are possible in auspicious and inauspicious *karmas* as well. The flavour of the inauspicious *karmas* is compared to the bitter flavour of the Nimba tree. That is, just as the flavour of the Nimba tree is bitter, even so the flavour of inauspicious *karmas* is bitter, i.e., painful or bad. And the flavour of auspicious *karmas* is compared to the sugarcane juice. Just as the sugarcane juice is sweet, even so the flavour of the auspicious *karmas* too is sweet, i.e., pleasant or good.

Attachment (*rāga*) and aversion (*dveṣa*) are covered by the four passions (*kaṣāya*), viz., anger, pride, deceitfulness and greed. As already explained, each of these four passions has four types, viz., *anantānubandhī, apratyākhyānāvaraṇa, pratyākhyānāvaraṇa* and *saṁjvalana.* The passions of the *anantānubandhī* type are the associates of unwholesome inclination or conviction (*mithyātva*) and the obstructors of the wholesome inclination or conviction (*samyagdarśana*). The passions of the *apratyākhyānāvaraṇa* type arrest even the partial abstinence from violence, etc. The passions of the *pratyākhyānāvaraṇa* type arrest only the total abstinence from violence, etc. And passions of the *saṁjvalana* type obstruct the conduct characterized by perfect non-attachment.[1] Thus, the passions of the first type are very intense, those of the second type are intense, those of the third type are moderate, and those of the fourth type are mild.

The duration of the bondage of karmic matter—auspicious or inauspicious—with soul will be long if the soul is afflicted with intense passions at the time when the karmic matter is being bound with the soul. And the duration of the bondage of karmic matter—auspicious or inauspicious—with soul will be short, if the soul is afflicted with mild passions at the time when the karmic matter is being bound with the soul. Thus the duration of bondage depends on the degree of intensity of passions. The stronger the passions, the longer is the duration of bondage. And milder the passions, the shorter is the duration of the bondage. The bondage of the longest duration taking place in respect of any *karma* is always possible in the case of inauspicious karmic matter alone.

But the case with the bondage of flavour is different. It is as follows: If the passions are intense, the flavour bound in the inauspicious karmic matter is more intense, while that bound in the auspicious karmic matter is less intense. And if the passions are mild, the flavour bound in the auspicious karmic matter is more intense, while that bound in the inauspicious karmic matter is less intense. The more intense the passions, the more intense is the flavour bound in the inauspicious karmic matter and the less intense is the flavour bound in the auspicious karmic matter. The milder the passions, the more intense is the flavour bound in the auspicious karmic matter and the less intense is the flavour bound in the auspicious karmic matter. That is, intense passions generate intense flavour in the inauspicious karmic matter and mild flavour in the auspicious karmic matter, while mild passions generate intense flavour in the auspicious karmic matter and the mild flavour in the inauspicious karmic matter. In short, in the case of the bondage of inauspicious karmic matter, the intensity of flavour varies directly in proportion to the strength of the

1. The *saṁjvalana,* etc.—the four types of each of the four passions—obstruct non-attachment, the complete self-discipline of a mendicant, the partial self-discipline of the convinced Jaina householder and the wholesome conviction/inclination respectively and cause celestial, human, animal and infernal births respectively. See the following verse:
vītarāga-yati-śrāddha-samyagdṛṣṭitvaghātakāḥ /
te devatva-manuṣyatva-tiryaktva-narakapradāḥ//—Ācārya Hemacandra's *Yogaśāstra,* IV. 8

passions, but in the case of the bondage of auspicious karmic matter, the intensity of flavour varies inversely in proportion to the strength of passions. The bondage of the most intense flavour taking place in respect of the auspicious karmic matter is always auspicious.

It has been repeatedly stated that the groups of material particles capable of being received by the souls are not called '*karma*', so long as they are not actually received by or bound with the soul. But as soon as they are received by the soul, some wonderful force is generated in them and assisted by mental states afflicted with passions they generate in themselves infinitefold flavour which causes obstruction, etc., of the spiritual qualities. It is this flavour alone that performs the function of giving various fruits to the soul or of making it experience various consequences and results. This flavour is the greatest calamity befallen on the soul. The auspicious flavour causes happiness and the inauspicious flavour causes misery.[1]

Dry grass is arid without any juice. But when it is eaten by a buffalo, a cow or a she-goat, it undergoes some process of transformation in their stomachs and turns into milk, and in this fluid milk we do find unctuousness in more or less degree. In other words, the buffalo, etc., eat dry grass and give milk. The milk of the buffalo is very dense and very unctuous, that of the cow is comparatively less dense and less unctuous, and that of the she-goat is still less dense and less unctuous. Thus, though the dry grass of the same type is eaten by them, it is transformed into milk of different kinds on being consumed in their stomachs. Similarly, the material particles capable of being received by souls acquire different flavours on coming in contact with different souls and consequently being assisted by their passions of different degrees. This is called *rasa-bandha, anubhāva-*

1. Knowing that it is very difficult to remain unattached while experiencing pleasures, the attachment-free Bhartṛhari wrote in his *Vairāgyaśataka* as follows:

vipākaḥ puṇyānāṁ janayati bhayaṁ me vimṛśataḥ /

Meaning: When I reflect on it, the fruition of the auspicious *karmas* frightens me. After this second metrical line, in the latter half of the verse, he makes a very significant observation in the following statement:

mahadbhiḥ puṇyaughaiś ciraparigṛhītāś ca viṣayā
mahānto jāyante vyasanam iva dātuṁ viṣayiṇām //

Meaning: Worldly objects that have been possessed and enjoyed since long on account of the great aggregates of the accumulated auspicious *karmas* go on greatly increasing as if to cause agonies to those attached to sensual pleasures.

bandha or *anubhāga-bandha* (bondage in respect of flavour). Of the milks of different kinds, some have more energy and some have less energy. Similarly, of all the auspicious or inauspicious *karmas*, some have intense flavour and some have mild one.

In his *Tattvārthasūtra* Maharṣi Umāsvāti states: *śubhaḥ puṇyasya / aśubhaḥ pāpasya /* (VI. 3-4). It means: the auspicious activity (*yoga*) causes the bondage of auspicious karmic matter, and the inauspicious activity causes the bondage of inauspicious karmic matter. But the science of *karma* declares that even at the time of auspicious activity, the bondage of inauspicious karmic matter takes place, and even at the time of inauspicious activity, the bondage of auspicious karmic matter takes place. So, the import, as shown by the Jaina thinkers, of the above-mentioned two aphorisms is that when the auspicious activity is intense (when the degree of passions is mild), then the flavour of high degree is bound in the auspicious karmic matter and the flavour of low degree is also bound at the same time in the inauspicious karmic matter. Conversely, when the inauspicious activity is intense (when the degree of passions is intense), then the flavour of high degree is bound in the inauspicious karmic matter and the flavour of low degree is also bound at the same time in the auspicious karmic matter. Thus keeping in view mainly the high degree of flavour bound in the auspicious karmic matter owing to auspicious activity as also the high degree of flavour bound in the inauspicious karmic matter owing to inauspicious activity, it is said in the above-mentioned two aphorisms that the cause of bondage of auspicious karmic matter is auspicious activity, and the cause of bondage of inauspicious karmic matter is inauspicious activity. Thus, the statement made in the above two aphorisms is to be understood from the standpoint of the high degree of flavour; in this context the low degree of flavour of the inauspicious karmic matter, bound owing to auspicious activity, and the low degree of flavour of the auspicious karmic matter, bound owing to inauspicious activity, are not taken into account; for, as is found in everyday intercourse and also in theoretical treatises, it is a rule that usage takes place on the basis of what is predominant. The rule in Sanskrit is: *prādhānyena vyapadeśā bhavanti.*

There are ten main states of *karmas*. They are as follows:

(1) Bondage (Bandha): Bondage is the state in which karmic material particles are assimilated by the worldly soul. It means interpenetration of the space-point of the soul and the fine particles of karmic matter like the interpenetration of the smallest units of milk and water. This state is compared to red-hot iron in which fire and iron become one with the other. The fine karmic particles are received by all the space-points of the soul and not by its some space-points lying in a particular direction. The karmic bondages of all the worldly souls are not uniform, because their activities of mind, speech and body are not uniform. This is the reason why the bondages-in-respect-of-the-quantity-of-the-karmic-particles differ with different souls in accordance with their different quanta of activity. Infinite molecules of each *karma*-type are bound to all the space-points of the soul. The molecules of the karmic particles of different groups, lying in the area pervaded by the space-points of the souls, enter into the bondage with the soul; those lying outside the area pervaded by the space-points of the soul can never enter into the bondage with the soul. The karmic molecules that are being bound with the soul are each formed of infinite times infinite atoms.

The first state of *karmas* is bondage. Without it, no other state is possible. Bondage has four types, viz., bondage-in-respect-of-nature, bondage-in-respect-of-duration, bondage-in-respect-of-flavour and bondage-in-respect-of-quantity. We have already explained these four types.

(2-3) Increased realization (Udvartanā) and Decreased realization (Apavartanā) : As we know, when the bondage of karmic matter with the soul takes place, at that very time the length-of-duration-of-time of its association with the soul and the intensity of its fruition (flavour) are also bound or fixed. But despite this fixation, a person can increase or decrease the length of duration and the intensity of fruition. The increase of the length of duration and the intensity of fruition is called *udvartanā*. Contrary to it, the decrease of the length of duration and the intensity of fruition is called *apavartanā*. After having bound the inauspicious *karmas*, if a living being performs auspicious acts, then he can reduce the length of their duration and the intensity of their fruition. From this one should learn a lesson that if a person who has made his soul impure by leading an evil life under the sway of ignorance and delusion realises his mistakes, improves his living, becomes righteous and performs auspicious acts, then by force of his auspicious mental states, good feelings and righteous conduct he can reduce the length of duration and the intensity of fruition of the formerly bound inauspicious *karmas*. The degraded and fallen man can very well elevate himself and ascend the ladder of spiritual progress. The great sinners who had bound *karmas* causing birth in a terrible hell woke up from the sleep of ignorance, saw the truth, and took to the path of spiritual welfare; by doing so, they destroyed the terrible evil *karmas* through the fire of their austerity and became great sages capable of attaining the state of Supreme Soul.[1] The soul in the spiritual slumber is a sleeping lion. When it really wakes up to the truth, and manifests and uses its infinite energy, then the mad and devastating elephant of delusion gets completely subdued and at last destroyed by the soul-lion's great spiritual power, assuming greater and greater brilliance. The reverse is the case with *udvartanā*. For instance, after having bound the inauspicious *karmas* of the short length of duration and of mild fruition, if a person performs even more evil acts and his mental states become more impure by more intense passions, then the length of duration and the intensity of fruition of those formerly bound inauspicious *karmas* get increased under the influence of his vicious mental states; and under the influence of the internal impure states, the length of duration and the intensity of fruition of the formerly bound auspicious *karmas* get reduced. On account of *apavartanā-udvartanā*, some *karma* gives its fruit earlier than the due time; some *karma* gives its fruit later than the due time; some *karma* gives its fruit of intensity higher than the due intensity and some *karma* gives its fruit of intensity less than the due intensity.

(4) Endurance (Sattā) : The existence in *potentia* of the assimilated *karmas* from the instant of the assimilation to the moment of the enjoyment is known as *sattā* (endurance). In other words, this is a state of dormancy. As we have already stated, a *karma* does not give its fruit as soon as it is bound, but it remains dormant for some time before giving its fruit. The period of its existence in a dormant state is called '*abādhākāla*'. When this period of time expires (either in a normal course or hastily through the process of *apavartanā*), the *karma* swings into action to give its fruit.

(5) Rise (Udaya): When the *karma* becomes ready to give its fruit at its due time, it is called the rise of *karma*. The *karma* comes into rise in order to give its fruit after the period of time called *abādhākāla* is over. This rise

---

1. *brahma-strī-bhrūṇa-goghātapātakān narakātitheḥ /*
Dṛḍhaprahāriprabhṛter yogo hastāvalambanam //—Ācārya Hemacandra's *Yogaśāstra*, I.12
Meaning: Having committed grave sins of killing a brāhmaṇa, a woman, an embryo and a cow, Dṛḍhaprahārī and such others who had earned guesthood of the hells have crossed the ocean of worldly existence with the help of spiritual and yogic practice.

continues uninterrupted till the end of fruition. Thus, rise here means actual showing of the activity of the *karma* and experiencing the actual result of the *karma*.

(6) Premature Rise or Realization (Udīraṇā) : At the end of the period of *abādhākāla*[1], the rise of the *karma* at its due time in a normal course is called rise or realization (*udaya*). But to drag forward by special efforts the bound karmic material particles that are to rise after some time, to mix them with those that have already attained the state of rise and thereby to experience them before their due time of rise or realisation is called *udīraṇā* (premature rise or realization). In the season of mangoes, to ripen mangoes quickly we pluck them from the tree and cover them with dry grass, etc. By this process, mangoes get ripe earlier than they would have become ripe on the tree itself. Similarly, the fruition of *karma* can also take place even earlier than its due time. This is called *udīraṇā.* In *udīraṇā,* first the due duration of *karma* is reduced by the process of *apavartanā.* And on account of reduction of the due duration, the *karma* rises even before its due time of rise. When a man dies before enjoying the full length of his due life-duration, then in the world we call this death 'untimely death'. The cause of it is the premature realization (*udīraṇā*) of the life-span-determining *karma.* And this premature realization (*udīraṇā*) takes place owing to the process of *apavartanā.* Barring certain exceptions, rise and premature rise of *karmas* continuously go on. Premature rise (*udīraṇā*) is possible in the case of the unrisen karmic particles of only that *karma* whose some particles have already risen; and it mostly accompanies the rise (*udaya*). In premature rise (*udīraṇā*), the *karma* comes into operation earlier than its natural due time of operation, on account of the special efforts by the soul.

(7) Transformation (Saṅkramaṇa): The state of transformation (*saṅkramaṇa*) is that state in which karmic particles are subjected to the process by which a sub-type of the main *karma*-type is transformed into another sub-type of the same *karma*-type. In other words, of the eight main *karma*-types, one cannot transform itself into another, but only a sub-type of any one main *karma*-type can transform itself into another sub-

1. The *karma* does not bear its fruit as soon as it is bound. It remains dormant (inactive) for some time before producing its good or bad result. This period of inactivity is called *abādhākāla.* Each *karma* has its fixed *abādhākāla.* And when it ends, the *karma* comes into rise to give its fruit.

type of the same main *karma*-type. That is, knowledge-obscuring *karma* can never transform itself into any of the remaining seven main *karma*-types; but pleasant-feeling-producing *karma* can transform itself into painful-feeling-producing *karma*, and *vice versa*. Thus the mutual transformation is possible in the case of sub-types of the same main *karma*-type. Of course, there are exceptions to this. As for instance, the four sub-types of the life-span-determining *karma* can never be transformed one into another; mutual transformation is not possible in their case. The bound infernal-life-span-determining *karma*-type can never be transformed into any of the remaining three life-span-determining *karmas*, viz., animal-life-span-determining *karma*, human-life-span-determining *karma* and celestial-life-span-determining. Similarly, mutual transformation is not possible even in the case of the two sub-types of deluding *karma*, viz., right-conviction-deluding *karma* and right-conduct-deluding *karma*.

(8) Subsidence (Upaśama): Subsidence is the state in which the already risen karmic matter is subsided, suppressed. It is like covering the burning charcoal with ashes. The rise (*udaya*), the premature rise or realization (*udīraṇā*), the transformation (*saṅkramaṇa*), the increased realization (*udvartanā*), the decreased realization (*apavartanā*), the *nidhatti* and the *nikācanā* are suspended by special spiritual efforts in the state of subsidence. The state of subsidence primarily means the state of the *karma* as it is pressed down or controlled by the will when it is felt to be rising.

(9) Nidhatti: *Nidhatti* is a state in which there is no possibility of *udīraṇā* and *saṅkramaṇa*. But in this state, there can take place *udvartanā* and *apavartanā*. Thus this state implies that the bondage of the *karma* is so tight that *udīraṇā* and *saṅkramaṇa* cannot take place, but not so tight that even *udvartanā* and *apavartanā* too cannot take place.

(10) Nikācanā: *Nikācanā* is the state in which even *udvartanā* and *apavartanā* are impossible. This state, thus, implies that the bondage is so tight that no change is possible in it. The *karma* in this state is unalterable. Barring some rare exceptions, it invariably gives its fruit when it rises, and the soul has to undergo its experience without fail.

(13)

Every birth of a soul is a rebirth in view of its previous birth. There can never be any birth which is not connected with the previous birth.

The series of a soul's births (i.e., of the different physical bodies assumed by the soul) has no beginning. This is but logical. If we were to maintain that a particular past birth is the soul's first birth, then we would have to believe that before that birth the soul was free from the birth-cycle and only at a particular point of time it was caught in the cycle, that is, it was born for the first time; and this contention would consequently force us to hold that it is possible that even a pure soul which has freed itself from the birth-cycle on account of its attainment of purity will have to take birth some time. This would lead us to further assume that even after the attainment of liberation, the soul will be possibly caught again in the birth-cycle in future. This would render the eternal, absolute and perfect liberation impossible. It would be quite illogical to believe that the soul remains free from births for some time and starts to assume births again. On the contrary, it is logical to hold that the series of births continues, if it continues at all, without interruption and that once it is snapped it is snapped for ever.

There never was a time in the past when the soul was without birth (i.e., without association with a physical body), because if we assume that it was, it would follow that after taking the trouble of freeing oneself from the cycle of births through mental and moral disciplines, after going through a lot of ordeals, one might be caught again in the cycle of births and come in contact with different physical bodies. The fundamental ground of the philosophy is that, so far as the past is concerned there was never a time when the soul was without any physical body or birth, but that there will be a time in future when the soul will be without body or birth, and once without it, will always be without it, perfect and liberated thereafter.

We find difference among the sons and daughters of the same parents. Not only that, but also we find difference between twin brothers born at the same moment. Though parents pay considerable attention to their bringing up and training, they differ in learning, education, intelligence, wisdom, experience and conduct. This shows that the difference in blood, semen and environment is not a sufficient ground to account for this difference. Influences of the impressions of the past births too have their place in causing the difference and inequality. It is proper, appropriate and logical to believe so. Worldly causes do produce their effects, but this consideration need not stop there only. Even these causes themselves beg some further cause governing them all. Underlying them there is some secret unseen driving force that brings these causes together and impels them to operate at proper time. In order to find out this original, fundamental cause, we shall have to go far beyond the circumstances of the present life or birth.

In this world, we find that the persons who indulge in immoral and cruel activities roll in riches and enjoy all the luxuries of life, whereas those who follow the path of morality and righteousness remain poor and miserable. What is the cause of this anomaly? Where is the rule of the law 'as is the act so is the fruit'? If we think of the connection of the present birth with the past births, we can find the solution to this problem. According to the impressions of the activities performed in the past births, the course of the present life is determined and the special circumstances are generated. Similarly, in accordance with the present life or birth, the future life or birth is going to be moulded. In other words, the effects or influences of the impressions of the activities performed in the previous birth manifest themselves in the present birth, and the effects or influences of the impressions of the activities performed in the present birth will manifest themselves in the future birth. Does it not so happen that some rascals, dacoits and murderers, even after committing heinous crimes, are not caught and consequently escape the punishment, and that the innocents are caught and punished? What a sort of justice! Where is the rule of the law 'as is the act so is its fruit'? But this intricate problem is solved by the doctrine of rebirth and pre-birth. Different and queer activities performed in the previous birth present their varied and queer fruits in the present birth.

But from this we are not to understand that those who accumulate wealth by immoral, unjust and cruel acts and enjoy prosperity and pleasures on the strength of the wealth accumulated thus have any right, from the moral and religious standpoint, to such enjoyments. Such persons have accumulated wealth by directly or indirectly cheating, by fraudulently or forcibly looting, or by exploiting the poor and the labour. No good government or enlightened and vigilant society can tolerate such a situation for long. If such a situation is tolerated and allowed to continue, the fault lies with the government first and with the lazy and slumbering society next. It is the responsibility of the government and the society to see that the wealth is properly and justly produced and distributed. No religion should approve and thereby nourish such disparity, disorder and anarchy. Nor should it award the reputation and prestige of the honestly and justly earned wealth to such wealth by allowing their use in activities considered to be religious, with the intention of spreading and strengthening religion. If it does so, it encourages immorality and cruelty. The first good quality of a householder is to earn wealth honestly in a just way. The only praiseworthy and auspicious path is the path of earning wealth in a just way and spending a portion of it for religious activities, according to one's capacity. It is wrong, unwholesome and unsalutary to remain always engaged in amassing wealth by fair means or foul with a view to spend it in religious activities and in great religious festivals in order to spread and strengthen religion. Authors of scriptures clearly teach us that it is better not to desire wealth than to desire it for the sake of religion. It is better not to soil one's legs with mud rather than to wash them after soiling them with it.[1] It is quite easy and simple to understand that if the religious activities are performed with the wealth earned in a just way, the purity of religion is preserved and maintained. This is the right way of spreading the greatness and glory of religion. We should not put at stake the purity of religion for the sake of external show and ostentation. If the wealth is earned honestly in a just way and only such wealth is used in religious activities, then it has good influence and impact on the society and on the public.

Again, another point worthy of note is that the rascal, decoit and murderer whom the government or society cannot catch and punish do have to experience the fruits of their evil acts inevitably and invariably according to the relentless law of *karma* (moral causation). Though we accept that the calamity or misery caused to the people by others is ultimately the result of their own acts, yet the society or government should take all the proper measures to avert it; this is but proper and just.

Now let us resume the main point. As stated earlier, of the twin brothers, though nourished and brought up in the same environment, the

---

1. *dharmārthaṁ yasya vittehā varaṃ tasya nirīhatā /*
prakṣālanād dhi paṅkasya dūrād asparśanaṁ varam //
(The *Mahābhārata, Vanaparva* 3, *Adhyāya* 2, Verse 49)
The variant available of the second metrical quarter is as follows: *tasyānīhā garīyasī/* Ācārya Haribhadra and Ācārya Hemacandra quote this verse with great respect and conviction in their works. The verse is well-known and very much quoted in the Jaina literature.

intelligence and memory of one are sharp while those of the other are dull; again, there is difference in their thinking and conduct. Though the same means and facilities are made available to them and their efforts too are of the same degree, one learns science or art in a short time while the other lags behind. Though the two undergo the same training, make the same practice and are brought up in the same environment and circumstances, one develops the faculties of oratory, poetic composition and music, while the other remains either destitute of all those faculties throughout his life or is very slow when compared to his brother in developing those faculties. A six or seven year old boy makes the appreciative audience spell-bound by his art of singing; a child reveals his brilliance in mathematics, another child is endowed with poetic genius which enables him to compose plays or dramas. Can all this be possible or explainable without the awakening of the powers lying dormant in the impressions accumulated through past births?

We come across instances of children whose intellectual capacities and skills are qualitatively different from those of their parents. A son of the uneducated parents becomes a great scholar. A boy becomes a great musician though his parents positively dislike music. Only external circumstances, conditions and environment do not constitute the sufficient cause to generate those excellences. If it be said that all this is the result of the wonderful nerves or brain cells of those boys, then there arises a question as to where from they enter into their brains, while they are absent in their parents whose blood and semen have developed their bodies. It is true that we find a child as intelligent as its parents, or a boy has a great poetic genius like his parents. But then there arises a question as to how there occurs a favourable incidence in their case. In other words, what is it that determines that they would be born of intelligent parents or of parents having poetic genius? And why does the child of highly intelligent parents remain dull or of ordinary intelligence in spite of their great efforts to make him intelligent? Innumerable such instances do call for our consideration.

A man is walking carefully. Suddenly a tile of a roof, a brick or a stone falls on his head. He is seriously injured. Is it his fault that he is put to this trouble? No, not in the least. How can there be any difficulty or calamity in the absence of any fault? A man suspects another man of something, becomes excited and thrusts a dagger into his belly. As a result, the victim dies. What is the fault of the man who dies? If he is really innocent and kind, why should he be the victim of that deadly attack? But the apparent anomaly of such cases disappears, if we take into account the acts performed in past births.

A child has to experience pains during the period between the inception of the embryo and the actual birth. Are they all the results of the child's acts? Or, are they all the results of its parents' acts? They could not be regarded as the results of its acts performed in the present birth, because it has performed no act—good or bad—in the state of embryo. And if they are regarded as the results of the acts of its parents, then it is also not proper because why should it experience the fruit of the good or bad act of its parents, without any reason? And it can never be maintained that it experiences pleasure or pain without any cause, because there can be no effect without its cause.

From all these instances we know that the primary cause of the varied diversity or inequality does not lie merely in the present birth, nor is the diversity or inequality the result merely of the training or culture imparted by the parents, nor is it the result merely of environment, situations or circumstances. So it is proper to maintain that the soul existed even prior to the inception of embryo. This prior existence itself is the previous birth. The present birth and the special capacities associated with it can very well be accounted for on the basis of impressions that are left on the soul by the desires entertained and the activities performed in the previous birth. The logic that proves the previous birth, proves also the birth prior to that birth, and even the birth prior to that one, and thus is proved the beginningless series of successive births prior to the present birth. Similarly, the same logic proves even the future birth of the mundane soul.

Even the fact that the new-born child that has yet learnt nothing in the present birth starts on its own sucking the milk from its mother's breasts, proves by inference the existence of soul or consciousness in the previous birth.

Some may raise a question: Why do we not remember our previous birth, if it really existed? In reply a counter-question is asked: Do we remember all the events that took place even in the present birth? No, many events are veiled by our forgetfulness. If we forget many events of the present birth, then what to talk of the previous birth itself and events thereof? In the present birth, we have undergone radical changes in the life-species, in body and in sense-organ; our entire life has radically and totally changed; so how can we remember our previous birth? And yet we do hear instances of the great saints remembering their previous birth. The details of such instances have also been published in the reputed Indian journals. These incidents of the memory of past births compel man to think about rebirth.

Doctrine of rebirth preserves and keeps intact man's moral responsibility. Some time even a great man has to experience calamity and suffer statutory punishment without any fault or crime. At that time, the doctrine of rebirth serves as a soothing balm and helps him much in his efforts of keeping his mind unagitated and peaceful. If the good acts of the present birth are not accepted as having continuation in or connection with the future life beyond the end of the present birth, then man would become disappointed and frustrated, and in the time of calamity he would be surrounded by the darkness of despair and despondency.

Not a few 'accidental' events take place in the life of man. They may be called 'accidental' on account of their having no connection whatsoever with the intelligent efforts of a conscious being. But how can they be causeless? There must be some cause of an 'accident'? Reflecting on the difficult search of the cause of an 'accident', we arrive at the law of the 'unseen', i.e., *karma*.

In the world some think: "There is no soul, etc. The days which I spend in sensual enjoyment are mine. After the end of this life, this body will return to the five elements and merge with them. As a result, the usage of 'I' will cease. Then what is the harm if I love or hurt beings, tell lies or speak truths, lead a restrained or an unrestrained life, or do as I wish? It is because there is nobody or no rule to give me punishment or reward of my acts."

But such a thinking or idea is totally wrong. Man may become rich by immoral and cruel acts, by robbery or bloodshed, and move happily. But he cannot escape the responsibility of those evil acts. If there is not some 'unseen' cause over and above the present circumstances behind the miserable state of the virtuous and the happy state of the wicked and the account of the state is closed here only, but does not remain open and continue even in future life, then that would be considered to be no less than anarchy in the spiritual world and the material world as well.

Rule of the law of *karma* (moral causation) is so universal, so sure, so exact and so just that it gives each and every being right fruits for its acts. Therefore, the law of *karma*, from which naturally follows the belief in rebirth, is extremely useful in improving the human society and making it righteous. The only object of the law is to urge man to refrain from evil acts and to perform good acts so that he may make gradual progress on the path of perfection and ultimately attain that perfection.

Doctrine of rebirth nourishes the feeling of benevolence and altruism and cultivates the tendency to perform duty readily and sincerely. The worldly fruits of benevolent activity and performance of duty are seen, yet if the miseries of life do not end, the upholder of the doctrine of rebirth is never disappointed and disheartened. Faith in the future life or birth keeps him firm on the path of duty and rectitude. He firmly understands that performance of duty can never be futile and fruitless. If it does not bear its fruit in the present birth, it will bear its fruit in the next one. Thus the belief in the better gain in the next birth keeps man engaged in wholesome activities. Moreover, one who is convinced of the fact of rebirth is not afraid of death. One who considers soul to be eternal and indestructible understands death to be nothing more than transfer of body. For him an event of death is like an act of putting off one coat and putting on another. He thinks that for those who are engaged in good activities death is a gate to the path of spiritual progress. In this way, when man conquers fear of death and understands the stream of life to be real, endlessly and eternally existent, continuously and uninterruptedly flowing, then he feels a strong urge—easily gained through power of discretion—to make his life more and more elevated and to devote firmly to the performance of duty. One who is convinced of the eternality and indestructibility of the soul thinks as follows: "To do evil to others is to do evil to one's own self. To hurt others is to hurt one's own self. Enmity breeds enmity. Impressions of the acts done remain associated with the soul through many future births and make it experience their fruits; sometimes the length of the duration of this experience is long." A person who believes in soul and has this understanding considers all souls to be like his. So he experiences the feeling of friendliness with respect to them. In the warm light of friendliness the ice of attachment and aversion melts away. In this manner, his feeling of equanimity and equality is fostered and his universal love goes on developing. Even in the midst of differences of sects, caste, class, nationality and race his outlook of treating all beings as equal remains unobstructed and unabated. He thinks as follows: "Can I say as to in which sect, in which caste, in which class, in which nation (country) and in which condition, I shall be born in the next birth? So to entertain ill-will towards a person belonging to a particular sect, caste, class, country or race, or towards a poor or so-called low person, to look down upon him, to take pride in one's family etc., and to hate other's family, etc. is not proper." Thus on account of the noble outlook resulted from the doctrine of rebirth and indestructibility of the soul, he never regards the beings high or low. He lives up to the great dictum, viz., '*paṇḍitāḥ samadarśinaḥ*' (i.e., the learned treat all beings equally) which for him is the motto or ideal of life. Therefore, he remains always engaged in doing good to others (irrespective of sect, caste, class, nationality, race, etc.) and thereby doing good to one's own self at the same time.

Many men claiming to be given to logic and reason have doubts about the existence of God and soul. But when a terrible calamity befalls them or an acutely painful disease attacks them, their vigour of logic and reason dwindles away and their mind gets absorbed in the memory of God (some incomprehensible, unseen, mysterious conscious power). Their heart then becomes inclined towards Him. They constantly recall Him and declare their total wretchedness by repeatedly confessing before Him their wickedness, weakness and helplessness. They solicit His shelter or refuge with the impatient heart full of fervent devotion. However intense be their mental obstinacy, it certainly wanes at the time of misery and calamity. During the time of merciless calamity, man's impudence melts away and disappears. And the impending death is the gravest calamity. At that time even the hard-core atheist becomes soft and his atheism withers away, and his eyes roll in search of some Supreme Soul whom he can beseech to free him from the jaws of misery, the only one who can give him shelter and mental peace.

If we do not accept the existence of soul, rebirth and God, and regard auspicious *karmas* and inauspicious *karmas* as mental figment, then we will be deprived of the best motivating force of spiritual development and the order of the world will lose its firm basis. The pilgrim of spiritual progress declares on the strength of his experience that man is robbed of his inner happiness and dark clouds of disappointment and despondency surround his mind as soon as he think that there is no soul, no God.

The pentad of soul, *karma* (auspicious and inauspicious), rebirth, liberation and Supreme Soul is such that the acceptance of one of them necessarily implies the acceptance of the rest. In other words, on the acceptance of one, the rest of them stand automatically accepted and on the rejection of one, all the rest stand automatically rejected. Once soul is accepted, rebirth stands automatically accepted. With rebirth, invariably go auspicious and inauspicious *karmas*. Liberation is nothing but perfect purity of the soul itself. So with the acceptance of soul goes also the acceptance of liberation. And liberation is identical with God. In other words, God is nothing but the pure liberated soul itself. So theism is implicit in the doctrine of soul.

Lengthy discussion is not necessary to prove the existence of God. We can easily prove it. Just as there exists in the world a dirty mirror, even so there exists a clean mirror too. Or, just as there exists impure gold even so there exists pure gold also. Similarly, the existence of pure soul stands logically established on the basis of the existence of an impure soul. The existence of a clean mirror or pure gold is necessarily inferred from that of a dirty mirror or impure gold. Similarly, the existence of pure soul can be inferred from that of impure soul. Just as an impure physical thing can become pure, even so the impure soul can also become pure. Again, we perceive the partial purity in living beings. From this, we can infer the possible perfect purity attainable by them. And the one who has attained it is Supreme Soul, the one who will attain it will become Supreme Soul. The attainment of the state of Supreme Soul is itself the manifestation of the state of God. The perfectly pure soul is the Supreme Soul, and the Supreme Soul itself is God.

(14)

It is not that this world is created altogether anew at a certain point of time. It exists from the beginningless time. Of course, it constantly undergoes change. Some changes are such as are brought about by sentient agency; and others are such as do not require sentient agency for their origination, that is, they are natural. The natural changes come into existence owing to the diverse combination of material atoms, molecules and aggregates. As for example, hills or mountains are formed on account of the combination of earth, stones, etc. A river comes into being on account of the commingling of streams of water flowing here and there. A jungle is formed when many plants, trees and creepers grow together. When vapour rises high, it cools and turns into water and comes down as rains. Again this water turns into vapour, and this cycle goes on.

It is rightly said that though *karma* is material, there is generated in it such a power owing to its peculiar association with the soul that it manifests its fruits on that soul at the due time. Every soul is sentient, and without its association with that sentient substance, the material *karma* is not capable of bearing its fruits. As are the acts performed by the soul, so are generated the thoughts in it. So, though the soul does not want bitter fruits of evil acts, it performs evil acts under the influence of ignorance or delusion and consequently experiences their bitter fruits. To perform an act is one thing, and not to desire its fruit is another thing. Merely by not desiring its fruit, one cannot avert the fruit of the performed act. As soon as all the casual conditions are gathered together, the effect automatically follows. As for instance, a man moves in the scorching sun, eats hot food and at the same time wishes that he may not feel thirsty; but then how can he remain free from the affliction of thirst? The point is that impressions of the nature of diverse material particles are imprinted on the soul according to its mental states, which is called the bondage of *karma*. The bound *karmas* acquire capacity on account of their association with the sentient soul, as a result they manifest their fruits on the soul at due time. Thus, the soul impelled by its own *karmas* experiences their fruits. This being the view of the upholders of the *karma* doctrine, they are not required to believe in God as a force impelling the soul to experience the fruits of its *karmas*.[1] The *Sāṁkhyas* and the *Mīmāṁsakas* also do not believe in God as the impeller. The Śramaṇa culture certainly does not accept God as the impeller.

Auspicious and inauspicious activities of mind, speech and body leave on the soul auspicious and inauspicious material traces called *karma*. Keeping in view the well-known universal law of *karma*, if man himself performs, inspires others to perform or praises others who perform good activities, he makes his future bright, good and happy. Contrary to it, if he denigrates others, cuts cruel and harsh jokes, speaks bitter and vulgar words, tells lies, then as a result of his evil activities of speech he becomes

1. *na kartṛtvaṃ na karmāṇi lokasya sṛjati prabhuḥ /*
na karmaphalasaṃyogaṃ svabhāvas tu pravartate //14//—*Bhagavad-Gītā, Adhyāya* 5.
God does not make man the doer of actions. That is, He does not force man to perform actions. Nor does he generate *karmas*. Nor does He join *karmas* with their fruits. In other words, He does not impel *karmas* to give their fruits to the soul; nor does He give the soul the fruits of its *karmas*. But *karmas* by their own nature proceed to give the soul their fruits. They do not require any intermediary.

dumb.[1] One who misuses one's mental powers invites madness. One who misuses one's hands gets one's arms or fingers severed. One who misuses one's legs becomes lame. An adulterous person becomes impotent.[2] So one who wants to be happy in all respects should remain always engaged in good activities of mind, speech and body.

If donation is given with the desire of earning fame, the charm of the act of donation disappears. If someone who donates his bungalow for the public use asks the public body to put a tablet bearing his name, then as a result of his infatuation with fame it may so happen that in his next birth he will be born of rich parents having a nice bungalow but his mind will remain so burdened with the worries of business and responsibilities that he will not be able to enjoy his stay in his bungalow.

Sometimes a person, though innocent, is trapped in a grave crime or calamity, but ultimately he is saved. It is because no court or no government is capable to punish him for the crime which he has not committed in this or the past birth. The powerful law of *karma* (moral causation) protects him.

When someone is held guilty of the crime which he has not committed and is punished, the cause of such punishment may possibly be such a crime committed by him in this very birth or in the past birth, the crime which he might have concealed or suppressed by unfair means. But that crime has not escaped the notice of the law of *karma.* So the *karma,* though late, rises to cause him experience its fruit in this manner.

Law of *karma* is the law of action and reaction (counter-action). Injustice done to others by you returns to you through somebody. It is

---

1. *manmanatvaṁ kāhalatvaṁ mukharogitām/*
vīkṣyāsatyaphalaṁ kanyālīkādy asatyam utsṛjet //53//
—Ācārya Hemacandra's *Yogaśāstra* II
This verse declares that the vice of untruthfulness causes dumbness, indistinct speech, stammering and other diseases of the mouth.
Read the following verse quoted by Ācārya Hemacandra in his auto-commentary on the above quoted verse:
mūkā jaḍāś ca vikalā vāghīnā vāgjugupsitāḥ /
pūtigandhamukhāś caiva jāyante'nṛtabhāṣiṇaḥ //
2. *napuṃsakatvaṁ tiryaktvaṁ daurbhāgyaṁ ca bhave bhave /*
bhaven narāṇāṁ strīṇāṁ cānyakāntāsaktacetasām //103//
—Ācārya Hemacandra's *Yogaśāstra* II
This verse tells us that the vice of adultery causes in the next birth impotency, misfortune and birth in the animal kingdom.

certain that good activity produces good results and evil activity produces evil results.

Sometimes we see that a cruel, treacherous, wicked and sinful person is happy while a good, virtuous and righteous one is unhappy. Let us solve this anomaly by an illustration. A man at present has wheat which he has formerly produced and stored. Therefore,at present he eats wheat (i.e., preparations of wheat) even though he is at present sowing *kodarā* (a kind of cheap coarse corn), but afterwards when all the stored wheat is used up he will have to eat *kodarā* only, which he is sowing at present. Similarly, a wicked man too can enjoy riches and luxuries earned on account of diverse auspicious activities performed by him in the past birth and accumulated in the form of material karmic traces, but afterwards at the end of the period of fruition of those accumulated auspicious *karmas* his vicious and wicked *karmas* with their grave and terrible fruits will rise before him. Take an example of a person who at present has *kodarā* which he has formerly produced and stored. Therefore, at present he lives on *kodarā* even though he is sowing wheat at present; but afterwards when all the stored *kodarā* gets exhausted, he will come to have wheat which he is sowing now. In the same manner, a virtuous and righteous man at present experiences miseries as a result of the evil acts performed by him in his past birth, though he is engaged in auspicious activities at present; but at the end of the fruition of the inauspicious *karmas*, that is, at the end of his hard times his auspicious *karmas* along with their auspicious fruits will rise before him.

Some particular result necessarily follows from certain situation or circumstance. Nothing else than this result can ever come into existence. This is called the 'Natural Law'. As is the situation or circumstance, so is the result. This is called the 'Natural Law'. This law never commands man to do this or not to do that. It simply lays down that if he wants to reap a particular result, he should perform a particular act. Nature prescribes that if he sows wheat, he will reap wheat; and if he sows seeds of thorny plants he will have thorns. But Nature never orders us to do either of them. One may sow whatever one chooses or likes. It is because Nature has given him freedom of choice from the very beginning. But once one has sown a particular seed, it is but vain to wish the fruit contrary to it. The law of Nature is unalterable. One who sows wheat will reap wheat only; and one who sows the seeds of thorny plants will get thorns. This is inevitable. Accordingly, if a man performs good acts, he will secure good results like happiness, prosperity, progress and peace; and if he performs evil acts, he will get bad or bitter fruits like unhappiness, poverty, degradation, defeat, sorrow, mental disturbance. This is the inexorable and relentless law of *karma.* The kind of influences the body receives from the food is determined by the kind of food it takes in. If it takes in nutritive food, it becomes healthy. And if it takes in harmful food, its health deteriorates. Similarly, the kind of activity determines the kind of its subtle influence. Good activity generates good subtle influences on the soul.

A person who does not care for his children will become barren in future in the next birth. One who misuses one's wealth thoughtlessly and extravagantly invites poverty in future. A man or a woman who disregards the love of his wife or her husband sows the seeds of future widowerhood or widowhood. A man who misuses his present power or authority given to him will have to suffer humiliation in future due to dependence and subordination. He who misuses his present leisure makes his future life hard. He who makes good use of his present opportunities and means will obtain better opportunities and better means in future. He who at present serves the people according to his means and circumstances will gain better means and more favourable circumstances in future. He who at present makes good use of his power and authority will in future attain greater power and greater authority. He who at present loves others unconditionally without the feeling of jealousy and passion will secure love of many in future. He who employs his present wealth in allaying the poverty of masses will become a benevolent rich man in future. He who is dishonest and accumulates wealth by intrigues, treachery and exploitation of others will invite his ruin in future. He who lives for his own self to the utter neglect of the interest of all others will be abandoned by all in future. In short, the wise man should always be vigilant to see to it that the given opportunities and means are not misused and are properly used for the good of his own self as well as of others and for the this-worldly and the other-worldly happiness as well.

When an individual hates someone, he binds the inauspicious *karma.* Similarly, when the whole family hates another family, it too binds inauspicious *karma.* And individual hatred gives rise to family hatred. So we can say that individual *karma* generates family *karma.* Thus auspicious and inauspicious individual *karmas* of the members of one family with respect to the members of another family, and *vice versa,* give rise to auspicious and inauspicious family-*karmas*. Similarly, when one village harasses the inhabitants of the neighbouring villages, destroys or damages their standing crop, steals or drives away their cattle, and gains its own selfish end at their cost, then it binds inauspicious *karma* with respect to them. This is the collective *karma*. And the entire village will have to experience its fruit collectively. In the same way, the entire country binds the corporate *karma* in accordance with the practice of good or bad customs, cherishing of right or wrong beliefs, following of right or wrong business and selfish or benevolent living—all this by the resident sects, classes and communities. And on account of the predominance of sins and vices, there often occurs in the country earthquakes, droughts, floods, excessive rainfall, famines and epidemics like plague, cholera, etc., or there breaks out internal civil war. Again, if one country or nation maintains good or bad relation with other countries or nations, then as a result it binds auspicious or inauspicious *karma*—which can be called international karmic bondage—and consequently will have to experience its good or bad results. Bitter or terrible results of the collective or corporate inauspicious *karmas* come upon the entire mass or class or community. And even in such adverse times of the country or nation, those who are extraordinarily holy and righteous can remain safe and secure.

In the society all members are not unjust, treacherous and cruel. But whatever be their number—great or small, there arises the situations and circumstances when the entire society has to suffer harassment and troubles on account of their evil deeds. Why should the entire society experience the bitter or bad fruits of the evil acts performed by only some of its members? If one reflects for a while on this question, one will find the answer. It is as follows: The society in which the wicked and cruel men freely indulge in evil activities without any opposition, objection and obstruction from the society and government, and in which the knowledgeable leading members do not exhibit moral courage to expose them before the government and society, and instead of putting forth efforts to oppose them, they ignore and tolerate them crestfallen meekly and thereby indirectly approve of their evil acts, that society has obviously to experience harassment and troubles on account of its such defect or fault.

Corporate or collective *karmas* are ultimately generated by individual *karmas*. So the improvement of the society depends on the improvement of its individual members. Paying heed to the power of the law of *karma* (moral causation), one should sincerely try to be good in thought, speech and behavior. Therein lies the prosperity, peace and happiness of an individual, a class, a society and a nation as well. If the people are moral and friendly, their entire country or nation is saved from varied troubles and calamities, and their life becomes happy, progressive, elevated and noble.

The fact that by industry and effort one can transform a sub-type into another of the same main *karma*-type and reduce the intensity of the fruits of the *karmas* that have risen to give their fruits, is proved even by observation. We observe that the schools for the blind, deaf, dumb and lame are established and therein they are trained to be self-reliant and self-dependent. In this way, many nations have lessened the hardness of the hard destiny or *karma* of their peoples by making great valiant efforts. Even an individual can improve his or her destiny by living a righteous and responsible life. Individual development and group development can reduce the hardness of the fruits of the *karmas* that are ready to give their fruits, and having overcome them make good advancement in the right direction. We should always remember here the following words of W.R. Alger: "Fate is the friend of the good, the guide of the wise, the tyrant of the foolish, the enemy of the bad."

(15)

(Special Interpretation of the term '*paraloka*')

The Sanskrit term '*paraloka*' is generally taken to mean 'the birth, after death, in any one of the main four classes of living beings', and we are asked to improve it. But, if the society or the class in which one is to be born in future is not cultured, then one cannot be happy in taking birth in such a society, however good one may be.

We are normally not able to establish in the present birth any contact with the celestial beings of the celestial class or the infernal beings of the infernal class. Hence, if we want to undertake reform activities, we can undertake them in connection with the human class and the animal class, living among human beings and animal beings. By doing so, we can gain benefits of the reformation or improvement in the present birth as also in the next birth (when we would be born in the human or animal class). So far as it concerns us, the term '*paraloka*' should, therefore, be taken in such special sense that we may become aware of our duty towards the human society and the animal world, perform it sincerely and thereby improve our present birth as well as the next birth. From this standpoint, we present the following idea or thought.

The term '*paraloka*' literally means 'another world', that is, living beings other than one's own self. Improving *paraloka,* therefore, means improving those other beings. For each and every man there are clearly two worlds with which he has contact, viz., human world and animal world. An attempt to improve them is the attempt to improve '*paraloka*'. If every man firmly understands that our visible '*paraloka*' is this human society and hence 'to improve our *paraloka*' means 'to improve this human society', then the human society will undergo radical transformation and become progressive, prosperous and happy. Similarly, he should make strong efforts to generate and foster good feelings in the human society for the animals and urge it to make arrangements for their fodder, drinking water and shelter. They have contributed greatly to the progress and comforts of the human society. They have been a constant and faithful aid to man in civilizing himself for ages. The human society owes a duty to them. If it has received so many benefits from the animal kingdom, it should reciprocate them by being kind to them, by taking care and attending those that are suffering.

It is not certain as to where a man will be born in his next birth, after the death of the present body. So he should always bear in mind that if the animal class is living in a bad state fraught with troubles and diseases, then he would have to be the victim of that bad state when he is born in the animal class. Therefore, from the standpoint of public weal as also from that of his weal, it becomes necessary for man to maintain his conduct so good and so righteous that it may have good, instead of evil, influence on both the societies—human and animal. Just as improvement of the city results in the happiness of all its residents, even so the improvement of the human and animal worlds would result in the happiness of all their members. Readiness to improve these two worlds is but the readiness to improve one's *paraloka.*

There is also another *paraloka.* It is one's own progeny. The live impressions of good or bad bodily activities performed by man are transmitted to his progeny through his blood and semen. If he is afflicted with the transmittable diseases like leprosy, tuberculosis, diabetes, cancer, his progeny will have to experience their fruits. Evil impressions of his vices like licentious behavior, drunkenness, etc., are transmitted to his progeny through his blood and semen, and this will ultimately lead to the grave degeneration and ruin of the whole human society. The meaning of 'improving one's *paraloka*' is, therefore, 'improving one's progeny' which necessarily implies 'improving one's own self'.

Just as man is reborn in his progeny through his blood and semen, even so he is reborn in his pupils, associates and neighbours through his thoughts. As are our conduct and thoughts, so is their influence on the minds of our pupils, associates and near ones. Man is such a social animal that knowingly or unknowingly he influences others and others influence him. He is no doubt responsible for his own improvement or degeneration, but at the same time he also contributes directly or indirectly to the rise and fall of the entire human society. The progeny procreated by man's semen and blood may, with its efforts, rid itself of the evil impressions received from its progenitors through their blood and semen. But the progeny created by man's thoughts can hardly regain its health, once a drop of poison of evil thought is transmitted to it. Each grown up man of the present time has his eyes fixed on the new generation. Some administer to it the intoxicant drink of sectarianism, others that of racism, still others that of family pride, so on and so forth. One knows not as to how many *isms* their perverse intellect has invented to produce intoxicants of different colours. They give these intoxicants to new generation to drink in the attractive bowls of religion, culture, society, nation, etc. and thereby deprave it in order to protect the superiority of their class, to strengthen and stabilize their power, and to further their vested interests. Under the influence of infatuation, they do not hesitate to perpetrate cruelty and oppression on their own brethren, forgetting the natural equality of all human beings. When in the present evil-ridden strange age, this is the condition of men in their mutual relationship, then where is the scope of our talking about man's duty to protect, feed and take care of animals?

The right knowledge of the real nature of the life-force or conscious principle is the supreme light. Once it flashes in the human mind, it removes all defilements and ignorance from it, enlightens it and leads man on the all-auspicious and all-blissful path.

CHAPTER 5

JAINA LOGIC

Perception

That by which a thing is known rightly is called *pramāṇa,* i.e., valid knowledge. On the rise of valid knowledge doubt, illusion and ignorance are removed and the nature of a thing is known or understood rightly to a considerable extent. So valid knowledge is regarded as *pramāṇa.* Having known a thing rightly, man decides to attain it, if it is desirable and to abandon it, if it is undesirable.

There are two types of valid knowledge, viz., direct and indirect. Objects, viz., colour, etc., are cognised through sense-organs, viz., eye, etc., assisted by mind. To be more explicit, colour or form is seen by the eye, flavour is grasped by the tongue, odour is smelt by the nose, touch is cognised by the skin, and the sound or word is heard by the ear. All these are the cases of perception. But they are the cases of sense-perception. The experience of pleasure, etc., generated by mind is mental perception.

The above-mentioned perceptions are called empirical perception. Each of them—the sense-perceptions and mental perception—passes through four gradual stages, viz., *avagraha* (grasping), *īhā* (cogitation), *avāya* (definite judgement) and *dhāraṇā* (retention). First there arises the general non-detailed knowledge of the object through sense-organs and mind. It is called *avagraha* (grasping). Then there takes place cogitation with respect to the very object with a view to arriving at definite judgement. This cogitation is called *īhā.* It is followed by the definite judgement called *avāya.* The consolidation or continuance of the judgement to such an extent that in future it may cause memory is a case of *dhāraṇā.*

Seeing a tall thing like a tree from a distance is *avagraha* (grasping). This is followed by a query or doubt: 'Is this a man or a stump of a tree?'—the doubt which urges the cogniser to cogitate on the basis of specific features in order to arrive at a definite judgement. This cogitation is a case of *īhā.* After cogitation, there arises a definite judgement like 'This is certainly a man'. This is called *avāya.* This determinate knowledge stays for some time. But afterwards, when the mind withdraws itself from its object and directs its attention to some other object, this determinate knowledge disappears, but it leaves behind its impressions. These impressions are such that in future on certain occasion they give rise to the memory of the thing determinately known in the past. The stream of judgement (determinate knowledge) continuously flowing for some time, the resultant emergence of mental traces and the recollection in future of the determinately known thing in the past—all these three operations of *matijñāna* constitute *dhāraṇā.* But it is noteworthy that recollection or memory falls in the class of indirect *pramāṇa* (valid knowledge) and not in that of direct *pramāṇa.*

These four gradual stages, viz., *avagraha,* etc. occur in each of the five sense-perceptions as also in the mental perception.

The perception-type which is different from the empirical perception, does not depend on sense-organs and mind, but depends solely on the spiritual power is called transcendental perception. Thus transcendental perception is derived directly from the self. It is not dependent on the services of the sense-organs and mind. The following three varieties fall in the category of transcendental perception. They are *avadhi* (direct perception of temporally and spatially remote material things), *manaḥparyāya* (direct perception of mental states of other persons) and *kevala* (perfect eternal perception—omniscience). *Avadhi* is found in all infernal and celestial beings from their very birth while human and animal beings attain it as a result of the spiritual practice of the ethical vows, self-imposed wholesome restrictions, etc. *Manaḥparyāya* manifests itself in only those human beings who are greatly self-controlled and saintly. *Kevala-jñāna* is the perfect, eternal and infallible knowledge. We have already expounded this in chapter III pp. 188-90.

The Jaina view regarding the sense-object contact in the generation of sense-perception is as follows:

When we taste the flavour with our tongue, our tongue is in direct contact with the flavour. When we grasp the touch of a thing, our skin is in direct contact of the thing. When we smell the odour, our nose is invariably in direct contact with the odorous substances. Even when we grasp the odour of a thing, which is considerably far away from us, our nose does have direct contact with the odorous subtle particles that proceed from the thing and reach the nose. When the sounds or words coming from a long or short distance strike the ear, we hear them with our ears. According to the Jaina view, words are the aggregates of the material atoms that have acquired capacity to convert themselves into speech. For the Jainas, therefore, the word or sound is a substance. Thus the tongue, the skin, the nose and the ear—these four sense-organs cognise their respective objects after having come in direct contact with them. But it is quite obvious that the things—whether distant or near—do not go near the eyes when they are seen with the eyes. This means that the eye perceives them without having come in direct contact with them.[1] So the Jainas call the eye '*aprāpyakārī*'. The term '*aprāpyakārī*' means 'that sense-organ which cognises its object (*kārī*) without reaching it (*aprāpya*), that is, without coming in its direct contact.'

Indirect valid-knowledge has five varieties, viz., memory, recognition, cogitation, inference and verbal testimony.

Memory and Recognition (Smaraṇa and Pratyabhijñā)

When we recollect a thing experienced in the past, it is a case of memory. When we find a lost thing we have the cognition of the form 'That certainly is this'; it is a case of recognition. On meeting again the person formerly seen, we recognise him 'That is this Candrakānta'. This is an instance of recognition.

Memory is caused by the past experience, while recognition is caused by both the actual experience and the memory operating together. When the impressions left on the mind by the past experience of a thing are revived by certain conditions, there takes place the phenomenon of memory of that thing. In recognition, the object recalled is actually before our eyes. When, on seeing a person, one recollects that he is the same person whom one saw before, it is a case of recognition. The actual experience of the thing or person is as much the cause of recognition as the impression left on the mind by the former experience of the same thing or person. In memory, the cognition takes the form 'That clock' 'That man' and the like. Thus, memory refers to its content by a form of the pronoun 'that'. This means that the object is not present before

---

1. The rays of light falling on a thing are reflected. Then the reflected rays reach the eye. This is the reason why we see the thing. This is the scientific view. Even in this view, it is obvious that there obtains no direct contact between visual sense-organ and its object.

the cogniser. In recognition, the cognition takes the form 'That necessarily is this'. The element of 'that' indicates memory and the element of 'this' indicates actual experience. Thus recognition is a synthetic unitary knowledge generated by the joint operation of actual experience and memory. Recognition of the form 'that necessarily is this' is the recognition of identity.

Someone has acquired the knowledge that Bos Gaveas (*gavaya*) is like a cow. On seeing it he remembers this piece of knowledge. As a result he comes to have the cognition 'This Bos Gaveas is like a cow', in other words, he recognises the similarity of this Bos Gaveas with the cow that he has already seen. When we happen to see an object which is similar to another that has already been experienced, the cognition of the form 'this is like that' emerges. This is a case of recognition of similarity. Similarly, when we happen to see an object which is dissimilar to another that has already been experienced, we come to have the cognition of the form 'this is dissimilar to that'. This is a case of recognition of dissimilarity. There are also other forms of recognition.

Hypothetical Reasoning (tarka) and Inference (anumāna)

In inference, knowledge of *vyāpti* (invariable concomitance) is necessary. It is a ground of inference. *Vyāpti* is the necessary universal relation of inseparability (*avinābhāva-sambandha*) or invariable concomitance (*niyata sāhacarya*). A thing is said to have the necessary universal relation of inseparability with another thing, if it does never exist without the other thing.[1] As for instance, non-existence of smoke in the absence of fire—this type of relation which smoke is having with fire is its necessary universal relation of inseparability with fire. As this *vyāpti* of the form of necessary universal relation of inseparability (i.e., invariable concomitance) subsists in smoke, smoke is called *vyāpya* (*vyāpya* of fire, i.e., pervaded by fire), because smoke is pervaded by fire. And as fire pervades smoke, it is called *vyāpaka* (*vyāpaka* of smoke, i.e., one that pervades smoke). Thus *vyāpti* is the relation of *vyāpya* with its *vyāpaka*. In other words, the characteristic

1. The term *avinābhāva* contains three words: *a* + *vinā* + *bhāva*. *Vinā* means without (i.e., in the absence of) probandum (*sādhya*); *a* and *bhāva* = *abhāva* means absence of probans (*sādhana*). Thus complete sense of the term is: non-presence (*abhāva*) of probans in the absence of (*vinā*) probandum. This constitutes the one and only defining characteristic of probans.

of being pervaded by the pervader (*vyāpaka*), which characterises the *vyāpya* (that which is pervaded) is called *vyāpti*. *Vyāpti* is a relation obtaining between two things or terms, of which one is pervaded (*vyāpya*) and the other pervades (*vyāpaka*). A thing is said to pervade another when it always accompanies the other. A thing is said to be pervaded by another, when it is always accompanied by the other. In this sense, smoke is pervaded by fire, since it is always accompanied by fire. But fire is not always accompanied by smoke, e.g., the red-hot iron ball. So fire is not pervaded by smoke. As the pervader is proved or established by the pervaded, the pervader is called *sādhya* (the thing to be proved, probandum, major term) and the pervaded is called *sādhana* (the thing that proves, probans, middle term) or *hetu* (logical reason). To know and ascertain *vyāpti* the joint method of agreement in presence (*anvaya*) and in absence (*vyatireka*) is very useful. The method of agreement in presence means the invariable presence of probandum in the presence of probans. The probandum is necessarily and invariably present where the probans is present. And the method of agreement in absence means the invariable absence of probans in the absence of probandum. The invariable presence of fire in the presence of smoke is a case of the method of agreement in presence. And the invariable absence of smoke in the absence of fire is a case of the method of agreement in absence. Thus, as smoke is having both *anvaya* (relation of agreement in presence) and *vyatireka* (relation of agreement in absence) with fire, we know and ascertain, on their basis, the invariable concomitance (*vyāpti*) of smoke with fire.

Smoke is pervaded by fire. But fire is not pervaded by smoke. In other words, wherever there is smoke there is fire; there is no exception to it. But it is not that wherever there is fire, there is smoke. That is, where there is fire, there may or may not be smoke. Therefore, we can infer fire from smoke, but can never infer smoke from fire. A *vyāpti* between two things or terms of unequal extension, such as smoke and fire, is called *asama-vyāpti* or *viṣama-vyāpti*. It is a relation of non-equipollent concomitance between two things or terms, from one of which we may infer the other, but not *vice versa*. We may infer fire from smoke, but not smoke from fire. As distinguished from this, a *vyāpti* between two things or terms of equal extension is called *sama-vyāpti* or equipollent concomitance. Here the *vyāpti* holds between two things or terms which are co-extensive, so that we may infer either of them from the other, e.g., flavour and colour. Wherever there is flavour, there is colour, and *vice versa.* In short, the *vyāpaka* is generally greater in extent than the *vyāpya,* though not necessarily so; for in some cases where both may be co-extensive, both are *vyāpaka* and *vyāpya* of each other.

The *vyāpti* (invariable concomitance) is grasped and ascertained by hypothetical reasoning or cogitation (*tarka*). As for example, 'Smoke is never present in the absence of fire, wherever there is smoke there is fire, there is not a single place where smoke is present but fire is not present'—this type of invariable concomitance of smoke with fire, which is called *vyāpti* can be established or proved by hypothetical reasoning. On seeing two things together in many places or on observing their successive occurrence in many places, we cannot establish or arrive at their invariable concomitance. But on exploring as to whether there is any logical or practical difficulty in separating the two or in not accepting their invariable succession, if we certainly find some difficulties—that is, the invariable concomitance is found without having any exception—, then the invariable concomitance between the two stands established or proved. This method of establishing or arriving at invariable concomitance (*vyāpti*) is hypothetical reasoning (*tarka*). The invariable concomitance of smoke with fire is grasped or established by the hypothetical reasoning as follows: 'Wherever there is smoke, there is fire'—this is the statement of *vyāpti* (invariable concomitance). If it is false, then its contradictory, viz., 'There are some places where smoke is present but fire is absent', must be true. This means that there may be smoke without fire. But this supposition is contradicted by the law of universal causation, for to say that there may be smoke without fire is just to say that there may be an effect without a cause. It is so because, fire is the only known cause of smoke. If any one has obstinacy to say that sometimes there may be effects without causes, he must be silenced by reference to the practical contradictions involved in his position. If there can be an effect without a cause, why do they who desire smoke seek fire?

Knowledge of invariable concomitance is the ground of inference. For any inference, the minimum condition is the knowledge of *vyāpti* between the middle (*sādhana, vyāpya, hetu*) and the major (*sādhya, vyāpaka*) term. We can infer fire from smoke only when we know that smoke is invariably connected with fire. Without the knowledge of invariable concomitance of smoke with fire, inference of fire from smoke is impossible. So long as one does not have the knowledge of invariable concomitance of smoke with fire, one cannot infer fire from smoke. This is quite obvious. This shows that for inference the knowledge of invariable concomitance is necessary and this knowledge of invariable concomitance one can have through hypothetical reasoning (*tarka*).

Inference is the knowledge of *sādhya* (probandum) through the instrumentality of *sādhana* (probans). This means that on knowing or perceiving probans and consequently remembering the invariable concomitance of probans with probandum, the cogniser infers probandum. As for instance, when one who has known the universal relation that obtains between smoke and fire, that is, one who has comprehended the invariable concomitance of smoke with fire, perceives smoke arising from some place, then at once he remembers the invariable concomitance of smoke with fire and consequently infers fire on that place. The emergence of inferential knowledge takes place subject to the fulfilment of two conditions, viz., perception or knowledge of probans and memory of the invariable concomitance of probans with probandum.

Let us study some cases of inference: (1) A particular place has fire on it because it possesses smoke. (2) Word is destructible because it is produced. (3) This is a tree because it is Nimba. (4) The constellation named Rohiṇī will rise because the constellation named Kṛttikā has already risen. (5) The constellation Bharaṇī rose before, because the constellation Kṛttikā is rising. (6) A particular fruit must have a particular colour because it has a particular flavour. Or, it must have a particular flavour because it has a particular colour.

In these cases of inference, the first probans is of the form of effect (*kārya*), because smoke is an effect of fire. The second and the third ones are of the form of essential identity of nature (*svabhāva*). The fourth one is the predecessor (*pūrvacara*) because Kṛttikā is the predecessor of Rohiṇī. The fifth one is the successor (*uttaracara*) because Kṛttikā is the successor of Bharaṇī. And the sixth one is co-occurrent or co-extensive (*sahacara*) because flavour and colour are co-occurrent or co-extensive.

From this we can have the idea of different types of probans. Again, we can see that it is not necessary that probans should be present when probandum is present. Kṛttikā that is rising enables us to infer Rohiṇī that is to rise as also Bharaṇī that rose before. This means that probans and probandum—belonging to the same time or different times and to the same place or different places—should have invariable relation between them. It is not necessary for the probans to be present at that very time and place at which the probandum is present. The only thing required of it is that it should have invariable concomitance with probandum. The present rise of Kṛttikā works as an instrument of inferring the posterior rise of Rohiṇī and the prior rise of Bharaṇī, because Kṛttikā is having a relation of sequence with Rohiṇī and Bharaṇī, which is an invariable necessary relation.

That which is contradictory of a particular thing acts as probans causing inferential knowledge of the absence of that thing. From certain facial changes we can infer the absence of the subsidence-of-anger. Here the probans of the form of certain facial changes is contradictory of the subsidence-of-anger or is the result of anger which is contradictory to the subsidence-of-anger. Therefore it acts as probans causing inferential knowledge of the absence of the subsidence-of-anger. From non-cognition of the bodily movements characterising health, we infer the presence of some disease in the body. The fact of our not seeing the bodily movements characterising health leads us to infer the lack of health, that is, the presence of some disease in the body. For our present purpose this is enough. We close this topic.

There are two types of inference, viz. *svārthānumāna* (inference intended for oneself) and *parārthānumāna* (inference intended for others). Without being instructed or taught by others, when one infers probandum from probans independently with his own reasoning, then that inference is called *svārthānumāna.* On the other hand, the inference employed by one to explain to others the truth of the conclusion one has arrived at is called *parārthānumāna.* To illustrate, when a man, having inferred or known the existence of fire in a hill, tries to convince another man, who doubts or questions the truth of his knowledge, he argues like this: "The hill must be fiery; because it smokes; and whatever is smoky is necessarily and invariably fiery, e.g. the kitchen; so also the hill is smoky; therefore it is fiery." The statement generally contains five members. They are: proposition (*pratijñā*), reason (*hetu*), example (*udāharaṇa*), application (*upanaya*) and conclusion (*nigamana*). In the above example, they are as follows:

(1) This place is fiery. (This is the statement of proposition or thesis or probandum).
(2) Because it is seen smoky. (This is the statement of reason or probans).
(3) All smoky things are fiery, e.g. the kitchen. (This is the statement of invariable concomitance, showing the necessary universal connection

between probans and probandum, as supported by a known instance).
(4) So also this place is smoky. (This is the statement of application).
(5) Therefore this place is fiery. (This is the statement of conclusion).

In *parārthānumāna,* one is required to follow this procedure.

Probans which does not have the relation of invariable concomitance with probandum is called pseudo-probans (*hetvābhāsa*). Pseudo-probans can never lead to valid inference.

Verbal Knowledge (Āgama or Śabda)

Knowledge generated through words of trustworthy authority (*āpta*) is called valid verbal knowledge (*āgama-pramāṇa* or *śabda-pramāṇa*).

Words that propound the pure Reality, that throw true light on spiritual development and its means, and that are not contradicted by other forms of valid knowledge, viz., perception, inference, etc. truly constitute *āgama* or scripture.

One who preaches and teaches the truth and reality as they are, for the benefit of all is called a trustworthy authority (*āpta*). And words of such a person are called scripture (*āgama*). The supremely trustworthy authority is that person who has totally removed all the defilements like attachment, aversion, etc., from his soul and who has preached the elevating and pure teaching on the basis of his perfect and pure knowledge. As he is absolutely free from the defects like attachment, etc., that soil the soul, his heart is full of universal love. He is the Compassionate *par excellence.* And impelled by universal love and compassion, he teaches Truth and Reality, especially the path leading to liberation, on the basis of his pure knowledge gained through spiritual and yogic practice.

The serene philosophy propounded in scriptures will possibly be totally misunderstood and will consequently do great harm instead of benefit, if it is not reflected on by one's impartial, discerning, discreet reason. Abandonment of obstinacy, love or predilection for truth, impartial attitude, judicious and sharp intellect, unagitated and calm mind, penetrating insight, pure desire for knowledge—if these qualities are cultivated by a person, then he can successfully and without any fear dive into the deep waters of the ocean of scriptural truths and realities.

When we think superficially about the thoughts of great sages, we feel that the thoughts of one are contradictory to those of another. But, if we adopt synthetic outlook and try to understand them from different standpoints, we find them not contradicting but supplementing one another, thus leading to one Grand Truth.

We have expounded, in brief, valid knowledge and its varieties. The opposite of it is called false knowledge (*apramāṇa, bhrama* or *mithyā-jñāna*). Valid knowledge cognises a thing as it is; while false knowledge cognises a thing as it is not. False knowledge cognises a rope as a snake, a shell as silver, etc. It mistakes one thing for another. It mistakes wrong view for right view, unwholesome conduct for wholesome conduct, insentient thing for sentient thing, sinner for saint, and *vice versa.* If we commit a mistake in understanding the nature of a thing or reality, know it as it is not, superimpose on it the nature which is not its own true nature and wrongly understand it to be having the nature which it actually does not have, then our activity based on such wrong understanding will naturally be not right or proper. When we mistake a rope for a snake, we shiver out of fear without any real cause for fear. When we mistake mirage for water, we run towards it to quench our thirst with great hope, but that attempt of ours does not succeed and we become downcast and dejected. If we mistake a friend for an enemy, and *vice versa,* then whatever activity we undertake with respect to them will certainly be improper and opposite of what it should be. These are the instances of activities generated by illusory or false knowledge. Illusory or false knowledge means wrong or perverse understanding. Hence it does not fall in class of valid knowledge.

As already stated in chapter III pp. 180-191, of the five types of valid knowledge, viz., *mati, śruta, avadhi, manaḥparyāya* and *kevala,* the last three are the cases of perception (transcendental perception). *Mati* and *śruta* are the cases of indirect valid knowledge or non-perceptual knowledge. *Śruta-jñāna* means *āgama-pramāṇa* (verbal knowledge) which is a variety of indirect valid knowledge. A sub-class of *mati-jñana,* which is formed by the knowledges of colour etc., generated by sense-organs (though regarded as indirect or non-perceptual from the ultimate standpoint on account of their being derived not directly from soul but indirectly through the medium of sense-organs) is called the class of empirical perception. And another sub-class of *matijñāna,* formed by memory, recognition, cogitation (hypothetical reasoning), inference, etc., is included in the class of indirect valid knowledge. Thus, the classification of valid knowledge into direct valid knowledge and indirect valid knowledge is reconciled well with the old scriptural classification of valid knowledge into five types, viz. *mati*, etc.[1]

Now let us explain the universally useful and important theory called

---

1. *Anuyogadvārasūtra* mentions four *pramāṇas* (types of valid knowledge), viz. *pratyakṣa* (perception), *anumāna* (inference), *upamāna* (analogy) and *āgama* (verbal testimony). Their treatment is similar to that found in Gautama's *Nyāya* philosophy.
Sthānāṅgasūtra (*Sthāna* 4, *Uddeśa* 3) also mentions the above enumerated four *pramāṇas*. But elsewhere (*Sthāna* 2, *Uddeśa* 1) it mentions two *pramāṇas* viz., *pratyakṣa* (perceptual or direct) and *parokṣa* (non-perceptual or indirect). And the mention of these two *pramāṇas* certainly occurs in *Nandīsūtra*.
Bhagavatīsūtra (*Śataka* 5, *Uddeśa* 3) mentions the above-mentioned four *pramāṇas*, referring to the authority of *Anuyogadvārasūtra*.
The special type of *pratyakṣa* (perception), viz., *sāṁvyavahārika pratyakṣa* (empirical perception) finds mention for the first time in Jinabhadragaṇi's *Viśeṣāvaśyakabhāṣya*. But it is based on *Nandīsūtra*, because *Nandīsūtra* includes sense-perception in both the divisions, viz., *pratyakṣa* and *parokṣa*.
From all the above discussion, we can arrive at the conclusion that the problem of knowledge has been treated in the Jaina tradition in two ways, viz., that based on the Āgamic classification, and that based on the logical classification. The treatment where knowledge is divided into *mati, śruta*, etc. is the one based on the Āgamic classification, the treatment where it is divided into *pramāṇas* like perception (*pratyakṣa*), etc., is the one based on the logical classification. The fivefold division of knowledge into *mati, śruta*, etc. is rooted in the scriptures and is very old. On the other hand, the classification of knowledge into *pratyakṣa*, etc. evinces the influence of the age of logic. At the time when *Āgamas* were edited (*saṅkalana*) portions containing the fourfold classification of *pramāṇas*, as also those containing the twofold classification, found entrance in *Sthānāṅga* and *Bhagavatī*. (In *Bhagavatīsūtra*, we come across portions where Rāipaseṇaia, Pannavaṇā, Nandī, Jīvābhigama, Anuyogadvārasūtra are found quoted by name in support, but these Rāipaseṇaia, etc., were composed very late after the composition of *Bhagavatīsūtra*. This shows that these portions were inserted in *Bhagavatīsūtra* when *Āgamas* were edited.) However, even though both these classifications had found place in the Āgamic texts, the Jaina teachers chiefly gave special thought to the twofold classification. The obvious reason for this is that the fourfold classification really belongs to the *Nyāya* system—and is therefore referred to by Umāsvāti in his *Tattvārthabhāṣya* (I. 6) as a *nayavādāntara* (view of another philosophical system)—, while the twofold classification is the Jaina teachers' own. The twofold classification has been accepted in *Tattvārthasūtra* and other Jaina works. And in this manner it has been firmly established in the Jaina tradition.
The same twofold classification is there in *Nandīsūtra*. But the speciality of *Nandīsūtra* is that it incorporated in its treatment an important point. The point is that *pratyakṣa-pramāṇa* is here sub-divided into two types, viz., *noindriya-pratyakṣa* (non-sensory perception which covers *avadhi*, etc.) and *indriya-pratyakṣa* (sensory perception). But it has been borrowed by it from the earlier work, *Anuyogadvārasūtra*. It is so because the author of *Anuyogadvārasūtra* divides *pratyakṣa-pramāna* into two types, viz., *indriya-pratyakṣa* and *noindriya-pratyakṣa* after having mentioned four *pramāṇas*, viz., *pratyakṣa*, *anumāna, upamāna* and *āgamá*. And it is on the basis of this classification of *pratyakṣa*

syādvāda or *anekāntavāda* formulated by the Jaina philosophy.

SYĀDVĀDA OR ANEKĀNTAVĀDA (THEORY OF MANY-SIDEDNESS)

The method of viewing or explaining a thing from different standpoints is *syādvāda.* It is also called *anekāntavāda.* The method of honestly accepting and reconciling the apparently contradictory attributes in a thing from different standpoints is called *syādvāda* or *anekāntavāda.* In a man, we accept seemingly contradictory attributes—that is, we call him father and son, uncle and nephew, son-in-law and father-in-law, etc.,—because they are reconcilable from different standpoints of different relations which he holds with different persons. Similarly, one accepts apparently opposite attributes, viz., permanence and impermanence, etc., in a thing, say a pot, because one reconciles them with one another from

---

into *indriya-pratyakṣa* and *noindriya-pratyakṣa,* presented in *Anuyogadvārasūtra* and *Nandīsūtra,* that Jinabhadragaṇi Kṣamāśramaṇa in his *Viśeṣāvaśyaka-bhāṣya* (*gāthā* 95) for the first time gave the name '*sāṁvyavahārika pratyakṣa*' to sensory perception (*indriya-pratyakṣa*) which is what people (and even logicians) understand by *pratyakṣa.* By doing so, he eliminated for the first time, the discrepancy—pointed out by the non-Jaina logicians—vitiating the twofold classification of *pratyakṣa* into *indriya-pratyakṣa* and *noindriya-pratyakṣa.* The discrepancy was as follows. When the Jaina system calls only that knowledge *pratyakṣa* which is born of *akṣa* (i.e., *ātmā* = soul) alone, it becomes self-contradictory to call sensory perception *pratyakṣa* (for sense-perception is not born of soul alone). Thus, Jinabhadra achieved two things. First, he removed discrepancy that was there in the previous *Sūtra* works and secondly he gave due respect to the popular view. After Jinabhadra, Akalaṅkadeva made even more firm the twofold classification of *pratyakṣa-pramāṇa.* Moreover, he showed his intellectual acumen in fixing the number of the sub-species of *parokṣa-pramāṇa* and in defining each of them. He maintained that the sub-species of *parokṣa-pramāṇa* are five only and they are (1) *anumāna* (inference), (2) *pratyabhijñā* (recognition), (3) *smaraṇa* (memory), (4) *tarka* (cogitation or hypothetical reasoning) and (5) *āgama* (verbal testimony). The result was that all post-Akalaṅka Jaina logicians—Digambara as well as Śvetāmbara—followed this classification made by Akalaṅka, and composed more or less lengthy texts basing themselves on Akalaṅka's very words (or their equivalents) and developing his very idea in this or that direction.

Siddhasena Divākara's *Nyāyāvatāra* is the product of that time when the academic atmosphere had started gathering stronger and stronger influence of logic and logical discussions. The term '*nyāya*' occurring in the title '*Nyāyāvatāra*' seems to be primarily suggestive of the meaning of *anumāna* (inference), because in this tiny treatise of 32 couplets too much space is devoted to the treatment of inference. *Nyāyāvatāra* treats of three *pramāṇas,* viz., perception, inference and verbal testimony.

different standpoints. The contradiction of opposite attributes in a thing is really apparent and can be removed by viewing the thing from different standpoints. Different standpoints yield contradictory attributes which are synthesised in a coherent whole by *syādvāda.* Thus *syādvāda* is a method of synthesis.

One and the same person is father with respect to his son and son with respect to his father, uncle with respect to his nephew and nephew with respect to his uncle, father-in-law with respect to his son-in-law and son-in-law with respect to his father-in-law, and so on and so forth. Accordingly, we accept all those opposite attributes—father and son, uncle and nephew, etc.—in one and the same individual from different standpoints of relations he is having with different persons. In the same way, why should we not accept in one and the same thing the opposite attributes, if on reflection we find them reconcilable from different standpoints?

What is a pot? It is well-known that earthen vessels like a pot, a bowl, etc., are produced from the same clay. After having broken a pot, a bowl is produced from the same clay; now, will anybody call the bowl a pot? No. Why? Is clay not the same? Yes, clay is the same but the form or mode has changed. As the form has changed, clay cannot be called 'a pot'. Well, then it is proved that a pot is a particular form or mode of clay. But one should remember that the mode or form is not absolutely different from clay. Clay itself is called 'a pot', 'a bowl', etc., when it assumes different forms or modes. So how can we consider clay and pot to be totally different? From this it is proved that the form-of-a-pot and clay both constitute the nature of the thing called 'pot'. Now let us see as to which of the two natures is permanent and which is impermanent. We observe that the form-of-a-pot is impermanent. So one nature of the pot, viz. the form-of-a-pot is established as impermanent. And how is the other nature, viz., clay? It is not impermanent. It is so because the forms or modes which clay assumes go on changing but clay as such remains the same. This is established by experience. Thus, we see that a pot has both these natures—one permanent, and the other impermanent. From this we can naturally maintain that from the standpoint of its impermanent nature, a pot is impermanent and from the standpoint of its permanent nature it is permanent. In this way to see and ascertain both the permanent and impermanent natures in one and the same thing from two different standpoints is a case of *anekānta* (synthetic or synoptic or many-sided) viewing.

Let us go a bit deeper into the problem in order to make the point more clear.

All things are characterised by origination, destruction and persistence.[1] Each and every thing has the triple character of origination, destruction and persistence. Take, for example, a golden necklace. After having broken it, a golden chain is made. At that time we clearly notice the destruction of the golden necklace and the origination of the golden chain. But the chain which is made out of the total gold obtained by breaking the necklace is not an entirely novel thing that has come into existence. It could be regarded as an entirely novel thing that has originated, only if nothing of the necklace has entered into its being. But when the total gold of necklace has entered into its being and merely the form-of-necklace is changed, then how can it be considered to be an entirely novel thing that has originated? By the same logic, we cannot say that the necklace is totally destroyed. We can say so, only if nothing of the necklace has persisted. When the total gold of the necklace has entered into the being of the chain and persists there, how can we say that the necklace is totally destroyed? From this we very well understand that destruction of the necklace is true insofar as the form-of-necklace is concerned, and the origination of the chain is true insofar as the form-of-chain is concerned. But gold of which the necklace and the chain are made is the same; it is common to both. The necklace and the chain are nothing but the different forms or modes of the same gold.

On the basis of this, anybody can say that when the chain is made after breaking the necklace, the form-of-chain originates, the form-of-necklace gets destroyed and gold persists; thus we rightly observe origination, destruction and persistence. In other words, we can say that gold in the form of necklace has been destroyed, gold in the form of chain has originated and gold *qua* gold has remained what it was (i.e., persisted); and all this at one and the same time. Such instances are present everywhere and at all times for one to observe. When a house collapses and gets destroyed, all the materials of which it was built are not totally destroyed. All those things or substances persist in the world in this or that form, subtle or gross; ultimately they do exist in the world in the form of ultimate atoms. So, the total destruction of the house is an impossibility and does not stand to philosophical reasoning. On the disintegration of

---

1. *utpāda-vyaya-dhrauvyayuktaṁ sat* /—*Tattvārthasūtra,* V. 29

a thing, its atoms or aggregates, give rise, independently or in combination with other things, to new transformation or effect. Worldly objects persist and move here and there in the world itself in their gross or subtle form and assume varied new forms. When a lamp is extinguished, it does not mean that it is totally destroyed. Its aggregate of atoms does exist all right. The very aggregate which manifested lamp (light) undergoes transformation; as a result it is not seen as the lamp and hence we experience darkness. The material atoms, according to the Jaina thinkers, assume the form of a lamp (light), but when the oil is exhausted or there is a blast of wind the atoms abandon the form of light and assume that of darkness. Thus the atoms persist as the original matter, that which changes being only their form. Water dries up, when rays of the sun fall on it. But that does not mean that it becomes totally non-existent. The elements of water do persist always in different form. When a gross form of a thing gets destroyed, the thing assumes a subtle form or gets itself transformed into another gross form, as a result of this the thing may not be perceived in its previously perceived form. A mere change of form does not mean total cessation. Clay, for instance, may take numerous forms, such as a jar, a bowl, etc., yet clay is recognised as the identical substance persisting through all the changes or forms. The transformation is not total destruction or cessation. The original thing or substance is not produced, nor is it totally destroyed. This is an unalterable universal law.

An absolutely non-existent entity can never come into existence. And an existent entity can never pass into absolute non-existence.[1]

It is only forms or modes that originate and get destroyed. Curd originated from milk is not a totally novel thing that has come into being. It is merely a transformation of milk. The dairy-product (*gorasa*) in the form of curd is produced on the destruction of the dairy-product (*gorasa*) in the form of milk. Both milk and curd are but forms of the dairy-product (*gorasa*).[2]

In the same manner, we have to understand that original substances or elements are eternal or permanent, and they assume different forms

---

1. *nāsato vidyate bhāvo nābhāvo vidyate sataḥ* /—*Bhagavad-Gītā*, II. 16
2. *payovrato na dadhy atti na payo 'tti dadhivrataḥ* /
   agorasavrato nobhe tasmād vastu trayātmakam //60//—Samantabhadra's *Āptamīmāṁsā*
   utpannaṁ dadhibhāvena naṣṭaṁ dugdhatayā payaḥ /
   gorasatvāt sthiraṁ jānan syādvādadviḍ jano 'pi kaḥ //
   —Upādhyāya Yaśovijayajī's *Adhyātmopaniṣad*, I. 44

or modes. In other words, in them the previous form is destroyed and another form is produced. Forms subsist in the persistent substance. There cannot be forms without substance, nor can substance be without this or that form. Everything is constituted of both substance and forms (modes). So, it is established that all things are of triple nature of origination, destruction and persistence. Those that are originated and destroyed are forms or modes. They are called *paryāyas* in the Jaina philosophy. The original element which persists and is eternal is substance. It is called *dravya.* The destruction or production of one form necessarily means the production or destruction of another form; and this necessity of one being dependent on the other suggests that there is some common bond between them and this is the persistent substance. Each and every thing is permanent from the standpoint of substance and impermanent from the standpoint of modes. This method of viewing and describing a thing as neither absolutely permanent nor absolutely impermanent, but as permanent-cum-impermanent is known by the term *syādvāda.*

Ācārya Hemacandra in his *Vītarāgastotra* (8th *Prakāśa*) writes:

ātmany ekāntanitye syān na bhogaḥ sukha-duḥkhayoḥ /
ekāntānityarūpe 'pi na bhogaḥ sukha-duḥkhayoḥ //2//
puṇya-pāpe bandha-mokṣau na nityaikāntadarśane/
puṇya-pāpe bandha-mokṣau nānityaikāntadarśane //3//

Meaning: If the soul is regarded as absolutely permanent (not permanent but absolutely permanent), then it would admit no change or transformation, would not assume different states, that is, we are constrained to accept it as absolutely changeless. And if the soul is regarded as absolutely changeless, then the experience of happiness and unhappiness, which is a felt fact, will be rendered impossible. For, there cannot be experience of happiness and unhappiness one after another, unless the soul could pass from one state to another. It will be possessed of either the happiness or the unhappiness for all time, if it is absolutely changeless. Furthermore, *puṇya* (merit or auspicious *karmas*) and *pāpa* (demerit or inauspicious *karmas*) are impossible on the hypothesis of absolute changelessness. For, the experience of happiness and unhappiness are brought about by *puṇya* and *pāpa,* which means that they should exercise a certain influence on soul, and this is impossible, if the soul is unchangingly eternal. Next bondage and liberation will be similarly inexplicable on the hypothesis of exclusive changelessness or permanence. Bondage is a kind of *saṁyoga* (conjunction) between the soul and *karma*. *Saṁyoga* is a relation of conjunction obtaining between two substances that were not conjoined previously. Thus, there are two distinct states involved in the notion of *saṁyoga*, the previous absence and the later presence—which are inconsistent with the hypothesis of absolute changelessness or permanence. Liberation is the dissociation of all the bound *karmas*. Thus bondage and liberation are the two states of the soul. One that is bound with the *karmas* becomes free from them. Thus, one and the same soul passes from the state of bondage to that of liberation. The absolutely changeless soul cannot have these two states. But if the soul is regarded as persistent through changes, that is, variable constant, then alone the different states of happiness and unhappiness, *puṇya* and *pāpa*, bondage and liberation, etc., become possible and explicable in its case.

As in the doctrine of the absolute permanence of the soul, so also in the doctrine of its absolute impermanence (momentariness) the above facts remain unaccounted for. So it is logical and reasonable to accept a persistent substance soul running through ever-changing modes, transformations, forms or states. Though the soul undergoes incessant changes, the soul *qua* soul persists through them all, remains eternal and unimpaired. For instance, a book, a piece of cloth, or an umbrella becomes dirty or gets spoiled with the splashes of filthy water or with the stains of excreta of birds, etc., or is decorated with colours, but on that account it does not cease to exist altogether. Similarly, the soul assumes different changes, but on that account it does not cease to exist altogether. A man, a horse, an elephant, etc., undergo bodily changes but on that account they do not cease to exist altogether. They themselves are said to have become fat or lean or to have assumed different bodily changes. In the same way, though the soul undergoes changes, yet on that account it does not cease to exist. Those changes, modes, forms or transformations being of the soul itself, the soul *qua* soul wholly persists through them all. Over and above the ordinary changes like dullness, brightness, etc., that gold may undergo, different changes, modes, transformations or forms like ear-rings, necklaces, bangles, bracelets, wristlets, waist chains, etc., are of gold itself, and through them all gold persists alright. Similarly, the soul wholly persists through different states not only of the present birth but also of different births. If this is the case, then alone can the soul experience the fruits of its good or bad actions in the present birth, the next birth, or the birth after many intervening ones, the moral responsibility of one's own actions can remain intact and unimpaired, the gradual progress can go on accumulating through different births; and then on account of the gradual accumulation of excellences of the spiritual practice, it can attain in some birth the lofty and elevated stage of spiritual welfare.

If instead of maintaining the soul to be a persistent unitary substance, it is regarded as a series of discrete moments coming into being one after another in close succession, without there being any principle of synthesis and unity lying behind them, then the moment which was responsible for a good or bad deed would pass away into nothingness, making the law of moral retribution impossible; and, similarly the moment which undergoes retribution would be so doing without having been the author of the deed of which it is supposed to be the retribution. This is contrary to the essence of the law of retribution (*karma*). In other words, if the soul is so absolutely impermanent, as to exist only for a moment and cease to exist absolutely in the next moment, the law of retribution which requires personal identity of the doer and the enjoyer, would not hold good, that is, the doer of the act will be one, while the enjoyer of the fruits thereof will be quite a different person. Again, in the doctrine of soul's absolute momentariness, the experiences of happiness and unhappiness one after another in the case of one and the same soul would become impossible. Similarly, such soul cannot be the author of *puṇya* (good deed) or *pāpa* (bad deed). For, the single instant is the length of time just sufficient for it to come into existence and there is nothing to spare for doing *puṇya* and *pāpa*. The bondage and liberation also will have no meaning, as they cannot be predicated of one and the same soul. The upholder of the soul's absolute impermanence cannot say that one who is bound becomes liberated. Bondage and liberation are two states. And a momentary soul cannot have two states.

As the soul is variable constant, it persists through all its incessantly originating and perishing modes. In such a soul, the different states or transformations taking place at different times in succession are possible, and such a soul can obtain fruits of its good deeds performed at different times after any length of duration of time—even after the interval of many births.[1] If the soul be taken as absolutely eternal

1. Once a thorn pierced through the sole of Gautama Buddha, a great saint, while he was walking. With reference to this event he said to his monks, "O Monks! in the 91st previous birth from the present one, I had killed a man with a spear. That the

(*kūṭasthanitya*)[1], there would be no possibility at all of its assuming different states, transformations or modes. Hence the different activities—good or bad—and the different states of happiness and unhappiness, etc., would also be absolutely impossible. Not only the sentient soul but also all the insentient things are in constant flux of momentary changes. Everything undergoes incessant changes. Modes or forms of a substance are changing every moment. This means that the sentient soul which is permanent should not be regarded as absolutely permanent, but should also be regarded as impermanent insofar as its changing modes are concerned. Similarly, the insentient objects like a pot, etc., which appear impermanent should also be regarded as permanent from the standpoint of original persistent substance (say, clay in the case of a pot). Thus the doctrine of permanence-cum-impermanence[2] is logical and cogent.

Ācārya Hemacandra gives a practical illustration in the context of his above-quoted two verses. He says: 'Jaggery (*guḍa*) and ginger (*nāgaram* or *suṇṭhi*)

---

thorn has now pierced through the sole of my foot is the result of that act of mine."
ita ekanavati kalpe śaktyā me puruṣo hataḥ /
tena karmavipākena pāde viddho 'smi bhikṣavaḥ //

1. Premanence (*nityatā*) is twofold—the absolutely unchanging permanence (*kūṭastha-nityatā*) and permanence amidst change (*pariṇāmi-nityatā*). The former is merely an abstraction, the latter is concrete reality. The term '*kūṭastha*' employed for the absolutely unchanging permanence is formed of two words, viz., '*kūṭa*' and '*stha*'. *Kūṭa* means 'a peak of a mountain' or 'a hammer'. And '*stha*' means 'abiding', 'stable'. So the term '*kūṭastha*' means 'abiding or stable like a peak of a mountain or a hammer'.
2. *jīvā ṇaṁ bhaṁte! kiṁ sāsayā asāsayā? Goyamā! jīvā siya sāsayā siya asāsayā / se keṇaṭṭheṇaṁ bhaṁte! evaṁ vuccai ...? Goyamā! davvaṭṭhayāe sāsayā, bhāvaṭṭhayāe asāsayā/*"
—*Bhagavatīsūtra, Śataka* 7, *Uddeśa* 2

Translation:
'Are the souls, O Lord, permanent or impermanent?
'The souls, O Gautama, are permanent in some respect and impermanent in some respect'. 'With what end in view, O Lord, is it so said...?'
'They are permanent, O Gautama, from the viewpoint of substance, and impermanent from the viewpoint of modes'.
syātām atyantanāśe'sya kṛtanāśākṛtāgamau /
na tv avasthāntaraprāptau loke bālayuvādivat //23//
tasmād ubhayahānena vyāvṛttyanugamātmakaḥ /
puruṣo 'bhyupagantavyaḥ kuṇḍalādiṣu sarpavat //28//
In the above two and other verses from his *Ślokavārtika* Kumārila Bhaṭṭa, a great *Mīmāṁsaka* thinker, explains the soul as permanent-cum-impermanent.

are said to cause phlegm (*kaphahetuḥ*) and bile (*pittakāraṇam*) respectively but when compounded (*dvayātmani*), they lose their respective defects (*doṣa*)'.[1] (Similarly, doctrine of absolute permanence and that of absolute impermanence are vitiated by logical defects while that of permanence-cum-change is free from them.)

Regarding the nature of reality, different systems of Indian philosophy have different views. The *Vedānta* maintains that *Brahman*, the only reality, is absolutely permanent. It considers reality to be absolutely static and dismisses all change as illusory or mere appearance. On the other hand, Buddhism contends that reality is momentary and discrete (i.e., characterised by origination and destruction alone). It conceives reality as pure change and declares all that is indicative of permanence or staticity to be illusory and unreal. The *Sāṁkhya* regards *Prakṛti* (Nature) as permanent-cum-impermanent (variable constant), while *Puruṣa* (the soul) as absolutely permanent. The *Naiyāyika* and the *Vaiśeṣika* philosophers maintain that of the real things, some like an atom, Time, soul, etc., are absolutely permanent while some like a jar, a piece of cloth, etc., are absolutely impermanent (i.e., characterised by origination and destruction alone). Thus, according to them, both the permanent and the changing are real but whatever is permanent is totally different from whatever is changing. For them one and the same thing is not both, permanent and changing. But the Jaina philosophy maintains that all things—sentient and insentient, tangible and intangible, subtle and gross—are of the triple nature of origination, destruction and persistence. Reality is both permanent and changing. Reality in the Jaina's view is a permanent subject of changing states.

As already stated, everything has always two aspects—one permanent and the other impermanent. On account of its permanent aspect, the thing is called permanent (unchanging, static). And on account of its impermanent aspect, it is regarded as undergoing origination and destruction (i.e., as constantly changing). When we pay attention to one aspect alone, we find the thing either absolutely permanent or absolutely impermanent. But when we pay attention to both the aspects, we know the thing in its entirety, as it is. It is only on the basis of these two standpoints that the Jaina philosophy describes reality as having a triple

1. *guḍo hi kaphahetuḥ syān nāgaraṁ pittakāraṇam /*
dvayātmani na doṣo 'sti guḍanāgarabheṣaje //6//

character of origination, destruction and persistence—from one standpoint (i.e., the standpoint of modes or impermanent aspect), it is of the nature of origination and destruction, while from the other standpoint (i.e., the standpoint of substance or permanent aspect) it is of the nature of permanence.

If all things are exclusively impermanent (momentary), then since a new thing originates and perishes every moment and since this thing has got no permanent basis, there should never have been experience of likeness in relation to the concerned series of momentary transformations—that is, on seeing again a thing that was seen earlier there should in no way take place recognition in the form 'this is the same thing', for recognition requires on the one hand permanence in the thing that acts as its object and on the other hand permanence in the soul that acts as seer.

The doctrine of absolute impermanence would render memory impossible. The moment that had experience has been totally destroyed. So, how can another moment which has no connection whatsoever with that lost moment remember what that lost moment had experienced? It cannot be that the person who had experience is one and the person who remembers is another. If the author of experience and that of memory were not required to be identical, X would experience a thing and Y would remember it. In other words, any man would remember any thing, irrespective of the need of previous experience. The impossibility of recognition and memory would make all money transactions pertaining to debtors and creditors impossible and all our worldly dealings inexplicable.

Similarly, if either the physical or conscious verity is exclusively changeless, then in the universe which is of the form of a commixture of these two verities there should never crop up that variety which is there to be seen every moment. Hence it is that the doctrine of permanence-cum-transience is treated as tenable by the Jaina system of philosophy.

The method of *syādvāda* synthesises the two standpoints which find exclusive existence and exclusive non-existence in a thing. One should think as to what are the factors depending on which man regards a thing as existent. Everything exists by its own qualities alone, and not by the qualities of another thing. A man is virtuous by his own virtues, and not by another man's virtues. A person is rich by his own riches, and not by another person's riches. Father is father by his own son, and not by another man's son. Similarly, each and every entity exists by its own qualities, and not by alien qualities. That it does not exist by alien nature means it is non-existent from the standpoint of alien nature.

One not endowed with literary faculty says, 'I am not a writer'. Another without oratory says, 'I am not an orator'. Here 'I am not a writer' means 'I do not exist as a writer'; and 'I am not an orator' means 'I do not exist as an orator'. Someone says, 'I am an orator but not a writer'. The statement means 'I exist as an orator but not as a writer'. To say 'I exist' and 'I do not exist' at one and the same time is tenable, because these two statements are made from two different standpoints. One and the same person exists as an orator and does not exist as a writer at one and the same time. From these simple examples, one can easily understand that even the existent could be regarded as non-existent from the viewpoint of that nature or quality which is alien to it.

Non-existence is nowhere said to belong to a thing from the standpoint of its own nature. If a thing were non-existent even by its own nature, it would then be absolutely non-existent. So, it cannot be non-existent by its own nature. But, if a thing were not non-existent even by alien nature, then one thing would be every other thing, i.e., anything would be anything, and there would be nothing like a thing's own nature. Therefore, a thing does exist by its own nature, but it does never exist by alien nature. The senstient soul exists by its own nature. If it were to exist even by the nature of the insentient substance, then it would not have its own characteristic nature. Here, we should note that the characteristic nature of everything or individual is constituted of its own substance, place, time and quality (or state). Everything exists by its own characteristic nature and does not exist by an alien nature. Thus existence and non-existence both the attributes are found together in all things—sentient and insentient—from two different viewpoints.

Let us take one more instance of the application of the method of *syādvāda.* A thing has both the general and particular characteristics. It is not that it is characterised by either general qualities alone or particular qualities alone. Along with particular characteristics, it also possesses general characteristics. With reference to different individual horses, we have cognition of identity, viz. 'this is a horse' 'this is a horse'. This cognition of identity proves that there is a common characteristic or similarity or identical nature in them. But from among a multitude of horses, their owners recognise their own horses as different from all others. This shows that each horse possesses differentiating traits or particular characteristics. Thus everything is possessed of two natures, viz., general and particular. These two natures are interdependent. One can never be found without the other. As the general and the particular are never found without each other, it can be concluded that a thing is of both the general and the particular natures. To understand each and every thing thus as possessed of both the natures, viz., general and particular is the result of the application of the method of *syādvāda.* Here *syādvāda* synthesises the two viewpoints, viz., one of generality and the other of particularity.

Really speaking, according to the Jainas, there are two kinds of universal (generality), one is called *ūrdhvatā-sāmānya* and the other *tiryak-sāmānya.* The universal which causes the cognition of identity in different individuals is called *tiryak-sāmānya.* As for example, horseness which causes the cognition of identity, viz., 'this is a horse', 'this is a horse' with reference to different horses is an instance of *tiryak-sāmānya.* This horseness is the general nature of all individual horses. By *ūrdhvatā-sāmānya,* the Jaina thinkers mean the permanent substance that persists through the past, present and future modifications. As for example, gold that persists through the different forms of golden ornaments like bracelet, ear-rings, bangles, etc., is an instance of *ūrdhvatā-sāmānya.* Similarly, the persistent individuality which remains the same in spite of its assuming different states of boyhood, youth, adulthood, etc., and causes recognition of the form 'this is the same individual' is another instance of *ūrdhvatā-sāmānya.*

Particular or specific characteristics (*viśeṣa*) are of two types, viz., quality (*guṇa*) and mode (*paryāya*). In other words, particular characteristics are found in the form of either quality or mode.

No material thing is without physical qualities (colour, odour, taste and touch). Thus physical qualities always exist in a material substance (*dravya*), they are co-extensive (*sahabhāvī*) with it. Though generally colour does always exist in matter, all the colours, viz., blue, yellow, etc., do not always exist in it, nor does a particular colour (say, blue) always exist in it. Modes or transformations of colour, viz., blue, yellow, etc., go on changing. Of the so many modes of colour, no two modes can co-exist. They exist in a material substance one after another (*kramabhāvī*). So, quality is regarded as co-extensive with its substratum (substance), while mode is regarded as not co-extensive with its substratum, i.e., as successive or changing (*kramabhāvī*). Thus quality is different from mode. Quality is that which always accompanies its substance, while mode is that which does not accompany its substance throughout its career. Despite their common substratum called substance, there is, between quality and mode, a considerable difference: a quality is a trait which is deeply embedded in the being of a substance and is therefore called '*sahabhāvī*', co-extensive with the substance or intrinsic to it. A mode, on the contrary, is a relatively extrinsic feature appearing in a substance for a time and disappearing later, giving place to another mode. It is, therefore, called '*kramabhāvī*'—successive or not co-extensive with the substance or extrinsic to it.[1] Thus, for example, sentiency (*cetanā*) is a quality of soul as it always accompanies the soul, while various forms of sentiency, viz. knowledge (*jñāna*), intuitive vision (*darśana*), etc., are its modes. Or, knowledge as a general faculty of soul is its quality, while its specific transformations such as the knowledge-of-a-piece-of-cloth, etc., are its modes.

That which is possessed of qualities and modes is called substance. Since to undergo transformation is the very nature of a substance, it goes on being variously transformed—that is, goes on undergoing various transformations. The capacity of a substance to produce transformations is called its quality, while the transformations produced by a quality are called modes. Thus, the quality is a cause and the modes are its effects; or the quality is a capacity and the modes are its manifestations. Now, qualities of the form of a capacity residing in a substance are infinite in number and they are in fact inseparable from the substance acting as their substratum or support, as also inseparable from one another. Similarly, in the case of each quality of the form of a capacity, the modes that emerge from time to time throughout the three phases of time are infinite in number. A substance as well as the capacities in question that act as its aspects, since they never originate or perish, are eternal—that is, beginningless and endless. On the other hand, all the modes, since they originate and perish every moment, are individually transitory—that is, they are possessed of a beginning and an end. However, viewed as a stream of successive states, even modes are beginningless and endless. Certainly, all those modes which are produced in a substance by one and the same capacity acting as a cause and which flow in the form of a stream running throughout the three phases of time, belong to one and the same class. The infinite capacities residing in a substance give rise to

1. *guṇaḥ sahabhāvī dharmaḥ. . .paryāyas tu kramabhāvī/—Pramāṇa-naya-tattvāloka*, V. 7-8.

infinite streams of modes and all these streams run their course simultaneously. Naturally, different modes belonging to different classes, since produced by different capacities, can be found to exist in a substance simultaneously, but different modes belonging to the same class, since produced by the same capacity, cannot be found to exist in a substance simultaneously. Thus in a material substance there can be found simultaneously the different modes belonging to the different capacities like colouration, smell, etc., but there cannot be found simultaneously the different modes blue, yellow, etc., belonging to the capacity for colouration. Similarly, in a soul there can be found simultaneously the different modes belonging to the different capacities like consciousness, joy, energy, etc., but there cannot be found simultaneously the different modes belonging to the capacity for consciousness, or the different modes belonging to the capacity for joy. This is so because in the case of each capacity, just one mode at a time can make itself manifest.

The term '*syādvāda*' is formed of two words '*syāt*' and '*vāda*'. The word '*syāt*' means 'in some respect, in a certain sense, from a particular viewpoint'. Here '*syāt*' is used as indeclinable particle signifying many (*aneka*) standpoints (*anta*). The word '*vāda*' means 'statement'. So, the meaning of the term '*syādvāda*' is 'the statement taking into account all the possible standpoints'. This is the reason why another name of *syādvāda* is *anekāntavāda*.[1] The term '*anekānta*' contains two words, viz., '*aneka*' and '*anta*'. '*Aneka*' means many. And '*anta*' is here used in the sense of attribute, viewpoint, respect. So the term '*anekāntavāda*' means 'examination conducted or statement made by taking into account all possible different standpoints or respects regarding any object'. Thus, the terms '*syādvāda*' and '*anekāntavāda*' are synonymous. The meaning or significance of *anekāntavāda* is manifest or obvious in its name. To view a thing from one standpoint only is called one-sided view (*ekāntadṛṣṭi*). So this is an imperfect view. On the other hand, to view a thing from all possible

---

1. *'syāt' ity avyayam anekāntadyotakam / tataḥ syādvādaḥ anekāntavādaḥ, nityānityādyanekadharmaśabalaikavastvabhyupagamam iti yāvat* /—Ācārya Hemacandra's *Siddhahemaśabdānuśāsana*, 2nd *sūtra*.
Meaning: *'Syāt'* is indeclinable particle which signifies many standpoints (*anekānta*). So *syādvāda* is nothing but *anekāntavāda*. Thus it is an acceptance of the fact that a single entity is variegated by a plurality of attributes, namely, permanence and impermanence, etc.

standpoints is non-one-sided view (*anekāntadṛṣṭi*). Hence this is an all-comprehensive view. It grasps a thing as it is, in all its totally.

Just as the blind men cannot have true knowledge of an elephant by touching its legs, ears, tail and trunk respectively, that is, by touching its one limb only, so also one cannot have true and comprehensive knowledge of a thing by grasping its one aspect or character alone. For the true knowledge of the elephant, each blind man should touch all its limbs. Similarly, to know a thing as it is, in its entirety, one should know its all possible aspects, should view it from all possible standpoints. A man who looks at a shield, standing on the side of its silvery side, says that the shield is made of silver, while another man who looks at it, standing on the side of its golden side, says that it is made of gold. Their knowledge is partially true, but it is not perfectly true. But one who examines it from both the sides, does have the true and complete knowledge, because he knows that one side of the shield is silvery and its other side is golden. So his statement that it is partly golden and partly silvery is perfectly true. Similarly, knowledge of a thing as it is, in its entirety, gained after taking into account all the possible standpoints, and the statement made strictly in accordance with this knowledge could be regarded as completely true.

One-sided view (*ekānta-dṛṣṭi*) can never give us complete truth. It is only non-one-sided, i.e., many-sided view (*anekānta-dṛṣṭi*) which takes into account all the possible standpoints, that can give us complete truth. It observes all the possible aspects of a thing, knows all the possible attributes of it from various standpoints. So it clearly, properly and truly grasps a thing as it is because it explores it from different angles, respects and viewpoints. It understands well the viewpoints of other men and tries to make such a synthesis as could never be contradicted. The true function of non-one-sided view is to effect synthesis of different or seeming opposite views, making them consistent with one another from different standpoints. This will give one an idea of its universality, utility and importance. By the divine force of this noble and liberal view, the quarrels and dissensions arising from the conflicting views subside and harmony is achieved in the entire human society. To spread and preach harmony, equality and friendliness is the object of the non-one-sided view. Thus non-one-sided view means synthetic view, and the idea of human equality and harmony is the good result that follows from it. This idea ultimately gives rise to universal friendliness and turns this human world into blissful and welfare world.

The non-one-sided view promotes reconciliation of all the conflicting views. It proves that all the conflicting views are tenable from different standpoints. Although the various views differ from and contradict one another, still there are certain aspects of truth in them which would harmonise if they are synthesised into an organic whole. And the function of non-one-sided view is to effect such synthesis. This non-one-sided view synthesises different aspects of truth and relates them to one another and finally arrives at one Grand Truth. It effectively demonstrates that the Truth consists in this very variety of its aspects which harmoniously co-exist with one another. It teaches us to understand the point that is being made by the opposite side. It wants us not to be dogmatic and obstinate about our own views. Thus it fosters intellectual toleration and induces man to respect the views of others. It makes a unique attempt to harmonise the persistent discord in the intellectual field.

Regarding *syādvāda,* some maintain that it is not a doctrine of certainty but it is a doctrine of doubt (uncertainty), i.e., scepticism. They say: "*Syādvāda* describes a thing as both permanent and impermanent, as both existent and non-existent, etc., at one and the same time. Can this be anything other than scepticism? The simultaneous predication of both permanence and impermanence, etc., of a thing is nothing but doubt. It shows that mind is unable to ascertain a thing's definite nature". But from our above exposition of *syādvāda* one can see that this criticism is wrong and baseless.[1] Those who know the nature of doubt can never rush to call *syādvāda* scepticism. In the dark night, one sees a rope and there

1. Anandshankar Bapubhai Dhruv, a renowned scholar of Gujarat, in his estimate of *syādvāda* states that it has been formulated for effecting synthesis of conflicting views. It is the doctrine or method of synthesis. Ācārya Śaṅkara's criticism is the result of his failure in grasping the original spirit of *syādvāda.* It is certain that one can never understand a thing perfectly, if one does not examine it from various standpoints. So, for gaining comprehensive knowledge, the method of *syādvāda* is very useful. Some opine that this Jaina doctrine of *syādvāda* is nothing but scepticism (*saṁśayavāda).* But I do not agree with them. It is not scepticism. On the contrary, it teaches us the universal art of viewing a thing from all angles or respects.
This opinion of Dhruv is published in the book entitled *'Jainetara Dṛṣṭie Jaina'.* Late Mahāmahopādhyāya Shriram Mishra Shastry of Kashi clearly brings out, with strong arguments, logical soundness and practical utility of *syādvāda* or *anekāntavāda* in his lecture entitled *'Sujana-Sammelana'* which has been published in the form of an independent book.

arises in his mind a doubt: 'Is this a rope or a serpent?' When one sees a stump of a tree from a distance, there arises in his mind a doubt: 'Is this a man or a stump of a tree?' Like these two, there are so many well known instances of doubt. In the above instances, the intellect goes on vacillating between two alternatives, viz., a rope and a serpent, a man and a stump of a tree, unable to ascertain one, excluding the other. But one does not find this nature of doubt in *syādvāda*. *Syādvāda* asks us to examine a thing from different standpoints and to ascertain a particular attribute in a thing from a particular standpoint. When one examines a thing from various standpoints, one understands that it is certainly existent from one standpoint and certainly non-existent from another standpoint; similarly, that it is certainly permanent from one standpoint and certainly impermanent from another standpoint. A thing is certainly existent from the standpoint of its own substance, place, time and attribute (or state), and certainly non-existent from the standpoint of alien substance, etc. It is certainly permanent from the standpoint of its substance, and certainly impermanent from the standpoint of its modes. *Syādvāda* which is of the nature of acceptance of seemingly opposite attributes in a thing when found consistent with one another from different standpoints, can never be regarded as scepticism or a doctrine of uncertainty. In fact, *syādvāda* is certainly not scepticism, but the doctrine of conditional certainty.

syād nitya eva ghaṭaḥ, syād anitya eva ghaṭaḥ/

From a certain point of view, or in a certain sense, the pot is certainly permanent; from a certain point of view, or in a certain sense, the pot is certainly impermanent.

The particle '*eva*' is here used in the sense of 'certainly' 'without doubt'. Thus the above sentences qualified by the particle '*eva*' are statements of certainty and not of doubt. The statement '*syād asty eva ghaṭaḥ*' means: 'the pot is existent, there is no doubt about it.' But this existence is not absolute and unconditional. Otherwise, the pot would exist as a pillar or anything else. The pot is certainly existent, but under certain conditions. This conditionality of existence is expressed by the term '*syāt*', which means 'from a particular viewpoint' 'in a certain sense' 'under certain conditions'. Thus the term '*syāt*' is not to be translated into English as 'may be' 'probably' 'perhaps' which yield the sense of doubt. What is the use of such words yielding the sense of doubt, in the statement or doctrine of certainty? Knowledge of the pot as permanent and impermanent from different standpoints is as much determinate and certain as is the knowledge of the pot as pot.

Wrong interpretation of the term '*syāt*' as 'may be' imparts a sceptical form to *syādvāda*. But in fact *syādvāda* is not scepticism. It is not the uncertainty of judgement, but its conditional or relative character, that is expressed by the qualifying particle '*syāt*'. Subject to the conditions under which any judgement is made, the judgement is valid beyond doubt. So there is no room for scepticism. All that is implied is that every assertion which is true, is true only under certain conditions. *Syādvāda* is not of the nature of doubt arising from the difficulty or inability of ascertaining the exact nature of a thing in regard to existence and non-existence, permanence and impermanence, etc. It is not the doctrine of uncertainty. It is not scepticism.[1]

---

1. Those who have widely studied the works of the different systems of philosophy know very well that those ancient systems of philosophy have also accepted and followed the non-one-sided viewpoint (*anekānta-dṛṣṭi*). The *Nyāya-Vaiśeṣika* system has adopted this non-one-sided viewpoint in accepting earth as permanent in the form of atoms and impermanent in the form of effects.
   And study the following verse :
   icchan pradhānaṁ sattvādyair viruddhair gumphitaṁ guṇaiḥ /
   sāṅkhyaḥ saṅkhyāvatāṁ mukhyo nānekāntaṁ pratikṣipet //—Ācārya Hemacandra's *Vītarāgastotra*
   Meaning: The *Sāṁkhya* system has accepted *syādvāda* in declaring that *Prakṛti* (the non-sentient ultimate entity) is constituted of the three mutually contradictory elements, viz. *sattva, rajas* and *tamas*.
   Again, understand the following aphorism (III. 13) from the Pātañjala *Yogadarśana*.
   etena bhūtendriyeṣu dharma-lakṣaṇa-avasthāpariṇāmā vyākhyātāḥ /
   Translation: Thus we have explained *dharma-pariṇāma* (change of characteristic), *lakṣaṇa-pariṇāma* (change dependent on time-variation) and *avasthā-pariṇāma* (change of state or condition) of the physical elements (*bhūtas*) and the senses (*indriyas*). While explaining various changes which a thing undergoes pertaining to characteristic, time and state, the *Yoga* system has provided an instance of *syādvāda*.
   The following observation made by Upādhyāya Yaśovijayajī is noteworthy.
   jāti-vyaktyātmakaṁ vastu vadan anubhavocitam /
   Bhaṭṭo vā'pi Murārir vā nānekāntaṁ pratikṣipet //49//—*Adhyātmopaniṣad,* I *Adhikāra*
   Meaning: Kumārila Bhaṭṭa and Murāri, the two great *Mīmāṁsaka* thinkers, respect the method or doctrine of *syādvāda,* when they declare, in accordance with experience, that a thing is of the nature of both universal and particular.
   On p. 335, we have presented the non-one-sided view of Kumārila Bhaṭṭa.
   And study the following remarks made by Upādhyāya Yaśovijayajī in his

Saptabhaṅgī (Sevenfold Judgement)

As we have already seen, *syādvāda* (*anekānta-dṛṣṭi*=non-one-sided view) makes a synthesis of many attributes, viz., existence and non-existence, permanence and impermanence, etc., in one and the same thing from various standpoints. This leads to the understanding that the nature of a thing should be expounded as it is, taking a comprehensive all-sided view of the thing. Someone desirous of knowing the nature of a thing asks a question: 'Is the pot impermanent?' If somebody, in answer, says, "Yes, it is certainly impermanent', then the statement is either untrue or incomplete. If he thinks that he has made the statement after full consideration, taking into account all the aspects of the thing, then the statement is not true. It is because when considered from the comprehensive standpoint, the pot is proved to be permanent as well as impermanent. And if the statement is made from one particular standpoint only, then

---

Adhyātmopaniṣad (I *Adhikāra*).
abaddhaṁ paramārthena baddhaṁ ca vyavahārataḥ /
bruvāṇo brahma vedāntī nānekāntaṁ pratikṣipet //50//
Meaning: The *Vedāntins* who regard *Brahman* as bound from the empirical standpoint and unbound from the transcendental standpoint recognise the importance of *syādvāda.*

Let us take a simple instance of the application of the method or doctrine of *syādvāda.*
kasyacid guṇakṛd dugdhaṁ doṣakāri ca kasyacit /
ekasyāpi daśābhede syādvādo 'yaṁ prakāśate //
eko 'rtha upayogī cānupayogī ca jāyate /
avasthābhedam āśritya syādvādo 'yaṁ prakāśate //
ekam eva bhaved vastu hānikṛl lābhakāri ca /
avasthābhedam āśritya syādvādo 'yaṁ prakāśate // (Author Nyāyavijaya)
Meaning: Milk is suitable to some and harmful to others. Not only that, but it is suitable and harmful to one and the same person at different times in his different conditions.

One and the same object is useful to a man in one state and useless to the same man in another state.

One and the same thing is beneficial to a person in one condition and harmful to the same person in another condition.

The purport of the above statement is made clear in the following explanation.

Someone asks a general question: Is milk beneficial or harmful? How can we say, in answer, categorically that it is beneficial? Or, how can we say categorically that it is harmful? In fact, it is proper to say that it is both beneficial and harmful from different standpoints. Of course, if we are required to make statement keeping in view a particular condition or occasion, we should give an answer in accordance with that condition or occasion.

it should contain some term suggesting that the statement is made from one particular standpoint. Without that term the answer appears incomplete. From this, it follows that while predicating a particular attribute of a thing, we should formulate a statement in such a manner that the opposite attribute which is there in the thing does not stand negated. This means that while describing a thing as permanent we should put such a word in the statement as would stop the rise of the suggestion that there is in the thing absence of the attribute impermanence. And while describing a thing as impermanent, we should use some such word in the statement as would stop the rise of the suggestion that there is in the thing absence of the attribute permanence. Similarly, one should be careful in the same way while describing a thing as existent, non-existent, etc. Such a word in Sanskrit is *'syāt'*. The meaning of the term *'syāt'*, as already pointed out, is 'from a particular standpoint'. So in the Sanskrit statement, the word *'syāt'* or its synonym *'kathañcit'* (meaning 'from a certain standpoint') is to be employed, as in the statement *'syāt anityaḥ eva ghaṭaḥ'* ('From a certain standpoint, the pot is certainly impermanent'); in this statement '*syāt*' is employed in order not to rule out the attribute permanence which is present in the pot from another standpoint.

The above presentation is philosophical. But all our worldly dealings are conducted through statements made from this or that standpoint (*nayavāda*). In worldly dealings, people make statements from one particular standpoint which is governed by the purpose in hand. Depending on the purpose aimed at, sometimes some one property and sometimes some other is desired to be expressed. Thus in our worldly dealings, it is this desire or intention of the speaker that determines the aspect (of a thing) which he expressly predicates of a thing. This is the reason why we do not employ the term *'syāt'* in the statements which we make in our worldly dealings. It is only to give the idea of a comprehensive (all-sided) view of reality that the term *'syāt'* is employed in a statement.

There are two fundamental answers to any question. In answer, we say 'yes' or 'no'. That is, we answer in affirmation or negation. As a matter of fact, a thing can be described by two fundamental propositions—one affirmative and the other negative. The sevenfold predication or judgement (*saptabhaṅgī*) is formulated on the basis of these two fundamental modes. The ways or modes of answering a question are called *bhaṅga*. There can be only seven modes or ways. And a set of these seven modes is called *saptabhaṅgī* ('a sevenfold statement or judgement or predication'). Technically *saptabhaṅgī* is defined as a statement in seven different ways—to be mentioned hereafter—of affirmation and negation, with the use of the word *'syāt'* (meaning 'from a certain standpoint'), singly and jointly, without inconsistency such as that arising from conflict with perception, etc., as the result of inquiry about each of the different properties of a thing such as existence, etc.

As against the seven modes (*bhaṅgas*) it may be urged, there will be infinite number of modes about everything in consequence of the infinite number of characters (*dharmas*) which can be affirmed or denied about that thing. The answer to that objection is: Surely, if you take all the infinite number of characters, the number of modes will be infinite. But in respect of each of the characters, the modes will be seven only.

There are only seven types of modes or propositions with regard to any one character of a thing. It is because there are only seven types of questions which give rise to these seven types of modes or propositions in the form of answers. Thus the number 'seven' of the modes of the sevenfold judgement is derived from the fact that the question is of seven kinds in respect of each character of a thing. The number 'seven' of the types of question is due to the fact that the curiosity from which the question springs is of seven kinds. The number 'seven' of the kinds of curiosity depends on the number 'seven' of the types of doubt. And the doubt is of seven kinds, because the facets of a character of a thing about which doubt arises are but of seven kinds. As is shown in this cause-effect chain, the number 'seven' of modes or propositions has ultimately been rooted in the seven facets of a character of a thing.

From this it follows that the seven modes or constituent statements of the sevenfold judgement are not mere words or purely imaginary or mental figments, but they are solidly grounded in the objective facets of an attribute of a thing. So we should bear in mind that the nature of each and every mode corresponds to one of the seven facets of an attribute of a thing.

The seven modes are as follows:

(1) It exists (It is). (2) It does not exist (It is not). (3) It exists and does not exist (It is and is not). (4) It is inexpressible. (5) It exists and is inexpressible. (6) It does not exist and is inexpressible. (7) It exists, does not exist, and is inexpressible.

But in the scientific way, they should be stated as follows:

(1) From a certain point of view, or in a certain sense, a thing is certainly existent.
(2) From a certain point of view, or in a certain sense, it is certainly non-existent.
(3) From a certain point of view, or in a certain sense, it is certainly existent and from another point of view, it is certainly non-existent.
(4) From a certain point of view, it is certainly inexpressible.
(5) From a certain point of view, it is certainly existent and from another point of view it is certainly inexpressible.
(6) From a certain point of view, it is certainly non-existent and from another point of view it is certainly inexpressible.
(7) From a certain point of view, it is certainly existent, from another point of view it is certainly non-existent, and from a third point of view it is inexpressible.

Now let us explain these seven modes.

First mode: The first mode is represented by the proposition, "From a certain standpoint a thing is certainly existent". Here, it is shown as to what a thing is. It is shown as follows. The thing is certainly existent, but from a certain standpoint. That is, it is certainly existent from the standpoint of its own substance, space, time and quality (or state). In this mode, the existence of any entity is affirmed from the standpoint of its own intrinsic characters. The existence predicated of a thing is not absolute but relative.

Second mode: The second mode is represented by the proposition, "From a certain standpoint a thing is certainly non-existent." In this mode, it is shown as to what a thing is not. It is shown as follows. The thing is certainly non-existent, but from a certain standpoint. That is, it is certainly non-existent from the standpoint of substance, place, time, quality (or state) of another thing. Here the non-existence of a thing is asserted from the standpoint of alien characters. The non-existence predicated of a thing is not absolute, unrestricted and unconditional, but relative, restricted and conditional.

If a thing were not to exist from the standpoint of its own substance, etc., it would be essenceless, mere void. And if it were not to non-exist from the standpoint of alien substance, etc., there would be confusion of things. For if a pot were not to non-exist as a piece of cloth, the pot would become the piece of cloth. That is, in that case anything would become everything. Apparently, it may seem that self-existence (*sva-sattva*) is identical with non-existence-of-others (*para-asattva*), that is, existence-of-x is identical with non-existence-of-non-x. But it is not so. They are different. Just as existence of a thing from the standpoint of its own nature is experienced independently, even so non-existence of a thing from the standpoint of the nature of others is experienced independently. By these two modes, one gains knowledge of two types. Knowledge generated by the first mode is different from that generated by the second mode. For example, when it is said, 'Mr. X is not in the market', from that proposition we cannot have the knowledge as to where he is. In spite of our knowledge that he is not in the bazar, our desire to know as to where he is persists; and for satisfying this desire the employment of the first mode is necessary. Even in practice, the employment of the mode pertaining to non-existence is necessary, though the mode pertaining to existence has already been employed. To say that there is a coin of a rupee in my hand is one thing and to say that there is not a coin of a dollar in my hand is another thing. Thus, the employment of both these modes is necessary.

An objection to treating the second mode as logical complement to the previous mode is that the two modes being mutually opposed are contradictory. In answer, it is sufficient to point out that the two elements, constituting the two modes, are not contradictory, but on the contrary are in fact mutually necessary complements. Contradiction would arise if the propositions 'the jar exists' and 'the jar does not exist' were absolute. As they are relative, contradiction does not arise. The objecter wrongly understands the latter proposition, viz., "the jar does not exist", as equivalent to "the jar does not exist as the jar". The true interpretation of it should be that "the jar does not exist as things other than itself". A thing does not exist from the standpoint of substance, etc., of another thing. In fact, it is the very point which the critics of *syādvāda* often miss and which the upholders of *syādvāda* make out in their defence.

Third mode: The third mode is represented by the proposition, "From a certain standpoint a thing is certainly existent, and from another standpoint it is certainly non-existent". In this mode, it is shown as to what a thing is and what it is not, successively. This mode predicates of a thing the existence and the non-existence successively from two different standpoints. It offers successive presentation of existence and non-existence. Here affirmation and negation are made conjointly.

Though this third mode is formed by taking together the first two modes, its function is different from those of the first two modes. The function which this third mode, pertaining to the existence-cum-non-existence, performs can never be performed by the mode pertaining to existence alone or by the mode pertaining to non-existence alone. Simple proposition is one thing and compound proposition is another thing. Though number 'three' is arrived at by adding number 'one' and number 'two', yet number 'three' is different from number 'one' and number 'two'. The necessity of such compound proposition lies in the need of comprehensive view of the positive and the negative characters of an object. The compound or conjunctive proposition presenting consecutive togetherness (of existence and non-existence) which is no less a unique or distinctive moment of factual significance than any other can never be regarded as redundant or superfluous.

Fourth mode: The fourth mode is represented by the proposition "From a certain standpoint, a thing is certainly inexpressible".

What is the standpoint from which a thing is certainly inexpressible? Or, what is the sense in which a thing is certainly inexpressible? We attempt to answer this question in what follows.

One can easily understand that a thing is inexpressible or indescribable from the standpoint of its nature of having infinite characters. But all the seven modes of a sevenfold judgement or predication apply or refer to one character only. So this fourth mode pertaining to inexpressibility of a thing is to be explained or interpreted with reference to any one of the infinite characters like existence, etc. If taking into account any one of the infinite pairs of opposite characters like existence and non-existence, permanence and impermanence, etc., we can describe a thing as of the nature of both existence and non-existence, etc., then how can it be inexpressible?

That the opposite characters in the pair of existence and non-existence cannot be expressed simultaneously is the reason why a thing is presented as inexpressible. The two words meaning existence and non-existence can never be uttered simultaneously.[1] As a result, it is impossible to predicate

1. And there is no one word in the language which means both existence and non-existence together. But supposing there were such a word, still it would present the two meanings to the mind one after another.

of a thing existence and non-existence simultaneously. Hence a thing is certainly inexpressible from this standpoint. Here someone may raise a question: What to talk of two words expressive of two characters? Even one word expressive of a single character cannot be uttered at a time in one moment in one sweep. Take, for instance, the word 'existent'. The letters constituting it can never be uttered simultaneously. In that case, even existence alone or non-existence alone could not be predicated of a thing in one sweep. Thus, if it were impossible for us to predicate of a thing any one character, a thing would become absolutely inexpressible.

Just as it is accepted that a word 'existence' expresses existence in one sweep, even though its letters are uttered successively, so also it should be accepted that two words 'existence' and 'non-existence' can express their respective meanings, viz., existence and non-existence simultaneously, even though they are uttered one after another. The characteristic existence is predicated of a thing in one sweep, and the characteristic non-existence is also predicated of a thing in one sweep. Similarly, both the characteristics existence and non-existence can also be predicated of a thing in one sweep. This being the case, how can a thing be inexpressible?

The existence of a thing is so unfathomable, so vast and so immense, and similarly its non-existence, since it is of the nature of exclusion from all other things, is so deep, so extensive and so great, that it is quite impossible for us to describe them as they are. And we can think in the same way in connection with other characters of a thing, viz., permanence, impermanence, generality, particularity, etc.

Apart from this, there are not as many words as are the characters of a thing. Again, all the characters can never be known by us. Even one who has gained the supreme knowledge cannot express in language all the characters which he knows. In this sense, a thing always remains inexpressible or indescribable. Let us think a little more about this point.

The characters of a thing are of two kinds—positive and negative. Positive characters are positive qualities or attributes. Negative characters are of the nature of absence of the characters of other things. A thing has infinite positive characters and infinite negative characters. So it is of the nature of infinite characters. When we describe a thing, we do so by stating some of its positive characters (I Mode), or by stating some of its negative characters (II Mode), or by stating some positive and some negative characters conjointly (III Mode). But in whatever manner we describe it, that description will always be incomplete, it will never be complete. It is so because of infinite characters those which are not describable can never be described. So, a thing can be partly called indescribable also (IV Mode). In short, when we describe a thing by expressing its positive characters alone, then also we can express only some of its positive characters, all other positive characters certainly remain inexpressible (V Mode). When we describe a thing by expressing its negative characters alone, then also we can express only some of its negative characters, all other negative characters certainly remain inexpressible (VI Mode). And when we describe a thing by expressing its both the characters positive and negative conjointly, even then we can express only some of its positive characters and only some of its negative characters, all other positive and negative characters certainly remain inexpressible (VII Mode). Thus, in whatever manner we may try to describe a thing, our description of it will never be complete. It will always remain incomplete.

The total nature of reality or a thing being impenetrable and incomprehensible, reality or one and the same thing is described by the seers variously. So, *Ṛgveda* declares: *ekaṁ sad viprā bahudhā vadanti* / That is, Reality is one but the wise describe it variously.

There is no question at all of expressing those characters in language, which we do not know. They are certainly inexpressible. But there are other characters also which are amenable to human experience, yet owing to the limitations of language they could not be expressed in words. Let us explain this point by illustration. Suppose somebody asks you: "How sweet is honey? What is the taste of clarified butter (*ghee*)? How is the feeling of pain?" You will have to say to the questioner: "They can never be described in language. You will have the answers to these questions through your own experience and not through words." The sweetness of honey is indescribable. Similarly, the taste of ghee and the feeling of pain are also indescribable. None can express in words the difference that is there in the sweetness of jaggery, honey and sugar. In this sense also, a thing is certainly inexpressible.

On account of its having infinite characters and various forms or aspects, a thing is certainly inexpressible, hence *Upaniṣads* call it indescribable or unutterable (*anirvacanīya*). Call it inexpressible (*avaktavya*) or indescribable, both mean the same thing.

In the fourth mode, it is shown that though the pot is expressible, it is also inexpressible from some other standpoint.[1]

The remaining three modes are obtained by combining successively each of the first three modes with the fourth. They are as follows:

Though a thing is certainly inexpressible, it is expressible also from other standpoints (Modes I, II and III). So, along with its inexpressibility when we want to present its expressibility also in some form, then the first three modes pertaining to any of the three forms of expressibility (e.g., existence, non-existence, existence-cum-non-existence) get combined with the mode pertaining to inexpressibility.

Thus by combining the first and the fourth modes successively we get the fifth mode, "A thing (say, the pot) is certainly existent from a certain standpoint and certainly inexpressible from another standpoint."

Similarly, combining again the second and the fourth modes successively we have the sixth mode, "A thing (say, the pot) is certainly non-existent from a certain standpoint and certainly inexpressible from another standpoint."

Lastly, combining successively the third mode with the fourth, we get the seventh mode, "A thing (say, the pot) is certainly existent from a certain standpoint, also is certainly non-existent from another standpoint, and inexpressible from a third standpoint."

A thing has infinite characters. Therefore, it is described as *anekānta* (manifold) or *anekadharmātmaka* (having manifold nature). In fact, it is infinitely manifold or its nature is infinitely manifold. If someone takes photographs of a house from all the four directions, then those photographs will not be identical. Even then they are the photographs of the same house, and we consider them to be of the identical house. Though the photographs relate to the identical house, they are different because they are taken from different angles or directions. Similarly, a thing appears varied from different standpoints. This is the only reason why our statements about it are also varied. We know that a particular man now in an elevated or high state was once in a low state or position. And we say: "Now this man is not that man, he has become a great artist or scholar."

---

1. According to the Jaina works on logic, a thing is inexpressible in the sense that the opposite characters like existence and non-existence, etc., embedded in a thing can never be asserted simultaneously with equal prominence. When existence and non-existence are, with equal primacy, predicated of a thing simultaneously, there being no proper word to meet the demand, the thing is said inexpressible.

Taking into account different conditions or factors, we make different statements about a thing. And we assert and negate a particular attribute of a thing from different standpoints. Nobody finds contradiction in them. A mango is smaller than a pumpkin and bigger than a berry. Here one and the same thing is called small and big in one statement, but from different standpoints. And nobody objects to it or sees any contradiction in it. These are the simple instances illustrating the theory of non-one-sidedness (*anekāntavāda*) or the doctrine of conditional judgement or predication (*syādvāda*). A thing exists and does not exist from two different standpoints. We do not know beforehand or from the very beginning as to which characters are contradictory. But when we find that the particular two characters cannot co-exist in a thing at a time, then only do we come to know that they are contradictory and consider them to be so. But if they are found co-existing in a thing at a time, then they are not contradictory at all. How can we regard them as contradictory? If a thing is regarded as both existent and non-existent from one and the same standpoint, then it is certainly a case of contradiction. But, if a thing is regarded as existent from the standpoint of its own substance, place, time and state (or quality) and as non-existent from the standpoint of alien substance, etc., it involves no contradiction. When one says that from the standpoint of persisting substance, a thing is eternal, but from the standpoint of modal changes, it is not eternal, he does not make any self-contradictory statement. As *syādvāda* or *anekāntavāda* is free from the defect of contradiction, it is also free from all those defects that are derived from that of contradiction.

On reflection, we find that the sevenfold judgement or predication (*saptabhaṅgī*) has only three primary modes (1) existent (is), (2) non-existent (is not), (3) inexpressible. The remaining four modes are derived from combining any two of these three primary modes in all possible ways. *Bhagavatīsūtra* mentions only these three primary modes. Therein we find: "*sia atthi, sia natthi, sia avattavvaṁ/*" And the sevenfold judgement or predication is the expanded, or rather developed, form of this threefold judgement or predication (*tribhaṅgī*).

While offering a reply to any question, we have to employ one of these seven modes. To make the point clear, let us take one ordinary gross illustration. Regarding a patient with his impending death a relative asks the doctor, 'How is his condition?' In reply, the doctor will give any one of the following seven answers:

(1) His bodily condition is good. (is)
(2) His bodily condition is not good. (is not)
(3) Compared to what it was yesterday, to-day it is good, but it is not so good that we may hope for his survival or cure. (is and is not)
(4) We cannot say as to whether it is good or bad. (inexpressible)
(5) Compared to what is was yesterday, today it is good, still we cannot say as to what will happen. (is and inexpressible)
(6) Compared to what it was yesterday, to-day it is not good, still we cannot say as to what will happen. (is not and inexpressible)
(7) Generally it is not good, but compared to what it was yesterday, to-day it is good, still we cannot say what turn it will take. (is, is not and inexpressible)

We can have the clear idea of the sevenfold judgement or predication (*saptabhaṅgī*) from this practical illustration. In this way, the method of the sevenfold judgement or predication is practicable. We can employ it in practice. In other words, it makes a very useful analysis of an event, condition or theory. We have already understood that regarding one and the same characteristic of a thing, these seven modes (statements) present seven different aspects from different standpoints and hence each of them has some speciality of its own.

We can apply this method of sevenfold judgement or predication to problems related to religion or ethics also. Study the following example:

(1) Killing is a sin (if it is committed through attachment-cum-aversion and negligence). (Is)
(2) Killing is not a sin, when we are constrained to kill a cruel and wicked man who perpetrates cruelty, terror and outrage on the innocent people. It is so because this killing is our duty.[1] (Is not)

---

1. In scriptures, there occur statements regarding medical treatment, etc. involving killing of six types of living beings (*cha-kāya*), to be given, in very rare cases of exception, to the sick and diseased monks etc., taking into account special place and time.

In scriptures there are injunctions, for monks, pertaining to matters such as may involve harassment to living beings, e.g., crossing a river.

Ācārya Haribhadrasūri in his commentary on the *Daśavaikālika-Niryukti, Adhyayana* I, *gāthā* 45, quotes the following verses:

uccāliammi pāe iriāsamiassa saṁkamaṭṭhāe /
vāvajjejja kuliṁgī marijja taṁ jogam āsajja //
na ya tassa taṇṇimitto baṁdho suhumo vi desio samaye /
jamhā so apamatto sā ya pamāo tti niddiṭṭhā //

(3) Intentional (*sāṅkalpika*) killing of innocent living beings without any purpose is a sin, but unintentional killing (*dravya hiṁsā*—formal violence which is not a mental defilement) that takes place in purposeful activity in spite of utmost care and vigilance is not a sin. Killing of the nature of injustice and violation of the rules of good conduct is a sin, but killing of the nature of duty is not a sin. (is and is not)

(4) Without taking into account the situation or circumstances we cannot say as to whether a particular killing is or is not a sin. (inexpressible)

(5) Killing is a sin, but without taking into account time, place and conditions we cannot say as to whether killing is or is not a sin. (is and inexpressible)

(6) As shown above, in extremely rare exceptional cases killing is not a sin, but without taking into account time, place and conditions we cannot say as to whether killing is or is not a sin. (is not and inexpressible)

(7) Killing is a sin, but there are special occasions when it is not a sin, and without taking into account time, place and conditions we cannot say as to whether it is or is not a sin. (is, is not and inexpressible)

Now let us apply this method of sevenfold judgement to truthfulness.

(1) To speak the truth is a virtue. (is)

(2) To speak the truth is not a virtue. For, to speak the truth before a hunter who asks you as to in which direction a deer has gone, or before a wicked man who is after a girl and asks you as to where she is, is a sin and not a virtue.[1] (is not)

The killing of living beings having two or more sense-organs, which may take place while walking carefully and without any passion of attachment and aversion is not mentioned in the scriptures as a cause of even the slightest bondage of karmic matter with soul, because that killing is not done through the act involving attachment-cum-aversion and negligence and it is specifically said that it is only attachment-cum-aversion and negligence that is violence or killing.

1. Regarding this point, we have quoted in our note on p. 114 *Ācārāṅgasūtra.* And study the following verse from the *Mahābhārata.*
bhavet satyam avaktavyaṁ vaktavyam anṛtaṁ bhavet /
yatrānṛtaṁ bhavet satyaṁ satyaṁ cānṛtaṁ bhavet //33// Karṇaparva Adhyāya 72
Meaning: At times, truth as such should not be spoken and on the contrary in its place untruth should be spoken. Thus at times untruth becomes truth and truth becomes untruth.
To elucidate the point made in the verse, the *Mahābhārata* narrates a story of an ascetic named Kauśika. His speaking truth led to the ruthless killing of many men.

(3) To speak the truth which is wholesome and conducive to welfare is virtue, but to speak the truth which is unwholesome and detrimental to welfare is not virtue. (is and is not)
(4) Without taking into account the situation or circumstances, we can never say as to whether truth-speaking is or is not a virtue. (inexpressible)
(5) To speak the truth is a virtue, but without taking into account circumstances or conditions we cannot say as to whether it is or is not a virtue. (is, and inexpressible)
(6) (As shown above in mode 2), to speak the truth is not virtue, but without taking into account circumstances or conditions we cannot say as to whether it is or is not a virtue. (is not and inexpressible)
(7) Generally, to speak the truth is a virtue, but there are certain special occasions when it is not a virtue, still without taking into account circumstances and conditions we cannot say as to whether it is or is not a virtue. (is, is not, and inexpressible)

Thus the method of sevenfold judgement will be a great help in bringing the different sects closer, if it is applied to the rules of conduct. If the rules of conduct are presented in the form of sevenfold judgement, followers of the different sects will realise that there exist, in fact, no difference between their codes of conduct. Once one knows as to under which circumstances or conditions a particular rule is applicable in its affirmative form (mode) and under which circumstances or conditions it is applicable in its negative form (mode), one can very well choose or select the modes (of the rules) appropriate to the present situation. This matter is very useful and beneficial to both the individual and the society. The application of the method of sevenfold judgement inevitably requires the use of the faculty of discretion. If the application of this method is attempted without using one's power of discretion, then it will not do any

---

So he had to take birth as an infernal being in a hell on account of his speaking the so-called truth.
There occurs the following verse in Ācārya Hemacandra's *Yogaśāstra* (*Prakāśa* II).
na satyam api bhāṣeta parapīḍākaraṁ vacaḥ /
loke'pi śrūyate yasmāt Kauśiko narakaṁ gataḥ //61//
Therein Ācārya Hemacandra refers to the story of this very Kauśika ascetic of the *Mahābhārata* to illustrate the point that the truth which causes harassment and injury to living beings should not be spoken.

good to either an individual or the society, but on the contrary may cause harm to both.

Much use has been made of the method of sevenfold judgement in the field of metaphysics and ontology. But from the above exposition, one can see that the primary object of this method should be nothing but to make human life as sweet as nectar. If the method permeates the entire field of conduct, then and then only can it be called 'live *anekānta*'.

NAYA (THEORY OF VALID PARTIAL KNOWLEDGE OR STANDPOINT)

Now let us deal with *naya. Pramāṇa* is an all-sided or comprehensive knowledge. And *naya* is one-sided or partial knowledge. Though both *pramāṇa* and *naya* are certainly of the form of knowledge, they differ from each other inasmuch as the former reveals a thing as a whole, while the latter reveals only a part of it. Thus Siddhasena Divākara notes in his *Nyāyāvatāra* (verse 29):

anekāntātmakaṁ vastu gocaraḥ sarvasaṃvidām /
ekadeśaviśiṣṭo'rtho nayasya viṣayo mataḥ //
Meaning: A manifold thing is the object of *pramāṇa,* while only an aspect of that very thing is the object of *naya.*

When a thing is revealed in its totality, it is a manifold object of knowledge. But when only one aspect abstracted from this very thing is primarily revealed, then it is called a one-sided object of knowledge. Knowledge that cognises a thing with all its aspects or characters is *pramāṇa,* while knowledge that cognises a thing with only one of its many aspects or characters is *naya.* Let us make this point clear by an illustration. When a horse is presented before our eyes, a particular form, a certain size and a specific colour—these special features are predominantly revealed; though these features are predominant at that time, the entire horse with all its non-abstracted other features becomes the object of visual cognition. At that time no feature is revealed as abstracted from other features or the entire horse entity. But through certain features, the entire horse is revealed, that is, the total horse becomes the object of visual cognition. This is the way how a thing becomes the object of *pramāṇa.* When a person who has thus known the horse through *pramāṇa* wants to convey this knowledge to others through words, he, the speaker, abstracts certain features from others through intellectual analysis and says that the horse is red, tall, or belongs to a particular breed. At that time though the horse is revealed to the speaker in his intellect as also to the hearer in his cognition, it is secondary. It is only those features which are stated after having separated or abstracted them from other features, that are primary. This is the reason why the horse, while becoming the object of knowledge, becomes its object as qualified by a certain aspect or character only. This is the way how a thing becomes the object of *naya.*

When knowledge gained with or without the assistance of sense-organs reveals a thing as it is, it is called *pramāṇa.* And the thought-activity touching, one by one, the different aspects of a thing in order to convey through words the very thing revealed to him through *pramāṇa* is called *naya.* In other words, knowledge that is being expressed in words is *naya,* and knowledge that precedes it is *pramāṇa.*

Naya is only a part of *pramāṇa.* Different currents of *naya*s spring forth from *pramāṇa.*

As already stated, comprehensive or all-sided knowledge (*pramāṇa*) grasps a thing in its entirety, while one-sided or partial knowledge (*naya*) grasps primarily only one of the many characters or aspects of a thing. One person sees or understands a thing in one form and another person sees or understands it in another form. So about one and the same thing different persons form different opinions. X does not understand the way in which Y understands a thing, and *vice versa.* But if they know each other's different understandings, rather standpoints or ways of understanding, their incomplete understanding will become complete. And they will try to understand each other's standpoints provided they are sincere truth-seekers. If one who knows the utility of only one of the two, viz., knowledge and practice, or understands only one of the two apparently opposite doctrines, viz., dualism and monism, directs his thought-activity to know and understand the other point or standpoint, he will surely accept it too.

Just as *pramāṇa* is pure knowledge, so also *naya* is pure knowledge. The only difference that obtains between the two is that the former grasps the entire thing, while the latter grasps only one of its many aspects or characters. Inspite of this difference, both are pure, rather valid, knowledge. Pure knowledge of the form of *pramāṇa* is utilised in worldly dealings or communication through the instrumentality of *naya,* because when it is expressed in words before others, it being put under certain special limitations becomes *naya.* The standpoint (one-sided knowledge, *naya*) which deals with one aspect of a thing may or may not have acquaintance with the other aspect of the same thing. Even if it is acquainted with the other aspect, it operates under the limitation of dealing with its own object only. And this is the only way of worldly dealings, practice or communication. For example, when the purpose on hand is to show the glory and utility of knowledge, whatever is said about the glory and utility of knowledge is governed by this purpose, i.e., by the standpoint of knowledge. At that time, though a person adopting the standpoint of knowledge knows that activity or practice too has its honoured place, i.e., glory and utility, he describes the glory and utility of knowledge alone. Thus depending on the purpose aimed at sometimes some one property, aspect or matter sometimes some other is desired to be spoken of, and depending on this desire sometimes some one property, aspect or matter sometimes some other is described or expressed. And in doing so, a standpoint (say, the standpoint of knowledge) does nothing wrong. Of course, it (the standpoint of knowledge) certainly goes wrong if in its obsession with the idea of the glory of knowledge, it completely effaces the place of utility due to practice or activity.

In fact, it is necessary to cultivate synoptic, many-sided outlook. On the strength of it, one can know different aspects or characters of a thing. And it is indispensable for a person to know different aspects of a thing, because then only (i.e., when he knows the other side or standpoint), it becomes, in practice, possible to use properly and profitably any aspect or character of a thing and at the same time to respect the similar proper use of another aspect or character by others. As a result, there may not arise any conflict of ideas or thoughts, which is ultimately rooted in ignorance. On account of the cultivation of the skill or faculty of properly harmonising one side, aspect or standpoint with other sides, aspects or standpoints, it becomes quite possible for the upholders of different ideas, thoughts and doctrines to agree with one another. The method of synthesis along with the synthetic outlook easily achieves mutual understanding and harmony. The method of non-one-sided knowledge, i.e., synthesis of many standpoints, progresses in the direction of the harmonious synthesis of different standpoints, and not in that of ignominious blind conflict of standpoints.

Different (right) opinions, ideas or concepts springing from different standpoints about the same thing are called *nayas*. One and the same person is uncle and nephew, son and father, son-in-law and father-in-law, etc., from different standpoints. From this practical example, one can have the idea of what *naya* is. A thing does not have only one character, it does possess many characters. There are as many opinions or intentions as are the characters of a thing. And there are as many *naya*s (standpoints) as are the opinions or intentions (*abhiprāya*s). All communication or exchange of ideas and thoughts is of the form of *naya*.

With the help of non-one-sided or synoptic view, one understands a thing in its comprehensive nature and realises that it is a treasure-house (substratum) of a great many different characters.

Now let us elucidate some examples of the theory of standpoints or one-sided views.

A pot is a thing. It is indestructible. In other words, it is eternal. But it is indestructible or eternal from the standpoint of its substance, viz., clay. On the other hand, it is destructible or non-eternal from the standpoint of its modes (i.e., changes). Thus it is regarded as eternal from one standpoint and as non-eternal from another standpoint. Both these standpoints are *naya*s.[1]

It is doubtless that the soul is eternal, because it is indestructible. But in its mundane state, it always undergoes changes or transformations. Sometimes it attains the state of animal existence, sometimes that of human existence; at one time it enjoys the pleasures of heaven assuming the state of celestial existence and at another time it is born into a hell as a hellish being. What great transformations it undergoes! How widely different are the states one and the same soul assumes at different times!! What does it suggest? It suggests that the soul is variable or changeable. Does it undergo only a very few transformations or changes even in a single birth? There continuously goes on in it the internal changes like varied thinking, feeling, willing, etc., and pleasure, grief, etc. Thus the embodied soul is caught in the ceaselessly moving cycle of transformations and changes. On this account (i.e., on account of its changeability), the eternal soul substance can be regarded as somehow non-eternal also. So we should regard the soul as neither absolutely eternal nor absolutely non-eternal, but as eternal-cum-non-eternal. When this is the situation, the standpoint from which the soul is eternal and the standpoint from

1. "Nothing extinguishes, and even those things which seem to us to perish are, in truth, but changed."

which it is non-eternal are called *nayas*.

In this connection one point is noteworthy. We should always remember that by the term '*ātmā*' ('soul') what is primarily suggested is a substance while by the term '*ghaṭa*' ('pot') what is primarily suggested is a mode. So the term '*ātmā*' ('soul') primarily generates the knowledge of an eternal element (*tattva*), while the term '*ghaṭa*' ('pot') primarily generates the knowledge of non-eternal object. As the soul is an original substance, it is certainly eternal. On the other hand, a pot is certainly non-eternal because it is a mode of matter.

The soul is certainly different from body. This is clear and beyond any doubt. But we should remember that the soul exists pervasively in its body just as butter exists pervasively in curds. From this, it is obvious that it is not different from its body just as sweet-balls are different from the pot in which they are. This is the reason why it experiences pain as soon as any part of the body is hurt. On account of this very close relation that obtains between the two, the Jaina thinkers maintain that though the soul is really different from the body, it should not be considered to be absolutely different from the body. It is because if it is regarded as absolutely different from body, it would not experience pain when the body is hurt just as of the two utterly different bodies one cannot experience pain when the other is hurt. But, in fact, the soul does experience pain as soon as the body is hurt. So it is necessary to regard the soul as somehow identical with the body. In other words, though the soul and body are really different, the conjunction of the two is so close and solid that they could be regarded as somehow identical from the standpoint of this close and solid conjunction. In this situation, the standpoint from which the soul and body are regarded as different and the standpoint from which they are regarded as identical are called *nayas*.

The standpoint which concentrates on knowledge and shows its achievements is the standpoint of knowledge (*jñānanaya*). And the standpoint which concentrates on practice (activity) and shows its achievements is the standpoint of practice (*kriyānaya*). Both these standpoints are called *nayas*.

A word, sentence, scripture (or scientific work) and doctrine—all these which present the speaker's intention or standpoint can be called *naya*. The standpoints (*nayas*) deserve our respect as long as they do not transgress their limits. But they cease to deserve our respect as soon as they start contradicting one another. For example, we can describe the achievements and gains one can attain through knowledge and we can also describe the achievements and gains one can attain through practice (activity), too. Both these views, ideas or descriptions are true in their own places and within their own spheres. If they attempt to prove one another false, they themselves turn false. Views or opinions formulated on the basis of different standpoints are called *nayas*. They are true insofar as they operate in their own spheres and relate to their own objects. As a standpoint (*naya*) grasps only a part or an aspect of a thing, it is a partial knowledge. Hence it is partially or relatively true. It is true relative to that aspect only. To regard one's partial knowledge as comprehensive knowledge and the partial truth as the whole truth is a form of obstinacy. A man afflicted with this obstinacy considers another's partial knowledge based on his intention or standpoint to be totally false, giving no thought to the other side of the matter. This type of obstinacy is harmful to the human society. Regarding any matter—financial, social, political and religious—one should examine it (the matter) from all possible standpoints and should not mistake the partial knowledge relative to a standpoint for the comprehensive all-sided knowledge. The resultant knowledge due to the synthesis of all those possible standpoints is worthy of being considered to be the whole truth.

Naya is so-called because it conveys (*nayati*) to the mind Reality as possessed of that particular attribute or aspect to which one desires to advert, although as a matter of fact that Reality is possessed of numberless attributes or aspects. Since *naya* operates upon Reality which has already been revealed by *pramāṇa, naya* follows *pramāṇa.* Here *pramāṇa* is viewed as a total unanalysed experience of an entire thing or Reality. So it is regarded as antecedent to *nayas* which analyse a thing or Reality into different aspects, parts or attributes in accordance with the different intentions or purposes of different knowing agents. *Pramāṇa* reveals the whole truth, while *naya* reveals but a part of the whole truth.

Nayas are the points of views which disclose only partial truths. *Pramāṇa* lays bear the whole truth which is the synthesis of fragmentary truths. Here *pramāṇa* is viewed as a synthesis of the aspects, parts or attributes abstracted or analysed by the *nayas*. So it is regarded as following *nayas*. In this sense, *naya* is the method of analysis, while *pramāṇa* is the method of synthesis.

A *naya* is defined as a particular intention or viewpoint—a viewpoint which does not rule out other different viewpoints and is thereby expressive of a partial truth about an object—as entertained by a knowing agent or speaker. *Nayas* do not interfere with one another or enter into conflict with one another. They do not contradict one another. They uphold their own objects without rejecting others' objects.

Naya becomes *durnaya* (pseudo-standpoint), when it denies all other standpoints, contradicts them, excludes them absolutely and puts forward its partial truth as the whole truth.[1]

From ancient times, men and intellectual pundits have been fighting with one another, because on their part they have not made any systematic attempt to understand one another's viewpoints as also because they have completely yielded to passions of pride and arrogance. If even the religious leaders and teachers had made sincere efforts to understand, with cool mind, one another's viewpoints, they would have grasped the positive and beneficial significance of one another's viewpoints and the wisdom embodied in them. In that case, they would have created and spread among the people the atmosphere exuding fragrance of accord and love. And as a result, we would have been blessed to witness today the sweet feeling of friendliness pervading the entire humanity. But we are not fortunate enough to see such a pleasing sight.

Generally, a man's cognitive operation is but partial in its coverage while he suffers from too much egoism and conceit. The result is that whatever little consideration he bestows on a subject tends to be treated by him as final and complete. And on account of the tendency in question he loses patience to give thought to the views of others. So ultimately he comes to mistakenly view his partial knowledge as complete knowledge. The mistaken view in its turn renders impossible a feeling of accord among persons holding true but different views concerning one and the same thing. The doctrine of standpoints (*nayavāda*) teaches us to see the truth in each and every view and to respect it.

Different systems of thought are formulated depending upon the different viewpoints about one and the same thing or Reality. These different systems of thought are *nayas*. The cultured, all-comprehensive and non-one-sided standpoint or outlook examines the different viewpoints

---

1. "All the standpoints (*nayas*) are right in their own respective spheres—but if they are taken to be refutations, each of the other, then they are wrong. But a man who knows the 'non-one-sided' nature of reality never says that a particular view is absolutely wrong."—*Sanmati-tarka,* I. 28

on which these different systems of thought are founded and thereby achieves a just (right) synthesis of them all, giving them their due place in the harmonious whole truth. The all-embracing philosophy of the doctrine of standpoints (*nayavāda*) is the method of synthesis.

Knowledge which touches upon a thing or Reality in all its aspects is *pramāṇa,* while knowledge which is content to touch upon one aspect of the same thing or Reality is *naya.* That is why *naya* cannot be independently called *pramāṇa* and yet it is not a *no-pramāṇa.* A drop of an ocean cannot be called an ocean, nor can it be called no-ocean, but can be called a part of an ocean.[1] The tip of a finger cannot be called a finger, and yet we cannot even say that it is no-finger—for after all it is a part of a finger. Similarly, *naya* too is a part of *pramāṇa.*

Whatever be the thing under consideration, the thought grasps it part by part and ultimately culminates in vast and all-comprehensive knowledge. Again, however complete be the knowledge relating to a thing, in practice this knowledge is invariably employed part by part. And this is the reason why it is in place to deal with *naya* separately independent of *śruta* (*pramāṇa*)—*naya* that is of the nature of thought which grasps the thing partwise and *śruta* that is of the nature of thought which grasps the thing in its totality.

The chief aim of the doctrine of *naya* is to look for the seed of compatibility among views that appear to be mutually contradictory but are not really so. So the doctrine of *naya* can be briefly interpreted as follows: It is a discipline which looks for the seed of real compatibility among views that appear to be mutually contradictory and which thus synthesises these views. For example, mutually contradictory views are found propounded concerning soul itself. Thus, at one place it is said 'the soul is one', at another place it is said 'the souls are many'. Now one-ness and many-ness appear to be mutually contradictory, and so the question arises: "Is this mutual contradiction among these statements real or not? If it is not real, Why?" The answer to this query has been found out by the doctrine of *naya* and the following is the synthesis it has worked out. *Quâ* individual units the souls are many, but if the attention is fixed on the aspect of pure consciousness, they are one. Working out such syntheses,

---

1. If a drop of an ocean were regarded as an ocean, then the ocean except the drop would be no-ocean or each and every drop of the ocean would be an independent ocean with the result that there would be crores of oceans in one ocean.

the doctrine of *naya* demonstrates the mutual compatibility—the possibility of standing together—among even such statements as are apparently contradictory. The seed of such compatibility lies in the viewpoint—the intention of the speaker or thinker concerned.

When on any topic—e.g. the nature of soul—a system of philosophy treats as wholly true the partly true view of a person deemed authoritative by it, then the other systems of philosophy which hold views that are true but opposite to its own are held in contempt by it and regarded as untrustworthy. Similarly, some other system of philosophy holds this first system in contempt, and both hold in contempt some third system. The result is that in place of mutual accord, there crops up discord which generates conflict. So it is with a view to opening the door for a true and complete knowledge and with a view to eliminating conflicts that the doctrine of *naya* has been established. The doctrine of *naya* effects logical and intelligible synthesis of apparently contradictory views. It generates among people the understanding of the various aspects of a thing or Reality and thereby removes conflicts, mutual discord and controversies and achieves harmony. Thus the doctrine of *naya* is the doctrine of synthesis. It is an art of how to effect synthesis of apparently opposite views. It is the doctrine of relative standpoint. It is also called the doctrine of *apekṣā.* The term '*apekṣā*' here stands for the standpoint or intention of the speaker or thinker.

Siddhasena Divākara declares that there are as many standpoints (*nayas*) as there are the ways of expressing Truth or Reality in words.[1] Two things follow from this—one that the standpoints are countless and the other that they are closely related to verbal expression. Each and every standpoint can be expressed in words. Therefore, it can be secondarily described as verbal. Thus we can maintain that there are two types of *nayas* (standpoints), viz., *bhāva-naya* and *dravya-naya. Bhāva-naya* means a *naya* that is cognitional or conceptual (*jñānātmaka*). *Dravya-naya* means a *naya* that is verbal (*vacanātmaka*).

In his *Tattvārtha-ślokavārtika* Vidyānandasvāmī says:

---

1. *jāvaiā vayaṇapahā tāvaiā ceva hoṁti ṇayavāyā /*
jāvaiā ṇayavāyā tāvaiā ceva parasamayā //—Sanmatitarka, III. 47
Meaning: There are as many standpoints (*nayas*) as there are ways of putting a proposition. And there are also as many views of non-Jaina philosophers as there are standpoints (*nayas*).

sarve śabdanayās tena parārthapratipādane /
svārthaprakāśane mātur ime jñānanayāḥ sthitāḥ //[1]

Translation : All the *nayas* (standpoints) are verbal when they are employed to convey their partial truths to others. On the other hand, those very *nayas* are cognitional or conceptual when they reveal their partial truths to oneself.

As all the *nayas* are of the form of knowledge with respect to oneself, they are cognitional or conceptual. On the other hand, as they are of the form of the cause of knowledge with respect to others, they are verbal. When the views or partial truths are discovered by a man without the help of others through his own experience or thought, the *nayas* are conceptual or cognitional. But when he imparts those views or partial truths to others through the medium of language, the *nayas* are verbal.

The delineation of *nayas* comprises classification of views; and the doctrine of *nayas* involves an investigation into views. There are innumerable *nayas*. Intentions of the speakers and modes of verbal expression are countless. And as the *nayas* are not different from them, they too are countless. Originally or fundamentally, there are only two types of *nayas*, viz., *dravyārthika-naya* (substantial standpoint) and *paryāyārthika-naya* (modal standpoint). *Dravya* means substance. For example, clay is a substance of a pot. And *paryāya* means modes, changes or transformations of a substance. For example, a pot is a form, mode or transformation of clay. All the changes—subtle or gross—that a substance undergoes are to be understood as its *paryāyas*. We do perceive or observe the gross changes. But it is impossible for us to perceive subtle changes that take place every moment. Though they are imperceptible, we can definitely know them through inference.

Dravyārthika-naya means the standpoint which concentrates on a substance (the generic and permanent aspect). *Paryāyārthika-naya* means the standpoint which concentrates on modes (changes or transformations). *Dravyārthika-naya* (substantial standpoint) considers all things to be permanent or eternal. For example, it states that a pot *quâ* substance clay is permanent or eternal. On the other hand, *paryāyārthika-naya* regards all things as impermanent, because they undergo changes (transformations). Hence it declares that all things are non-eternal or momentary

1. Verse No. 96 in the *vārtika* on the *Tattvārthasūtra* I. 33.

from the standpoint of modes or changes. The standpoint which grasps the generic aspect is *dravyārthika-naya.* And the standpoint which grasps the specific aspect is *paryāyārthika-naya.*

Human intellect inclines sometimes towards the generic aspect of things, and sometimes towards their specific aspect. When it grasps the generic aspect, its view is called *dravyārthika-naya.* But when it grasps the specific aspect, its view is called *paryāyārthika-naya.* It is not that *dravyārthika-naya* does not grasp the modes at all, or that *paryāyārthika-naya* does not grasp the substance at all. In other words, it is not that the former grasps the substance exclusively and the latter the modes exclusively. As a matter of fact, both the *nayas* grasp substance as well as modes, but one grasps substance primarily and modes secondarily, while the other grasps modes primarily and substance secondarily. In *dravyārthika-naya,* substance is predominant and mode subordinate. On the other hand, in *paryāyārthika-naya* mode is predominant and substance subordinate.

Let us explain these two standpoints with the help of the following illustration:

When at any time or place or under any condition, the eye is fixed on the ocean and what is attended to are not the specific features of water like its colour, taste, depth or shallowness, extent and limits, but only water as such, then we have before us a generic consideration having only water for its subject-matter; and this precisely is the *dravyārthika-naya* pertaining to water.

On the contrary, when what is attended to are the specific features of water like its colour, taste, etc., then the consideration in question, inasmuch as it has the specific features of water for its subject-matter, is called the *paryāyārthika-naya.*

What has been said concerning water can be understood also in the case of all other physical things. Thus, just as in relation to the different things of an identical nature that are located in different places—e.g., in relation to all water—it is possible to have both a generic and a specific consideration, similarly in relation to a single thing that is spread out on the limitless time-plank with its three divisions past, present and future—e.g., in relation to a soul—it is possible to have both a generic and a specific consideration. When the different formations resulting from a difference of time and condition are not attended to and attention is fixed on pure consciousness, then we have before us the *dravyārthika-naya* pertaining to consciousness; when attention is fixed on the different states of consciousness resulting from a difference of place, time, etc., then we have before us the *paryāyārthika-naya* pertaining to consciousness.

There is neither substance without mode nor mode without substance. The one can never be without the other. The relation of identity-cum-difference obtains between a substance and its modes. Though a substance is different from its one particular mode, it is identical with it from the standpoint of a continuum of modes.

For the detailed treatment of the doctrine of *naya,* we explain and expound seven types of *nayas*. They are *naigama, saṅgraha, vyavahāra, ṛjusūtra, śabda, samabhirūḍha* and *evambhūta.*

Naigama: Nigama means *kalpanā* (resolve, imagination). All our communications that are governed by it are called *naigama.* It has three main types, viz., *saṅkalpa-naigama, aṁśa-naigama* and *āropa-naigama.*

(1) *Saṅkalpa-naigama: Saṅkalpa* means resolve, purpose, end, intention. *Saṅkalpa-Naigama* concentrates on the resolve or purpose. For instance, a person is putting his clothes in his bag. At that time, his friend arrives and asks him, "What are you doing?" In answer he says, "I am going to Bombay". This answer is from the standpoint of his resolve. His friend does not object to his answer, because it is an accepted popular convention.

A man has decided to perform an act of theft. The religious works regard him as defiled by the sin of theft, though he has actually not performed the act of theft. The standpoint adopted by the religious works is that the act which is sought to be undertaken is as good as being accomplished (*kriyamāṇaṁ kṛtam*). This is also an instance of *saṅkalpa-naigama.*

Again, a person carrying fuel, when asked "What are you doing?", says "I am cooking" instead of saying "I am carrying fuel". The answer given is from the standpoint of *saṅkalpa-naigama.* This standpoint concentrates on the general purpose for which a particular act is being performed. This mode of communication or expression has the sanction of popular convention.

(2) *Aṁśa-naigama: Aṁśa* means a part. This standpoint takes a part for the whole. For example, when a spark falls on a saree put on by a lady, she gets frightened and at once says, "My saree has been burnt". Similarly, when a leg of a chair is broken, we say, "The chair is broken".

(3) *Āropa-naigama: Āropa* means superimposition. This standpoint superimposes one time-division on another, one state on another, etc. For

example, we say, "Today, the Deepāvali day, is the day of Lord Mahāvīra's *nirvāṇa* (liberation)", or "Today, the thirteenth day of the bright half of the month of Caitra, is Lord Mahāvīra's birth-day." Here we superimpose the past on the present.

When the rice is about to be cooked, we say, "The rice has already been cooked". Or, when the bed is about to be spread out, we say, "The bed has already been spread out". Here we superimpose the future on the past. This superimposition is related to time.

Somebody says, "Here is a brāhmaṇa-monk". Strictly speaking, a monk cannot be a brāhmaṇa for he is supposed to give up his caste-privileges. But the above statement is easily understandable as it refers to one who was a brāhmaṇa before he became a monk. Here the past state is superimposed on the present one.

Upacāra-naigama is included in *āropa-naigama. Upacāra* means metaphorical or figurative use of words. When we make figurative statements, we do so from the standpoint of *upacāra-naigama.* The following are the instances in point. 'Kavi Kālidāsa is the Shakespeare of India.' About a friend who stands by us in good or bad days we say, "He is my right hand". About our beloved daughter we say, "She is a pupil of my eye". About a beautiful lady we say, "She is a beauty incarnate".

"tvaṁ jīvitam tvam asi me hṛdayaṁ dvitīyaṁ
tvaṁ kaumudī nayanayor amṛtaṁ tvam aṅge /"

"You are my life; you are my twin heart; you are the moon-light of my eyes and nectar against my body."

All these are the instances of *upacāra-naigama.*

Thus, whatever views or verbal usages originate on account of varied popular conventions, they all are collected together under the title *naigama-naya.*

The *naigama-naya* subordinates one of the two—substance and quality—to the other. For example, in the description of soul, the qualities, viz. cognition, etc., are subordinated to the soul, while in that of qualities, viz. cognition, etc., the soul is subordinated to them. This *naya* does not touch upon the identity that obtains between a substance and a quality, a substance and activity, a part and a whole, a universal and an individual. It notices the difference that obtains between them. It is a method which makes one member of each of these pairs principal and the other subordinate.

Saṅgraha-naya (*Class view*) : The word *'saṅgraha'* means collection. Thus, this standpoint is a method which collects and brings together different things or individuals under one class on the basis of a common feature.

When one keeps in view the one generic feature 'existence' that is common to the numerous particular things of a physical or conscious type—thus quietly overlooking the specific features that are equally present there—and treating all these things as of one form reflects, "The entire universe is of the form of existence—for there is nothing that is devoid of existence—and hence one", then what we have before us is *saṅgraha-naya.*

The statement 'The soul is one' does not mean that in reality there is only one individual soul. There is a plurality of souls. Each body has a separate soul.[1] But concentrating on a common quality, viz., consciousness which is found in all souls, one can say that there is one soul.[2] This is an instance of *saṅgraha-naya.*

Similarly, when paying no attention to the variety of types and the multiplicity of units characterising the pieces of cloth that are present there, one keeps in view just one generic feature clothness and reflects, 'What is present here is just cloth', then too what we have before us is *saṅgraha-naya.*

In accordance with the greater or lesser extent of the concerned generic feature, one can construe numberless illustrations of *saṅgraha-naya.* Thus, the more extensive the concerned generic feature, the more extensive will be the resultant *saṅgraha-naya;* similarly, the less extensive the concerned generic feature, the less extensive will be the resultant *saṅgraha-naya.* The idea is, whatever views operate by unifying various things on the basis of a generic feature are fit to be placed in the category of *saṅgraha-naya.*

Vyavahāra-naya (Practical Standpoint): Even after various things have been subsumed under one form if it is required that they be introduced to someone in a specific form—or if the occasion arises for making a practical use of them—then they have to be distinguished from one another on the basis of a specific form. For example, by being told of just cloth one cannot be made acquainted with the various types of cloth taken separately. Again, he who wants *khādī* (the handspun and handwoven

1. *vyavasthāto nānā /—Vaiśeṣikasūtra,* III (last but one *sūtra*). This aphorism propounds the doctrine of the plurality of souls.
2. *Ṭhāṇaṁga, Sūtra* 2.

cloth) cannot get it without introducing distinction among cloths; for certainly cloths are of numerous types. Hence it is that distinctions like the *khādī* cloth, the mill-cloth, etc., too, have to be introduced. Similarly, in the field of philosophy one says: 'The thing of the form of existence is of two types, viz., the physical and the conscious; again, the conscious thing is of two types, viz., one entangled in the worldly life and the other emancipated from it'. And further distinctions of the same sort have to be made. All such views tending towards making distinction are to be placed in the category of *vyavahāra-naya*. In short, the synthetic operation of intellect is *saṅgraha-naya,* while the analytic operation of intellect is *vyavahāra-naya.*

Ṛjusūtra-naya (The 'Straight-thread' standpoint): It is called *ṛju* (straight) because it does not bend towards the past or the future. It recognises the reality of the present only, neither of the past nor of the future, as the two latter are no more real than the 'horns of a hare'—which do nothing and, therefore, are nothing.

Though human imagination cannot absolutely ignore what is past or what is future, it often happens that human intellect, keeping its attention fixed on an immediately present consequence, begins to operate only in relation to what is present. Under such a situation, man's intellect begins to suppose as if only that which is present is real and efficacious, while that which is past or that which is future being not efficacious at present, is as good as void. Thus, a prosperity that is present can alone be called prosperity, because it alone is a means of happiness; on the other hand, the memory of the past prosperity or the anticipation of the future prosperity can never be called prosperity, because neither is a means of happiness at present. Similarly, a son who is present and who serves his parents is a son; on the other hand, a son who existed in past or will exist in future but does not exist at present is not a son at all. This is all *ṛjusūtra* standpoint. Again, this standpoint recognises only the present state of pleasure or pain. For it, what is present is real. It concentrates on the present state, condition or mode of a thing. For this view, even a householder is a monk, when he possesses auspicious mental states characteristic of a real monk. On the other hand, it regards even a monk as *avratī* (one who does not observe the vows) when he possesses mental states of unrestraint. Moreover, when a man who has taken a vow of keeping mind equanimous for fortyeight minutes, sitting at one place, indulges in evil thoughts, this view considers him to be one who has broken his vow and has gone to a very dirty place.

The *ṛjusūtra-naya* has got two sub-types, viz., *sūkṣma* (subtle) *ṛjusūtra* and *sthūla* (gross) *ṛjusūtra*. That *ṛjusūtra* which recognises or grasps the present momentary state is the *sūkṣma ṛjusūtra*. And that *ṛjusūtra* which recognises or grasps the present state existing for many moments is the *sthūla ṛjusūtra*. The life-span of the present human state (*manuṣyaparyāya*) of the soul, which is of the duration of one hundred years, is an instance of the *sthūla ṛjusūtra*.

The four standpoints which we have treated above are called *artha-naya*, because they chiefly consider an *artha* or a thing. Now let us study the three *śabda-naya*s. They are so-called, because they chiefly consider a *śabda* or a word. They consider as to which word is appropriate for expressing a particular thing.

Śabda-naya (the 'Verbal' standpoint): This standpoint maintains that the synonymous words convey the same meaning or thing, provided they are not different in tense, case-ending, gender, number, etc. In other words, it states that two synonymous words can never convey the same thing if they have different tenses, case-endings, genders, numbers. Thus this view comes to posit a difference in meaning of the two synonymous words on the basis of a difference in tense, gender, etc.

For example, in a particular work, there occurs the statement: "There was a town named Rājagṛha." The broad meaning of this statement is that the town named Rājagṛha had existed there in the past, but did not exist in the days of the author. However, as a matter of fact, Rājagṛha existed even in the days of the author. If it were present there in the days of the author, then why was it written 'It was there'? This question is answered by *śabda-naya* by maintaining that Rājagṛha that existed in the days of the author was different from Rājagṛha that had existed in the remote past, and that since the context requires an account of the latter, the statement made was 'Rājagṛha was there'. This is an illustration of the difference of meaning based on a difference of tense.

As an example of the difference of meaning based on a difference of gender, take the words *kuvo* (Gujarātī for Sanskrit *kūpa* meaning 'well') and *kuī* (Gujarātī for Sanskrit *kūpikā* meaning 'a diminutive well'). Here the first word is in masculine gender, the second in feminine gender. The two are regarded as two different words meaning two different things, though the base behind them is the same.

This view takes care in the use of words. It employs only that word which is expressive of the intended object. The object intended may be an individual (a substance), a quality, an activity or a relation. This view employs different words to convey different sex of living beings of the same class; for example, *nara, nārī; gardabha, gardabhī; kukkura, kukkurī; mayūra, mayūrī; putra, putrī;* etc. Again, it employs different words to convey different magnitudes of the things of the same class; for example, *loṭo* (a Gujarātī word meaning 'a jug' or 'a pitcher'), *loṭī* (a diminutive jug or pitcher); *ṭekaro* (a Gujarātī word meaning hill), *ṭekarī* (a diminutive hill); *pahāḍa* (mountain), *pahāḍī* (a diminutive mountain); etc. A man holds different relations with different persons. Different words are employed to convey these different relations; for example, uncle, nephew; father, son; son-in-law, father-in-law; etc. (All these are the instances of relative terms.) This view is very particular in using different words to convey different tenses. It uses past tense, if the action took place in past (e.g., *agacchat* = went), uses present tense, if the action takes place in present (e.g., *gacchati* = goes), and uses future tense, if the action is to take place in future (e.g., *gamiṣyati* = will go). It employs the word in plural number to convey the plurality of the thing. And it employs the word in singular number, if the thing to be conveyed is one only. [In Sanskrit language, the word is used in dual number, if the things to be conveyed by the said word are two in number. Plural number is employed when things to be conveyed are more than two.] Moreover, it employs a word with an appropriate case-ending in order to convey a particular type of relation[1] that the intended thing holds with the activity expressed by the verb. '*Rājñaḥ putraḥ*' ('a king's son'); here the genitive case expresses the relation which the king holds with his son. '*Rājñaḥ prāsādaḥ*' (a king's palace'); here the genitive case expresses the relation of possession which the king holds with his palace. '*Mṛdāṁ ghaṭaḥ*' ('a pot of earth or clay'); here the genitive case expresses the relation of material cause with its effect. '*Mama hastaḥ*' ('my hand'), '*Siṁhāsanasya pādaḥ*' ('a leg of a throne'); here the genitive case expresses the part-whole relation. All these relations are conveyed by the genitive case.

At this juncture, it is useful to point out incidentally that the standpoint which is useful and appropriate at a particular time or on a particular

1. *Kāraka sambandha* means the relation subsisting between a noun and a verb in a sentence. There are six such *kāraka sambandhas* belonging to the seven cases (*vibhaktis*) except the genitive: (1) *kartṛ,* (2) *karma,* (3) *karaṇa,* (4) *sampradāna,* (5) *apādāna* and (6) *adhikaraṇa.*

occasion should be principally adopted at that time and on that occasion. If we were to employ the *saṅgraha-naya* on the occasion demanding the adoption of *vyavahāra-naya,* there would be no difference between wife and mother, master and servant, etc., and there would ensue great confusion. If we were to employ the *vyavahāra-naya* on the occasion appropriate for the application of *saṅgraha-naya,* then there would be difference and discrimination everywhere and the noble sentiment of love and friendliness would be totally effaced from the heart of man, giving rise to conflict, violence and quarrels. If one were to adopt *naigama-naya* on the occasion appropriate for the adoption of *śabda-naya,* then one would call a man an ascetic, merely because he is clad in the dress of an ascetic, though he may be quite lacking in spiritual qualities essential for an ascetic. And if one were to adopt *vyavahāra-naya* on this occasion, which is appropriate for the adoption of *śabda-naya,* then one would call a man an ascetic, simply because he performs external activities (rites) prescribed for an ascetic, in addition to wearing a dress of an ascetic, though he may be lacking in spiritual qualities essential for an ascetic. But the one who adopts *śabda-naya* considers him to be a hypocrite and calls him a pseudo-ascetic; he regards only that man an ascetic, who has cultivated in himself the true spiritual qualities essential for an ascetic. On such occasion, *śabda-naya* is principal. On every occasion, therefore, we should use our power of discretion to decide as to which *naya* is appropriate for that particular occasion.

A man may be ugly, though his name is Sundarlal (= handsome). And a lady may be poor, though her name is Lakṣmī (= wealth). But one whose viewpoint is *naigama,* naturally calls him and her by their respective names. And a person whose viewpoint is *śabda-naya* has to adopt the *naigama* and to call him or her by their respective names, however hard he may feel to do so, because on such an occasion *naigama-naya* is appropriate.

Śabda-naya does not consider it to be wrong to employ any one of the synonyms to convey or express the concerned meaning or thing. But, as stated above, it maintains that the meaning or thing differs with the difference in tense, gender, etc., of the words which are regarded as synonymous.

Samabhirūḍha-naya (Etymological standpoint): According to this standpoint, each word has its own meaning. There is only one word for one meaning. No two words mean the same thing. *Śabda-naya* accepts the difference in the meaning of the synonymous words when they have different tenses, different genders, etc., but does not accept the difference in their meaning when they have the same tense, the same gender, etc. For example, the synonymous words like *rājā, nṛpaḥ, bhūpaḥ* (all meaning 'king') express the same thing or meaning. On the other hand, *samabhirūḍha-naya* maintains that different words have different meaning. That is, for it even the synonymous words having the same tense, the same gender, etc., do not mean the same thing. This standpoint does not recognise any synonymous terms. It asks us to make a subtle distinction in the meanings of words which are supposed to denote the same object. Such distinction is based on the etymological derivations of words concerned.

Thus *samabhirūḍha-naya* attributes, on the basis of etymology, different meanings to the synonymous words like *rājā, nṛpa, bhūpa,* etc., (all meaning 'king'). Its contention is that one who is decorated with royal insignia is *rājā,* one who protects the people is *nṛpa,* one who maintains the earth—i.e., makes it prosperous—is *bhūpa.* Thus this view which, on the basis of etymology, posits differentiation within one and the same thing that is denoted by the three synonymous words in question is called *samabhirūḍha-naya.* All suppositions which posit a difference of meaning in the case of the different synonymous words are to be placed in this category of *samabhirūḍha-naya.* Each word originally had its own separate meaning. But with the passage of time and through the usage by individuals and groups they became synonymous with other words. As shown above, the *samabhirūḍha* grasps its original (etymological) meaning, overlooking its synonymity.

Evambhūta-naya (*The 'Thus-happened' Standpoint*) : This standpoint reflects that when a difference in etymology can yield a difference in meaning, then it too should be conceded that a word stands for a thing only in case this thing satisfies the etymology of this word and that only in such a case—not otherwise—this thing has to be denoted by this word.

On this supposition a man is not to be called *rājā,* if he has only earned the right to be decorated by royal insignia at some time or other, nor is he called *nṛpa,* if he has only been entrusted with the responsibility to protect the people. But to add a further requirement, he is to be called *rājā* only in case he is actually carrying the royal sceptre and is shining with glory on that account; similarly, he is to be called *nṛpa* only in case he is actually protecting the people. All this is to say that it would be proper to call a man *rājā* or *nṛpa* only in case he is actually satisfying the etymology of the word concerned.

Similarly, only at a time—or at the times—when a person is actually performing some service is he to be called *sevaka* (Sanskrit for 'one who serves'). Thus all the suppositions which employ a word standing for some qualifier or one standing for some qualificand, only in case the activity with which this word is related is actually being undertaken, are to be called *evambhūta-naya.*

As already noted, the *samabhirūḍha-naya* maintains that all words—even synonymous words too—have their own different meanings. Each word means or conveys a different thing. But *samabhirūḍha-naya* does never object to our applying the term '*yoddhā*' (Sanskrit for 'one who fights in war') to a warrior even when he is not actually engaged in the activity of fighting in war (but is living in his house peacefully when there is no war). Contrary to this, *evambhūta-naya* objects to it. It says that a man can be called *yoddhā,* only when he is engaged in the activity of fighting in war, and not at any other time. Similarly, a person can be called *pūjārī* (Sanskrit for 'one who worships'), only when he is engaged in the activity of worship, and not at any other time. All words connote some activity. So when a thing is engaged in the activity connoted by the etymology of a particular word, then and then only that thing is to be denoted by that word. Each and every word is derived from some verbal root, hence it is connected with some activity. If *samabhirūḍha-naya* some time observes a thing engaged in the activity connoted by a particular word, it employs that word to denote that thing always at all times, whether that activity is present there in that thing or not. But *evambhūta-naya* employs the word to denote the thing when and as long as that activity is actually present in the thing. In the absence of that activity, it regards that word unfit to be employed for denoting that thing.[1] According to this *evambhūta-naya* all words are action-words, that is, derived from some verbal root.

While *samabhirūḍha-naya* insists upon making distinctions of meanings or things conveyed by words in accordance with the different etymologies of words, *evambhūta-naya* confines the word to the thing just while it performs the activity which it connotes.

1. In practice, we see that the Government takes the side of its servant as long as he is on duty, if somebody ill-treats him. But at other times, the Government treats him as it treats any other common citizen. This method of treatment which the Government adopts in regard to its servants is in accordance with the *evambhūta* standpoint. 'I did not meet the Governor, but I met my friend', 'I am not a king, but a guest'—in all such modes of expression we have a glimpse of *evambhūta-naya.*

We have briefly dealt with the seven standpoints. The subject-matter of *naigama-naya* is both Existence (Being) and non-Existence (non-Being), because the object of resolve, conception or popular convention is both Existence and non-Existence. The subject-matter of *saṅgraha-naya* is more limited in extent than that of *naigama-naya,* because its subject-matter is Existence (Being) alone. And the subject-matter of *vyavahāra-naya* is divisions of Existence. *Ṛjusūtra-naya* is subtler than *vyavahāra-naya. Śabda-naya* is subtler than *ṛjusūtra-naya*[1]. *Samabhirūḍha-naya* is subtler than *śabda-naya,* and *evambhūta-naya* is subtler than *samabhirūḍha-naya.* Thus every succeeding *naya* exhibits more subtlety than every preceding *naya.* In other words, every succeeding *naya* is more limited in extent than every preceding *naya.* As the first three *naya*s are gross, they grasp the generic aspect of things. *Ṛjusūtra-naya* accepts only the present phase—not the past or the future; hence it is obvious that its subject-matter comes into view not as something generic, but as something specific. And of the three *naya*s coming after *ṛjusūtra,* each succeeding one is subtler than the preceding one; hence the subject-matter of the succeeding one is more specific than that of the preceding one.

Every preceding *naya* is wider than every succeeding *naya. Naigama-naya* deals with both Being and non-Being, while *saṅgraha-naya* with only Being. *Naigama* is thus wider than *saṅgraha. Vyavahāra-naya* deals with particular forms or entities of Being, while *saṅgraha-naya* with general Being. *Saṅgraha* is, therefore, wider than *vyavahāra. Ṛjusūtra-naya* is concerned with present only, while *vyavahāra-naya* with past, present and future. *Vyavahāra* is thus wider than *ṛjusūtra. Śabda-naya* deals with the *artha*s (meanings, things) which it regards as differing according to differences of time (tense), gender, etc. *Ṛjusūtra-naya* makes no such distinction and is, therefore, wider than *śabda-naya. Samabhirūḍha-naya* distinguishes between the *artha*s of even synonymous words, according to their varying etymologies. *Śabda-naya* does not do so. *Śabda-naya,* therefore, is wider than *samabhirūḍha-naya. Evambhūta-naya* is confined to *artha*s only while they perform a particular activity and thus it distinguishes between *artha*s according to the activities connoted by the terms. *Samabhirūḍha-naya* distinguishes between the meanings of words according to their varying etymologies, but it applies the term to the thing which

1. As *śabda-naya* recognises distinctions of meanings of even synonymous words on the basis of distinctions of time (tense), etc., it is subtler than *ṛjusūtra.*

has performed the activity connoted by the etymology of the term, but is not at present engaged in that activity. *Samabhirūḍha* is thus wider than *evambhūta.*

Here it too must be understood that among the seven *nayas*, when every succeeding *naya* is said to be subtler than every preceding *naya,* then to that extent every preceding *naya* is more directed towards the generic than every succeeding *naya.* As the generic aspect and the specific aspect are inseparable and indissoluble, all the *nayas,* in fact, grasp both the aspects; and yet a *naya* is regarded as *dravyārthika,* if it grasps the generic aspect more than the specific aspect, and as *paryāyārthika* if it grasps the specific aspect more than the generic aspect. This is so because names are given to things taking into account the predominant element or aspect of those things (*prādhānyena vyapadeśā bhavanti*)

When the first three *nayas* are called *dravyārthika* and the last four *paryāyārthika,* the idea is that in the first three the generic element and a consideration of it are relatively more obvious inasmuch as they are relatively crude; on the other hand, the last four *nayas* are relatively subtle and in them the specific element and a consideration of it are relatively more obvious. It is on the basis of this obviousness or non-obviousness of the generic and specific elements—and on the basis of their dominant or subordinate status—that the seven *nayas* are divided into two types, viz., *dravyārthika* and *paryāyārthika.*

The comprehensive non-one-sided knowledge (*pramāṇa*) establishes that a thing or Reality is characterised by innumerable attributes as also that it is of the nature of both substance and mode (form or transformation). And *nayas* (standpoints or partial knowledges) analyse a thing or Reality into many parts or aspects. As already shown, *nayas* are divided into two main types, *dravyārthika* (substantive standpoint) and *paryāyārthika* (modal standpoint). The seven *nayas* are included in these two divisions.

Having given the subordinate status to the diversity or manifoldness which is the object of *paryāyarthika-naya, dravyārthika-naya* deals with the identity or generality which is its own object. For example, from the *dravyārthika* standpoint a master says to his servant, 'Bring gold'. If the servant brings and presents before the master any ornament of gold—a bracelet, an ear-ring, a waist-band or a neck-chain—, he will be considered to have followed his master's order. It is so because any of these golden ornaments, viz. bracelet, etc., is nothing but gold. We think that by presenting before his master any of these ornaments the servant has presented only gold in accordance with his master's order.

Having given the subordinate status to the identity or generality which is the object of *dravyārthika-naya, paryāyārthika-naya* deals with the diversity or manifoldness. For example, on hearing the statement, 'Bring an ear-ring' spoken by his master from the *paryāyārthika* standpoint, the servant brings only an ear-ring, leaving all other golden ornaments like bracelet, etc. It is so because though the substance viz., gold is the same in all these ornaments, they being different forms of gold are different from one another. Therefore, if the servant brings only that form of gold which he is asked to bring, he will be considered to have obeyed his master's order.

From this it follows that from the *dravyārthika* standpoint, gold is one while from the *paryāyārthika* standpoint it is manifold. It is so, because though the same gold substance is present in all its different forms, yet these forms of gold are different from one another. The method of seven-fold judgement deals with this pair of one-many (identity-diversity) with respect to anything. And from the two different standpoints of *dravyārthika-naya* and *paryāyārthika-naya,* we can establish oneness and manifoldness of anything always and everywhere.

If we reflect deeply, we can understand that there are only two main standpoints—the standpoint of identity or generality and the standpoint of diversity or particularity. *Dravyārthika-naya* is the standpoint of identity or generality, while *paryāyārthika-naya* is the standpoint of diversity or particularity. All the *naya*s beginning with *naigama-naya* are but the expansion of these two *naya*s. Siddhasena Divākara has included the *naigama,* that concentrates on or deals with identity conceived by the popular convention, in *saṅgraha-naya,* while the *naigama* that concentrates on or deals with diversity or distinction conceived by the popular convention is included in *vyavahāra-naya.* He does not regard *naigama-naya* as an independent *naya.* According to him there are only six *naya*s.

Pseudo-standpoints (Nayābhāsa)

Now let us treat of pseudo-standpoint (*nayābhāsa*).

Pseudo-*naigama*: The view that regards substance and attribute, substance and quality, etc., as absolutely different is pseudo-*naigama.* It accepts only the difference, totally rejecting the identity. An instance of this fallacious standpoint is the *Nyāya-Vaiśeṣika* philosophy which maintains absolute difference between categories (substance, quality, activity, universal, etc.).

Pseudo-*saṅgraha: Saṅgraha-naya* is of two types, viz., *para-saṅgraha* and *apara-saṅgraha.* The subject-matter of *para-saṅgraha* is the highest universal, viz. Existence. *Para-saṅgraha* says, "The entire universe as Existence is one." It takes into account pure substance in its highest universality (Existence) and remains indifferent to particulars or forms. But when it becomes aggressive and absolutely rejects particulars, it turns into pseudo-*para-saṅgraha.*

Apara-saṅgraha-naya brings proper things together under any of the lower universals and regards them as one or identical, remaining indifferent to their differentiating traits. It regards all the substances, viz., the soul, matter, time, etc. as identical, because they all possess *dravyatva* (substancehood) in common; it remains indifferent to their differences; But when, however, it does not rest content with grouping soul, matter, etc., together in one class, viz. substance class, but goes a step further and totally denies particular distinguishing features, it degenerates into pseudo-*apara-saṅgraha.*

Laying such an exaggerated and undue emphasis on the universal as to leave no room at all for the particular leads to pseudo-*saṅgraha,* a fallacy of which the *Sāṁkhya* and the *Advaita* schools of philosophy are notable instances.

Pseudo-*vyavahāra*: Existence which is the subject-matter of *saṅgraha-naya* is divided and subdivided into various types by *vyavahāra-naya* in the following manner: "That which exists is either *dravya* (substance or universal) or *paryāya* (mode or particular); that which is *dravya* (substance) is either soul, or matter, or medium-of-motion, or medium-of-rest, or time, or space; that which is soul is either emancipated or bound (= worldly, transmigratory); and so on." But if you go further and insist upon an absolute difference of *dravya* (universal) and *paryāya* (particular), you commit the fallacy of pseudo-*vyavahāra.* When the generic correlative of a specific feature is entirely ignored, the resultant fallacy comes to have only semblance of the *vyavahāra* standpoint. The materialism of Cārvāka in Indian philosophy is an instance of pseudo-*vyavahāra.*

Pseudo-*ṛjusūtra: Ṛjusūtra-naya* accepts only the mode or state of the present moment. When, however, it goes further and denies the persistent substance altogether to which this mode or state belongs it degenerates into pseudo-*ṛjusūtra.* It is generally held that the Buddhist philosophy accepts the momentary evanescent modes or states to be real and absolutely rejects substance which persists in all the three divisions of time and serves as the substratum of these momentary modes. Some such philosophy is given as an instance of pseudo-*ṛjusūtra.* The philosophical system that accepts only the fleeting aspect to the absolute exclusion of the persistent aspect of concrete reality is an instance of this pseudo-*ṛjusūtra*.

Pseudo-*śabdanaya*: When *śabdanaya* insists that different meanings or things conveyed by different (synonymous) words in accordance with different tenses, genders, etc., are absolutely different, it degenerates into pseudo-*śabdanaya*. The view that maintains that Rājagṛha having the past-tense predication and Rājagṛha having the present-tense predication are utterly different is an instance of pseudo-*śabdanaya*.

Pseudo-*samabhirūḍha: Samabhirūḍha-naya* is one in which meanings of even synonymous words are distinguished in accordance with their different etymologies. But when it considers them to be absolutely different, it becomes pseudo-*samabhirūḍha*. In other words, if anybody thinks that corresponding to the different etymologies of synonymous words there are different individuals, he commits the fallacy of pseudo-*samabhirūḍha*. If we construe the difference in meaning as implying difference in things, we will be indulging in pseudo-*samabhirūḍha*. *Samabhirūḍha* is a true standpoint as long as it accepts the distinction in the connotation of synonymous words in accordance with their different etymologies. But when it goes further and makes distinction in the denotation of the synonymous words on the basis of their different etymologies, then it becomes pseudo-*samabhirūḍha*.

Pseudo-*evambhūta: Evambhūta-naya* maintains that we can call a person or a thing by a particular name or word when and only when he actually performs the activity connoted by its etymology. When it stubbornly sticks to this view and obstinately insists that *rājā* cannot be called *rājā* when he is sleeping, then the view degenerates into pseudo-*evambhūta*.

The *evambhūta* standpoint asks us to apply the word '*pācaka*' ('cook') to a person only when he is actually cooking, but not when he is sleeping or walking. If we absolutely maintain that a cook does not remain a cook unless he is cooking at the present moment, we will commit the fallacy of pseudo-*evambhūta* standpoint.

From the above exposition, it is clear that the non-one-sided view or *syādvāda* grasps or describes the multitude of various attributes of a thing, while one-sided view or *naya* thinks of any one attribute of the thing and primarily makes presentation of that attribute only. The former refers to the entire, undivided Reality or thing, while the latter to a fragment or an aspect of the same. The former is synthetic, while the latter is analytic. In the former, the entire Reality or a thing is comprehended synthetically i.e., with all its attributes taken simultaneously; in the latter, Reality or a thing is treated analytically, i.e., with its attributes taken one by one. Therefore, the former is called comprehensive or full-orbed statement (*sakalādeśa*), whereas the latter is called incomprehensive statement (*vikalādeśa*). It is because the former grasps the whole Reality or a thing through one attribute which is related to or united with all other attributes, while the latter grasps only one attribute as abstracted from all others. The former is, therefore, known as *pramāṇa-vākya* or Proposition of the whole Truth, while the latter is called *naya-vākya* or Proposition leading to the whole Truth, i.e., the proposition of a particular viewpoint. In other words, the former depends upon *pramāṇa,* i.e., the view of the whole Truth or full-orbed Reality, while the latter depends upon *naya,* i.e., the view of the partial Truth or fragments of Reality. For example, the term *'jīva'* ('soul') causes the knowledge of the concrete *jīva* with all its special characteristics like knowledge, intuitive vision, etc., with all its common characteristics like existence, knowability, etc., and with all its special-cum-common characteristics like incorporeality, possession of innumerable space-points, etc. In this all these attributes are grasped as one undifferentiated whole. Hence the intention of the speaker to present these attributes or characteristics in primary and secondary relation gets absorbed in his mind. The incomprehensive statement or the statement of a particular viewpoint presents one attribute primarily or principally and all others are subordinated to it. For example, '*cetana jīva*' ('sentient soul') or *'jñātā jīva'* ('knower soul') generates the knowledge of soul's quality of sentiency or knowledge principally and all other attributes of the soul are subordinated to it.

Thus, we see that the statements are of two types, viz. statement of the whole Truth (*pramāṇa-vākya*) and statement of a particular viewpoint or a partial Truth (*naya-vākya*). The statement that presents concretely or synthetically a thing in its entirety is called *pramāṇa-vākya.* And the statement that presents a thing partly, abstracting some aspect of it is called *naya-vākya.* The difference between these two statements is to be known not on the basis of outward verbal forms, but on the basis of the speaker's internal mental states or intentions. When we present synthetically the whole Reality or a thing in words, the statement is called *pramāṇa-vākya.* On the other hand, when we present some one aspect or attribute in words, the statement is called *naya-vākya. Naya-vākya* (incomprehensive statement—*vikalādeśa*) presents Reality or a thing through some one aspect or attribute of it. But *pramāṇa-vākya* (comprehensive statement—*sakalādeśa*), instead of presenting Reality or a thing through some one aspect or attribute of it, presents it concretely or synthetically in its entirety.

Let us understand the point with an illustration. Take the statement—'The worldly prosperity or objects are momentary like a lightning'. In this statement by the term 'lightning', the thing lightning is presented through its one character or attribute, viz., momentariness. The lightning is not presented concretely as an unanalysed whole. But one character, viz., momentariness is abstracted from it and through it, the thing lightning is presented. So, the term 'lightning' here presents the thing lightning partly, not wholly. This is the case of incomprehensive statement (*vikalādeśa*). On the other hand, keeping in mind many characters of a girl we say, 'This girl is a lightning'. Here the term 'lightning' presents the entire concrete thing lightning with all its characters. The girl is compared to lightning in all respects. The lightning is not only fickle but also dazzling, etc. Similarly, when we use the term *'jīva'* ('soul') to convey the concrete thing *jīva* with all its characteristics like knowledge, intuitive vision, etc., our statement is full-orbed or comprehensive (*sakalādeśa*); on the other hand, when we use the term *'jīva'* to convey merely one attribute viz. *jīvana* (life or sentiency) of a *jīva*, our statement is incomprehensive (*vikalādeśa*).

The comprehensive knowledge (*pramāṇa*) is expressed in the statements like 'It is existent from a certain standpoint' (*'syāt sat'*) or 'It is certainly existent from a certain standpoint' (*'syāt sad eva'*). Therein the employment of the particle *'syāt'* (meaning 'from a certain standpoint') is to suggest other attributes from other standpoints. When modified by the particle *'syāt'*, the statement becomes *syādvāda* (non-one-sided). This is the statement of the whole Truth. The incomprehensive or partial knowledge (*naya*) is expressed in the statements like 'It is existent' (*'sat'*). It presents or states the intended attribute alone. It does not consider other attributes. In other words, it does not exclude or deny attributes other than the intended one. This is the statement of partial truth or a particular viewpoint. But the statement which rejects or denies other attributes along with the acceptance of the intended one is not a *naya* (a true viewpoint) but a *durnaya* (a pseudo-viewpoint). *Durnaya* is expressed in the statements like 'It is only existent' (*'sad eva'*).[1] Here the

1. *sad eva, sat, syāt sad iti tridhārtho mīyeta durnīti-naya-pramāṇaiḥ* /—Hemacandra's *Anyayogavyavacchedikā*, verse 28.

use of 'only' (*eva*) excludes non-existence, etc., and makes the absolute predication of existence. *Durnaya,* thus, is one-sided (absolute one-sided) view. It does not recognise the fact that there are other aspects of truth, in the object, than the one reflected by it. It is a dogmatic absolute assertion. This is the only difference between *naya* and *durnaya.* Though there may not be outward verbal difference between the two, yet there is certainly the difference between the intentions of their speakers.

Just as a statement of an attribute without definitive particle *'eva'* (meaning 'certainly') is *naya,* as 'It is existent' (*'sat'*), even so a statement of an attribute, with definitive particle *'eva'* is also *naya,* if it is not absolute but relative to a particular standpoint. The example in point is the statement, 'It is certainly existent from a certain standpoint' (*'syād sad eva'*). In this statement, existence is definitely predicated of a thing from a particular standpoint. In other words, though existence is definitely predicated of a thing, the predication is not absolute but relative to a particular standpoint. This relativity is known from the particle *'syāt'* either understood (*adhyāhāra*) or actually used in the statement. Similarly, just as the statement, 'A pot is impermanent' which is a statement of an attribute, without the employment of the definitive particle *'eva'*, is *naya,* even so the statement 'A pot is certainly impermanent from a particular standpoint' which is a statement of an attribute, with the use of the definitive particle *'eva'*, is also *naya* because it is relative to a particular standpoint. This is the reason why Svāmī Samantabhadra says: "*nayās tava 'syāt'-padalāñchanā ime*" (For you, O Lord, these statements of viewpoints are characterised by the use of *'syāt'*).

Again Svāmī Samantabhadra observes:

anekānto'py anekāntaḥ pramāṇa-nayasādhanaḥ /
anekāntaḥ pramāṇāt te tadekānto'rpitān nayāt //103//—*Svayambhūstotra*

The verse means: Even non-one-sided view, rather Reality, is not absolutely non-one-sided. This means that when it is an object of *pramāṇa* (comprehensive or full-orbed knowledge) it is non-one-sided, but when it is an object of *naya* (incomprehensive or partial knowledge) it is one-sided. From the standpoint of *pramāṇa* it is non-one-sided and from the standpoint of *naya* it is one-sided.

From this we clearly understand that as the statement of *naya* (partial truth or an aspect of Reality) is the statement of relative one-sided view, it is the right one-sided view. And a garland of the harmoniously arranged such one-sided views is but the statement of non-one-sided comprehensive whole Truth or Reality.

Study the following verse from Siddhasena Divākara's *Sanmatitarka*:

bhaddaṁ micchādaṁsaṇasamūhamaiassa amayasārassa /
jiṇavayaṇassa bhagavao saṁviggasuhāhigammassa //3.69//

In this verse, the word of Jina is described as a collection of wrong views. In other words, the teaching of Jina, pure on account of its being based on non-one-sided outlook, is but a compendium of harmoniously synthesised false views. This means that the view which is regarded as false is partial knowledge of an aspect of Truth or Reality. Even Ānandaghana's metrical statement '*ṣaḍdarśana jina-aṅga bhaṇīje*' means the same thing. To mistake the partial truth, the object of the partial knowledge or one-sided view, for the whole Truth is the wrong or false view.

This reminds us of the oft-quoted parable[1] of the elephant and the seven blind men. One can grasp the elephant when it is examined from all sides. It is foolish to grasp only a limb of it and regard it as the whole elephant. The seven blind men of the parable mistook a limb for the whole elephant. How foolish they were! This was the reason why they quarrelled among themselves. Those who obstinately stick to their views and regard their partial truths as the whole Truth, never try to understand the views of others and to grasp their partial truths. As a result, they disregard and disrespect the views of others, enter into conflict and quarrel with them. We see all this happening around us. It is ignorance (partial knowledge coupled with obstinacy) that breeds intellectual intolerance and conflict.

Just as one cannot perceive the elephant by knowing only a limb of it, even so one cannot know the whole Reality or Truth by knowing only an aspect of it. When one knows all the possible aspects of a thing, one knows the whole thing. Knowledge that grasps all the limbs of the elephant is called the comprehensive knowledge about it. Similarly, knowledge that grasps Reality or a thing in all its aspects is the comprehensive knowledge about it. That is to say, perfect or comprehensive knowledge of a thing is not generated when only a part or an aspect of it is grasped, but it is generated when all the possible parts or aspects are grasped. Will there be any conflict among them if the philosophers properly understand the sentient and the insentient substances in all their aspects? They

1. This parable occurs in *Udāna, vagga* VI, *Titthiyasutta*.

quarrel because like the blind men of the parable they too mistake their partial truths for the whole Truth. The different aspects of Truth, accepted by different schools of philosophy, when related to one another, all together form the whole Truth.

But in worldly dealings, we have to mostly adopt any one standpoint or view in accordance with the situation or circumstance. In practice or worldly dealings this is the only way. As particular standpoints or views are useful in practice, one has to select, from among many present in the treasure of *anekānta*, some one view proper for and favourable to a particular occasion.

The *syādvāda* or the principle of non-one-sidedness is such a comprehensive principle that it examines a thing from different standpoints. The examination conducted by it proves that one-sided views are incomplete, narrow and closed. At the same time it synthesises into one harmonious whole, these different (apparently conflicting) views yielded by different standpoints. As properly related pearls make a beautiful necklace, so properly synthesised one-sided views make one Grand Truth. The principle of non-one-sidedness (*anekāntavāda*) is therefore a real art of reconciliation and synthesis, which pacifies the conflicts arising from one-sided partial views and inspires feelings of equality and equanimity. When one who upholds a particular view depending upon a particular standpoint understands and grasps the truth of the seemingly opposite view, one's undue obstinacy and quarrel about it subside. It is necessary for us to have comprehensive knowledge, if we want to make our minds calm and to generate mutual love in our hearts. And for the comprehensive knowledge we should cultivate comprehensive outlook or viewpoint, which is called in the Jaina philosophy *'anekāntadṛṣṭi'*. This *anekāntadṛṣṭi* is the essential ingredient of the cultured life. It is useful in the worldly dealings and the spiritual discipline as well. It is beneficial to the men of practical world as also to the pilgrims on the Path of Liberation. It purifies the mind of the impurities of attachment and aversion, charges it with universal love and friendliness, generates serenity in it and thereby makes it competent enough for the spiritual concentration and trance.

On account of the comprehensive outlook or viewpoint, the feelings of tolerance and liberality are manifested. Let us understand this point with the help of an illustration.

One religious sect maintains that there exists the world-creator God. Another sect declares that there does not exist the world-creator God or that God is not the creator of the world. It is doubtless that either of the two views is false. But the important point which one should consider here is as to what is the purpose behind these two views. The upholders of the former view state that if you do evil acts, God will punish and send you to hell and if you do good acts He will be pleased with you, make you happy and send you to heaven. The Jainas who subscribe to the latter view say that if you indulge in evil acts, you will bind inauspicious *karmas* which will give you unpleasant or painful fruits like the unwholesome food eaten by you and will cause you to go to hell; and if you perform good acts, you will earn auspicious *karmas* which will give you auspicious or pleasant fruits like the wholesome food eaten by you. By instilling into men the faith in the world-creator God, one sect causes them to perform the same type of activity which another sect causes them to perform by making them opposed to the view of the world-creator God. But here we should ask ourselves: Do these two views differ on the point of religious, righteous or good conduct? No, they agree on the point that the results which one has to experience of one's bad acts are bad and the results which one has to experience of one's good acts are good. They differ only on the point as to how the bad or good results come upon the doers of the bad or good acts. But this difference is trifling. Why should it be the cause of conflict? The conflict is understandable, if the aims or purposes of the two sects are contradictory. But here their purpose is one and the same. Even if we regard the view of the creator God as scientifically untrue, we cannot say that it urges men to indulge in evil activities. Those who are temperamentally emotional rather than intellectual are attracted to this view; they consider it to be more beneficial. They think that if we leave everything to the will of God and surrender ourselves completely to His will, we become free from worries. The belief in the world-creator God subdues and destroys our egoism as to the agentship of acts and makes us discreet about what is good and what is evil. Those who are temperamentally more rational do not believe in the creator God, because to them such God does not stand to reason and logic. They think that instead of believing in the creator God and depending on Him, we should be self-reliant and ever vigilant, and should make sincere efforts for the cultivation of spiritual powers; again, instead of irrationally devoting ourselves to God and making absurd efforts to please Him it is better to get engrossed in the performance of our duties. They think that there is no one who can forgive us for our sins. So we should be afraid of doing evil deeds; we should abstain from them.

We clearly see that those who have accepted the world-creator God have done so in order that man might not indulge in evil activities, and those who have rejected Him have done so to achieve the same purpose. The aim of the propounders of the two doctrines is the same. Their aim is that man may become righteous and consequently happy.

Those who subscribe to the doctrine of spiritual monism maintain that ultimately there is only one Reality. It is One Soul. They say that the idea of duality is the cause of transmigratory existence. A believer in the doctrine of One Soul is not soiled by narrow, selfish thoughts. He never thinks in terms of his own and of another's interest. He has no self-interest, nor selfish motives. He understands that his interest is included in the interest of the entire world. He thinks that his welfare or good can never be different from that of all beings. He, therefore, does not commit sins which one who hankers after one's own individual interest commits. As a result, he remains free from sins or evil acts and thoughts. On the other hand, those who uphold the doctrine of dualism contend that ultimately there are two fundamental elements or substances—the sentient and the insentient. He thinks: "I am soul. Though I am soul, I am associated with non-soul matter. My soul is soiled with the foreign substance. On account of my association with matter, I am subdued by passions, I make a fool of myself, I do not behave justly and honestly with other living beings who are sentient like me, I do injustice to them and oppress them. This is not good for me. As I am caught in the infatuating and enticing net of matter and material objects, I behave as their slave. As a result of it, I myself become miserable and cause misery to others. So, I must break this painful bondage of maddening matter."

Thus, the spiritually beneficial results that follow from these two doctrines, viz., monism and dualism are the same.

I would like to reproduce here some verses from my *Dvātriṁśikā* entitled '*Anekānta-Vibhūti*' (='Greatness of Non-one-sided View or Outlook'):

Dvaitādvaitavāda (Dualism and Non-dualism)

dvaitaṁ yathārthaṁ jaḍa-cetanābhyām advaitam apy ātmavikāsadṛṣṭyā /
itthaṁ dvayaṁ tat paṭu saṅgamayya śāntas tvayā tāraka ! tadvirodhaḥ //9//

Dualism is true because the world is really constituted of two fundamental substances—one sentient and the other insentient. As the soul is the only Reality or substance which one should realise and attain, the enunciation of non-dualism is also right from the standpoint of spiritual progress. The spiritual non-dualism is propounded in order to emphasise the fact that it is absolutely necessary for man to devote himself wholly to spiritual discipline if he wants to realise and attain soul; he should think of nothing else. Thus, effecting rightly the synthesis of these two views, O Savior, you have resolved their conflict. (9)

Ekātmavāda-Anekātmavāda (Spiritual Monism and Spiritual Pluralism)

ekātmavādo hi samātmavādaḥ sa sarvabhūtaiḥ samabhāvavādaḥ /
itthaṁ sudhīr bhāvayati śrito'pi nānātmabhāvaṁ paramārthasiddham //10//

According to one view there is but one soul. According to another view there are many souls. The former is called *ekātmavāda*, while the latter *anekātmavāda*. None can have any objection to the former, but *quâ* individual units the souls are really many. It is proper to understand the spiritual monism as the doctrine of the equality of individual souls. And the doctrine of their equality means that all souls are identical in nature, though numerically different. From the standpoint of their common nature of pure consciousness they are one. This doctrine teaches us to cultivate an attitude of viewing all living beings as equal and of viewing others as one views oneself. The wise reflect on the essential unity of all individual souls in the manner as indicated above, though they maintain the view that the individual souls are many. (10)

Avatāravāda (Doctrine of Incarnation)

muktasya bhūyo na bhavāvatāro muktivyavasthā na bhavāvatāre /
utkṛṣṭajanmāna udārakāryair mahāvatārā uditā mahāntaḥ //11//

The soul is not born again after having attained the state of liberation. If it is accepted that the liberated soul is born again in the world, it will contradict liberation itself and liberation will no longer remain liberation. So such a doctrine of incarnation is repugnant to reason. The birth of the great men is regarded as great due to the great works they perform in the birth. And the meaning of *avatāra* (incarnation) being *janma* (birth), they are regarded as *avatārī, mahān-avatārī* (those having great birth or incarnation). (11)

Kartṛtvavāda (Doctrine of the Soul as Agent)

sopādhir ātmā jagati pravṛtto 'nupādhir ātmā na vahed upādhim/
evaṁ hi kartṛtvam akartṛtāṁ cāśrityodbhavantaḥ kalahā vyapeyuḥ //12//

The soul associated with adjuncts like body, sense-organs, etc., does perform activities. But the soul which has attained its pure and pristine nature of Existence, Consciousness and Bliss, which has consequently freed itself from adjuncts, and which has gained the state of Supreme Soul, has not to bear the burden of adjuncts and as a result has not to get involved in any activity. Thus the controversy as to whether the soul is the agent (*kartā*) or not is resolved. (12)

Sākāravāda-Nirākāravāda (Doctrines of Supreme Soul with and without form)

sākārabhāve saśarīratāyāṁ nirākṛtitve ca videhatāyām /
saṅgacchamāne parameśvarasya virodhabhāvo 'navakāśa eva //13//

The Supreme Soul did have form in the state when it assumed bodies. But it does not have any form in the state when it has absolutely freed itself from body. Thus, as both the views are reconcilable from two different standpoints, there is no scope for them to contradict one another. (13)

Ātmavibhutvavāda (Doctrine of all-pervasiveness of soul)

śarīramāno'sti śarīradhārī vibhuḥ punar jñānavibhutvayogāt /
itthaṁ budho 'vaibhava-vaibhavasya samanvayaṁ satkurute tvadīyam //14//

So long as the soul assumes bodies, its size is equal to the body it inhabits. And when it shines with the all-pervading (i.e., all-comprehending) light of knowledge, it can very well be regarded as all-pervading from the standpoint of its all-pervading knowledge. Thus, the wise respectfully accept the synthesis effected by you of the two apparently opposite views, one maintaining that the soul is all-pervasive and the other that it is not all-pervasive. (According to the Jaina philosophy, the soul possesses innumerable space-points. So when they expand and spread, they pervade the whole universe (*loka*) which too has innumerable space-points. From this standpoint also, the soul is all-pervasive). (14)

Śūnyavāda (Doctrine of Void) and Kṣaṇikavāda (Doctrine of Momentariness)

jagat samagraṁ khalu sārahīnam iti prabuddho nijagāda śūnyam /
vinaśvaraṁ ca kṣaṇikaṁ tad eva jñātvā" śayaḥ kaḥ kurutāṁ virodham //15//
Those who realised the worthlessness or essencelessness of the whole world called it 'Void' (*Śūnya*). And those who found it to be evanescent described it as momentary. Who will oppose these two views, if thus understood? (15)

Digambaravāda (Doctrine of Ascetic Nudity) and Śvetāmbaravāda (Doctrine of Ascetic Clothing)

śvetāmbarā digvasanāś ca hanta! kathaṁ mithaḥ syuḥ kalahāyamānāḥ /
āśritya nagnetarabhāvabhūmiṁ bhavaty anekāntadhurandharatve //16//
Śvetāmbara and Digambara Jainas are the strong supporters and propagators of *anekāntavāda* (the doctrine of non-one-sidedness). Then, why should they quarrel on the point as to whether or not nudity is necessary for the attainment of salvation? (16)

kaṣāyamuktāv avagatya muktiṁ buddhvā 'py anāsaktisamarthayogam /
jñātvā kramaṁ sādhanasaṁśrayaṁ ca muneḥ sacelatvam api pratīyāt //17//
Having known that true liberation consists in the freedom from passions, having realised the strength of the spiritual practice of non-attachment and having understood the gradual order of undertaking the practice of the means of liberation, one can very well understand a monk's acceptance of clothing. (17)

kiṁ muktisaṁsādhanayogamārgo vastraṁ vinā"viṣkurute na muktiṁ /
ced vītarāgatvam udeti pūrṇaṁ nagno 'py anagno 'pi labheta muktim //19//
Does the yogic practice, the supreme means for the attainment of liberation, not manifest the state of liberation, if the practiser is without clothing? Does the absence of clothing (i.e., nudity) prevent the state of liberation from manifesting itself? No, not at all. The only essential point is that when one attains the state of perfect non-attachment, one definitely attains liberation, irrespective of one's being a nude or not. (Clothing is not an obstacle to salvation. It is attachment that acts as an obstacle to salvation.) (19)

Mūrtivāda (Doctrine of the Worship of Jina Image)

sadbhāvanā jāgrati mūrtiyogād upāsakās tāṁ tata āśrayanti /
yogāpramatta-sthiramānasānām āvaśyakaḥ syān na hi mūrtiyogaḥ //22//

If we take recourse to the worship of Jina image, good meritorious spiritual feelings are roused in our hearts. This is the reason why householders worship Jina image. For those who have attained the state of firm spiritual vigilance and hence whose minds are stable and serene, the worship of Jina image is not necessary. (22)

sadbhāvanodbhāvanasādhanānāṁ mūrtyātmakaṁ khalv adhikaṁ ya ekam /
śrayed yathāśakti vivekayuktaṁ karoti naivānucitaṁ sa kiñcit //23//

Among the means for rousing good meritorious spiritual feelings, worship of Jina image is one important means. If one discreetly takes recourse to the worship of Jina image, does he do anything improper? No, not at all. (23)

kaṣāyarodhāya hi mūrtiyogaḥ samāśrayaṁs taṁ tam anāśrayadbhiḥ /
sārdhaṁ virodhācaraṇaṁ dharec cet kutas tadā tasya sa sārthakaḥ syāt//24//

We take recourse to the worship of Jina image for the sake of achieving subsidence or destruction of passions. If those who resort to the worship of Jina image bear feeling of enmity towards those who do not accept the worship of Jina image, then how can their worship of Jina image bear its proper fruit? (24)

Kriyāvāda (Ritualism)

na karmakāṇḍāśrayadurgrahasyā'nekāntadarśī dadate 'vakāśam /
sarvāḥ kriyāḥ śuddhibhṛtaḥ suyogāḥ śubhāvahāḥ ko 'tra satāṁ virodhaḥ//25//

One who possesses non-one-sided view never gives scope to obstinacy or stubbornness with regard to the performance of rituals and rites. Any rite or ritual does bring spiritual good or welfare, if it is performed with the pure or auspicious operations of mind, speech and body. Does any wise person have any objection to this view? (25)

There is a vast and baffling multitude of philosophical views. Some believe in soul, others do not. Even among those who believe in soul, some hold that there is but one soul while others maintain the plurality of souls. Similarly, there is a variety of views about God. All these views conflict with one another and give rise to controversies. In spite of all this, one thing is self-evident and firmly established in the eyes of all men. It is that all living organisms or beings experience I-consciousness. No living being is without the experience of I-consciousness. On the basis of this unanimously accepted phenomenon of the experience of I-consciousness, the teaching of 'Live and let others live' has become universally acceptable. Even the hardcore atheist or materialist individual or institution accepts this teaching and considers it to be a duty of man to put it into practice. This teaching has spread far and wide among all human beings to such an extent that all men have come to understand that to achieve one's own individual interest at the cost of others' is immorality, defect and sin and that as I-consciousness is uniformly and universally present in all living beings they should live and behave with one another amicably and friendly. Welfare and happiness of all consist in such living and behaviour. In short, the whole edifice of morality and good conduct is rightly erected on the firm foundation of the universally accepted entity 'I'. Even a man who is greatly puzzled by the philosophical controversies and hence has become averse to the terrible storm of conflicting philosophical views can achieve welfare and peace through the practice of morality and good conduct solidly established on the foundation of the universally accepted entity 'I'. In fact, on account of this practice one gradually attains more and more purity of mind and at last mind becomes so pure and brilliant that the truths which have remained covered and incomprehensible till then become clearly manifest to one's inner vision.

There are some persons who do not believe in soul yet practise good conduct. Their practice of good conduct should be regarded as spiritual practice (i.e., the practice resulting in the realisation of soul). Their practice of good conduct leads to the purification of their souls, without their knowledge (of the soul as an independent substance). Such persons are, therefore, the believers in soul from the standpoint of their conduct, though they are called 'non-believers in soul' from the standpoint of their opinion. On the other hand, there are some persons who believe in soul, yet their conduct is not good, not purified through righteousness. So they are in fact non-believers in soul though they uphold the view that there exists soul. They are believers in soul in name only, but virtually they are non-believers in soul, they are really harmful to themselves as also to others. The same logic can apply to theism. God or the Supreme Soul commands us to practise good conduct, to be righteous, to be pure in thought, speech and action. There are some persons who do not believe in God yet follow His command, that is, tread on the auspicious path of righteousness and rectitude. Are they not the devotees of God? Virtually they are devotees of God, believers in God, though they are regarded as atheists from the standpoint of their opinion. It is so because though they do not uphold the view or idea of God, they do follow the path of righteousness which God has commanded all beings to follow. God who pervades and sustains the whole world expects nothing from His devotee. If at all He expects, He expects this much from him that he may be a very human person. If He were to command him, He would command him simply this much: "Be human. Remove all impurities, defects and evils from life. Be virtuous. Be righteous. Be kind and good unto others. Perform good acts." It is only with a view to inspiring man to lead such a life that spiritual monism instructed him to shed off all infatuation with worthless material worldly objects, to realise unity and identity of all living beings, to cultivate spiritual disposition and to practise spiritual discipline for the realisation of soul. Dualism instructed us to clearly distinguish the insentient material element associated with soul from the soul and to completely dissociate the former from the latter. In other words, it taught us to attain the state of non-attachment and thereby to reveal pure consciousness. Momentarism demonstrates the fleeting nature of all worldly objects and thereby impresses on our mind that it is not wise to get attracted to and infatuated with them. In this way, it has contributed to the wise teaching of how to destroy attachment and infatuation. *Śūnyavāda* (the theory of Void) explains how all worldly objects are decaying and perishing every moment and propounds that all things are of the nature of void, that is, they are essenceless or worthless. The theoreticians enunciated such a theory on the basis of universal experience of all-pervading Emptiness or Void, with a view to uprooting attachment which is the main cause of all miseries and wickedness. *Jñānavāda* puts emphasis on right knowledge and declares that it is the main and direct cause of liberation. It considers Nescience or Ignorance to be the cause of bondage or transmigratory existence. Under the influence of Nescience, mind mistakes happiness for unhappiness, good for evil, the beneficial for the harmful, and *vice versa.* Mind of the ordinary worldly men imagines non-existent attributes and superimposes them on the external objects. Thus Nescience causes miseries. *Jñānavāda* teaches us to see through the workings of Nescience, to know things as they are, and thus to destroy Nescience. On the rise of right knowledge, Nescience is destroyed, practice of truthfulness and righteousness reaches perfection, mind becomes completely purified, and pure experience or consciousness manifests itself. And peace and bliss of life depend on this pure experience or consciousness. This is the positive contribution of *jñānavāda* to the spiritual wisdom. The doctrine of the world-creator God describes Him as omnipotent, teaches us to cultivate devotion to Him and states explicitly that the true result of this devotion is righteous conduct, meaning thereby that without righteous conduct there can never be true devotion to God and *vice versa*, one without the other is impossible. On the other hand, the view that does not accept such God describes the soul itself as possessed of infinite energy by its own innate nature and propounds that it should employ its infinite energy to ward off attacks of *karmas* that obscure natural faculties of soul. The ancient propounders of these mutually conflicting philosophical views had only one main purpose in view in propounding them. And that purpose was to make man's life virtuous, righteous and altruistically active. Adherents of any of these views can well achieve this purpose and thereby attain their own welfare and at the same time make praiseworthy contribution to the efforts of converting this miserable world into happy, lovely, lovable and liveable one.

Let us take one more instance where the method of non-one-sidedness or synthesis is fruitfully applied. Various views have been propounded to explain the occurrence of events. They give mutually conflicting answers to the question as to what determines the happening of events. The views in point are as follows:

(1) *Time (Kāla)*

The auspicious and inauspicious *karmas* that are bound with the soul due to its auspicious and inauspicious activities do not rise to give their fruits immediately when they are bound. But when they mature, they rise to give their fruits. For, *karmas* have to depend on Time to present their fruits. Human effort favourable to the accomplishment of the undertaken work requires some time for being fruitful or successful. One cannot have mangoes the very moment the mango-tree is planted. A steamer or car does not reach the destination as soon as it starts moving. An aeroplane does not reach the destination the moment it takes off. Though the stone (*goṭalo*) of the mango-fruit has the inherent nature to grow into the mango-tree as also other favourable conditions like human effort, etc., are available to it, yet it cannot grow into the mango-tree without passing through the required duration of time. It cannot neglect the temporal limitation set out by time for its transformation into the mango-tree. For, even inherent nature has to depend on time for its manifestion or actualisation. The climate becomes cold in winter and hot in summer, it rains in rainy season, in spring trees have soft young sprouts, in youth moustache and beard appear on the face of men, etc.—all these and such things make us realise the power of time as an important instrumental cause of all occurrences.

Time is a controlling principle. Without it temporal order could not be accounted for. But for it, all serial effects would take place simultaneously and thus there would ensue chaos instead of order. If there were no time, a sprout, a stem, a stalk, a flower and a fruit—all would emerge and exist simultaneously. We cannot but acknowledge the fact that time plays an important role in the events of one's life. Importance of time is recognised even in the attainment of liberation. It is explicitly stated in scriptures that one can attain liberation only when one's transmigratory state (*bhavasthiti*) attains its maturity (*paripāka*). This also is nothing but a case where time shows its power and strength.

(2) *Nature (Svabhāva)*

If rice grains are sown, rice will grow. And if wheat grains are sown, wheat will grow. This is the glory of the inherent nature of a thing. Though duration of time has its undeniable place in the process of growth, yet the fruit will necessarily be in accordance with the inherent nature of the seed sown. Man obtains mangoes after a certain period of time by sowing a stone of a mango-fruit and putting forth proper human effort, only because the stone has inherent nature to grow into a mango-tree. Nothing can generate an effect against its own inherent nature, though all other causal conditions, viz., time, human effort, etc., are present there. An insentient or sentient thing produces an effect strictly in accordance with its own inherent nature. Undoubtedly, the place of inherent nature is very important in the production of an effect or in the occurrence of an event. It is the inherent nature of a thing that determines the effect it would generate.

(3) *Past Karma (Pūrva-karma)*

Happiness, misery and various conditions related to them depend on the diverse *karmas*. Sometime we notice that good deeds yield bitter fruits and evil deeds yield sweet ones. Behind this apparent anomaly, it is the force of *karmas* that is at work. Accidental or sudden gain and calamity are the crucial instances displaying the power of *karmas*. As all the transmigratory souls are souls bound with the diverse *karmas*, they are accordingly placed under diverse circumstances and have to pass through various states. All know and recognise power of *karma*.

kṣmābhṛd-raṅkayor manīṣi-jaḍayoḥ sadrūpa-nīrūpayoḥ
śrīmad-durgatayor balābalavator nīroga-rogārtayoḥ /
saubhāgyāsubhagatvasaṅgamajuṣos tulye'pi nṛtve'ntaraṁ
yat yat karmanibandhanaṁ tad api no jīvaṁ vinā yuktimat //
(Quoted in the auto-commentary of Devendrasūri's *Karmagrantha*, Part I)
Meaning: The king and the meek servant, the wise and the fool, the beautiful and the ugly, the rich and the poor, the strong and the weak, the healthy and the diseased, the fortunate and the unfortunate—all of them differ widely from one another in this manner, though they are all human beings; this diversity among human beings is due to their *karmas*. And how can there be *karmas* in the absence of soul? So the existence of soul gets automatically established as soon as the existence of *karmas* is established.

The entire chapter four of this book is devoted to the exposition of *karma*. Therein we have dealt with the auspicious and inauspicious *karmas* called *puṇya* and *pāpa* respectively.

Man is naturally imperfect. However skillful and clever he may be, he is more or less hampered by unmindfulness and bodily restlessness—both natural to the class of human beings. Hence it is that sometimes he falls victim to imperfection and defects; sometimes he accidently and unknowingly hurts his eye with his own finger, crushes his tongue with his own teeth, and as a result suffers pains. Sometimes, he falls victim to such an accident for which none can put a blame on his carelessness. Very often it so happens that he goes to a certain place and is suddenly caught in a tragic accident, or performs wrong and harmful acts inspite of his being very wise and clever.

There occur inexplicable or strange events in the life of an individual or of a group, which are described as 'determined or controlled by God or Fate'. From such events, we can have the idea of the existence of *karma.*

(4) *Human effort (Puruṣārtha)*

We cannot help but recognise the importance of human effort. Those who regard *karmas* as supreme should question themselves as to who generates *karmas*. It is the soul who generates *karmas.* The soul binds *karmas* to itself. Human effort helps *karma* to rise (*udaya*). It can convert the auspicious *karmas* into inauspicious ones, and *vice versa.* It rules supreme there where the *karmas* cannot reach and function. The *karma* (the '*adṛṣṭa*'—'Unseen') makes the soul wander in the transmigratory cycle, whereas human effort wages war against *karmas*, destroys their entire force and leads the soul to the Abode-of-the-Liberated. It is not the force of *karmas* that brings about the manifestation of the state of liberation. In fact, it is the destruction of *karmas* that is the only cause of liberation. And it is only human effort that can destroy *karmas*. When one directs one's attention to this uncommon characteristic of human—rather spiritual—effort, one finds improper to give sole importance to *karma.* This is the reason why the knowledgeable and wise saints have taught us that the only means for improving and destroying *karmas* is one's firm determination to keep one's mental, vocal and bodily operations auspicious (wholesome) or pure while performing good, auspicious and praiseworthy acts. Those who depend solely on *karmas* become despondent and indolent; hence they are deprived of success, they are unable to remove their 'poverty' or 'destitution'. Wealth chooses and favours those who are industrious and brave.[1]

---

1. *ārabhetaiva karmāṇi śrāntaḥ śrāntaḥ punaḥ punaḥ /*
karmāṇy ārabhamāṇaṁ hi puruṣaṁ śrīr niṣevate //300//—Manusmṛti IX
Tired and tired over again, he should begin his activities; for fortune favours the man who undertakes activities.
Schopenhaur, a German philosopher, says: "Our happiness depends in a great degree upon what we are, upon our own individuality."
"It is the prerogative of man to be, in a great degree, the creature of his own making"—Burke.
"The poorest have sometimes taken the highest places; nor have difficulties apparently the most insuperable proved obstacles in their way. Those very difficulties, in many instances, would even seem to have been their best helpers by evoking their

Though human effort has to depend on time, nature, etc., it is the most efficient to bring victory to man. In the modern age, many wonderful things have been invented, viz., railway, motor-car, telegraph, wireless, phonograph, aeroplane, radio, atom-bomb (atomic energy), etc. They are widely used. And more and more new things are being invented. These inventions serve as brilliant instances of the efficacy of human effort. Individuals or nations that put forth great efforts make progress and attain prosperity and welfare. On the other hand, idle individuals and nations fall behind and degenerate on account of their lack of vigour and vitality, and consequently they become slaves of others and subject themselves to their oppressions. (If the achievements attained or inventions made by human effort are misused, it is the persons who misuse them that are at fault, and not the achievements or inventions. This is quite obvious.)

(5) *Destiny (Niyati)*

Destiny means that the future is unalterable. The future is as unalterably fixed as the past. Future events will take place without fail. What is to happen will certainly happen. The course of future events cannot be changed. It is firmly fixed. Rich and ready crop is standing. And suddenly it gets destroyed by frost-fall, attack of locusts or some other unavoidable natural calamity. This illustrates the working of destiny. Suddenly one falls seriously sick or some such powerful obstruction crops up at a very critical time when one is just about to reap the fruits of one's sincere efforts. In this way, one is deprived of one's just fruits. This is another instance of destiny. One wins in lottery or speculation and suddenly becomes a very rich person. This incident is also attributed to destiny. Destiny can be regarded as identical with the unalterable *karma*, a special type of *karma*. In the Jaina terminology, it is called '*nikācita karma*'. The *nikācita karma* is that which is mostly unalterable and which most certainly causes the experience of pleasure or pain to the concerned soul at the time of its fruition. The fruit or result of such type of *karma* being *niyata*

---

powers of labour and endurance, and stimulating into life faculties which might otherwise have lain dormant."—S. Smile's *Self-help*

"Slumber not in the tents of your fathers. The world is advancing. Advance with it."—Mazzini.

(fixed and unalterable), the *karma* is known by the name '*Niyati*'.

We have seen above the power of the five causal factors. All the five are useful in their own places. All contribute to the production of an effect. We should not give exclusive importance to any one of them, rejecting all others or relegating them to utterly insignificant place. The believers in the doctrine of time are under the sway of illusion, if they accept time to the exclusion of all others without properly evaluating their contribution. That view is the right view, which accords proper place to all the causal factors. Contrary to it, that view is the wrong view, which regards anyone of them as the sole cause, neglecting the rest.

We have before us many instances of the cooperation of all the five causal factors in the production of an effect. All these five factors co-operate in bringing about the birth of a baby. Without the due period of time (i.e., before the completion of the period of time that an embryo requires for its full development) a baby is certainly not born. This is quite obvious. Again, it is quite clear that only a fertile woman can give birth to a baby. This means that the inherent nature as a causal factor is present there to make its necessary contribution in bringing about the birth of a baby. Moreover, it goes without saying that human effort is certainly present there in the aggregate of the causal factors. And a baby is born to a woman, only if the past *karmas* or destiny of the parents are favourable. Thus, the union of all the five causal factors is necessary to bring about the birth of a baby.

Let us take another example. A student secures first class in the examination. It is noticed that all the five causal factors jointly cause the occurrence of this event. Certain duration of time for the continuous study is noticed to be present there as one of the causal factors. Without effort conducive to development, the student cannot secure the first class. Thus human effort is also noticed there as a causal factor contributing to the occurrence of the event. The studious nature of the student is also there as a necessary causal factor. And the favourable *karma* or destiny is also to be taken as present in the causal aggregate.

But we are not to understand that in the production of each and every effect, all the five causal factors are equally important. Of course, all of them are necessarily present there to produce an effect. But with respect to a particular effect a particular causal factor acts as a principal one and the rest act as subordinate to it.

The period of time can be changed through effort, etc. The period of time that a particular crop or fruit requires for its ripening is not unalterable or fixed. It differs with different countries. It is shorter in countries that employ machines in farming than in those that do not. When things are made by hand, their production takes much time. But when the same things are manufactured by machines in factories, their production takes very little time. In the medieval age when there were no railways, it took months for a traveller to reach Banaras from Viramgam, whereas in the modern age by railways he can reach Banaras within three days and by aeroplane he can reach a distant country within a few hours only. All know this. We observe that the duration of time required by a particular effect to come into being can be thus changed. Even then generally long or short duration of time is necessarily required by every effect for its production or emergence. Time is not independent or sole cause of an effect. But it is proper to grant it as much importance as it deserves, when it produces an effect depending upon effort, nature, etc. If man understands that time is one of the important factors that produce an effect, he will learn to be patient during the whole period from the inception of the work to its completion or accomplishment. Otherwise, he will wrongly expect success or accomplishment or fruit the moment the work is started or before its due time; he will lose all hope on account of not attaining success or the result at once or before time; this will make him slack in his efforts; and as a result he will be certainly deprived of success or result. But as soon as he recognises the fact that time is one of the factors that are necessarily required in the production of an effect, he comes to have an understanding that the fruit or success can be secured only in due course of time; and consequently he remains firmly engaged in the work till it is accomplished.

The due duration of time can be changed. But the nature cannot be transgressed. From the practical standpoint, even the nature can be transgressed. (In practice, what is regarded as the nature of man is in fact not his pure nature but impure nature, hence there is possibility of change in it.) Angry nature of a person can become mild on account of his association with the calm and composed saint or can be totally exterminated by the force of spiritual and wholesome reflections. Under the influence of good company, the wicked may turn into saintly persons. And under the influence of bad company, even the good persons become wicked. When different things are mixed with one another, their original natures get changed and in their place new natures emerge in them. For example, jaggery and ginger which have the nature to cause phlegm and bile respectively, when compounded, lose their respective harmful natures.

Even *karmas*—past *karmas*—can be changed by effort. One can increase or decrease their duration and flavour. One can make one's *karmas* rise earlier than their due time. One can subject one's *karmas* to the process of subsidence (*upaśama*), increased realisation (*udvartanā*), decreased realisation (*aparvartanā*) and transformation or conversion (*saṅkramaṇa*)[1].

---

1. We have dealt with the main states of the '*karma*' on page 295 ff. We mentioned there a state called *upaśamanā* (subsidence). This state has two types, viz. *deśa-upaśamanā* (a state of partial subsidence) and *sarva-upaśamanā* (a state of complete subsidence). In the state of *deśa-upaśamanā,* the subsided *karmas* can undergo the processes of increased realisation, decreased realisation, and transformation (conversion). But in this state, the *karmas* cannot undergo the process called '*nidhatti*' and '*nikācanā*' which tighten the bondage of *karmas* with soul. On the other hand, when the *karmas* are in the state of *sarva-upaśamanā,* they cannot undergo any of the above-mentioned processes. Of course, this state of *sarva-upaśamanā* does not last long. And within a very short period of time, the subsided *karmas* rise again and consequently the *upaśānta* soul that had spiritually risen starts falling down.
Ultimately, the destruction (*kṣaya*) of *karmas* alone is the means to the highest Good (liberation). (Destruction of *karmas* means dissociation of material karmic particles from the soul.) The destruction (*kṣaya, nirjarā*) of *karma* that takes place as a result of the experience of its fruit cannot lead a living being on to liberation, because this type of destruction is necessarily accompanied with the binding of ever new *karmas* with the soul. If a living being, having made the *karmas* rise before their due time by force of pure conduct and austerity, dissociates them from the soul without experiencing their fruits, the dissociation or destruction (*kṣaya, nirjarā*) of *karmas* is good and acts as an effective means for liberation. The more elevated the power of spiritual practice, the greater is the dissociation or destruction of *karmas*.
Thus, dissociation (*nirjarā*) of the bound karmic matter is of two types, viz., involuntary and voluntary. The involuntary dissociation takes place automatically on account of the effective rise (*vipākodaya*). In other words, the bound karmic matter gets automatically dissociated as soon as it rises and gives its fruits. On the other hand, the voluntary dissociation is effected by the soul through spiritual effort. When the voluntary dissociation takes place, there is the rise of flavourless simple karmic particles. This is called *pradeśodaya* which ultimately means nominal rise.
The process called *saṅkramaṇa* is already explained. By the process of *udīraṇā* a living being drags forward the unrisen karmic particles through special spiritual effort and mixes them with already risen ones and thereby experiences their fruits along with those of the latter, that is, before their due time. In this way, the soul advancing towards the final goal of liberation experiences through the process of *udīraṇā,* the

One can destroy the *karma* by force of strong spiritual efforts without experiencing their fruits through effective rise (*vipākodaya*). If we do not cultivate our bodies, sense-organs, etc., which we have come to possess as a result of our past *karmas*, they cannot develop their powers. Thus the development of the instruments acquired on account of *karmas* require efforts. Without efforts their powers cannot develop. When a person properly develops the powers of his body, sense-organs, mind, intellect and heart through training and education, he achieves welfare, prosperity and happiness through such praiseworthy wholesome efforts. Just as those who solely depend on destiny or *karma* cannot progress in life on account of the lack of effort and as a result of their idleness they become powerless and make their lives worthless and vain, even so those who altogether reject *karma*—past *karma*—tumble and fumble in the pithy darkness of ignorance and illusion. We have already expounded the arguments adduced in favour of the doctrine of *karma* and demonstrated its utility. Those who disregard the doctrine are necessarily not convinced of the existence of soul, a very important entity; and at the time of calamity and troubles they cannot remain calm and endure them peacefully. It is very difficult for them to experience the pure feeling of universal love. Hence even on the occasion of trifling conflict, they become restless, confounded and unhappy. Elevated feelings of calmness and blissfulness are difficult for them to attain. The original and real ground (source) of welfare and bliss being unknown to them it is simply impossible for them to make real progress in life.

Destiny (*niyati*) in indomitable. As already pointed out, the *karma* which suddenly causes or obstructs gain can be regarded as destiny. This *karma* is such as can never be altered. On account of its speciality of unalterability or fixity, this type of *karma* might have been separated from all other *karmas* and given a special name '*niyati*' ('destiny'). Other *karmas* can be altered, but this *karma* cannot be altered.

As stated in chapter three, the store of *karmas* is well concealed, incomprehensible and beyond the reach of our intellect. There are various types of *karmas* in it. Not all the *karmas* belong to the *nikācita* (unalterable) type. Many *karmas* and obstructions that they might cause are

---

fruits or karmic particles of all the remaining bound *karmas* simultaneously at the last moment of its last birth, thereby dissociates them all simultaneously and attains the disembodied state of liberation (*videhamukti*). Thus *udīraṇā* is also one of the processes that effect dissociation or destruction of *karmas*.

such as could be altered or destroyed by the special spiritual effort. So, when we do not attain the desired thing or success immediately, we should not think that it is certainly not there in our destiny. We do not know the veils of *karmas* and their types. Again the workings of the *karmas* are beyond our comprehension and understanding. Then why should we regard the desired thing or success as obscured and obstructed by the unalterable *karma* when we do not attain it within a certain period of time? Why should we leave all hopes and discontinue our efforts? Sincere effort with firm determination brings us success. The powers of our brilliant austerity do fructify our wishes and desires.

As time, etc. produce an effect not singly, but jointly mutually depending on one another, they are called '*samavāyī*' ('associate') cause. The original pure nature of the soul is constituted of Existence, Consciousness and Bliss. So one should always make continuous efforts to remain equanimous while experiencing fruits of *karmas* and also to exterminate all desire that is the root-cause of the transmigratory cycle. By doing so one can attain the highest Good, the Liberation. Time will never deny us its cooperation, when we zealously make our sincere efforts to attain our goal. Thus, we see the mutual and joint cooperation of these factors in the attainment of spiritual welfare.

The following is a very nice quotation which denounces the conflicts and controversies in a debate, but at the same time throws light on its good and lovely aspect.

"Disagreement is refreshing when two men lovingly desire to compare their views to find out truth. Controversy is wretched when it is only an attempt to prove another wrong."—F.W. Robertson.

Now let us see how knowledge (*jñāna*) and practice (*kriyā*) mutually cooperate with one another to attain the desired end or thing.

Knowledge and practice are closely related. Attainment of anything—even Liberation—depends on both knowledge and practice. Mere knowledge is cripple and mere practice is blind. So one cannot attain the desired end or thing by mere knowledge or mere practice.

Let us understand the point with the help of illustrations. There is a man suffering from malaria. He knows that quinine is the sure remedy for it. If he does not take it as medicine in right proportion, he cannot cure himself of the disease. He cannot drive away the disease, if he does not put into practice his right knowledge of medicine. Similarly, in the absence of right knowledge of the proper medicine, if he takes any useless and irrelevant substance as medicine, then also he cannot remove his malarial fever. Thus, both the knowledge of the proper medicine and the activity in accordance with this knowledge are necessary for the patient to cure himself of the disease. The same thing applies to a person who wants to attain liberation. He knows that one cannot progress on the path of liberation, if one does not refrain from immorality, injustice and hypocrisy. If he does not act or behave according to his knowledge, he cannot progress on the path of liberation. On the contrary, he moves in the opposite direction, getting more and more away from the goal of liberation. This means that if knowledge is not put into practice, it is useless, that is, it does not bring about the desired fruit. Similarly, mere practice without right guidance of knowledge cannot bear the desired fruit or bears the undesired and unfavourable one.

A hungry man can never satisfy his hunger by merely seeing or praising the meal presented before him. To satisfy his hunger, he should move his hand and mouth, that is, he should actually eat the meal. Similarly, it will not do for us to merely listen to the beneficial teaching of the great saints, but in addition we should put it into practice after having properly understood it. How can a man who has the knowledge of the way to his destination reach there, if he does not walk forward on the way? And what would happen if he, in the absence of right knowledge of the path, takes to and moves on the wrong path? In that case, the destination would certainly remain far off and in addition he would wander here and there, without moving a step forward in the direction of the destination.

Regarding the mutual cooperation of knowledge and practice, *Viśeṣāvaśyakabhāṣya* declares.

hayaṁ nāṇaṁ kiyāhīṇaṁ hayā annāṇao kiyā/
pāsaṁto paṁgulo daḍḍho dhāvamāṇo a aṁdhao// 1159 //

—*Viśeṣāvaśyakabhāṣya (Āvaśyaka-Niryukti gāthā)*

Meaning: Futile indeed is knowledge without practice. Even so is practice without knowledge. A lame man was burnt inspite of his sight while a blind caught fire even though fleeing.

This illustration is elucidated in the following verse:

saṁjogasiddhi phalaṁ vayaṁti na hu egacakkeṇa raho payāi/
*aṁdho ya paṁgū ya vaṇe samiccā te saṁpauttā nagaraṁ paviṭṭhā//*1965//

—*Viśeṣāvaśyakabhāṣya (Āvaśyaka-Niryukti gāthā)*

A desired fruit is brought about only through the cooperation of knowledge and practice. A chariot cannot move on one wheel alone. Once in a forest there burst out a conflagration. At that time a cripple and a blind man were there in the forest. They cooperated with one another. So they could save themselves and reached the city safely. The lame man sat on the shoulder of the blind man and the latter walked as directed by the former. Thus they helped one another. Hence they were saved. If they had not cooperated with one another, they would have been devoured by the conflagration. Knowledge is compared to the lame man and practice to the blind man. When they associate with one another and cooperate mutually, they certainly attain the desired end or success. But, if they remain separate and single, they will become powerless and hence will not be able to attain success or desired end.

Even though possessed of right knowledge, one does not attain the desired fruit, if one fails to act in accordance with the knowledge. Although competent due to knowledge possessed by it as its guide, the soul does not attain liberation in the absence of spiritual practice. Knowledge without practice does not lead to liberation. Nor does practice without knowledge lead to it. One without the other is powerless. One finds its fulfilment in the other. Without this fulfilment mere knowledge is cripple and mere practice is blind. Knowledge enlightens practice. And practice makes knowledge efficient and dynamic. Knowledge and practice are equally necessary for success. This is, in brief, the mutual relation between knowledge and practice.

Now we propose to deal with definitive standpoint (*niścaya-naya*) and empirical standpoint (*vyavahāra-naya*).

We can perceive, through sense-organs, a soul and matter in their empirical form. Matter is atomic in its ultimate original form. Hence in this form it is not perceptible. But matter in its empirical form is always in the state of an aggregate, which is formed by the combination of infinite-times-infinite number of atoms. So in its empirical form it is amenable to sense-perception. As, in its pure state, the soul is beyond sense-perception, it can never be experienced through sense-organs. But being associated with matter in its empirical state, it is amenable to sense perception. The ultimate spiritual aim of a living being is to purify the impure soul by removing all impurities that soil it on account of its association with matter. The standpoint that concentrates on the original pure nature of a thing is called the definitive standpoint (*niścaya-naya*). On the other hand, the standpoint that concentrates on the empirical state of a thing is called the empirical standpoint (*vyavahāra-naya*). The definitive standpoint directs its attention towards the subtle and touches upon what is essential and purely natural, while the empirical standpoint directs its attention towards the crude, adventitious and that in which there is predominance of transfer of epithet. The former concentrates on the natural properties or states of a substance, while the latter concentrates on the contingent or adventitious properties of it. An account of a soul in terms of what happens to it all by itself is its account from the definitive standpoint, while an account of it in terms of what happens to it as a result of its association with matter is its account from the empirical standpoint. In other words, the definitive standpoint penetrates into the transcendental or ultimate nature of soul, whereas the empirical standpoint studies the empirical nature of it, which is the result of its association with matter. The standpoint which recognises the soul as pure Existence, pure Consciousness and pure Bliss is the definitive standpoint. And the standpoint that recognises it as deluded, ignorant, soiled with passions like anger, greed, etc., is the empirical standpoint. In short, the empirical standpoint touches upon the conventional, gross and empirical aspect of a thing, whereas the definitive standpoint concentrates on the ultimate original pure nature of a thing. The empirical standpoint presents the popular or conventional truth, while the definitive standpoint presents the ultimate truth. As the definitive standpoint sees the Supreme Consciousness equally present in all living beings, it is permeated through and through with universal love and friendliness.

Cherishing definitive viewpoint in our heart, that is, entertaining feeling of pure affection and friendliness towards all living beings, we should perform all our worldly activities and duties. The wise describe such living as *kalyāṇa-vihāra* ('a blissful trip in the region of Spiritual Welfare').

The definitive standpoint makes our everyday life or worldly practice (*vyavahāra*) pure by removing impurities or evil elements already crept into it as also by preventing those that are about to creep into it. Just as in the dark night in the mid-ocean, the helmsman saves the sailing ship from colliding with a big rock with the help of light from the lighthouse and sails it on the danger-free route, even so the definitive standpoint having removed the darkness of delusion and ignorance spreads the light of discretion, saves our conduct from being impure and evil, and makes the way to liberation easy, clearing it of all obstructions. In the transmigratory state, one cannot escape from worldly conduct or practice that one has to undertake for the benefit (material, mental and spiritual) of oneself as well as of others. One should undertake such worldly practice as one's duty. This worldly conduct or practice continues as long as the body is alive. If it is pure and associated with pure love, it does not act as an obstruction to the attainment of liberation.

One can easily imagine how greatly the light of the definitive standpoint which is but the pure spiritual standpoint, enlightens and guides the outward life—the worldly dealings, behaviour or practice—of a man in whose temple of innermost heart burns the lamp of this pure spiritual standpoint. Such a good person behaves righteously and affectionately with his or her spouse, servants or master, customers or relatives, or anyone who comes in his or her contact. Such noble behaviour is possible then and then only, when one has already attained a lofty spiritual stage. It is the true pilgrimage to the spiritual Good.

The learned saints teach us to harmoniously employ both these standpoints in our life and direct us to keep both our outer and inner lives pure.

There occurs in *Ācārāṅgasūtra* (*Adhyāya* 4, *Uddeśa* 2), a Jaina canonical work, the following *sūtra* which enunciates the non-one-sided viewpoint (*anekānta-dṛṣṭi*): *je āsavā te parissavā, je parissavā te āsavā* / Meaning: What acts as the cause of bondage (*āsava*) can act as the cause of release (*parissava*), and *vice versa.*

To explain, that very activity which causes bondage of *karmas* in the case of the ignorant and indiscreet causes dissociation or destruction of *karmas* in the case of the learned and discreet. Conversely, that very activity which causes dissociation or destruction of *karmas* in the case of the learned and discreet causes bondage of *karmas* in the case of the ignorant and indiscreet.

Whatever activity the learned and wise undertake, they undertake with a view to doing good to all living beings. They wish welfare of all beings. They have no pride or egotism. They do not think that they are obliging others. They do not desire fame, reward or award. Of course, they eat and drink, enjoy the comforts of life, and keep their body fit and healthy. All this they do in order that their mind remain sound and unagitated as also that they can continue to be bodily and mentally efficient to do more and more good to others. They consider their body and mind to be the prime instrument for bringing good to others. It becomes their nature to help others, to do good to them. And when they behave according to their true nature, they find no difficulty at all. Not only that, they do not have the slightest thought that they have performed great acts; they do not have any feeling of pride or self-praise. As a result, no activity acts as a cause of bondage in their case.

Though the activity of an ignorant person results in the good of living beings, he has in fact no intention to do good to them. He undertakes the activity with the sole intention of achieving his own selfish end. He desires to eat delicious dishes, to drink fragrant sweet drinks, to enjoy all comforts and luxuries, to build palatial bungalows, to own luxurious car, and to indulge in pleasures of sex, etc., and for fulfilling all these desires he tries to amass wealth by any means, fair or foul. Even if his activity brings good to others, he is afflicted with pride at the time of that activity, thinks that he is putting others under his obligation, and there is a burning desire in his heart for fame, reward and award. Though he performs activities regarded as religious, viz. continuous muttering of a sacred formula, observance of austerities, meditation, study of spiritual works, service of the people, observance of rites of *sāmāyika* (equanimity) and *pratikramaṇa* (confession), worship of Tīrthaṅkara images, veneration of teachers and elders, etc., he is puffed up with pride, thinks that he performs great many religious activities, and entertains the feeling of self-praise. On this account, even the activities considered to be religious act as the cause of bondage in his case. The learned and wise mainly intend to do good to others and are very humble, whereas the ignorant are mainly selfish and afflicted with pride and egotism.

The very same activity which acts as the cause of bondage, if performed with ignorance, infatuation and passion, acts as the cause of release if performed with wisdom, discretion and pure feeling of universal friendliness and non-attachment. A wicked man attacks a person and cuts off his hand. A surgeon amputates a hand of his patient. Outwardly both perform the same act. But the intention of the former is cruel and evil while that of the latter is kind and good. The former wants to harm the victim, while the latter wants to do good to the patient. Thus one and the same act causes the bondage of the grave inauspicious *karmas* in the case of the former and the bondage of the auspicious *karmas* in the case of the latter. When a man touches a woman with the feeling of devotion, affection and compassion, it is not a defect or sin. But when he touches her with the feeling of lust and passion, it is certainly a defect or a sin.

Two men eat sweet dishes. But one eats with attachment and the other without attachment and with' the noble purpose of sustaining his body for the good of others. Though their activity of eating food is identical, the former binds *karmas,* whereas the latter keeps his inner life sublime (even while eating). It is because the former is indiscreet and under the sway of attachment and infatuation, while the latter is discreet and free from attachment and infatuation. Similarly, two persons visit a holy place of pilgrimage and stay there for a few days. But one does all his activities with mindfulness and thinks good thoughts, while the other does all his activities carelessly and thinks deceitful and wily thoughts. So, the pilgrimage acts as the cause of release in the case of the former, while the same acts as the cause of bondage in the case of the latter. The mental states of all those who visit a temple for worship are not uniform. Those whose mental states are good and pure earn spiritual merit, and others who entertain cruel, evil or wily thoughts bind inauspicious *karmas*. Thus, worship of *tīrthaṅkaras* acts as the cause of the spiritual good in the case of the former, while the same acts as the cause of the bondage of the inauspicious *karmas* in the case of the latter.

Thus we explain the above quoted statement of *Ācārāṅgasūtra.*

We can also explain it somewhat different. A wise and discreet man does not stick to the general rule always on all occasions without using his power of discretion. He takes into account the various conditions, viz. the place, time, etc., then decides as to what is right action and what is wrong action, or what is duty or otherwise under present conditions, and accordingly acts or behaves. On the other hand, a stupid and indiscreet person blindly follows the general rule and considers an act to be right or wrong strictly in accordance with the general rule. He does not take into account the conditions and circumstances of the concerned place and time. As a result, though he has the intention to perform duty and act rightly, he performs what is not duty and acts wrongly.

In his observance of austerity, a person has completely given up food and water. Now it so happens that he becomes very much thirsty, longs for water, constantly utters 'water' 'water', and tosses about with pain and restlessness. If, at that time, our sense of duty and religion does not offer him water and allows him to die, then it is really not the sense of duty and religion.

A man has taken the vow of *covihāra* (renunciation of food and water during the whole night.) Suddenly his body is overpowered with the unbearable and fatal heat, and as a result he faints. How can it be the sense of duty and religion, if in such a condition it does not offer him ghee, etc., to eat as treatment for the cure?

At this juncture, I would like to narrate the following story of a stupid man.

There was a stupid villager. A kind, rich man from a city visited him. The villager welcomed him and devotedly served him with hospitality. It was the month of Pauṣa in winter. It was severe cold. The villager sprinkled water on the ground and requested the guest to sit there for dinner. For him, he got prepared the sweet dish made of concentrated curds and sugar. He gave him ice-cold water to drink and fanned him. He said to the guest, "How can a person like me properly entertain a great man like you with proper hospitality?" In reply, the rich man said, " Brother! your hospitality is matchless. But my vital breath is so strong that it cannot come out of the body in spite of great efforts."

Now let us deal briefly with the subject of a general rule (precept) and its exceptions.

The understanding that pertains to a general rule and its exceptions is identical with that which pertains to substance, place, time and state of a thing. That understanding is useful in acquiring the right knowledge of a thing as also in deciding as to which action is right and which action is wrong and in realising their respective consequences.

The general rules (precepts) about conduct are formulated, keeping in view the general or ordinary circumstances. They constitute the path or code of general rules (precepts), called in Sanskrit '*utsarga-mārga*'. And the exceptions which man is required to follow in changed or special circumstances constitute the path or code of exceptions, called '*apavāda-mārga*'.

It is very necessary for a person to reflect on a question or problem taking into account the conditions of substance, place, time and state in order to decide as to whether he should follow the path of general rules or that of exceptions. Substance means the concerned person, place means favourableness or otherwise of place, time means favourableness or otherwise of time, and state means efficiency or otherwise of the present state of the person concerned. To express briefly the meaning conveyed by the phrase '(conditions of) substance, place, time and state', we generally use the terms 'situation' or 'circumstances'.

This means that though science of ethics or law has laid down as a general rule that man should do certain things or behave in a certain way and, as a corollary of it, he should not do the opposite things or behave otherwise, it is really wrong and one-sided to understand that the positive and negative rules or injunctions are applicable always in all conditions. Whether a particular act is proper or not in a particular place and at a particular time is to be decided only after taking into account the conditions of substance, place, time and state (i.e., only after taking into account circumstances) pertaining to that occasion or event. The act or behaviour which is considered, as a general rule, to be a duty in normal conditions becomes opposite of duty in the changed or special situation or circumstances; conversely, the act or behaviour which is considered, in normal conditions, to be not worth doing becomes worth doing (a duty) in the changed or special situation or circumstances. This is called the path of exceptions. Here the general rule is not violated. But the very purpose which one achieves by following the general rule in normal conditions is achieved by following the exception in special conditions. Or, one may even achieve some noble end by following the exception in special circumstances. But one should be very vigilant and judicious while abandoning the path of general rules and accepting in its place the path of exceptions.

Regarding the conditions of substance, place, time and state, or regarding a general rule and its exceptions, what the following verse observes, is noteworthy:

utpādyate hi sā 'vasthā deśakālāmayān prati /
yasyāṁ kāryam akāryaṁ syāt karma kāryaṁ ca varjayet //[1]

Meaning: Due to place, time and disease, one attains such a state that in

---

1. Jineśvarasūri has quoted this verse in his commentary on the fifth verse of Ācārya Haribhadra's 27th *Aṣṭaka.* And Malliṣeṇasūri too quotes it in his *Syādvādamañjarī,* a commentary on Ācārya Hemacandra's *Anyayogavyavacchedikā Dvātriṁśikā* (verse 11). While explaining it, he says that according to the Indian science of medicine (*Āyurveda*), in the case of one disease at a certain stage, some substance is unwholesome, and that very substance is wholesome in the case of the same disease at another stage. Giving up food is prescribed for a person who is suffering from one type of fever, while another person who is suffering from another type of fever is advised to take food. Relative to certain place, time, etc. even eating of curds, etc. is wholesome for one stricken with fever. This means that avoidance of a particular substance in food cures a person of a particular disease in one condition, whereas eating of that very substance acts as the cause of the cure of the same disease in another condition.

it the very act which is generally regarded as unworthy of doing becomes worthy of doing, and *vice versa.* So, the act which we perform in normal conditions should be avoided in special conditions.

The path of exceptions is certainly conducive to the path of general rules, it is never detrimental to it. It is with the help of the injunction of exception that the path of general rule can develop and gather strength. Both together can achieve the original and final goal. For example, food and drink are certainly for the sustenance and nourishment of life, but we also observe that sometimes even giving up of food and drink saves life. Thus, when the apparently opposite practices strive to achieve the same goal, they fall under the category of *utsarga-apavāda* (general precept and exceptions). If we call *utsarga* (general precept or rule) a soul, then we should call *apavāda* (exception) its body. Their joint or common purpose is to make life harmonious. By following both the paths judiciously one can live a harmonious life.

Both the paths—one of general rule and another of exception—have the same end in view. The purpose for which a general rule is formulated is the same for which exceptions are made. In other words, the purpose for which a general rule operates is the same for which its exceptions operate. We explain the point by an example. For the practice of monastic discipline, there is a general rule that a monk should accept only pure food. Similarly, there is an injunction of exception for monks to accept even the unacceptable food (unacceptable due to certain reasons like its being specially prepared for monks) on special occasions (there being no other way on those occasions like monk's illness, etc.) for the sake of the practice of monastic discipline. Thus general rule and exception have the same end in view.

Ācārya Hemacandra in his auto-commentary on the verse III. 87 of his *Yogaśāstra* writes as follows:

> *kambalasya ca varṣāsu bahir nirgatānāṁ tātkālikavṛṣṭāv apkāyarakṣaṇam upayogaḥ/ bāla-vṛddha-glānanimittaṁ varṣaty api jaladhare bhikṣāyai niḥasaratā kambalāvṛtadehānāṁ na tathāvidhā apkāyavirādhanā / uccāra-prasravaṇādipīḍitānāṁ kamabalāvṛtadehānāṁ gacchatām api na tathāvidhā virādhanā/*

Meaning: It is rainy season. A monk is out on begging tour (for food) and suddenly it starts raining. At that time, he should cover his body with a woollen blanket or shawl with a view to protecting waterbodied beings. Or, it is raining and a monk goes out to bring food for a child monk, an old monk or a sick monk. Then he should go out after covering his body with a woollen blanket or shawl. By doing so, he does not cause that much injury to waterbodied beings as does he cause without covering his body with it. Or, a monk goes out to answer call of nature, while it is raining. At that time too, he should cover his body with a woollen blanket or shawl in order to avoid injury to waterbodied beings as far as possible. (It is strictly forbidden to suppress the urge to pass urine and stools. "*vacca-muttam na dhārae*" *Daśavaikālika* V. 19).

Thus scriptures forbid, as a general rule, a monk to touch unboiled water. But they command him, as exception, to go out while it is raining, with the above-mentioned purpose in view. (And this is the only use of a woollen blanket or shawl Ācārya Hemacandra has mentioned. He has mentioned no other use of it.)

Religion, or science of good conduct, commands us, as a general rule, to speak truth. But it forbids us, as exception, to speak truth, when we are asked by a hunter as to in which direction an animal has gone and there is no other way to save its life. It is our duty to speak untruth on such exceptional occasions, with the sole purpose of non-violence.[1] Thus general rule and exception have the same end in view.

Again, it is a general rule that a monk should not touch a woman. But when she is drowning in a river or is caught in fire or any other dangerous calamity, it becomes his duty to save her by lifting, etc., which necessarily involve touching. The purpose behind the general rule that a monk should avoid touching a woman is to help him protect his celibacy which is but a form of non-violence and hence is covered by the field of non-violence. And the exceptional touching of a woman is also meant for fostering non-violence which serves as a strong foundation of celibacy. Thus both the general rule forbidding a monk to touch a woman and the exceptional injunction commanding him to touch her aim at the same goal.

jaṁ davva-khetta-kālāisaṁgayaṁ bhagavayā aṇuṭṭhāṇaṁ/
bhaṇiyaṁ bhāvavisuddhaṁ nipphajjai phalaṁ taha u //778//
na vi kiṁci vi aṇuṇṇātaṁ paḍisiddhaṁ vā vi jiṇavariṁdehiṁ/
titthagarāṇaṁ āṇā kajje sacceṇa hoyavvaṁ//779//

—*Uvaesapaya* by Haribhadrasūri

---

1. *yas tu saṁyamaguptyarthaṁ na mayā mṛgā upalabdhā ityādikaḥ sa na doṣāya* /—*Vṛtti* on *Sūyagaḍa, Adhyayana* 8, *gāthā* 19.

Meaning: Lord has commanded us to do that act which is suitable to substance, place, time and state, keeping our mental states pure. He has commanded us to act and behave in such a manner that we cause good to ourselves as well as to others. (778)

Lord *tīrthaṅkara* has not commanded us to perform a particular act absolutely always in all circumstances. Nor has he forbidden us to perform a particular act absolutely always in all circumstances. His command is only this much that one should behave and act honestly and sincerely keeping in view the welfare of oneself as well as of others. (779)

Before closing the topic of *anekānta-vāda*, we would like to warn all against the misuse of the theory.

It is certain that the meaning of *anekānta-vāda* is to examine all sides or views and to effect proper synthesis of those sides or views which are consistent with one another. But an attempt to synthesise inconsistent or discordant views is childish. An attempt to prove what is wrong to be right, and *vice versa* is foolish. That way *anekānta-vāda* becomes theory of chaos instead of that of synthesis and harmony.

When our faculty of discretion considers the activity to be improper and positively harmful in certain circumstances, to seek support of *anekānta-vāda* for it, to try to make it consistent with *syādvāda* and under the pretext of *anekānta*, synthesis and liberality to establish it as proper and respectable is the misuse of *anekānta-vāda*. It is a mockery of *anekānta-vāda*. *Anekānta-vāda* does not ask us to surrender to each and every view, though it is not consistent with the whole Truth. It is nothing but a theory of judicious synthesis. It is not a hotch-potch theory.

Nikṣepa (Four Meanings of a Word)

Language is a means of communication. All practical intercourse or exchange of knowledge has language for its chief instrument. When it is couched or embodied in language, intangible knowledge becomes tangible and hence conveyable. Language is made up of words. One and the same word is employed to yield several meanings depending on the purpose or context. In any case, four meanings at least are had by each and every word. These four meanings are called *nikṣepas*. They are *nāma* (name), *sthāpanā* (representation), *dravya* (substance) and *bhāva* (present state). (1) The meaning that is not derived etymologically, but is gathered on the basis of convention set up by the father, mother or some other people is meaning of the type called *nāma-nikṣepa*; for example, a person who possesses no qualification appropriate to a *rājā* (Sanskrit for king), but whom somebody has given the name Rājā. (2) The meaning which has in view a copy, statue or picture of the real thing is the meaning of the type called *sthāpanā-nikṣepa.* We call a statue, picture or photograph of the real thing *rājā rājā,* just as we call an image of God God. Here we employ the term *'rājā'* in the sense of the representation of the real *rājā.* In this usage we superimpose the real thing on its representation, viz., a statue, photograph, picture, etc. (3) The meaning which has in view a past or future state of a thing is the meaning of the type called *dravya-nikṣepa.* For example, a person who was *rājā* in the past or is going to be *rājā* in future is called *rājā,* though at present he is not *rājā.* The term '*dravya*' in the word *'dravya-nikṣepa'* has the sense of worthiness (*pātratā*). From the standpoint of worthiness he is *rājā.* He is *dravya-rājā.* Here we should take the term '*dravya*' in the sense of worthiness. This means that the person who was *rājā* in the past or who is going to be *rājā* in future is worthy of being *rājā,* but is actually not *rājā* at present. (4) The meaning which satisfies the etymology of the concerned word is the meaning of the type called *bhāva-nikṣepa.* It is well-known that a person is called *rājā,* when he is actually carrying the royal sceptre and is shining with glory on that account.

Thus a word, when employed, yields four meanings, viz., *nāma, sthāpanā, dravya* and *bhāva.*

We worship Supreme Soul (God) by respectfully remembering and muttering His name, or worshipping His image. We can also worship Him by devotedly serving the spiritual teacher, because the real spiritual teacher can be regarded as Supreme Soul (God) in *potentia.* In this way, these meanings, viz., *nāma-nikṣepa, sthāpanā-nikṣepa* and *dravya-nikṣepa* (rather our activities performed with respect to these three meanings) lead to *bhāva-nikṣepa* (rather the activity with respect to the *bhāva-nikṣepa,* or the actual attainment of the actual thing or state corresponding to the actual etymological meaning of the concerned word).

CHAPTER 6

NON-SECTARIAN AND LIBERAL OUTLOOK

The great Jaina spiritual teachers of ancient times have composed great many works to elucidate the principles of Jaina religion and philosophy. Therein they have mainly kept the object of the welfare of all people before them, while impartially and honestly expounding Reality and Truth. In the original Jaina canonical works one notices the great currents of pure equanimity and equability. Even the works composed by the later Jaina teachers are not less important, in this respect. Take, for example, *Śāstravārtāsamuccaya* by Ācārya Haribhadra. Therein one finds that great author saint's noble qualities of equanimity and universal love. We cannot help quoting some excerpts illustrating these qualities, though, we know, this is not the place to quote them.

In the third section (*stabaka*), after having logically established the Jaina doctrine that God is not the creator of the world, the author writes as follows:

tataś ceśvarakartṛtvavādo'yaṁ yujyate param/
samyagnyāyāvirodhena yathā"huḥ śuddhabuddhayaḥ //10//
īśvaraḥ paramātmaiva taduktavratasevanāt/
yato muktis tatas tasyāḥ kartā syād guṇabhāvataḥ //11//
tadanāsevanād eva yat saṁsāro'pi tattvataḥ /
tena tasyāpi kartṛtvaṁ kalpyamānaṁ na duṣyati //12//

Meaning: Even the view that God is the world-creator can be established by adducing in its favour the argument of the following type. None but the Supreme Soul who is completely free from attachment, aversion and infatuation, perfectly non-attached and omniscient, is God. By following the path of spiritual welfare propounded by him, one can attain liberation. So, secondarily he can be called liberator. And by not following it one has to wander in the transmigratory existence.

Thus, transmigratory wandering is the result of one's not following the teachings of God (Supreme Soul).[1]

Some have cultivated attachment or love for the statement 'God is Creator'. The saint philosophers have preached that God is the creator of the world, keeping in view these persons. This is what Ācārya Haribhadra has said in the following verse:

kartā'yam iti tadvākye yataḥ keṣāñcid ādaraḥ /
atas tadānuguṇyena tasya kartṛtvadeśanā //13//

Now he shows how God is the agent or creator in the primary sense.

paramaiśvaryayuktatvān mata ātmaiva veśvaraḥ/
sa ca karteti nirdoṣaḥ kartṛvādo vyavasthitaḥ //14//

Meaning: Or, it is maintained that the soul itself is God (*Īśvara*), because in its pure pristine state, it is possessed of divine faculties of omniscience etc. (*aiśvarya*). And there is no doubt that the soul is really the agent or doer. In this way we can make the doctrine of God as creator cogent.

While closing the topic, Ācārya Haribhadra concludes with these words:

---

1. When we gain profit by following the advice of someone, we call him the doer of good (in the form of profit) to us. If we incur losses by not following his advice or by acting against it, we do not call him—even in worldly intercourse—the doer of evil (in the form of losses) to us. Similarly, we attain liberation by following the path propounded by the Supreme Soul. So, we can consider him our liberator or doer of good to us. (This consideration is certainly secondary, yet cogent and attractive and appealing). But it is not proper to regard him even secondarily the giver of miseries to us, even if we suffer miseries of transmigratory wanderings on account of our not following the path preached by him. We neither like nor approve of even such secondary usage as calling Supreme Soul, the giver of miseries to us. This is the reason why Upādhyāya Yaśovijayajī has to write as follows, while commenting on the above quoted verse 12: "*aṅgulyagre kariśatam' ity ādivad yathākathañcid upacāreṇa vyavahāranirvāhāt.*" (Meaning: This statement is like the worldly statement 'There are one hundred elephants on the tip of a finger' and like the latter, it is to be tolerated somehow even secondarily.)

According to Jaina philosophy, there are two types of supreme souls, viz. *bhavastha* (those in the embodied state) and *bhavātīta* (those beyond the embodied state). As supreme souls who are in embodied state have mind, spech and body, they perform activities like walking, speaking, etc. They are the discoverers and propagators of the path of spiritual welfare, that is, liberation, as also the founders and organisers of the Order of aspirants. On the other hand, as supreme souls who are beyond embodied state are totally free from body, they are engrossed in their natural pure light of knowledge. They are called *siddhas*.

śāstrakārā mahātmānaḥ prāyo vītaspṛhā bhave/
sattvārthasaṁpravṛttāś ca kathaṁ te'yuktabhāṣiṇaḥ //15//
abhiprāyas tatas teṣāṁ samyag mṛgyo hitaiṣiṇā/
nyāyaśāstrāvirodhena yathā"ha Manur apy adaḥ //16//

Meaning: The great seers who have composed scriptures were mostly free from desires and well disposed to do good to all people. So, why should they preach wrong, improper and harmful principles? Hence we should examine their intention in such a manner as it would become consistent with logic or reason; even Manu has stated to this effect.

In this very section, after the topic of God, the author examines the doctrine of *Prakṛti*, propounded by Kapila. Having pointed out defects in the doctrine as expounded by the *Sāṁkhya* thinkers, he brings out the object behind Kapila's propounding it and in conclusion declares:

evaṁ prakṛtivādo 'pi vijñeyaḥ satya eva hi /
Kapiloktatvataś caiva divyo hi mahāmuniḥ //44//

Meaning: From the standpoint of its purpose or significance, the doctrine is to be regarded as true. Again, Kapila was a great divine sage; so his teaching must be true and wholesome, it can never be false and harmful.

In the sixth section, Ācārya Haribhadra critically examines the doctrines of momentariness (*kṣaṇikavāda*), void (*śūnyavāda* or nihilism) and subjective idealism (*vijñānavāda*), shows their defects and finally reveals their propriety in the following verses.

anye tv abhidadhaty evam etad āsthānivṛttaye /
kṣaṇikaṁ sarvam eveti Buddhenoktaṁ na tattvataḥ //51//
vijñānamātram apy eveṁ bāhyasaṅganivṛttaye /
vineyān kāṁścid āśritya yad vā taddeśanā 'rhataḥ //52//
evaṁ ca śūnyavādo'pi sadvineyānuguṇyataḥ /
abhiprāyata ity ukto lakṣyate tattvavedinā //53//

Meaning: The impartial saints maintain that it is not from the factual or real standpoint that Lord Buddha taught that everything is momentary.[1] He enunciated the doctrine of momentariness with a view to rous-

---

1. There is neither substance without mode nor mode without substance. Everything undergoes change every moment. The whole substance is subjected to constant transformation. The Jaina and almost all other Indian thinkers agree on this point. We experience these momentary changes or transformations. Hence it is highly probable that Lord Buddha declared all things to be momentary from this stand-

ing in man the feeling of detachment towards worldly objects and thereby eradicating longing for worldly pleasures which causes attachment to sensual objects. Even the theory which admits *vijñāna* or consciousness as the only reality and rejects the reality of external world is propounded with the sole object of destroying attachment for external objects and is addressed to the qualified pupils or audience only. And even the doctrine that everything is void or essenceless seems to have been taught to the qualified pupils only, with a view to fostering in them feeling of detachment.

In the eighth section, Ācārya Haribhadra examines the *Vedānta* monism as explained by *Vedānta* philosophers and points out the logical defects that vitiate it. But in conclusion, he says the following words to do justice and thereby brings out the practical utility of it in the cultivation of equanimity and universal love.

anye vyākhyānayanty evaṁ samabhāvaprasiddhaye /
advaitadeśanā śāstre nirdiṣṭā na tu tattvataḥ //8//

Meaning: Other great sages declare that *Vedānta* monism is taught not to present the true picture of reality, but to help man cultivate and attain the state of equanimity.

Let us explain the point. As the worldly souls are under the sway of infatuation and delusion, they are attached to some and averse to others. All this is the result of nescience. To convince man of this fact, to prevent him from falling prey to these defects and to cultivate in him equanimity, the teaching of *Vedānta* monism is propounded and propagated through the great propositions like *'ātmaivedaṁ sarvam'* ('All this is Soul'), *'sarvaṁ khalv idaṁ brahma'* ('All this is really *Brahman*'), etc. The scriptures of *Vedānta* monism teach to regard the world as essenceless, unreal and illusory as also to look upon all living beings as upon oneself. [For the object of these theories, see p. 389 ff.]

In *Śāstravārtāsamuccaya*, the author impartially evaluates doctrines of other philosophical systems and effects their synthesis with pure mind. This provides us a laudable example of the innately affectionate temperament and pure heart. Again, he mentions the prominent thinkers of

---

point. The whole world is in constant flux. We notice changes wherever we cast our glance. So it is quite natural for any philosopher or seer sage to express from a certain standpoint the view that all things are momentary.

other philosophical schools with highly respectful terms like *'maharṣi'* ('great seer'), *'mahāmuni'* ('great sage'), *'jñānī'* ('wise and learned'), *mahāmati* ('highly intelligent'), etc. Moreover, even while criticising the logically defective doctrines, he does not use derogatory terms for their propounders, but employs pure and elevated style evincing politeness and culture. By doing so, he awakens them to spiritual good. It displays great liberality and nobility of the Jaina sages that they treat affectionately and friendly the theoreticians of other schools of philosophy and pay respects to them. How pure that mind will be which remains equanimous and calm even while conducting religious and philosophical discussions with the thinkers of the opposite camps.

Study Ācārya Hemacandra's following utterance evincing high nobility and liberality.

bhavabījāṅkurajananā rāgādyāḥ kṣayam upāgatā yasya /
brahmā vā viṣṇur vā haro jino vā namas tasmai //

It is a traditional story that he uttered this verse, while reciting the devotional song before the image of Somanātha Mahādeva in Somanātha Pāṭaṇa.

This verse declares: 'I offer my respectful salutation to him who has completely destroyed all the mental defects beginning with attachment, the cause of transmigratory cycle—may he be Brahmā, Viṣṇu, Śaṅkara or Jina.'

An image is a symbol of the Supreme Soul, the highest ideal of non-attachment. It reflects perfect non-attachment. We can worship the ideal (the Supreme Soul) through the medium of its image. Droṇācārya refused a low caste Ekalavya to teach archery. So Ekalavya made an idol of Droṇācārya as he could and superimposed on it Droṇācārya as his teacher. With great devotion to Droṇācārya he started learning archery. As a result, he learnt archery and surpassed even Arjuna, the most favourite pupil of Droṇācārya. How suggestive the illustration is!

The verse in point throws light on the question as to by which name one should worship the ideal. It is not that one can worship the ideal by uttering or muttering one particular name only. As a matter of fact, one can worship the ideal giving it any name and uttering or muttering it. Upādhyāya Yaśovijayajī observes in his *Paramātma Paccīsī:*

budho jino hṛṣikeśaḥ śambhūr brahmā "dipūruṣaḥ /
ityādināmabhede 'pi nārthataḥ sa vibhidyate //

Meaning: Though Buddha, Jina, Hṛṣīkeśa, Śambhu, Brahmā, Ādipuruṣa, etc. are different names, the meaning for which they stand is identical. All these different names denote the same Supreme Soul.[1]

Whatever image and whatever name one may accept as means to spiritual perfection, there is no reason for or sense in quarrelling with others, simply because they employ different names for the same ideal and worship different images symbolising it. Not only that, but on that account there should be no adverse change in one's friendly behaviour or attitude with respect to them.

Non-attachment should be the ultimate goal of each and every man. Without sacrificing this main object, Jaina religion respects philosophical views as well as codes of conduct or systems of rituals of other religious sects. This is clear from the following verse:

jitendriyā jitakrodhā dāntātmānaḥ śubhāśayāḥ /
paramātmagatiṁ yānti vibhinnair api vartmabhiḥ //

Yaśovijayajī's *Paramātma Paccīsī*

Meaning: Those who have control over their sense-organs, have subdued passions like anger, etc., have equanimous and calm mind, and

---

1. The name 'Buddha' means one who has attained pure spiritual knowledge or is the knower of ultimate reality. The term 'Jina' has the sense of one who has conquered (removed) all the mental defects beginning with attachment. The name 'Hṛṣīkeśa' yields the meaning 'lord of sense-organs' (i.e., one who has completely subdued sense-organs. '*Hṛṣīka*' means sense-organs, and '*īśa*' means lord). The name 'Śambhu' means the source of supreme bliss. The term 'Brahmā' has the meaning 'an embodiment of pure knowledge'. 'Ādipuruṣa' yields the sense of Supreme Soul. The name 'Viṣṇu' means one who pervades the entire universe by his all-encompassing perfect knowledge. The term 'Śaṅkara' conveys the sense of 'one who causes happiness to others or one who shows the path of happiness'. Names 'Hari' and 'Hara' mean one who destroys miseries of living beings. 'Mahādeva' has the meaning 'one who shines with perfect light'. The name 'Arhat' means the supreme object of adoration and veneration.
rāgādijetā bhagavan ! Jino'si
Buddho'si buddhiṁ paramām upetaḥ /
kaivalyacidvyāpitayā'si Viṣṇuḥ
Śivo'si kalyāṇavibhūtipūrṇaḥ //[Author's *Anekāntavibhūti-Dvātriṁśikā*]
Meaning: O Lord ! You are Jina because you have conquered passions like attachment, aversion, etc., you are Buddha because you have attained the supreme knowledge, you are Viṣṇu because you are all-pervasive by your all-comprehensive omniscience, and you are Śiva because you are an embodiment of perfect spiritual good.

have good intentions, do attain the highest spiritual state, though they follow different paths of purification.

The aspirant of this highest ideal certainly attains liberation if he is equanimous, may he belong to any religious sect and may he be known by any sect name. This thing is presented in the following verse:

seyaṁbaro ya āsaṁbaro buddho ya ahava anno vā /
samabhāvabhāviappā lahaī mukkhaṁ na saṁdeho //2//

Saṁbohasattari by Jayaśekharasūri

Meaning: If a person is equanimous, he attains liberation without fail—no matter whether he is a Śvetāmbara, or a Digambara, or a Bauddha or a follower of any other religious sect.

There is no harm in one's being known by this or that sect name. But if he thinks that practice of nudity is the sole condition of liberation, or that practice of wearing pieces of cloth is the sole condition of liberation, or that metaphysical speculation or logic-chopping is the means of liberation, or that philosophical debate leads to liberation, or that service of bigotry is the cause of liberation, then such views are all wrong and pernicious to spiritual welfare or liberation. In fact, freedom from passions (attachment, aversion, infatuation) is the real spiritual freedom. Teaching of this type is found in the following verse:

nāśāmbaratve na sitāmbaratve na tarkavāde na ca tattvavāde /
na pakṣasevā"śrayaṇena muktiḥ kaṣāyamuktiḥ kila muktir eva /

Regarding the question as to what type of teaching should be, Ācārya Haribhadra observes:

citrā tu deśanā teṣāṁ syād vineyānuguṇyataḥ /
yasmād ete mahātmāno bhavavyādhibhiṣagvarāḥ //132//

Yogadṛṣtisamuccaya

Meaning: The teaching of those great sages [Kapila, Sugata, etc.] exhibits diversity of types parallel to the diversity of levels possessed by the understanding of the disciples concerned; for, these great personages are competent physicians in relation to the ailment called worldly existence.

Let us explain the point. The teaching should be different in accordance with the different qualifications or grades of the hearers so that they can digest and put it into practice. It is because spiritual elevation cannot be attained all at once. It is attained gradually. One can advance step by step only. There is a great danger of breaking one's leg if one tries to take a big leap. And many have broken their legs in such attempts. A good physician first diagnoses the different diseases of his patients, then prescribes different medicines for them in accordance with their different diseases or the different intensities of one and the same disease, and advises to take different fluid vehicles of medicines and suggests different diets accordingly. Similarly, even the greatly competent physicians in relation to the ailment called worldly existence first determine the intensity of the disease their hearers suffer from and then offer different teachings in accordance with their different qualifications and grades.

In his auto-commentary on the verse in point Ācārya Haribhadra says, "The diversity of the teaching of the omniscient Kapila, Sugata (Buddha), etc., is due to the diversity of the type of their pupils or hearers, because those great omniscient sages were the distinguished physicians in relation to the disease called worldly existence."

The difference that we notice between the philosophical teachings of the great sages is due to the different standpoints they have adopted while propagating their teachings. They have adopted different standpoints keeping in view the different types of their disciples. Thus, the diversity that we find in their teaching is apparent, while in reality their teaching is not diverse or conflicting. As they were the great physicians in relation to the disease called worldly existence, they have propounded and propagated the wholesome teaching which can effectively cure the living beings of the disease of worldly existence.[1]

---

1. Yoga philosophy mentions fourfold classification, viz. *heya* (that which is fit to be abandoned), *heyahetu* (the cause of what is fit to be abandoned), *hāna* (abandonment or destruction of what is fit to be abandoned) and *hānopāya* (means of abandoning or destroying what is fit to be abandoned). It is misery (*duḥkha*) that is fit to be abandoned (*heya*). Nescience (*avidyā*) is its cause (*heyahetu*). Complete destruction or removal of misery is the destruction of what is fit to be abandoned (*hāna*). And the means to the destruction or removal of misery (*hānopāya*) is knowledge of the distinction between the self and the non-self (*vivekakhyāti*). According to Buddha, the fourfold classification is *duḥkha* (misery), *duḥkhasamudaya* (rise, i.e., cause of misery), *duḥkha-nirodha* (destruction of misery) and *mārga* (means of destroying misery). The cause of misery is desire or craving (*tṛṣṇā*). This sense is intended by the term '*duḥkhasamudaya*'. *Mārga* (means) of destroying misery is the destruction of desire. And even the *mārga* (means) by which one can destroy desire can also be regarded as the *mārga* of destroying misery. The *Nyāya-Vaiśeṣika* and the *Vedānta*

Ācārya Haribhadra's thought related to this verse is worth studying.

When we acquaint ourselves with the essence of Jaina religion, we find that it is not a factional religious sect, but that it is a way of living. Of course, *tīrthaṅkara* Mahāvīra has established the fourfold Order (of monks, nuns, laymen and laywomen) and has formulated a code of conduct. In order to lay down a practical path for the good of the people at large and to guide them properly, he could not but present before them the constitution of the Order as also the code of conduct. But this certainly does not mean that only that person who has entered the Order and observes that code of conduct is called Jaina. The verdict of Jaina religion, *tīrthaṅkara* and his scriptures is that even a person who has not entered the Order and does not follow that code of conduct is no doubt a Jaina and can attain Ultimate Release (irrespective of his country, caste, race, family lineage, and religious sect), if he follows the path of truth and non-violence. We have already dealt with this point elsewhere in this work.

There are two aspects of life—thought and conduct. To improve them Lord Mahāvīra has prescribed two remedies. They are non-one-sided standpoint/outlook (*anekāntadṛṣṭi*) and non-violence (*ahiṃsā*). The former purifies thought and makes it right, while the latter purifies conduct and makes it friendly.

There are three noteworthy features that characterise the religion of Lord Mahāvīra. They are non-one-sided standpoint/outlook (*anekānta*),

---

schools of philosophy recognise the fourfold classification, but they use different terminology. The former employs the terms *saṁsāra* (transmigratory existence), *mithyā-jñāna* (wrong knowledge), *tattvajñāna* (true knowledge of Reality) and *apavarga* (liberation), while the latter employs the terms *saṁsāra, avidyā* (Nescience), *Brahma-bhāvanā* (meditation on *Brahman*) and *Brahma-sākṣātkāra* (realisation of *Brahman*). In Jaina terminology, *bandha* (bondage of material karmic particles with the soul) is what is fit to be abandoned or destroyed (*heya*); the cause of bondage (*heyahetu*) is the influx of karmic particles (*āsrava*); *saṁvara* (stoppage of the influx of karmic particles), *nirjarā* (partial dissociation of the bound karmic particles) and *mokṣa* (total dissociation of the bound karmic particles)—these three constitute *hāna* (destruction or removal of what is fit to be abandoned); and *manovākkāyagupti* (restricted or controlled activities of mind, speech and body), *satya* (truthfulness), *saṁyama* (self-control), *tapa* (austerity), *tyāga* (renunciation), etc., are the means to the destruction of what is fit to be abandoned or destroyed (*hānopāya*).

non-violence (*ahiṁsā*) and non-possession (*aparigraha*).[1] We have already expounded the non-one-sided standpoint. There we have pointed out that the non-one-sided standpoint makes it easy for us to achieve mutual love and friendliness in the human society. The non-one-sided standpoint springs from non-violence which, in turn, is made more vigilant by the non-one-sided standpoint. Thus there obtains close mutual relation between them. Violence includes in its fold all defects and vices like untruth-

1. *Tīrthaṅkara* Pārśva taught *cāujjāma* (Sk. *cāturyāma*) *dharma* (the law of four restraints). Buddhist *Tripiṭaka* and Jaina *Uttarādhyayanasūtra* (*adhyāya* 23, *gāthā* 23) mention it. The term '*yama*' or *yāma*' means restraint or vow. Thus *cāturyāma* is said to involve restraint from four sorts of activities: injury, non-truthfulness, taking what is not given and possession. In other words, *cāturyāma* means four vows, viz. non-violence (*ahiṁsā*), truthfulness (*satya*), non-stealing (*asteya*) and non-possession (*aparigraha*). From this, it follows that in the vows accepted in the Order of Lord Pārśva, that of celibacy (*brahmacarya*) was not separately mentioned. Regarding this point, it is said that the vow of celibacy was included in that of non-possession. Study the following verse:
no apariggahiāe itthīe jeṇa hoī paribhogo /
tā tavviraīe ccia abambhaviraitti paṇṇāṇa //
Meaning: One cannot enjoy a woman, if one does not possess her. This means that enjoying a woman is included in or covered by possessing her. Thus restraint from sexual activity is included in restraint from possession.

If we reflect a little more on this matter, we find that in olden days the term '*parigraha*' was used in such a broad sense or it yielded such a variety of meaning that the sense of wife was included in it. Not only that, but Sanskrit lexicons and great classical poems employ the term in the sense of wife. The following are instances in point.
patnīparijanādānamūlaśāpāḥ parigrahāḥ //237//—Amarakoṣa, Nānārtha Varga
parigrahaḥ kalatre ca..../—Ajaya
... jāyā parigrahaḥ //276//—Haima Abhidhānacintāmaṇi, Kāṇḍa III
parigrahaḥ parijane patnyām //353//—Haima Anekārthasaṅgraha, Kāṇḍa IV
kā tvaṁ śubhe? kasya parigraho vā?—Kālidāsa's *Raghuvaṁśa*, XVI.8
Its meaning is: O auspicious one! Who are you? Whose wife are you?
From this we can see that by '*parigrahavirati*' occurring in the four *yamas* (*mahāvratas* = great vows) accepted in the Order of Lord Pārśva was intended renunciation of both material things and wife. Both the senses—the sense of material things and that of wife—are primarily yielded by the term '*parigraha*'. So, both these senses were primarily understood by the people from the term '*parigraha*'.

fulness, stealing, etc. Passion or craving for possession gives rise to evils like violence, untruthfulness, theft, deceitfulness, cunningness, etc. Again, it is passion for possession that generates disparity in human society, and leads to class-war entailing riots, disorder and confusion. It is the root-cause of all vices, evils, wantonness and lust. Practice of non-violence is impossible without renouncing attachment for possession and limiting one's possessions. Therefore control over one's desire to possess and consequent voluntary cut in one's possessions constitute the fundamental condition for the good of both an individual and the society. If man does not limit his possessions, there can be no friendliness, happiness and peace in the society and among the people. It is desire to possess more and more things or wealth that leads man to indulge in exploitation, forgery, misappropriation, falsehood, theft, smuggling, illegal trade, tax-evasion, intrigue, cheating, use of false weights and measures, adulteration, corrupt practices, etc. In lust for gain, son murders father, and brother kills brother. It is for this reason that men bear false witness and rob on the highways. This is the reason why Lord Mahāvīra, the great sage, has put great emphasis on limiting one's possessions. He himself renounced all his possessions and preached the people at large to curtail their possessions to the minimum or as far as possible.

Thus he made sincere efforts in the direction of making their practical life pure, peaceful and happy. At present, we witness the movements of communism and socialism in different parts of the world. But 2,500 years ago, Lord Mahāvīra eminently propagated pure form of communism by loudly proclaiming the necessity of limiting one's possessions as also of cultivating universal friendliness.

Lord Mahāvīra was a great sage. His wealth was austerity. He observed severe austerities and taught the people at large lessons of equality in order to abolish inhuman institution of slavery prevalent in his days. He emancipated human mind. He purified man's faculty of reason and understanding by presenting rational philosophy against infatuation with scriptures, misunderstanding about God and blind ritualism which was based on the temptation of heaven, etc., given in the name of religion. He was an embodiment of compassion. He brought about a great revolution by non-violently and peacefully opposing the killing of animals in sacrifices, done in the name of religion, through his discourses and sermons exuding universal love and friendliness. As a result, an epidemic of violence had to suffer a severe blow, and the principle of non-violence and universal love spread among the people.[1] Even Buddha, a great saint, who was contemporary of Lord Mahāvīra made highly praiseworthy efforts in propagating the grand principle of non-violence and universal love. The Venerable Ascetic Mahāvīra taught the people:

kammuṇā baṁbhaṇo hoi kammuṇā hoi khattio /
vaisso kammuṇā hoi suddo havai kammuṇā //

—*Uttarādhyayana, Adhyayana* 25

Meaning: One becomes brāhmaṇa, kṣatriya, vaiśya or śūdra by one's actions.

Thus he emphasised the principle that caste should be determined by one's actions. This is the best principle that can establish harmonious social order. Not subscribing to it and accepting the wrong principle in its place that caste should be determined by birth, the Indian society lost its vigour and vitality. The invidious feeling of discrimination of high and low was so strong at that time that those who were regarded as 'low' were

1. *Vīro yadājāyata Bhāratasya*
sthitir vicitrā samabhūt tadānīm /
mūḍhakriyākāṇḍavimohajāle
nibadhyamānā janatā yadā"sīt //28//
When Lord Mahāvira was born, the condition of Bhāratavarṣa (India) was shocking. The people were being ensnared in the deluding net of blind ritualism.
'dharmāgraṇī'bhiś ca jano yadā'ndhaśraddhāvaṭe'bhūt paripātyamānaḥ /
uccabruvā nīcapade'vagamya parān yadānalpam adūdavaṁś ca //29//
The self-styled religious leaders were pushing people in the deep dark valley of blind faith. Those who considered themselves 'high' ('superior') looked down upon others, regarded them as 'low' and oppressed them.
yadāpajahur mahilādhikārān anyāyataḥ pauruṣagarvamattāḥ /
dharmāya yajñādiṣu bhūrihiṁsāpāpānalaḥ prajvalito yadā"sit //30//
Men who were infatuated with the pride of their manliness were unjustly depriving women of their rights. Fire of sin of killing animals in sacrifices in the name of religion was dangerously flaring up.
etādṛśe Bhārata-dausthyakāle devāryadevo viṣaye Videhe /
khyāte pure 'Kṣatriyakuṇḍa'nāmni prājāyata kṣatriyarājagehe //31//
At that time when Bhārata (India) was in such bad condition, Lord Devārya (Vardhamāna alias Mahāvīra) was born in the royal palace of kṣatriya king in Kṣatriyakuṇḍa, a well-known town of the ancient kingdom of Videha (modern Bihar). [These verses are from the author's poem *Vīra-vibhūti*]

subjected to excessive cruelty and oppression.[1] The doors of religion were tightly closed to them. Against all this cruelty and injustice, the Venerable Mahāvīra declared:

ucco guṇe karmaṇi yaḥ sa ucco
nīco guṇe karmaṇi yaḥ sa nīcaḥ /
śūdro'pi cet saccaritaḥ sa uccaḥ
dvijo'pi ced duścaritaḥ sa nīcaḥ //

[That person is really high who is high in quality and action, and that person is really low who is low in quality and action. Even a śūdra is high if his conduct is good and virtuous, while even a brāhmaṇa is low if his conduct is evil and vicious.]

Declaring thus, he taught that highness or superiority of a man is based on and determined by the good and cultured thought and conduct. Not only by preaching it but also by putting it into practice he taught the principle. He threw open the doors of his religious Order to the untouchable, low-caste and down-trodden people. Having been initiated into the Order of Jaina monks, they attained the high spiritual titles of *ṛṣi* (sage), *maharṣi* (great sage) and *mahātmā* (great soul). The biographical accounts of such persons are found in the twelfth and thirteenth chapters of *Uttarādhyayanasūtra.* In his days the status of women was very low. The Vedic tradition treated them with contempt and disregard. Their condition was pitiable and miserable. As against this, he declared women equal to men in status, elevated them to the same position as men held in the field of religion, regarded them as qualified for ascetic life and accepted them to the monastic Order.[2] The religion taught by

1. *atha hāsya vedam upaśṛṇvatas trapujatubhyāṁ śrotraparipūraṇam, udāharaṇe jihvācchedaḥ, dhāraṇe śarīrabhedaḥ /—Gautama-Dharmasūtra.*
Meaning: If a śūdra listens to the recitation of the *Veda,* his ears should be filled with hot lead and lac. If he recites the *Veda,* his tongue should be cut off. And if he commits the *Veda* to memory, his body should be chopped up.
na śūdrāya matiṁ dadyān nocchiṣṭaṁ na haviṣkṛtam /
na cāsyopadiśed dharma na cāsya vratam ādiśet //—Vāsiṣṭha-Dharmasūtra.
Meaning: One should not impart knowledge to a śūdra, should not give him remainder of food or offerings in sacrifices, should not teach him religion and should not command him to observe vows.
2. Candanabālā who was once a princess had to pass her days as a female slave. Lord Mahāvīra freed her from slavery and made her an ascetic nun (i.e., initiated her into the spiritual discipline of total abstinence from violence, etc.). Thus he established the Order of nuns with this noble lady as its first member.

the Venerable Ascetic Mahāvīra was highly revolutionary. The path he showed can well be regarded as the religion of man in its true form. It looks upon all human beings as equal and discriminates none. It enjoins justice to all, men and women. Any man can follow it according to his capacity, circumstances and conditions. As it is taught by a Jina,[1] it is called Jaina religion. Otherwise, looking to its object of welfare of all and its universal appeal, it can truly be called religion of the people at large (*janadharma*).

There were *śramaṇa*s (non-Vedic ascetics), *brāhmaṇas, muni*s (mendicants) and *tāpasa*s, who were lax and hypocritical. Universal friend Mahāvīra took them to task. He observed in *Uttarādhyayana* (chapter 25) as follows:

na vi muṁḍieṇa samaṇo na oṁkāreṇa brāhmaṇo /
*na muṇī raṇṇavāseṇa kusacīreṇa na tāvaso //*30//

Meaning: One does not become a *śramaṇa* (non-Vedic ascetic) by mere shaving one's head, a *brāhmaṇa* by mere muttering *Oṁ*, a *muni* (mendicant) by mere living in uninhabited woods, or a *tāpasa* by mere wearing garments made of bark or *kuśa* grass.

We should acquaint ourselves with the inner life of a man. We should not be misled by his dress, external appearance or overt behaviour, and should not think that he certainly possesses qualities which they suggest. This verse warns us against the danger of being deceived by the outward appearance and overt behaviour of a man. Again, the following verse throws a flood of light on this matter.

samayāe samaṇo hoi baṃbhacereṇa baṃbhaṇo /
nāṇeṇa ya muṇī hoi taveṇa hoi tāvaso //31//

Meaning: One becomes a *śramaṇa* by equanimity (*samatā*), a *brāhmaṇa* by the spiritual practice for the realisation of the Supreme Soul (*brahmacarya*), a *muni* by knowledge (of soul as distinct and different from body, etc.), and a *tāpasa* by austerity (judiciously observed without any desire for fruit and with the sole object of the good of oneself and others).

1. 'Jina' is not a proper name of any one individual. It is a generic term applied to all those who have conquered the passion of attachment and become perfect seer (i.e., omniscient).

[*Samatā* (equanimity) means to regard all living beings as equal and also to look upon them as upon oneself. It also means to keep one's mind unagitated and calm on occasions of misery and happiness, gain and loss, victory and defeat, etc., without losing its balance or evenness.

Brahmacarya means not to crave for objects of senses and sensual pleasures, to have control over mind, to remain absorbed in the Supreme Soul and to follow wholeheartedly the Good Path leading onward to the state of Supreme Soul or Highest Bliss.]

Experience shows that Jainism is a system of spiritual philosophy. It puts great emphasis on the practice of spiritually good life. It mainly deals with ascetic culture and ethical behaviour. The sole object of its entire literature dealing with various subjects is to bring man to the Path of non-attachment, to instruct him how to advance on it and ultimately attain the state of perfect non-attachment. It repeatedly and emphatically proclaims that Supreme Good or Welfare solely depends on non-attachment. Its chief teaching is that man should live in such a manner that his passions of attachment and aversion may gradually decrease and ultimately suffer complete destruction.[1] This instruction presents the final and highest message its entire literature delivers. It loudly proclaims that there is no harm in following any system of philosophy and practice, if it helps man to cultivate righteous conduct and to progress in the direction of the final goal of non-attachment. The guiding principle of one's life should be: *mitti me savvabhūesu* (May I have a friendly relation with all beings). One may adopt any system of thought and practice which suits one's temperament, the only condition being that it should foster universal friendliness and love.

Conclusion

I have expounded in the present work, to the best of my ability and understanding, the main topics of Jaina philosophy and religion. I have treated of nine 'reals' (soul, non-soul, auspicious karmic matter, inauspicious karmic matter, influx of karmic matter, stoppage of the influx, bondage of karmic matter, partial dissociation of karmic matter from

1. *kiṁ bahuṇā? iha jaha jaha rāgaddosā lahuṁ vilijjanti /*
taha taha payaṭṭiavvaṁ esā āṇā jiṇiṁdāṇaṁ //
—Yaśovijayajī's *Adhyātmamataparīkṣā,* last verse.

soul, and total and absolute dissociation of karmic matter), six substances (soul, medium of motion, medium of rest, matter, space and time), the path of liberation and its three constituents (right inclination, right-knowledge and right conduct), spiritualness, stages of spiritual development, code of conduct for laymen, logic and epistemology, doctrine of relative judgement, doctrine of standpoints and theory of non-absolutism. The third chapter deals with the miscellaneous topics related to metaphysics and ethics. The fourth chapter is devoted to the detailed exposition of *karma* philosophy (theory of moral causation). Both the chapters present various thoughts. Here ends my exposition. At last, I would like to express my wish that as a result of reading this book there may arise in the mind of readers desire to know further about religion and philosophy and they may become eager to read great works of great men.

May peace prevail everywhere in the whole world.

GOSPELS OF MAHĀVĪRA

True Sacrifice

susaṁvuḍā paṁcahiṁ saṁvarehiṁ iha jīviaṁ aṇavakaṁkhamāṇā /
vosaṭṭhakāyā suicattadehā mahājayaṁ jayaī jaṇṇasiṭṭhaṁ //

—*Uttarādhyayanasūtra,* 12.42

Those who are well protected by the five vows and are not attached to the life of sensual pleasures, who dedicate their body to the performance of good actions, who are pure-hearted and righteous are indeed continuously engaged in the performance of supreme sacrifice which brings them victory in the field of good conduct.

tavo joī jīvo joiṭhāṇam jogā suyā sarīraṁ kārisaṁgaṁ /
kamme ehā saṁjamajogasaṁtī homaṁ huṇāmi isiṇaṁ pasatthaṁ //

—*Uttarādhyayanasūtra,* 12.44

Austerity is my fire; soul my fire-place; threefold activity of mind, speech and body is my sacrificial ladle; the body the dried cowdung; *karman* is my fuel; self-control, good activity and tranquillity are the oblations, praised by the sages, which I offer. As this sacrifice is of the form of pure self-restraint, it brings peace and happiness to the sacrificer. It is this sacrifice that is extolled by the great sages.

True Brāhmaṇa

jahā paumaṁ jale jāyaṁ novalippai vāriṇā /
evaṁ alittaṁ kāmehiṁ taṁ vayaṁ būma māhaṇaṁ //

—*Uttarādhyayanasūtra,* 25.26

He who is not defiled by cravings for sensual pleasures as a lotus growing in the water is not wetted by it, him we call a brāhmaṇa.

jāyarūvaṁ jahāmaṭṭhaṁ niddhaṁtamalapāvagaṁ /
rāga-dosa-bhayāīaṁ taṁ vayaṁ būma māhaṇaṁ //

—*Uttarādhyayanasūtra,* 25.21

He who is free from attachment, aversion and fear, and as a result who shines forth like burnished gold, purified in fire, him we call a brāhmaṇa.

Holy Ablution

dhamme harae baṁbhe saṁtititthe aṇāile attapasannalese /
jahiṁsi ṇhāo vimalo visuddho susītibhūo pajahāmi dosaṁ //

—*Uttarādhyayanasūtra,* 12.46

The good and righteous conduct is my pond, celibacy my holy bathing place which is not turbid and throughout clear for the soul; there I make ablutions; pure, clean and thoroughly cooled I get rid of hatred (or impurity).

Charity or Donation

jo sahassaṁ sahassāṇaṁ māse māse gavaṁ dae /
tassāvi saṁjamo seo adiṁtassāvi kiṁcaṇa //

—*Uttarādhyayanasūtra,* 9.40

A man who gives no alms but controls himself is better than one who gives, every month, thousands and thousands of cows.

True War

jo sahassaṁ sahassāṇaṁ saṁgāme dujjae jiṇe /
egaṁ jiṇejja appāṇaṁ esa se paramo jao. //

—*Uttarādhyayanasūtra,* 9.34[1]

A man who conquers nobody but himself is the greater victor than one who conquers thousands and thousands of valiant enemies.

appāṇam eva jujjhāhi kim te jujjheṇa bajjhao /
appāṇam eva appāṇaṁ jaittā suhamehae //

—*Uttarādhyayanasūtra,* 9.35

---

1. The fourth *gāthā* in the *Sahassavagga* of *Dhammapada,* a Buddhist work, is very similar to this one. Many *gāthās* of *Uttarādhyayanasūtra* are found in *Dhammapada,* with some minor changes; many other statements from the *Jaina Āgamas* closely resemble those that occur in *Dhammapada.*

Fight with your own self; why fight with external enemies? He who conquers himself through himself will attain happiness.

se asaiṁ uccāgoe, asaiṁ nīāgoe, no hīṇe, no airitte,....
ko goyāvāī ? ko māṇāvāī?

—*Ācārāṅgasūtra,* 2.3.77

A soul has been born in high families and low families innumerable times. So, who is high and who is low? Who is *gotravādī* (believer in family lineage) and who is *abhimānavādī* (believer in family pride)?

jahā puṇṇassa katthai, tahā tucchassa katthai;
jahā tucchassa katthai, tahā puṇṇassa katthai /

—*Ācārāṅgasūtra,* 2.6.101

The saint or the wise should speak to the poor, the wretched and the miserable the way they speak to the fortunate, the rich and the kings; and they should speak to the fortunate, the rich and the kings the way they speak to the poor, the wretched and the miserable.

purisā ! saccam eva samabhijāṇāhi /
saccassa āṇāe se uvaṭṭhie mehāvī māraṁ tarai /

—*Ācārāṅgasūtra,* 3.3.118

O men! understand Truth rightly. The intelligent person who obeys the commands of Truth crosses death.

savvao pamattassa bhayaṁ, savvao appamattassa natthi bhayaṁ /

—*Ācārāṅgasūtra,* 3.4.123

One who is unmindful and careless has fear from every quarter, while one who is mindful and vigilant has fear from nowhere.

SELECT BIBLIOGRAPHY

Bhargava, Dayananda

1968 *Jaina Ethics*, Delhi: Motilal Banarsidass

Bhattacharya, Harisatya

1958 *The Philosophy of the Jainas*, Bombay

1950 *Reals in the Jaina Metaphysics*, Bombay

1976 *Jain Moral Doctrine*, Bombay: Jain Sāhitya Vikāsa Maṇḍala

Bhattacharya, N.N.

1976 *Jaina Philosophy, Historical Outline*, New Delhi: Munshiram Manoharlal

Caillat C., Upadhye A.N and Patil B.

1974 *Jainism*, Delhi: MacMillan Company of India

Chakravarti, A.

1957 *The Religion of Ahiṁsā*, Bombay

Deo, Shantaram B.

1956 *History of Jaina Monachism*, Poona: (Deccan College Dissertation Series, 17)

Devendra Muni Shastri

1983 *Source-Book in Jaina Philosophy*, Udaipur: Sri Tarak Guru Jain Granthalaya

Diwakar, S.C.

1970 *Glimpses of Jainism*, Delhi

Dixit, K.K.

1978 *Early Jainism*, Ahmedabad: L.D. Institute of Indology

1971 *Jaina Ontology*, Ahmedabad: L.D. Institute of Indology

Gandhi, V.R.

1993 *Religion and Philosophy of the Jainas*, Ed. by Nagin J. Shah. Ahmedabad: Lalit Shah, Trustee, Jain International, 21 Saumya

Apartments, Navrangpura, Ahmedabad-380014

Gopalan, S.
1973 *Outlines of Jainism,* New Delhi: Wiley Eastern.

Guseva, N.R. (Mrs.)
1971 *Jainism,* translation from Russian by Y.S. Redkar, Bombay: Sindhu Publications

Jain, C.R.
1974 *Fundamentals of Jainism,* Meerut: Veer Nirvan Bharati (originally published in 1916 as *Practical Path*)

Jain, Jyoti Prasad
1983 *Religion and Culture of the Jains,* New Delhi: Bharatiya Jnanapith

Jaini, Jagmandar Lal
1916 *Outlines of Jainism,* Ed. by F.W. Thomas. Cambridge

Jaini, Padmanabh S.
1979 *The Jaina Path of Purification,* Delhi: Motilal Banarsidass

Marathe M.P, Kelkar M.A. and Gokhale P.P. (Eds.)
1984 *Studies in Jainism,* Poona: I.P.Q. Publications, Department of Philosophy, University of Poona

Matilal, B.K.
1981 *The Central Philosophy of Jainism,* Ahmedabad: L.D. Institute of Indology

Mehta, Mohan Lal
1954 *Outlines of Jaina Philosophy,* Bangalore
1955 *Jaina Psychology,* Amritsar: Sohanlal Jaindharma Pracharak Samiti

Mookerji, Satkari
1978 *The Jaina Philosophy of Non-Absolutism.* 2nd edition, Delhi: Motilal Banarsidass

Nahar P.C. and Ghosh K.C.
1937 *An Epitome of Jainism,* Calcutta

Padmarajiah, Y. J.
1963 *Jaina Theories of Reality and Knowledge,* Bombay: Jaina Sāhitya Vikāsa Maṇḍala

Paul Marett
1985 *Jainism Explained*, Leicester: Jain Samaj Europe

Schubring, Walther
1962 *The Doctrine of the Jainas* (translation from the revised German edition by Wolfgang Beurlen), Delhi: Motilal Banarsidass

Sogani, K.C.
1967 *Ethical Doctrines in Jainism*, Sholapur: Jaina Samskriti Samrakshaka Sangha

Stevenson, Sinclair (Mrs.)
1970 *The Heart of Jainism*, New Delhi: Munshiram Manoharlal

Talib, G.S. Ed.
1975 *Jainism*, Patiala: Punjabi University

Tatia, Nathmal
1951 *Studies in Jaina Philosophy*, Benaras: P.V. Research Institute

Warren, Herbert
1983 *Jainism in Western Garb, as a solution to Life's Great Problems*, Edited, with notes, by Nagin J. Shah, Bombay: Shree Vallabhsuri Smarak Nidhi

Williams, R.
1983 *Jaina Yoga*, Delhi: Motilal Banarsidass

AUTHOR INDEX

TITLE INDEX

WORD INDEX

SUBJECT INDEX

Karmic traces